Homelessness in America

Edited by Jim Baumohl

For the National Coalition for the Homeless

ORYX PRESS
1996

The rare Arabian oryx is believed to have inspired the myth of the unicorn. This desert antelope became virtually extinct in the early 1960s. At that time several groups of international conservationists arranged to have 9 animals sent to the Phoenix Zoo to be the nucleus of a captive breeding herd. Today the oryx population is over 1,000, and over 500 have been returned to the Middle East.

© 1996 by The Oryx Press
4041 North Central at Indian School Road
Phoenix, Arizona 85012-3397

Published simultaneously in Canada
Printed and bound in the United States of America

∞ The paper used in this publication meets the minimum requirements of the American National Standard for Information Sciences—Permanence of Paper for Printed Library Materials, ANSI Z39.48-1984.

Library of Congress Cataloging-in-Publication Data

Homelessness in America / edited by Jim Baumohl for the National
   Coalition for the Homeless.
      p. cm.
   Includes bibliographical references (p.   ) and index.
   ISBN 0-89774-869-7 (cloth : alk. paper)
   1. Homelessness—United States. 2. Homelessness—Government policy—United States. I. Baumohl, Jim. II. National Coalition for the Homeless (U.S.)
HV4505.H652 1996
362.5'8'0973-dc20   96-30244
                                                                      CIP

In memory of Janet Fitchen, Jack Graham, and Elliot Liebow,
whose work honored the dispossessed.

CONTENTS

• • • • • • •

FOREWORD

· · · · · · ·

Kai T. Erikson
Professor of Sociology and American Studies
Yale University

The homeless poor can be said to constitute a distinct population (and thus serve as the subject of a volume like this), at least in the sense that they have in common the condition of being unhoused. No problem there. Persons who, for an appreciable span of time, find themselves without a home of some kind—a place, an address, a more-or-less settled niche— obviously share a special experience and relate to the larger social order in a special way. And yet, as most experts on homelessness are quick to point out, to draw too abrupt a line between those poor who are for the moment housed and those who are not may pose more questions than it answers.

Do the homeless poor form a discrete class in any other respect? That is a very difficult question to approach sensibly, never mind to answer satisfactorily. For one thing, the variety of people who qualify as homeless at any given moment is so great as to defy even the simplest of generalizations. For another, people move into and out of the ranks of the homeless with such fluidity that it is far easier to focus on the destitute in general as the population pool from which the temporarily unhoused are drawn.

Because both of those things are so, little of importance can be learned from assuming, as is so often done, that homeless people as a class tend to have experienced more abuse as children, taken more drugs as adults, suffered more from mental illness, spent more time in prison, seen more of the horrors of war, had flimsier educations—or that they have proven to be more damaged vessels than their housed counterparts along any other dimension. To say that they are more vulnerable to misfortune is only to note that they have dropped out of the bottom of the housing market—which is about as useful as declaring that someone who breaks a limb or comes down with the mumps must have been susceptible to such an outcome all along.

Homelessness, then, as specialists have been insisting for years, has to be seen as a social circumstance rather than a personal characteristic. The homeless have been swept away from the settled shore, so to speak, by a cruel and unrelenting undertow. For that reason, the proper study of homelessness has to at least begin with questions about prevailing socioeconomic tides rather than about the personalities or life histories or physical constitutions of the people caught in them.

The most important questions one can ask about homelessness, then, are two: What is the nature of that undertow? And what can be done to reverse it? The papers brought together in this collection deal primarily with those matters, especially with the second of them. All I can say here by way of introduction is that the chapters to follow constitute the most important gathering of fact and insight and wisdom on the subject we are likely to have for a very long time.

I would like also to reflect for a moment on yet a third point of emphasis: What are the consequences of sustained homelessness for the persons who experience it? The question being asked here is not, what kinds of persons are drawn into the ranks of the homeless; rather, what happens to them as a result?

Our society in general often seems to view homeless people as living on the other side of a divide so deep and so wide that they look as if they were alien, of another place and kind, maybe even of another species. It is extremely important that we understand the nature of that divide correctly (to the extent that it exists at all), and it is equally important that we find ways to describe it that do justice to the realities of the world in which homeless people live. On the one hand, as I just noted, there are no reasons in the world to assume that persons who become homeless were originally a sorrier or more disreputable lot than the rest of the desperately poor. We need to be very clear on that point because there are masses of people out there, many of them in positions of public responsibility, who would be very relieved to be able to think that the homeless were destined by their own shortcomings and misdoings for the fate that now claims them. At the same time, however, sustained homelessness in particular and sustained poverty in general have the potential for doing a great deal of damage to the human spirit, and, thus, to create divides where none existed before. We need to be very clear on that point, too, because there is no better way to convey what the costs of homelessness are to society and to the individuals drawn into it.

I want to address two matters here—and, as befits the fact that I probably have had less experience thinking about homelessness than a majority of the persons whose work appears here, I will do so by raising questions.

First, to what extent can one say that sustained exposure to homelessness is traumatizing in the sense that it can induce the kind of demoralization and numbed despair often found among people who have experienced some kind of crushing blow? I have been studying the effects of disasters on the people who survive them, and it seems logical to me that the experience of finding oneself without a home over any stretch of time must be of much the same *kind* as the experiences that follow exposure to emergencies of a more acute sort.

Victims of disasters, like victims of homelessness, are drawn from an immense variety of backgrounds and seasonings, and it makes no sense at all to begin research on them by asking what individual traits placed them in the path of a hurricane or what disabilities were responsible for their presence on an endangered floodplain. They were simply in the wrong place at the wrong time. But disasters can *induce* differences among at least a sizable portion of those who encounter them—bringing in their wake a sense of bleakness and depression that can deaden whatever personal resources victims might otherwise have at their disposal. Does sustained homelessness produce a similar result? We may have to define homelessness as a *chronic* disaster for the purposes of this question to distinguish it from more immediate catastrophes—the storms and explosions and collisions and eruptions and other sharp turns of fate that punctuate the flow of everyday life and are reported in newspapers. But it is a disaster all the same, and the evidence I have seen so far suggests that it can inflict emotional wounds of the same kind one finds wherever people have suffered a traumatic injury of significant proportions.

Second, to what extent can one say that exposure to homelessness (or to desperate poverty in general, for that matter) not only damages the spirit in some individual way but creates a distinct and deleterious communal atmosphere? The experience of other disasters has been that the connections drawing people together can also become deadened afterward, and that the spiritual texture of the air people breathe, so to speak, as well as the spaces through which they move, almost seem to engender feelings of disorientation and humiliation. Whatever we want to call this dark and heavy sense of things—"mood," "temper," "climate," even "culture"—it seems to give form to the outlooks of the people caught up in it. Does the social climate of the world of the homeless help produce numbers of people who are largely without hope, have little faith in human institutions, and no longer know how to envision (never mind plan for) a secure future? Do such people often come to feel that they live outside the social world spoken of in schools and portrayed on television? Outside the world where life is governed by order and where a sense of human charity reigns?

The answer to both sets of questions, I would guess, is yes, and that brings us back to the question of divides. If one looks at the gulf separating the homeless from the rest of us through the cold, ungenerous lens of a social conservative, it offers a logic for cutting whatever lifelines we still maintain with the desperately poor and letting them drift like so many damaged hulks out to sea. To offer any empirical comfort to so ruthless a view as that, of course, would be a great pity from any moral standpoint as well as a serious misreading of what evidence we have been able to gather on the subject. If we were to speak of the homeless as if they were a different order of being, occupying a different kind of social space, we would run the risk of promoting an impression we know to be flatly wrong—that the differences between us and them are so deeply ingrained and so close to the heart of things that a fairer distribution of the country's resources will not help very much. We cannot let people forget for even an instant that the homeless are of our kind and live but a moment away. And yet we also need to convey that the costs of the indifference with which the problem is being treated in many quarters is incalculable, and, indeed, that the grotesque disproportions of power and wealth that characterize the social landscape we now live in is producing a rot for which we shall all pay dearly.

The papers in this volume do an extraordinary job of describing the contours of that problem and offering suggestions for what we can only hope will prove to be a warmer future.

A NOTE FROM
The National Coalition for the Homeless

. . . .

The National Coalition for the Homeless is indebted to the Melville Charitable Trust, who gave us a grant to produce this book to enlighten the public dialogue about homelessness in America and to help stimulate the thrust toward real change. We are grateful to the individual authors for the contributions of their reflections and insight born of their own experience and research, and for the donation of their royalties to further public education on this issue. We thank Jim Baumohl for his constancy and his commitment to this work, to informed public opinion, and to challenging us all to "reckon with poverty."

Mary Ann Gleason
Executive Director

INTRODUCTION

·······

This book is about homelessness rather than homeless people. The distinction is important, for like most social problems, homelessness involves socioeconomic arrangements that exist quite apart from those troubled by them. Moreover, in the meaning I want to invoke here, *social problems* do not exist without politics; they do not arise *spontaneously*, even from widespread and visible suffering. Rather, they result from a *collective definition* of distress: Interested people and organizations bring private troubles to public attention by broadcasting claims about what such phenomena mean and why they're worth worrying about, and they recommend what should be done. In response, other interested parties contest these interpretations and prescriptions. We citizens come to recognize social problems and the possibilities of social policy largely through such public discourse. We pick up news and commentary from the radio or television and read newspapers or books like this one, and we discuss these opinions over coffee with friends or colleagues, in the neighborhood bar, around the family dinner table, or in any of the primal scenes of democracy.

Not all opinions have the same weight, of course. Because they are persuasive and have access to audiences, some people wield influence. In popular parlance, they are often called opinion makers, and to the extent that they influence elected and appointed officials, they shape public policy. Understanding this, would-be opinion makers of similar views frequently coalesce into organizations dedicated to asserting their claims about the nature of social problems and appropriate responses to them. Whatever their political hue, these advocates, as they are called in social policy circles, are scouts of misery and unrest and promoters of some plan of social betterment (even if that plan is merely to leave things alone). Unlike lobbyists, advocates do not write checks to political action committees, but they do orchestrate constituencies to pressure officials, and they are always ready to educate politicians, bureaucrats, and media representatives about their causes. As they spread the word, some turn up frequently in sympathetic newspapers and magazines, on television, in court cases, and in public hearings. Depending on the political climate, advocates of one stripe or another sometimes serve as political ghostwriters and editors, drafting and vetting legislation.

There is a fine line between ideological affinity and outright political partisanship, and, occasionally, an advocacy organization crosses it. The resulting political relationship sometimes becomes quite controversial and perhaps even subject to scrutiny by the Internal Revenue Service, which patrols the domain of nonprofit/nonpartisan status.[1] Recently, conservatives have been apt to characterize liberal advocates (in particular, what they call the "poverty industry") as quintessentially nefarious, privilege-seeking "special interests" that undermine the democratic process. (Given the immensely greater resources and influence of conservative advocates, this is disingenuous, indeed.) But advocates are better understood as indispensable animators of modern democracy. They are special pleaders, to be sure, but neither elected officials and their staff members, nor civil servants in the "permanent government," can (or should) supply all of the points of view relevant in the consideration of a complex issue. Nor can they adequately motivate and organize citizens to participate in the debate about policy—a debate more often about justice than technical measures. Rather than usurping democracy, advocates promote a political diversity and vitality generally squandered by Republicans and Democrats, preoccupied as they are with the merely inoffensive. Advocates often amplify the voices of aggrieved citizens who would otherwise be unheard. Short on funds and information technology, lacking access to the mainstream media, and persuaded that it is sometimes valuable to shock the "squares," some advocates, some of the time, raise hell and stop traffic—and that is as it should be.

Antihomelessness Activism and Advocacy in America

Political activism by homeless people, and advocacy on their behalf, has a long history in the United States. Local demonstrations by the dispossessed were a common feature of the depressions that followed the cyclical economic "panics" of the years between the end of the Civil War and the beginning of World War II.

Whole decades, notably the 1870s, 1890s, and 1930s, were shaped by mass dispossession and civil unrest. The federal government first became a target of such protest in the spring of 1894, when several "industrial armies" of unemployed, often shelterless men—some assembled as far away as Los Angeles and San Francisco—converged on Washington by foot, rail, and riverboat to demand a program of public road building.[2]

The contemporary era of antihomelessness activism and advocacy also began locally, often in college towns, where pools of unemployed, ill-educated, and often homeless young adults—mostly White—had formed by the deep "stagflation" recession that began in the mid-1970s. This portentous reappearance of homelessness was noticed briefly even by *Time* and the *Washington Post,* and some of today's antihomelessness agencies—from Berkeley-Oakland Support Services in northern California to the Daily Planet in Richmond, Virginia—were established in the early seventies.[3] But the local advocates of those years—and I was one of them—had little sense of how to capitalize on provincial gains, nor did they effectively connect what they saw on the streets with the grinding inner-city poverty of African Americans, conditions that would yield a renaissance of homelessness within just a few years (see Chapter 11). Homelessness remained a latent social problem, a growing but little-remarked phenomenon awaiting promotion to public view by more talented organizers more strategically placed.[4]

If one event were to be identified as the catalyst for the takeoff of contemporary national advocacy, it would have to be the occupation of the National Visitors' Center (now part of the Union Station complex in Washington, DC) by the Community for Creative Non-Violence (CCNV) in November 1978. Federal police rousted them after a few nights, but antihomelessness work had moved into a new phase.[5]

Few other advocacy groups could match CCNV in temerity, style, or commitment to organized confrontation, but they could demand that the public face up to the shame of homelessness, and shortly reports, broadsides, newspaper articles, and scholarly publications began to echo them. Indeed, within a few years, a revived documentary tradition flourished. In March 1981, Ellen Baxter and Kim Hopper's hugely influential monograph, *Private Lives/Public Spaces*, was issued in New York City by the Community Service Society. This was followed by detailed reports on homelessness published in Baltimore and Phoenix. After circulating a shorter but substantively similar draft for two years, CCNV published *Homelessness in America: A Forced March to Nowhere* in December 1982. (The title of the present book pays homage to that document.) Testimony and supporting material from Congressional hearings in 1982 and 1984 filled five volumes of proceedings. In the next few years, dozens of local studies followed, producing a literature on homelessness quickly surpassing in volume even that of the Great Depression.[6]

These early documentary efforts were complemented by a series of political actions and organized demonstrations. Throughout the 1980s, CCNV remained the nerve center of political theater, organized street vigils, punishing fasts, disruptive mischief, and determined evangelizing. In 1980, its members embarrassed District of Columbia religious leaders by vainly seeking shelter for homeless people in churches during a snowstorm. In November 1984, moral brinksmanship (a 51-day fast that brought CCNV's Mitch Snyder near death) effectively extorted a White House commitment to renovate a federal building for use as a shelter, but it would take two more publicized fasts before the promised funds were released a year and a half later.[7]

Whether undertaken by CCNV or other groups, less extreme measures were the rule, however: In December 1981, a memorial service was held across from the White House for people who had died on the streets. In January 1983, over 150 demonstrators were arrested in Washington, DC, for occupying the Capitol building to protest the lack of shelter for poor people. A year later, 100 homeless people and their advocates occupied the mayor's office in Columbus, Ohio, to demand the use of a public facility for shelter. On Christmas Eve 1986, advocates in Atlanta marched in procession behind a black crucifix (the "vagrant Christ") to protest a proposed "derelict-free" zone; 14 months later, a national March for the Homeless drew thousands of homeless poor, their advocates, and civil rights veterans from across the country to the same venue. Later that summer, campaigns were mounted in Washington, Atlanta, Boston, Cincinnati, San Francisco, and other cities to "take off the boards" and reclaim abandoned housing. In March 1988, civil rights leaders joined thousands of homeless people and activists in Atlanta to promote homelessness as an issue in the upcoming elections. In October 1989, a quarter-million advocates, homeless people (some of whom had marched hundreds of miles to get there), and ordinary citizens, converged in Washington under the banner of "Housing Now!" And since 1992, the National Coalition for the Homeless has been spreading the message "You Don't Need a Home to Vote" to disfranchised citizens everywhere.

These actions originated in the local anti-homelessness coalitions that proliferated during the 1980s. In July 1980, the Coalition for the Homeless was formed in New York City, and in the next two years, similar organizations took shape in Massachusetts, Atlanta, San Francisco, Phoenix, and Minneapolis/St. Paul. Allied efforts soon followed in Chicago, Columbus (and then throughout Ohio), Denver, Los Angeles, Richmond, Seattle, and Tucson. These built on the isolated efforts of the seventies, creating for the first time the possibility of nationwide activity. In April 1982, a group of advocates declared their intent to form a National Coalition for the Homeless (NCH), made real by an organizational meeting in Chicago a year and a half later. Executive directors Bob Hayes (in New York) and Maria Foscarinis (in Washington, DC) coordinated an advocacy effort on several fronts, including litigation, legislative work, and public education. By the early 1990s, thanks largely to country-wide organizing (chiefly by Michael Stoops), NCH represented advocates in virtually every state.

In 1989, Foscarinis left the National Coalition's Washington office to form a separate advocacy group, the National Law Center on Homelessness and Poverty (NLCHP). Along with NCH and NLCHP, the major forces in national antihomelessness advocacy have been the National Low-Income Housing Coalition, the National Housing Law Project, the Legal Services Homelessness Task Force, the U.S. Conference of Mayors, and the National Alliance to End Homelessness (see the appendix listing information clearinghouses, national organizations, and state organizations, at the end of this volume). Campus activists formed Students to End Homelessness (now, the National Student Campaign against Hunger and Homelessness) in the late 1980s, whose members have done direct service and advocacy in communities across the country.

Organizations of homeless people took shape as well—notably in San Francisco (1982) and Philadelphia (1983)—and a national Union of the Homeless was launched in 1985. By the end of 1988, it had established chapters in 14 cities. Local groups staged demonstrations, conducted strikes at mandatory work programs, organized marches, and engaged in mass sleep-ins to dramatize the plight of their members (see also Chapter 19).

In 1986, CCNV and NCH collaborated with nine other groups to draft a comprehensive relief bill, the Homeless Persons' Survival Act, to guide and give substance to a federal role in ending homelessness. The following spring, after a vigorous legislative campaign coordinated by Foscarinis and Snyder and a winter street vigil led by Snyder and Stoops—briefly joined by Congressional leaders and Hollywood celebrities—Congress approved a portion of that act; essentially, the emergency relief provisions. In July 1987, it was signed into law by a reluctant President Reagan as the Stewart B. McKinney Homeless Assistance Act. It was the first significant piece of federal antihomelessness legislation in 50 years. Between 1987 and 1994, appropriated funding for programs sponsored under McKinney increased tenfold, from $180 million to nearly $1.8 billion (see Chapter 15).

About This Volume

The present volume is a benefit for the National Coalition for the Homeless. All of the authors have contributed their royalties to further the Coalition's aim of public education. Indeed, this book is a form of public education, and as such, it is a form of claims-making about the nature of a social problem. It is not propaganda, however. The contributors are serious, fair-minded, and in many cases, skeptical veterans of years of research and/or advocacy.[8]

Moreover, although this book is written for citizens who are not scholars, it is not a "dumbed down" venture into McTruth. In fact, it is intended as an antidote to the oversimplification of homelessness, which though making the issue amenable to talk show chat, 10-second news clips, campaign rhetoric, and the pie charts beloved of bad newspapers, also conceals the real issues and impedes our ability to do anything meaningful about them. To understand homelessness and what to do about it, the contributors examine carefully not merely the characteristics of the homeless population, but the social and economic arrangements that shape individual experiences. While minimizing dense professional jargon and academic formulations, they have also taken care to avoid sentimentalism and oversimplification. Readers looking for lurid stories and easy solutions won't find them here.

The book is organized into three parts. The first, "History, Definitions, and Causes," includes chapters that address fundamental questions about homelessness: What is it? Have we seen it before? How many people might be considered homeless? Why does it happen? Chapter 1 offers a historically informed, theoretical interpretation of the ambiguous meaning of homelessness. Chapter 2 provides a discussion of definitions of homelessness used in research and puts the numerous and controversial estimates of the size of the homeless population in proper perspective. Chapter 3 discusses the complex and interrelated causes of homelessness and some common oversimplifications of them. Chapters 4 through 6 examine housing policy, employment, and income maintenance.

The second part of the book, "Dimensions of Homelessness," takes up social and demographic aspects of the problem. Chapter 7 summarizes the case of rural homelessness. Chapter

8 probes the economic logic of street life, discussing in detail how homeless people make do. Chapters 9 through 12 analyze homelessness among veterans, families, African Americans, and Latinos, teasing out common and distinctive features.

Finally, Part 3, "Responses to Homelessness," concerns public attitudes about homelessness, what we have done about it, and what we might do in the future. Chapter 13 reports the findings of public opinion surveys about homelessness. The authors reject on the evidence the notion that the citizenry's compassion has been "fatigued," a popular theme in national media. Their findings also refute the most recent calumny from the political right, which asserts that as a result of personal encounters with homeless people, the citizenry has decided that they are not worth helping.[9] In fact, public opinion is quite consistent with American charitable tradition: Americans want both social welfare and public order.

Following on this point, Chapter 14 examines the political and legal controversy over one form of social control, the regulation of public space. Chapter 15 provides a detailed history of the McKinney Act, the legislation that has guided the federal response to homelessness since 1987. Chapter 16 briefly describes the important features of states' responsibility. Chapter 17 takes up programmatic responses to homeless people with serious alcohol, drug, and/or mental health problems, and Chapter 18 analyzes approaches to preventing homelessness. Finally, Chapter 19 considers the circumstances of local antihomelessness movements—collectively, the backbone of activism and advocacy over the last 20 years.

Each chapter is meant to stand on its own, so that a reader interested in a particular subject will find a thorough treatment in one essay. At the same time, the book aims to be coherent from cover to cover and to have substantive integrity as a whole. Thus, numerous cross-references are provided to send curious readers to related discussions in other chapters or to chapters where similar points are considered in greater depth.

An Agenda for the Present and Future

If one theme unites the book, it is this: To end homelessness, we must reckon with poverty. While poverty is not all there is to homelessness, there is precious little homelessness without it.

Advocates have always understood this. From the beginning of the national antihomelessness movement, advocates have seen homelessness as "a symbolic Trojan horse in a renewed war on poverty."[10] At the same time, the explicit goals of the movement have not always reflected this understanding, and there are logical reasons for this. As Rosenthal points out in Chapter 19, local movements cannot achieve fundamental antipoverty goals because the resources and authority of local and state jurisdictions are limited, no matter how politically sympathetic such targets might be. Thus, circumscribed goals pertaining to shelter and relief from official harassment are in order. Similarly, because Reaganomics was in full sway by the advent of the national movement, advocates working at the federal level turned to a strategy of piecemeal, incremental reform focused on the right to shelter and the moral urgency of that claim. In the short run, it was remarkably successful, but the long-term effectiveness of this strategy is doubtful. Indeed, the large shelter industry in the United States alerts us to the failure of advocacy as much as it demonstrates its success.

The current political climate does not augur well for broad-gauge reform, however. As this book goes to press, universal health care remains a pipe dream; there is a declining commitment to low-income housing; welfare reform is balkanized and unsettled but likely will be a draconian affair; and no politically feasible increase in the minimum wage would approach achievement of a living wage. These days, rather than real work for real wages, public employment means the occupation of prisoners or desultory make-work, created to exact repayment from welfare mothers. Moreover, the looming devolution of political, administrative, and fiscal authority from the federal government to the states—and in some states, to the counties—likely will be a debacle for poor people. Most states have neither the tax bases, the fiscal mechanisms, the administrative capacities, nor the political inclination to provide equivalent services at the same standards. In sum, all of the conditions are right for continued dispossession, American style. The contributors to this volume light some lamps, but they should be excused when they curse the darkness.

But political circumstances notwithstanding, what does it make sense to do? The contributors to this book provide ample evidence of the pressing need for a broad set of policies to create livable incomes and decent, affordable housing. These seem like logical goals to pursue first if the aim is to reach the early twenty-first century without mass homelessness.

Because it provides support while simultaneously promoting interdependence and social order, *employment* is the best means to raise incomes. But as Hardin discusses in Chapter 5, it is very unlikely that the market will provide, anytime soon, living-wage jobs for all who need them. The problem of redundancy is most acute for those who do not graduate from high school or otherwise bring minimal human capital to the labor market. Given the myriad poverty-related problems that have turned parts of American cities into war zones and have filled prisons as fast as federal and state authorities can build them, it seems both just and prudent to invest considerable public funds in the creation of work for those whose modest or undeveloped talents might still be used to their own satisfaction and the benefit of society. A national program might create both training programs in and out of public school systems and living-wage jobs in housing construction, the repair of the country's decaying urban infrastructure, and personal care, to name but three areas that obviously need attention and can absorb large numbers of unskilled and semiskilled workers. Such a program would also have large potential benefits for civility and tolerance, for it would employ people frequently condemned as parasites at work of visible public value.

Even with an ambitious scheme of public job creation, *income maintenance* programs must provide a decent standard of living for those unable to work for short or long periods of time. As discussed in Chapter 6, and as evidence in other chapters bears out, the demographic shape of the homeless population owes a great deal to the coverage boundaries and benefit inadequacies of America's crazy quilt of income support programs. The disproportionate presence among homeless people of adults without children is testimony to the limits of General Assistance; the rarity of homeless people over 65 years old is mainly due to their eligibility for housing assistance, Social Security, Supplemental Security Income, Medicare, and Medicaid benefits. Categorical cutbacks in coverage—eliminating disability benefits based on addiction to alcohol or other drugs, hiking the age of eligibility for Social Security, or eliminating old-age benefits to elderly noncitizens, for instance—will affect what the homeless population looks like in the future. A federally administered system of guaranteed income, relying in part on a more generous Earned Income Tax Credit expanded to support adults without children (see Chapter 6, note 6), would be preferable to the current system of federal categorical aid and state and local General Assistance.

As Dolbeare makes clear in Chapter 4, America's largest *housing* program consists of tax benefits for homeowners. Such benefits represent 80% of federal housing expenditures, and in 1994 almost 80% of such benefits accrued to the top 20% of households—those with annual incomes over $60,600. Only 20% of lowest-quintile households (those with incomes under $13,100) got *any* housing support, whether in the form of tax benefits or housing assistance.

To address the problem of homelessness, housing assistance must be made far more widely available to those at the bottom of the income pyramid. The principles enunciated in the Federal Housing Trust Fund proposal summarized by Dolbeare are good guidelines. Simply put, they encourage an initial focus on very-low-income households with critical housing problems, and they recommend support for a variety of housing arrangements ranging from home ownership or cooperative membership to group tenancy or tenancy in a humble single-room-occupancy hotel. Determination of which mix of structural and household configurations best suits the needs of a given community is left to local planning processes.

There are numerous financial mechanisms by which to make housing assistance more widely available. It would be useful, for instance, to expand the role of secondary mortgage market institutions like Fannie Mae and Freddie Mac, utilize the Community Reinvestment Act to enhance private capital, and expand state and local housing trust funds and low-income housing tax credits. It would also be useful to pursue substantial "social ownership" of the housing stock. Although social ownership can involve public ownership (by housing authorities, for example), it can also involve ownership by nonprofits or by private individuals obligated to abide by strict resale provisions. Social ownership—currently practiced more widely in Canada than in the United States—intends to "decommodify" housing; that is, to limit or eliminate its handling as a product traded for profit. Social ownership intends to promote a combination of security of tenure, resident control, and affordability. It is a curb on speculation, not autonomy.[11]

Particularly in connection with social housing mechanisms, it would be wise to further develop systematic connections between funding streams in housing, health, mental health, and substance abuse treatment. Although the contributions of mental disorder and substance abuse to the creation of homelessness have been greatly overstated, particularly by those intent on framing homelessness as a problem of troubled and troublesome people, such contributions are not negligible (see Chapter 3). They are mediated by public policy, however. Whatever else was intended, the depopulation of state mental hospitals, the tightening of commitment laws, and the decriminalization of public drunkenness represented de facto changes in housing policy. Community care, a logical but hardly necessary consequence of such policies, has failed a great many people—not for lack of

imagination by its proponents, but as the result of a critical shortage of resources that combine housing and appropriate therapeutic support. Any sensible local housing mix must include such resources.

In Chapter 17, Oakley and Dennis review what seems to work with homeless people with severe mental illness and/or substance abuse, and any effective approach to rehousing them must heed such wisdom. Beyond this, however, it is important to view health and health care generally in the context of making a living and maintaining a home. The Health Care for the Homeless (HCH) program, which approaches its patients as people in environments, not merely as bodies with medical problems, has taught valuable lessons about what good health care can be: universally accessible (both financially and culturally), alert to profoundly important social aspects of care, and effectively embedded in a network of services through which nonmedical needs can be addressed quickly. Some HCH providers even operate housing and respite or hospice programs for patients with debilitating illnesses or conditions from which they cannot recover while living on the street or in shelters.

HCH is successful in some part because it is funded by a combination of federal grants and a Medicaid reimbursement formula based on actual costs and allowing for HCH's comprehensive approach. Thus, HCH is in a position to combine funds for what are generally considered medical and nonmedical purposes, including forms of therapeutically appropriate housing. Managed care arrangements, now becoming popular in many states as cheap mechanisms to provide health care to poor people, do not seem likely to foster such a useful approach. Short of establishing a comprehensive social medicine model based in public agencies (as partially realized in the Canadian province of Québec, for instance), it would seem wise to preserve at all levels of government grant mechanisms that encourage the widespread creation of social medicine programs by capable nonprofits.

In the end, raising the incomes of very poor people and making housing assistance more widely available would allow American cities to dismantle their systems of mass shelters and use the funds to support other forms of housing. Even so, new housing initiatives would require far more money than is currently available and almost certainly would entail some redistribution of housing benefits away from the well-to-do. A variety of proposals to do the latter have been floated, some of which cap the deductibility of mortgage interest based on the amount borrowed, some of which peg deductibility to income. Redistributive reforms of estate and property tax policies have also been suggested, and some housing analysts have recommended the use of public funds to promote unmortgaged social ownership.

But such proposals meet formidable opposition from elite interests far more powerful than antihomelessness advocates, particularly the National Association of Realtors and its local affiliates. The organized realtors view any limitation on mortgage interest deductibility as an assault on the middle class; they even opposed former Republican Senator Robert Packwood's modest 1995 plan to eliminate deductibility on any portion of a loan over $250,000—despite the fact that only a vanishingly small fraction of American households earn the six-figure income required to borrow such an amount at prevailing mortgage rates.

Appeal to a beleaguered middle class has become the rhetorical hallmark of contemporary American politics. But, in truth, what does the lifestyle of a family of four with an income of $120,000 per year have in common with a similar family living on $40,000 per year, which is, statistically speaking, the American middle? Not much. And yet, in the Orwellian world of politics, both are dubbed middle class, for in political parlance, middle class has no fixed sociological meaning, whether used as a noun or an adjective. The term does important political work, however: it legitimates the protection of broad constituent groups from redistributive assessments. Indeed, Republicans are truly ecumenical in this regard, inclined as they are to extend various "middle-class" tax benefits to families with annual incomes up to $200,000!

Many homeless people, no doubt, find great (if caustic) humor in this state of semantic affairs. And they have a message for the rest of us: A society can see its necessities clearly only when it calls things by their proper names.

Acknowledgments

Introductions to books customarily end on a personal note, and this one is no exception. This book has a tortuous history. It was conceived during the early months of the Clinton administration. Nearly complete, it was sidetracked by the 1994 Congressional elections, which threw social policy up for grabs for a protracted period. As a result, some chapters were completely rewritten, others were substantially revised, and all were revisited to be sure they were current. Given this history, being the editor has been quite a ride. That the long process has been fun, as well as demanding and occasionally frustrating, says a lot about the intelligence, forbearance, and humor of the people involved.

This volume was originally planned to include several essays that do not appear, due to considerations of length and timing. The National Coalition for the Homeless intends to publish that material in a separate volume. The topics concern homelessness among Native Americans, older people, and juveniles on their own; shelters; the legal regulation of shelters; and health care for homeless people, along with a fuller treatment of rural homelessness. Thanks are owed to Louisa Stark, Carl Cohen, Marjorie Robertson, Russell Schutt, Martha Fleetwood, Minouche Kandel, Matthew Menes, Charmaine Panikar, Kevin Stein, Wayne Anderson, and John Lozier for their valuable contributions on these subjects.

I also want to thank the organizations that made this project possible. First of all, the National Coalition for the Homeless hired me to edit this book and then let me do it without interference. A grant to the National Coalition from The Melville Charitable Trust allowed me to give up summer work to tend the editing. The Bryn Mawr College Graduate School of Social Work and Social Research gave the project a woodsy home complete with copier, telephone, fax machine, and e-mail. My own research has been generously encouraged by The Lindesmith Center and faculty grants from Bryn Mawr College and McGill University.

Money solves a lot of problems, but I owe equally important if less tangible debts to those who commented on manuscripts and provided intellectual and technical support of one kind or another: Anita Beaty, David Beriss, Gary Blasi, Callie Cole, John Donahue, Barbara Duffield, Kai Erikson, Mary Ann Gleason, Joel Handler, Dana Harris, Fred Karnas, Julia Littell, Gloria Marti, Beverly Merrill, Sue Watlov Phillips, Louisa Stark, Michael Stoops, Anne Thompson, Nancy Travers, and Matias Vega. Elizabeth Welsh, the book's editor at Oryx Press, was unfailingly smart, witty, and sympathetic. My friend and intellectual running buddy, Kim Hopper, is coeditor of this book in all but name. Truth be told, though, I am responsible for whatever is wrongheaded or inelegant about it.

Finally—Smitty, Jake, and Chris: It's finished, guys. Time to play.

Jim Baumohl
May 1996

CONTRIBUTORS

· · · · · · ·

Leon Anderson, Ph.D., is an associate professor of sociology at Ohio University, Athens, Ohio. He is coauthor (with David A. Snow) of *Down on Their Luck: A Study of Homeless Street People,* and he has written numerous articles on various aspects of homelessness. Dr. Anderson has served as a research fellow for the Ohio Department of Mental Health and is currently involved in ethnographic research on social service agencies.

Laudan Y. Aron works for the Urban Institute in Washington, DC. Her research interests span a wide range of social welfare subjects; currently she is studying how child welfare agencies address domestic violence. Her book, *Serving Children with Disabilities: A Systematic Look at the Programs,* was recently published by the Urban Institute Press. Ms. Aron holds a master's degree in demography from the University of Pennsylvania.

Susan González Baker is an assistant professor of sociology at the University of Texas at Austin and a research affiliate at the UT Population Research Center. She specializes in the demography of homelessness, international migration, and social policy analysis. She is currently analyzing policy responses to undocumented immigration in Spain and the United States, and the place of Mexican immigrant and U.S.-born women in urban Southwestern labor markets.

Jim Baumohl is an associate professor in the Graduate School of Social Work and Social Research at Bryn Mawr College. Between 1970 and 1986 he was, among other things, a street worker, a shelter director, and an organizer of single-room-occupancy hotel tenants. He has written about homelessness since 1973. Professor Baumohl holds a doctorate in social welfare from the University of California, Berkeley.

Michaeline Bresnahan is a doctoral candidate in the Division of Epidemiology at Columbia University. She is interested in posttraumatic stress disorder and in the implications of expanding knowledge about genetic risks for disease on the lives of people found to be at such risk.

M. Audrey Burnam holds a Ph.D. in social psychology from the University of Texas at Austin.

She is a senior behavioral scientist and codirects the Drug Policy Research Center at RAND, a nonprofit policy analysis and research institution in Santa Monica, California. She is also a visiting professor to the Department of Psychiatry at the University of Arkansas for Medical Sciences. Dr. Burnam has been involved in mental health and substance abuse research for over 15 years.

Martha R. Burt, Ph.D., is the director of the Social Services Research Program at the Urban Institute in Washington, DC. She received her doctorate in sociology in 1972 from the University of Wisconsin-Madison and has done research in a variety of areas. Her work on homelessness began in 1983. She is the author of *America's Homeless: Numbers, Characteristics, and the Programs that Serve Them*, and *Over the Edge: The Growth of Homelessness in the 1980s*.

An-Me Chung, Ph.D., is a postdoctoral fellow at the School of Public Health of Columbia University and director of research and evaluation at the Yale Bush Center in Social Policy and Child Development. She has done research on women, work, and stress.

Daniel Cress, Ph.D., is an assistant professor of sociology at the University of Colorado at Boulder. He and David A. Snow are currently examining mobilization campaigns among the homeless across a number of American cities. His research interests encompass marginalized groups, their political responses to their marginalization, and the organizations relevant to them.

Deborah L. Dennis, M.A., is a senior research associate with Policy Research Associates in Delmar, NY, and the director of the National Resource Center on Homelessness and Mental Illness, which is operated by PRA under contract to the federal Center for Mental Health Services. For the past six years, she has both coordinated and provided technical assistance to the Center for Mental Health Services and the National Institute of Mental Health demonstration projects for homeless people with serious mental illnesses.

Cushing N. Dolbeare began her housing career in 1952 with the Baltimore Citizens Planning and Housing Association and spent 15 years with the Housing Association of Delaware Valley (formerly the Philadelphia Housing Association). She has been a consultant on housing and public policy since 1971, and is the founder of the National Low Income Housing Coalition and its sister organization, the Low Income Housing Information Service. She was executive of those organizations from 1977 to 1984, and from 1993 to 1994. She has also served as interim director of the National Coalition for the Homeless and as executive director of the National Rural Housing Coalition.

Kai T. Erikson is a professor of sociology and American studies at Yale University and author of several books, the most recent being *A New Species of Trouble: Explorations in Disaster, Trauma, and Community*. He is past-president of the American Sociological Association.

Janet M. Fitchen, Ph.D., was a cultural anthropologist who concentrated on the rural United States. She was the author of two books on rural America, a member of several national and state advisory boards on rural poverty, and a consultant to numerous social agencies. After teaching for many years in the anthropology department of Ithaca College, she joined the Department of Rural Sociology at Cornell University. Professor Fitchen died in the spring of 1995.

Maria Foscarinis, M.A., J.D., is the founder and executive director of the National Law Center on Homelessness and Poverty. She has been active in legal issues affecting homeless people since 1984. She was a primary advocate for major legislation affecting homeless people, including the Stewart B. McKinney Homeless Assistance Act, and has litigated to enforce legal rights of homeless persons. Before founding the Law Center, Ms. Foscarinis established and directed the Washington, DC, office of the National Coalition for the Homeless.

Linda K. Frisman, Ph.D., is an associate director of the Northeast Program Evaluation Center, and the Project Director for the Evaluation of the Department of Veterans Affairs' Health Care for Homeless Veterans Programs. She is also an associate research scientist in the Department of Psychiatry, Yale University School of Medicine. She is a mental health services researcher specializing in cost-effectiveness analysis.

Mark H. Greenberg is a senior staff attorney at the Center for Law and Social Policy (CLASP) in Washington, DC. CLASP is a national nonprofit organization focusing on issues pertaining to family poverty. Prior to joining CLASP in 1988, Mr. Greenberg represented low-income clients on a broad range of public benefits matters at the Western Center on Law and Poverty in California and Jacksonville Area Legal Aid in Florida. Mr. Greenberg is a graduate of Harvard Law School.

Bristow Hardin received his Ph.D. in sociology from the University of California, Santa Cruz. He has worked for advocacy organizations at the state and national levels and is now with the Legal Services Corporation in Washington, DC. He is the author of numerous analyses of U.S. economic, budgetary, and military spending policies.

Kim Hopper is a medical anthropologist who works as a research scientist at Nathan S. Kline Institute for Psychiatric Research and lectures at the Columbia University School of Public Health. Since 1979, he has conducted ethnographic and historical research on homelessness, chiefly in New York City. A cofounder of both the New York Coalition for the Homeless and the National Coalition for the Homeless, he served as president of the latter organization from 1991 to 1993.

Paul Koegel holds a Ph.D. in anthropology from the University of California, Los Angeles. He is a behavioral scientist at RAND, a nonprofit policy analysis and research institution in Santa Monica, California, where he currently directs a study of public sector service use among homeless adults in Houston, Texas. For the last 15 years, his research has concerned the community adaptation of socially and economically marginal populations in urban settings.

Julie A. Lam, Ph.D., is an associate director of the Northeast Program Evaluation Center and project director of the client-level national evaluation of the Access to Community Care and Effective Supports and Services Program of the federal Center for Mental Health Services. A sociologist, she coauthored the national report on the Robert Wood Johnson-sponsored Health Care for the Homeless program.

Catherine A. Leda, M.S.N., M.P.H., is an associate director of the Northeast Program Evaluation Center and project director of the Evaluation of VA Domiciliary Care programs, Work Therapy programs, and Veterans Benefits Outreach programs at the Department of Veterans Affairs in West Haven, Connecticut. She is also an associate research scientist in the Department of Psychiatry, Yale University School of Medicine. She has authored many articles about homeless veterans.

Eric N. Lindblom, a policy analyst and writer based in New York City, was formerly Deputy Special Assistant on Homelessness to U.S. Department of Veterans Affairs Secretary Jesse Brown. He authored the federal government's 1990 and 1991–1992 reports on the federal response to homelessness.

Bruce G. Link is an associate professor of public health at Columbia University and a research scientist at New York State Psychiatric Institute. His interests include the consequences of stigma for people with mental illness and the effects of socioeconomic inequality on health.

Norweeta G. Milburn is an assistant professor of psychology at Hofstra University. She holds a Ph.D. in community psychology from the University of Michigan in Ann Arbor.

Robert E. Moore is a research scientist at New York State Psychiatric Institute. His current research, on a project funded by the National Institute of Mental Health, involves the analysis of children and adolescents' need for and use of mental health services.

Deirdre Oakley, M.A., is a research associate for the National Resource Center on Homelessness and Mental Illness, operated by Policy Research Associates of Delmar, NY, under contract to the federal Center for Mental Health Services. She holds a master's degree in urban geography and serves as an adjunct lecturer at the State University of New York at Albany.

Jo C. Phelan is an assistant professor of sociology at the University of Southern California. Her research interests include homelessness, social stigma, and attitudes about the legitimacy of inequality.

Theron Quist, Ph.D., is an assistant professor of sociology at Bowling Green (Ohio) State University. He is currently engaged in research on crime among homeless people, and on the relationship between homelessness and police work. His research interests include attribution processes and their relevance for social policy, and the relationship between power and justice in society.

Robert Rosenheck, M.D., is the director of the Veterans Administration's Northeast Program Evaluation Center and a clinical professor of psychiatry at Yale Medical School. Dr. Rosenheck has conducted studies of the causes of homelessness among veterans, and outcome studies of a variety of programs for homeless persons. He also has studied the causes of post-traumatic stress disorder among Vietnam veterans and has evaluated the cost-effectiveness of specialized programs for veterans with a variety of mental health problems.

Rob Rosenthal, Ph.D., is an associate professor and chair of the sociology department at Wesleyan University and is the author of *Homeless in Paradise* (1994). He was a founder and member of the Santa Barbara Homeless Coalition from 1983 to 1987. He is working on a book (with Dick Flacks) on the use of music in social movements.

Marybeth Shinn, Ph.D., is a professor of psychology at New York University and associate editor of the *American Journal of Community Psychology*. With Beth C. Weitzman, and with funding from the National Institute of Mental Health, she is conducting a five-year longitudinal study of homelessness among public assistance families in New York City. She has authored or coauthored a number of articles on homeless families, and was a member of the American Psychological Association Advisory Panel on Homelessness.

Harry Simon is a staff attorney with the National Health Law Program in Los Angeles, and coordinator of the Criminalization Working Group of the Legal Services Homelessness Task Force. He was previously staff attorney at the Legal Aid Society of Orange County, California, and served as lead counsel in a series of lawsuits against the City of Santa Ana, challenging that city's efforts to drive out its homeless residents.

David A. Snow, Ph.D., is a professor of sociology at the University of Arizona, Tucson. He is coauthor (with Leon Anderson) of *Down on Their Luck: A Study of Homeless Street People,* and has written numerous articles on various aspects of homelessness, on social movements and collective behavior, on religious conversion, and on ethnographic research methods. Dr. Snow is a former president of the Society for the Study of Symbolic Interaction, and is president-elect of the Pacific Sociological Association. He is also vice-president of the Primavera Foundation in Tucson, a nonprofit organization that provides a range of services for the homeless.

Elmer L. Struening is the director of the Epidemiology of Mental Disorders Research Department, New York State Psychiatric Institute. His research has focused on epidemiological surveys of residents of shelters for homeless adults, the evaluation of treatment programs for people with mental illness, and on the influence of attitudes toward mental illness on the welfare and behavior of people with mental disorders.

Ann Stueve is an assistant professor of public health at Columbia University. Her research interests include the relationships among stress, social support, and psychopathology, and the impact of mental illness on family caregivers.

Vicki Watson is a program associate with the Council of State Community Development Agencies. Her position involves assisting executives of state executive community development agencies through technical assistance and advocacy on various housing issues. She holds a master's degree in public administration from George Mason University.

Beth C. Weitzman, Ph.D., is an associate professor of public health administration at New York University's Wagner Graduate School. Her research has focused on the health and social services needs of urban poor families. With Marybeth Shinn, she coedited a 1990 issue of the *Journal of Social Issues* entitled "Urban Homelessness." Dr. Weitzman has authored or coauthored a number of articles on homeless families.

PART
1
· · · · · · · · · ·

HISTORY, DEFINITIONS, AND CAUSES

CHAPTER 1

Redefining the Cursed Word: A Historical Interpretation of American Homelessness

Kim Hopper
Jim Baumohl

> *"Home" has become such a scattered, damaged, various concept in our present travails.*
> *There is so much to yearn for. . . . How hard can we expect even a pair of magic shoes to work?*
> *They promised to take us home, but . . . will they permit us to redefine the blessed word?*
> —Salman Rushdie, "At the Auction of the Ruby Slippers"

INTRODUCTION

Americans have used the word "homeless" in something like its modern sense for roughly 150 years. Most often, its meaning is literal and prosaic: the absence of a domicile. Thus, we employ it to describe those sleeping outdoors in any of a variety of makeshifts, or residing in temporary accommodations like the police-station lodgings of earlier generations or the emergency shelters of the present day. But we also invoke the word to indicate something poignant and diffuse: the absence of belonging, both to a place and with the people settled there. In this sense, we sometimes call homeless those who are just passing through, or who, like exiles and guest workers, are never quite at home where they live.

Thus, homelessness is a term that covers a big territory. Indeed, as we reviewed the record of the past, we were struck by the disparate phenomena indexed by the term at one time or another. It seems that homelessness is at best an odd-job word, pressed into service to impose order on a hodgepodge of social dislocation, extreme poverty, seasonal or itinerant work, and unconventional ways of life. Moreover, it is often employed, as a matter of bureaucratic expedience, to describe the clientele of institutions intended to settle homeless people. And, to complicate matters further, the poor historically—and their homeless contemporaries, in particular—make use of relief institutions in ways that may be quite at odds with the official rationale for their existence.[1]

These definition problems are well known; however, discussion usually ends with their acknowledgment, or, as Martha Burt takes up in Chapter 2, with certain operational compromises. Thus, the esteemed sociologist Peter Rossi writes of homelessness: "It is easy to get bogged down in academic exercises in definition. I will resist the temptation." Then, like other analysts, he proceeds to use the word to cover a variety of historical stations, circumstances, practices, and accounting devices.[2] At the risk of running a fool's errand, we will yield to the temptation. In our view, to subsume such an array under the rubric of homelessness is to emphasize a surface commonality that fails to do justice to the miscellany beneath. With a nod to Salman Rushdie, we attempt in this essay to redefine the *cursed* word.[3]

To do so, we borrow two concepts from anthropology and historical sociology—liminality and abeyance, respectively—that force us to move away from surface appearance in favor of more essential underlying processes. Although we raid the past for evidence, we aim less for a comprehensive historical narrative than for a theoretically coherent account that may prove useful to understanding both the past and the present. We begin by outlining our theoretical scheme. Then we provide a short narrative of American homelessness to put flesh on its bones. In the last sections of the chapter, we develop further our interpretation of what homelessness means, or, perhaps more accurately, we try to track "what the term *does*, given its ambiguity."[4]

THEORETICAL FRAMEWORK: LIMINALITY AND ABEYANCE

Liminality (from the Latin word for threshold) is a term anthropologists use for a variety of *states of passage*, through which designated members of a given culture travel at specified times.[5] For the duration of passage, such people are "betwixt and between," suspended between the familiar social niche they have left behind and the one they have yet to assume. Because they occupy no fixed status in the liminal state, they are considered ambiguous beings—even dangerous—and their presence is subject to ritual regulation. Special precautions are taken to separate them from ordinary social life. Deputized "guides" (who have already made the passage) are on hand to expedite the process and safeguard its completion.

Initiation rites are one such transition. Often undertaken in secret or in ritually segregated settings, these ordeals mark the initiates for life and certify their passage to adulthood. Other critical transitions—entering marriage, assuming leadership, taking religious vows, apprenticing in a profession—often are similarly regulated by ritual. One other feature deserves mention here: during the liminal period, the usual markers of social distinction among participants are erased. Such leveling, coupled with the experience of shared ordeal, makes possible intense group solidarity. But no matter how rigorous the ordeal or sublime the solidarity, the expectation of return to ordinary life and a settled status is implicit in the process.

The ascription of liminality can be extended to the situation of others who temporarily remove themselves from the sway of conventional demands. Pilgrimages, religious retreats, secular festivals, even wilderness treks partake of similar "time out." Crises, too, can exempt from ordinary demands. Consider the suspension of routine that follows natural disasters (epidemics, floods), civil disturbances (wars, revolutions), or private misfortunes (a death in the family). Even sickness has been analyzed as a liminal state. They all share a suspension of the commonplace; intermingling with unfamiliar others in strange settings; and a heightened sense of uncertainty, of things being unfinished and in process.

Although liminal passages are usually undertaken in well-mapped territory from which the voyager is expected to return, *occasionally the process stalls*. For a variety of reasons, the liminal period of being betwixt and between can become extended. If this liminal period becomes sufficiently long, we may see the expectation of return (both by voyagers and those who wait) give way to *the routinization of displacement*. A kind of forgetfulness sets in; the becalmed voyager is set aside, and liminality becomes institutionalized in its own right. What began as a temporary moratorium on business as usual is transformed over time into another way of life, a status understood to be potentially long lasting by its occupants and by others—though defined as an anomaly, fit only for misfits. Refugee camps, established in the wake of civil war, are a common contemporary instance of how displacement can be routinized without recreating homes.[6] The bands of "wandering scholars" who roved the medieval countryside are a colorful but more distant example. Having taken minor orders in the church but unable to secure employment as tutors, they turned to the minstrel life. In exchange for the hospitality of accommodating abbots, they performed ribald parodies of liturgical hymns—to the amusement of their hosts and the distress of the established Church, which eventually cracked down on the practice.[7]

Such routinization of displacement creates a social and cultural *limbo*, a place of forgotten confinement supposed by Catholic theologians to be situated on the border of hell—and not without reason. Indeed, the pain was singular because limbo was an invention of logic, not justice: it was reserved for those anomalous souls, born too soon in history (admirable pagans) or dying too early in life (unbaptized infants), to whom the usual options of final judgment did not apply. Put bluntly, limbo was a celestial holding mechanism.[8]

Liminality refers to the sometimes perilous passage from one social "status slot" to another; *abeyance*, on the other hand, has to do with the absolute scarcity of status slots in a given society at some time.[9] Specifically, when there are too few social positions available to accommodate the potential claimants, various mechanisms (abeyance measures) are devised to provide supplemental status slots to absorb the surplus. Whether these surrogate occupations are provided under the auspices of the state (frontier settlements, public works, compulsory education), the church (monasteries, breakaway religious orders), or even countercultural groups (communal experiments), the effect is the same. Such measures provide for—and control—redundant people who, in their restive idleness, might undermine public order. Abeyance measures work by providing forms of livelihood devised to be materially uncompetitive with the marketplace, though not on that account unproductive. Their "value" ranges from the strictly utilitarian to the manifestly symbolic.

In contemporary American society, abeyance measures exist in a variety of forms and degrees of completeness. The simplest and most fragmentary measures constitute what is now commonly called the "safety net": the income maintenance programs intended to provide a minimum subsistence to the poor or unemployed whose labor is not required or is grossly under-remunerated in the market. But more powerful and effective abeyance measures exist, too; these provide enveloping social roles—even, sometimes, whole communities—to absorb surplus people. In these robust forms, abeyance mechanisms establish not merely where people will sleep at night, but what they will do once the sun is up. Equally important, such measures attend to the restraining (or "social control") effects of the company in which such activities are performed. Abeyance measures reckon not only with subsistence, but with the social order produced by interdependence. Thus, in its more robust forms, abeyance links the domains of labor, housing, and community. The fire-fighting camps established in California during the late 1920s, the Civilian Conservation Corps (CCC) and many projects of the Works Progress Administration (WPA) of the 1930s, or today's Job Corps are examples of such measures. Whatever their differences, these government projects, along with countercultural communes and standing armies, have in common this feature of *completeness*—the provision of an encompassing way of life.[10]

Let us now put these two concepts in working order. Liminality refers to a state of transition from one status slot to another in a society. It is a guided passage from one set of activities and responsibilities to another, and the voyager expects to complete it. Indeed, it is in the interest of the whole society that this passage be successful, for extended liminality results in people without a settled relationship to the social order. As outsiders, such ambiguous people, individually or collectively, are unpredictable and even dangerous.

And yet, the passage stalls on occasion, and when it does, intervention is necessary. Liminal persons must not be left betwixt and between: either they must be rerouted toward an alternative outcome, or the liminal state must be incorporated into the social order. When a particular state of liminality is routinized, abeyance enters the play: abeyance mechanisms may create status slots to resolve stalled liminality; or, they may serve, in effect, to institutionalize the passage as an alternative way of life in itself. Abeyance measures reckon with liminality gone wrong, as well as with an absolute scarcity of status slots. *We will argue that what unites the phenomena gathered up in the term homelessness is liminality (resolved or stalled) and abeyance gone awry.*

A BRIEF NARRATIVE OF HOMELESSNESS IN AMERICA

In what follows, we track the shifting contours of American homelessness. We pay particular attention to the stability of the state or transitional status at issue; its visibility and the cultural reception accorded it; the degree to which it is formally recognized, even institutionalized as an alternative lifeway or accepted transition; and, where possible, whether it represents the direct result of unexpected misfortune, the strategic use of an earmarked resource, or the predictable by-product of uncertain livelihood. Such a reckoning will necessarily capture a wide range of utilities, auspices, and coherencies. Some break, others embody statute. Some defy, others enforce convention. Some cater to outcasts, others cope with superfluous souls.

Vagrancy in the Pre-industrial Era

Colonial American poor relief was a jumble. It mixed local and county control, appealed to canonical and secular authority, and tapped church collections as well as disbursements from public treasuries. But however patchwork the apparatus of relief, few went begging. When family resources failed or proved insufficient in times of especially demanding need, community members anted up; religious duty and frontier solidarity demanded provision for those who could not provide for themselves. Such an arrangement proved adequate so long as numbers remained small and settlements stable. But as 16th-century Europe had learned, a large and mobile needy population could easily overwhelm the capacities of casual relief. In America, as well, local custom proved unequal to the demands of circulating strangers whose numbers grew steadily.

In the late 17th century, for example, New York City, in concert with local churches, rented a building for use as emergency housing for kinless—and otherwise homeless—residents. In 1734, the city erected a formal almshouse whose residents were considered members of a substitute "family," and whose responsibilities were detailed in the posted rules of the house.[11] However, not all the needy were seen as deserving; vagrants and slaves in particular were of dubious worth in the social calculus of colonial culture. Even so, runaway slaves no less than the kinless poor were frequent occupants of such catchall facilities as the original almshouses. "Here," as one historian put it tersely, "slaves were kept for correction, and the very poor sheltered."[12]

From the outset, then, the structural response to "homelessness" betrays what a later analyst called a "hybrid" character.[13] "Transgression" (here, both outlaw fugitive slaves and suspect rootless men) mixes under a single roof with "simple need" (the penniless poor who lacked friends or family). The almshouse took on a host of custody and care responsibilities that had previously been widely (and informally) distributed throughout the community. It nursed the terminally ill, took in the deranged and disabled, put up deserted children and newly arrived strangers and—not infrequently—punished those whose behavior fell outside the jurisdiction of penal institutions. Into so broad a compass fell not only the luckless and the criminal, but also (if only for short periods of "Hard Labour") "friendless laboring people and vagabonds."[14]

It isn't long before relief gives way to rehabilitation, and a grudging eye settles upon those who would live on the bounty of local government. By the end of the 18th century, a complaint is raised that will recur throughout the following century and extend well into our own: that the poorhouse is rife with fraud. According to the New York Common Council of 1789, it had become "too much a common receptacle for idle, intemperate vagrants, many of whom have no lawful residence," people who "by pretended illness or otherwise" displace the proper objects of charity.[15] As time passed, similar concerns were expressed from Boston to Chicago. A century later and a continent away, the San Francisco almshouse was described as a "free hotel" catering to "men who for years past have never done a stroke of work or earned an hon-est dollar, but whose time has been passed be-tween begging on our streets, guzzling in our whiskey dens and fattening in our Almshouse."[16]

By the 1840s, idleness had become abhor-rent to almshouse keepers, as befits the manag-ers of a fully encompassing abeyance mech-anism, and efforts were made repeatedly to find ways to occupy the residents usefully. This proved easier to advocate than to achieve. Household chores and simple subsistence labor were one thing; attempts to contract out pau-per labor, or to turn it to productive effect in public works projects, were quite another. Like convict labor later in the century, pauper labor was regularly opposed by "free labor." Nor was it true that the almshouse held vast reserves of untapped labor. Many of its residents were mothers with children, or were elderly or dis-abled—people for whom work outside the home was impractical.[17]

In any event, neither the almshouse nor any facility subsequently set up to harbor the indi-gent managed to solve the problem of people whose predicament could not be neatly classi-fied, let alone those who preferred to slip the strictures of official relief altogether. Belonging nowhere, their stake in the social order was unclear and their claim to material support sus-pect. Benighted paupers; the insane poor; the hapless victims of illness, addiction, desertion or old age: for surplus populations such as these, the almshouse and its satellite facilities (bridewells, asylums, inebriate institutions) were well suited (if meanly appointed). Accidents of nature, victims of neglect and cruelty whose burden of support wore out the resources of kin—these could be accommodated. But more elusive groups—casualties of uncertain labor markets, frontier workers, wandering fortune-hunters, confidence men, and defiant tramps: the whole ragtag collection that came to be known as homeless after the mid-19th century and wore the label well into the 20th—these proved more troublesome. By the 1870s, an entire culture was experiencing the sustained dislocations brought on by a civil war and a nascent industrial order. Many would be left by

the wayside; not a few would choose to make their own way, however humbly.

Industrialization, Urbanization, and Homelessness

In the first half of the 19th century, the rela-tively stable coincidence of livelihood, family, and place still provided a basis for community and social order, and nurtured local traditions of mutual aid and regulation of troublesome behavior. Whether by intention or tricks of for-tune (or a mischievous combination of the two), homeless people fell outside this web of sup-port and control. They were "unsettled," lacked critical moral as well as material anchors, and were best dealt with by being relocated to parts elsewhere. It was not simply the burden of sup-port they posed, it was the message they sent. Visible, abrasive, intrusive, defiant—or merely unsettling in the nakedness of their need—their existence called into question the promise of social harmony and material progress.

Nineteenth-century Americans understood homelessness to reflect the declining cohesive-ness of their society; it signified the splintering forces of modernity. Although colonial-era sea-ports had their share of mobility, an explosion of migration was ignited in the early 19th cen-tury by rapid population growth, innovations in transportation, the diffusion of production for markets, the rise of waged employment, and the relentless extension of the frontier. By mid-century, novel economic vulnerabilities and opportunities had created a new logic of liveli-hood for many common citizens that was at odds with community stability. Indeed, economic expansion and modernization demanded legions of rootless workers. Pioneering required pio-neers—swarms of unsettled men, women, and families. Early industrialization was rife with hard, dirty work in far-flung regions, and thus itinerant men dug canals, built levees, laid track, cut timber, punched cattle, and worked mines. With the westward spread of wheat and cotton and the growth of large-scale agriculture, men, women, and families together followed the har-vest, forming battalions of pickers, threshers, and cannery workers from coast to coast. Late in the century, the Alaskan salmon fisheries absorbed thousands of workers each spring, only to disgorge them in the autumn. As opportunities for farm work declined for women after the Civil War, and as the demand for labor in booming, exciting cities rose, rural young women moved cityward to become servants, factory workers, sales clerks, and secretaries. Some sang, danced, and waited tables or tended bar in beer halls and honky-tonks, and some became prostitutes. For all of these people, home was where—for the time being—they hung their hats.

By the mid-19th century, burgeoning American cities were worlds of unreliable strangers "on the make" (as the contemporary expression had it). Cities were bustling, atomized, anonymous, licentious, and their inhabitants moved in and moved on with startling frequency. Those attempting to reckon with these circumstances—the men and women who first named the condition of homelessness—were concerned not merely with poverty, crime, and viciousness, but with recreating in the city the stability and moral order of the village.[18]

But American culture has never been known for uniformity, and the dislocations of the latter part of the 19th century also were interpreted as the rude hearths on which opportunity and freedom could be forged by the wily and intrepid. Upheaval and moral peril were understood by some as concomitants of progress, even necessary tests of individual and national character. "Tramps" and their frontier counterparts found some refuge in a long-standing romantic strain in the interpretation of American homelessness. The Maine logger, the California forty-niner, and the Southwestern cowboy quickly became the stuff of legend. By World War I, the "new" woman who worked and lived on her own was no longer portrayed as a "woman adrift," an "innocent and weak" victim, "torn from the protective shelter" of rural and small-town family and community life and "exposed to the muscle of the city." She had become a familiar and even admirably sophisticated urbanite who could take care of herself.[19]

The attractions of tramping should be noted. For men at least, the road was an equal opportunity employer. Confirmed veterans of the tramp, men who chose to work on their own terms while dodging the discipline of the factory and shop floor, mixed with men whose jobs required frequent moves and rootlessness (the gandy dancers, canal diggers, and bridge workers who built the transportation infrastructure, for example). But the road also drew men who were at loose ends, happy to postpone hard decisions about livelihood. For most in this latter group, tramping was a late adolescent adventure, even an unofficial rite of passage, before assuming the usual settled way of life.[20] But for some, this transitional period was extended. Whether from enthusiasm for an eventful life and colorful company, or aimlessly, after disappointment with failed jobs and marriages, these men persisted in a footloose way of life on the margins of established society. Anti-tramp publications and the proceedings of many conferences in the field of "charities and corrections" were filled with warnings about the siren call of the road.

Here, then, is an example of *liminality stalled*. Like their medieval counterparts—the permanent pilgrims and shifting miscellany of traveling tradesmen who perfected "wayfaring as a way of life"[21]—late-19th-century tramping assembled a motley mix of people in sometimes tumultuous transition: demobilized soldiers and emancipated slaves,[22] disillusioned workers unwilling to buckle to the time demands and discipline of the new industrial order, stubborn practitioners of vanishing skills (umbrella repair, for instance), and venturesome adolescents lured, like young Jack London, by the novelty and danger of it all. Of such material was the turn-of-the-century, semi-outlaw category of "tramp" composed.

Similarly, makeshift institutions may be set up to handle mundane liminality—accommodations intended for those *temporarily* betwixt and between—only to become permanent fixtures on the urban landscape as the need persists. (That this is a commonplace in our day, when Red Cross "disaster response offices" have evolved into substantial providers of contracted shelter services in many municipalities, hardly needs argument.) Take, for example, police-station lodgings. These were typically a room set aside in the precinct house for holding transients overnight. Officially endorsed virtually everywhere in the mid-19th century, they rapidly developed into the de facto shelter system of that time, housing the temporarily stranded or newly arrived stranger, as well as the inebriated and chronically vagrant.[23] Steady users effectively converted these improvised quarters into satellite units of the almshouse (that is, into another abeyance measure). And yet, as if to erase evidence that a new facility had been created (let alone that a serious problem required attention), the rooms were closed and hosed down each morning when the sun rose.

Casualties of the Industrial Juggernaut

After about 1890, social reformers began to rapidly discard traditional arrangements based on sentiment in favor of business-like systems of "scientific" intervention. In this climate of rationalized innovation, municipal lodging houses proliferated as the preferred public alternative to the "indiscriminate aid" of police-station lodgings, especially in larger cities where the ranks of both transients and "scientific philanthropy" were concentrated. But despite brave hopes and ambitious plans, municipal lodging houses (like their improvised predecessors) soon proved vulnerable to the separate agendas of both their users and sister institutions. Unaccountably, institutional castoffs—people who, by the logic of professional classification, "belonged" in specialized care facilities—began to show up, dispatched as nuisances by other keepers.[24] So did men whose only (and unanswerable) "complaint" was that they could find no sustained work: lack of shelter led them to seek public assistance, but it was for want of work that they were in such straits to begin with. In times of industrial depression, too, demand for shelter easily outstripped supply, and large numbers of people (reaching well into the thousands in New York City) took to sleeping "rough" (in saloons, on docks, in public waiting rooms, on

the streets, even in garbage dumps). From these and other signs, it was clear that the new abeyance mechanism was overtaxed.

Nor were matters improved much during the Great Depression, when police-station lodgings were revived in cities that had not employed the practice for years, and when the largest "warehouse" shelters ever seen in the country were added to the inventory. (Philadelphia had one that held over 4,000 men.) Once again, unemployment found expression as lack of shelter, in the main to be treated as though homelessness were the only concern. There were, of course, exceptions: the CCC camps, referred to earlier; some WPA projects; the short-lived Federal Transient Program (1933–1935), which had preceded both; and in western states, particularly California, state or joint state and federal work camps for single men (1932–1941). (Beginning in 1936, the federal Farm Security Administration also operated camps for migrant families.) But for the most part, homeless men proved as much the disposable advance corps of work relief projects as they had been the ignorable vanguard of the unemployment problem. Deployed by Eleanor Roosevelt, for example, to demonstrate the feasibility of small construction projects (they built lodges and trails in a New York State park), they succeeded so well that they worked themselves out of contention. Subsequent projects, like most work relief before the Depression, were restricted to local ("resident") men with families. Only the more isolated and demanding work sites would draw upon transient, unattached men. Indeed, whether in the California fire-fighting camps first opened in the late 1920s, or similar nationwide projects of the New Deal, the use of single, drifting men to do work in far-flung locations was praised as a boon to them and to the good order of communities.[25]

Forgotten Men

Just as preparation for World War I closed the books on an unruly period of widespread homelessness between 1913 and 1916, mobilization for World War II all but emptied the shelters and relief offices of the 1930s, leaving behind only the elderly and seriously disabled. By late 1942, there was so little slack in employment that the Kaiser shipyards in Richmond, California, accepted a busload of 74 "skid road sherry winos" from the Los Angeles County Jail to be trained as welders in lieu of their 90-day sentences.[26]

Skid row, an amalgam of old age, poverty, and addiction, had been in the making since the 1920s, when mechanization and other changes in the occupations that had afforded livelihood to unskilled men began to cut deeply into the economies of the lively workingmen's districts often called "hobohemias" (after the hard-living, itinerant laborers who constituted their dominant group of residents). For unskilled workers, the Depression began long before 1929, and by the mid-1930s, the degradation of hobohemia was virtually complete. Further, with post–World War II prosperity, no new cohorts of young unemployed workers lightened the gloom. The skid row of the 1950s and 1960s was a close approximation of pure redundancy. The *Saturday Evening Post* called the place a "junk heap for human beings."[27]

Skid row men posed the same sort of "threat" as 19th-century tramps: they were affronts to the work ethic and notions of a settled, orderly community. But if tramps were chastised mainly for the work they refused to do, skid row men were faulted, by sociologists, at least, mainly for the homes they failed to make. These were "disaffiliated" men, who had severed (or had never sustained) ties to family, workplace, church, or community, presumably because there was something profoundly wrong with their socialization and/or their personalities.[28] But it is noteworthy that very few postwar "homeless" men, defined in this fashion, met the criteria of "literal homelessness" in common use today (see Chapter 2). In fact, researchers agreed that only a minority of "homeless men" actually resided on skid row. Nonetheless, for that visible portion of the disaffiliated, skid row functioned as something like a reservation, its denizens more akin to a tribal people than to a forgotten cadre that had outlived its usefulness.[29] (Urban geographers, however, referred to such districts as "dead land."[30]) The proxim-

ity of places like New York City's Bowery was both a boon to sociologists ("For the price of a subway token, [the researcher] can enter a country where the accepted principles of social interaction do not apply"[31]) and a tourist draw (buses had been ferrying the curious through the Bowery since the 1930s). There was, in short, something safely fascinating—yet repellent—about the figure of the captive bum. Such men knew the drill, and they rarely ventured off the premises. Skid row's collection of rough taverns, shoddy lodging, pick-up work, and haphazard entertainment may have fallen far short of complete abeyance, but like their modestly upscale counterparts in cheap residential hotels and rooming houses in less stigmatized sections of a city, the men of skid row lived out their lives in a "social and cultural limbo."[32]

Thus, the threat was largely symbolic—and laced through with ambivalence.[33] Contrast that relatively settled cultural attitude of fascination with the quiet horror evoked by the figure of the "shopping bag woman," shuffling along on city thoroughfares a mere decade later. Hers was the anomalous, "out-of-place," classification-defying status of something that was not supposed to happen. Like other "women on the outside,"[34] there was something undeniably unsettling, even threatening, about her. This sight was neither titillating nor edifying, it didn't draw stares for long, and nobody thought to phone the tour guides.

To the Present

As the remainder of this volume attests, the largely invisible, sequestered homelessness of skid row was transformed beginning in the 1970s into the intrusive sort that has become a staple of urban life in the 1990s. Early analysts of this transformation were impressed both by the explosive growth of displacement and, absent serious employment and rehousing efforts, by the likelihood that such dislocations would stabilize—that homelessness would become a "captive state."[35] Had that happened in sufficient numbers, it would have meant a new (and historically unprecedented) addition of large numbers of families to the ranks of those consigned to limbo. But subsequent research showed just how commonly bouts of homelessness occurred in the makeshift economies of the urban poor especially. More recent analyses (reviewed in Chapter 3) have stressed both the high turn-over rates seen in shelters and what appear to be relatively successful efforts at rehousing. This suggests that, at least in some places, homelessness is reverting to transitional form: it disrupts ties of support and affiliation, erodes self-esteem, even traumatizes, but it is thankfully short lived for most.

That prospect, in turn, raises the awkward question of success. The durable testament of the shelters and the streets notwithstanding, it is no small irony that so much of the rehousing that has been accomplished in the last decade has since receded into unremarkable poverty. There, despite the continuing inquiries of small armies of researchers, it has gone largely unnoticed.[36] This should not surprise, for once people manage to escape from the streets and shelters, they typically prefer to resume their new lives as "neighbors," "workers," and "citizens"—not as tagged specimens of the "formerly homeless" (or even, as Rosenthal shows in Chapter 19, as movement activists). A brief bout of homelessness is far more common in contemporary American lives than most of us appreciate, just as it was remarkably common among poor Americans long before the Great Depression. But if once rehoused, the markers of that experience are not such as to attract attention—if the "formerly homeless" choose to pass rather than be "out"—then evidence of successfully resolved homelessness (likely all around us) is bound to be difficult to detect.[37] Unseen, it can offer little reassurance of the value of social investment in shelter or rehousing efforts.

THE LESSONS OF ANOMALIES

Elsewhere, we have made the case that certain anomalies in the historical record of homelessness—shelters functioning as "warehouses" for surplus populations—as well as some missing from that record—peacetime military service, for example—are better accounted for as aspects of (sometimes incomplete) abeyance mechanisms.[38] In the same way as the official

unemployment rate is but a pale index of either the full range of joblessness or the myriad alternatives to working, so do official homelessness figures fall far short of capturing both the depth of houseless poverty and the improvisations of shadow shelter. Here, we concentrate on the additional interpretive power brought by the notion of liminality. Several instances of liminal phenomena ("tramping" by young adults, for example) have already been noted. But what other anomalous instances of homelessness might be cited?

In 20th-century America, life-course transitions in general have become more individualized and less tied to strategic family decisions, let alone subject to strict cultural regulation.[39] Liminality, in consequence, is riskier; more susceptible to being derailed or stalled. Two examples may suffice to illustrate this. Late adolescence—a time when young adults enter the labor market, undertake additional schooling, and/or set up independent households—has become an increasingly uncertain period of transition. Successful completion of high school (itself a classic abeyance mechanism[40]) is a less secure ticket to livelihood than ever before—even the army is downsizing. Prone to drift, prey to the temptations of illicit commerce, hard pressed to locate reason to hope, and increasingly ineligible for public assistance, poor young men in particular may find themselves effectively stranded. Adapting to that uncertainty, not only when kin resources are unavailable but also when they are finite,[41] increasingly seems to entail use of public shelter as an accessory. Their counterparts, young mothers with children, may find public shelter the most expeditious route to housing assistance and establishment of a household of their own.[42] When such transitional arrangements get congested and the process stalls, the results can resemble "refugee camps for the American poor."[43]

Women fleeing abusive domestic situations offer another example. Sanctuary housing—probably the best example of shelter serving as support structure to a forced transition—emerged in the late 1970s as a distinctive response to a particular kind of displacement. The very availability of such resources not only helped destigmatize the status but made the transition feasible for many women.

In addition to the above life-course transitions, contingent (temporary) labor, used with increasing frequency as employers seek to minimize their long-term manpower commitments and fringe benefit payouts, represents a different kind of transitional status susceptible to stalling. Day labor and migrant work always have played important roles in the livelihood of the betwixt and between, and as Snow and his colleagues demonstrate in Chapter 8, this continues to a lesser extent today. But all sorts of work have been rendered temporary in recent years, and most of the people doing it are looking for something permanent, the claims of the "temp" industry notwithstanding.[44] If history is any guide at all, the relationship between temporary work and temporary shelter bears watching.

TAKING STOCK: WHAT'S IN A NAME?

The puzzle of American homelessness, that which makes tracing its continuities and discontinuities over time so difficult, is that it is not one thing but many, gathered up under a common heading that masks as much as it discloses. If we set aside the vagaries of situational classification for the moment, the genus homelessness is made up of unequal—and changing—proportions of poverty, mobility, joblessness, housing scarcity, preference, and household tolerance. Character (indolence, addiction, incorrigibility), kinship difficulties (no family, or frayed family ties), and the economy (cyclical employment, structural unemployment) are the usual culprits invoked to explain the range of homelessness. But the story proves more complicated than that.

But classification anomalies abound. To this day, for example, strategic application of the term occurs, as when bureaucracies, chasing earmarked funds, categorize certain forms of dispossession as homelessness (even imminent eviction) but not others. For similar strategic reasons—qualifying for assistance that would otherwise be out of reach—self-designation of one's own hardship as "homeless" may occur.[45] Others, hunkered in their homemade street dwellings, defiantly reject the term as applicable to them. Some circumstances that appear to meet surface criteria of homelessness turn out to be occupational hazards of particular lines of work—sometimes recognized by the locals and their chroniclers (temporarily jobless men gathered on the curbs of hobohemia's "main stem," for example), and sometimes not (as with the boatmen and cannery workers of the fishing industry or prostitutes who followed the railroad gangs). For a generation of postwar researchers, the term "homeless" was interpreted through a purely sociological lens: it meant "disaffiliation," the shearing of attachments to family, community, or (for the most part) work.[46] So construed, it overlapped only partially with the more familiar domain of "shelterless poverty." And historically, as this brief review has shown, whole categories of relief (the almshouse and allied institutions) clearly forestalled what would otherwise have been the wholesale destitution of their occupants, but did so in a way not usually considered part of the antihomelessness apparatus—except by those of its charges who chose to do their time on the installment plan.

These are familiar problems in both historical and cross-cultural work. When deciding how to read an unfamiliar (or, worse, a deceptively familiar) world—how "to ferret out the unapparent import of things"—we fret over how best to translate native categories of distinction so as to preserve the meaning of another time and place.[47] To translation difficulties, we have here added another: whether "homelessness" is the most appropriate construct for comparative analysis. Put differently, we might say that ambiguities exist on both sides of the need equation: in determining what should count as "homeless" and in deciding what forms of relief are to be considered "shelter." Accordingly, we have sought conceptual assistance elsewhere.

The notion of *abeyance* helps us get at the larger dynamic of society's management of potentially troublesome redundancy. In the process, it alerts us to administratively camouflaged domains of need—met and unmet—that might otherwise go unnoticed.[48] So, for example, we were able to detect unexpected kinship between the respectable and disreputable poor: both are charges of a "Welfare State [through whose] agency . . . the 'useless' are made useful or are, at least, kept out of the way."[49] At the same time, we see how important distinctions are smudged when the useful mobility of the seasonal worker of the 19th and early 20th centuries and the redundant stasis of the skid row denizen are both classified as "homeless." The first fulfilled an essential economic function; the latter occupied a permanently marginalized status. That two so differently valued conditions can be captured by the same term says something about the undiscriminating reach (and brief memory) of ordinary language.

Abeyance gone awry—shelters warehousing redundant men and women, careless of their morale, inured to demands for useful work—is still only part of the picture. We introduce an additional concept—*liminality*—to draw attention to the more dynamic and transient forms of displacement. As Chapter 3 documents, for all the attention attached to the exotic figures of the street-dwelling homeless,[50] longitudinal analyses of the arguably larger complement of the officially homeless (shelter users) have shown that most are there for a short-term, transitional stay.[51] For these people, homelessness represents a crisis that, while disruptive and unexpected, has proven remarkably susceptible to remedy, at least in the sense of resolving their transitional status. In New York City, for example, the vast majority of homeless families who entered the public shelter system in the late 1980s appear to be stably housed five years later.[52] For some of these families, shelters bolstered a bid for independence: over two-fifths of those mothers had never run a household of their own. In a fashion both unplanned and unexpectedly successful, that is, homelessness served in effect as a rite of passage to adulthood.

For others, the passage stalls and the liminal state persists. Historically, as we have seen, two things usually happen. Either the state of extended liminality is itself routinized as a legitimate alternative form of livelihood in its own right (structurally, it is "resolved" by converting it into a recognized abeyance mechanism); or, it endures in that state of suspended animation and suspect status we have called *limbo*. With respect to the officially homeless, the first alternative is perhaps best represented by the lucky few who escaped the warehouse shelters of the 1930s for the work crews of the WPA or the CCC. The second is illustrated by longstanding observations of "shelterization" (or "demoralization") among men confined to barracks for the homeless.[53] A third should be mentioned as well: the ranks of the unsettled dispossessed may be emptied by the launching of a new abeyance measure—as happened in 1916–1917 and during the early 1940s with the inauguration of war efforts.

Even for those whose shelter stays are prolonged and/or repeated, the notion of botched transitions may apply. Consider those shelter residents who come directly from hospitals, psychiatric facilities, jails and prisons, or foster care placements: their homelessness is an artifact of careless or cynical institutional practice, with shelters serving as substitutes for (and thus reasons to neglect) "discharge planning."[54] For some, the official status of being homeless opens access to goods and services (drug rehabilitation programs, psychiatric treatment, subsidized housing) otherwise unavailable. For young, African American men, stuck in prolonged periods of adolescent "drift," public shelters are simply another port in what promises to be a continuing storm (see Chapter 11).[55]

FORWARD TO THE PAST

A final caution is warranted at this point. If we raid history for one purpose, others are free to do so for contrary ones. We have in mind especially government bureaucrats freshly impressed by the untapped wealth of an old virtue. In early 1995, the new commissioner of social services for the State of New York announced her intention to shut down the state's homeless relief apparatus, arguing that it allowed kin to default on their responsibility to support their own and to resolve problems by ejecting the troublesome household member. Her memorable assertion: "Everyone has friends or family."[56] On the federal level, Congress seems bent on returning to some imagined beneficent past. House Speaker

Newt Gingrich: "We must replace the welfare state" with "a strategy of dramatically increasing private charities." Homelessness could be greatly reduced, he continues, if "every church and synagogue in America" were to "adopt one homeless person."[57]

Though we have argued here and elsewhere for the centrality of productive, socially valued activity—and not just a rack to sleep in—to any lasting solution to homelessness, we would caution as well against taking counterfeit programs for the real thing. In an era rediscovering supposed Victorian charms, when the word "character" has been placed once again above the family hearth and the value of sheer toil has been raised to a civic virtue, it is well to recall Orwell's warning of some 60 years ago: "this instinct to perpetuate useless work is, at bottom, simply fear of the mob."[58]

CHAPTER 2

Homelessness: Definitions and Counts

Martha R. Burt

In social science methodology books, survey research begins with ideas and hypotheses. These are clarified into conceptual and operational definitions, then survey instruments are assembled and tested, and the data are collected. Rarely discussed is the issue of *who to include* in a study, nor are the biases inherent in different inclusion criteria usually addressed.

It is always easier in the books than in real life. Homelessness is but the latest of many research topics in which the population of interest is not clearly defined. Even when the goal was to describe "the homeless," early studies collected data without developing precise guidelines for who should and should not be included as respondents. They did not propose definitions, did not use screening questions to be sure that the people they interviewed were indeed homeless, and did not make major efforts to cover the universe of homeless people. In large part, they adopted de facto definitions based on where respondents were located, such as in shelters and street-sleeping locations. Anyone encountered in one of these locations was assumed to be homeless by virtue of their presence at the site.

This might have been an acceptable strategy if all researchers had picked the same types of locations for their studies, but of course they did not. Of 24 studies conducted between 1983 and 1991 that included interviews with homeless individuals, 1 sought respondents only on the streets, 1 went only to soup kitchens, 5 went only to shelters, 1 went to streets and soup kitchens, 7 went to streets and shelters, 3 went to shelters and soup kitchens, and 6 went to all 3 types of locations. Even within a single type of location, such as shelters, some researchers included battered women's shelters or youth shelters and some did not. Or, within street searches, some included people in vehicles or in all-night commercial establishments and some did not; some diligently searched "hidden" places such as abandoned buildings and railroad cars but most did not. Therefore, readers of the early studies who wanted to draw conclusions from the entire body of work on homelessness found themselves faced with a collection of studies that could not be compared. The situation has changed a bit in recent years, but not as much as it must if research results are to be readily interpretable.

A good part of the problem is the slipperiness of definitions of homelessness. As we go from the core meaning of the term to its periphery, there is less and less agreement about who should be included and who should not. We do quite well at counting and describing people in shelters, assuming we have some agreement on what types of facilities should be included as shelters. We do reasonably well at counting and describing people who use other services, after adopting some criteria for who should be included as homeless. We do far less well at including people who are not in shelters or using other services for homeless people—those who are on the streets are missed because they do not want to be found or because finding them might be dangerous, and others, including the rural homeless and the "doubled up," are often not included because we cannot agree on definitions.

WHAT IS HOMELESSNESS?

Defining who is homeless is one of the hardest aspects of conducting a study of the population, and understanding the definitions used in research is one of the most challenging tasks for people who want to use its results. All too often, a study fails to satisfy the information needs of one or more groups who want to use the data.

Most would agree that people in shelters or literally living on the street are homeless, but there is less agreement regarding people in the following circumstances:

- Youth on their own, with no permanent residence or even a usual place to sleep, who spend each night in a different hotel room paid for by a "john" or "trick" (prostitution client)

- Children who have been separated from their homeless parents and are in foster care or are living with relatives

- A young mother and her children who have lived for two or three months at a time with different relatives during the past year or so, and who expect that, within the next few months, they will have to leave where they now live

- A family or single person who migrated to a new town looking for work, lives with relatives, does not pay rent, cannot find work, and does not know how long the present arrangement will last or where to go if it terminates

- A family or single person whose previous housing was lost recently, is staying with relatives or friends, is not contributing to the rent, and expects this arrangement to continue for less than two months until other housing can be found

- A family or single person whose previous housing was lost recently, is staying with relatives or friends, is contributing to the rent, and expects this arrangement to continue for less than two months until other housing can be found

- A family or single person who left their previous housing and returned to live in their parents' house, with no clear expectation of when this arrangement will end

- A teenager and her baby who remain in her mother's house, with the expectation that they can stay as long as they need

- People living in stable but physically inadequate housing (having no plumbing, no heating, or major structural damage, for example)

Which of these people should be considered homeless? There is no right answer; there can only be agreement on a convention. At the beginning of the 1980s, as awareness of the phenomenon was first surfacing, no two scholars saw it the same. Researchers and advocates alike struggled with these definitions, which often were at the heart of arguments about the size and nature of the homeless population.

By the 1990s enough experience had been accumulated to develop some common understanding about who should be considered homeless. In a project on methods to count homeless children supported by the Department of Education, for which the advisory group included state and local government officials responsible for programs to combat homelessness, service providers, and advocates, a set of definitions and a methodology based on them was developed that met the needs of all involved.[1] Subsequently, in work for the Department of Housing and Urban Development (HUD), the definitions were refined and expanded to include adults. These have become the working definitions for preparing the antihomelessness components of a Comprehensive Housing Affordability Strategy (CHAS), Consolidated Plan, and other HUD-related work.[2]

The categories presented below are taken from *Practical Methods for Counting Homeless People*.[3] They are designed to address all of the situations described earlier. Members of the first two categories would be considered "literally homeless"—that is, living on the streets or in shelters. The remainder are considered "at imminent risk" of literal homelessness—that is, if their current precarious housing arrangements fail, or if an institutional stay comes to a predictable end, they have neither prospects nor resources to keep themselves from literal homelessness. A more expansive definition of literal homelessness might include the institutionalized who have no usual home elsewhere, the most unstable group among the precariously housed, or both. An ideal study includes as many segments as feasible of the population of interest, makes clear who is included and excluded, gains agreement from interested parties that obtaining information on the remainder is prohibitively expensive, and reports results separately for different segments of the population studied.

Components of the Homeless and At-Risk Population

Adults, children, and youth sleeping in places not meant for human habitation. "Places not meant for human habitation" include streets, parks, alleys, parking ramps, parts of the highway system, transportation depots and other parts of transportation systems (e.g., subway tunnels and railroad cars), all-night commercial establishments (e.g., movie theaters, laundromats, and restaurants), abandoned buildings, squatter sites, building roofs or stairwells, farm outbuildings, caves, campgrounds, vehicles, and other similar places.

Adults, children, and youth in shelters. "Shelters" includes all emergency shelters and transitional shelters for the homeless, all domestic-violence shelters, all shelters and residential centers or programs for runaway and homeless youth, and any hotel, motel, or apartment voucher arrangement paid because the person or family is homeless.[4]

Adults, children, and youth at imminent risk of residing on the streets or in shelters.

- Children in institutions. Children or youth who, because of their own or a parent's homelessness or abandonment, reside temporarily and for a short anticipated duration in hospitals, residential treatment facilities, emergency foster care, detention facilities, and the like, and whose legal care has not (yet) been assumed by a foster care agency.

- Adults in institutions. Adults currently residing in mental health facilities, chemical dependency facilities, or short-term criminal justice holding facilities, who at time of entry had no home of their own, no known address, or whose address was a shelter for the homeless or another facility such as a soup kitchen serving the homeless.

- Adults, children, and youth living "doubled up" in conventional dwellings.[5] One category is the "precariously housed." For people sleeping in conventional dwelling units to be considered "precariously housed," their housing situation must have arisen from an inability to pay for their own housing due to an emergency,[6] and the arrangement must be of short anticipated duration (less than 60 days). The other category, which involves people more severely at risk, includes precariously housed children, youths, adults, or families, with the additional characteristics of no plans or prospects for stable housing and no financial resources to obtain housing.

DEFINITIONS IN THE ABSTRACT AND IN PRACTICE

A review of research practices in eight recent studies of the homeless gives some idea of the pitfalls that await the researcher and the user of research even after an "official" definition of homelessness has been accepted.[7] These eight studies each used a reasonably sophisticated method to count the homeless. They can be considered second-generation studies, in that they followed the very simple efforts undertaken earlier in the 1980s. They are: (1) Barrett Lee and the Nashville Coalition for the Homeless's repeated enumerations of Nashville's homeless, beginning in December 1983; (2) Rossi's 1985–1986 studies of homelessness in Chicago; (3) the Urban Institute's study of homeless users of soup kitchens and shelters in U.S. cities with populations of 100,000 or more; (4) the Rand Corporation's study of the homeless mentally disabled in 3 California counties; (5) James's 2 studies of homelessness in Colorado; (6) the Census Bureau's count of the homeless on S-night 1990;[8] (7) Research Triangle Institute's (RTI) study of the homeless as part of the Washington, DC, Metropolitan Area Drug Study; and (8) the Kentucky Housing Corporation's 1993 statewide homeless count. The following discussion focuses on screening procedures, locations searched, and search procedures.

Screening Procedures

When reading a report of a study of homeless people, it is important to look for the "screener"—procedures the researchers used to identify the homeless and separate them from the non-homeless. A reader attempting to compare one study to another is often unable to determine whether the researchers counted the same types of people, because screening procedures often are not described clearly enough.

Two of the studies, Lee's and the Census Bureau's S-night count, used no screener. Lee used the expert judgments of Nashville Coalition for the Homeless enumerators to identify homeless persons. The Bureau of the Census took another tack entirely: it refused to define homelessness. Instead, it identified locations where homeless people were likely to be found and counted people in those locations, excluding from these counts only those people "engaged in money-making activities" and people in uniform for work. Users of these data take any position they want as to who among those counted should be defined as homeless, and they aggregate the counts from different locations.[9] Analysts will be able to use different definitions for different purposes, but they will have to make their inclusion/exclusion decisions explicit and defensible to their audiences. In some ways this is the most flexible approach, since it allows the user to make the definitional decisions. The Census Bureau's enumeration is made even more valuable by coupling enumerations in treatment facilities and other institutions with a screener determining whether the person had a usual place to live elsewhere. In the S-night count, inclusion of people sleeping in cars or other vehicles would also have been useful, but the Census Bureau decided that to do so would involve too much risk to enumerators.

The remaining six studies used screeners. Since Rossi's was one of these and three of the remaining five (the Urban Institute, Rand, and RTI) adapted Rossi's screener with some modifications, it is not surprising that they selected similar people as homeless. They counted as "homeless" people who had no home or permanent place to stay of their own (meaning they rented or owned it themselves) and no regular arrangement to stay at someone else's place. Rand and RTI, which did street searches, also excluded from enumeration people "engaged in money-making activities," people in uniform, and people obviously carrying out service jobs (e.g., janitors and newspaper delivery people). The Urban Institute did not do a street search and had no exclusion rule other than that implied by the screener.

All screeners proceeded with step-by-step questions that clarified most potential points of confusion before classifying someone as homeless or not homeless. For example, if someone said he or she had a place of his or her own, but that place turned out to be a park bench or a bed in a shelter, the person was counted as homeless. None of the screeners asked people explicitly whether they considered themselves homeless. None of the studies validated their screeners; that is, the information given by respondents was not checked to determine its accuracy.

The Kentucky Housing Corporation study used a very simple three-question screener: "In what type of place are you now staying?" "Is that your permanent place to stay?" and "Are you living with someone else?" If the answer to the first question was a conventional dwelling of some type, and the answer to the second was yes, the person was not considered homeless and was asked the third question but not asked to complete the remainder of the questionnaire.

The studies by James used different screening methods. The 1988 study interviewed all people at soup kitchens, then separated the homeless from the non-homeless based on their interview responses to a question about having a permanent place of their own. They were counted as homeless if they said no, or if they said yes, but it was someone else's place, they did not contribute to the rent, and they used soup kitchens. In the 1990 study, respondents were screened prior to interviewing and were included as homeless if they said they had no permanent place to stay. If they said they did have a permanent place, even if that place was a shelter, they were *not* counted as homeless.

Locations (and Categories of People) Included or Excluded

Selection of search locations is another dimension of an operational definition of homelessness. If battered women's shelters, voucher hotels, and conventional dwelling units are excluded, then battered women, homeless families staying in hotels on vouchers, and the precariously housed "doubled up" will be excluded from the homeless population studied. Locations or types of people may be excluded for several reasons. As noted, some exclusions are clearly related to a particular definition of homelessness; thus, more narrow definitions exclude people in doubled-up situations or those in treatment or criminal justice facilities. Commonly, however, resource constraints determine exclusions. For example, it is very expensive to do a thorough street search.

Doubled up. Of the studies reviewed here, only James in the 1988 Colorado study and Hutcheson in the more recent Kentucky study attempted to include people in doubled-up situations. The Kentucky study identified and reported separately those who were literally homeless and those who were doubled up. A recent Houston study is the only study of which I am aware that attempted a systematic, probability-based approach to estimating the precariously housed doubled-up population.[10] This study first randomly selected blocks in low-income neighborhoods, then randomly selected buildings within blocks, and then dwelling units within buildings. Once in a dwelling unit, the researchers conducted a personal interview with household members to obtain information that was used to separate the stable doubled up from the precariously doubled up.

Youth. Most of the studies considered here either seriously undercounted youth (under 18 years of age, but on their own; i.e., not with a parent) or explicitly excluded them. Rand was explicit in screening out anyone under 18; so was Rossi in his fall 1985 data-collection period. Several studies did not include shelters designed to serve runaway or homeless youth in their sampling frames, although they may have encountered and interviewed some homeless youth in their street searches or during interviews in other service sites.

Vehicles. The Bureau of the Census explicitly excluded people sleeping in vehicles. All other studies that used street searches *did* count people sleeping in vehicles. The Urban Institute study included some people who slept in vehicles if they also used soup kitchens or periodically used shelters.

Voucher programs. Several studies did not include voucher hotels or motels—or similar arrangements—in their sampling frame of shelters, even though the study locations included programs that paid for hotels or motels for homeless people.

Battered women's programs. Most studies included battered women's shelters in their homeless shelter sampling frames; Rossi did not, although there were such facilities in Chicago; Rand did not because there were no such facilities in its study area.

Residential treatment or criminal justice facilities. Four of the studies included people in these types of facilities. Lee, RTI, and the Kentucky study used a screener to separate those who did not have a usual home elsewhere (the homeless) from those who did. The census, in its Group Quarters enumeration on 1 April 1990, also used a screening question to determine if someone had a usual home elsewhere.[11] If the answer was no, the people were included in the homeless count under the separate Group Quarters categories.

Generic services. Only the Kentucky study searched for homeless people in welfare offices, community action agencies, charity food pantries, food stamp offices, mental health agencies, law enforcement agencies, social service agencies, libraries, housing programs, community health centers, and similar places.

Geographical areas of city. Some studies (e.g., Lee) did not include locations beyond downtown areas, while others (e.g., Rand) did not search blocks where there seemed little likelihood of finding homeless people ("low-probability" blocks) or that had not been identified prior to the evening of the count (e.g., Census, James).

People not using services. Except for the Urban Institute study, all of the studies considered here used some type of search procedures for street, outdoor, and nonservice locations. It is impossible to "add up" across studies, because the categories of locations and people used in different studies are not mutually exclusive. For instance, the Urban Institute included people who used soup kitchens but did *not* use shelters (29% of the sample), and these people slept in all the places usually thought of as "street" locations: parks, cars, bus stations, tents, and highway tunnels, for example. It is impossible to tell precisely what proportion of the street population (i.e., those homeless not using shelters) was thus included in the Urban Institute estimate, but it

certainly was higher than in studies that went only to shelters.

In any event, there is an unknown and probably unknowable amount of category-overlapping across studies. And, as I will discuss below, even individual studies may include some duplication of counts across locations.

Policy Implications of Definitions

Definitions are absolutely critical to policy decisions about homelessness. Different problems arise and different potential solutions pertain depending on whether policy is being developed for the literally homeless or also for those at imminent risk. The size of the population will increase tremendously if the at-risk people are included. This increase may appeal to those who are trying to convince policy makers that the problem is important; however, by lumping together people facing very different circumstances, the problem of developing solutions is made significantly murkier and more difficult. Targeted programs—those for substance abusers, for example—require clear target populations. Furthermore, eliminating the distinction between the literally homeless and those at risk makes it impossible to examine the factors that push people into literal homelessness from unstable residence in conventional dwellings. Therefore, it would be impossible to use research evidence to prevent this final transition. For all these reasons and more, definitions matter for social policy.

NUMBERS AND COUNTS

250,000–350,000. 500,000–600,000. 2 million–3 million. And lately, 7 million. We are bombarded by different estimates of the size of the homeless population. Which numbers should we believe? How can we tell whether an estimate is credible? Why is one estimate so different from another?

This section provides a practical guide for the consumer to the "homeless" numbers game. It tells you what you need to know about a number before you make a judgment about its accuracy or a decision about using it. The section is organized around a series of questions that will help you assess what a number means.

When was the estimate made, or, when were the data collected on which the estimate is based? All other things equal, numbers produced in the early 1980s will be lower than those produced later in the decade or in the 1990s, simply because the extent of homelessness grew during those years. The commonly cited HUD number, 250,000–350,000, was developed for 1984. It is the lowest of the frequently cited numbers, and should be considered obsolete at this time.

Where did the enumerators go to search for homeless people? All other things equal, counts that rely solely on shelter data or that are based on research conducted only at shelters will be lower than counts that search for homeless people in non-shelter locations. Many studies search outdoor locations as well as shelters; other studies supplement their shelter data by searching at soup kitchens, locations providing health care for the homeless, and sites offering similar services. Some do both. There is some evidence that studies that include non-shelter services for homeless people actually find more "street" people than studies using a late-night, street-search methodology. However, studies that go to several different types of services must include a way to correct for the duplication that will undoubtedly occur because many homeless people use more than one service within a type (e.g., they go to more than one soup kitchen) and also may use more than one type of service during the study period (e.g., shelters and soup kitchens, or soup kitchens and health care services).

Who helped? Assuming that data collection included a search of outdoor areas, counts will be higher if homeless people themselves were enlisted to guide interviewers to locations where homeless people congregate and to help interviewers gain their trust and willingness to be interviewed.

How long did the data collection period last? Data collection can be done in one night or one day, or it can extend over several days, a week, several months, or for a year or more. If the data collection extended for more than one day, it

---

EXHIBIT 2.1

THE THREE MOST COMMONLY CITED ESTIMATES FOR THE NUMBER OF HOMELESS PEOPLE IN THE UNITED STATES AT A SINGLE POINT IN TIME

250,000–350,000

1-day estimate by HUD, 1984
(based on projection of expert opinion in 60 randomly selected geographical areas)

500,000–600,000

1-week estimate by the Urban Institute, 1987
(based on projected results from systematic random sample of homeless people in cities over 100,000 population)

2 million–3 million

1-day guess by Mitch Snyder, activist, 1983
(no known statistical basis)

---

could still be producing only a one-day estimate. The RTI study, for example, collected data during a four-month period, but the estimate it produced was the number of people homeless on an "average day." The Kentucky study collected data for two months and produced two numbers: (1) the number of people homeless on the first day of the count, and (2) the number of people (unduplicated) homeless during the entire two-month period.

The rationale for the "blitz" type of study, conducted in shelters and outdoor locations on a single night, is that it avoids duplication (people are assumed to stay in one place during the relatively short period of data collection). Increasingly, however, it is clear that one-night studies miss a lot of the unsheltered homeless.

Taking more time to collect data gives homeless people more chances to be included. Someone who uses a shelter only once a week would be included in a shelter-only count if the count lasted a week, but has only a one-in-seven chance of being counted in a one-night effort. Also, someone who spends a few days in an institution (e.g., a detoxification facility or a jail) will be back on the street or in a shelter—and countable—if the data collection lasts a week or more. However, extending the time period also increases the chances that some people will be counted more than once. Therefore, these strategies of taking more time to collect data must be supplemented by one or more ways to adjust for duplication.

Taking more time to collect data also makes it possible to include some people in the count who were homeless when counted, but who were not homeless when the count began. If they are to produce data that can be compared with most other studies, longer data-collection strategies therefore must also be supplemented by some method to produce a one-day count, as well as a count for whatever time period was actually covered.

If the methodology can produce an unduplicated count and if it can also produce a one-day count, then all other things equal, a longer time period for data collection will result in a higher count even for the one-day base period.

Was the count corrected for duplication? Obviously, any estimate that lets some people be counted more than once will be higher than one that corrects for duplication, but it will also not be accurate or helpful in telling us the size of the homeless population. Duplication can occur because the same person uses a single service (e.g., a shelter or soup kitchen) or stays in the same street location on more than one day and is counted two or more times during the course of data collection. It can also occur because the same person appears in several places (e.g., uses both a shelter and a soup kitchen, or more than one shelter) and is counted in each of them. To get an accurate count of the number of people who are homeless, this duplication must be eliminated, and any study using methods that risk duplication should discuss what was done to eliminate duplication before producing an estimate. If the report does not discuss duplication and it seems likely there was some risk of it, the estimate is probably too high.

On the other hand, policy makers and service providers have a legitimate need to know about the number of service contacts, in addition to knowing the number of people who are homeless. Service contacts include, for example, number of nights of shelter provided, number

of meals provided, number of admissions, and number of medical visits. Service contacts do not have to be unduplicated—with respect to resources needed, it does not matter to a soup kitchen operator who serves 300 meals a day if those meals go to the same 300 people every day or to 300 different people every day. It is useful for a study to report its duplicate data, which it can present as an indicator of the level of service demand. It is only necessary that this information not be presented as a count of the number of homeless people in a jurisdiction.

What time period does the estimate cover? Point prevalence versus longer time periods. "Point prevalence" refers to the number of people who are homeless at a single point in time—usually one day or one night. "Period prevalence" refers to the number of people who have been homeless during some longer time period. For example, annual prevalence refers to the number of people who are homeless at some time during the period of a year—whether they started the year homeless or became homeless after the year began.

Most studies of the homeless collect data over a very short time period and produce estimates of point prevalence. They give a count and provide descriptions, based on the people who are homeless on a single day or single night. There have been some attempts, using interview data from point-in-time studies on how long people have been homeless, to estimate the number of people who might be homeless during the course of a year. In light of recent evidence on annual prevalence from the few jurisdictions in the country that can produce an unduplicated count for the entire jurisdiction, it is clear that these annual projections were much too low.

Until recently, lack of jurisdiction-wide computerized data systems made it impossible to get accurate annual or longer-term counts for whole cities or counties. Some shelters could produce unduplicated counts just of their own users over a year's time, but they could not tell whether people had used more than one shelter during that time period. Table 2.1 gives unduplicated counts of homeless persons receiving shelter

---

TABLE 2.1

RECENT ESTIMATES OF HOMELESSNESS DURING 1-YEAR, 3-YEAR, AND 5-YEAR PERIODS

	Philadelphia 1990–1992 all residents (data system*)	New York City 1988–1992 all residents (data system*)	United States 5 years prior to date of interview in 1990 and reinterview in 1994, adults (telephone survey†)
1 year	0.96% 15,000 people	1.17% 86,000 people	
3 years	2.77% 45,000 people	2.21% 162,000 people	
5 years		3.27% 239,000 people	2.4%–3.1% 4.4 million–5.7 million adults

*Culhane, et al., "Public Shelter Admission Rates."
†Link, et al., "Lifetime and Five-Year Prevalence of Homelessness."

---

during the course of one year and three years in Philadelphia and New York City, and for five years in New York City.[12] These are compared with results using a totally different method—a random telephone survey of all U.S. adults.[13] The results from the two cities for the three- and five-year periods correspond surprisingly well with the rough estimates from the random telephone survey. Approximately 3% of each population appears to have been homeless during these extended time periods.

Policy Implications of Counts

No one has done the perfect study of homelessness, and no one is likely to do so. Both resource constraints and the slipperiness of the definition of homelessness (and its different meanings in different policy contexts) make this prediction almost certain. Also contributing are the different sources of data for counting homeless people and the different legitimate uses to which such numbers can be put. There is no one right number. Different types of counts serve different purposes, and all are useful. Someone interested in service planning needs to know about the expected level of service contacts on a given day and will not care so much whether the contacts are made repeatedly by a relatively

small group of people or only once each day by a very large number of different people. Someone who wants to create permanent housing for the most long-term homeless with disabilities will need to know the actual number of such persons, not just at one point in time. And someone who wants to stop family homelessness through prevention efforts needs to know how many families might be at risk of homelessness during a particular time period such as a year and whether they need temporary, crisis assistance or more long-term supports to remain in housing.

The 1980s began with only the crudest ways to estimate the level of homelessness. Throughout the decade and into the 1990s the assessment of homelessness has become more sophisticated, both in the need for numbers for different purposes and in the ability to determine these numbers. It is critically important for those who wish to make policy, or to influence it, to have a very clear understanding of what they are trying to do and for whom they want to do it. It will then be much easier to identify the right number for that specific purpose. It is also important to realize that bad policy will result from using the wrong numbers or from using numbers that confuse rather than clarify the nature of the policy task.

CHAPTER 3

The Causes of Homelessness

Paul Koegel
M. Audrey Burnam
Jim Baumohl

INTRODUCTION

Imagine the children's game of musical chairs, but played with both an individual aim to keep a chair and a collective goal to keep everyone seated. Imagine, as well, that in this game not only are seats gradually removed, but the number of players is progressively increased.

At the start of the game, adjustments are made easily enough, and for a short time the collective goal is achieved. True, the number of seats decreases and the pool of individuals competing for them gets bigger, but those sitting down accommodate the others by sharing their chairs or allowing them onto their laps. The seats are small, however, and there are limits to how much weight people can bear. Inevitably, some people find themselves standing, their number growing as time passes.

As the game continues, many small dramas unfold. Some of those seated on laps are pushed off, then allowed back again. Seats are periodically relinquished, and the appearance of an empty seat precipitates a scramble among those outside the circle. Indeed, many people move back and forth between standing up and sitting down, but the total number of people standing

continues to grow, and the collective goal of the game becomes untenable.

Who gets left standing is not determined merely by chance. Some players are fast and strong; some are impaired. Some are unpleasant and disruptive, and others are very heavy: these players are unlikely to be invited onto an occupied chair. Some are timid, ashamed to enlist help, or perhaps just don't know any of the other players. Still others don't understand the rules of the game and wander through the scene.

The grossly disadvantaged are the first to lose their seats and the least likely to grab replacements; they are disproportionately present among those on their feet, particularly at the early stages of the game. Later, as there are fewer and fewer chairs and more and more people vying for them, they are joined by players whose disadvantages are more subtle. Inevitably, as the competition becomes even fiercer, they share the floor with large numbers of the hale, hearty, and sociable.

So it has been with homelessness. A host of problems in society's needs-meeting mechanisms established the context in which homelessness was inevitable. Those affected first and most profoundly were drawn from the most vulnerable of the poor. They were single minority males with little education and few occupational skills; they were those with severe mental illnesses and habits of substance abuse; they were those whose early childhood experiences left them ill prepared to take their place in a competitive world; they were those without friends and family to help them, or whose kith and kin were no better off. And more often than not, they did not have just one of these vulnerabilities.

THE CAUSES OF HOMELESSNESS: AN INTEGRATED PERSPECTIVE

When widespread homelessness emerged in the early 1980s, explanations were of two sorts. On the one hand, the large numbers of troubled and troublesome people among the homeless poor suggested to some observers that homelessness was best explained by the personal limitations of those who became homeless. According to this perspective, people were homeless because something was wrong with them. They were severely mentally ill, for instance, or end-of-the-line substance abusers—people incapable of caring for themselves, unable to keep themselves housed, and newly visible because of drastic changes in policies that had previously kept them institutionalized in hospitals or jails. Or, they had trouble maintaining relationships and therefore lacked the protective buffer of supportive family and friends. Or, worst of all, they rejected conventional responsibilities and had chosen homelessness.

Liberal advocates of this perspective tended to see homeless people sympathetically: as victims of circumstances over which they had little control. Emphasis was placed on the role of failed mental health and substance abuse treatment policies, and advocates pressed for rehabilitation programs and better networks of community care. On the other hand, conservatives were more likely to impute willfulness and choice to homeless people. To press people to shoulder responsibility, they advocated policies designed to make homelessness less attractive, such as controlling the availability of subsistence services and stepping up legal sanctions against being homeless. And while allowing that the homeless mentally ill deserved society's help, they favored a return to widespread institutionalization of mentally ill people and substance abusers, to protect both these persons and the public at large.

The other explanation put forward was that pervasive and rising homelessness was caused by structural factors; that is, that it was a function of the way our society's resources are organized and distributed. Those who favored this explanation emphasized a dramatically widening gap between the availability of low-cost housing and the income-generating ability of those on the lowest rungs of the housing ladder. They observed that the number of available low-income housing units was rapidly diminishing just as the population of poor people in need of such housing was growing. Their equation was simple: too few housing units for too many poor people meant that growing numbers of the poor were unable to afford housing. The solution that was proposed was to expand the supply of low-income housing.

Public rhetoric in the 1980s about the causes of homelessness was characterized by strident and generally sterile debate between defenders of these two positions. Many on the political left dismissed personal problems as inconsequential to the creation of homelessness, branding as apologists for inequality those who focused on the causal contributions of mental illness and substance abuse. In their view, this medicalized—or, worse, moralized—a fundamentally economic problem. While conceding that some among the homeless had serious personal problems, they denied that most homeless people were anything other than well-adjusted people who had fallen on hard times. Homeless people were "just like you and me," except that they were suffering the consequences of a breakdown in the needs-meeting structures of society. The rest of us were "just a paycheck away."

Their opponents cited the existence of a large proportion of homeless people with severe mental health, substance abuse, or behavioral problems as evidence that the structural arguments must be flawed. Many homeless people, they claimed, *were* fundamentally different from ordinary citizens. Pointing to studies documenting high rates of these debilitating conditions, they argued that the structuralists "normalized" homeless people in order to elicit public sympathy and advance a policy agenda that had far more to do with eliminating poverty among housed individuals than with providing needed help to the homeless. This point of view, stated most pointedly by Alice Baum and Donald Burnes,[1] asserted that the structuralists encouraged the nation to remain deeply in "denial" regarding the "true" nature of homelessness and promoted policies that deprived homeless individuals of the treatment and rehabilitative services without which they would never be able to secure and maintain housing.

In fact, neither of these positions independently could accommodate a growing body of evidence. Narrowly defined structuralist arguments did not satisfactorily explain the high rates of mental disorder and substance abuse documented in carefully designed studies. But by the same token, arguments claiming that individual limitations caused homelessness turned a blind eye toward a well-developed body of scholarship suggesting a close historical relationship between homelessness and broader economic conditions, and ignored the changing social contexts in which poor people—including poor, non-institutionalized mentally ill and substance-abusing adults—lived their lives. Moreover, they could not explain the distinctive demographics of contemporary homelessness, which did not resemble the broader group of those troubled by mental health and substance abuse problems, but instead, those groups at greatest disadvantage in our socioeconomic system (see Chapters 10 and 11). While acknowledging the contributing influences of structural events like deinstitutionalization (without necessarily recognizing their structural character), they continued to frame their explanations of homelessness largely in terms of the limitations of *people*. They ignored one of history's clear lessons: that the lives of all people, disabled or not, are embedded in circumstances shaped as much by structural factors as personal

and biographical ones, and that in a permissive environment full of cheap flops and undemanding work, even outcasts largely remain housed.[2]

This chapter offers a structural explanation of homelessness that gives individual limitations their due. We will be concerned with the effects of the patterned deployment of society's resources, and within this framework will suggest why the ranks of the homeless are disproportionately filled with troubled and troublesome people.

PERVASIVE HOMELESSNESS: THE STRUCTURAL BASIS

The rise in homelessness over the last 15 years has accompanied 2 broad trends, each of which has exacerbated the impact of the other. First, there has been steady erosion of the supply of rental housing affordable to those falling at or below the poverty level. Second, the pool of poor people competing for these increasingly scarce units has swelled at precisely the same time.

The Decline in Low-Cost Housing

The nation's supply of low-cost rental housing has been shrinking for over 20 years. During the 1980s, changes in the federal tax structure, rising interest rates, and new financing practices removed incentives for private investors to produce new low-cost housing, and this occurred just as the federal government was dramatically scaling back the production and maintenance of public housing. Simultaneously, first-time buyers faced substantial difficulty in purchasing single-family homes and thus remained renters. This intensified competition in the rental market and rapidly drove up rents. Further, low-income housing units were lost to demolition, conversion, abandonment, and arson as redevelopment and gentrification reclaimed some inner-city areas previously ceded to the poor. Others were lost as it became fiscally prudent for owners to disinvest and warehouse low-income properties, especially in blighted areas. Contemporary building codes and land-use regulation have made their replacement an ever-more-costly and arduous affair.

While there is room to question the precise mechanics of these processes and their relative importance, the end result is uncontroversial. Ample growth took place in the national housing stock throughout the 1980s, but not at the lower end of the market. The number of units renting for more than $500 per month (in 1987 dollars) increased by 86% between 1981 and 1987, but those renting for less than $300 *fell* by more than 13%.[3] This continued a trend begun in the 1970s, when 6% of units renting for less than $300 were lost. Making a bad situation worse, the rental market was *tightest*[4] among units renting for less than $300. The vacancy rate among units renting for less than $150 stood at 3.8% in 1987, well below the 5% threshold that housing analysts usually consider essential to the normal functioning of the market. As Dolbeare notes in Chapter 4, this dismal situation was somewhat mitigated by a marked increase during this period in the number of renters receiving housing subsidies from the federal government, despite the draconian cuts experienced by the Department of Housing and Urban Development. Still, approximately two-thirds of poor renters received no such subsidies and thus remained extremely vulnerable to the impact of rising housing costs.

National figures mask extremes and local scarcities, of course. The availability of surplus elsewhere in and of itself is no incentive to move. (Generally speaking, a vacancy in Houston does no good for someone queued up for public housing in San Francisco or New York.) For instance, in Los Angeles, the cost of housing shifted to a much greater degree than national figures would suggest. After correcting for inflation, the proportion of units renting for more than $500 in Los Angeles County grew from 14% in 1974 to 45% in 1985. But this occurred at the expense of low-end units, which fell from 35% of the rental stock in 1974 to only 16% by 1985. While the number of units renting for upwards of $750 per month rose by 320% in this time period, the number of units renting for $300 or less fell by 42%, with vacancy rates in this low-end sector hovering around 1%. This

bleak picture continued throughout the 1980s, during which time no net additions to the public housing stock occurred, and approximately 4,000 low-cost housing units (which had cost less than $350/month) were demolished or converted annually.[5]

Not only the stock of multi-room units typically inhabited by poor families suffered significant losses during this period. Even more precipitous losses befell the stock of single-room-occupancy (SRO) hotels, the housing of last resort for those on society's margins, and a particularly important source of housing for poor single persons, including the severely mentally ill and down-and-out substance abusers.[6] This was especially the case in large cities. New York, for instance, lost 87% of its $200 per month or less SRO stock between 1970 and 1982. Chicago, in addition to experiencing sharp losses in SROs, experienced the complete eradication of cubicle hotels that had previously housed thousands of near-homeless individuals in its skid row area. By 1985, more than half the SRO housing that had existed in Los Angeles's downtown area had been destroyed, a process that was arrested only when the city's Community Redevelopment Agency placed a moratorium on downtown SRO demolition.[7]

A Growing Pool of the Vulnerable Poor

A decrease in the supply of housing units at the lower end of the market is not necessarily bad, of course. Were the absolute number of people falling below the poverty level shrinking, a decline in low-end housing units could be interpreted as a healthy response of the housing market to changing demand. This was not the case in the 1970s and 1980s, however, when just as the supply of low-cost housing began to decrease, the demand began to rise. Between 1970 and 1988, the number of poor people grew from 25.4 million to 31.9 million, an increase of almost 26%.

Several factors were responsible for increasing poverty during these years. For one, this period coincided exactly with the coming of age of those born during the "baby boom," the post-World War II birth explosion that lasted through 1964. But during the 1970s and 1980s, when huge numbers of good new jobs were required to absorb the boomers successfully, the American occupational structure was transformed by intensification of an older process called "deindustrialization." Deindustrialization refers to a shift from a predominance of relatively high-paying, often unionized manufacturing jobs to lower-paying, often part-time or temporary service jobs that lack the same level of benefits and security. Ultimately, deindustrialization created a growing pool of young workers, particularly poorly educated women and people of minority status, who became mired in chronic unemployment or in jobs that kept them below the poverty line. As Hardin shows in Chapter 5, wages, work opportunities, and employment levels for these individuals fell precipitously between 1979 and 1993, even during periods of economic recovery.

A steady erosion of the real dollar value of public entitlements other than Social Security also contributed to growing poverty in the 1970s and 1980s. For instance, the monthly purchasing power of a family receiving Aid to Families with Dependent Children (AFDC) fell by almost one-third, from $568 in 1970 to $385 in 1984, a time during which rents increased significantly. (In Chapter 4, Dolbeare shows the current relationship between entitlement levels and prevailing rents.) A related development was the systematic tightening, particularly during the Reagan administration, of eligibility requirements for federal entitlements, which are more generous than aid provided by states and counties (see Chapter 6). This process left almost 500,000 previous recipients of AFDC without access to benefits in 1981 and an additional 300,000 with reduced benefits.[8] It also resulted in almost a half million disabled individuals being removed from the Supplemental Security Income (SSI) and Social Security Disability Insurance (SSDI) programs between 1981 and 1984.[9]

Yet another factor underlying the growing numbers of the poor was deinstitutionalization, which during the 1960s and 1970s propelled into the community a severely mentally ill population—once housed in state institutions—and foreclosed the option of prolonged hospitaliza-

tion for their present day counterparts. The reliance of these individuals on public entitlements for income consigned most to poverty. Thus, a new and socially marginal population of poor individuals entered the pool of those competing for low-cost housing. Similarly, the decriminalization of public drunkenness in many states ensured that public inebriates, most of whom had previously spent considerable time in county jails and state hospitals, now sought housing in their communities.[10] Both of these groups made heavy use of the SRO hotels that, at the time of deinstitutionalization, were sufficiently plentiful to house them. But the rapid erosion of this housing in the 1970s did not bode well for such people or their successors.

Nor did the changing urban landscape. The skid-row neighborhoods that had previously served as zones of tolerance for such people increasingly shrank. Moreover, loss of physical space was accompanied by a decimation of the *vocational* space they occupied. Day labor, which allows people to work intermittently as their functioning and motivation permit (see Chapter 8), was increasingly in short supply. At the same time, changes wrought by deindustrialization and both legal and illegal immigration created a larger, more competent, and more tractable pool of individuals vying for spot work. The growth of the temporary help industry meant that an increasing amount of temporary light industrial work—traditionally important to poor people and skid-row denizens—was controlled by agents who screened out the least presentable job seekers.[11]

Increasing Rent Burden and Its Consequences

The inevitable consequence of sharply rising housing prices and simultaneously decreasing wages and benefits was a growing mismatch between the supply of low-cost housing and the demand for it. As Chapter 4 details, in 1970, a substantial surplus of housing units affordable to households in the bottom quartile of income was available. By 1989, however, there was a deficit of 5 million units—2.8 million units for 7.8 million bottom-quartile renter households.

In other words, there were nearly three poor households for every one unit affordable to them (costing 30% of their income, or less).

Because of the dearth of low-cost housing, poor households began to spend more of their income on rent, increasingly becoming "shelter poor."[12] By 1978, 72% of poor renter households across the nation were spending at least 35% of their income on rent. By 1985, this percentage rose to almost 80%. Even more disturbing, 64% spent more than half their income on rent. Again, these national averages mask regional extremes. In areas of the country where the low-income housing market was particularly tight, the situation was worse. For instance, by 1985, 74% of poor households in Los Angeles spent more than half their income on rent.[13]

To cope with their growing inability to afford housing, poor households found it increasingly necessary to double up, reversing a trend toward smaller households that was apparent until 1978. Even worse, they devoted higher proportions of their income to rent, dangerously stretching their ability to meet basic needs and seriously compromising their ability to cope with even minor financial crises.[14] As their situations worsened, poor households increasingly experienced many of the problems that leave people most vulnerable to homelessness (such as substance abuse and domestic violence). Over time, too, the strain reduced their capacity to support unproductive household members. This latter point is worth highlighting. In good times, when households are less crowded, when budgets are less tight, and when levels of stress are low, it is far easier for an unemployed relative or friend to feel welcome on the couch, or for a severely mentally ill relative to feel comfortable within the household, just as it is easier for household members to accommodate them. Under adverse conditions, such makeshift arrangements are prone to unravel, either because the tense household climate prompts such peripheral household members to leave, or because the household's diminished capacity to provide support leads to their expulsion.

We see, then, that throughout the 1970s and 1980s, poor people—particularly the impaired among them—faced a growing set of pressures that included a dearth of affordable housing, a disappearance of the housing on which the most unstable had relied, and a diminished ability to support themselves either through entitlements or conventional or makeshift labor. Households barely making do increasingly found themselves under financial and interpersonal stress that only made a bad situation worse. Such pressures have a cumulative impact, culminating in the pervasive homelessness we have begun to take for granted.

Once homelessness became an established phenomenon, it fed on itself, not only because the structural forces responsible for it were intensifying, but because the very pervasiveness of homelessness robbed it of some stigma. This is not to say that homelessness became acceptable or that people chose it, but rather that those in intolerable situations could now more easily think about letting go. As Hopper and Milburn point out in Chapter 11, public shelters increasingly became incorporated into the coping strategies of poor individuals and households, particularly African American households. For a young, unemployed man struggling against an uneasy welcome in a relative's household, a municipal shelter could provide an alternative that lessened the possibility of permanently exhausting an important resource. For a woman with young children, cramped in her mother's apartment and unable to afford market housing, a few months in a homeless shelter might provide access to public or subsidized housing, offering her a chance to form her own household (see Chapter 10). With the establishment of homelessness as a social reality, then, new possibilities were added to the myriad makeshifts upon which poor people always had relied for survival. From safety valve to resource in times of transition, the function of shelter was changing.

FRAMING CONSTRAINTS: THE CONTEXT OF LIFE CHANCES

Before reviewing data on life histories and personal characteristics associated with heightened vulnerability to homelessness, it is useful to consider how individual factors can be more or less consequential, depending upon historical trends and local circumstance. Even individual *choices* are swayed by the limits and pressures of changing times, in addition to whatever baggage a person carries from the past. Such constraints not only determine the alternatives that are realistic in a given life, but also establish to a significant extent how the field of choice is structured. Survey research rarely considers such matters. Even more insidious, the formative power of changing contexts in constraining choice, or reckoning its consequences, often passes unnoticed or ill-appreciated by the actors themselves. Koegel, for example, found in his research that although subjects tended to explain their fall into homelessness as a function of their individual problems or specific events, analysis of their life histories revealed that such problems had long existed, and that such events had happened to them many times before, without resulting in homelessness. It was the times that had grown unforgiving, a fact lost on those whose (culturally encouraged) habit was to blame themselves.[15]

Even studies that allude to the general relevance of the housing, income, and policy factors discussed earlier, too often ignore them in their examination of proximate (or immediate) causes of homelessness. We need to decipher and trace the larger structural arrangements that organize the local contexts within which our research is situated and where the relevant dramas of misfortune, from epidemics to homelessness, unfold. We need, that is, to track those persistent "fundamental causes" built into our social structure that determine an individual's relative risk of exposure to hazards, as well as the access to resources for coping with or escaping them.[16] Doing so will alert us to the need not only to contextualize risk factors and behavior, but to watch how the *expression* of continuing stressors (e.g., poverty) changes over time.

With this in mind, let us move on to consider what leaves certain individuals at particularly high risk for homelessness in a context defined by low income and housing scarcity. A methodological caveat is in order first, however.

Taking the Measure of Disorder in Homeless Populations

Epidemiologists distinguish between "point-in-time" counts and "period prevalence," the latter being a measure of people experiencing a given condition over the course of some defined interval of time (see Chapter 2). Obviously, where turnover is great, period prevalence may be many times the magnitude of a single "snapshot" count (as happens, for example, with "demand" in a hospital emergency room). But more to the point here, if "exit" (or recovery) rates are not uniformly distributed throughout the group of sufferers, a point-in-time measure can yield a distorted picture of the whole.

Recent studies of shelter occupancy over time in Philadelphia and New York show that in a given year roughly 5% of the poor population in each city uses the shelter system at some time.[17] Indeed, in New York City, of the 73,000 single persons using the system during a 3-year period, nearly 60,000 used it once or twice, staying less than 2 months on average, and disappeared thereafter.[18] Nor, to judge from comparable analyses of other shelter systems, are these rates unusual. Analysis of available figures from jurisdictions in 6 additional states (Ohio, Minnesota, California, New Hampshire, Rhode Island, and Kentucky) found that between 4.4% and 13% of the local poor made use of public shelter annually in the early 1990s.[19]

With respect to measures of disorder, the point is straightforward. To the extent that disabilities or disruptive habits not only help precipitate homelessness, but extend the duration of a person's homelessness by making it more difficult to secure replacement housing, the rates of disability in cross-sectional studies will be biased upward.[20] The longer-term homeless or shelter users are simply more likely to be captured in any brief sampling procedure. Such a rate inflation tendency should be borne in mind when reading the results reported below.

Three other factors also skew the findings reported. First, most estimates are derived from studies consisting largely of homeless adults who are unmarried or without children in their care. While this group still predominates among the homeless poor in most places, to the extent that studies underrepresent adults in families—whose mental health problems are less severe (see Chapter 10)—they overestimate the prevalence of mental health and alcohol and drug disorders among the total population of homeless adults. Moreover, such studies generally exclude the large numbers of children who become homeless with their parents. Including them would further the lower the prevalence rates.[21] Second, studies commonly report "lifetime" rates, which are invariably inflated relative to current rates of disorder, especially depression and substance use.[22] Finally, summary averages are sometimes taken to yield a "magic number" for prevalence, when close examination of methodologically rigorous studies suggests that great variability exists in rates of mental illness and substance abuse across regions and points in time.[23]

With such caveats in mind, we turn now to a summary of what the data show.

The Prevalence of Disorder

Since the early 1980s, when they first examined the contemporary homeless population in earnest, survey researchers have consistently documented high rates of both severe mental illness and severe substance abuse. Admittedly, early studies suffered from egregious methodological flaws that occasionally surface even now: a woeful lack of precision in the definitions of homelessness used, an even greater degree of variation in definitions of mental illness and substance abuse, an over-reliance on inadequate measures of these disorders, and a failure to draw representative samples of homeless people. As a result, estimates of these disorders across studies have varied enormously, ranging from 1% to 70% in the case of mental health problems, 4% to 86% in the case of alcohol problems, and 2% to 90% in the case of drug problems.[24] Such variability did little to promote consensus on the actual prevalence of these disorders and only fed suspicions that data were

being manipulated to medicalize a social problem.

More precise examination of these studies narrows this range considerably, however. Once we dismiss studies with gross methodological flaws, and once we control for the way in which mental illness and substance abuse are defined and measured, it seems that between 20% and 25% of those homeless people studied have at some time experienced severe and often extremely disabling mental illnesses such as schizophrenia and the major affective disorders (clinical depression or bipolar disorder). The prevalence of substance abuse is even higher. As many as half of the homeless people studied have had diagnosable substance use disorders at some point in their lives, with alcohol use disorder being more prevalent (almost half of all homeless, single adults) than drug use disorder (approximately one-third).

Still, these are lifetime prevalence figures derived from short-term studies of primarily single adults. They are doubtless significantly higher than current prevalence figures would be from, say, a year-long study of a homeless population that included significant numbers of families. Even so, there is no doubt that mental illness and substance abuse, singly or together, are much more common among homeless as opposed to domiciled adults.[25] It is true that we often diagnose as pathological behavior that which is in fact adaptive within the context of homelessness, though more sophisticated diagnostic instruments have been designed to take such factors into consideration, especially those modified to be sensitive to the particularities of homeless life.[26] It is also the case that some homeless adults experience these problems after, rather than before, becoming homeless—a fact that has been used to suggest that homelessness itself causes these problems. While this occurs in a minority of cases, these in no way prove that homelessness is at the root of the disorders observed. It is possible that both homelessness and disorder are to some extent twin products of a complicated set of factors apparent in the life histories of homeless people.

The Contribution of
Long-Standing Misery

Several studies have shown that homeless adults experienced very high rates of out-of-home-placement as children (in foster care, juvenile hall, orphanages, and treatment facilities)—rates that average approximately 20% but reach as high as 40% in some samples.[27] These extraordinarily high rates may be tied to other indicators of family disruption: disproportionately high rates of mental health, substance abuse, and physical health problems among their parents and/or other adult members of their households; physical or sexual abuse in the household; and jail time among adult household members.[28] Fully half of the homeless adults in Koegel and Burnam's Los Angeles sample came from families in which such problems existed. Two-fifths experienced housing problems while living with their families between the ages of 6 and 18 (this at a time when the low-income housing market was far more forgiving): they doubled up with other households because of difficulty paying their rent, experienced evictions, and (in much smaller numbers) experienced literal homelessness with their families before such a phenomenon became common.[29]

On the basis of such findings it is tempting to conclude that vulnerability to homelessness in adulthood has important childhood antecedents, but caution is in order. First, the mechanisms are not clear. Foster placement, for instance, may be related to adult homelessness because it reflects serious psychological damage to children in their original homes (or in foster care, for that matter), or it may be related to adult homelessness because these children are deprived of the material and emotional supports of kinship when they struggle with life as adults. Second, not all studies that assemble comparison groups find stark differences between homeless and domiciled people,[30] especially when it comes to families.[31] One logical reason for this is that the two groups—homeless and housed—do not constitute distinctive populations, as the figures on shelter turnover reviewed earlier suggest. When comparison groups are drawn from other vulnerable, low-

income people living in similar circumstances, the overlap is especially clear.[32]

Similarly, the immediate situational precipitants of homelessness are difficult to interpret because of the absence of good comparison groups. In Koegel and Burnam's Los Angeles research, they asked detailed questions about events that occurred in the year before the members of their sample first became homeless. Some of these events had clear structural roots. For instance, in the year before first becoming homeless, half of the individuals experienced a drop in income, either because they lost a job or lost the public benefits on which they relied. Approximately one-third experienced a major increase in expenses during that period, such as in rent or health care. Other events spoke more pointedly to problematic interpersonal relationships. More than two-fifths reported that they had become separated or divorced, or that they had experienced a break in a relationship with someone else with whom they had been close. Somewhat more than a third faced a situation in which someone on whom they had depended for housing, food, or money was no longer willing or able to help them out. Still other events spoke more directly to individual disorders and their sequelae. Almost half of these adults admitted that they were frequently using alcohol and drugs in the year prior to first becoming homeless. A quarter had spent time in a hospital, jail or prison, group care or treatment facility in that year. Fully one-fifth acknowledged serious physical or mental health problems during that period. Nearly 90% of the sample reported at least one of these various experiences, but multiple experiences were the rule. On average, sample members reported three such problems.

Clearly, there is a plausible argument to be made that some sharp shock to stability, or more likely, some cumulative burden of calamity, finally results in displacement and subsequent homelessness. But without studies that ask such detailed questions of both homeless people and "vulnerable" but for the time being housed people, the case cannot be made with certainty.

Further, to complete the causal picture, we would need to show why certain risk factors for homelessness—whether distal (in childhood) or proximate (precipitating)—are more likely to occur, and with greater disruptive effect, in the lives of some people for whom the game seems rigged at the outset. Certain environments are more likely to breed the sort of events that are associated with later homelessness. Such environments are not randomly distributed across a population with vastly unequal degrees of access to resources or gradients of exposure to hazard. It is this larger, persisting scaffolding— the social structures that "organize the defining encounters"[33] between host and pathogen (or person and risk factor)—that we need to construct, and its relation to more immediate causes to untangle.

CONCLUSION

Given a structural context that fosters homelessness, people may be at risk because of their economic situations, their demographic characteristics, their disabilities, their childhood histories, their access to family and friends, their personalities, or their experience of any number of situational crises. Conceivably, any of these alone can trigger homelessness. Most often, however, they act in combination, probably because they are all so interrelated. Risk factors, in other words, are almost invariably bundled; very rarely does one alone cause homelessness. And the chances that one will acquire such bundles are not evenly distributed at the outset of the game. Nor do they even out over time.

While available knowledge does not allow us to assign definite probabilities of becoming homeless to vulnerable people based on the particular bundle of risk factors they exhibit, it is clear that the extent to which a given risk factor predisposes an individual to homelessness is a function of the overall vulnerability load he or she bears. In other words, there may be a common threshold beyond which one's summed vulnerability translates into extremely high risk of homelessness.

The lesson here is that there are no simple solutions to the problem of homelessness. Effective policy responses must at a minimum address both the vulnerabilities that leave certain individuals at risk for homelessness and the structural conditions that differentially distribute such vulnerabilities and make their consequences more serious. Thus, rehabilitative and economic responses must be *paired* so that affordable housing is provided along with the jobs, services, and supports that will allow vulnerable people to stay housed. More challenging still would be to address the terrific imbalance of resources and opportunity in the starting gate. The political task is to recognize that homelessness is not an isolated crisis requiring an independent set of solutions, but is one of many symptoms—like the crack epidemic or the foster care debacle—which point to the growing failure of the needs-meeting structures of our society. We cannot address homelessness at its sources until we recognize that it is inextricably connected to other social ills—as the biographies of homeless people amply attest. As Rosenheck and Fontana recently noted, we would be wise to view homelessness as "the proverbial miner's canary."[34]

CHAPTER 4

Housing Policy:
A General Consideration

Cushing N. Dolbeare

The one thing all homeless people have in common is a lack of housing. Whatever other problems they face, adequate, stable, affordable housing is a prerequisite to solving them. Homelessness may not be *only* a housing problem, but it is *always* a housing problem; housing is necessary, although sometimes not sufficient, to solve the problem of homelessness.

A CHANGING PROBLEM

In 1940, when the first housing census was taken in the United States, 46% of all households lived in units that either lacked basic plumbing facilities or were classified as dilapidated. Crowding and doubling up were also at far higher levels than today. These conditions continued through World War II.

At war's end, the nation sought to make good on a commitment to provide returning veterans with educations and homes. Through the 1950s—when long-term mortgages were available and interest rates were low—the balance between housing costs and incomes was such that almost any White man with a steady job could afford to buy a new house. The economy was good and construction boomed. During this period, the focus of federal housing policy was on the quantity and quality of the supply, not on affordability.

During the postwar decades, suburbs expanded dramatically. In 1950, 42% of the metropolitan population lived outside of central cities. By 1960, the proportion had risen to almost half (49%), and by 1980, the figure had reached 60%, roughly the current level.[1] Suburban growth was fueled by Federal Housing Administration (FHA) and Veterans Administration (VA) mortgage insurance, and by road and highway construction that meant housing no longer needed to be near jobs or public transportation. Employment and business opportunities eventually followed the migration to the suburbs. But minorities were excluded from suburbanization, as were low-income Whites. With diminished tax bases, central cities were left to cope with the needs of the households left behind. Thus, the housing trends that expanded the suburbs were also a major cause of the social and fiscal crisis that now affects many central cities.

During the 1960s, housing needs began to shift, though the change was little noticed by housing advocates and policy makers. Quality and supply problems were being addressed; growing affordability problems were not. Indeed, the 1968 Report of the President's Committee on Urban Housing, which proposed the goal of constructing or rehabilitating 26 million units over a 10-year span, 6 million for low-income households, based the latter number on its estimate of occupied, substandard units. The report acknowledged affordability problems almost in passing, but it recommended an experimental program of housing allowances. The Housing and Urban Development Act of 1968 incorporated the major recommendations of the committee. It now seems the high-water mark of the federal commitment to housing.

The 1970s was a period of struggle over housing policy. In 1973, President Nixon imposed a moratorium on additional low-income housing commitments, which lasted until late 1974. The controversy generated by that action has overshadowed both the substantial low-income housing achievements during that decade and the fact that the number of additional commitments for low-income housing reached its highest level ever during 1976, the last year of the Ford administration. It took from roughly 1937 to 1970 to complete the first million subsidized housing units (excluding housing in rural areas financed by the Farmers Home Administration of the U.S. Department of Agriculture). Between 1970 and 1980, the number almost trebled, to 2.8 million. Most of the increase after 1980 was in rental assistance through the Section 8 program, which enabled low-income households to afford rents in privately owned units.[2]

During the 1980s, in spite of savage budget cuts, the number of occupied, low-income units subsidized by the Department of Housing and Urban Development (HUD) increased by another 50%, and stood at roughly 4.6 million in 1990.[3] Despite some modest increases during the early 1990s, it appears unlikely that the number of households occupying HUD-subsidized low-income housing will reach 5 million

in the foreseeable future, if ever. Indeed, because most of the subsidy contracts expire, the amount of HUD-subsidized, low-income housing is almost certain to decrease in the near future.[4]

The majority of low-income renters receive no subsidies, however. In 1993, only a relatively small proportion of low-income renters lived in public or privately owned federally subsidized units: 37% of the 3.1 million households with incomes below $5,000, 37% of the 5.4 million households with incomes between $5,000 and $10,000, and 19% of the 3.7 million households with incomes between $10,000 and $15,000. The proportion declines further as incomes rise.

Furthermore, most low-rent housing is in the unsubsidized stock. Except for units with gross monthly rents[5] below $250, most housing that rents for less than fair market rents[6] is not subsidized by the federal government. While 79% of the 0.9 million units costing less than $125 monthly in 1993 were federally subsidized, the proportion dropped to 54% for the 3.1 million units costing between $125 and $250, and to 12% for the 12.3 million units costing between $250 and $500, with the proportion dropping further for higher-cost units.[7]

AFFORDABILITY: THE KEY ISSUE

While problems of quality and shortage persist, the overriding housing problem today is affordability. During the 1970s, the loss of private, unsubsidized, low-cost rental units far outweighed the increase in subsidized units. Many households, particularly renters, have such low incomes that they cannot possibly pay what it costs to provide housing.[8] The key facts about low-income housing affordability are outlined below.

The Rental Affordability Gap

A useful (though over-simplified) way to gauge the extent of the affordability changes during the 1970s and 1980s is to compare the number of households in the bottom quartile of the renter income distribution with the number of units that fall in the range they can afford at

30% of income.[9] This simple comparison of the poorest quarter of renter households and the number of units they can afford shows the trend. In 1970, there were 500,000 more units in the bottom quartile affordability range than households. By 1989, there were 7.8 million bottom-quartile renter households, but only 2.8 million affordable units. In other words, there was a gap of 5 million units.

The gap was caused by a combination of falling real incomes of renter households and rising real housing costs. Also, the number of renter households increased, while much of the private, unsubsidized, low-rent housing that existed in 1970 was lost either because of rent and utility increases, abandonment, or conversion to other uses. In constant 1995 dollars, the 25th percentile renter household income dropped by 30% between 1970 and 1989, and the affordable housing cost for this household, at 30% of income, dropped from $240 to $169 per month. Meanwhile, median inflation-adjusted gross rents increased 31% between 1970 and 1989, from $317 to $416. The number of occupied units with costs below the affordable threshold dropped dramatically, from 5.8 million in 1970 to only 2.8 million in 1989. The decline in affordable units for these poorest households was primarily caused by the loss of privately owned, unsubsidized, low-cost housing units, together with the failure of subsidized housing programs to offset the shortfall. In 1970, only 10% of the bottom-quartile units were subsidized; by 1989, 74% were subsidized.

This analysis refutes the contention of some that housing affordability has little to do with the dramatic increase of homelessness. The low-cost units did not disappear because the public demanded larger units with more amenities. Instead, they vanished because of the pressure of rising energy costs and other costs of maintaining and operating housing, together with the demolition of many older units and the gentrification of others.[10]

This analysis also refutes the widespread assumption that the affordability gap was generated primarily by the cuts made in low-income housing programs by the Reagan administration. It is accurate to say, however, that those cuts

reduced the *rate of increase* in the number of occupied subsidized housing units. Between 1970 and 1980, the number of occupied subsidized housing units rose from 1 million to 3.2 million. By 1990, the total number of subsidized units was 4.4 million. The number of subsidized units occupied by households in the bottom quartile rose from an estimated 0.6 million in 1970 to an estimated 1.6 million in 1989. The remaining subsidized units were occupied by households whose incomes, although low, were above the bottom quartile.

Despite the growing number of subsidized bottom-quartile units, only a small proportion of eligible low-income households are, in fact, living in subsidized housing. Just over one-quarter (26%) of "very-low-income" renter households—the group eligible for housing assistance—lived in federally assisted housing. Overall, in 1993, 13% of the nation's 33.5 million renter households occupied subsidized housing.[11]

The foregoing "housing gap" analysis seriously understates real housing needs because it ignores many basic housing facts: At least a third of the inexpensive units were occupied by people with incomes above the bottom quarter. The cost of many of the units classified as inexpensive was near the ceiling used, whereas many renters had incomes that were much lower. Many of the units were substandard. Many were of the wrong size or in the wrong location. Many were unavailable to minorities or families with children, for example, because of discriminatory renting practices. Somewhat offsetting this, the calculation ignores vacant units on the assumption that if they were suitable and available, they would be occupied.

A major consequence of the affordability gap is that many renters are forced to pay very high proportions of their incomes for housing. Obviously, the validity of using percent of income paid for housing as a measure of affordability depends on the level of income in the first place; for example, a household with an income of $1 million after taxes could pay 90% of it for housing costs and still have $100,000 left for nonhousing needs.[12]

A sounder (but more complicated) method to measure housing affordability is a "residual" or "market basket" criterion, under which the affordable housing amount is the remainder after subtracting the cost of other basic necessities. An estimated 1.9 million renter households had incomes so low in 1989 that, using this approach, they could not afford *anything* for housing. They are the people most at risk of homelessness. An additional 7.9 million renter households could afford something for housing, but generally far less than they actually paid. Ironically, it is the households who can least afford to pay substantial portions of their incomes for housing who have the highest ratios of housing costs to income. Half of all shelter-poor renters paid more than 50% of their incomes for housing in 1989; only 17% paid less than 30%.[13]

Except for renters living in subsidized housing, there is a high correlation between low incomes and high housing cost burdens. In 1993, 69% of unsubsidized renters with incomes below the poverty level paid more than half their incomes for housing. Only 14% paid less than 30% of income. Almost two-thirds (64%) of all renters paying over half their incomes for rent in 1993 had incomes below the poverty level. Only 12% had incomes above 200% of poverty.

The affordability problems of those owning homes were far less critical. Only 3.8 million owners, or 7% of the 55.1 million owner households, spent more than half of their incomes on housing costs. Two million of these, or 4%, spent more than 70% of their incomes on housing. Another 7.1 million owners spent between 30% and 49% of income on housing costs. Half of all owners paid 18% or less of their incomes for housing.

Whether renters or owners, most U.S. households that pay substantial percentages of their incomes for housing have very low incomes. Thus, housing costs exacerbate differences in income distribution in this country. For example, the median income of renter households paying 50% or more of their incomes for housing in 1993 was $7,000, about 12% of the median income of renters paying less than 10% ($58,200). But after paying housing costs, the median renter household paying less than 10% of income had 48 times as much income for other needs as the median high-cost-burden household ($53,800 compared to $1,100).

"Worst Case" Housing Problems

Federal housing law gives preference for admission to subsidized housing to households who are displaced, living in severely inadequate housing, homeless, or paying more than half their incomes for housing costs. These are known as "priority problems."[14] Unsubsidized renter households with incomes below 50% of area median who have one or more of these problems have "worst case" housing needs.

A HUD study of 1993 American Housing Survey (AHS) data (which do not include homeless people) found 5.8 million renter households and another 4.7 million owner households with priority problems. Of these 10.5 million households, 5.3 million were renters with incomes below 50% of their area's median who did not receive housing assistance. These "worst case" households comprised 5.6% of all households. Significantly, high rent burden was the *only* problem of 78% of the worst case households, although the incidence of multiple problems was higher among worst case households than among other very-low-income households.

The HUD study found both that worst case needs had been growing dramatically and that they were increasingly concentrated among extremely low-income households—those with incomes below 30% of median. Worst case needs grew by 1.1 million between 1978 and 1991, and by another 400,000 between 1991 and 1993, a time of steady economic expansion. The increases since 1978 were solely because more very-low-income renters paid over 50% of income for rent. Fewer than 9% of worst case households in 1993 lived in inadequate housing; 95% paid over half their incomes for housing. This growth in worst case needs reflects declining incomes at the lowest levels, particularly families with children—many of whom depended solely or partly on Aid to Families with Dependent Children (AFDC). Forty-three percent of worst case households have incomes below 20% of median, and another 29% have incomes below 21% and 30% of median. Over 70% of unassisted renters with incomes below 30% of median have worst case problems, compared with 23% of those with incomes between 31% and 50% of median. Only 5% of renters with incomes between 51% and 80% of median have comparable problems.

Worst case needs increased by 1.25 million between 1978 and 1993 for extremely poor households (incomes below 30% of median), but by only 250,000 for households with incomes between 31% and 50% of median. Comparable problems fell slightly for households with incomes between 51% and 80% of median. In large part because of federal preferences, federal housing subsidy programs are well targeted to addressing worst case needs: more than 70% of public housing and Section 8 units—the bulk of federally subsidized housing—are occupied by extremely poor households.[15]

Families with children constitute 42% of worst case households; childless elderly households, 21%; childless, disabled households, 3%; and "other" households, 34%. The striking rise in the number of households with children with worst case needs accounted for 76% of the increase in extremely low-income households.

Overall, the private, unassisted housing market has been increasingly able to meet the needs of households with incomes above 50% of median, although shortages persist in many areas. In addition, the Housing Partnership (HOME) and Low Income Housing Tax Credit programs have substantially increased the supply of units affordable for households with incomes between 51% and 80% of median. However, more deeply subsidized housing, including rental assistance, is the primary source of affordable units for extremely poor households. In 1993, the housing gap for extremely low-income households stood at 1.6 million, and many of the available units were occupied by households with higher incomes. The result: there were only 46 afford-

able units per 100 extremely low-income households that were actually occupied by or available to these households. Moreover, affordable housing for extremely low-income households is "filtering up" to higher rent levels far more rapidly than higher cost housing is filtering down.[16]

Single-Room-Occupancy Housing

A key housing trend with particular impact on homelessness has been the loss of single-room-occupancy (SRO) housing in many urban communities. Indeed, it was not until the visible rise in homelessness that SRO housing was recognized as playing a significant role in meeting an otherwise unmet housing need. Prior to this, SRO units typically were considered substandard; for instance, many housing codes prohibited housing units without private bathrooms. Moreover, federally subsidized housing programs did not generally admit single persons—unless they were elderly or handicapped, or the housing could not otherwise be filled—until the definition of "family" was revised in 1990 to include them.

Meanwhile, urban renewal and other efforts dramatically reduced the number of SRO units, although no good information is available on how many have been lost. Certainly a major thrust of many urban renewal efforts was downtown revitalization and the elimination of skid rows. The most widely used estimate is that at least one million SRO units were demolished between 1970 and the mid-1980s. Census and AHS data are of little use in attempting to quantify the losses, because much SRO housing does not appear to meet the operational definition of "housing unit."

Clearly, however, efforts to reverse this trend and provide decent SRO units have been minimal compared to the number of people displaced by earlier demolition. The HUD moderate rehabilitation program for SRO units, for example, subsidized fewer than 7,000 units between 1988 and 1991, after which HUD stopped reporting the number of units funded by the annual appropriations available. The $105 million appropriated in 1991 produced 2,995 units. From

1992 through 1995, an additional $457 million was appropriated for this program.

Since 1994, HUD has pressed for consolidation of all of the McKinney Act programs it administers (see Chapters 15 and 16) into a formula grant program, which will give recipient states and local governments discretion over how funds to aid homeless people are spent, with the focus to be on a "continuum of care." But, as with other forms of needed federal housing assistance, there is little likelihood that the scale of the program will meet more than a tiny fraction of the need.

State Variations in Affordability

The national data cited above obscure wide local variations in housing affordability. No other major component of the cost of living index shows as much variation from state to state and metropolitan area to metropolitan area. Moreover, the differences in incomes as well as housing costs mean that some states with relatively high costs—and high incomes—have fewer affordability problems than states with low costs—but even lower incomes. For example, West Virginia, which ranked 50th in housing costs and renter incomes, ranked 6th in the median percent of renter income spent on housing. Conversely, Alaska, which ranked 6th in housing costs and 2nd in renter income, ranked 50th in percent of income spent on housing costs.

For several years, I have used HUD's fair market rents for existing housing and HUD's estimates of household income to estimate the extent of housing affordability problems for states and metropolitan areas. Since fair market rents, which include utilities, are based on costs of recent movers into unsubsidized housing more than two years old, they tend to be higher than median rents. So estimates of the proportion of households who cannot afford fair market rents differ from those based on actual cost levels. But they are a good indication of the direction in which housing costs are moving and, more important for homeless households, they indicate the amount that households seeking housing can expect to pay to obtain decent units.

Based on 1994 fair market rents (FMRs) and renter income estimates, at least one-third of all renter households in every single state cannot afford the HUD fair market rent for a one-bedroom unit.[17] In the median state, an estimated 39% of renter households cannot afford the $417 FMR for a one-bedroom unit. More than half of all renter households in three states (Hawaii, New York, and Illinois) and the District of Columbia cannot afford their FMRs, which range from $537 to $909.

Half of all renter households need at least a two-bedroom unit, but they cost even more. In the median state, an estimated 47% of renter households cannot afford the $523 FMR for a 2-bedroom unit. Three out of 5 renter households in Hawaii, the District of Columbia, and New York cannot afford the fair market rent for a 2-bedroom unit. More than half the renters in 14 additional states cannot afford to rent such units. Even in Kansas and Utah, the "most affordable" states, the FMR for a 2-bedroom apartment is beyond the reach of 40% of all renter households.

Worst of all, and most relevant to homeless people, are the disparities between AFDC and Supplemental Security Income (SSI) payments and fair market rents. The FMR for a 2-bedroom unit is higher than the entire maximum AFDC grant for a mother with 2 children in every state except Alaska. In seven states (Mississippi, Texas, Alabama, Tennessee, Louisiana, South Carolina, and Arkansas) and the District of Columbia, the grant is less than *half* the FMR (see Figure 4.1). Households dependent on Supplemental Security Income also have critical affordability problems, although they are somewhat better off than those on AFDC. The SSI grant for a single person is below the fair market rent for a 1-bedroom unit in 15 states and the District of Columbia. In the states where the SSI grant exceeds the FMR, FMRs range from 64% to 96% of the grant.[18]

FIGURE 4.1

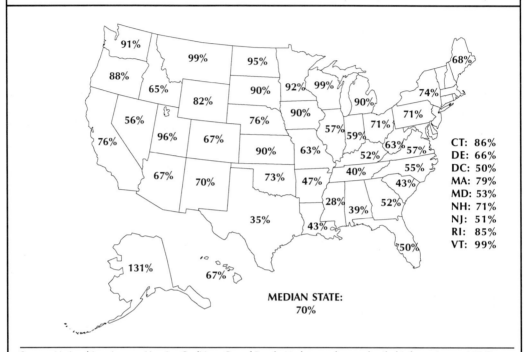

PERCENT OF RENT FOR 2-BEDROOM UNIT COVERED BY ENTIRE MAXIMUM AFDC GRANT, 1994 (FOR 3-PERSON HOUSEHOLD)

91%
99%
95%
68%
88%
65%
90%
92% 99%
74%
82%
90%
56%
76%
90%
71%
76%
96%
67%
90%
63%
57% 59%
71%
63% 57%
52%
67%
70%
73%
47%
40%
55%
43%
28%
52%
35%
39%
43%
50%

CT: 86%
DE: 66%
DC: 50%
MA: 79%
MD: 53%
NH: 71%
NJ: 51%
RI: 85%
VT: 99%

131%
67%

MEDIAN STATE:
70%

Source: National Low Income Housing Coalition, *Out of Reach*. Updates and more detailed information on AFDC grant levels compared to fair market rents can be obtained from the National Low Income Housing Coalition/Low Income House Information Service, 1012 Fourteenth Street, N.W., Washington, DC 20005 (202-662-1530).

FEDERAL SPENDING FOR HOUSING

Federal spending for housing is done in three ways. First, before any spending commitments can be made, Congress must make an appropriation of the necessary *budget authority*. Budget authority authorizes the government to incur a financial obligation that will result in *outlays*, which are payments to discharge the obligations that have been incurred. Budget authority for housing is generally calculated as the cost of the commitment over the life of the subsidy contract; outlays are the payments made under all contracts and commitments currently in force. *Tax expenditures* are the cost to the U.S. Treasury of income deductions and deferrals contained in the various provisions of tax law. Each year, the federal budget states the cost of all budget authority and outlays by agency, program and function, and the estimated cost of all tax expenditures.

An example may be helpful. If you are buying a house, your down payment and total payments incurred over the life of the mortgage would be your *budget authority*. To get your total budget authority, you would add the down payment and the monthly mortgage payments over 360 months (if it were a 30-year mortgage). Thus, the bulk of the budget authority would come when you purchase the unit. But there would also be some additional budget authority each year for maintenance, utilities, and other expenses not included in the mortgage. Your *outlays* would be the payments for all of these costs that you make in any given year. And the amount you save by deducting your mortgage interest and property taxes from your income tax would be your benefit from federal housing-related *tax expenditures*.

Patterns of Federal Housing Spending

In inflation-adjusted 1996 dollars, budget authority for federal low-income housing programs peaked in 1978 at $98 billion. This was 6.4% of all federal budget authority. Moreover, 80% of this amount was spent for providing additional subsidized units or households. In that year, outlays for low-income housing assistance cost $17 billion. Housing-related tax expenditures, primarily homeowner deductions, cost $73 billion.

In contrast, the Clinton administration's current budget request calls for $17 billion in low-income housing budget authority. This is only 1.4% of total budget authority. Worse, less than 25% of this amount is to be used for assisting additional households through vouchers and the HOME, rural housing, homeless, elderly, and other special-needs housing programs. Federal outlays for low-income housing assistance are projected to cost $28 billion, and tax expenditures in 1997 are estimated at $101.8 billion.

TABLE 4.1

FEDERAL HOUSING EXPENDITURES AND BENEFITS, 1994

Estimated Federal Housing Expenditures, in Millions of Dollars

	Income Quintile					
	Lowest	Second	Third	Fourth	Top	All
Estimated Quintile Income Limit	13,100	25,500	38,200	60,600	—	—
Mortgage Interest	52	380	2,117	9,753	39,533	51,835
Property Taxes	15	96	541	2,397	10,816	13,865
Capital Gains	20	133	747	3,375	14,421	18,695
Investor	13	90	503	2,274	9,719	12,600
Total, Tax Expenditures	100	699	3,909	17,799	74,488	96,995
Low-Income Housing Outlays	20,786	2,416	504	120	14	23,840
Total Housing Costs	20,886	3,115	4,413	17,919	74,502	120,835

Estimated Households Receiving Housing Benefits

	Income Quintile					
	Lowest	Second	Third	Fourth	Top	All
Tax Benefits*	124	707	2,992	8,471	16,127	28,422
Housing Assistance*	3,567	829	346	165	47	4,954
Total*	3,690	1,536	3,338	8,636	16,175	32,771
Percent of Quintile	20%	8%	18%	46%	87%	—
Average Amount per Household Receiving Subsidy	$5,660	$2,027	$1,322	$2,075	$4,606	$3,620
Average Subsidy per Household in Quintile	$1,121	$167	$237	$962	$3,999	$1,297

Source: National Low Income Housing Coalition
*Thousands of households

The entitlement to deduct mortgage interest from income for tax purposes is this nation's most expensive housing program. It is a subsidy provided to all homeowners with mortgages and enough income to itemize their income tax deductions. About 40% of all homeowners use this entitlement; the rest either do not have mortgages or their incomes are too low for them to benefit from itemized deductions. In 1996, the mortgage interest deduction is estimated to cost the U.S. Treasury $51 billion. Additional homeowner deductions for property taxes and exclusion or deferral of capital gains on home sales will bring the total to $86 billion.[19]

For every dollar of outlays for low-income housing programs, the federal treasury loses four dollars to housing-related tax expenditures. In 1994, more than three-quarters of these expenditures benefited households in the top fifth of the income distribution. The top fifth got an estimated 61% of all housing benefits—both tax and direct—compared to only 18% for the bottom fifth. Only 19% of the households in the bottom fifth—about 3.7 million in all—got federal housing assistance, although two-thirds of the households in this quintile had housing problems. In contrast, 87% of the households in the top fifth got homeowner deductions. Households in the middle three-fifths were least likely to get federal housing benefits. Table 4.1 summarizes the data on the inequity of our housing subsidy system. The top panel gives the distribution of housing outlays and major tax expenditure categories, and the bottom panel shows the number of households receiving assistance.

In short, as low-income housing needs have grown, our performance has withered—but tax expenditures, which primarily benefit upper-income people, have not been restrained. Yet, for about half of what the federal government "spends" on tax benefits to people in the top fifth of the income distribution, it would be possible to provide permanent, affordable housing not only for all the homeless families and individuals in the United States, but also for housed people who must skimp on other necessities in order to pay for their housing, or who live in housing that does not meet minimum standards of decency.

The Federal Housing Trust Fund Proposal

Clearly, homelessness and other housing problems will grow unless we change the scale of low-income housing programs. In part because low-income housing and homeless advocates have had so many proposed cuts to fight over the last 20 years, there has been little organized effort to mobilize public support for the scale of effort needed. Therefore, in 1994, the National Low Income Housing Coalition launched a national effort to do this through a Housing Justice Campaign. The major long-term goal of this campaign is the establishment of a Federal Housing Trust Fund to generate an estimated $25 billion annually to provide housing assistance and to expand and improve the stock of affordable housing.

The purpose of the Federal Housing Trust Fund is to make access to decent, affordable housing a reality for low- and moderate-income people. The trust fund would be created by *reducing*, but not eliminating, the benefits of homeowner deductions to upper-income households. Funds would be allocated, by formula, to state and local entities to carry out eligible housing activities, including rental and home-ownership assistance, affirmative fair housing efforts, and improvement and expansion of the housing supply to provide affordable units and a range of quality housing choices for low- and moderate-income people.

The proposed Federal Housing Trust Fund would be based on the following principles:

- Trust fund resources would be used for rental and home-ownership assistance, for increasing and improving the housing supply, and for community-based work to overcome segregation and other barriers to affordable housing. The fund would be targeted first at the needs of very-low-income people with critical housing problems. It would be a flexible source of funds usable for both tenant-based and project-based assistance, as well as assistance for fee-simple homeowners, co-op members, and others, and for production and rehabilitation of housing of all types needed.

- Fair housing and counseling activity by community-based organizations would be an integral component of trust fund activity throughout the nation.

- Modifications of housing-related tax deductions to support the fund would be carefully drawn to meet the following conditions:

  1. Only taxpayers in households in the top fifth of the income distribution would be affected, and all taxpayers would continue to be able to take substantial deductions.

  2. The proposal would not penalize taxpayers living in areas with high housing costs, or produce significant disincentives to home buying or housing mobility.

  3. Because it would affect only high-income taxpayers and would be phased in, the proposal would not drastically and suddenly reduce the value of housing currently occupied by homeowners.

  4. The proposal would provide sufficient income to the trust fund, when fully phased in, to support the estimated cost of providing an adequate supply of housing, opportunity for housing choice, and assistance to cover the gap between 30% of income and the cost of housing needed in the market area.

- A major objective is to strengthen community-based nonprofit organizations, particularly those involved in fair housing, in counseling, and in enforcement, litigation, and advocacy for greater housing opportunity for low-income people. The trust fund would provide significant support for these activities.

The Federal Housing Trust Fund would supplement and complement existing housing programs, not replace them, recognizing that current programs frequently are responsive to special conditions, and also that in many cases community-based groups have expertise in dealing with such programs. Current programs and the housing opportunities created by current and former programs represent a valuable and often irreplaceable resource for meeting low-income housing needs.

THE OUTLOOK FOR FEDERAL HOUSING PROGRAMS

Since reaching its peak in 1976, the rate of expansion of federal low-income housing programs has declined dramatically. While Presidents Bush and Clinton expanded programs of housing assistance to homeless people, neither attempted to reverse the effects of cuts in the overall housing budget achieved during the Reagan administration. Both, moreover, faced public and congressional support for reducing federal expenditures generally, and neither made expanding low-income housing programs a personal priority.

The election of 1994 threatened the viability, and perhaps the existence, of any federal low-income housing efforts. HUD itself has proposed "re-inventing" or reconfiguring its housing and community development programs in an effort to keep them alive. Some members of Congress, in key positions to influence the substance of housing legislation or the level of funding, have urged that the federal government substitute block grants—with few or no strings attached—for the current array of federal housing programs. Others have developed their own approaches for significant changes. At this writing (February 1996), two things are clear: first, funding for low-income housing will be significantly reduced; second, there will be major changes in program structure and substance. However, the specifics of these changes are still unclear.

Several trends can be identified, however. First, federal funds for expanding low-income housing and other HUD programs will almost certainly decline—or even disappear—under all of the scenarios currently under consideration for the overall federal budget for the 1996–2002 period. Second, the total number of households living in federally subsidized, low-income housing is likely to decrease, with far more reliance placed on tenant-based assistance and a steady reduction in the number of very-low-income units with project-based assistance. Third, targeting requirements mandating priority for "worst case" households will be relaxed or repealed. Fourth, HUD will be reduced in size, and states and local governments will be given far more flexibility in carrying out HUD-funded programs.

Less Federal Money for Housing

As this is written, the Clinton administration and Congress have agreed to balance the federal budget by 2002, but they have reached no conclusion on the specifics of how to do it. Under all proposals being seriously considered, the level of funding for discretionary programs will decline. Some programs will probably expand to some degree, however, with the specific programs and amounts depending on the outcome of the negotiations. But housing programs are not included in the priorities articulated by the president or any of the congressional parties to the negotiations.

Fewer Households Helped

Since 1974, the number of units assisted with either project-based or tenant-based subsidies has increased, although the increases have diminished to a fraction of their 1970s levels. Just as most homeowners get a mortgage when they purchase—to spread the cost over a number of years—HUD project-based subsidies have traditionally been provided under contracts to make annual contributions (the subsidy) for a specified period. The amount of the subsidy and the length of the contract have varied, but the pattern has been the same. Initially, the contracts were for 40 years, but the duration has been shortened so that the standard for project-based subsidies recently has been 15 years. Subsidies for tenant-based assistance are now normally provided for a five-year period.

Several years ago, the early subsidy contracts began to expire, and HUD and the Congress renewed them. However, subsidy contract expirations have become bunched, with most 40-year, 15-year, and 5-year contracts due to expire by 2005. HUD estimates that during this period, contracts for about 800,000 units of Section 8 project-based housing and about 1,000,000 tenant-based vouchers and certificates will expire. Project-based Section 8 subsidy contracts covering about 200,000 units will expire each year from Fiscal Year 1996 through Fiscal Year 1999. The cost of renewing these contracts is currently estimated at $14 billion in 1999. HUD is therefore proposing, and Congress is currently considering, a "mark to market" approach, under which rents on most projects would float to market levels, and residents would be given vouchers or certificates and the choice of remaining in the unit or using their vouchers to move elsewhere. As necessary, the outstanding mortgages on the properties would be reduced so that projects would be financially viable at market rents.[20]

The devils here are, first, in the details. Assuming that the concept is sound, inevitable, or both, how can it be carried out without displacing tenants and/or providing windfalls to some owners and penalizing others? Second, what assurance is there either that residents will continue to receive rental assistance or that they will be able to find decent, affordable housing in neighborhoods where they wish to live?

Already, there is resistance at the Office of Management and Budget and in Congress to adding rental assistance units, given the pressures on discretionary funds. HUD is persisting in its efforts to expand rental assistance, but it seems improbable—to put it mildly—that low-income housing will compete successfully with other more popular activities for the additional appropriations needed to maintain the current subsidized level.[21]

Targeting Relaxed

The federal preferences giving "worst case" households priority for subsidized housing have been effective in increasing the proportion of very-low-income households receiving assistance. The number of such households living in subsidized housing has increased significantly faster than the number of subsidized units. Once living in subsidized housing, these households are unlikely to leave unless their economic circumstances improve. All too often, this is precluded by the location of the housing and the absence of employment and education opportunities. Meanwhile, most households with one or two steadily employed members, even when wages are low, are able to afford unsubsidized housing and often choose to move there.

This situation has led to a concerted effort by housing owners, HUD, and many policy makers to relax the targeting requirements. Indeed, housing laws adopted in 1990 and 1992 significantly eroded targeting requirements, reducing them from 90% of new admissions to 50%. Legislation currently pending in Congress, and likely to be adopted in some form during 1996, would repeal the federal preferences, including the preference for homeless people. Instead, local housing agencies would adopt their own preferences, although there would still be some income targeting required, including some percentage of available units allocated to households with incomes below 30% of area median. However, given the increase of extremely low-income households—particularly families with children—with worst case needs, any relaxation of targeting is likely to have a major impact on homelessness.

More State and Local Discretion

The current Republican majority in Congress has made devolution of the substance and administration of many federal programs a primary theme. At the same time, the success of the HOME and Community Development Block Grant (CDBG) programs has led both HUD and many advocates to support programs that combine federally mandated goals with local flexibility in achieving them.

Shortly after the 1994 election, HUD unveiled the first of a series of "re-invention" pro-posals, which called for restructuring HUD's major housing subsidy programs and consolidating a multitude of small programs and some larger ones into several major block grants. Meanwhile, the House and Senate are working on legislation to reshape the public housing program, giving most local authorities (except "troubled" public housing agencies) far more flexibility. Congress is expected to consider the still-evolving proposals for block-granting homeless programs and consolidating other programs into block grants for housing assistance, HOME, and CDBG. Under HUD's own proposals, the department would be reduced in size. A likely component of any legislation, given the commitment of the congressional leadership to reducing federal mandates, will be a relaxation of many current targeting and planning requirements. Thus, the extent to which state and local governments use federal housing funds to address the needs of homeless people may well depend less on federal requirements than on the sensitivity of state and local governments and on the effectiveness of advocacy directed at them.

CONCLUSION

The problem of homelessness is rooted in the failure of this nation to address its low-income housing problems, particularly the gap between housing costs and income available to pay them. No matter how dedicated and creative those attempting to deal with homelessness may be, the problem cannot be significantly diminished without a fundamental shift in national priorities and a resolve to allocate spending for low-income housing on the basis of dealing with actual housing needs.

CHAPTER 5

Why the Road off the Street Is Not Paved with Jobs

Bristow Hardin

The dream of reason did not take power into account.
—Paul Starr, *The Social Transformation of American Medicine*

INTRODUCTION

This chapter analyzes labor market trends and related developments affecting homeless people's employment options and the viability of an "employment strategy" for mitigating homelessness. It emphasizes two points that are highlighted throughout this volume. First, homeless people are the most dispossessed and disfranchised members of American society. Not only are they financially destitute in a society where freedom is fundamentally determined by access to material resources, but in losing their homes, they frequently lose their possessions, their connections to critical social networks and institutions, and the rights "that legitimate one in the eyes of society and government."[1] Second, analyzing social problems such as poverty and homelessness by focusing on the attributes and characteristics of "the poor" or "the homeless"—a distinctively American tendency—is of limited usefulness if the goal is to eliminate or mitigate such problems and their effects. Analysts elsewhere find this approach "bizarre,"[2] not least because it obscures the nature and causes of these problems and thereby undermines the efficacy of policies to address them. A more fruitful strategy is to analyze the structural conditions and dynamics that create and perpetuate these problems, and then to examine the characteristics of those most affected by them *within the context of* these conditions and dynamics.

With this in mind, the chapter first examines the labor market conditions that determine the demand and rewards for workers generally and for those at the bottom of the occupational structure in particular. It profiles the labor market transformations that, since the early 1970s, have diminished opportunities for nearly all workers, especially those who—like most homeless people—are less educated and less skilled. The analysis does not elaborate the difficulties homeless people face in the labor market; it should be emphasized, however, that homeless workers' limited skill and education levels usually consign them to, at best, temporary employment at very low wages. Compounding these liabilities are those resulting from homelessness itself, which undermine a prospective worker's ability to present herself or himself and to perform in ways that employers expect (see Chapter 8).

The analysis next places labor market changes and employment options in a broader historical and social context. Upheavals such as those transforming the U.S. labor market are inherent in capitalist development and are conditioned by a society's unique political and economic dynamics. The chapter concludes with a discussion of policy measures that could increase employment opportunities enough to mitigate the problem of homelessness. Regardless of their merits, however, such policies will not be seriously considered—let alone implemented—in the present political climate. The more germane issue is the extent to which current policy developments will further increase extreme poverty and its attendant consequences, including homelessness.

LABOR MARKET TRANSFORMATIONS FROM THE 1960s TO THE 1990s

Since the late 1960s and early 1970s, when the long post–World War II economic boom ended, labor market transformations in the United States and other major industrialized nations have significantly reduced the opportunities available to large segments of the workforce. These transformations have had disparate effects on different groups of workers: especially hard hit have been people of color, those with lower skills and educational levels, and younger workers.[3] As noted in Chapter 3, these economic upheavals are at the bottom of widespread homelessness.

The eroding labor market opportunities produced by these changes are reflected in a variety of indices, especially unemployment and underemployment rates, and income and wage levels. Salient trends during the last quarter-century are highlighted in the accompanying tables, most of which provide data for the peak years of economic cycles—1967, 1973, 1979, and 1989—as well as the most recent year. Data for peak years of the business cycle are appropriate benchmarks for two reasons. First, they minimize variances due to cyclical conditions, thus providing a consistent comparative standard. (This minimizes invalid uses of such data to support particular policy objectives or theo-

retical perspectives.) And second, economic benefits typically are greatest and most widely distributed in those years; that is, during peak years the material well-being of the mass of the population—and the "average" worker or family—is greatest.

Unemployment and Underemployment

Official unemployment levels in the United States have increased consistently since the late 1960s. This trend is illustrated in Table 5.1, which provides data on unemployment rates and the numbers of unemployed.[4] In 1967, the unemployment rate was 3.8%, which meant that some 2,975,000 people were unable to find work. In 1989, after a 7-year upswing, the rate stood at 5.3%. With the workforce much larger than 20 years earlier, this translated into a more than two-fold increase in the number of workers—some 6,528,000—who sought employment without success. And in 1994, despite 2 years of economic "recovery," the unemployment rate averaged 6.1%, as nearly 8 million workers could not secure employment.

Even though unemployment abated somewhat from 1979 to 1989, declining from 5.8% to 5.4%, this was not associated with commensurate improvement in workers' well-being. Instead, as elaborated in more detail below, the decline in the unemployment rate reflected the significant increase in the proportions both of workers who had given up looking for work (and thus were not included within the official definition of unemployment), and of those who were employed at less than a living wage.[5]

A broader and more useful measure of workers' limited labor market opportunities is provided by the "underemployment" rate, which includes the unemployed, involuntary part-timers (who would like to work full time but cannot because of "economic reasons"), and "discouraged workers" (those who have given up looking for work). Underemployment has increased significantly since the early 1970s (see Table 5.1). The underemployment rate was 8.2% in 1973, when an average of 7,397,000 workers were underemployed, and steadily worsened thereafter: underemployment reached

---

TABLE 5.1

UNEMPLOYMENT AND UNDEREMPLOYMENT IN THE U.S., ANNUAL AVERAGES, 1967–1994

	1967	1973	1979	1989	1993	1994
Unemployment						
Rate (percent)	3.8	4.9	5.8	5.3	6.8	6.1
Number (1,000s)	2,975	4,365	6,137	6,528	8,734	7,996
Underemployment						
Rate (percent)	N/A	8.2	9.7	9.8	12.6	N/A
Number (1,000s)	N/A	7,397	10,281	12,281	16,211	N/A

Sources: U.S. Department of Labor, Bureau of Labor Statistics, *Employment and Earnings, January 1996*, Table A-1; and Mishel and Bernstein, *The State of Working America*, Table 4.2.

12.6% in 1993, when underemployed workers exceeded 16 million.

These trends were especially problematic for men at the bottom of the occupational structure. As McFate observes, the increase in unemployment levels was

. . . almost entirely the result of an increase in joblessness among low-skilled males. Unemployment rates among higher skilled males have remained fairly constant . . . while the proportion of unskilled males who are unemployed or out of the workforce has grown significantly. . . . The unemployment rate of the unskilled . . . is five times the rate of college educated workers.[6]

Moreover, low-skill workers were unemployed 8.5 weeks longer in 1987–89 than were their counterparts in 1967–69, and "the share of men who have 'permanently withdrawn' from the workforce was 50 percent higher in the late 1980s than in the late 1960s."[7]

The problems of severe and worsening unemployment and underemployment are not limited to the United States, but plague the entire "developed" world.[8] The Organization for Economic Cooperation and Development (OECD), the leading industrialized nations' major economic research organization, reported in 1994 that:

There are 35 million people unemployed in OECD countries. Perhaps another 15 million have either given up looking for work or un-

willingly accepted a part-time job. As many as a third of young workers in some OECD countries have no job.[9]

The OECD noted that these problems had significantly worsened since the early 1970s. For example, while the total number of unemployed averaged less than 10 million throughout the 1950s and 1960s, "from 1972 to 1982, this number tripled." The economic expansion in the 1980s "only trimmed back the unemployment total to 25 million people in 1990. Since then, it has risen sharply."[10]

Conditions are far worse in the so-called "developing" countries, where 1 in 3 people (1.3 billion) live below the poverty line, nearly 800 million people do not get enough to eat, and more than one-third of children are malnourished and underweight. To meet the growing demand for employment in those countries, some 1 billion new jobs must be created in the next decade.[11]

Income and Wage Levels

Levels of unemployment and underemployment reveal only part of the labor market's failures. Trends in wages and other compensation are also critically important measures of the opportunities and rewards available to workers. As the data in Table 5.2 illustrate, after decades of robust growth the "real" (inflation-adjusted) wages and incomes of most workers have declined or stagnated since the early 1970s. Median family income leapt from $18,099 in 1947 to $31,579 in 1967, a 2.8% annual growth rate, and then to $36,893 in 1973, a 2.6% annual growth rate. But it reached only $38,248 in 1979 (a 0.6% annual increase) and merely $39,696 10 years later (0.4% annual growth). It then fell during the most recent downturn, and by 1993 had rebounded only to $36,959, barely more than its level 22 years earlier. The data on changes in annual wages paint a similarly bleak picture. The annual wage or salary of the average worker increased from $18,418 in 1967 to $21,423 in 1973 (a 2.5% annual increase), but then stagnated, reaching only $21,582 in 1979 (a 0.1% annual increase), $23,079 10 years later (a 0.7% annual increase), and then fell back to $22,370 in 1992 (a drop of 1% annually). The impact of this trend is that the compensation of a typical full-time worker in 1993 would have been 56% higher if it "had continued to grow at the same rate after 1973 as it had in the previous 25 years."[12] While there is no reason that real wages should increase inexorably, this expectation has been widespread in the United States, and underlies our historically optimistic assumptions about intra- and intergenerational mobility.

However sobering these data for median family income and annual wages, they understate the increasing hardships workers confronted during this period, because income and wage levels would have been lower but for the significant increases in households' work effort. Several indices highlight this: the average worker toiled 106 more hours (the equivalent of over 2.5 weeks) in 1989 than in 1973;[13] parents worked 139 more hours—almost 3.5 more weeks—in 1989 than in 1969;[14] the portion of working-age women in the workforce increased by half during the last 30 years;[15] and the annual hours worked by wives increased more than 32% from 1979 to 1989.[16]

The declining fortunes of the typical worker are profiled somewhat more accurately by the remaining entries in Table 5.2—"average hourly earnings" and "average weekly earnings" of nonsupervisory and production workers, who comprise more than 80% of all wage and salary employees. During the 1947–73 period, average hourly wages increased from $6.75 to $12.06

TABLE 5.2

Wage and Income Trends, 1947–1993 (In 1993 Dollars)

Year	Median Family Income*	Annual Wages†	Average Hourly Earnings‡	Average Weekly Earnings‡
1947	18,099	N/A	6.75	272.16
1967	31,579	18,418	10.67	405.40
1973	36,893	21,423	12.06	455.10
1979	38,248	21,582	12.03	429.42
1989	39,696	23,079	11.26	389.50
1993	36,959	22,370	10.83	373.64
Change (Annual Growth Rates, percent)				
1947–67	2.8	N/A	2.3	2.0
1967–73	2.6	2.5	2.0	1.6
1973–79	0.6	0.1	0.0	-0.6
1979–89	0.4	0.7	-0.7	-1.0
1989–93	-1.8	-1.0	N/A	N/A

*Mishel and Bernstein, *The State of Working America*, Table 1.1.
†Mishel and Bernstein, *The State of Working America*, Table 3.1.
‡Mishel and Bernstein, *The State of Working America*, Table 3.3.

TABLE 5.3

CHANGE IN HOURLY WAGES BY OCCUPATION CATEGORY, 1979–1993

	Percent of Workforce 1989	Percent Change		
		1979–89	1989–93	1979–93
Men				
White Collar	43.5	0.0	-3.4	-3.3
Service	9.9	-9.2	-1.8	-10.8
Blue Collar	43.8	-9.3	-5.8	-14.6
(Laborers)	(7.0)	(-14.9)	(-8.3)	(-22.0)
Women				
White Collar	71.2	9.0	3.0	12.2
(Admin/Clerical)	(29.6)	(4.0)	(1.2)	(5.3)
Service	15.1	-6.7	2.6	-4.2
Blue Collar	11.8	-3.9	-2.4	-6.2

Source: Mishel and Bernstein, *The State of Working America,* Table 3.5.

TABLE 5.4

PERCENT CHANGE IN REAL HOURLY WAGES FOR ALL WORKERS BY WAGE PERCENTILE, 1973–93 (IN 1993 DOLLARS)

Period	Wage Percentile				
	20	40	Median	60	80
1973–79	-1.0	-1.3	-3.0	-0.1	3.2
1979–89	-10.3	-5.5	-2.1	-4.1	0.4
1989–93	-0.6	-2.4	-2.6	-0.8	-0.9
1973–93	-11.7	-9.0	-7.5	-4.9	2.7

Source: Mishel and Bernstein, *The State of Working America,* Table 3.6.

(an annual increase over 2.2%), while average weekly earnings increased from $272 to $445 (an annual increase of nearly 2%). From 1973 to 1979, however, hourly earnings were little changed at $12.03, while weekly wages fell to $429 (a 0.6% annual decline). Then, from 1979 to 1989, hourly wages fell to $11.26 (a 0.7% annual decline) and weekly earnings dropped to $390 (a 1% annual decline). And in 1993, both were significantly less than their 1989 levels, and far less than they had been 20 years before.

Of course, data about "typical" workers obscure the varying consequences of these economic transformations for different segments of the workforce. As noted above, these changes have had especially harsh consequences for people of color, workers with lower skill and education levels, and younger people. These disparate impacts are highlighted in Tables 5.3–5.8.

The data in Table 5.3 profile the changes from 1979 to 1993 in hourly wages for men and women in the major occupational categories. The wages for men in service industries and blue-collar industries—which generally have lower skill and education requirements—fell 10.8% and 14.6%, respectively, in contrast to the 3.3% drop for white-collar male workers. Moreover, the wages of laborers, the least skilled blue-collar workers, fell 22%. Even though the wage declines for women in service and blue-collar jobs during these years were less than those for men, this was in large part because women's wages were already far lower than men's, and remained so in all major industry categories.

Table 5.4 shows the changes from 1973 to 1993 in the real hourly wages received by workers in different percentiles. While most workers' wages declined in this period—only those at the top of the pay scale saw their wages increase—the pay of lower wage workers fell the most. Indeed, the more meager one's wages, the more they declined. For example, those at the 20th percentile experienced wage losses of 11.7% and those at the median sustained a 7.5% loss. In contrast, those at the 80th percentile saw their wages rise by 2.7%.

Another salient dimension of the changing wage structure during the 1973–93 period is highlighted by the data in Table 5.5, which show the portion of the workforce with wages below the poverty line. In those years, the proportion of all workers earning wages below the poverty

level rose from 23.9% to 26.9%. Moreover, the percentage of the workforce earning very low wages—less than 75% of the poverty line—*doubled*, from 6.8% to 13.3%.[17] These data are especially disturbing when we keep in mind that many scholars and a large portion of the American people believe that the official poverty line is much too low to reflect the true state of deprivation in the country.[18]

These data reveal significant differences between men and women and among members of different race and ethnic groups. The proportion of all male workers receiving only poverty wages increased from one in eight in 1973 to one in five in 1993, while the proportion of women workers receiving less than a poverty-line wage dropped somewhat, from two in five to one in three. Among Whites, the portion of male workers with subpoverty wages increased from 11.1% to 17.6% during this period, while the portion of women with such wages fell from 37.5% to 30.8%. Among Blacks, the percentage of men paid subpoverty wages increased from 24% to 33.2%, while the percentage of women with such wages fell from 49.7% to

TABLE 5.5

WORKERS WITH WAGES LESS THAN POVERTY, 1973–1993 (PERCENT OF TOTAL WITH POVERTY WAGES)

	1973	1979	1989	1993
All Workers				
All	23.9	22.8	25.3	26.9
Men	13.1	12.9	18.4	21.4
Women	39.5	35.8	33.0	33.0
White Workers				
All	21.8	21.1	22.6	23.9
Men	11.1	11.0	15.1	17.6
Women	37.5	34.4	31.1	30.8
Black Workers				
All	36.0	31.5	34.5	36.4
Men	24.0	22.6	29.2	33.2
Women	49.7	41.1	39.7	39.4
Hispanic Workers				
All	34.7	32.5	39.0	42.5
Men	25.7	22.6	34.6	39.0
Women	50.2	47.7	45.5	47.7

Sources: Mishel and Bernstein, *The State of Working America*, Tables 3.10, 3.11, 3.12, 3.13.

TABLE 5.6

CHANGE IN REAL HOURLY WAGE BY EDUCATION, 1973–1993 (1993 DOLLARS)

	Year	High School	High School Graduate	Some College	College Graduate	College Graduate with 2+ Years
Real Hourly	1973	10.16	11.63	12.86	16.99	20.91
Wages (dollars)	1979	10.06	11.23	12.24	15.52	18.80
	1989	8.44	10.21	11.82	15.90	20.36
	1993	7.87	9.92	11.37	15.71	19.93
Percent Change	1973–79	- 1.1	- 3.5	- 4.8	- 8.6	10.1
	1979–89	-16.1	- 9.1	- 3.5	2.4	8.3
	1989–93	- 6.7	- 2.8	- 3.8	- 1.2	- 2.1
	1973–93	-22.5	-14.7	-11.6	- 7.5	- 4.7
Share of Workforce*	1973	28.5	41.8	15.1	8.8	3.6
(percent)	1979	20.1	42.2	19.1	11.1	4.9
	1989	13.7	40.5	22.3	14.0	6.9

*Sums do not total 100% because shares for those with one year of schooling after college graduation are not shown.
Source: Mishel and Bernstein, *The State of Working America,* Table 3.18.

TABLE 5.7

ENTRY-LEVEL WAGES AND EMPLOYMENT SHARES FOR WORKERS AT DIFFERENT EDUCATIONAL LEVELS, 1973–1993 (1993 DOLLARS)

	Year	High School Graduate	College Graduate
Entry Level	1973	8.82	12.55
Wages* (dollars)	1979	8.75	12.01
	1989	7.17	12.43
	1993	6.61	11.67
Percent Change	1973–79	-0.8	-4.3
	1979–89	-18.1	3.5
	1989–93	-7.8	-6.1
	1973–93	-25.0	-7.0
Share of Employment**	1973	42.7	13.8
(percent)	1979	42.7	14.8
	1989	35.8	19.0
	1993	N/A	N/A

* Wages of workers with 1–5 years work experience.
** Share of those with 1–5 years of experience by educational level.
Source: Mishel and Bernstein, *The State of Working America,* Table 3.22.

TABLE 5.8

UNEMPLOYMENT, POVERTY, AND INCOME DATA BY RACE AND ETHNICITY

	1967	1973	1979	1989	1994
Unemployment (Percent)					
White	3.4	4.3	5.1	4.5	5.3
Black	7.4	9.4	12.3	11.4	11.5
Hispanic	N/A	7.5	8.3	8.0	9.9
Ratio: Black/White	2.2	2.2	2.4	2.5	2.2
Ratio: Hispanic/White	N/A	1.7	1.6	1.8	1.9
Poverty (Percent)					
White	11.0	8.4	9.0	10.0	11.7
Black	39.3	31.4	31.0	20.7	30.6
Hispanic	N/A	21.9	21.8	26.2	30.7
Ratio: Black/White	3.6	3.7	3.4	3.1	2.6
Ratio: Hispanic/White	N/A	2.6	2.4	2.6	2.6
Median Family Income (1994 Dollars)					
White	30,412	34,592	34,565	36,340	34,028
Black	17,657	20,362	20,293	21,612	21,027
Hispanic	N/A	25,571	26,119	26,199	23,421
Ratio: Black/White	.581	.589	.587	.595	.618
Ratio: Hispanic/White	N/A	.739	.754	.721	.688
Year-Round, Full-Time Male Workers' Earnings (1994 Dollars)					
White	30,195	34,603	34,855	34,111	31,598
Black	19,503	24,742	25,310	24,412	23,742
Hispanic	N/A	N/A	24,793	21,941	20,314
Ratio: Black/White	.646	.715	.726	.716	.751
Ratio: Hispanic/White	N/A	N/A	.711	.643	.643

Sources: U.S. Department of Commerce, Bureau of the Census, *Current Population Reports, Consumer Income, Series P60-189;* Unpublished data from the Census Bureau P-60 Series; U.S. Department of Labor, Bureau of Labor Statistics, Employment and Earnings, Table 11. Ratios are author's calculations.

39.4%. And among Latinos (or Hispanics, as some prefer to denote the same population), the number of men earning subpoverty wages increased from 25.7% to 39%, while for Latinas, this amount declined somewhat, from 50.2% to 47.7%. In sum, *while 1 in 6 White male workers earned only subpoverty wages in 1993, roughly 1 in 3 White women and Black men, about 2 in 5 Black women and Latino males, and nearly 1 in 2 Latinas earned wages below the poverty line.*

The data in Table 5.6 show the extent to which the wages of—and demand for—less-educated workers declined from 1973 to 1993. For example, the real hourly wages of high school dropouts and high school graduates fell 22.5% and 14.7%, respectively. In contrast, the wages of college graduates and those with two or more years of postgraduate education only fell 7.5% and 4.7%, respectively, and these declines were due to the effects of the 1990–91 downturn and its aftermath. Moreover, while those with less than a high school degree comprised 28.5% of the workforce in 1973, 20 years later their share was less than half that amount (13.7%). At the same time, the portion of workers who were high school graduates declined slightly (from 41.8% to 40.5%), but there were significant increases in the portion of workers with some college education (from 15.1% to 22.3%), college degrees (8.8% to 14%), and graduate work (3.6% to 6.9%). In short, job opportunities are becoming increasingly more limited for those without a high school degree or even some college.

Table 5.7 provides another perspective on changes in the structure of the labor market. It shows the changes during the 1973–93 period in the entry wages paid and the share of entry-level workers who were high school or college graduates. While entry-level wages fell for both groups in this period, the drop for high school graduates was more than 3.5 times greater than for college graduates (25% versus 7%). Also, the portion of entry-level workers who were high school grads fell from almost 43% in 1973 to less than 36% in 1989, while the share with a college degree increased from less than 14% to 19%. Thus, the premiums attached to high levels of education are especially important for young workers now entering the labor force.

As with unemployment and underemployment trends, wage inequalities and declining wages for those at the lower end of the occupational structure have been common throughout the developed world since the 1960s. However, conditions have been significantly worse for less-skilled individuals in the United States than for their counterparts elsewhere. As economist Steven J. Davis notes:

> . . . the duration and extent of increases in overall wage inequality, the comparatively sharp increase in educational differentials, and other aspects of the United States experience during the past two decades place it at the upper extreme among the advanced economies.[19]

The Proximate Causes of These Trends

While the exact reasons for the declining fortunes of American workers are debatable, scholars agree that four factors are most significant in exerting downward pressure on wages and the demand for labor, and that these factors have had particularly adverse consequences for lower-skilled and less-educated workers. First is the decline in economic growth rates, a development that typically depresses employment and wage levels. The growth in real per capita output in the developed countries averaged 4% from 1960–70 but only 2.2% in 1970–80 and 1980–90.[20] Second is the growing integration of the global economy and corporations' incessant drive and increasing capacity to obtain the lowest prices for all of their inputs, including labor.[21] This trend "places less-skilled U.S. workers in competition with less-skilled (and typically lower-paid) foreign workers."[22]

Third are technological changes that have eliminated entire categories of unskilled and semiskilled jobs in many industries and have "accelerated the demand for more-skilled workers."[23] It should be emphasized, however, that while the demand for higher education and skill levels has increased for many workers, many jobs require far fewer skills than their incumbents provide, and in some respects the workforce is overeducated. In 1990, for example, only one-fourth to one-third of U.S. jobs required a college or advanced degree. The Bureau of Labor Statistics recently emphasized that "a college degree does not guarantee success in the labor market" and projected that in the 1992–2005 period, about one-fourth of college graduates would not find jobs requiring a degree.[24]

"Institutional factors" represent the fourth major proximate cause of recent changes. Most important are the declining value of the minimum wage and significant erosions of the "social wages" (i.e., income assistance payments) that serve as wage floors, and decreasing rates of unionization, which herald workers' weakness in negotiations with employers. Research consistently demonstrates that real wage declines are associated with declining union density and erosions of the minimum wage and the social wage.[25]

THE SOCIAL AND HISTORICAL CONTEXTS OF RECENT LABOR MARKET UPHEAVALS

Recent labor market transformations are best understood in social and historical context. Several points should be noted. First, economic upheavals and their effects are endemic features of capitalism. Not only are short-term business cycles inherent in capitalist development, but so too are longer waves of prosperity and crisis as well as shifts in relative economic power among nations.[26] Indeed, the unprecedented opportunities for *individual* economic advancement that have shaped two centuries of American reality and mythmaking were based on historically specific and unique conditions.[27] After World War II, the overwhelming dominance of U.S. corporations and related factors propelled the extraordinary increases in workers' incomes until the early 1970s. These, too, were products of historically specific developments.[28] While analysis of these conditions and their demise is beyond the scope of this chapter, we should note here that the labor market transformations described above were but one consequence of their dissolution.

Second, chronic, widespread unemployment also has been a fundamental feature of capitalist development.[29] The relatively low unemployment in the United States and other industrial countries during the postwar era was exceptional, as recent labor force upheavals have again demonstrated. A large and ever-growing portion of the U.S. workforce is now effectively redundant in the ever more integrated global economy. As the data elaborated above indicate, the declining value of the commodity that less-skilled and less-educated workers can offer in the labor market—the bundle of their skills and talents—makes them increasingly unemployable, *except at less than a living wage*. Furthermore, the dispensability of these work-

ers will only increase in the foreseeable future.[30] Because of this and related developments, many scholars have concluded that "there is little hope that the 'problem of unemployment' will ever be solved by everyone becoming employed," and that it is therefore necessary "to rethink the concepts of both work and leisure, with the aim of achieving a comfortable reduction of employment."[31]

Third, these transformations intensified the economic insecurity and threatened the quality of life of nearly all workers in the United States, and left the income growth and consistently improving material well-being that President Ronald Reagan deemed Americans' "birthright" beyond the reach of much of the population. As Elliot Currie observes:

> Never before in our recent history have so many been excluded from the realistic prospect of living the good life as their society defines it; never have so many been subjected to such severe and pervasive social and economic stress and such persistent insecurity; never have the public and private sources of help been so uncertain.[32]

Fourth, while workers' fortunes have been declining since the onset of the global economic funk some 25 years ago, they markedly worsened during the last 15 years with the implementation of the "supply side" policy regime.[33] Trumpeted as remedies for the economic problems in the United States and other leading industrial nations, these policies appear to have created or exacerbated several trends that emerged in or since the late 1970s.

One of these trends was falling income and wage levels across much of the income and wage structure during periods of economic expansion. Indeed, "America has never experienced falling real wages for a majority of its work force while its per-capita G.D.P. [Gross Domestic Product] was rising."[34] Another was the relative decline in the income and wages of those at the bottom of the occupational structure. As Nobel laureate James Tobin notes: "the rise in the wages of unskilled and less-educated workers relative to skilled and better-educated workers, a stylized fact of past business cycle

TABLE 5.9

WORKERS WITH WAGES BELOW THE POVERTY LINE DESPITE FULL-TIME WORK AND YEAR-ROUND ATTACHMENT, 1974–1993 (PERCENT)

	Prime Age Workers		Workers and Families with Children	
Year	Male	Female	All	Female-Headed
1974	8.1	26.4	17.2	37.5
1979	9.0	24.6	18.6	34.4
1989	12.3	23.8	20.3	34.4
1993	16.3	26.7	23.9	42.2

Source: Mishel and Bernstein, *The State of Working America*, Figures 6I and 6J.

TABLE 5.10

WAGE TRENDS AFFECTING LOW-INCOME WORKERS, 1973–1993 (PERCENT CHANGE IN HOURLY WAGES)

	Male Workers		Female Workers	
Percent Change by Tenths	1973–79	1979–93	1973–79	1979–93
Lowest Tenth	-1.6	-20.7	12.6	-14.1
Second Tenth	-1.9	-19.1	2.9	-7.6
Third Tenth	-0.5	-18.0	0.9	-1.7
Fourth Tenth	0.3	-14.7	0.3	1.6

Source: Mishel and Bernstein, *The State of Working America*, Table 6.24.

recoveries, did not take place in the 1980s."[35] A third was worsening inequality during cyclical upswings. This is illustrated by the data in Table 5.11, which show the income shares of the bottom, middle, and top quintiles (i.e., fifths of the population) and the top 5%, as well as Gini Ratios, for 1947–93 (Gini Ratios are a measure of inequality, with 0 indicating total equality and 1 indicating total inequality). These data show that income inequality declined from 1947 to the late 1960s and early 1970s, as the income shares of those at the bottom and middle of the income distribution grew while the share of those at the top fell. Even though inequality increased somewhat in the 1970s, income distribution was almost as equal in 1979 as it had been 30 years before. In the 1980s, however, inequality grew. Indeed, by the end of the decade it was at its highest level at a business cycle peak for any time since World War II; it worsened significantly during the

1990–91 downturn and its aftermath. Moreover, a recent study of OECD countries found that the extent of inequality in the United States is the greatest among all industrial countries.[36]

A fourth unprecedented trend that emerged in the 1980s was the failure of economic growth to significantly reduce poverty. Contrary to the claims of conservative analysts such as Charles Murray and Lawrence Mead, this was not due to low-income people's declining work effort, which, it is asserted, resulted from "welfare" and other social programs.[37] In fact, the hours worked by low-income people in the 1980s were greater than in previous periods. As discussed above, the problem was declining wages for those at the bottom of the earnings distribution.

Another point to emphasize about recent economic transformations is that they reflect the outcomes of social and political conflicts. As such, they must be understood not as inevi-

TABLE 5.11

SHARES OF INCOME GOING TO VARIOUS GROUPS, AND GINI RATIOS, 1947–1993

| Year | Share of Income | | | | |
	Lowest Fifth	Middle Fifth	Top Fifth	Top 5%	Gini Ratio
1947	5.0	17.0	43.0	17.5	0.362
1967	5.5	17.9	40.4	15.2	0.358
1973	5.5	17.5	41.1	15.5	0.356
1979	5.2	17.5	41.7	15.8	0.365
1989	4.5	16.5	44.7	17.9	0.402
1993	4.2	15.9	46.2	19.1	0.420

Source: Mishel and Bernstein, *The State of Working America*, Tables 1.6 and 1.7.

TABLE 5.12

REAL FAMILY INCOME GROWTH BY INCOME GROUP, 1947–1993 (AVERAGE ANNUAL CHANGE)

Year	Lowest Fifth	Middle Fifth	Top Fifth	Top 5%	All
1947–67	3.0	2.8	2.5	2.3	2.6
1967–73	2.8	2.5	2.4	1.6	2.5
1973–79	0.0	0.7	1.0	1.0	0.7
1979–89	-0.4	0.4	1.7	2.3	1.0
1989–93	-2.9	-1.5	5.5	10.3	2.1

Source: Mishel and Bernstein, *The State of Working America*, Table 1.7.

table consequences of inexorable "natural" processes, but as the results of policies pursued over time by political and economic actors. Many developments underscore this reality, but the following examples are especially salient. Just as "free markets" have always been created and maintained by—indeed, they have been fundamentally dependent on—state policies,[38] the globalization of the economy has been aided and abetted by government policies that disproportionately benefit different social classes and groups.[39] Similarly, the conservative, market-oriented regimes that assumed power in most of the developed world in the late 1970s and 1980s ushered in policies that made the 1980s "an era of labor fragmentation and insecurity," and left "many more insecure, in numerous ways."[40] Also, levels of unemployment in the United States (and elsewhere, because of the importance of the dollar to the international financial system) are directly affected by policies of the Federal Reserve Board ("the Fed"). When the Fed raised interest rates six different times in 1994 alone, these measures had the direct and *intended* effects of curbing economic growth and increasing (or preventing reductions in) the U.S. unemployment rate.[41] Another example: the low (and declining) unionization rates in the United States are due in part to government policies, specifically labor laws that are less conducive to worker organization than any in the industrialized world.[42] Finally, among the forces fueling the growth in low-wage work in the United States are policies that have allowed steep declines in the values of the minimum wage and the social wage, already penurious by standards of the developed world.

In considering these examples, as well as the broader economic transformations that have been the subject of this discussion, we should

recall that the defining feature of the U.S. political landscape during the last two decades has
been a "business political mobilization of historic scale"[43] intended to reverse a profit squeeze
that began in the mid-1960s. This has incorporated efforts on several related fronts, such as
increased and targeted campaign contributions
to secure receptive legislatures, resurgent trade
associations to mobilize members, new or expanded think tanks to shape policy discussions,
and public relations initiatives to mold public
opinion. The objective has been to eliminate
any and all barriers to maximizing profits by
overturning the gains made by popular movements in the 1960s and early 1970s. While the
centerpiece of this campaign has been getting
"people to accept lower wages, fewer benefits,
and less job security,"[44] it also has entailed assaults on worker safety and health protections
and environmental regulation. In workplace
relations, the "implicit contract between owners and workers"—in which the latter could
expect rising real wages and relatively secure
employment as long as firms were profitable—

> has been smashed by companies with high and
> rising profits that are nonetheless reducing
> wages, eliminating fringe benefits and perma-
> nently laying off hundreds of thousands of
> workers from what had been society's best
> jobs.[45]

In short, the labor market transformations
discussed in this chapter are in large measure
the consequence of economic and political policies pursued by the business community.

A final point to note about recent economic
transformations is their entwinement with the
dynamics of racism. Racial inequality continues to consign peoples of color to subordinate
status in American society. The costs of economic dislocation and deprivation have always
been imposed on those who were not native
Whites, whether they were (depending on the
historical period) African Americans, Native
Americans, Latinos, Asian Americans, or newly
arrived immigrants from Ireland or Southern
and Eastern Europe. This pattern continues
today. As shown in Table 5.5, for example, Black
and Latino workers are far more likely than

Whites to work for wages below the poverty
level. And as the data in Table 5.8 reveal, Blacks
are more than twice as likely as Whites to be
unemployed, are almost three times as likely to
be poor, and have far lower incomes, even when
working full-time, year-round. While Latinos
are somewhat less likely than Blacks to be unemployed or poor, and median family income is
somewhat higher, the wages of full-time, year-
round Latino workers have declined steadily
over the last two decades, and by 1993 they were
the lowest among America's major racial groups.
Moreover, in the face of eroding employment
opportunities and wage levels, Black workers
are more likely than Whites to have withdrawn
from the workforce.[46] And Blacks and Latinos
of all educational levels are more likely to be
unemployed and to receive lower wages than
their White counterparts.[47] Finally, Blacks and
Latinos have far less wealth holdings than
Whites,[48] thus limiting their likelihood of en-
trepreneurial success, as well as leaving them
more vulnerable to the adverse consequences
of job and income loss.

The racial impact of recent economic transformations also has had important consequences for political conflicts and policy making.
We turn to this subject in the next section.

THE POLITICS OF POLICIES TO MITIGATE POVERTY AND HOMELESSNESS

Policies that would meaningfully address poverty and homelessness are neither unknown nor
mysterious.[49] An appropriate policy repertoire
would include measures to increase employment
opportunities by fostering stronger, sustained
economic growth; greatly expand the stock of
affordable housing; markedly increase the minimum wage; in the absence of available jobs that
pay a living wage, provide wage supplements
and income assistance; and ensure the availability of affordable health care, child care, and
other supports individuals and families require
to meet their basic needs.[50] The nations that
are the major economic competitors of the
United States have demonstrated that the lev-

els of relative deprivation countenanced in this country are neither inevitable nor unavoidable.

We can also readily identify policies to expand employment options generally, and for lower-skilled workers in particular. These include expansionary monetary and fiscal policies to stimulate growth and job creation; expanded education and training programs to enhance workers' skills; increases in the minimum wage and the provision of wage supplements to raise the wage floor of the lowest-paid workers; the expansion of work-related services (such as child care and transportation); and reforms of income support and other social assistance programs to reduce work disincentives. However, given the integration in the global economy, institutional measures must be developed to coordinate these policies within and among nations. Otherwise, nations pursuing such policies would incur disadvantages in world trade as competitors adopt a wage-cutting, "race to the bottom" strategy. As the International Labor Organization (ILO) emphasizes, the "alternative of seeking individual solutions will lower world welfare and lead to a more divided, unequal, and politically turbulent world."[51]

A persuasive case can be made for the efficacy and efficiency of such policies;[52] the obstacles to enacting them are political, not technical. The overriding problem is that these initiatives would require increased market intervention or regulation by government entities, a course of action clearly at odds with the approach favored in the current political climate of allowing the "market" (corporations and investors) to dictate economic and social outcomes.

The current parameters of international and multilateral economic policies are embodied in measures such as the North American Free Trade Agreement (NAFTA) and the General Agreement on Tariffs and Trade (GATT), and the policy initiatives and prescriptions of the World Bank, International Monetary Fund (IMF), and the OECD. The former provide for cooperation primarily to reduce tariffs and other barriers to "free trade," while the main thrust of the IMF and World Bank initiatives are the imposition of "structural adjustment" policies

on developing countries, the centerpiece of which is the elimination of "inefficient" state employment, and income and food subsidies. Measures such as those suggested by the ILO to coordinate essential social assistance and proactive employment policies are not seriously considered. To the degree these are considered, it is to follow recent OECD suggestions to deregulate labor markets and reduce the benefits to workers provided through policies that protect job security or replace or enhance wages.[53] Even more beyond the pale are measures to coordinate monetary policies, a prerequisite for significantly reducing unemployment in the industrialized world, or to establish meaningful minimum standards for workers' rights to organize, worker safety and health, compensation levels, and environmental protections. Without such standards, however, conditions in investment and employment-starved developing countries will exert constant, inexorable downward pressure on the wages and working and living conditions in the industrial nations.

No less daunting are the barriers to domestic policies that would diminish unemployment and increase incomes. To comprehend these obstacles, it is useful to recall why corporations and investors are leery of full employment, in spite of its benefits for society as a whole. Not only can it fuel inflation, which erodes the value of financial assets and redistributes income downward,[54] but it can undermine labor discipline and shift political power from capital to labor.[55] Accordingly, the American business community has tenaciously opposed full employment policies except under the most extraordinary circumstances, such as World War II. (While the business community is not of one mind on this or any other policy matter, certain preferences clearly have been dominant.)

This opposition is reflected in prevailing orientations toward the monetary and fiscal policy measures that constitute the primary means of influencing rates of economic growth and levels of aggregate demand and employment. (The need for countercyclical policies and stimulus to maintain minimal levels of aggregate demand has been widely acknowledged since the 1930s.[56]) Lower interest rates foster higher growth, demand, and employment by reducing the costs to businesses and consumers when they borrow to make investments and purchases. All government expenditures—whether for military procurement, roads, education, or social security—also increase growth, demand, and employment, but different types of expenditures have different consequences for the capital accumulation process because some subsidize capital intensive investments (e.g., military spending) while others can directly increase workers' bargaining power (e.g., a high social wage) or compete with private enterprise (e.g., direct provision of low-income housing or student loans). Accordingly, the business community typically has opposed monetary polices that might fuel inflation or generate too little unemployment and has instead preferred fiscal policies, such as military spending and tax cuts, which have the fewest redistributional effects and least interfere with capitalist social relations.[57]

The policy developments of recent years have reflected great sensitivity to these concerns. Under the leadership of Alan Greenspan, the Federal Reserve Board has steadfastly maintained interest rates at levels that have fostered "moderate" growth, with unemployment above 5%, a course favored by most business leaders and major investors. As for investment policies, President Clinton's meager stimulus package of $30 billion in 1993 was defeated by opposition from most of the business community and a single-minded focus on federal deficit reduction. Current levels of government stimulus (as a percent of gross national product) are nearing historic lows for the postwar era, a development directly related to the reductions in military spending at the end of the cold war. It is not coincidental that the 1990–91 recession began after the Reagan-era military expansion crested in 1989 (when real military spending—in 1995 dollars—peaked[58]) and that growth has been stagnant as military spending has declined. Economic growth is likely to remain halting, and overall unemployment is likely to remain at current levels, unless and until the Fed alters its policies and an alternative government stimulus program to military spending is developed.[59]

The prospects are hardly more auspicious for the enactment of employment and training programs and related initiatives that would meaningfully improve the labor market prospects of disadvantaged groups, including homeless people. Many analysts, among them current Labor Secretary Robert Reich, advocate such measures to enhance workers' "human capital" (skill and educational levels). As discussed above, not only can increases in educational and skill levels yield significant employment and wage premiums, but those lacking necessary human capital will have little likelihood of obtaining jobs that pay a living wage. Given the average skill and educational levels of homeless people, they are especially in need of appropriate employment and training programs.

Although it may be necessary to increase workers' skill levels, the major lesson from the last quarter century of employment and training programs is that such programs are not sufficient to improve significantly participants' employment prospects. In early 1995, the Department of Labor published a report that "summarize[s] the best quantitative evidence that is available from the evaluation literature on the impacts of past and existing programs on such tangible outcomes as employment, earnings, and educational achievement."[60] It was based on an analysis of all major employment and training programs, such as those funded under the Comprehensive Employment and Training Act (CETA), the Job Training Partnership Act (JTPA), Jobs Corps, the Jobs Opportunities and Basic Skills Program (JOBS) of the Aid to Families with Dependent Children (AFDC) program, as well as numerous special demonstration projects. While the analysis determined that some programs were more effective than others, it concluded that "at least some services have been successful for every population examined" and that many programs are "cost-effective investments" (that is, they provide net benefits to society). However, while the "gains created by training programs are important, and represent real gains for society and the individuals involved," they "are often not enough to accomplish the goals set out for them." Among their shortcomings, training programs could not offset the incomes workers lost when they were laid-off in corporate downsizings; very successful "programs with a substantial positive effect [on earnings] haven't greatly reduced poverty rates among participants"; and JTPA adult training, "a highly cost-effective program which created significant earnings gains," still left participants with low incomes.[61]

The inability of employment and training programs to overcome broader labor market conditions, most notably the insufficient number of jobs that pay a living wage, does not mean that they are failures and should be eliminated. Instead, if such programs are to address problems such as poverty and homelessness in a meaningful way, they must be expanded and complemented by measures to increase both employment and wage levels. Policy trends are running in the opposite direction, however. Spending for all federal employment and training programs in Fiscal Year 1996 are projected to be $7.9 billion, 10% less than Fiscal Year 1995, and 66% less than 1979.[62]

The prospects are equally bleak for other policies necessary to increase viable employment opportunities for low-skilled workers. At this writing (May 1996), the ascendant political Right in Congress has blocked efforts to increase the minimum wage, even though it is at a historic low and despite the fact that such an increase is critical for raising wage levels for the 30 million people in the lower quarter of the workforce.[63] The Right is also significantly cutting the Earned Income Tax Credit, the major wage supplement available to low-wage workers (see Chapter 6, note 6). According to one estimate, nearly 8 million households with low-wage workers, including over 3 million families with children, would lose income as a result of the recent budget reconciliation bill. Families with children would lose an average of $508 a year under this measure.[64] At the same time, "welfare reform" initiatives being considered by Congress likely will increase significantly poverty and deprivation (see Chapter 6).

It should be emphasized that the related problems of poverty, homelessness, unemployment, and the absence of jobs that pay a living wage have consistently worsened since the mid-1970s, regardless of which party controlled the White House or the Congress. To be sure, the supply-side regime under President Reagan significantly exacerbated these problems, and the policy repertoire of the current Congress will likely have the same consequences, or worse. But as the economic security of the majority of the U.S. population worsened over the past two decades, policy initiatives that would reverse this trend have not been politically viable, regardless of the party in power. The fundamental issue is that the enactment of such policies would fundamentally alter the American political economy. While other capitalist nations have been able to guarantee their populations income and services that meet socially defined minimum standards of decency, the business community and its allies have always been able to checkmate such initiatives in the United States, and they are intent on continuing to do so.

Opposition to social democratic policies by the business community and the most affluent is quite understandable, but it seems curious that broad sections of the population who would benefit from social democratic policies nonetheless oppose them, or at least fail to mobilize for their support. Though scholars debate the reasons for the weakness of social democratic forces in this country, there is consensus that no factors are more significant than the racial and ethnic divisions in the U.S. working class.[65] Indeed, though there have been multiracial struggles for economic and social justice in the United States since White indentured servants and Black slaves from Africa fought together against the dominant class in colonial Virginia, all these efforts have ultimately foundered on the shoals of racism and nativism.

The future may be no different. Polling data and focus group discussions consistently reveal that many Whites, especially males, see "welfare" and related government initiatives to provide income security and necessary services as benefiting "minorities," especially Blacks and immigrants, at their expense.[66] The popularity of anti-affirmative action and anti-immigrant measures are further examples of the enduring strength of these sentiments.

The potential for an effective multiracial movement for social and economic justice exists, however, if only because a significant and growing portion of the White population is seeing its living standards erode and future prospects grow dim as never before. While the policies of the "Gingrich revolution" of the 104th Congress *could* improve the economic opportunities and well-being of the majority of the population, White and "non-White" alike, the first-phase results of the supply-side experiments indicate that these policies are far more likely to make things worse—indeed, much worse. While such conditions may fuel reactionary responses, they might also lead to new political movements that pursue social and economic justice for the entire population. The limited ability of social science to satisfactorily explain events—let alone predict them—is well known, but we can say with equal confidence and sadness that without the emergence of such movements, the problem of homelessness will little abate, however long or hard the toil of the nation's dispossessed.

CHAPTER 6

Income Maintenance: Little Help Now, Less on the Way

Mark H. Greenberg
Jim Baumohl

For over a decade, studies have reported that many homeless people receive no aid from government cash assistance programs.[1] At first glance, this may seem puzzling. If, as many Americans believe, we spend so much on "welfare," why do homeless people so infrequently receive aid? The answer is that the current income maintenance system offers less than meets the eye. Federal, state, and local governments make income support available in ways that are highly constrained. A family with no income may or may not be eligible for cash aid. In many states, a non-elderly single individual with no income and no demonstrable disability will not qualify for any form of cash assistance. Further, programs often create substantial procedural and other barriers to initial and ongoing eligibility. Moreover, the receipt of cash aid may not prevent or ameliorate homelessness. Benefit levels are often so low that recipients sometimes cannot even pay rent consistently.

This chapter begins with a brief overview of American income maintenance and then discusses five key programs of cash and near-cash assistance: Aid to Families with Dependent Children (AFDC), the Food Stamps program

(FS), Supplemental Security Income (SSI), Unemployment Compensation (UC), and General Assistance (GA). To understand these programs is to appreciate the large gaps in the American safety net and how these gaps contribute to homelessness.

This chapter has been written at a time of great uncertainty about the future of some of the principal programs of cash or near-cash assistance to the poor. In 1995, Congress passed—and President Clinton vetoed—legislation to repeal AFDC (providing states instead with block grants of federal funds) and to curtail the Food Stamp program and SSI in ways that would have significantly restricted program access for many homeless and near-homeless individuals. It remains unclear whether Congress will enact welfare legislation in 1996. We close this chapter with a discussion of the potential impact of legislation along the lines of the vetoed bill.

A PERSPECTIVE ON "WELFARE" PROGRAMS AND SPENDING

When a person has no income and needs help to pay the rent, will a government program provide assistance? To answer that question, and to comprehend the structure of the income maintenance system in the United States (as it exists in May 1996), it is helpful to map the differences among programs based on five dimensions: whether a program is based on *categorical eligibility*, whether it is based on the principle of *entitlement*, whether it is grounded in the principle of *insurance*, whether it is *means tested*, and which *level of government* is responsible for the program.

Categorical eligibility. Governmental cash assistance in the United States often operates on the principle of categorical eligibility. This means that to be eligible for assistance, a person must be in the right category. Very few public benefits programs (of which FS is the principal exception) are open to all (or nearly all) poor persons simply because they meet income eligibility standards. More typically, the threshold question is whether a person fits into the category that the program intends to address. For example, the two principal federally assisted cash assistance programs are AFDC and SSI, but to qualify for AFDC, a person must be part of a family with children under age 18, and to qualify for SSI, an individual must be elderly, blind, or disabled. No matter how poor, a person who cannot establish categorical eligibility for AFDC or SSI will generally not qualify for federally assisted means-tested cash aid (see below).

Entitlement programs. A second key distinction among programs derives from the principle of entitlement. In law, an entitlement means that a person who qualifies for assistance under program rules has a legal right to receive aid; the government cannot lawfully deny assistance simply because spending has been high and the program is running low on funds.[2] Both AFDC and SSI are examples of entitlement programs; therefore, if there were a sudden surge in applications for either program, the government could not (without changing the law) impose a cap on new entrants or put new applicants on a waiting list. In contrast, there is no entitlement to public housing or housing assistance, and it is quite possible—indeed, it is usual—for a qualified individual to wait for months or years without receiving assistance.

Entitlement programs may or may not be targeted at the poor, and may or may not be means tested. For example, the largest cash entitlement program in the United States is Social Security. Social Security benefits are not targeted at the poor, though their availability does play an important role in reducing poverty.[3] An individual (and, in some circumstances, his or her dependents) qualifies for Social Security if he or she has worked a specified period in "covered" employment and then becomes aged or disabled, or dies.

Insurance-based programs. A third key distinction concerns whether a program is grounded in the principle of insurance. In an insurance-based program, the individual qualifies for assistance because he or she (or an employer or relative, in his or her behalf) has made contributions to the fund. For example, an individual may qualify for Social Security disability benefits because he or she has worked for a sufficient period of time in covered employment, during which both the individual and employer made contributions through payroll taxes. An equally disabled individual who did not work long enough in covered employment will not qualify for Social Security disability benefits. An entitlement program may (as in Social Security) or may not (as in SSI) be insurance based, but an insurance-based program will be structured as an entitlement.

In the public mind, a sharp distinction is often made between insurance-based benefits, which are considered "deserved" or "earned," and benefits not based on an insurance program, which may be labeled pejoratively as "welfare." As a practical matter, the difference can be overstated: the benefits received in an insurance-based program may be vastly greater than the total amount paid in payroll taxes on the individual's behalf. Nevertheless, the line between insurance-based and non-insurance-based programs is quite important in public perceptions of differences among programs and among program beneficiaries.

Means-tested programs. A fourth key distinction concerns whether a program is means tested; that is, whether eligibility depends on income or resources. A means-tested program may or may not be based on categorical eligibility (for example, FS is means tested but not limited to a particular category of persons, whereas AFDC is means tested but limited to families with children). A means-tested program may or may not be an entitlement (AFDC is a means-tested entitlement, while Low-Income Energy Assistance is means tested but not an entitlement). Finally, a program may be means tested but not limited to the poor. For example, a student loan program may be means tested, but eligibility for assistance may extend far above the poverty line.

Level of government. One final dimension of differences among programs concerns which level or levels of government are responsible. Federal, state, and local governments each play a role in income maintenance, and programs often involve a complex mix of governmental roles. For example, in FS, the entire cost of benefits is borne by the federal government, and virtually all program rules are set by the federal government. The cost of administration, however, is shared by federal and state governments, and the program is administered on a day-to-day basis by state or local public assistance offices. In AFDC, the costs of benefits and administration are shared by federal and state (and in some states, county) governments, with some rules established federally and some established at the state level. In GA, there is no federal role, and the program (if it exists) may be state, local, or some combination of the two.

With the above distinctions in mind, it is easier to analyze eligibility for governmental cash assistance: in the current income maintenance structure, a homeless person may qualify for Food Stamps but will not qualify for cash assistance unless he or she satisfies one of the following conditions:

- Is elderly or disabled

- Resides with a minor child and meets all other requirements for AFDC

- Is recently unemployed and satisfies all requirements for unemployment compensation

- Happens to live in a locality that operates a GA program for which he or she is eligible

How, then, can this rather large hole in the safety net be reconciled with the public perception that our nation spends much of its budget on a broad (and to many, over-broad) set of programs for the poor? A brief examination of the amount and nature of government spending on income support demonstrates the limits in available assistance. Although "entitlement spending" makes up more than half of the federal budget, most entitlement spending is not specifically targeted at the poor. Only 20% of all entitlement spending in 1990 was for benefits to families with incomes below $10,000. Most federal entitlement spending (60%) in Fiscal Year 1994 was for Social Security and Medicare (neither of which is means tested); less than one-quarter (22%) of federal entitlement spending in Fiscal Year 1994 was for means-tested entitlements. Taken together, AFDC, FS, and SSI represented only 8% of entitlement spending and about 4.5% of all federal spending.[4]

Of course, spending on the poor is not limited to entitlement spending; there is a broad array of means-tested programs. The claim is often made that government spends more than $300 billion a year on "welfare." This claim appears to be based on the totals contained in a periodic inventory of government spending on "needs-tested benefits programs" conducted by the Congressional Research Service (CRS).[5] Table 6.1 shows the CRS totals for Fiscal Year 1994.

As Table 6.1 demonstrates, almost half (47%) of means-tested spending involves medical care: Medicaid (the means-tested counterpart to Medicare) alone accounted for over $161 billion in spending in Fiscal Year 1994 ($94 billion federal, $67 billion state and local) and exceeded the combined total of all spending for cash, food, and housing assistance.

Only about one-quarter (24%) of means-tested spending involved *cash* aid to the poor. Many non-cash programs are means tested, but

TABLE 6.1

EXPENDITURES ON MAJOR MEANS-TESTED BENEFITS PROGRAMS, FISCAL YEAR 1994 (IN BILLIONS OF DOLLARS)

Category	Federal Spending	State-Local Spending	Total Spending	% of Total Spending
Medical Care	93.9	67.2	161.1	46.7%
Income Support	61.5	22.3	83.7	24.3%
Food Benefits	36.2	1.9	38.1	11.0%
Housing Benefits	25.7	.4	26.1	7.6%
Education Aid	14.8	.9	15.7	4.6%
Services/Other	7.4	5.2	12.6	3.7%
Jobs/Training	4.9	.6	5.5	1.6%
Total	246.2	98.6	344.9	100.0%

Note: Amounts within categories are rounded, so totals may not equal sums of data reflected in table.

these programs probably do not represent what many people think of as welfare. For example, "Medical Care" includes spending for community health centers and family planning services. "Food Benefits" include the School Lunch Program and the Nutrition Program for the Elderly. "Education Aid" includes student loans, Pell Grants, and the work-study program. The "Jobs/Training" category includes the Job Corps and the Foster Grandparents Program.

In the area of cash aid, CRS identifies 11 different programs of needs-based assistance. Table 6.2 demonstrates that most (about 83%) needs-based cash assistance involves three programs: AFDC, SSI, and the Earned Income Tax Credit.[6]

While a larger number of programs exist, most are quite small and serve narrowly defined groups. Moreover, even if one totals all federal, state, and local spending for means-tested income support for the poor, federal spending for Social Security benefits in Fiscal Year 1994 ($317 billion) reached an amount nearly four times as great.

In sum, most government spending on income assistance is not targeted at the poor, and much means-tested assistance is neither limited to the poor nor intended to help families or individuals pay the rent. The remainder of this chapter describes the programs that could provide income support to help pay the rent, and examines the extent to which they are designed to do so.

AID TO FAMILIES WITH DEPENDENT CHILDREN (AFDC)

AFDC is America's basic income support program for families with children.[7] Almost one in seven children receives AFDC. In Fiscal Year 1993, an average of 5 million families, including 9.5 million children, received AFDC each month.

AFDC involves both federal and state responsibilities. No state is required to participate in the program, but every state does so. Half or more of program costs are paid by the federal government, and federal law establishes the basic program framework. States must comply with federal requirements in order to receive federal participation in program costs, but states have great discretion concerning eligibility and benefit levels.

In recent years, the array of state choices in the AFDC program has increased dramatically. Starting in 1992, the federal government routinely began to grant states permission to depart from federal requirements in order to promote "welfare reform" activities. Since that time, most states have applied for one or more "waivers." These waivers enable a state to operate a program that is inconsistent with federal requirements in some or all parts of the state.[8] As a result, almost any statement about federal AFDC rules no longer applies to at least some states, or parts of states. Accordingly, there may be significant exceptions to the following description of program rules.

TABLE 6.2

FEDERAL AND STATE-LOCAL SPENDING ON MEANS-TESTED INCOME SUPPORT, FISCAL YEAR 1994 (IN BILLIONS OF DOLLARS)

Category	Federal Spending	State-Local Spending	Total Spending
Aid to Families with Dependent Children (AFDC)	14.1	11.8	25.9
Supplemental Security Income (SSI)	23.5	3.8	27.3
Earned Income Tax Credit	16.5	—	16.5
Pensions for Needy Veterans, Their Dependents, and Survivors	3.2	—	3.2
Foster Care	2.7	2.4	5.2
General Assistance (Non-Medical)	—	3.3	3.3
Adoption Assistance	0.3	0.3	0.6
Emergency Assistance	0.8	0.8	1.6
Assistance to Refugees and Cuban/ Haitian Entrants	0.1	—	0.1
Dependency and Indemnity Compensation and Death Compensation for Parents of Veterans	0.05	—	0.05
General Assistance to American Indians	0.08	—	0.08
Total	61.5	22.3	83.7

Note: Amounts within categories are rounded, so totals may not equal sums of data reflected in table.

Categorical eligibility requirements must be met to qualify for AFDC. In AFDC terms, this means the applicant family must have a child who is "living with a specified relative" and is "deprived of parental support or care." Each of these elements potentially limits who is eligible for assistance:

- There must be a *child* in the home. The child must be under age 18, though states may provide aid to an 18-year old who is still in high school but expects to graduate by age 19.

- The child must be living with a *relative*. Along with parents, relatives such as grand-parents, aunts, uncles, and cousins qualify.

- The child must meet the *deprivation* require-ment. A child is considered deprived of pa-rental support or care if a parent is absent, dead, or incapacitated. In limited circum-stances, the deprivation requirement is met if a parent is unemployed. However, to qualify on the basis of unemployment, the

parent must satisfy requirements for demon-strating a prior work history and must be unemployed or working less than 100 hours a month.

Financial eligibility must also be established. This involves satisfying both a resource test and an income test.

- To satisfy the *resource* test, a family must have less than $1,000 in countable resources. Any equity in an automobile in excess of $1,500 is counted against the resource limit. This means that if a family has more than $2,500 equity in a car, the family is ineligible for aid.

- To satisfy the *income* test, a family's count-able income must be below the state's "stan-dard of need." In theory, a standard of need reflects a state's determination of the basic and special needs it recognizes as essential for applicants and recipients, but there are no enforceable federal standards for setting a standard of need, and in practice, states are essentially free to set their need standards wherever they choose. Most states set their need standards well below the federal poverty line. In addition to satisfying the standard of need test, in most states, a family's countable income must be below the AFDC payment level to a family with no income. In the median state, the payment level to a family of three with no income is $367 a month; thus, if a family's countable monthly income exceeds $367, the family is ineligible for aid. A set of complicated rules are used to determine "countable income" when a family has earnings from employment. In most states (except where the state is operating under a waiver), the practical effect of the rules is to ensure that after the first four months of employment, all earnings after the first $120 result in a dollar-for-dollar reduction of aid. For example, in a state with a payment level of $367 per month, a family with gross monthly earnings exceeding $487 would probably be ineligible for aid after the first four months of employment.[9]

If a family does meet the eligibility requirements for AFDC, for what does it qualify? Under federal law, each state sets its own benefit level, and these vary widely: Alaska pays $923 a month to a family of three with no income, while Mississippi pays $120. As noted above, the median state pays $367 to a family of three with no other income. There is no requirement to adjust benefit levels based on inflation, and in real terms, the value of AFDC assistance in the median state dropped by 47% from 1970 to 1994.[10]

Even if a family meets categorical and financial eligibility requirements, it still may not successfully establish or maintain eligibility. Under federal law, when a family applies for assistance, the state is allowed 45 days in which to act on the application, and the state has no duty to provide aid more rapidly when the family has no income or is otherwise in an emergency situation. Thus, a family without income can become homeless while awaiting a decision on its case.

In addition, applicants and recipients often face daunting *procedural* requirements in their efforts to demonstrate eligibility. A state risks a federal fiscal penalty if its error rate exceeds federal standards. To avoid federal sanctions, states often impose extensive verification procedures: for example, applicants may be required to show birth certificates, rent receipts, social security number verifications, verification of living arrangements, verification of income, and verification of no income.[11] Most denials of AFDC assistance are for failure to meet procedural requirements rather than based on a finding that the family is substantively ineligible for aid. Similarly, most AFDC terminations are for reasons other than a finding that the family is no longer substantively eligible.[12]

In addition to the procedural requirements, families may be subject to a range of *behavioral* requirements that, if not met, may result in reduction or termination of aid. Under federal law, there are two principal behavioral requirements: a duty to cooperate with child support enforcement efforts, and a duty (unless exempt) to participate in state-specified work-related activities, such as job search efforts, education and training programs, and work programs. Generally, if an individual (usually a parent) subject to these requirements fails to comply without good cause, then that person is removed from the AFDC grant for a period of time and a reduced grant is provided for the other family members; the practical effect is to reduce the amount of income available to meet the family's basic needs. In addition, a number of states have used the AFDC waiver process to add behavioral requirements, expand the circumstances under which individuals are subject to participation requirements, and increase the penalties for noncompliance.[13]

In light of this basic structure, four principal reasons can be identified to explain why a homeless family might not qualify for AFDC, or why a family receiving AFDC might nevertheless be or become homeless:

- First, a very poor family may not meet AFDC *categorical* eligibility requirements. For example, there may be no young children, or the children may not be related to the adult with whom they are living. Or, a two-parent family may not satisfy the work history requirements.

- Second, even if in an eligible category, a family may be deep in poverty yet not able to meet AFDC *financial* eligibility requirements. For example, the family may have no income, yet have a car that disqualifies it. Or, a parent may have a minimum-wage job that results in income exceeding AFDC guidelines, though still leaving the family in poverty.

- Third, even if the family meets both the categorical and financial qualifications, it may be unable to establish or maintain eligibility due to *procedural* requirements, or may become homeless while the state agency is processing its case. Or, the family may receive a reduced grant—or no grant—as a result of violation of program *behavioral* requirements.

- Fourth, even if the family qualifies for and receives the full amount of aid to which it is entitled, the *amount of assistance* may be insufficient to meet basic needs.[14] As Dolbeare observes in Chapter 4, the fair market rent for a two-bedroom unit is higher than the maximum AFDC grant for a mother with two children in all but three states.

In addition to the reasons listed above, a new issue is now arising in the waiver process: a rapid increase in the number of states seeking to impose time limits on assistance. Under current federal law, a state must provide aid to an eligible family as long as the family satisfies program rules; a state may not limit the number of months or years for which a family may receive aid. However, through the waiver process, a group of states has received federal permission to conduct "demonstrations," in which aid for some families is limited to a period of time, typically two years. As of May 1996, 16 states have approval—or pending applications—to operate programs in which aid to some families will be terminated after a time limit (typically, 24 months or less). Each approved waiver includes a range of exemptions (families not subject to the time limit) and extensions (provisions for continuing aid after the time limit). The first time-limited demonstrations began operating in 1994, so it is not yet known what will happen

to those families who reach a time limit, although the families most likely to reach the time limits are those with the greatest barriers to employment.[15] A principal objection to time limits derives from the concern that if families reaching the time limit are unable to obtain or sustain employment, the result could be a dramatic increase in family homelessness.[16]

THE FOOD STAMP PROGRAM (FS)

The Food Stamp program is the principal federal means to provide food assistance to poor people.[17] Strictly speaking, FS is not an income support program; rather, an eligible household receives coupons that can be used to purchase food. In Fiscal Year 1994, total FS spending (for benefits and administration) reached $27.4 billion, and the program provided assistance to 28.9 million participants each month, making it the largest program providing assistance to poor individuals (both in its cost and in the number of participants).

In contrast to AFDC, the full cost of FS benefits for eligible households is paid by the federal government; the program's administrative costs generally are divided evenly between the federal government and the states. Unlike AFDC, benefit levels and eligibility requirements for FS are set nationally.

The FS program aids eligible *households*. Generally, a household consists of persons residing together who purchase and prepare food together. Under certain circumstances, relatives living together must constitute a single FS household, even if they do not purchase and prepare food together. A single individual, even if living with others, can constitute a separate FS household if he or she purchases and prepares food separately and is not subject to one of the rules requiring that he or she be counted in the household of another.

FS is the only federally assisted program that does not impose categorical restrictions on eligibility; it aids all poor individuals who apply and meet eligibility conditions such as income and resource requirements. While a household must meet numerous procedural requirements, an individual will not be denied Food Stamps because he or she is single, has no work history, or is employable but has no job. Most eligible households receive Food Stamps. The most recent analysis of FS participation, using August 1993 data, concluded that 64% of eligible households and 76% of households with incomes below the poverty line were receiving Food Stamps. However, participation rates varied considerably with household characteristics, and among eligible households without children, only 40% were participating in the program.[18]

To qualify for FS, a household must satisfy both a gross income and a net income eligibility test. A household with gross income exceeding a specified level is ineligible no matter how low its net income (i.e., countable income) might be.[19] A household satisfying the gross income eligibility test will still be ineligible for assistance unless its net income falls below the program's net income eligibility limits. In Fiscal Year 1996, the monthly gross income limit for a single individual is $810, and the net income limit is $623.[20]

The FS benefit level is calculated based on the expectation that a household should spend 30% of its countable cash income on food.[21] Benefits are intended to make up the difference between the household's expected expenditure level and the amount needed (in theory) to furnish an adequate, low-cost diet. A single individual receiving the maximum allotment in Fiscal Year 1996 would receive $119 in Food Stamps each month; a three-person household receiving the maximum allotment would receive $313.

In addition to having a more generous income eligibility standard than AFDC, FS also has more responsive application processing rules. Generally, an application must be acted on within 30 days of the date of application. However, in four situations, the state has a responsibility to provide *expedited service*, in which the household's application must be processed and benefits provided (if eligible) within five days of application. A household qualifies for expedited service if:

- It has less than $150 in gross monthly income and $100 or less in liquid resources.

- It is composed of destitute migrant and seasonal farm workers with liquid resources of $100 or less.

- All members of the household are homeless.[22]

- It is considered at risk of becoming homeless because the combined monthly income and liquid resources of all members is less than the household's monthly housing and utility costs.

The principal data on Food Stamp receipt by homeless people comes from research on who qualifies for expedited service. During Fiscal Year 1992, over one-third (35%) of approved FS applicants qualified for expedited service. Of approved expedited cases, 24% met the definition of "homeless," and another 56% were considered "at risk" of homelessness because monthly shelter costs exceeded monthly income and liquid resources. In general, households qualifying for expedited service were in desperate circumstances: 81% reported having no assets; for those with any assets, the average level of liquid assets was $128; most (54%) reported no income; and for those households with income, the monthly average was $334. Most (59%) indicated that in the last month, there were days in which the household had no food and no money to buy food. Nearly one-quarter (22%) reported that they were temporarily sleeping at a friend's or relative's place; an additional 15% reported that in the last week they had slept in a shelter or welfare hotel, outdoors, or an indoor setting such as a bus station or abandoned building.[23]

A homeless individual or household with minimal income or resources probably will qualify financially for FS. However, this does not ensure that assistance will be provided. As with AFDC, there may be a formidable set of verification requirements. In addition, a Food Stamp program office may impose job search requirements on theoretically employable applicants or recipients, and a household can be disqualified from receiving Food Stamps for 60 days if the principal earner fails without good cause to comply with job search requirements. Federal rules contain a built-in incentive to impose these sanctions: each year a state must meet a participation rate, and an individual will count toward the participation rate *either* if he or she participates *or* if the state imposes a sanction on him or her.

Even if a homeless household qualifies for FS, the receipt of coupons may do little to alleviate homelessness. Food Stamps cannot legally be used to purchase housing or other nonfood items. Sometimes, desperate recipients sell their coupons at a discount to generate cash to purchase shelter or other necessities. However, this leaves them with less ability to acquire food, and often with only short-term shelter.

In short, if a household has other income, FS can help meet its food needs so that the other income can be used to pay shelter costs. If a household has no other income, FS will likely do little to help its members avoid homelessness.

SUPPLEMENTAL SECURITY INCOME (SSI)

SSI is the basic federal program providing cash assistance to low-income people who are elderly, blind, or disabled.[24] There are uniform federal eligibility standards, and a basic federal benefit level. Some states supplement federal benefits. While SSI provides an important source of income to those who meet its stringent eligibility standards, many people with some level of disability or substantial barriers to employment do not qualify. In 1994, there were 6.4 million SSI recipients receiving $27.3 billion in assistance ($23.5 billion in federal funds, and $3.8 billion in state supplements).

To qualify for SSI, an individual must meet categorical (aged, blind, or disabled) and financial qualifications. To qualify based on age, an individual must be 65 or older. To qualify based on disability, an individual must be unable to engage in any "substantial gainful activity" because of a medically determined physical or mental impairment that is expected to result in death or is expected to last at least 12 months. Most individuals (77%) receiving SSI do so on the basis of disability; the remainder qualify by virtue of age (22%) or blindness (1%).

Why might aged or disabled people receive SSI instead of Social Security benefits? The answer is that some people are sufficiently aged or disabled to qualify for Social Security but are not eligible because they did not work for a long enough period in covered employment. Some also qualify for and receive Social Security benefits, but at a level so low that they qualify for SSI to augment them; in fact, 39% of SSI recipients also receive Social Security.

To be financially eligible for SSI, an individual must have countable resources not exceeding $2,000, or $3,000 in the case of a married couple. The basic assistance level is considerably higher than that of AFDC—in fact, the difference between the two benefit levels has grown over the years, as SSI benefits have been adjusted for inflation and AFDC benefits have not. In 1995, the federal SSI benefit level for a single individual with no income was $458 if the person lived alone; for a couple living alone, the SSI level was $687. A lower benefit level is provided to SSI recipients who reside with others. The benefit level is reduced by one-third when an SSI recipient lives in the household of another person and receives support and maintenance in kind from that person. However, this reduction is not supposed to apply to an individual who owns or rents, buys food separately, eats meals out rather than eating with the household, or pays a pro rata share of the household's food and shelter expenses.

In addition to receiving federal SSI benefits, recipients in some states receive a state supplement. In many states, the amount of the supplement is not large; in 1994, the amount of the state supplement exceeded $100 in only three states for an aged individual living independently, and the median supplement for such an individual in "supplement states" was $31.

Why don't all impoverished, disabled adults receive SSI? In a word, stringency. SSI eligibility standards are rigorous, and the determination process is lengthy and complex. The factors used to calculate whether an individual is disabled make it significantly more difficult for an individual to qualify when of prime working age, even if, as a practical matter, the individual is unlikely to find employment in the local labor market. Moreover, the durational requirement—that disability must be expected to last at least a year or end in death—excludes some seriously disabling conditions.

A recent change in federal law will have a substantial effect on homeless and near-homeless individuals who suffer from a substance use disorder. On March 29, 1996, President Clinton signed The Contract with America Advancement Act of 1996 (P.L. 104-121). Among its provisions, the act denies SSI and Social Security Disability benefits (and, by extension, access to Medicaid and Medicare) to people whose addiction was a "material factor contributing to the [Social Security Administration's] finding of disability."[25] However, because the disabled substance abuser group is very unevenly distributed, some states (notably, California and Illinois) probably will feel the terminations much more acutely than others.[26]

UNEMPLOYMENT COMPENSATION (UC)

Unemployment Compensation makes it possible for many people to avoid welfare during times of unemployment. However, UC is often unavailable to homeless persons, even those with a recent work history. Indeed, restrictions on the availability of UC do not affect just the homeless; in recent years, less than 40% of the unemployed have received UC benefits each month.[27] To understand why, UC's structure must be considered.

Every state operates a UC system[28] with federal participation in the costs. States have broad discretion in determining individual qualification requirements, disqualification provisions, and benefits. In general, to qualify for UC, a person must:

• Have sufficient qualifying wages or employment

• Be able and available for work

• Not be disqualified from eligibility

To have sufficient qualifying wages or employment, the claimant must have worked a

specified number of weeks and earned a specified amount of money during a "base period." The earnings required to qualify for a minimum weekly benefit often are not large; in 1994, they exceeded $2,000 in only 11 states.[29] However, earnings typically need to be spread over two quarters in the base year. In addition, states sometimes impose additional requirements regarding the distribution of wages, which have the effect of making it more difficult for low-wage workers to satisfy the requirements.[30] Further, in most states, the base year is *not* the most recent period before which the claimant seeks assistance. Rather, most states define the "base year" as the first four of the last five completed quarters. Thus, even in states where base-year earnings requirements do not appear substantial, the requirements for how earnings must be distributed over the year, or the way in which the base year is determined, may keep a recently unemployed worker from eligibility. Generally, the use of any earnings requirement (as opposed to an hours-of-work requirement) discriminates against low-wage workers because higher-wage workers always will satisfy base-year earnings requirements more easily.

To be eligible for UC, a person's qualifying wages must be in "covered employment"; that is, employment covered by the UC taxation system (see note 27). Most workers (98%) are in covered employment, but not those who work in the day-labor market or in the informal economy—as many homeless people do (see Chapter 8).

Individuals who meet the monetary eligibility requirements for UC must also meet state requirements for being "able and available for work." Thus, if an applicant had worked previously but is now ill and unable to return to work, he will not meet UC standards.

Finally, individuals who meet all other requirements will still be denied UC if disqualified from eligibility. The three major reasons for disqualification are: having been discharged from prior employment due to misconduct, having voluntarily quit prior employment without good cause, or having refused suitable work. Depending on the state, a disqualification may result in a waiting period before receipt of benefits, or may result in disqualification for the entire period of unemployment. In addition, a disqualification may result in cancellation of a worker's wage credits, making it more difficult for that person to qualify for UC after subsequent employment.

The amount and length of UC benefits vary from state to state. Most states calculate the benefit amount based on a percentage of the earnings in the highest quarter of the base period; others use a percentage of annual wages, or an average weekly wage. As to the length of benefits, in some states all eligible claimants receive benefits for the same number of weeks; in most, the length of benefits depends on the claimant's wages or employment in the base period, up to a maximum number.

In 1993, the average UC benefit nationwide was $172 a week. However, each state has a minimum and maximum weekly benefit. Typically, an eligible worker employed consistently at the minimum wage for 40 hours a week might anticipate a UC check of 50% of that amount; that is, about $85 a week. In all but a few states, individuals may not receive more than 26 weeks of regular benefits. However, in periods of high unemployment, a federal program of extended benefits, activated by Congress and subject to presidential veto, can stretch this to 39 weeks.

The limitations of UC as a source of assistance to homeless people should be apparent from the structure of the program. First, it is only a source of support to those who have worked in covered employment. Second, the monetary qualification requirements tend to screen out the lowest-paid workers and those with an irregular work history. Finally, even if an individual does qualify, the benefit structure generally will provide the least assistance for the shortest period of time to those who have earned the least.

Not surprisingly, unemployed individuals who do not receive UC tend to be poorer than those who do. A Congressional Research Service study concluded that the poverty rate for unemployed persons receiving UC was 18.4% (based on monthly income), while the rate for those not receiving UC was 39%. For unem-ployed single adults, the poverty rate of those not receiving UC was a staggering 73.5%.[31]

GENERAL ASSISTANCE (GA)

What about the non-elderly person who has no minor children, is not completely disabled, does not qualify for (or has exhausted) UC, and cannot find a job? The federal system of categorical eligibility makes no provision for non-elderly, non-disabled adults without minor children. However, in some jurisdictions, such a person may qualify for a program often called General Assistance or General Relief.[32] In many jurisdictions, however, such a person does not qualify for *any* public cash assistance.

There is no federal duty to run a GA program, and there is no federal participation in its costs. States decide whether to run such programs, who should be eligible, under what circumstances they should be eligible, and what they should be eligible for. In some states, there is a constitutional requirement to operate GA. In others, there is no constitutional duty, and the decision is in the hands of the legislature. In some states, a GA program is administered by the state with relatively uniform requirements throughout the state's political subdivisions. In other states, counties have a duty to operate GA, and there may be substantial variation among their programs. In yet other states, no one has a duty to operate GA, and counties may or may not do so.

Since there is no federal monitoring of GA, it is difficult to compile clear and consistent information about the scope and coverage of these programs. A 1992 survey by the National Conference of State Legislatures and the Center on Budget and Policy Priorities[33] found that:

- In 42 states, there was a formal GA program in at least one county.

- In 22 states, GA was administered under uniform statewide regulations.

- In 20 states, there was no statewide GA, but some or all counties or localities operated a program.

Although there has been no comprehensive survey since 1992, there is clear evidence that the availability of General Assistance has contracted dramatically since that time.[34]

GA programs often differ on two key dimensions: *who* is eligible, and *how long* an eligible person can receive assistance. According to the 1992 survey, 11 states (including 2 with statewide programs) imposed no categorical eligibility restrictions. Each of the remaining states had some form of categorical restriction. For example, GA often is limited to those who are considered "unemployable." In some cases, the program may apply a disability standard as stringent as the SSI standard; other GA programs are designed to cover people who have a work-limiting disability but who cannot qualify for SSI, or who are aged but have not yet reached the age of qualification for Social Security or SSI.

According to the 1992 survey, about half of the states that had GA (22 out of 42) imposed no time limits on assistance. In 10 states, benefits were time limited for certain categories, while in another 10, benefits were time limited for all recipients.

Despite their diversity, GA programs share one fundamental characteristic: low benefit levels. The 1992 survey reported that the monthly benefit for a single person was less than $400 in all but 2 reporting jurisdictions; it was less than $200 a month in 12 jurisdictions. Thus, the GA payment level typically is far below that of SSI, and often far below that of AFDC. An analysis of GA in 20 cities concluded that in 18, the benefit for a single person was less than the fair market rent for a single-room-occupancy (SRO) housing unit; in the 2 remaining cities, an SRO with rental costs equal to the fair market rent would consume at least 97% of the GA benefit.

In part, the meagerness of GA benefits may be attributable to the lack of federal participation in program costs and absence of any federal standards governing provision of GA benefits. In part, it is likely attributable to the characteristics of those associated with General Assistance. While the caseload is often far more diverse, the public perception of the typical GA recipient is that of the most culturally suspect figure among the poor: an able-bodied single man without children. This describes the majority of homeless people, of course.

In recent years, a number of states have eliminated or sharply reduced the availability of GA. When states were under fiscal stress due to the recession of the early 1990s, GA was a particularly inviting target because there was no federal participation in program costs and no federal requirement to operate a program. When a program has a federal financial match, a state loses federal dollars for every state dollar withdrawn. GA lacks this disincentive. In addition, some key federal programs affecting the poor include a "maintenance of effort" requirement; that is, a penalty is imposed if the state reduces its spending below a particular level. GA is not protected in this way, either.

The availability of GA in a community appears to reduce the prevalence of homelessness. A study of homelessness in 147 cities during the period from 1981 to 1989 concluded that the cities with the highest rates of homelessness were ones in which no general assistance program existed, the next highest rates were in cities where general assistance was provided only for the disabled and families, and the lowest rates of homelessness were found in cities where general assistance benefits were also available to able-bodied individuals.[35]

Only a few studies have examined the effects of GA eliminations or curtailments. While the magnitude of the effect varies among studies, a review of the experiences of Michigan, Ohio, and Pennsylvania found consistent evidence of increases in the prevalence of homelessness after GA reductions or eliminations.[36]

INCREASED HOMELESSNESS THROUGH "WELFARE REFORM"?

We have described American income maintenance as a patchwork structure with serious gaps in coverage and often inadequate assistance for those who do qualify. It is quite possible, however, that the situation will deteriorate further in the near future.

In December 1995, Congress passed H.R. 4, the Personal Responsibility and Work Opportunity Act of 1995. This legislation was subsequently vetoed by President Clinton, and it is unclear whether any federal welfare legislation will be enacted in 1996. The specifics of any enacted legislation could differ from H.R. 4; however, to appreciate the current dimensions of the welfare reform debate and its likely impact on homelessness, it is helpful to look at some of the act's key features.

There has long been broad support for "welfare reform" without clarity about what the term means. In recent years, the focus of many "welfare reform" efforts has been to turn the income maintenance system into a work-focused system. Some proposals have emphasized linking employable recipients with job search and education programs, some emphasize the creation of work programs for employable recipients or for those who need aid for more than a brief period of time. In 1994, the Clinton Administration's welfare reform legislation—which was introduced but never acted on—would have required states to create work programs for families receiving AFDC in excess of two years and would have required AFDC parents to participate in a work program as a condition of receiving further aid after two years. A number of proposals—including the Clinton plan—have foundered because cost estimates project that the work-centered approaches cost more than the current system (at least in the short run, and perhaps in the long run, as well).[37]

In 1995, the terms of the debate shifted as Republican Congressional leadership advanced a proposal (H.R. 4) organized around three principles: reducing projected federal spending, ending individual entitlements, and devolving responsibilities to states. The key features of the legislation included:

- Repeal of AFDC; elimination of the federal entitlement to assistance for needy families with children; and provision instead of a "block grant" of federal funds to states, with broad state discretion to determine who receives assistance, and with a mandate that federal funds not be used to provide cash aid to a family for more than five years (with limited exceptions)

- Sharp reductions in future Food Stamp program spending, along with an option for a state to receive an FS block grant

- Curtailment of eligibility for assistance for legal immigrants

- Block granting of a set of child protection and child care programs

- Restrictions on SSI eligibility for children with disabilities

Legislation of this type could result in expanded homelessness, simply by reducing the availability of cash assistance to poor individuals and families. For example, nearly half a million elderly and disabled persons would be terminated from receipt of SSI benefits because of the bill's restrictions on benefits for legal immigrants. In addition, had H.R. 4 been enacted, about 320,000 low-income children who would qualify for SSI under current law would not receive assistance in 2002, and an additional 650,000 children in 2002 would receive SSI at a level 25% below what would have been provided under current law.[38]

Two legislative provisions likely to result in increased homelessness or increased desperation for those who are already homeless are the AFDC block grant and the restructuring of the Food Stamp program. Under H.R. 4, AFDC would have been repealed, and each state would have instead received a "block grant" of federal funds. The block grant would have been set based on the amount of recent federal spending for the state, and for most states, this level would have been frozen or near-frozen for a seven-year period. In AFDC, states have been required to contribute state funds to receive federal matching funds, so about 45% of current program spending represents state money. Under H.R. 4, states would have been permitted to withdraw up to 25% of state funding without penalty, and would have been permitted to transfer up to 30% of their block grant funding to block grants for other social services.

Under H.R. 4, the federal entitlement to AFDC assistance would have been eliminated, and states would have had no responsibility to provide assistance to needy families. States would have been free to restrict eligibility for aid in any manner they chose; the principal federal mandate was that a state could not use federal funds to provide aid for a period in excess of five years (with exceptions permissible for 15% of the caseload). However, a five-year limit, in itself, could result in massive curtailments of assistance. Recent research on AFDC caseload dynamics estimates that 35% of new applicants—and 76% of those receiving AFDC at any point in time—could eventually be expected to receive AFDC for five years. However, since there would be no entitlement to assistance, states under H.R. 4 would have been free to impose time limits on aid far more severe than a five-year limit, and there is clear evidence that a number of states would do so if given the opportunity.[39]

Apart from time limits, a block grant structure would seem likely to increase the prevalence of homelessness because it simultaneously increases state incentives to cut aid while eliminating any responsibility to assist needy families. A block grant structure alters fiscal incentives profoundly. Under current law, the federal and state governments share in each dollar of program costs. For example, in wealthier states, the federal match rate is 50%. This means that if costs increase, the federal government bears 50 cents of each additional dollar, and if costs go down, the federal and state governments share equally in savings. In a block grant structure, all costs beyond the federal contribution must be borne by the state alone. Thus, if there is a surge in need, the effective cost of responding is twice as high as under current law, because federal participation is unavailable. Conversely, in the block grant structure, if the state reduces aid by a dollar, the state keeps the entire dollar. In effect, the financial return to the state from cutting aid is doubled. All together, the combination of new fiscal incentives to reduce aid, authority to withdraw state funding, authority to transfer federal funding, and no responsibility to aid poor families likely will result in a very sharp curtailment of aid.

Changes in FS like those proposed in H.R. 4 could increase the prevalence or severity of homelessness in at least three different ways.

First, H.R. 4 would have permitted states to elect a block grant for FS, and a state so choosing would have been free to end FS for entire categories of persons. With this discretion, there is reason to fear that some states would eliminate aid for the least politically popular constituencies; for example, single persons. Second, H.R. 4 included a provision under which FS for able-bodied persons between age 18 and 50 without dependents would be limited to 4 months out of 12 *unless* the individual was working or participating in a work program after the 4-month point. However, states would have had no responsibility to offer work slots to individuals wishing to work but unable to find a job. Third, one of the principal ways in which FS assistance is currently targeted at families with higher shelter costs is through the "excess shelter deduction." Households whose shelter costs exceed half of the household's net income (after other deductions) are allowed to deduct these excess shelter costs, resulting in additional FS benefits. Historically, the amount of the excess shelter deduction has been capped (except for the elderly and disabled), but under current law, the cap was scheduled to be removed. H.R. 4 would have permanently frozen the current level of the cap and would have provided states an option to eliminate the excess shelter deduction altogether.

While no study has estimated the likely aggregate impact of H.R. 4–type legislation on homelessness, the Clinton Administration did estimate the legislation's poverty impacts. Using a set of conservative assumptions, the Office of Management and Budget concluded that, if H.R. 4 were enacted, it would increase the number of children in poverty by 1.5 million, raise the child poverty rate from 14.4% to 16.5%, increase the poverty gap for families (i.e., the amount by which families in poverty fall below the poverty line) by one-third, and increase the total number of persons in poverty by 3 million.[40] Further, with the devolution of authority to states (and in some states, further devolution to counties), a set of new fiscal pressures would emerge that could result in even greater pressure to reduce or eliminate remaining GA programs.

CONCLUSION

In a number of important ways, the current structure of income maintenance in the United States fails to provide needed assistance for homeless people. There is a fundamental mismatch between the categorical requirements of federally assisted income maintenance programs and the relevant characteristics of the homeless population. Many homeless people are single men and women who are neither sufficiently old nor disabled to qualify for SSI or Social Security, and who lack the work history to qualify for UC. As a result, such persons may be eligible only for GA—in the declining number of jurisdictions where GA exists.

Even sufficiently impoverished people in favored categories face daunting procedural barriers to assistance, and these are particularly discouraging to homeless people, whose lives are constantly at loose ends and whose daily priorities may crowd out full compliance with bureaucratic expectations.

Finally, the low benefit levels of AFDC, GA, and in some places, SSI and UC, do not allow recipients to pay anything close to fair market rents (see Chapter 4), even when combined with FS to offset the cost of food. This is a principal reason why even the receipt of assistance often fails to ameliorate or prevent homelessness.

In many respects, the current state of the welfare debate is profoundly troubling. Our nation's income maintenance programs provide no aid for many in need, and yet much of the public seems to believe that a principal problem is that we provide too much to too many. There is a broad-based belief that those who can work ought to do so, yet a reluctance to fund work programs. There is a belief among many that "the states can do it better," yet the experience of GA offers no basis for confidence that the states will do more if current federal requirements are reduced or eliminated.

If the current trend toward devolution—whether through waivers or block grants—continues, perhaps the best hope is that a set of states will step back, acknowledge the patchwork nature of the current structure, and develop an approach to income maintenance that establishes appropriate terms for assistance, addresses public concerns for accountability, and yet does not arbitrarily exclude categories of needy persons. States have often decried the procedural complexity and categorical restrictiveness of current law. The question now, in a world of reduced federal requirements and reduced federal resources, is whether states will have the political will, economic capacity, and administrative ability to do better.

PART
2
· · · · · · · · · ·

DIMENSIONS OF HOMELESSNESS

CHAPTER

Rural Homelessness: A Synopsis

Laudan Y. Aron
Janet M. Fitchen

Much of what we know about home-lessness is based on research conducted throughout the 1980s in urban areas across the country: homeless people are more numerous, visible, and geographically concentrated in cities; so, too, are the institutions designated to serve them. In rural areas, by contrast, we are still at the early stages of understanding how to identify and serve homeless people. Indeed, it is only in recent years that the presence of homeless people in rural America has been widely acknowledged.[1]

Rural *poverty*, on the other hand, is the stuff of legend; a stubborn vestigial feature of that "other America" Michael Harrington described as "invisible . . . hidden . . . off the beaten path."[2] And it persists: nationally, rural poverty rates reached a recent peak of more than 17% in 1986 and declined to 16.3% in 1990 (when the metropolitan poverty rate stood at 12.7%). Four trends account for its persistence: the erosion of rural employment and earnings, an increase in single-parent families, the migration of low-income urban people to small towns, and, in some areas, the failure of family farms.[3] Such poverty sometimes includes episodes of home-lessness.

PROBLEMS OF DEFINITION

Rural advocates for homeless people often note the difficulties they encounter with the usual interpretation of "literal homelessness"—conventionally defined as people living on the street or in shelters (see Chapter 2). Rural communities have few official shelters and fewer public places such as heating grates and subway or train stations at which urban people without housing congregate. However, they do have woods, campgrounds, and remote hills and valleys where literally homeless people may be found, albeit with difficulty. It has been argued that "homelessness" in rural areas should include people who are precariously housed: those in homes that fall below minimal standards of habitability, as well as those whose tenure is so brief and uncertain that remaining housed becomes a preoccupying endeavor.[4] This approach has the advantage of circumventing the obvious fallacy of acknowledging the existence of homeless people only where services exist to accommodate them, but the disadvantage of being equally applicable to urban areas. Adopting a more flexible and inclusive definition of homelessness has consequences. Characterizing "doubled-up" families and individuals as home-less, some suggest, can lead to poor targeting of scarce resources, sometimes to the detriment of those whose circumstances are more press-ing.

In a recent series of conferences,[5] advocates and service providers alike argued in favor of dispensing with certifying definitions and rec-ognizing instead that individuals can fall any-where along a continuum of housing distress. For the most part, though, the definition of homelessness included in the McKinney Act (see Chapter 15) was considered adequate by advocates, although they suggested that it should be applied more flexibly. What service providers have learned in cities applies equally in rural areas: "In the final analysis, the total number of homeless persons, when homeless-ness has [such] a broad definition, is really less important than segmentation of the homeless population into meaningful components, so that policy makers can design appropriate programs for specific groups."[6]

ESTIMATES OF SCALE

Studies to determine the prevalence of rural homelessness must clearly define "homeless" and the rules of inclusion and exclusion. Two studies have yielded estimates of rural home-lessness based on extensive inventories of places where homeless people may be found. Their findings differed considerably from the data obtained during the Census Bureau's 1990 S-night count, a survey done over a brief time period and in a much more limited number of locations (see Chapter 2).

An Ohio study[7] attempted to count all homeless persons in a sample of rural and non-urban counties over a six-month period. Home-lessness was defined broadly, and included people whose residential arrangements afforded less than 45 days of security. Intensive fieldwork was conducted to find and count all those who met the definition, and local service providers, advocacy groups, and knowledgeable residents participated in the effort. The results show that the 1-week prevalence of homelessness in nonurban counties was 5.7 per 10,000, and the

6-month prevalence was 14 per 10,000. Al-though about half of the 921 adults interviewed had spent the previous night in the home of a friend or family member, most of them had been "literally" homeless (sleeping in a shelter or a place not meant for human habitation) at some point in the 6-month period. Significantly, too, mental health problems were not found to be prominent, although about one in six had sought help for drinking. Respondents most of-ten cited family conflict, inability to pay rent, and unemployment as causes of their homeless-ness.

A 1993 Kentucky study used an extended period of data collection to cast a wide net among service providers, local governments and health agencies, and community organizations. Outdoor searches of likely camping areas were also made. The 1-day rate of homelessness for rural areas of the state was 12.9 per 10,000, compared with 22.1 per 10,000 in 3 urban coun-ties.[8] Rates based on data from the Census Bureau's 1990 S-night counts were 1.2 and 17.5 per 10,000, respectively, showing the multiple influences of the Census Bureau's more re-stricted set of search locations, a shorter data-collection period, and a narrower operational definition of homelessness. Because the Ken-tucky study employed a very broad definition of homelessness, which included people who were doubled up or living in crowded or inad-equate housing, it found that homeless rural women were twice as prevalent as homeless rural men, and that homeless families were more common in rural areas. Distinctive causes were cited for rural homelessness: rural respondents were more likely than their urban counterparts to identify domestic violence and alcohol or other substance abuse (both groups cited un-employment and inability to pay rent).

SPECIFIC FEATURES OF RURAL HOMELESSNESS

Several types of rural areas generate higher-than-average levels of homelessness. Among these are regions that are primarily agricultural, regions with economies that center on declin-ing extractive industries (such as mining or timber) and that are located in long-standing pockets of poverty, and areas experiencing economic growth.[9] Rural areas with growing economies include those with new or expanding industrial plants (which attract more job seekers than are needed or can be absorbed), and areas on the urban fringe that attract new businesses and higher-income residents (which drives up taxes and other living expenses, to the detriment of long-time residents). In regions with persistent poverty (such as Appalachia), the young and able-bodied often leave to relocate in urban areas in search of employment. If after several years they return home because they have no work, they may find themselves homeless. Residents in impoverished or primarily agricultural areas may lose their livelihood as a result of changing economic conditions—a lower demand for farm labor because of mechanized and corporate farming, or a shrinking service sector because of declining populations. Finally, many communities alongside major transportation routes receive homeless people literally "off the interstate"—people on the road looking for work, or simply on the move, who have run out of resources.

At the same time, the stock of low-rent housing in rural America has shrunk dramatically. Although housing costs are generally lower in rural areas than in cities, rural incomes are lower, resulting in a "shelter burden" nearly as high. As Fitchen's research in New York State[10] revealed, the rural housing problem is characterized by:

- Worsening supply and demand imbalances (more people of limited means shopping for fewer affordable units).

- A decline in home ownership. Whether acquired through inheritance, cheap purchase, or co-ownership with relatives—and although often of questionable quality—secure, owner-occupied housing at very low maintenance costs (usually unmortgaged) had long been seen as a rural birthright, but the rate has declined in recent years.[11]

- Restrictive land-use regulations and housing codes. Stringent building codes make it difficult for the rural poor to obtain and oc-

cupy cheap (often rundown) dwellings while they "fix them up." Used building material—the stock-in-trade of "handyman specials"—is also proscribed, placing a severe crimp in the makeshift, piecemeal patterns of construction in homemade housing.

- Rising rent burden. Low wages and low public-assistance benefit levels mean that many rural households are devoting half of their income to rent. Irregular earnings increase the likelihood of eviction and make the costs of moving more difficult to meet.

- Insecure tenancy. Sudden changes in the local real estate market uproot long-time tenants when dwellings are sold out from under them; a distinctive form of rural homelessness occurs when trailer park owners displace occupants—leaving people with a roof over their heads, but no place to put it.

Rural areas also have some distinctive—if not unique—populations susceptible to homelessness; groups with which urban researchers and service providers have relatively little experience. The largest Native American populations are in rural areas, as are most migrant farmworkers. Rural veterans, too, present singular challenges of outreach and engagement to service providers.[12]

COPING STRATEGIES

Like their urban counterparts, rural poor people often resort to a variety of makeshift arrangements in order to maintain housing. Most are reluctant to use shelters or welfare-paid motels. Instead, they make use of three common strategies to fend off literal homelessness:

- Doubling up in short-term arrangements. Researchers have frequently found that people tend to move in temporarily with parents or other relatives as a first—and, not uncommonly, a last—defense against literal homelessness. But doubling up has become more difficult as increasingly restrictive land-use regulations outlaw certain makeshifts (such as siting a trailer in the back yard, or adding a room), and as landlords or welfare officials limit the options of kin-based aid (enforcing lease agreements, for example, to restrict overcrowding). A woman with children may resort to a less easily detectable form of doubling up when she moves in with a boyfriend; despite concerns that the arrangement may not be good for either her or the children, she may simply have nowhere else to go.

- Recourse to seriously inadequate or unsafe housing. In nonmetropolitan America as a whole, 23% of poor homeowner households and 27% of poor renter households live in inadequate housing. These figures are somewhat higher than those for their urban counterparts (17% and 22%, respectively).[13] With an ever-larger proportion of the rural poor living in rented housing, substandard conditions in low-cost dwellings may become an even greater problem. As demand outstrips supply, prospective tenants must accept whatever the market offers, paying higher prices for lower quality. Structural or physical problems in dwellings—problems that jeopardize health or safety—commonly figure as precipitants of displacement.

- Residential mobility. Frequent moves are increasingly common among the rural poor. Residential narratives collected by researchers show that poor people with unsatisfactory housing tend to move suddenly, shifting from one rented small-town apartment to another, from one village to another, from trailer park to trailer park, from village to trailer park and back to village, and from open country to village and back to country. Friends and relatives are frequently the sources of referrals.

CONCLUSION

For service providers, rural areas offer some distinct advantages in mobilizing local resources to combat homelessness. The system of assistance is likely to be informal and personal; agency staff tend to be well-acquainted with the stories of local residents; sharing information and coordinating activity across agencies tend

to be easier to accomplish; and, in some areas at least, a sense of belonging, of "taking care of our own," enhances the assistance efforts. New measures to enhance rural service delivery capacity would do well to build upon such indigenous resources.

On the other hand, efforts to build an efficient service delivery network for homeless people can be hampered by the isolation of rural areas, huge distances to cover, paltry social service assets, ignorance of successful efforts in other communities, and, in some areas, denial that a problem exists or that "outside" assistance is needed. Communication upgrades are urgently needed in many areas if a better-informed and better-coordinated approach is to be made possible. A more aggressive case-finding attitude is required, too—outreach, under a variety of auspices, to locate people in need who rarely find their way to formal assistance.

But care should be taken not to replicate the specialization of services for homeless people so often found in urban areas. Most rural communities rely on generic service agencies—welfare offices, community action agencies, public housing authorities, police and mental health departments—to assist homeless people. This makes an integrated approach easier to mount. At the same time, generic approaches can fail to address certain problem areas that in the past have been either less urgent or have been ignored (or even kept hidden). Mental health and substance abuse services, and even assistance in parenting skills and budgeting, are examples of such neglected needs.

Prevention promises to be the most challenging task of all, for virtually no resources are available. Long-term prevention would entail improvement and expansion of the rural housing stock, retraining of rural workers, and local economic development to supply jobs at wages sufficient to meet housing costs. In small towns, more scatter-site public housing is needed, especially for young families. Additional rent subsidies, funded under federal auspices, are also critical. Revolving loan funds to help people with security deposits could ease the transition out of doubled-up quarters. And measures are surely needed to modify land-use regulations and building codes that needlessly restrict home ownership possibilities for lower-income people. More flexibility is needed in government programs to assist low-income families to purchase, hold onto, or renovate their homes, taking into account the actual conditions of their dwellings and budgets. Greater coordination would be welcomed, as well, between Department of Housing and Urban Development programs and the Department of Agriculture's Rural Economic and Community Development Administration, for example.[14] Rural areas are notably rich in social capital, and formal efforts to prevent or arrest homelessness should build upon the many existing bonds of informal support in such communities. This will not be easy, however, nor should the availability of such supports be hailed as evidence that "outside assistance" is therefore unneeded (see Chapter 1).

Finally, it should be emphasized that rural areas differ widely in their characteristics and needs. Significant differences are found in the types of housing problems experienced from one region to another and in how those problems contribute to homelessness. Affordability, habitability, and availability are distinctive problems, and determining which is the salient one in a given community is the first step in crafting a response.

CHAPTER 8

Material Survival Strategies on the Street: Homeless People as *Bricoleurs*

David A. Snow
Leon Anderson
Theron Quist
Daniel Cress

> *The "bricoleur" is adept at performing a large number of diverse tasks.*
> —Claude Levi-Strauss, *The Savage Mind*

Thinking about homelessness and its eradication has been conditioned primarily by two genres of research: the first, which includes the bulk of the voluminous literature on homelessness, consists of cross-sectional (i.e., single-point-in-time) surveys of the demographics and disabilities of homeless individuals; the second consists of macrolevel studies of the relationships among rates of poverty, unemployment, median rents, and the like, and rates of homelessness across cities.[1] Although both genres illuminate the characteristics of the homeless and the causes of their plight, they also unwittingly generate several erroneous assumptions about homelessness. One is that homeless people can be described and understood adequately in terms of their demographic characteristics and personal disabilities or blemishes, which generally are discussed as if they precede the onset of homelessness; the other is that identification of the precipitating causes—structural, individual, or a combination of the two—holds the key to resolving the problem.

Glossed over in both cases is how the experience of homelessness shapes the behavior of homeless people and their street careers, and how it affects their prospects for getting off the street. In this chapter we assess what the bulk of the research has neglected: the adaptive strategies of the homeless, variations in the use of these strategies, and their implications for facilitating or impeding escape from the street. We begin with a discussion of our data sources and research methods. Next, we take up the issue of adaptive behaviors, focusing on material survival strategies.[2] We then turn to a consideration of factors associated with variation in their use. And finally, we briefly consider some implications of these observations.

DATA, METHODS, AND RESEARCH CONTEXTS

This chapter derives from two research projects. The first was a multimethod case study of homelessness in Austin, Texas, in the mid-1980s. This was based on a year and a half of intensive field-work intended to develop an understanding of street survival strategies and variations in their use among the homeless. Two of us spent over 400 hours "hanging out" with homeless people in a variety of settings central to their subsistence and everyday routines (e.g., a Salvation Army shelter, soup kitchens, day-labor sites, the city jail, and plasma centers). We supplemented these observations with life history interviews of 20 key informants who had been on the street for lengths of time ranging from 2 months to 14 years. We also spent 200 hours with the personnel of social service agencies, police officers, local political officials, and neighborhood activists, all of whom dealt with the homeless in one fashion or another. In addition to the fieldwork, we tracked a random sample of 767 homeless individuals through the network of institutions with which they had frequent contact in Austin, including the Salvation Army, the state employment office, the city hospital, the police department, state and local mental health facilities, and a private welfare service.[3]

The second project was a national study of collective action campaigns by homeless people. The component most relevant here consisted of structured interviews with 400 homeless people in Detroit, Philadelphia, and Tucson. These three cities were among eight in which several of us had conducted case studies of homeless activists and their organizational allies and targets in order to learn about the factors that influence homeless activism. During the structured interviews noted above, one objective was to understand the biographies and experiences of homeless people. We draw on these interviews, and those conducted in Austin, to examine material survival strategies.

In each of the three cities, we interviewed homeless people in a variety of settings so as to capture a broad range of biographies and experiences.[4] Thus, in Philadelphia, we interviewed people in shelters, parks, subway stations, on the street, on heating grates, and in malls; in Tucson, we conducted interviews in parks and campgrounds, on the street, and in a shelter. In Detroit—where the temperature was 10 degrees below zero for most of the week we interviewed,

and virtually no one was on the street—we conducted our interviews in the principal drop-in center in the area of the city with the greatest concentration of homeless people. This proved to be a reasonable alternative, as a variety of homeless individuals had crowded into the center to avoid the cold and to receive shelter assignments.

In each of the settings, interviewees were screened by their responses to a number of initial questions, one asking if they currently regarded themselves as homeless, and several asking about their sleeping arrangements during the past 60 days. In all, we interviewed 162 homeless people in Detroit, 102 in Philadelphia, and 136 in Tucson.

Although there were a number of conspicuous differences in the demographic characteristics of the homeless in the 3 cities, as an aggregate they were predominantly male (85%), minority (72.4%), unattached (85.5%), and in the age range of 31 to 50 years (mean age of 34.9 years). Even though these figures are not representative of homeless people in the three cities because of our sampling strategy, they are consistent with those of other studies that aggregate findings across cities.[5] The same is true of our findings about sleeping arrangements, which showed a decided tendency toward sleeping in shelters or other such facilities over sleeping in public places. Yet, a significant percentage of individuals in each of the cities had slept in both shelters and public places, suggesting that there may be no tidy relationship between the sleeping arrangements of the homeless and their other characteristics, as sometimes assumed.[6]

MATERIAL SURVIVAL STRATEGIES

Like people everywhere, the homeless must eat, sleep, eliminate, make ends meet, socialize, and secure a measure of meaning and self-respect. However, they must attend to these basic human needs without the resources and social support that most people take for granted. Additionally, street life is shot through with uncertainty. There are no guarantees that what promoted survival today will work tomorrow. Consequently, the homeless must frequently ad-lib to stay afloat. They are not only people with needs, but "grudging players in a rough theater of improvisation."[7]

Improvisation is a constant requirement of the abject poverty in which the homeless live. One of the most pressing daily problems for homeless people is to find a way to get some money almost immediately. Whether they wake in a shelter, a motel room, a building alcove, an abandoned building, a car, a weed patch, an encampment, a tunnel or sewer, or under a bridge, they usually face each day broke—or nearly so. Even though food and shelter can often be procured for free, amenities such as cigarettes, coffee, soft drinks, and beer must be purchased or acquired through some effort. This unrelenting problem raises the question of how the homeless make do, apart from the loosely coupled network of shelters and soup kitchens in most cities. An answer to this question requires consideration of other questions: What strategies do homeless people fashion or adopt to acquire money or material goods for personal use or exchange? How does their use of these strategies vary, and what accounts for such variation?

At the outset of such a discussion, it is important to keep in mind that the survival routines of homeless people in any locale are embedded in specific organizational, political, and ecological contexts that encourage some strategies while making others less likely. Variation in the pursuit of employment from one city to the next, for example, is probably not due so much to differences in the work orientation of the homeless as it is to differences in local economies and markets for certain kinds of labor. Variation from city to city in the number of shelters, soup kitchens, and other street facilities will also yield different adaptive repertoires, as will local ordinances that, for example, ban panhandling or require padlocks on dumpsters to make scavenging more difficult. Such policies not only exacerbate the plight of the homeless by narrowing their survival options, but may unwittingly push them toward more-criminal activities like theft and prostitution.[8] The point is that survival repertoires are not fashioned

willy-nilly. Rather, they are the product of the interplay of the resourcefulness and ingenuity of the homeless and local organizational, political, and ecological constraints. A thorough understanding of the experience of homelessness thus requires consideration of the strategic improvisations of the homeless and the community context in which they are embedded.[9] We address only the former in this chapter.

Exhibit 8.1 provides a composite taxonomy of material survival strategies pursued by homeless people in Austin, Detroit, Philadelphia, and Tucson—and presumably elsewhere. Three generic strategies are noted: institutionalized assistance, wage labor, and shadow work. We consider each in turn.

EXHIBIT 8.1

TAXONOMY OF MATERIAL SURVIVAL STRATEGIES

Institutionalized Assistance
    Institutionalized Labor (Working for Street Agencies)
    Income Supplements
        Public Assistance
        Assistance from Family and Friends

Wage Labor
    Regular Work
    Day Labor

Shadow Work
    Selling/Peddling (Sales Work)
        Selling Junk and Personal Possessions
        Selling Illegal Goods and Services
            Selling Drugs
            Prostitution
        Selling Plasma
    Soliciting Public Donations
        Panhandling
        Performing in Public
    Scavenging
        Scavenging for Food
        Scavenging for Salable Goods
        Scavenging for Money
    Theft

Institutionalized Assistance

We begin with institutionalized assistance because the homeless, like most of the extremely poor, are often perceived to be on the public dole. We use the term institutionalized assistance more broadly, however, to refer to established or routine monetary assistance patterned in accordance with tradition, legislation, or the mission or operational requirements of organizations. One type of institutionalized assistance can be understood as *institutionalized labor*, in that it is provided by organizations such as shelters, soup kitchens, and drug and alcohol "rehab" programs that sometimes pay homeless clients for work related to operation of the facility. The number of homeless people employed by these agencies is minuscule in relation to the homeless population, however, and it is probably never a significant subsistence alternative for more than a handful of people in any one community. In Austin, for example, only 7 of the 168 homeless in our field sample worked for a street agency. When the local Salvation Army opened a new facility in 1988, many more homeless were employed, but they still constituted only a small proportion of the local population. Moreover, their pay—usually room, board, and a small stipend—typically tied them to the organization rather than providing the means to escape the street.[10]

A far more common type of institutional assistance takes the form of *income supplements* provided by the government or by family and friends. These supplements are funneled through such federal programs as Social Security (Old Age, Survivors, and Disability Insurance; OASDI), Supplemental Security Income (SSI), Unemployment Compensation (UC), Aid to Families with Dependent Children (AFDC), and state and local programs usually called General Assistance (GA). Relatively few homeless people receive such benefits in spite of their dire poverty. As indicated in Table 8.1, only 27% of the 400 homeless people interviewed in Detroit, Philadelphia, and Tucson had received some form of income assistance during the previous month, with AFDC and GA the most common. Further, only 17.7% said that these programs provided their major source of

income. These figures are comparable to the Urban Institute's finding that 20% of 1,704 homeless surveyed nationally in 1987 received AFDC, GA, or SSI.[11]

Such aggregate figures hide a great deal of variation, however. In Philadelphia, for example, two-thirds of our respondents received government assistance (mostly AFDC and GA) during the previous month, and 50% counted it as their most important source of income. In Detroit and Tucson, by contrast, only 6.8% and 21.4%, respectively, received such assistance during the previous 30 days, and less than 10% in each city claimed it as their most important source of money. In Austin, an even smaller number of homeless people received any kind of income assistance, and only about 4% of our 168 field informants named it as their major source of income.

For the most part, such variation results from two factors: the differential availability of GA programs across the United States and wide variation in their benefit levels, and local differences in the composition of the homeless population. In Austin, for example, our sample included only unattached homeless men and women who were rarely elderly or obviously disabled. GA, the only income assistance program for able-bodied, non-elderly individuals and childless couples, did not exist in Texas, and the characteristics of the homeless population did not match the qualifying categories of federal programs (AFDC, SSI, and Social Security).[12] But even if GA had been available, its benefits would have been meager and insufficient to sustain survival on the streets—much less enough to get off them.

The same can be said about *cash from family or friends*. As shown in Table 8.1, 40% of the 400 homeless interviewed in Detroit, Philadelphia, and Tucson received money from family or friends during the previous month, but less than 5% rated it as their most important resource. This suggests that while a significant number of the homeless may receive financial assistance from family or friends, it is seldom substantial.[13] Thus, given the unavailability or insufficiency of the various forms of institutionalized assistance, the majority of the homeless—

TABLE 8.1

Sources of Income during Past Month (in Percent)

Income Sources	Detroit (N=162)	Philadelphia (N=102)	Tucson (N=136)	Totals (N=400)
Income Assistance	6.8	66.6	21.4	27.1
AFDC/GA	2.5	61.7	14.1	21.5
OASDI/SSI	1.2	6.4	6.6	5.0
Unemployment Compensation	3.1	1.9	0	1.8
Cash from Family or Friends	43.8	55.9	24.5	40.3
Wage Labor	27.3	25.0	48.5	33.9
Shadow Work	55.6	54.9	61.0	57.3
Selling/Peddling	37.7	35.3	40.7	38.1
Selling Junk	9.9	24.5	19.3	16.8
Selling Drugs	3.1	8.8	9.6	6.7
Selling Plasma	29.0	13.7	20.0	22.0
Panhandling	22.8	30.4	21.5	24.3
Scavenging	16.1	24.5	24.5	21.0
Theft	6.8	19.6	11.1	11.5
Other	4.3	4.9	3.0	4.0

Since we will examine the relationship between family status (e.g., men and women with children) and the receipt and/or pursuit of these income sources, it is important to keep in mind the percentage of adults with children in the samples for each of the three cities: 1.8% in Detroit; 23.5% in Philadelphia; and 4.4% in Tucson. Overall, 33 (8.2%) of the 400 homeless men and women in our sample were with children.

particularly homeless men, as we will see—must pursue alternative subsistence strategies to make do.

Wage Labor

One alternative is wage labor. Wage labor customarily refers to work that involves the exchange of labor for money. Wage-labor jobs can vary considerably in actual wages, how wages are determined, the regulation of the time and place of work, and the extent to which they are monitored by governmental authorities. Usually, wage-labor jobs have regulated and prearranged rates of pay and times and places of work. Typically, wage labor also is enumerated and monitored by a governmental agency, as reflected in the figures generated by the U.S. Department of Labor on changes in the occupational structure and unemployment rates. We refer to this variety of work as *regular work.*

Regular work does not figure significantly in the lives and routines of the homeless, as it is typically unavailable or inaccessible. In Austin, for example, over 90% of our tracking sample of 767 indicated that they were unemployed when they checked into the local Salvation Army for the first time, a finding comparable to other studies.[14] To be sure, some of the homeless hold regular jobs; in Austin, we found that about 9% of our tracking sample secured regular jobs out of the local branch of the Texas Employment Commission (TEC). Although it is possible that some found regular work by checking want ads and "beating the pavement," this probably was uncommon since the TEC was the funneling point for such jobs locally. Our research in Detroit, Philadelphia, and Tucson six years later revealed similarly that pursuit of regular work was not a reliable strategy: two-thirds of the homeless claimed that they had not worked for pay during the past month and only about 8% counted regular work as their most important method to make ends meet.[15]

So, some of the homeless do work at regular jobs, but in nearly all of the cases we examined, the wages received were not sufficient to allow escape from the street. Moreover, homelessness poses serious obstacles to securing and maintaining regular work. These include the absence of a permanent address or a telephone where an individual can be reached directly, the difficulty of meeting employers' expectations for dress and appearance, the problem of finding transportation to and from the work site, and the difficulty of coordinating regular-work schedules with the schedules and strictures of shelters and other street agencies.

Consider the experience of a homeless man in Austin who managed to get two dishwashing jobs, one in a fraternity house and the other at a restaurant located seven miles from the shelter at which he slept. He worked the two jobs eagerly for a couple of weeks, bragging, "I'm in good shape now, and all on jobs nobody else wants." However, his hours at the restaurant conflicted with the schedule of the local shelter. He claimed it was not hard to find a place to sleep, but one evening when one of us was giving him a ride to the shelter before it closed, he fell asleep in the middle of a conversation. Within two weeks he had quit both jobs and talked of moving to another city. He scuttled these plans when he secured another kitchen-helper position at a downtown restaurant, but his initial optimism was dampened again by his inability to sustain his work routine without a place to stay that accommodated his employment schedule.

Because of such obstacles, the homeless must pursue other strategies for securing employment. One such strategy is *day labor*. Day labor is wage labor secured on a day-to-day basis, usually in changing locales, and typically at pay lower than regular work. In spite of its irregular character and low pay, day labor tends to fit better than regular work with the situation of the homeless because transportation is provided to the work site, and neither a neat and clean appearance nor a recent work history or job references are required for employment. Perhaps most impor-

tant, day labor pays cash at quitting time and thus provides immediate pocket money. Many of the homeless actively pursue day labor, but its availability from city to city is highly variable, depending on shifting economic conditions, corresponding changes in labor markets, and seasonal changes. Fueled by a construction boom, there was considerable demand for day labor in Austin during the first half of the 1980s, and, not surprisingly, it was the preferred subsistence strategy among the majority of the homeless during this period. Between 300 and 400 homeless adults, usually men, showed up daily at the city's 3 central day-labor sites. Research conducted in other southern cities during the 1980s also notes the importance of day labor to the subsistence of the homeless.[16] We found that the homeless in Detroit, Philadelphia, and Tucson used day labor as well, but it was not as common as it had been in Austin several years earlier, as less than 20% named it their most important means of survival.

However robust the day-labor market in a particular city, and however dependent some homeless are on it, day-labor jobs are, by definition, without a tomorrow. This quintessential feature of day labor, coupled with its notoriously low pay, makes it an improbable basis for getting off the street. As a homeless man working out of the Austin Labor Pool told us despairingly:

> If you're working the labor pool, you're making at most, say, $25. Meals cost you $4.50 or so and cigarettes are over a buck. Then a bunk at the Bunkhaus is $6.50 a night. If you drink, forget it. You can't make it. And if you don't go to work the next day, there goes your bankroll.

Clearly, day labor can facilitate survival on the street, but, sporadic and uncertain, alone it is rarely sufficient. Consequently, many of the homeless turn to shadow work.

Shadow Work

By shadow work we refer to a set of compensatory subsistence tactics such as panhandling and scavenging, fashioned or pursued in the shadow of regular work.[17] While such activities do not constitute work as traditionally conceived, they nonetheless focus attention and energy on procuring money or other material goods for personal use or exchange. Unlike wage labor, though, shadow work involves no routine exchange of labor for money, and there is no official sanction or formal control.

Besides being unofficial, unenumerated work outside the wage economy, shadow work is highly opportunistic and innovative. It involves, at minimum, the recognition and exploitation of whatever resources and unofficial markets happen to be available whenever a few dollars are needed. As suggested by the shadow work activities itemized in Exhibit 8.1, the homeless trade or sell their possessions, peddle illegal goods and services, sell their plasma, solicit donations from passersby, scavenge refuse in search of usable and salable items, and, on occasion, steal.[18] Seldom does a homeless person engage in all of these activities consistently, but as need and opportunity arise, he or she combines a number of them into a distinctive repertoire to augment institutionalized assistance and day labor. As reported in Table 8.1, nearly 60% of the homeless interviewed engaged in some shadow work during the previous month, and shadow work was the most widely pursued survival strategy in Detroit and Tucson, and the second most common in Philadelphia. Additionally, the type of shadow work pursued is not purely a function of opportunity but reflects some selectivity. As suggested by Table 8.2, shadow work is ranked in a preference hierarchy of sorts. For example, when the homeless surveyed in the three cities were asked which activities they were most likely to pursue when short on cash and unable to find regular work or day labor, they generally mentioned some form of street sales first, most often selling plasma, followed in descending order by panhandling, scavenging, and theft.

That some varieties of shadow work are preferred over others is not surprising, since some are less dangerous, easier to master, and less humiliating or less immoral. But recourse to one activity over another is not merely a matter of choice. Indeed, this is the case with the entire repertoire of material survival strategies. As we noted previously, no single strategy, whether day labor or shadow work, can ensure survival on the streets, and no matter how strongly one activity is preferred, there is no guarantee from one day to the next that it will remain available. Day labor is not sufficiently abundant to ensure paid work day after day, and it is vulnerable to bad weather and is usually unavailable on weekends. Plasma centers, too, are typically closed on weekends. And in many cities, Sundays are bad for panhandling because few nonhomeless pedestrians are about. Survival, then, is facilitated by a mix of strategies. For example, while many of the homeless frown on scaveng-

	TABLE 8.2			
SHADOW WORK ACTIVITIES MOST LIKELY PURSUED WHEN SHORT ON CASH (IN PERCENT)				
Income Sources	Detroit (N=101)	Philadelphia (N=53)	Tucson (N=94)	Totals (N=248)
Selling/Peddling	59.4	35.8	60.6	54.8
Selling Junk	10.9	15.1	17.0	14.1
Selling Drugs	3.0	9.4	11.7	7.7
Selling Plasma	45.5	11.3	31.9	33.1
Panhandling	24.7	28.3	14.9	21.8
Scavenging	6.9	9.4	13.8	10.1
Theft	5.9	20.7	8.5	10.1
Other	3.0	5.6	2.1	3.2

ing because it involves rummaging through garbage and discarded materials, necessity may leave little choice.[19] Thus, the majority of homeless people (54%) who engaged in shadow work in Detroit, Philadelphia, and Tucson pursued 2 or more varieties in the previous month, with 25% resorting to 3 or more types.

As a result, we think many of the homeless can be described metaphorically as *bricoleurs*. *Bricoleurs* are persons who are "adept at performing a large number of diverse tasks." However, they do so not with the tools or know-how of the skilled craftsman or professional, but with whatever resources and means are at their disposal. As traditionally understood in France, *bricoleurs* do odd jobs "with 'whatever is at hand,' that is to say with a set of tools and materials which is always finite and is also heterogenous" because it bears no conventional relation to the current project.[20] Used metaphorically, *bricoleur* can designate any individual who devises unconventional but pragmatic solutions *(bricolages)* to pressing problems. We think the homeless—at least many of them—qualify for such designation because of their inventive and opportunistic cobbling together of a mix of income sources and survival routines from limited possibilities. It is this repertoire or *bricolage* that enables them to make do under very trying circumstances. Other researchers have made similar observations. As Jacqueline Wiseman noted in her study of skid row in the 1960s:

> When the skid row man thinks of getting money, he . . . must show ingenuity in creating something out of nothing. Thus, he thinks in terms of objects, relationships, or short-term tasks that can be converted into enough cash to take care of current needs—liquor, food, shelter, incidentals.[21]

To understand the homeless as *bricoleurs* is not only consistent with the character of material survival on the streets, but shifts attention from their widely chronicled disabilities to the practices by which they survive. Viewed this way, homeless people look more like resourceful, fully human actors than mere incompetents.

INDIVIDUAL VARIATION IN SURVIVAL STRATEGIES

In examining their material survival strategies, we have focused on the homeless in general, thus glossing over individual variation in adaptive behaviors. We now turn to an examination of this issue.

Time on the Street

A central finding of our Austin research was that the more time homeless people spent on the street, the less likely they were to pursue wage labor and the greater the probability that they engaged in various forms of shadow work.[22] This also was evident among the homeless in Detroit, Philadelphia, and Tucson when we examined the correlations among various survival strategies and the predictor or independent variables of time on the street, gender, age, race, and being with or without accompanying children. We found that time on the street was negatively and significantly related to involvement with regular work and receipt of cash from family or friends, and was positively related to shadow work in general, as well as to each variety of shadow work with the exception of selling plasma. In other words, the longer they were on the street, the homeless in Detroit, Philadelphia, and Tucson, like the homeless in Austin, appeared to drift away from regular work and from kith and kin, toward the world of shadow work.

Gender, Family Status, Age, and Ethnicity

Since behavioral patterns and life opportunities often vary significantly by gender, the presence or absence of dependent children, age, and ethnicity, it is reasonable to wonder if the above findings and observations hold in spite of such differences. The answer is both yes and no. When we looked at the correlations for the 60 homeless women with or without children, we found that being female was negatively related both to time on the street and to age, meaning that homeless women were not as likely to be on the street as long as men, and that typically they were younger than the men. Further, being female was negatively related to engaging in wage labor, as well as to regular work and to day labor individually, and it also was negatively related to shadow work in general, indicating that homeless women were not as likely as homeless men to pursue these strategies. However, being female was significantly and positively correlated with receiving income assistance and cash from family or friends. Taken together, these findings suggest that homeless women and homeless men have different survival repertoires, with various forms of institutionalized assistance being more salient for homeless women, and shadow work figuring more prominently in the survival of homeless men.

However, the presence of children made a difference. For the 33 homeless women and men with children, as with all females, the significant negative correlations remained for time on the street and age, as well as for shadow work in general, but they disappeared for wage labor. The significant and positive correlations with income assistance and the receipt of cash from family and friends remained, but the correlation with income assistance became particularly strong. Taken together, the entire pattern of associations suggests that the correlations between being female, time on the street, and material survival strategies were really artifacts of having children.

These findings suggest that differences in the material survival strategies and street careers of homeless men and women depend largely on the presence of children. In comparison to unattached homeless men, homeless women with children have distinctively different street careers and survival repertoires: they are not on the street as long, they depend much more on various forms of institutionalized assistance, and they rely very little on shadow work. The survival routines of childless homeless women, on [no kids] the other hand, are more similar to those of homeless men than those of homeless women with children, but with two exceptions: they are more likely to receive assistance from family or friends, and they are less likely to pursue wage labor. Burt and Cohen's conclusion, based

on their analysis of differences among homeless single women, homeless women with children, and homeless single men, bears repetition here: "In many ways homeless women with children differ from homeless single women even more than the latter differ from homeless men."[23] This appears to be the result of the culturally privileged position of dispossessed women with children. They are advantaged by being eligible for public assistance, particularly AFDC, and their families appear to be more inclined to lend a helping hand than are the families of homeless men.

Age does not appear to have much influence on survival strategies, at least not for the non-elderly homeless adults who comprised more than 95% of our sample.[24] Aside from being positively correlated with time on the street and being female, age varied significantly with only two material survival tactics: cash from family and friends, and theft. In the case of cash handouts, the relationship was negative, meaning that as age increased, the receipt of such handouts declined. The relationship between age and theft was also negative, indicating that theft was practiced more by the younger homeless.[25]

The relationship between race and survival strategies was even less remarkable. Categorizing the homeless according to their race (White or Black),[26] we found a significant correlation only with time on the street: Black homeless persons tended to have longer street careers.

Thus, race and age have relatively little influence on individual variation in material survival strategies in comparison to time on the street, gender, and the presence of children. More specifically, homeless women with children rely more on various forms of institutional assistance, while homeless men who have been on the street for awhile are more dependent on various forms of shadow work.

Given these findings, we are left with an intriguing question: What accounts for the inverse relationship between time on the street and pursuit of wage labor among the homeless? Why does shadow work figure more prominently in the survival repertoires of those who have been on the street longer?

Two contrasting answers warrant consideration. One is rooted in conventional wisdom, and holds simply that the greater emphasis upon shadow work among the long-time homeless is due to a decline in work orientation. That is, street life disinclines people toward conventional work; it makes them lazy. Such an explanation strikes us as wrongheaded, though. As emphasized earlier, shadow work is like all work insofar as it involves the concentration of energy and attention on procuring money or other material goods for personal use or exchange. It differs in that it is neither formally sanctioned nor regulated as to time, place, or wage. But it is work, nonetheless. To scavenge involves no less toil than most kinds of manual labor, and to panhandle effectively requires the interactional mettle and interpersonal skills necessary to many kinds of sales work.

An alternative explanation seems more plausible: it is not a decline in work orientation per se that accounts for the greater prominence of shadow work among those with longer street careers, but rather a change in orientation from the world of regular work to the world of shadow work. The incentive to work remains but it is directed toward a different order of work. Moreover, this shift in orientation is quite reasonable in view of the demoralizing nature of the wage-labor jobs available to homeless people. Because of their irregularity and low pay, these jobs rarely provide either a reliable basis for surviving or a means off the street. As a consequence, experience with wage labor frequently leads to alienation from it, especially as familiarity develops with the various forms of shadow work and the possibility of cobbling together alternative measures. Thus, when one of our homeless informants found a dollar one morning on the way to a labor corner and said, "Forget it; I'll get a cup of coffee and go donate blood," it was not a decline in work orientation that prompted him to forego his job-hunting expedition but the realization that it was unlikely to yield anything anyway, and that he was likely to fare better pursuing shadow work. He cast his lot with the world of shadow work not because he was uninterested in regular work but because he had lost faith in its capacity to sustain him. Further, shadow work has some advantages: control over the pace of the work and the way it is done, and the possibility of teaming up with friends when doing it, as we observed often with panhandling and scavenging. Still, the benefits of shadow work do not promote the shift of focus, at least not initially.[27] Rather, this shift seems rooted in a sense of futility nurtured by unrelenting failure to find regular work at a living wage.

It might be argued, of course, that if the homeless only looked beyond the moment—if they were not so oriented to present impulses—they would see the advantages of playing the wage-labor game.[28] But the issue is not so much one of orientation to time—whether the homeless are less future-oriented than those of higher status—as one of articulation between the present and the future. Elliot Liebow understood this well when he wrote that the difference between Black streetcorner men of the 1960s and their middle-class counterparts "lies not so much in their different orientations to time as their different orientations to future time or, more specifically, to their different futures."[29] For most people, the immediate present corresponds with the future; they have a reasonably strong sense that what they do today will yield a better tomorrow. Psychiatrist Robert Coles has referred to this as a sense of entitlement, and has observed that its salience increases with movement up the status system.[30] But clearly, such a sense is not prominent among the homeless. Most homeless people have little confidence that their individual actions today will yield a better tomorrow.[31] As we have seen, the wage-labor jobs that await them, if any, typically are jobs without a future. The tomorrows they can realistically imagine do not inspire either the investment of whatever limited resources they have scrimped to save, or strategies that go beyond the world of shadow work. For many of the homeless, then, the inability to secure wage labor, or its repeated failure to yield a fair return on the time and energy invested, forces upon them the *bricoleur* mentality and pushes them into the cobbled-together world of shadow work.

IMPLICATIONS

This portrait of many homeless people as *bricoleurs*—people who "do this and that" in order to make do—suggests several implications for dealing with homelessness. First, the fact that most homeless people are active agents in pursuit of subsistence suggests that a good number of them may benefit directly and immediately from programs that build on that agency—for example, by providing training that builds on existing skills and jobs that pay a living wage. This is not to deny the need of many for substance abuse treatment, for mental health services, or for social services of other sorts, but it does suggest that intervention programs that stereotypically homogenize the homeless as helpless and dysfunctional are likely to be of limited success.

Second, if material survival strategies vary with time on the street, and if some homeless people become habituated to street life, then it follows that homeless people may be differentially amenable to social service assistance and intervention. Clearly, veterans of street life who are anchored in it behaviorally, socially, and cognitively will be more difficult to "rescue"

from homelessness than those who have been on the street for a relatively short time. Street life can become taken for granted. Like the rest of us, homeless people can find it difficult and daunting to change routines and associates, even when it is in their interest to do so. A formerly homeless alcohol and drug counselor made the point well when he told us:

> After awhile, the streets are all you know. And you may think about getting back in society and what you would like to do, but you don't really know. And it scares you when you really think about trying to do it—fear of the unknown, and not being able to make it. That's what stops a lot of guys from even trying.

Such observations suggest an approach to the homeless that appreciates such features of socialization and caution us not to rely so heavily on distinctions of demography and disability. More specifically, perhaps homeless people who have adapted to street life need transitional resocialization programs more than programs that thrust them headfirst back into the conventional, domiciled world.

CHAPTER 9

Homeless Veterans

Robert Rosenheck
Catherine A. Leda
Linda K. Frisman
Julie Lam
An-Me Chung

INTRODUCTION

For as long as there have been armed forces, homeless veterans have been subjects of public concern. The first soldiers' hospitals were established in the 12th century to care for homeless Crusaders returning from the Holy Land, and one of the first veterans' homes was built to house 16th-century English sailors living vagabond lives after long years at sea.[1] From the soldiers of Andrew Jackson's army, marooned in New Orleans years after their famous battle, to the Vietnam veterans who camp nightly across from the White House, homeless veterans have been recognized as having a special place in the social fabric of our country and special claim to public sympathy.

In spite of the long history of homelessness among veterans, the appearance of large numbers of them during the 1980s was not easy to understand. Since World War II, U.S. veterans have been offered a broad range of special benefits, including educational assistance, home loan guaranties, pension and disability payments, and free health care. In fact, veterans consistently have higher median incomes, lower rates of poverty and unemployment, and are better educated than U.S. males in similar age groups.[2] Veterans should have been *less* vulnerable to homelessness than other Americans.

As surveys conducted during the 1980s indicated that perhaps half of homeless veterans served during the Vietnam era (compared to only one-third of veterans in the general population), many suggested that their homelessness might be yet another consequence of military service during the Vietnam War and, more specifically, of combat-related post-traumatic stress disorder (PTSD). But although some Vietnam veterans have suffered prolonged psychological problems related to their military service, the assumption that homelessness among veterans is largely related to Vietnam service seems more consistent with painful collective recollections of our longest and least popular war than with available scientific evidence. A November 1993 headline in *USA Today*, for example, described "a shattered army: 500,000 homeless veterans most of whom served in Vietnam"; but, according to studies reviewed in this chapter, this estimate is probably 2 to 4 times the actual figure.[3]

In contrast to exaggerated and sensational reports on homeless veterans, a number of scientific studies have been undertaken during the last decade, many of them by the Department of Veterans Affairs' Northeast Program Evaluation Center. In this chapter we review these and other studies, and we present previously unpublished data that address: (1) the antecedts of homelessness among veterans, especially the role of military service, (2) the distinctive characteristics of homeless veterans as compared to nonveterans, and (3) the scope and focus of services provided to homeless veterans by the Department of Veterans Affairs (VA) and by voluntary veterans' service organizations (VSOs).

MILITARY SERVICE AND HOMELESSNESS

The Proportion of Veterans among Homeless Americans

The first effort to summarize current knowledge about homeless veterans reported a wide range of estimates of their representation among homeless persons (18% to 51%).[4] A more systematic synthesis indicated that 40% of homeless men report past military service, as compared with 34% in the general adult male population.[5] This study concluded that male veterans were 1.4 times more likely than nonveteran men to be homeless. Using a generally accepted 1987 estimate of 512,000 homeless men in America on an average night,[6] we can estimate the number of literally homeless ("houseless") male veterans to have been at least 200,000 per night in those days, a figure which may be higher now.

Although homelessness among women and children has been a distinctive and alarming feature of contemporary homelessness (see Chapter 10), limited attention has been directed to our 660,000 female veterans, probably because this group makes up less than 1% of adult women, less than 3% of all veterans, and only 1.6% of homeless veterans.[7]

Military Risk Factors for Homelessness

Data on the overall proportion of veterans among the homeless do not, of course, address

the question of principal interest: whether specific aspects of military service, and particularly combat exposure, are associated with increased risk of homelessness.

During the years since the end of the Vietnam War there has been considerable interest in, and extensive scientific study of, the psychological consequences of traumatic war-zone stress. In the early 1980s, the VA commissioned the Research Triangle Institute to conduct a major national survey to determine the exact prevalence and causes of PTSD among Vietnam era veterans. The resulting study, the National Vietnam Veterans Readjustment Study (NVVRS), was conducted from 1987 to 1988. It found that more than a decade after the last U.S. soldier left Vietnam, 15.2% of those who served in the Vietnam theater suffered from PTSD, as compared to only 2.5% of veterans who served in the military during the Vietnam era but did not serve in the war zone, and only 1.2% of a matched sample of civilians. The study also indicated that, among Vietnam veterans, PTSD was significantly related to high levels of war-zone stress and to other postwar readjustment problems such as substance abuse, troubled interpersonal relationships, and unemployment—problems frequently identified as risk factors for homelessness.[8]

In considering the relationship between military service and homelessness, it is important to distinguish three related but distinct military risk factors: (1) PTSD, (2) service in a war zone or in combat, and (3) service during a wartime era, regardless of combat exposure or PTSD. During the period from 1987 to 1988, an estimated 472,000 Vietnam era veterans were suffering from war-zone related PTSD, 3.1 million living veterans had served in the Vietnam theater during the war, and 8.2 million veterans had served during the Vietnam era (August 1964–March 1975).

To assess the relationship between each of these military service factors and homelessness, the VA's Northeast Program Evaluation Center conducted a series of studies in which homeless and non-homeless samples were compared on each of these risk factors. To the extent that wartime military service, war-zone exposure, or

PTSD are risk factors for homelessness, we would expect to find a significantly higher prevalence of these risk factors in homeless as compared to non-homeless samples.[9]

PTSD. Using standardized instruments, a systematic study of homeless persons found that 39% of those who reported past combat exposure met diagnostic criteria for PTSD.[10] Intake assessment data on tens of thousands of veterans from the VA's Homeless Chronically Mentally Ill (HCMI) program, involving combat veterans of all wartime eras, reveal that the same proportion, 39%, appear to be suffering from PTSD related to their combat experiences. Although they are based on initial diagnostic impressions and must, therefore, be used with some caution, they suggest that among homeless veterans who report combat service, about 45% of Vietnam veterans, about 12% of Korean conflict veterans, and about 8% of World War II veterans are suffering from PTSD. When compared with rates of PTSD in the general population of combat veterans treated in VA outpatient mental health clinics (Table 9.1), these help-seeking homeless veterans appear to be no more likely than other veterans to have received a clinical diagnosis of PTSD. Comparisons with other sources of data on rates of PTSD among

treatment-seeking World War II and Korean War veterans yield similar results.[11]

Service in combat. The imprecision in the diagnostic data on PTSD can be compensated for, to some extent, by addressing a more objective indicator of military stress, exposure to combat. Among homeless veterans who served during wartime, 41% of Vietnam era veterans, 36% of Korean era veterans, and 55% of World War II era veterans report combat service. When compared with national survey data on combat service among male veterans who served in wartime (Table 9.2), homeless veterans appear *less* likely than veterans in the general population of domiciled veterans to have served in combat.

Combat exposure, PTSD, and homelessness in the NVVRS. An additional source of information on the role of PTSD and combat exposure as antecedents of homelessness comes from the rich data available from the National Vietnam Veterans Readjustment Study (NVVRS). In a recently published study, these data were carefully reanalyzed to evaluate the relationship of military stressors, health status, and social adjustment factors to past homelessness among Vietnam era veterans.[12] Among the factors examined were personal experiences prior to military service, degree of exposure to war-zone

---

TABLE 9.1

DIAGNOSED PTSD AMONG HOMELESS COMBAT VETERANS COMPARED WITH PTSD AMONG COMBAT VETERANS SEEN IN VA MENTAL HEALTH OUTPATIENT CLINICS, BY SERVICE ERA

	Homeless Combat Veterans in the VA's HCMI Program			General-Population Combat Veterans in the VA Outpatient Clinics				
	All Veterans	PTSD	Percent PTSD	All Veterans	PTSD	Percent PTSD	Odds Ratio*	95% Conf. Interval
Vietnam War Era	11,670	5,267	45.1%	20,486	9,446	46.1%	0.96	(0.82–1.11)
Korean War Era	1,386	163	11.8%	4,683	663	14.2%	0.81	(0.67–0.97)
World War II Era	1,176	89	7.6%	12,388	2,079	16.8%	0.41	(0.32–0.51)

*The odds ratio reflects the relative risk of homelessness among veterans diagnosed with PTSD. If the odds ratio (and both ends of its 95% confidence interval) are above 1.0, the presence of the factor is thought to significantly increase the risk of homelessness. If the odds ratio is less than 1.0, the presence of the factor is thought to be associated with a significantly reduced risk of homelessness.

TABLE 9.2

COMPARISON OF COMBAT EXPOSURE AMONG HOMELESS AND NON-HOMELESS VETERANS, BY SERVICE ERA

	Homeless Combat Veterans in the VA's HCMI Program		1987 Survey of Veterans*			
	All Veterans	Percent Combat	All Veterans	Percent Combat	Odds Ratio†	95% Conf. Interval
Vietnam War Era	28,712	40.6%	1,031	50.4%	0.67	(0.58–0.77)
Korean War Era	3,870	35.8%	637	42.7%	0.75	(0.63–0.89)
World War II Era	2,129	55.2%	1,234	67.1%	0.61	(0.52–0.78)

*Includes only veterans whose personal incomes are below the median for service era.

†The odds ratio reflects the relative risk of homelessness among veterans exposed to combat. If the odds ratio (and both ends of its 95% confidence interval) are above 1.0, the presence of the factor is thought to significantly increase the risk of homelessness. If the odds ratio is less than 1.0, the presence of the factor is thought to be associated with a significantly reduced risk of homelessness.

stress, current PTSD, other psychiatric disorders, and substance abuse. PTSD had no statistically significant relationship to homelessness *independent* of other factors. Premilitary experiences had the strongest relationship to homelessness, with especially notable influence from adolescent conduct disorder (i.e., antisocial or delinquent behavior) and childhood physical and sexual abuse. Taken together, military experiences had only a *modest* relationship with past homelessness, with the strongest contribution coming from participation in abusive violence. Overall, social isolation (for example, being unmarried or having had no one to talk with after discharge from the military) had a stronger relationship with homelessness than did psychiatric disorders (psychiatric diagnosis, PTSD, and substance abuse).

Service in wartime eras. A final study relied on secondary analyses of data from several well-designed community surveys of homeless people to look—beyond war-zone stressors and PTSD—at the relationship of homelessness and service during different eras. Since nonveterans cannot be classified into military service eras, these analyses compared the risk of homelessness among veterans and nonveterans in age groups selected to correspond to specific military service eras.[13] These analyses reveal a significantly greater risk of homelessness among veterans who

were in the 20- to 34-year-old age group in 1987 (those who served during the post-Vietnam era) and veterans in the 45- to 54-year-old age group (those who served in the peacetime era between the wars in Korea and Vietnam). In contrast, veterans in the 35- to 44-year-old age group (most of whom served during the Vietnam era), or in the 55- to 64-year-old and the 65-and-older age groups (those who served during the Korean or World War II eras), showed no greater risk of homelessness than nonveterans.[14] Thus, while younger veterans have a high risk of homelessness, older veterans have a reduced risk.

The Census Bureau's March 1990 S-night enumeration of homeless persons (see Chapter 2) provides an opportunity to confirm these findings, for they allow us to subdivide veterans who served during the post-Vietnam era into 3 age groups (20–24, 25–29, and 30–34) and those who served during the Vietnam era into 2 age groups (35–39 and 40–44). Since people generally enter military service at about 19 years of age, these groups can be used to reflect recruitment during 2 segments of the Vietnam era—1965–1969 and 1970–1974—and 3 different segments of the post-Vietnam period—1975–1979, 1980–1984, and 1985–1989.

Table 9.3 shows that the census data generally confirm the previous finding that the risk of homelessness among veterans is greatest among those who served during the post-Vietnam era and during the latter part of the Vietnam era.[15] It is especially notable that the increased risk of homelessness (higher odds ratio) is greatest among veterans who were in the 30- to 34-year-old and in the 35- to 39-year-old age groups in 1990 (and who are presumed to have entered the military from 1970 to 1974, and

from 1975 to 1979). The risk of homelessness declines progressively among those aged 25 to 29 (who likely entered the military between 1980 and 1984) and those aged 20 to 24 (who probably entered between 1985 and 1990). The reasons for this declining risk will be addressed below.

TABLE 9.3

VETERANS AMONG HOMELESS MEN AND AMONG MEN IN THE GENERAL POPULATION, BY AGE: 1990 CENSUS DATA

Age in 1990, in Years (Corresponding Service Era)	Homeless Males		Non-homeless Males*		Percent Veterans		Odds Ratio†
	Total	Veteran	Total	Veteran	Homeless	Non-homeless	
20–24 (Post-Vietnam War: 1985–89)	9,317	656	8,897	357	7.0%	4.0%	1.8
25–29 (Post-Vietnam War: 1980–84)	16,227	2,784	10,256	929	17.2%	9.1%	2.1
30–34 (Post-Vietnam War: 1975–79)	19,697	5,857	10,783	1,321	29.7%	12.3%	3.0
35–39 (Vietnam War Era: 1970–74)	17,859	6,675	9,698	1,761	37.4%	18.2%	2.7
40–44 (Vietnam War Era: 1965–69)	13,787	6,247	8,620	3,421	45.3%	39.7%	1.3
45–54 (Peacetime Era between Korean War and Vietnam War)	18,753	8,180	12,376	4,972	43.6%	40.2%	1.2
55–64 (Korean War Era)	10,392	5,811	9,952	6,485	55.9%	65.2%	0.7
>64 (World War II Era)	4,810	2,612	12,514	6,830	54.3%	54.6%	1.0
Total	110,842	38,822	83,096	26,076	35.0%	31.4%	1.2

*In thousands

†If the odds ratio is above 1.0, the presence of the factor is thought to significantly increase the risk of homelessness. If the odds ratio is less than 1.0, the presence of the factor is thought to be associated with a significantly reduced risk of homelessness. Confidence intervals are not included because the data are from a census, not a sample.

Vulnerability for Homelessness among Post-Vietnam Veterans

The studies we have reviewed consistently show that veterans at greatest risk for homelessness are those who entered the military during the late Vietnam and post-Vietnam eras; that is, during the wind-down phase of the Vietnam War and the initial period of the All Volunteer Force (AVF). These veterans had little exposure to combat, since military forces in Vietnam dropped sharply after 1971 and the last U.S. soldier (other than prisoners of war) left Vietnam in March 1973. Psychological sequelae of combat can therefore be largely ruled out as affecting those veterans' vulnerability to homelessness.

Socioeconomic characteristics. To explore possible explanations for the high risk of homelessness among younger veterans, 1987 Current Population Survey data on employment, education, income, and marital status were examined. Comparison of White post-Vietnam veterans and matched nonveterans revealed few differences and does not suggest an explanation for the strikingly different risk of homelessness among veterans and nonveterans in this age-race group. Data on Black veterans in this age cohort, however, show them to be substantially *better* off than Black nonveterans: they have higher incomes, lower poverty and unemployment rates, and a lower probability of living alone.[16] These data are consistent with the fact that the overrepresentation among the homeless of post-Vietnam Black veterans is significantly smaller than the overrepresentation of their White peers (see note 14).

Mental health. Data from the Epidemiological Catchment Area study, a five-city study of psychiatric illness in the United States, show striking differences in rates of mental illness between veterans of the post-Vietnam era and nonveterans matched on age and race. Among White men in the 20- to 34-year-old veteran cohort, non-substance use psychiatric disorders and substance use disorders were 2 to 3 times more prevalent among veterans than among nonveterans. Rates of antisocial personality dis-

order in this cohort were five to six times as high among White veterans as among nonveterans. Differences are far less dramatic among Black veterans, although rates of substance abuse are almost twice as high among Black veterans aged 20 to 35 as among Black nonveterans.[17] It thus appears that in the cohort of veterans at greatest risk for homelessness, it is mental illness and substance abuse, rather than combat exposure or economic disadvantage, that are most strongly associated with increased risk for homelessness.

Military Recruitment in the Post-Vietnam Era

The shift to an all-volunteer force in 1973 marked a major change that was accompanied by widespread concern that the military would become an employer of last resort for impoverished youth who lacked adequate skills to succeed in the competitive job market.[18] Recruitment during the later years of the Vietnam War, when there was widespread disillusionment about its purposes, was especially difficult. Because of these experiences, many studies have compared characteristics of AVF recruits with those of age-matched civilians. These studies focused on three issues: socioeconomic status, intellectual aptitude test results, and substance abuse.

Socioeconomic status. A 1977 study reported that post-Vietnam military recruits tended to come from lower-income neighborhoods than their civilian peers, but that the differences were small. A 1980 study, in contrast, found AVF recruits to be *better* educated and *more likely* to be married than age-matched civilians, and failed to identify significant differences in socioeconomic background between recruits and age-matched civilians employed full time. That study also noted, however, that Black recruits tended to come disproportionately from *higher* socioeconomic strata of the Black community and appeared to use military service as a stepping stone to better opportunities. A 1990 comprehensive review of studies of the socioeconomic status of the AVF concluded that "military members tended to come from backgrounds that were somewhat lower in socioeconomic status than average, but the differences . . . were relatively modest."[19]

Military aptitude tests. A major problem in interpreting studies of socioeconomic status among participants in the AVF is that the methods of these studies often were flawed and not consistently applied over the years. Systematic longitudinal data are available, however, from the Armed Forces Qualifying Test (AFQT). The AFQT is a test of verbal and quantitative aptitude that is used to screen out recruits with low potential for success in the military. Longitudinal comparisons (comparisons over time) are made possible because the AFQT is standardized to a World War II era reference population. In 1981, it was discovered that between 1976 and 1980 the AFQT had been misnormed (unqualified candidates were inadvertently scored as qualified). As a result, over 300,000 low-aptitude "potentially ineligibles" had entered the military. Thus, between 1976 and 1981, during the first phase of the post-Vietnam era, average AFQT scores among military recruits were lower than at any time since 1960.[20]

Substance abuse. Responding to reports of high levels of substance abuse in the military, a series of studies conducted during the 1970s and 1980s compared the prevalence of substance abuse in military and civilian populations. A 1972 study concluded that "enlisted men drink much more and get into considerably more trouble than civilians of same age." Studies conducted during subsequent years also reported consistently higher levels of alcohol use and alcohol-related problems among military personnel, even when age and marital status were controlled.[21]

In sum, although veterans who entered the military during the post-Vietnam era do not appear to have come from households of lower socioeconomic status than their nonveteran peers, they do appear to have had lower aptitude scores on standardized tests and more severe substance abuse problems, both during their military service and subsequently. The high risk of homelessness among veterans who entered the military between 1970 and 1979 thus appears to reflect the recruitment of less-well-adjusted men during that period of time.

It should be emphasized that we do not believe that these risk factors "caused" homelessness among the veterans, but rather that, with the severe recession of 1982, the declining availability of affordable housing during the 1980s, and the redistribution of wealth away from low-income Americans, these veterans were at greater risk for homelessness than those who had fewer vulnerabilities (see Chapter 3).[22]

During the early 1980s, the recruiting situation changed substantially. The misnorming error on the AFQT was corrected and aptitude scores rose sharply. At the same time, military service became more attractive as military salaries increased and employment opportunities in the civilian workforce declined. As a result, the quality of recruits began to improve.[23] Indeed, the combination of higher recruitment standards and the attractiveness of military employment—not the absence of combat exposure or war-related PTSD—best explain the declining risk for homelessness among veterans who entered the service during the 1980s.

Homelessness among Black Veterans

Virtually every scholar who has considered risk factors for homelessness has observed that Blacks are overrepresented among the homeless. Recent studies have also shown that Blacks were more likely than Whites to suffer negative psychiatric effects of military service in Vietnam. By many accounts, the exceptionally painful and alienating service experiences of minority group members has resulted in considerable distrust of the government, its leaders, and its institutions.[24] At the same time, there have been reports that Black military recruits come disproportionately from *higher* socioeconomic strata of the Black community and have used the special benefits associated with military service as stepping stones to better opportunities, thus suggesting that the risk of homelessness may be lower among Black veterans than among Black nonveterans. It is important, therefore, to consider available evidence on whether the military experiences of Black veterans are related to a greater or lesser risk of homelessness, as compared to Black nonveterans.

Data from studies summarized previously indicate that 47% of homeless men are Black, as compared to only 11% of all adult U.S. males. These data suggest as well that the relative risk for homelessness among Blacks is 7.3 times that for Whites. Much of this difference, it is reasonable to assume, is due to the greater rate of poverty among Blacks and their concentration in urban centers where homelessness is most prevalent.

To adjust for the influence of these factors, we estimated the relative risk of homelessness among impoverished, urban-dwelling Black veterans and nonveterans as compared to comparable White veterans and nonveterans. For this analysis we used data on homeless men from the Urban Institute's 1987 national survey of homeless service users in cities of over 100,000,[25] and comparison data on domiciled Americans living in poverty in Standardized Metropolitan Statistical Areas (urban areas by a fixed definition) from the 1987 Current Population Survey (the Census Bureau's annual employment survey of the U.S. population). After adjusting for the influence of poverty or urban residence, these analyses revealed that Blacks are still 2.1 times more likely than Whites to be homeless (Table 9.4).

When veterans and nonveterans are compared, Black veterans are 1.4 times more likely to be homeless than White veterans. In contrast, Black nonveterans are 2.9 times more likely to be homeless than White nonveterans. It thus appears that in spite of the harshness of their military experiences, veteran status attenuates race-related vulnerability to homelessness among Blacks to at least a modest degree. This reduced risk is most likely due to the special educational opportunities and other benefits to which veterans are entitled, and indirectly attests to the value of government programs in reducing the risk of homelessness.

CHARACTERISTICS AND NEEDS OF HOMELESS VETERANS
Male Veterans

Studies conducted during the 1980s consistently reported that homeless veterans were older and more likely to be White than other homeless men, and some studies reported that they had more often been in jail and were more likely to have problems related to alcohol use or to have been hospitalized for a psychiatric or substance abuse problem.[26] Our reanalysis of data from

TABLE 9.4

URBAN, POOR, AFRICAN AMERICANS: RISK OF HOMELESSNESS

	Homeless Men*			Urban Poor Men†			Odds Ratio‡
	Whites/Others	Blacks	Percent Blacks	Whites/Others	Blacks	Percent Blacks	
Total	85,159	54,541	39.0	2,695,964	818,833	23.3	2.11
Veterans	43,433	17,289	28.5	583,302	162,564	21.8	1.43
Nonveterans	41,726	37,252	47.2	2,112,662	656,269	23.7	2.87

*Data from Urban Institute survey: Burt and Cohen, "Feeding the Homeless."

†Data from U.S. Department of Commerce, Current Population Survey (1987); males in poverty residing in standardized metropolitan statistical areas (SMSAs)

‡If the odds ratio is above 1.0, the presence of the factor is thought to significantly increase the risk of homelessness. If the odds ratio is less than 1.0, the presence of the factor is thought to be associated with a significantly reduced risk of homelessness.

three surveys of this period found that home-less veterans were older than nonveterans, more likely to be White, better educated, and previously or currently married. These data also showed that veterans did not differ from nonveterans on indicators of residential instability, current social functioning, physical health, mental illness, or substance abuse. Differences between homeless veterans and nonveterans in age, race, and education were largely explained by differences between these groups in the general population.[27]

On the other hand, a review of diagnostic data from the 19-city Robert Wood Johnson-Pew Memorial Trust Health Care for the Homeless Program showed veterans to have more frequent health problems than nonveterans. Significant differences were identified for AIDS, cancer, seizures, hypertension, and trauma. The proportions of veterans suffering from alcohol abuse (24%) or mental illness (16%) were also greater than among nonveterans (17% and 12%, respectively).[28] Comparing homeless veterans who used the VA system and those who did not, this study reported that system users were 1.7 times more likely to have a chronic illness and 1.5 times more likely to have alcohol problems.

Finally, a study of 1,431 homeless adults in Santa Clara County, California, had a unique feature worth noting here: it considered the elapsed time between discharge from the military and initial homelessness. Seventy-six percent of combat veterans and half of noncombat veterans first became homeless more than a decade after leaving military service.[29]

In sum, research findings about homeless male veterans are not altogether consistent. There is some evidence that quite apart from differences explained by age, homeless veterans may be in poorer health than nonveterans and have somewhat more severe problems with alcohol, but in general, their service needs are not substantially different from those of other homeless men.

Female Veterans

Clinical assessment data from the VA's HCMI program have been used to conduct a series of comparisons between male and female homeless veterans. The women were younger, more likely to be married, and less likely to be employed. They were also more likely to suffer from a serious psychiatric illness (52% versus 41%), but less likely to have a substance use disorder (43% versus 72%).[30] Comparison of mental illness and substance use rates among homeless female veterans and other homeless women showed no differences.

SERVICES FOR HOMELESS VETERANS
VA Programs

The Department of Veterans Affairs assists homeless veterans both through its regular programs and benefits and through specialized programs.[31] Like domiciled veterans, the homeless may be eligible for compensation for medical and psychiatric conditions precipitated by military service, for pensions, and for other benefits such as education and housing. As a result of their extreme poverty, they almost always qualify for free medical services at the 172 VA medical centers throughout the United States. A 1993 survey conducted at a large VA medical center in California found that 30% of psychiatric inpatients were homeless at admission.

Since 1987, VA has sponsored two major specialized programs to assist homeless veterans: the Domiciliary Care for Homeless Veterans Program (DCHV) and the Health Care for Homeless Veterans Program (HCHV, the largest component of which is the HCMI program). DCHV operates at 33 VA medical centers across the country and has provided 16,000 episodes of care since it began. HCMI currently operates at 57 VA medical centers. Between 1987 and 1993, HCMI teams evaluated 62,000 homeless veterans and provided 12,000 episodes of residential treatment.

Although HCMI and DCHV differ in several respects, both involve five core activities: (1) *outreach*, to identify veterans among homeless persons encountered in shelters, soup kitchens, and other community locations; (2) *psychosocial assessments*, to determine the needs of each veteran seen by the team and to give priority to those who are most vulnerable;

(3) *referral* to medical and psychiatric inpatient and outpatient treatment; (4) time-limited *residential treatment* in domiciliaries (for DCHV) or community-based halfway houses (for HCMI); and (5) *follow-up case management*, as permitted by available resources, to help veterans identify resources to facilitate their community integration. The main differences between HCMI and DCHV are that HCMI places an emphasis on outreach and provides residential treatment through contracts with non-VA providers, whereas DCHV accepts more self-referred and VA medical center-referred cases and provides treatment in residential facilities on VA medical center grounds.

Treatment outcome studies show that both programs promote significant improvement in housing, psychiatric status, substance abuse, employment, social support, and access to health services. Studies comparing the two programs have revealed few significant differences in services delivered or outcomes. However, a recent study reported that veterans believe that the VA-based DCHV program offers a more active treatment environment, perhaps because—unlike the HCMI programs, which mix veterans and nonveterans—DCHV is exclusively for veterans.

To enhance these core programs and to create a continuum of care, VA expanded the housing, financial support, and rehabilitative dimensions of its services by establishing formal collaborative relationships with other federal, state, and local providers. At the national level within VA, an outreach program was established within the Veterans Benefits Administration to facilitate access of homeless veterans to VA benefits, and VA's Compensated Work Therapy (CWT) program was expanded. In CWT, private industry contracts with VA for various types of work done by disabled veterans at standard wages under trained supervision.

Special programs were also initiated in collaboration with other federal agencies such as the Social Security Administration and the Department of Housing and Urban Development. Links with state and local governments were forged in many cities, and service contracts were made with community-based, nonprofit organizations across the country. A small number of Comprehensive Homeless Centers also were established to integrate the broad range of services provided to homeless veterans at selected sites.

Veterans' Service Organizations (VSOs)

Since the Civil War, veterans have joined together in large, independent advocacy and support groups like the Grand Army of the Republic, the American Legion, and the Veterans of Foreign Wars. Many of these VSOs have become prominent forces in American life and have made important contributions to assisting homeless veterans, often through donations to support national VA programs.

The growth of homelessness stimulated the creation of numerous smaller VSOs specifically to help homeless veterans. Often these groups adopted a nonprofessional, "veterans helping veterans" philosophy. In 1993, the National Coalition for Homeless Veterans (NCHV) was formed by organizations providing services to veterans. A survey sponsored by VA and conducted by the NCHV identified over 150 organizations across the country that operate specialized programs for homeless veterans. One of the best known of these is the Vietnam Veterans Workshop, sponsor of the New England Shelter for Homeless Veterans. Since its founding in 1988, it has grown from a small group of committed comrades to a multimillion-dollar enterprise that occupies a 10-story building in downtown Boston.

The programs at the New England Shelter for Homeless Veterans, and in those modeled after them, draw heavily on veterans' sense of fellowship and commitment to one another, a commitment originally developed in military training and on the battlefield. At the New England Shelter, veterans are organized into platoons, each led by a staff counselor, many of whom are formerly homeless veterans who have advanced through the program. At each stage of the program, residents are expected to contribute to the maintenance of the program and must demonstrate their capacity for responsible action.[32]

Other veteran-run programs (such as Base Camp in Nashville, Tennessee; Swords to Ploughshares in San Francisco, California; and the Veterans Clearing House in Roxbury, Massachusetts) have successfully combined the veterans' mutual-aid philosophy with a strong community-service orientation. These programs often facilitate veterans' access to VA services and provide sustained guidance and support to veterans who are mistrustful of more traditional service providers.

CONCLUSION

Despite abundant evidence that wartime trauma can result in prolonged PTSD and other associated adjustment problems, homeless veterans, including combat veterans, are much like other homeless Americans. Although PTSD affects a portion of the veteran population, and although some homeless veterans suffer from it, homelessness among veterans is not clearly related to military experience. Rather, it is the result of the same interrelated economic and personal factors that cause homelessness in the civilian population (see Chapter 3).

Since wartime military service is not a major independent cause of homelessness, and since homeless veterans suffer from the same problems as other homeless Americans, what consideration should be given to past military service and to PTSD in the treatment of homeless veterans? What implications does past military service have for public policy? To take the most specific matters first, it is important to note that while military service may not be a major independent *cause* of homelessness among veterans, many homeless veterans do suffer from combat-related PTSD. These veterans clearly deserve the treatment and compensation for illnesses related to their military service to which any veteran is entitled.

It is also important to recognize that veteran status, and especially wartime service, may play an important role in treatment and rehabilitation. Virtually all homeless people must overcome demoralization and self-doubt as they attempt to rebuild their lives. Military service was a time of effective functioning for many vet-

erans, and even more important, a time they recall with pride, particularly if they coped successfully with severe hardships. Clinical programs that tap and enlarge this reservoir of pride can both enhance participation in treatment and increase the likelihood of exiting homelessness.[33] The fact that veterans find the treatment environments in the all-veteran, VA-based DCHV program to be more active than those of the mixed-population HCMI may reflect the special value of concentrated support for a positive veteran identity. We would expect to find similar effects in mutual-aid programs run by VSOs.

Finally, we must consider broader matters of public policy, particularly the special status veterans enjoy because of their past national service. Since the era of the Plymouth Colony, Americans have, in the European tradition, recognized a public obligation to assist veterans injured in the course of military service and even to provide assistance to those who served but were not injured while in arms. Since the end of World War II, the VA's health-care system has grown to 172 facilities, and these provide services to millions of indigent veterans each year even when their conditions are not service-connected. In addition, $2.4 billion in non-service-connected pension payments are provided to over 600,000 wartime veterans each year.[34]

Some critical policy scholars assert that such special programs for veterans perpetuate the traditional distinction between the "deserving" and "undeserving" poor, a distinction, so the argument goes, that keeps us from committing ourselves as a nation to eradicating poverty among all Americans. Like the allied argument that homelessness itself has become a privileged category whose members have access to resources foreclosed to more ordinary poor people, this is a troubling claim and must be taken seriously.[35]

Our view is pragmatic. Neither homelessness nor poverty more generally are problems that can be solved locally. We believe that the special claim of veterans helps to elevate homeless poverty to a problem of national significance. In the current climate of political

decentralization and the related decentralization of tax burdens, we think this is an important asset to the antihomelessness movement.
Further, we do not believe that special programs
for homeless veterans deflect us from the larger
issue of poverty in America. Rather, by linking
the issue of poverty to honored and respected
members of the community, additional attention can be drawn to the plight of all poor
people. In February 1994, Department of Veterans Affairs Secretary Jesse Brown, cochair of
the Interagency Council on the Homeless, sponsored a two-day summit of service providers to
consider new approaches to the problems of
homeless veterans and new ways of fostering
collaboration between government and private
agencies at the federal, state, and local levels.
At a Senate hearing prior to the summit, Brown
said that homelessness among veterans "is an
American tragedy—and it must not be allowed
to stand. . . . The way a society treats its veterans is an indication of who we are as a nation."
If we are successful in caring for homeless veterans, we may not only assist people who once
served us all, but also develop new confidence
in our ability to extend our efforts more widely.

CHAPTER 10

Homeless Families Are Different

Marybeth Shinn
Beth C. Weitzman

In this chapter, we argue that parents in homeless families, while similar to parents in other poor families, are different from home-less adults who are not part of family units. Some differences mirror distinctions in the general population between people who come together and stay together as families and those who do not; others reflect the ways shelters and social service systems sort potential clients.

We begin by discussing how social policy shapes our understanding of homeless families. We then survey characteristics of homeless fami-lies in comparison to both poor housed families and homeless single adults. Next, we examine how poverty and the shortage of low-income housing contribute to family homelessness. We then describe effects of homelessness on chil-dren who are part of families, and close with discussion of policies to reduce homelessness and its adverse consequences for families. For these purposes, we define homeless families—in the fashion of most shelters and social ser-vices—as one or more adults with one or more children currently in their charge. Pregnant women are sometimes also included.

HOW POLICIES AFFECT WHAT WE KNOW ABOUT HOMELESS FAMILIES

Homeless families are more likely than home-less single adults to seek shelter where it is avail-able, both because parents feel it is important to protect their children from the elements, and because shelter policies for families typically are more generous, or less onerous, than those for single adults. Because of this, most studies of homeless families are limited to those in shel-ters, and both the composition of families and what we know about them are shaped by shel-ter policies.[1]

Proportion of Homeless People Who Are in Families with Children

Even estimates of the proportion of families among the homeless are shaped by social policy. A recent report by the U.S. Conference of May-ors suggests that families make up 43% of home-less people, reaching equivalence for the first time in 1993 with the numbers of homeless single men. Because the mayors base their data largely on people making use of shelters and city services, and because families are more likely to be eligible for shelters and to use them, this number is likely an overestimate.[2]

Using a far more sophisticated sampling strategy, Burt and Cohen estimated that in 1987, 10% of homeless *households* (not individuals) were families, and Jencks, using these data, calculated that 18% of homeless *people* were in families with children present. These figures are based on estimates of people who are homeless at a single point in time. But homelessness is more like a river than a lake. Most people do not stay homeless forever: on any given day, some find housing and others become homeless. Thus, far more people are homeless over an extended period of time than on any given night. To estimate the numbers of people homeless over a period of time, we must examine both the capacity of the river and its speed of flow. Single adults are likely to remain homeless for longer periods than families—2.75 times as long in Burt and Cohen's data—in part due to the greater generosity of welfare and housing programs for families. Because families leave homelessness faster than do single individuals (their river is smaller but flows more rapidly), the ratio of the number of families who are homeless over the course of a year to the number who are homeless on a given night is larger than the same ratio for single adults. Combining Burt and Cohen's data on counts and length of time homeless suggests that 38% of those who became homeless in 1987 were members of families, although they were only 18% of those who were homeless on a particular night that year.[3]

Even these figures are likely to be underestimates because Burt and Cohen drew their shelter sample from facilities housing at least 10 adults. To be counted, a family shelter—with an average of 2.2 children per family—had to serve about 3 times as many people as a shelter for single adults. A 1988 U.S. Department of Housing and Urban Development (HUD) survey showed family shelters housing only two-thirds as many adults, on average, as shelters for single adults, so Burt and Cohen's procedure would lead to a relative undercount of families.[4] Thus, a conservative estimate might be that two-fifths of people who become home-

less do so as members of families, although only about one-fifth of those homeless on any given night are homeless with their families. In addition, many women and men in shelters for single adults are parents whose children are no longer with them, as described below. If all these people were included in the count of families, the proportion of families among the homeless would be substantially larger.

Composition of Families

What we know of the composition as well as the numbers of homeless families is affected by shelter and welfare policies. As a result of eligibility requirements, it is often more difficult for two-parent rather than one-parent families to obtain welfare benefits (see Chapter 6). Poor mothers who have received entitlements as single parents may fear loss of benefits if they acknowledge the presence of a father in the family. Because many family shelters exclude men, or permit them only if they can prove their legal marriage to the woman or paternity of a child, families are often split up at the point of applying for shelter. The men are sent to a shelter for single adults or are admitted but not counted as part of the family unit. Thus, we systematically underestimate the proportion of men in homeless families.[5]

Families may be broken up for reasons other than shelter policies. Mothers may leave children with relatives who cannot house the entire family, in order to spare children the ordeal of homelessness or to permit them to continue to attend their usual school. Children in homeless families may be especially likely to be placed in foster care. It is not clear to what extent this is due solely to the fact that their families are homeless, to family problems that may have precipitated both the episode of homelessness and the foster care placement, to stressors that may be consequences of homelessness, or to the scrutiny to which homeless families are subjected by shelters and social services.

There is some evidence for each of these explanations. In New Jersey in 1986, 18% of children in foster care were there only because their families had no place to live. But as we shall see below, some homeless mothers have serious substance abuse or mental health problems that impair their ability to care for their children, and rates of domestic violence are also high. Economic stressors are associated with child abuse in non-homeless samples, and it is likely that the more extreme stressors of homelessness, compounded by crowding and lack of privacy in shelters, lead some parents to abuse their children. Research also shows that observers rate behaviors of low-income parents as more abusive than the same behaviors by middle-income parents, and it is likely that homeless families are accorded even more biased assessment. Model child welfare guidelines recommend against intervention if parents use resources available to them, even if they cannot support their children adequately, and several states have ruled out placement of children due to homelessness alone. Nonetheless, in the case of minor problems, protective service workers may remove children from a homeless family more readily than if the family had adequate housing.[6]

Loss of a child to foster care may precipitate homelessness if a family thereby loses welfare benefits that allow purchase of housing. Later, if the situation detrimental to the child is resolved, a family may be in a double bind: parents cannot obtain housing or welfare benefits without the child, but the child cannot return if the parents have no housing. Some states have made money available to address this dilemma, but the amounts often are insufficient for a family to regain housing.[7]

Although the relative importance of these factors in the break-up of homeless families is not clear, the phenomenon has been documented in study after study. In New York City, a survey found that 60% of residents in shelters for single adults (61% of men and 51% of women) had children who were not with them. In 71% of cases, the youngest child was below age 14. An earlier study in the same city found that 51% of women in shelters for single adults had children under 18. Three-fifths of the children (62%) were with relatives and one-third were in foster care. Of 94 parents in a sample of 25 shelters in Maryland, only 43% had children with them. The majority had children living with relatives or friends, suggesting voluntary placement, and 9% had children in foster care. Of 186 "street homeless" people interviewed in Washington, DC, 39% had dependent children not with them. In Chicago, 54% of a combined street and shelter sample were parents, but 91% were homeless alone. In a particularly mobile group of families and single individuals who sought help from Travelers Aid in 8 cities, 20% of families had left children behind, half with the former spouse, a third with relatives or friends, an eighth with the current spouse, and only a small number (3%) in foster care. About a fifth of homeless single adults also had children living elsewhere; two-thirds with a former or current spouse, and a quarter with relatives. Again, only a tiny minority (6%) of their children were in foster care.[8]

Even families in shelter as family units may have lost some of their children. In a study of 700 families requesting shelter in New York City, families reported having an average of 2.2 children, but there was an average of only 1.8 children under 18 currently in the household. The whereabouts of these "missing" children is unknown; given the relative youth of the mothers, it is likely that only a small proportion had grown to adulthood before leaving their families.[9]

Shelter policies shape our understanding of family characteristics in other ways. Family shelters often exclude those who use drugs or alcohol or have mental illnesses.[10] Thus, shelter policies may lead to *underestimates* of such problems among homeless families. On the other hand, most studies of people in shelters—indeed, most studies of homeless people—are based on snapshots of a cross section of people homeless at a given time. These studies overrepresent those who remain homeless for long periods and underrepresent those who are homeless only briefly. To the extent that substance abuse or mental health problems make it difficult for homeless people to find housing, cross-sectional studies of shelter residents *overestimate* the extent of such problems among all people who become homeless. Interestingly, a study that avoided both problems by sampling homeless families at the point they requested shelter in New York City, where families had a right to shelter irrespective of mental health or substance abuse problems, found the lowest rates of prior mental hospitalization (4%) of all studies in the literature.[11]

In the end, though, screening out substance abusers and mentally ill people is difficult, for these conditions are often not readily apparent to shelter staff. Certainly, such restrictions are harder to impose than those based on family composition, and thus we believe they introduce far less bias to research findings. Child welfare practices may be more consequential, for if child welfare agencies are more apt to permit homeless parents without substance abuse or mental health problems to keep their children (and go to family shelters), but remove children from parents with more problems (so that these parents must go to shelters for single adults), the agencies indirectly sort homeless parents into single or family shelters partly on the basis of mental illness and substance abuse. This may help account for why residents of shelters for single adults have higher levels of mental illness and substance abuse than residents of family shelters (see below). In the words of one service provider in New York City, "you have to be pretty together to hold onto your kids through an episode of homelessness."[12]

CHARACTERISTICS OF HOMELESS FAMILIES

This section describes America's homeless families and compares them with homeless single adults and housed, poor families. In general, homeless families are more similar to their housed counterparts than to homeless people outside of family units. While there is evidence that problems such as substance abuse and mental illness are more prevalent among poor families who are homeless than among those who are housed, studies have repeatedly demonstrated that only a minority of homeless families have any of these problems; the proportion is far lower than among homeless single adults.

Before describing homeless families, we should emphasize the striking similarities found across studies in Boston, Detroit, Los Angeles,

Minneapolis, New England, New York City, northern California, Philadelphia, and St. Louis. This consistent profile of homeless families in urban America suggests that family homelessness is embedded in national conditions.[13]

Demographic Characteristics

Homeless mothers in shelters are young, poor, and often from ethnic minority groups. Study after study has placed the average age of homeless mothers between 25 and 30—about the same age or younger than housed poor mothers, and younger than homeless single adults.[14]

Although people of color are disproportionately represented among both poor families and homeless adults, homeless families are even more likely to be from minority groups.[15] Because comparison groups are often matched to homeless families on either ethnicity or some other characteristic that is associated with ethnicity (like neighborhood), studies are not always in a good position to determine whether ethnic differences exist between homeless families and other poor families in the same area. A study in New York City found that homeless families were more likely than a random sample of the public-assistance caseload to be African American.[16]

In contrast to the homeless single adult population, which is largely male, the majority of adults in homeless families are female. Because the majority of homeless families are headed by single mothers, some conclude that single motherhood is a risk factor for homelessness.[17] No doubt it is a risk factor for poverty; however, findings from appropriately designed studies (those that had comparison groups and did not sample on the basis of marital status) do not suggest that single parenthood contributes to homelessness among poor families. Some studies found no difference in marital status between housed poor and homeless mothers.[18] Others found men present more often in homeless than in housed poor families.[19] Further, as mentioned above, the absence of men from many homeless households may be an artifact of shelter policies that exclude men or fail to record them as part of the family unit.[20]

In New York City, mothers in homeless families were far more likely to be pregnant or to have experienced a recent birth than mothers who were housed, although their family sizes were comparable after adjusting for the mother's age. Homeless families tend to be small. Across studies, the average number of children ranged from 1.7 to 3.3, with a median of 2.3.[21]

Education and Job Histories

Poor educational attainment and minimal job histories predominate among homeless and housed poor families. In most studies, homeless and housed poor mothers did not differ with regard to rates of high school graduation, which ranged from 35% to 58%.[22] Several studies have also shown that mothers in homeless families (most of whom receive public assistance) differed little from housed poor mothers in recency or frequency of employment.[23] For example, adjusting for age differences between the groups, homeless and housed mothers in New York City were equally likely to have worked full time for a year or more.[24] Of note, among mothers in this study with full-time work experience, the homeless were more likely to have held a job within the past two years than those who were housed. In a national comparison of homeless individuals and families, Burt and Cohen found low educational attainment and short job histories across the board, but noted lower achievement among women with children. In a New York City study, 35% of family shelter residents and 24% of single shelter residents had neither completed high school nor had any recent employment experience.[25]

Disruptive Experiences

Mothers in homeless families have had more disrupted childhoods than mothers in poor but housed families. In Boston, 69% of homeless mothers and 57% of poor housed mothers reported a major family disruption (for example, divorce or death of a parent) during childhood.[26] Foster care and other forms of separation from the family in childhood were more common among homeless than among domiciled mothers in Los Angeles and New York. Similarly,

three studies found that homeless mothers were more likely to have been battered as adults and abused as children. A New England study using a more detailed interview found no difference in domestic violence between housed and homeless mothers: rates in both groups were extraordinarily high.[27]

Although homeless women in families have had more disrupted childhoods than housed poor women, they have had more stable childhoods than women in shelters for single adults. In each of 2 New York City studies with different comparison groups, comparable percentages (10%) of respondents in homeless families had been in foster care as children. The number was much lower (2%) among housed poor mothers but higher (17%) among women in shelters for single adults. Similarly, the proportions of adults in homeless families who had experienced childhood sexual abuse (9%–10%) and abuse by a partner as an adult (23%–27%) were higher than for housed poor mothers but substantially lower than for women in shelters for single adults.[28] These figures are likely to be underestimates because questions were relatively crude and because some women who experience domestic violence go to specialized shelters whose residents are not counted as homeless.[29]

Mental Illness

There is little evidence that hospitalization for psychiatric disorders is common among homeless families. Parents in homeless families are far less likely than single homeless adults to have had such experience, but more likely than parents in housed, poor families. Fourteen percent of homeless mothers in Los Angeles, as compared to 6% of those who were housed, reported histories of psychiatric hospitalization. In New York City, the numbers were 4% among homeless mothers and 1% among those who were poor and housed. Indeed, most studies have found percentages of mental hospitalization in the single digits for homeless mothers, whereas hospitalization rates for samples composed primarily of single homeless adults have ranged from 10% to 35% and average 24%. In Burt and Cohen's national sample of homeless people, 8% of women with children reported a psychiatric hospitalization, as compared with 27% of single women and 19% of single men. A St. Louis study reported a similar difference (6% versus 25%) between women with and without children.[30]

But psychiatric hospitalization is an uncertain measure of mental illness. Because hospitalization has been limited to the most severe cases in recent years, it underestimates the prevalence of mental disorders. In a Boston study, only 8% of homeless mothers and 4% of housed mothers reported psychiatric hospitalization, yet based on a psychiatric interview, 22% of homeless mothers and 6% of housed mothers were diagnosed with a major psychiatric syndrome. (The study included mental retardation and substance abuse among such syndromes, however.) Of 49 homeless mothers interviewed, 3 (6%) were determined by the researchers to be schizophrenic, while none of the 81 housed mothers were so diagnosed. On the other hand, homeless and housed mothers did not differ on self-reported psychiatric symptoms in Minneapolis or on depressive symptoms in New York City; both homeless and housed but poor mothers in these cities had high scores compared with general population norms.[31]

As with hospitalization, rates for psychiatric disorders except depression are much higher among single homeless individuals than among adults in homeless families. But these estimates, too, are shaped by social policy. As discussed above, many homeless single women are mothers whose children are no longer with them, and this separation may have been occasioned by serious mental illness.[32]

It is also possible that many cross-sectional studies overestimate the extent of mental illness among homeless people. As noted earlier, if mentally ill people are more likely to be chronically homeless, they will be oversampled in such studies. Static portraits of homeless people may also confuse the causal relationship between homelessness and mental illness. Sometimes mental disorder antedates homelessness, but depression, in particular, may be the result of it. Moreover, depression is more common among women and is more likely than schizophrenia to be a consequence of poverty and stressful circumstances.[33]

Substance Abuse

As with estimates of mental illness, estimates of substance abuse in homeless or housed poor populations vary as a result of sampling strategies and different definitions of the problem. In a New York City study, 8% of mothers requesting shelter and 2% of housed poor mothers had been in detoxification. In a cross-sectional study of shelter users in the same city, 23% of the women and men in family units reported having been in alcohol or drug rehabilitation as compared to 38% of homeless single adults. In a national study of shelters and soup kitchens, 19% of single women and 37% of single men reported inpatient treatment for chemical dependency, whereas only 7% of women with children had such a history. These studies had no comparison groups of housed poor families or individuals; they relied on treatment history as an indicator of problems. It is difficult to interpret differences in rates of treatment for substance abuse because they are influenced by many factors, notably, variation in the availability of treatment.

In general, however, homeless parents report substance abuse more frequently than parents in housed poor families, but far less often than homeless individuals. Three percent of the adults in homeless New York City families reported daily drug use, as compared to 11% of single men and 7% of single women. In Los Angeles, where 32% of homeless mothers and 26% of housed mothers reported substance abuse, the difference was not statistically significant. In northern California, a history of substance abuse was related to family homelessness only among non-Hispanic Whites. Substance abuse, like mental illness, may be both a cause and a consequence of homelessness.[34]

Social Networks

Findings about the relative quality of social networks and social supports among homeless and housed mothers are quite variable. Some studies indicate that homeless families have few people to rely on, while others indicate that homeless families relied on families and friends before becoming homeless but eventually "used up" their reservoir of goodwill. In Los Angeles, 66% of homeless mothers reported 1 or no adult supports, while 48% of housed mothers indicated such a low level of support. In Boston, similar differences between housed and homeless families were found. In contrast, studies in New England and New York City found no differences between homeless and housed mothers on a number of measures of social networks and social support. In another New York City study, families requesting shelter were *more* likely than housed poor families to have had recent contact with relatives and friends, but they were less likely to indicate that relatives and friends had room for them. Given that nearly all families had spent some time doubled up before requesting shelter, it appears that many simply exhausted the resources in their social networks. To the extent that network members shared the poverty of families who became homeless, these resources were limited to begin with.[35]

Looking solely at homeless individuals might lead one to conclude that homelessness results directly from such problems as mental illness, drug addiction, alcohol abuse, or lack of social support, yet characteristics of homeless families suggest otherwise. Since only a small proportion of homeless families experience such problems, other factors must be at work. Similarly, if one looks only at homeless families, neglecting to compare them to other poor families, one might conclude that single parenthood or weak employment histories cause families to require emergency shelter. But as most poor families are housed despite high rates of single parenthood and lack of substantial employment experience, something else must be at the root of family homelessness.

Housing

Families who become homeless—that is, enter shelters—frequently have experienced extended periods of unstable housing. In a Boston study, families averaged 3.6 moves in the year prior to their current shelter stay. In Los Angeles, homeless families averaged nearly 6 moves during the prior 5 years, as compared to only 2.3 among poor housed families. Often,

these moves are from the home of one friend or family member to another: 81% of homeless families requesting emergency shelter in New York City had been doubled up at some previous time.[36]

Many homeless families have always relied on others for housing. In New York City, 44% of families requesting shelter had either never been primary tenants, or had been so for less than a year; in comparison, only 12% of housed families had always been doubled up. Homeless singles may be more likely than homeless families to have had their own place at some point; for example, in a study of New York City shelter users, 31% of families had never had their own apartments, as compared to 18% of single women.[37]

To understand homelessness among families, it is important to appreciate both the type and quality of their prior housing. In New York, families requesting shelter were less likely to have lived in the city's housing projects or in subsidized housing than were poor families randomly sampled from the public assistance caseload. This suggests that these "regulated" units offer some protection from homelessness. Compared to housed poor families, families requesting shelter reported more housing problems such as lack of heat for a week or more, or feeling unsafe due to crime or drugs. Frequently, they also come from substantially more crowded homes.[38]

Research in northern California and in New York City indicates that most formerly homeless families can remain out of shelters if they are provided with dwellings that are decent and affordable. Among 169 formerly homeless families in New York City considered at high risk for repeated homelessness, only 8 returned to shelters during the first year after being given their own apartment. The type and quality of the housing, and families' comfort level in their new neighborhoods, were among the strongest predictors of who would become homeless again. Families placed in public housing were less likely to return to shelters than those placed in other housing situations. Once families had subsidized housing and income support from welfare, case management services made only a small additional difference.[39]

THE CONTRIBUTIONS OF HOUSING AND POVERTY TO HOMELESSNESS AMONG FAMILIES

The persistent housing problems in the backgrounds of homeless families—along with the success of housing assistance in preventing homelessness (see Chapter 18) or helping families to extricate themselves from it—suggest the need to look at the housing market in order to understand family homelessness (see Chapters 3 and 4). A shortage of affordable housing arises when there are insufficient inexpensive housing units for households that need them. Loss of housing units, increases in rental prices, and increases in the numbers of poor households and the depth of their poverty all contribute. Thus, to understand the rise of homelessness in the 1980s, we must examine changes in both housing and poverty. Families and single adults compete for housing in the same market, although families need larger units. Although affected by the same economic trends, poverty plays out somewhat differently for single adults than for adult family members, largely because of differences in access to public assistance.[40]

Housing Poor Families

How do families react to unaffordable housing? Probably the most common response is to double up with others. By 1987, three million households were doubled up, a level not seen since immediately after World War II. This included an increase from 1980 to 1987 of 98% in households with related subfamilies and an increase of 57% in households with unrelated subfamilies. In New York City, 38% of a random sample of 524 families receiving public assistance reported doubling up at some point, and as noted, 12% never had a place of their own for as long as a year. A quarter (26%) reported excessive crowding (3 or more people per bedroom). Histories of doubling up and crowding were far more common among homeless families, contributing to the frequency with which they moved before turning to shelters.[41]

Another common response to the lack of decent affordable housing is to live in housing that is affordable but deficient. Although the quality of the housing stock has improved in the last two decades, poor renters still face tradeoffs between affordability and decency. Among 3.78 million households with incomes less than 25% of the area median and no rent subsidy in 1989, 70% paid over half their income on rent and another 22% lived in housing classified as inadequate by the American Housing Survey. Only 8% had housing that was both adequate and cost less than half of household income. Poor families in New York City had high rates of inadequate housing: 38% had endured 2 or more serious building problems such as lack of heat in the winter, lack of running water, or rats. Although conditions were significantly worse among families who sought shelter, there is a vast reservoir of poorly housed families at risk of homelessness.[42]

Recently, Christopher Jencks questioned whether lack of housing could be at the root of homelessness, considering that during the 1980s national vacancy rates for apartments renting for less than $250 per month were at least as high as vacancy rates for more expensive apartments.[43] This evidence is misleading for several reasons. First, the typical family looks for housing in a limited geographic area, and vacancy rates for low-income housing were much lower than the national rate in cities like New York, where large numbers of families became homeless during the 1980s. Second, moving into an apartment costs far more than a month's rent: typical expenses include first and last month's rent, a security deposit, funds for furniture, and moving expenses. Such costs are beyond the reach of many poor families who are starting out. Third, a unit listed as vacant may not be available to all potential renters. HUD documented ongoing racial discrimination against African American and Latino renters in its 1989 study of 25 metropolitan areas. When African American and White testers with comparable personal characteristics asked about the same apartments, African Americans received no information 15% of the time, received less information 39% of the time, and were offered less favorable terms and conditions 41% of the time.[44] Finally, some housing offered for rent and reported vacant is not truly habitable.

Poverty among Families

Because affordability of housing depends on both its cost and household income, the rise in poverty in the 1980s exacerbated the housing crisis. Some analysts have questioned the link between poverty and homelessness, because the surge in homeless families in the second half of the 1980s coincided with a decrease in overall poverty from 15.2% of the population in 1983 to 12.8% in 1989. (Overall poverty then increased again, reaching 14.2% in 1991.) However, the recovery never extended to single mothers with children: the poorest 20% of this group had incomes that stagnated at about a quarter of the poverty line throughout the period from 1983 to 1989.[45]

Overall, the number of poor people in the United States increased 41% between 1979 and 1990; from 21.6 million to 30.5 million. Families with an unmarried head-of-household and children under 18 accounted for nearly half (49%) of that increase. The U.S. House of Representatives' Committee on Ways and Means studied this change, and their findings are startling: The lion's share of the increase, in the committee's analysis, was due to changes in social programs. Welfare program changes, including both erosion of benefits and tightening of eligibility requirements, accounted for 43% of the total rise in numbers of poor people in single-parent families. Changes in other social insurance programs, such as Social Security and disability insurance, accounted for an additional 13% of the increase. The increase in births out of wedlock accounted for a much smaller portion of the total increase than did changes in government programs: this factor was included by the committee in the category of demographic and other changes, which accounted for a little over a quarter of the increase (27%). Finally, average population growth accounted for 23% of the increase. (These numbers sum to over 100%, because offsetting changes in market income and in federal taxes each reduced the number of poor single-parent families by 3%.) Since 1990, benefits have eroded or have been cut further. In 1991, 40 states either slashed Aid to Families with Dependent Children (AFDC) or failed to adjust benefits

for inflation; in 1992, 44 states did likewise. Both Congress and many states are now proposing to terminate or reduce welfare benefits for particular subgroups of families (see Chapter 6).[46]

All of these figures have been given in terms of the "poverty line." It is thus important to understand what the poverty line is and how it is calculated.

The poverty threshold was first defined in 1955. Based on survey data indicating that poor families spent about one-third of their income on food, the poverty level originally was set at three times the amount necessary to purchase the lowest-cost, nutritionally adequate diet (as calculated by the U.S. Department of Agriculture) for a family of a particular size and composition. The poverty threshold—actually, the collection of thresholds for families of different sizes and compositions—is adjusted for inflation each year.

The poverty line has been criticized because it fails to account for all of the government benefits given to poor people, such as food stamps and Medicaid.[47] Whereas some of these benefits are equivalent to cash (e.g., food stamps), others are not (e.g., Medicaid). Advocates for poor people argue that increases in these funds go to service providers such as doctors and to social service bureaucracies, not to the poor.

A number of other problems with the poverty line have also been noted. First, when originally calculated, a family at the poverty threshold had about half the income of the median family of the same size, but by 1986 the family at the poverty line had only about one-third the median family's income.[48] Thus, in the decades since the line was first drawn, families at the poverty line have lost ground in comparison with other families. The poverty threshold alone fails to capture this growing economic distance between poor and middle-income families.

Second, poverty statistics state how *many* families fall below the poverty threshold, but do not show how *far* below the threshold they have fallen. The amount by which family income fell short of the poverty line (controlling for inflation and family size) was larger in the 1980s than in any previous decade, especially for families with female heads-of-household. In 1991, the *average* poor, female-headed family was surviving on an income of about half the poverty line.[49] As we have seen, the *poorest* fifth of single mothers with children had incomes at about a quarter of the poverty threshold.

Third, although the poverty line has been adjusted for inflation, it has not been adjusted for the changing ways in which families spend money. In 1989, the majority (56%) of poor families spent at least half their income on housing.[50] With a third of a poverty-level income spent on food and one-half on housing, there is little left for clothing, transportation, medical expenses, and other necessities. Jencks suggests that the problem of rent burdens is overstated because the Labor Department's Consumer Expenditure Survey shows that poor people spend 50% to 75% more than they report in income. He argues that because the excess of expenditures over reported income grew in the 1980s, the burden of housing costs as a portion of total expenditures did not increase.[51] But the Consumer Expenditure Survey data reported by Jencks are confined to families who rented their own homes and remained in the survey for four quarters. Thus, the survey was likely to miss the majority of families on the verge of homelessness, who are doubled up with others and move frequently. Also, as Edin observes (and Jencks acknowledges), when poor people spend more than they report earning, it is likely to be because they supplement their reported income with jobs that are "off the books" or with help from friends or relatives. Such unreported income is more precarious than income from reported sources.[52]

In sum, in the past 15 years there has been enormous growth in both the numbers of very poor families and the depth of their impoverishment. A weakened economy, loss of government benefits, and an increase in the relative cost of housing have left many poor people vulnerable to homelessness. Although substance abuse and mental illness increase the risk of homelessness for the small fraction of families who experience these conditions, they do not explain a large portion of family homelessness. Factors such as single parenthood, poor educa-tion, and scanty job histories no doubt contribute to poverty, but these factors do not increase the risk of homelessness among families who are already poor.

EFFECTS OF HOMELESSNESS ON CHILDREN

Stability is central to children's growth and development, and times of transition are times of risk. Data from the National Health Interview Survey show that children who have moved three or more times are more likely to have emotional and behavioral problems, to repeat a grade, and to be suspended or expelled from school. Excessive changes in schools are also problematic: high rates of school mobility are associated with poor academic performance, repetition of grades for elementary school children, and low self-esteem for adolescents. Even ordinary transitions from elementary school to junior high and from junior to senior high are frequently associated with declines in self-esteem, academic motivation, and grade point average. Stable child-care arrangements are associated with higher levels of play, with lower levels of aggressiveness and withdrawal, and with later academic competence.[53]

It should come as no surprise, then, that compared with housed poor children, homeless children have worse health; more delays in development; more anxiety, depression, and behavioral problems; poorer school attendance; and lower educational achievement.[54] As observed earlier, homeless families often have moved several times before they turn to shelter. Adding to instability are shelters that limit the length of time families may stay and shelter systems that move families from place to place. Every move has the potential to increase children's insecurity, disrupt their schooling, dissolve their friendships, and make it harder for them to hold on to their few possessions.[55]

Health

Research suggests that homeless children's risk for health problems starts before birth. Compared to mothers in public housing, homeless mothers are less likely to receive prenatal care and more likely to have low-birth-weight babies. Rates of infant mortality among children born to women in shelters are one-and-a-half times higher than among children born to families in public housing. Homeless children are more likely than other poor children to be hospitalized, to have delayed immunizations, and to have elevated levels of lead in their blood. Studies without comparison groups of poor children have found that homeless children experience high levels of upper respiratory infections, asthma, minor skin ailments, ear infections, anemia, gastrointestinal disorders, chronic physical disorders, diarrhea, and infestation ailments. Rates of such conditions for children using clinics for homeless people are higher than among children served by private physicians.[56]

Several studies that have relied on parents' reports of health conditions, rather than medical records or examinations by physicians, have not found differences between homeless and housed samples; both homeless and housed groups have high rates of symptoms. In one of these studies, homeless children were more likely than other poor children to have gone hungry, and were more likely to be obese due to poor diet. In another study, homeless children were found to have received fewer medical services.[57]

The poor health of shelter children may be due to poor nutrition, to communicable diseases spread in congregate living environments, to inadequate sanitary facilities, and to noise and light that disrupt sleep. Shelters in many cities require families to leave during the day, making it difficult for young children to nap or for sick children to recuperate.[58] Homeless children who live in cars, abandoned buildings, or in the open may suffer from exposure to the elements and are even less likely than shelter children to have adequate nutrition, sanitary facilities, and places to sleep. In many areas, health care for homeless children is provided by special programs operated by Health Care for the Homeless, but elsewhere, access to timely care and a consistent health-care provider may be difficult.

Mental Health and Behavioral Problems

Homeless children are more likely than housed poor children to experience mental health and emotional problems—particularly depression and anxiety—and behavioral problems including aggression. Housed poor children also have greater problems than children in general population samples. Studies without comparison groups have found that homeless children have abnormally elevated scores (i.e., clinically significant scores) on self-reported symptoms of depression or on parental reports of behavior problems.[59]

Masten and her colleagues describe these results as indicating a continuum of risk: poor children are at greater risk than children who are not poor, and homeless children are at greater risk than other poor children. In their school-age sample in Minneapolis, differences between homeless and housed children on behavioral problems and depression rarely reached statistical significance, but the homeless sample was more often significantly different from general population norms. A study of preschool-age children in New York City found a nearly identical pattern of results for behavioral problems. Both studies found mothers' psychological symptoms—and in Minneapolis, recent stressful life events—to be better predictors of children's behavioral problems than current housing status.[60]

The long-term consequences of homelessness for children are unknown; however, in one study, a sixth of formerly homeless parents reported that their children's behavioral and emotional problems engendered by homelessness persisted after a move to permanent housing.[61]

Developmental Delays

Homeless children in Boston and Philadelphia were more likely than housed poor children to experience developmental delays, including delays in language, in reading for school-age children, in personal and social development, and in motor development. In a New York City study, both housed poor and homeless preschool children scored below general population norms

CHAPTER 10
120

on a measure of development, but the two groups did not differ from each other. Early childhood education protected both groups against developmental delays. In other studies without comparison groups of poor children, homeless children have shown delays relative to test norms for general population and low-income samples.[62]

Homelessness may impede access to quality early childhood education programs that are associated with children's developmental functioning. Homeless children not in shelter are least likely to be enrolled in child care, and the transitory nature of many shelter stays makes stable child care less likely than for housed poor children. Children in shelters—and even more so, homeless children who are not in shelters—lack developmentally appropriate toys and may not have suitable places to play. Because homeless families do not have a stable residence, children do not have a regular set of playmates to foster their social development.

Educational Impairments

Homeless children of school age suffer educational impairments relative to housed poor children or general population samples. In several studies they had poorer school attendance and they more often repeated grades. Homeless children also scored lower on tests of educational achievement and had lower expectations for future educational and occupational attainment.[63]

Many of these problems are plausibly related to the instability in homeless children's lives. Students who switch schools in midyear may not experience a coherent curriculum; skipping, for example, from subtraction to long division without having studied multiplication. School retention is likely to have long-term adverse consequences for academic achievement, self-concept, and even delinquency.[64]

Many homeless children and adolescents have difficulty obtaining and maintaining access to schools. In recent years, barriers such as residency requirements have fallen, but other problems remain, such as the inability to obtain past school records, transportation prob-

lems, lack of clothing or supplies, and hostility from teachers or other pupils. Children who become homeless frequently lose any specialized educational services they received prior to losing their homes (such as remedial assistance, bilingual services, or gifted-and-talented programs) because new schools typically require students to undergo the bureaucratic process of reestablishing eligibility for such services.[65]

The educational problems documented for shelter children are likely to extend to children who are not literally homeless (i.e., in shelter or on the street) but are precariously housed (i.e., doubled up and mobile). Problems are likely to be exacerbated for homeless children who are not even in shelter.

IMPLICATIONS FOR POLICY

Homelessness is an extreme manifestation of poverty. Over the past two decades, Americans at the bottom of the economic ladder have become increasingly impoverished. Women with children have been disproportionately affected. Thus, we believe that policies to redress this increased social and economic inequity would make marked inroads into the problem of family homelessness. Unfortunately, pending or foreseeable state and federal legislation is likely to worsen the problem. Time limits on welfare entitlements, reductions in Medicaid expenditures, and the replacement of federal nutrition programs with block grants all will place poor families at risk of deeper poverty. In contrast to many proponents of "welfare reform," we believe that economic policies that foster employment at livable wages are more likely to end the crisis of homelessness. Policies such as an increase in the minimum wage, and expansion of jobs subject to it, would be especially beneficial to women, who are concentrated in jobs at or below the minimum wage.[66] Welfare reform should aim to move families out of poverty by further expanding earned-income tax credits for low-income households (see Chapter 6, note 6), providing more effective job training programs with the guarantee of job placement, enforcing the payment of child support, and guaranteeing access to high-quality day care and health care.

In the absence of a more equitable distribution of the nation's wealth, the amelioration of family homelessness is most likely to grow out of policies to expand the number of decent and affordable housing units. Current tax expenditures (such as the deductibility of mortgage interest and property taxes) provide substantial government housing subsidies to many wealthy and middle-class Americans (see Chapter 4). Such government support needs to be expanded among the poor.

Targeted efforts to provide emergency aid to keep families housed, and transitional money to move families into apartments of their own, have shown promise in preventing homelessness (see Chapter 18). More rigorous research is needed to determine whether the effectiveness of such efforts is enhanced by case management services and to compare the cost effectiveness of targeted efforts to prevent homelessness with broader efforts to expand low-income housing.

Focusing resources on low-income housing—especially if coupled with efforts to improve the financial condition of low-income families—would reduce the number of families requiring emergency shelter and the time spent there. This does not mean that the myriad problems faced by poor families would suddenly disappear; rather, these problems would not be exacerbated by homelessness. To emphasize the overarching need for housing is not to deny the service needs of many homeless families. But there is evidence to suggest that such services can be provided without recourse to elaborate systems of graduated shelters. In New York City, a pilot program delivering community-based service to high-risk families leaving shelter for permanent housing demonstrated that such families can be engaged in a range of services without segregation in "transitional" housing or shelter.[67] Such models allow problems to be addressed within the families' own homes and communities.

We believe that policies and programs to address only such problems as substance abuse or mental illness are doomed to have minimal impact on the overall problem of family homelessness. First, such problems affect relatively few homeless families. Second, these programs simply do not address a family's need for decent and affordable housing. A young mother in recovery from substance abuse continues to face an enormous risk of homelessness if she is poor, has experienced a great deal of mobility and disruption, and lives in a city with few affordable housing options. Substance abuse treatment may help this young mother address her substance abuse problem; it will not allow her to obtain permanent housing.[68] New models for housing people in recovery from problems such as substance abuse need to be considered and tested.[69]

Within the current systems of services for homeless families, which vary enormously from city to city, we urge that policies be adopted to minimize the negative effect of homelessness for both parents and children. First, families with children must be legally entitled to receive emergency shelter; children should not be forced to endure a single night sleeping on the street, under a highway, or in a "tent city." Even in cities like New York, where families have benefited from this entitlement, the right to shelter is under attack.

Second, shelter should be stable and adequate. Policies should aim to minimize the time spent in shelter and maximize families' access to needed services in the community. Policies that allow greater stability and continuity during the time of homelessness should be supported. Frequent, forced moves—which result, for example, from limits on shelter stay—needlessly increase the suffering of homeless families, especially the children in them.

As we have shown, family dismemberment too frequently has resulted from homelessness. Policies should be adopted to minimize this risk. Emergency housing must be available for single-parent and two-parent families. All children should be safely accommodated with their family unit, regardless of age or gender. And homelessness should never be sufficient reason to remove a child from his or her family.

Such policies will not reduce the number of families needing emergency shelter. However, until broader solutions are at hand, they will improve the "management" of the problem and may reduce its negative consequences.

Finally, homelessness has too often become a barrier to the receipt of other needed services. School systems must continue to grapple with the problem of how best to accommodate those children who move frequently and experience bouts of homelessness. Travel vouchers, for example, may be critical to ensure regular attendance. With regard to health, targeted medical services (such as those offered by Health Care for the Homeless projects) have greatly eased barriers to needed care. But efforts must be made to ensure that such services do not become fragmented. Given the typical mobility of homeless families, policy should encourage families to maintain a "medical home." Again, while such policies will do little to house families, they will promote educational services and health care.

SUMMARY AND CONCLUSION

Homeless families are more similar to other poor but housed families than they are to homeless single adults. Although a small proportion of mothers in homeless families have mental health or substance abuse problems that contribute to their homelessness, these problems do not explain family homelessness. Observers who conclude that single parenthood is the primary cause of homelessness among families ignore the fact that other poor families are at least as likely to be headed by single mothers. Thus, we are left with the increase in poverty and decrease in affordable housing as the principal reasons for the growth of homelessness among families.

Homelessness has serious consequences for children—for their physical health, mental health, development, and school achievement. However, in many studies, comparison samples of housed poor children also fared badly. As many children's problems are plausibly explained by instability, policy should aim to prevent homelessness, promote stability in shelters, and facilitate rapid transition to permanent housing.

CHAPTER 11

Homelessness among African Americans: A Historical and Contemporary Perspective

Kim Hopper
Norweeta G. Milburn

Among the more distinctive features of the resurgence of American homelessness in the 1980s was the overrepresentation of African Americans.[1] One authoritative review of 60 studies conducted in the 1980s, for example, found that Black Americans accounted, on average, for 44% of the homeless populations surveyed by the studies. The 1990 S-night count by the U.S. Bureau of the Census netted nearly a quarter of a million people in shelters or on the street on a given night in March; 41% of the shelter group and 39% of the street group were reported to be African Americans. The disproportionate representation of Blacks seems to be especially prominent among younger homeless persons. Recent analyses of shelter use over time in Philadelphia and New York City yield striking data on longitudinal trends: in the 3 years studied (1990–1992), 6% of the African American population in each city made some use of its public shelter system, compared with less than 0.5% of the White population.[2] Studies of homeless families, which usually focus on mothers and their children, suggest that Black Americans are also overrepresented in that population, both nationally (reckoned at 54% of homeless families) and within specific

locales (e.g., 54% of homeless families in New York and 57% in Los Angeles).[3]

This chapter will consider why African Americans are overrepresented in the American homeless population today. We want to acknowledge at the outset, however, that the literature on African American communities in recent decades (from 1975 on) is rather sparse, reflecting the disengagement of many social scientists in the wake of the acrimonious "culture of poverty" debate of the early 1970s.[4] As a result, this discussion is weak on detail when it comes to describing the contemporary state of traditional alternatives to public shelter—especially the accommodating tendencies of extended networks of kin. Although we review trends in the labor market, households, and housing, we leave the relevant details of the present context to others (see Chapters 4, 5, and 6). Because of their salience in contemporary debates, some cultural issues are examined more closely. The discussion takes shape, as well, against the persisting backdrop of both institutional and attitudinal racism (sometimes subtle and unconscious) in American society.[5] We begin with a historical perspective on African American homelessness[6] and then move to contemporary issues, including discussion of the possible causes of homelessness among American Blacks.

HISTORY OF AFRICAN AMERICAN HOMELESSNESS

Although persistent poverty would seem to have put African Americans at increased risk of homelessness, historically a number of obstacles have worked against them being literally homeless (especially visibly). In the first place, centuries of slavery made homelessness tantamount to a crime: homeless Blacks were "masterless" and, with rare exceptions, that meant they were fugitives. Indeed, in the colonial era, the social statuses of vagrants and runaway slaves were closely allied.[7] In the years after Reconstruction, when mobility was inseparable from the newly acquired sense of freedom, many former slaves took to the roads, though prospects were hardly conducive to an easy life there. The post–Civil War period saw the emergence of widespread "tramping" as a distinctive—and sometimes defiant—form of homelessness (see Chapter 1), and public sympathy rapidly reached exhaustion in many communities. If anything, African American men on the road had a harder time of it: they were more likely to be arrested for vagrancy, they were discriminated against by proprietors of businesses catering to transients, even menial work could be tough for them to come by, and the casual hospitality of individuals or households encountered en route was uncertain at best. Nonetheless, although documentation is spotty, the current widespread impression that Black homeless men were extremely rare before the 1980s is not supported by the evidence.[8]

In the late 19th century, for example, available records show that African Americans were a significant presence among arrested tramps, lodging house residents, and transients, in cities as diverse as Philadelphia, Kansas City, and Washington, DC.[9] In Chicago, where the impact of the Black migration northward was especially strong, proprietors in the city's freewheeling "hobohemia" may have restricted African American transients to segregated "col-

ored men's hotels," while other establishments simply directed inquiries to the Urban League, but both practices attest to the presence of a substantial number of homeless Blacks.[10] Abundant evidence also can be seen in records from the Great Depression. By the winter of 1932–33, nearly one-quarter of Philadelphia's homeless transients were Black, as were one-tenth of Chicago's sheltered men, one-fifth of Buffalo's "landsmen" transients (i.e., non-seamen), and one-sixth of New York City's public shelter clientele.[11] Across the country, between 7% and 12% of the local caseloads of "unattached" transients (not part of family groups) served by the Federal Transient Relief Program were African American. Such percentages are all the more striking when it is recognized that Black men on the move tended to take extra precautions against detection because of the costs of discovery: as one former migrant worker recalled, "When I was hoboing, I was in jail two-thirds of the time." African American men make frequent appearances in road memoirs of this period, although the color-blind brotherhood of the road reported by some sociologists is not consistently supported by first-person accounts.[12]

But most surprising of all is the unmistakable presence of African American men in and around traditional skid rows in the post–World War II era. Again, their appearance is in much smaller numbers than would be anticipated by looking only at figures of poverty and unemployment among African Americans at this time, a discrepancy rightly attributed to the robust networks of support (both kin-based and neighborhood-based) that had long characterized Black communities in northern cities.[13] Nonetheless, a steady Black presence—ranging from 9% to 40% in the studies we examined[14]—attests to the limits of even these long-standing sources of support. Unaccountably, even when their own research turned up such evidence, social scientists sometimes were remarkably blind to it. Take, for example, the case of New York's infamous skid row district—that mile-long corridor of the lower east side known as the Bowery. In 1964, fieldworkers on the Columbia Bowery Project consistently found a substantial minority (29%) of Bowery men to be African American. Four years later, the same research group estimated that Black men accounted for nearly one-third of the entire Bowery population, more than twice the proportion it had been a decade earlier. African Americans even made up a quarter of the inmates in a city-run shelter annex some 60 miles north, and were noticeably younger than their White counterparts. Such findings were novel enough to be picked up by the local press at the time. Oddly, though, in the definitive book on the project, the lead investigators remark only that New York City's skid row is "probably darker" than those of most northern cities.[15]

The Bowery was a well-defined area of flophouses, second-hand stores, cheap taverns, and eating joints, and its denizens were a distinctive, segregated group. Far more numerous were those "skid row-like men" who could be found among "the more amorphous destitute residents of the slums," and whose extreme poverty, frequently combined with addiction to alcohol or drugs, made them indistinguishable from their more readily identified counterparts in such urban "dead lands" as the Bowery.[16] The striking thing about such men was that despite such obvious inducements to instability, they were not often homeless in the literal sense of living on the street or in shelters.[17]

CONTEMPORARY AFRICAN AMERICAN HOMELESSNESS

By the mid-1970s, the numbers of homeless African Americans were such that they could no longer be ignored. In cities like New York, young African American men were appearing in steadily growing numbers in public shelters; by the early 1980s, they made up the majority of the residents. Trends elsewhere, although not quite as marked, are nearly all in the same direction. In 17 studies of homeless *women* (mostly in shelters), at least half were minority women, most of whom were mothers with an average of 2 children.[18] Studies of homeless *families* (also mostly in shelters) exhibit similarly telling divisions: a recent review found that African Americans (mostly mothers with an average of 2

children) made up half of their respective samples.[19]

The few studies that have addressed racial differences in homelessness offer several clues to why extreme poverty in the African American community should increasingly take the form of homelessness in the 1980s and early 1990s, especially in light of the robust legacy of the Black extended family.[20] Although the evidence from these and other studies is still slim, a few themes recur. First, like the pattern of African American poverty generally, recurrent homelessness among the Black poor tends to be less event-driven and more a matter of reshuffling. Reliance upon the "social capital" of kinship is commonplace, both as an alternative to shelter and as a way of staving off the inevitable turn to emergency public relief.[21] Although extended families provided a wide range of support in the past—material, informational, emotional, and (less frequently) financial—they have been experiencing increasing strains of late and are no longer able to prevent literal homelessness as effectively. The increasing marginalization of inner-city areas and the resultant loss of support systems (both personal and economic) have depleted resources that traditionally buffered against the negative aspects of poverty. Second, unemployment and underemployment invariably play a large part in life histories of Black homeless men. Decades-old trends of discrimination that have relegated African Americans to less desirable jobs have been abetted by the growth of the "informal" economy and influx of new immigrants competing for cheap housing and the menial jobs that remain. Third, racial discrimination remains the rule in many (though not all) of the remaining institutions that cater to homeless men. Finally, mental health problems, alcohol and drug abuse, and involvement with the criminal justice system have also been linked to literal homelessness among some African Americans.[22]

What, then, changed in the 1970s and 1980s—and in many places, changed markedly—that transformed a minority presence into a substantial if not a definitive one? Several interlocking developments are relevant. Restructured labor markets and tightened government assistance have not only driven up general poverty rates but also have hurt the informal support system (the capacity of households to feed and house an additional member, for example). Diminished work opportunities further undercut informal mechanisms of social control (the local cultural authority lost and access to entry-level jobs foregone, for instance, when older men are no longer connected to the job market), and boosted the appeal of alternative sources of livelihood (such as dealing drugs or trafficking in stolen goods). These changes, in turn, took place under tightened conditions of housing availability, persisting racism, and—in the 1980s especially—hardening attitudes toward poor people.

In some places, for some people, the functions of public shelter have also changed. For African American families, evidence suggests that shelters continue to serve as an emergency makeshift, set up in response to unforeseen adversity (as with relocation efforts occasioned by fire), the cumulative tensions of doubling up, the inevitable day of reckoning after rent has been deferred, and family subdivision (such as a new mother's bid to establish a household of her own). In New York and Philadelphia, for example, most such public shelter stays (80% of users) are transitory, and relocations appear to be fairly stable.[23] For single people, the contrast with the old institutions of skid row is especially striking. No longer a grubby terminus for spent lives, nor simply an emergency recourse in straitened times, public shelter also functions as a prosthetic extension of the marginal housing stock. Like their rapidly disappearing relatives—the old flophouses and cheap residential hotels that used to crowd central business districts[24]—shelters may not be the most reputable of abodes, but they will suffice during extended bouts of residential instability. For more resourceful residents, the shelters offer not only free lodging but also places of trade, shadow work (see Chapter 8), convalescence, and even transient community. For families struggling to make ends meet, the decision by one of their members to resort to public shelters can mean the kind of temporary respite formerly available chiefly through kith and kin.[25] And in some areas, doubled-up families have learned that the temporary indignities of applying for emergency shelter, participating in mandatory therapeutic programs, and enduring unsavory quarters is simply the going price for preferred access to affordable housing.[26]

STRUCTURAL CAUSES OF RECENT AFRICAN AMERICAN HOMELESSNESS

As suggested above, if we are to trace the changes that have led to the sustained rise in African American homelessness in the 1980s, we will need to examine a host of factors that affect both the availability of work and the viability of extended families. Gradually, evidence has mounted that allows us to make a plausible case for the factors at work on a number of fronts. In summary form, that case runs as follows:

The Role of Labor Markets

African American males have long paid a higher toll in unemployment and underemployment than their White counterparts.[27] What is extraordinary about the past quarter century is that a bad situation has gotten worse. Joblessness has increased, relative earnings declined, and the return on schooling has slipped in value (see Chapter 5). The period between the early 1960s and the late 1980s saw a *fivefold* increase (from 6.89% to 32.7%) in the percentage of Black men of laboring age who are idle.[28] The driving forces are not difficult to identify. Deindustrialization (which hit northern Black factory workers early and hard), the globalization of the workforce, plant closures and relocations, employer preferences, and an exploding "informal economy" have each played a part.

Two "cultural" aspects of the changing work environment merit note in this connection. The first, alluded to above, is the secondary disadvantage that a dearth of laboring men imposes on a local neighborhood. Fewer workers means a reduced supply of those vital informal connections to entry-level positions for the upcoming generation of job seekers. It also means a loss of visible embodiments of respectability, of handy means to enforce informal social sanctions, and of object lessons dispelling the notion that playing by the rules is just for chumps. Second, service sector work imposes a different kind of discipline than that demanded by blue-collar work. Proper attitude and comportment matter more. Performance standards are more personalized. Greater visibility and more frequent customer contact not only up the ante of appearance and demeanor, they also restrict the time and space available for compensatory, face-saving maneuvers, and curtail the worker's ability "to stamp [the job] as his own."[29] At the same time, labor market conditions are such that high turnover rates are tougher on circulating workers than on hiring firms.

Changes in the African American Extended Family

Framed as it was by the legacy of slavery, the resiliency and adaptability of the African American extended family (from captivity to the present) has been justly celebrated.[30] It was the crucial social capital that made possible the Great Migration north; it welcomed boarders and lodgers (turning some into "fictive kin") and provided solace and contacts. The extended family buffered the effects of uncertain employment, and anchored the lives of intermittently working men, whose loves and livelihoods were otherwise marked by repeated failure. It elevated sub-subsistence welfare benefits through the medium of mutual aid. Even in households where the nuclear family was customary, the extended family functioned as what one historian has termed "a private institution to redistribute the poverty of the nuclear family by way of the kinship system."[31] Our concern is with the health of that informal system today.

In the 1970s, the residential pattern of extended households became more common among the urban poor and jobless, while being buffeted by a number of economic developments that severely weakened its carrying capacity. If one ignores public transfer payments (e.g., welfare payments and unemployment compensation) and considers only pooled household income, the ability of such households to rise above poverty was nearly halved in that decade. In 1969, the income of household heads alone put 30% of them above poverty; adding income of additional household members lifted another 39% above that level. By 1979, the comparable figures were 24% and 22.5%. If anything, trends have worsened since. The "antipoverty effectiveness" of such households had been badly degraded,[32] and public benefits (which peaked in the early 1970s) have not stepped in to fill the gap created by the erosion of job security and social margin.

Although typically their kin "credit accounts" are much stronger, women too have found that the elasticity of kinship is not without limits. For African American women, domestic violence and the hardship associated with multiple-family occupancy appear to be the most common precursors of homelessness.[33] In New York City, African American mothers with children applying for emergency shelter report not a dearth of family ties, but a dire shortage of kin with the capacity to put them up—usually because they had already relied upon such kin for a place to live or for help with rent in the previous year. Findings in St. Louis and Boston were similar.[34]

Housing

As detailed elsewhere in this volume (Chapters 3 and 4), the lot of the low-income tenant has grown increasingly tenuous in the last decade. But many urban African American households have faced additional hardships, owing to the legacy of racism and to a deliberate federal policy in the postwar years to favor suburban development at the expense of inner cities. This de facto race-based housing policy can be seen as part of a larger social apparatus devoted to the containment of Black ghetto communities—a pattern two analysts have referred to as "American apartheid."[35] African Americans may well have been disproportionately affected by cuts in targeted federal subsidies for low-income housing in the 1980s (see Chapter 12).

By the usual indices of habitability, the housing of Black Americans fares poorly. Blacks are more likely than Whites to live in dwellings that are physically deficient or overcrowded. Nearly three-quarters of poor African American households pay more than 30% of their income (the usual ceiling of "affordable") for housing. A more telling measure of affordability, one that takes into account household size as well as income, is provided by the notion of "shelter poverty." This refers to the situation of households that, having met their housing costs, lack sufficient income to meet other necessities at a minimal standard of decency. By this reckoning, approximately half of Black households were shelter poor in the period 1972–1991, compared to roughly one-third of households in the general population. Put differently, although African Americans make up 11% of all households, they account for 19% of shelter-poor households.[36]

The loss of single-room-occupancy (SRO) hotels and lodging houses in the postwar years— a loss catalyzed by private profit-seeking and government policy—merits special note. Such places had provided a cheap alternative for generations of lodgers of questionable repute and means. It is not difficult to recognize similar individuals— "unattached to a family, they had few possessions, enjoyed recreational drinking, worked intermittently, and traveled often"[37]— in shelter rosters today. Although accurate figures do not exist for the pre-1970 era, the loss of SRO units in major cities alone is estimated in the millions; since 1970, scores of thousands more have fallen victim to demolition, conversion, arson, and warehousing (removal from the market).[38] The depletion of these lodgings increases competition for the remaining affordable housing, paring back the excess residential stock that was part and parcel of the extended household's elastic ability to accommodate additional members.

The Disputed Role of "Culture"

Many commentators have seized upon the convenient device of a reputed "underclass" culture to explain the persistence of apparently self-destructive behaviors[39] and, by extension, entrenched poverty. The argument merits a serious response. A closer look reveals that both

the underlying premises and the evidence summoned are open to serious question.

Few observers deny that some African American poor people (at least some of the time) "hold values and take actions far outside the mainstream;"[40] that, for some, these can become characteristic patterns; and that such behavior adds to the injuries and exacerbates the captivity of ghetto life. But how widespread such behavior is, how best to interpret it, how tightly it is coupled to local context, how long it persists in the absence of specific generative conditions, where critical loci of control lie— all of these remain hotly disputed items. As was true of the "culture of poverty" debate in the 1960s and early 1970s, the most divisive issue remains that of self-perpetuation: the extent to which "some cultural traits may take on a life of their own for a period of time and thereby become a constraining or liberating factor."[41]

Still, it has yet to be established that stable, distinctive patterns are there to be studied. Anomalies abound in the ethnographic record, making dubious the claim of any single finding to be representative of African American "culture." Consider the competing versions of young Black fatherhood offered by Anderson and Sullivan: the first sees it in terms of "sex codes" (chiefly, "the peer-group ethic of 'hit and run'"); the second, using a comparative design that varied configurations of class, ethnicity, and social ecology, identifies a dominant pattern of quietly honored paternity among young Black fathers.[42] Striking differences appear in accounts of schooling, as well. Ogbu and Fine both offer densely textured, persuasive accounts of oppressive high schools and defiant, disengaged students for whom race has become a caste status.[43] But MacLeod tells the more compelling story of inner-city Black students for whom the same legacy of race has become a liberating force.[44] Not that finishing high school, even completing some college, guarantees success: MacLeod's bleak extended ethnography confirms that service economy jobs place a premium on "good attitude" in exchange for "low wages, infrequent raises, awkward working hours, minimal training, and high turnover."[45] But it is the disaffected

White teenagers he follows into the labor market—and not their Black counterparts—who turn in substantial numbers to the drug trade.

Close examination of the work habits and consumption "values" of poor Blacks that the dominant culture finds most disturbing reveals further ironies. Hochschild, for one, has argued that it would be a mistake to set aside certain features of what passes for "underclass" life as merely strange, menacing, or pitiable. To the contrary: the discipline and work ethic of the drug trade, the wiles devoted to outwitting government regulations, the taste for pain-numbing pastimes—these characteristics make their practitioners "not only inhabitants of an alien culture or innocent victims of the capitalist juggernaut . . . [but] in an exaggerated and distorted way, us."[46]

Such distorted-mirror effects should not be allowed to obscure a larger point. Like "beliefs," values do a job.[47] Durable dispositions to act they may be, but they are also subject to modification, hedging, and reinterpretation as circumstance (and self-respect) demand. Whether they match those of the dominant or mainstream culture seems largely beside the point. The anthropological literature is full of accounts of how dissonance, born of unaccommodating circumstance, gives rise to doubled lives.[48] Resistance is not without its costs, separate is rarely equal, and refusal may serve to perpetuate that same structure of exclusion. Mimicking the mainstream, too, can exact "hidden injuries" of its own.[49]

Culture (however construed) can never be severed from local context. Several lines of inquiry in psychological research make the case that both differential exposure and differential vulnerability to sources of psychological stress are needed to account for the joint effects of race and class.[50] This body of work has shown that not only are African Americans subject to more episodes of undesirable "stressful life events," but that their resources for coping with them (internal and external) are compromised, leaving them more susceptible to negative impacts.[51] Understanding exactly how such variables as coping and adaptation strategies affect resistance to stress must await further study, but it is clear that the operation of such strategies must be examined over time and across contexts. It would be a mistake, for example, to treat "available social support" as simply another personality "trait" to be assessed on intake. Nor is "social capital" (the turn to voluntary associations, networking, and mutual aid) the sort of civic good that thrives best under conditions of benign neglect—an especially vital observation in these days of "devolution" and government shrinkage.[52]

In summary, then, the role of culture is complex and remains to be fully explicated. But it would be foolish to avoid mounting evidence of disturbing developments that may be grouped under that heading. We have in mind research findings that suggest:

- In some ghetto communities, sources of embodied respectability in males have become scarce.[53]

- Absent males (and gone with them, connections to the world of work) mean that effective informal sanctions for controlling antisocial behavior are often absent as well, shifting the disciplinary burden to female heads of households.[54]

- Cultural suspicions and misunderstandings bred by segregation in everyday life are intensified by the high visibility and extensive customer contact of service sector work.

- Minority status interacts with social class to increase psychological distress.[55]

- Although a flourishing drug trade may offer a way to regain the self-esteem, respectability, and purchasing power denied by legitimate work opportunities, that fact does not cancel the damage done to self, family, and neighborhood by that illicit commerce.[56]

To the extent that any of these factors further hobbles an individual's prospects on the job market, or erodes informal sources of aid in times of crisis, it will increase the risk of homelessness.

DISCUSSION

The evidence summarized above suggests that a sound answer to the question of why home-lessness has increased among poor African Americans must be multifaceted. In the past two decades, labor and housing markets have grown progressively more hostile to men of low skill and modest means. Already reeling under the impact of concentrated poverty, many ghetto neighborhoods saw commercial invest-ments decline, public services cut back, and sectors of the physical landscape reduced to ruins.[57] Extended households found it progres-sively more difficult to make ends meet, as household-member earnings and government benefits both declined in value.[58] When we shift focus from the material base of support and look instead at informal mechanisms of social regu-lation, another factor moves into prominence. With legitimate work opportunities severely cur-tailed, the social regulatory function of work itself is degraded, and the disciplinary role for-merly played by older males in the community atrophies.[59] Responsibility for wielding informal control thus shifts progressively to women, and one of the most effective sanctions they exer-cise is ejection from the household. The up-shot: when market losses in affordable housing and decent work combined with the mounting strains on extended households, feminization of familial discipline, the growth in the drug trade, and continued failures of community-based men-tal health treatment and drug treatment,[60] homelessness was virtually a foregone conclusion.

Although in the life histories of some home-less poor people, family ties are absent or long dormant,[61] for many others—and especially, it appears, for those whose homelessness is local and episodic—such ties are not only main-tained, but effectively spell the difference (sometimes repeatedly) between a berth amid kin or friends and one among strangers. Far from suffering from "a pathology of connectedness," as some observers continue to insist,[62] these people are able to avoid homelessness (or to "exit" from it periodically), owing to the resil-iency of such networks. As was the case in the late 1930s,[63] it is the generosity of African American extended households today that stands out.[64]

But clearly, even obligations rooted in kin-ship have their limits. Putting up with the de-mands of relatives or overcrowded situations is easier if they are expected to be short-lived. That, in turn, depends upon the availability of alternatives. When the bridgework essential for a successful transition to adulthood is in severe disrepair—absent mentors, a succession of "en-try-level" jobs that lead nowhere, the lure of illegal work and collateral risk of incarceration, housing costs that a keep a place of one's own out of reach[65]—many young Blacks are stuck in cultural limbo (see Chapter 1). Under such circumstances, doubling up may still serve as an extended way station, but it does so under increasingly hostile circumstances. Household resources are badly stretched and sorely tried by disruptive guests.[66] In many places, the sup-ply of affordable housing, whose low costs and routine vacancies were so vital to the ability of households to expand and contract as need demanded, has suffered huge losses.[67] The op-tions of circulating family members are limited; whatever "slack" remained in household carry-ing capacity is soon exhausted.[68]

In strained households, a kind of "triage" may be resorted to.[69] With resources insufficient to meet the needs of all, those who are better able to fend for themselves are expected to do so. For good reason, such decisions are gender-bi-ased. Women are more valued and versatile as household members and, until recently, were less likely to have disabling drug or alcohol prob-lems.[70] In short, women's investment in the so-cial capital of kinship—and thus their expected return—is greater and more durable than that of men;[71] it is surely stronger than that of young men, many of whom have yet to secure jobs that would enable them to perform as "responsible" and "respectable" members of the family. Not surprisingly, for women—much more so than for men—a lengthy sojourn with family imme-diately preceded their homelessness.[72]

But men, too, are prey to the nagging claims of kinship and bristle at prolonged periods of dependency. For them, leaving a sorely strapped household and seeking public shelter may be a way of repaying hospitality.[73] Given the scarcity of affordable lodging and the pressure on shared or doubled-up arrangements, the appeal of non-market alternatives for both livelihood and residence grows. Military service was one such option, but it came at the cost of a heavy commitment.[74] In the late 1970s, another appeared. Concurrent with a decline in its traditional clientele, the use patterns in public shelter began to shift markedly. Formerly a terminal option for elderly, poor, and friendless White men, the shelters became way stations for young Black men in flux—a modern, relatively unstructured version of the 19th-century police station houses for tramps (see Chapter 1).

A novel pattern of intermittent "official" homelessness is the result, one that can make strict distinctions between housed and "houseless" poverty quite difficult. The confusion is evident in the following 1989 press excerpt: "Although he described himself as homeless when he was arrested Monday, friends and neighbors at his parents' house . . . said yesterday that he had been living there off and on recently."[75] Indeed, over half of New York City shelter residents report that they make use of the system on a part-time or occasional basis; one in seven residents currently considers the shelter his "home," and nearly a third do so from time to time.[76]

To sum up: among the more important "complexities of need"[77] slighted by advocates and analysts of homelessness alike in the 1980s was the element of race. But, as we have seen, they were hardly the first to do so. Despite their steady presence in the ranks of skid row men and transients, African Americans have been largely absent from this country's chronicles of homelessness. In the past, that absence was easier to understand: Black men were, after all, a minority population among skid row men (though not nearly as negligible as some commentators have led us to believe). But the persistent overlooking of homeless Blacks, which at least one group of researchers detected as early as 1978,[78] is harder to account for in the years since then.

Some have argued that a short-sighted strategic decision by advocates in the early 1980s—to emphasize the "just-like-us" aspects of the homeless—had the inadvertent consequence of erasing the element of race from the roiling politics of the issue.[79] At the same time, the African American political leadership was hardly eager to embrace so thorny an issue while doing battle on so many other fronts during these increasingly conservative times. Both developments had the effect of further marginalizing Black homelessness and of distorting perceptions of the dynamics of African American poverty in the process.

The necessary corrective to such ideological segregation will demand a good deal of work. Different tasks can be discerned. For African Americans, the critical task today is not only that of securing standing as cultural observers, but the broader one of "rethinking the larger structures that constrain and enable our agency"—as everyday actors as well as privileged commentators.[80] For other Americans, the initial task is simpler. It will mean recovering the lesson that Ralph Ellison tried to teach nearly half a century ago—that invisibility is not an accident, but the product of a determined refusal to see.[81] Dispelling invisibility, we slowly learned (only to rapidly forget), is not so much a matter of shedding light as it is one of choosing, deliberately, to look.

CHAPTER 12

Homelessness and the Latino Paradox

Susan González Baker

Although research on homelessness through the 1960s revealed a predominantly White population, today's street surveys and shelter counts include a greater share of racial and ethnic minorities than we see in the general population—an "overrepresentation" of these groups. This simple statement, however, obscures a more interesting finding. While nearly all studies find that African Americans are overrepresented among the homeless, Latinos—of diverse national origins—tend to be underrepresented, in areas as diverse as Los Angeles, San Antonio, and New York.[1]

If Latinos and African Americans share many socioeconomic characteristics that place both groups at higher risk for poverty than non-Hispanic Whites, why do studies find these two groups not comparably represented among the homeless? This chapter examines two competing explanations for this "Latino paradox." The first asserts that the difference in African American and Latino homelessness rates is not real—that it is, instead, a result of using flawed methods to assess the composition of the homeless population. The second accepts the valid-ity of the discrepant rates that have been reported and asserts that differences in African American and Latino risk factors explain the paradox.

I begin with a review of findings about race and ethnicity in studies of homeless populations. Next, I examine biases in homelessness studies that may result in African American oversampling and Latino undersampling. If sampling biases are pervasive, we can question whether the patterns reported by researchers about the racial or ethnic composition of homeless populations reflect genuine differences.

I then examine evidence supporting the view that the risk factors associated with homelessness truly differ by race/ethnicity. I compare three sets of risk factors: (1) characteristics of individuals, such as mental illness and substance abuse; (2) structural influences, such as economic position, housing availability, and residential segregation; and (3) "middle-range" factors, including the availability of support through interpersonal social networks. If these risk factors vary by race/ethnicity, it is more likely that homelessness research reveals true differences, and that Latinos are less likely than African Americans to experience "literal" homelessness.

LATINOS IN THE HOMELESS POPULATION: EVIDENCE FROM LOCAL STUDIES

Most local homelessness studies are small sample surveys. Typically, researchers sample homeless people in locales where the homeless are likely to congregate—shelters or public parks, for example—or sample from inner-city census tracts. Interviews usually collect demographic information, socioeconomic data, and a report of social service use, such as welfare receipt or shelter use. Many include a mental health assessment. The data usually distinguish between the "street" and "shelter" components of the homeless population, although considerable overlap often exists.

For this chapter, I examined the racial/ethnic composition of samples of homeless people in 24 studies conducted in 18 U.S. cities. I found that, on average, the African American share of the homeless sample exceeded the African American share of the metropolitan population by 25.5 percentage points. In areas for which Latino data were available, Latino homeless were underrepresented relative to the Latino general population by 3.5 percentage points, on average. This underrepresentation was even more dramatic in areas with large Latino populations of Mexican origin. In Albuquerque, for example, where the Latino portion of the general population was 37.8%, Latinos constituted only 24.9% of a homeless population studied in 1985—an underrepresentation of 12.9 percentage points. A study the same year found a similar degree of Latino underrepresentation in San Antonio, and other studies of the same period found significant underrepresentation of Latinos in Austin, Los Angeles, San Francisco, and Chicago.[2]

A few homelessness studies have compared racial and ethnic groups on other dimensions: usually demographics, "street careers," socioeconomic characteristics, and social networks.

On each dimension, I summarize distinctions between minorities and non-Hispanic Whites, then review differences between Latinos and African Americans where evidence permits.

Demographic Features

Age structure is a key distinction among racial and ethnic groups within the homeless population. Latino and African American homeless people are significantly younger than their White counterparts. However, despite their relative youth, African American homeless are more likely than non-Hispanic Whites to have graduated from high school, at least in studies conducted in Ohio, Texas, and Los Angeles. In contrast, a Texas homelessness study found that Latinos were less likely than either non-Hispanic Whites or African Americans to have completed high school.[3]

Any analysis of Latino-origin groups invites the question of birthplace and immigration status. None of the studies reviewed identify immigration status. However, a Texas census of the homeless did identify Latino immigrants indirectly. Fifteen percent of the Latino respondents identified "lack of documents or identification" as their primary barrier to employment—a reason virtually absent for non-Hispanic White and African American respondents. Clearly, some subset of the Latino homeless consists of immigrants, but there is scant direct evidence on the immigrant share of the total.[4]

Variation in "Street Careers"

African Americans and Latinos seem to experience brief episodes of homelessness more often than non-Hispanic Whites. Rossi notes that for all homeless people, a time gap exists between their last steady job and the onset of their current homeless spell. For Latinos and African Americans, this time gap is longer than for non-Hispanic Whites, suggesting that they may avoid homelessness longer on inadequate incomes. But, once homeless, both minority groups are more likely than non-Hispanic Whites to slip into numerous episodes of homelessness.[5]

Socioeconomic Variation

Rossi found little racial and ethnic variation in monthly income level among the homeless. All groups in his Chicago study reported minimal monthly income, from $97 for Native Americans to $197 for African Americans.[6] Some racial/ethnic variation does exist in income sources, however. Among single adults, African Americans have reported heavier use of welfare than have Whites. In a nationwide study by Martha Burt and Barbara Cohen, single mothers (a category that was over 80% "non-White") reported welfare as their primary income source, consistent with welfare eligibility criteria that privilege single-parent families (see Chapter 6). Only 15% of these families received any income from employment.[7]

Still, members of all groups express a willingness to work. In the Texas homeless census, two-thirds of the men and half of the women in each racial/ethnic group reported that they were "able to work." Indeed, in several studies, minorities were more likely than Whites to attribute their homelessness to economic factors like unemployment or lack of affordable housing than to poor health or problematic behavior. In Austin, Snow and his colleagues found that 43% of the people in their sample sought job referrals from the state employment office—more contact than was made with any other social service agency in the city. These efforts often met with frustration, however, as referrals were obtained only for sporadic, low-paying, day-labor employment.[8]

Social Network Variation

Researchers agree that homelessness imposes great strain on the relationships between homeless individuals and their domiciled families and friends. Lengthening time on the street can exacerbate these tensions until a homeless person stops linking personal identity to traditional social roles—those of sibling, parent, spouse, or coworker—but instead constructs meaning and identity from the homeless experience itself.[9]

Homelessness research is only now beginning to examine social network structure and social support supplied through networks. Little attention has been devoted to racial and ethnic variation in the social networks of the homeless. Researchers continue to speculate that the apparently small homeless Latino population derives from Latino "cultural patterns" of extended household formation and community support. But there is little evidence with which to test this hypothesis.

Summing Up

We can glean a few insights on the relationship between race or ethnicity and homelessness from research that has already been conducted. Homeless Latinos and African Americans are younger than homeless non-Hispanic Whites, more likely to be homeless with children, and more likely to endure frequent spells of homelessness. In other ways, Latinos and African Americans clearly differ: homeless Latinos are less educated than homeless African Americans, are more likely to be foreign born (and less likely to speak English), and may be less likely to use public assistance. As to the comparability of the personal social networks of Latinos and African Americans—during or after the homeless spells that bring them into a researcher's sample—there is virtually no direct evidence.

Thus, the homelessness literature does not provide evidence to account clearly for the Latino paradox. The question of why researchers have recorded such a low proportion of Latino homelessness remains open to the methodological and substantive explanations outlined at the beginning of this chapter. I now turn to an evaluation of these explanations.

EXPLAINING THE LATINO PARADOX: BIASED RESEARCH SAMPLES?

Homelessness research relies heavily on cross-sectional or "one-time-only" surveys of shelter users. Such samples are biased in an important way: ethnic or racial groups that use shelters more often and for longer periods of time are most likely to be included; in technical terms, they are "oversampled." Homeless people who use shelters infrequently or briefly are correspondingly "undersampled" (see Chapter 2).

At the same time, patterns of poverty, residential segregation, zoning, and neighborhood political activism typical of American cities make homeless shelters more likely to be in areas that are both extremely poor and disproportionately African American. Under such circumstances, we would expect African Americans to be more likely to patronize shelters and thus to be overrepresented in shelter studies. Latinos might not use shelters as often because of less ready access, and thus they would be underrepresented in such studies. Unfortunately, we know too little about racial and ethnic variation in shelter use to evaluate such selection effects. Until shelter use patterns are analyzed by race and ethnicity, and until we examine carefully the effects of shelter location on their patronage, we cannot rule out such selection bias as an explanation for the Latino paradox.

If a large number of Latino homeless are not using shelters, where are they? Several possibilities exist. First, in the more hospitable climates of the southwestern United States, homeless Latinos may have greater options for "sleeping rough" in parks, in campgrounds, on hillsides, and in abandoned buildings. Researchers have made efforts to augment shelter surveys with samples of "street" populations, in an attempt to account for those using alternative sleep sites. To date, however, there is no compelling evidence that Latinos are more heavily represented in "street" samples than in "shelter" samples. Further, the underrepresentation of homeless Latinos is comparable in Chicago and Austin, implicating more than climate in the differences we see.

There is evidence, however, that non-shelter-based living arrangements are quite important for one Latino subgroup: newly arrived undocumented immigrants in southern California. Chavez documents whole campsite communities in the canyons and hillsides of the San Diego area. From such bases, immigrants work in agriculture or as domestics in the wealthy bedroom communities on the outskirts of the city. Not connected to the shelter network, these "hidden homeless" tend to move directly

from their campsite communities to private residences, either doubling up with other immigrants or securing their own housing.[10]

If such patterns exist in other areas or with other Latino populations, researchers are missing some of the "gray areas" between urban and suburban space in which some Latinos might be found. Even so, the underrepresentation of Latinos among the homeless cannot be explained solely by undocumented immigrants making use of non-shelter-based living arrangements: most Latinos in the United States are U.S.-born or legally resident aliens, and furthermore, Latino undocumented immigrants demonstrate great resourcefulness in finding and maintaining housing in U.S. communities.[11]

With these caveats, it bears repeating that the modest level of Latino presence among the homeless can be seen across a wide range of locales using a variety of sampling methods. Unlike African Americans, nowhere are Latinos dramatically overrepresented. Methodological critiques, though necessary, may be insufficient to explain the Latino paradox. Thus, we turn to substantive explanations for ethnic and racial variations in homelessness.

EXPLAINING THE LATINO PARADOX: ETHNIC VARIATION IN RISK FACTORS FOR HOMELESSNESS?

Researchers frequently identify three sets of homelessness risk factors: individual behavioral factors, economic and structural factors, and "middle-range" factors that fall between individual characteristics and macrolevel processes.

Behavioral Explanations

Mental illness. I will set aside the debates on the measurement and prevalence of mental illness among the homeless (see Chapter 3). The more pertinent question here is whether this risk factor varies by race or ethnicity. Specifically, are Latinos less likely to be homeless because they are less likely to be mentally ill, and are African Americans at greater risk for homelessness due to higher levels of mental illness?

Mental illness does not vary across racial and ethnic groups in ways consistent with the observed variation in homelessness. Latino and African American mental health profiles imply that both should be overrepresented among the homeless, since both show higher levels of psychological distress in tests administered to the general U.S. population. Moreover, if African American homelessness were attributable to higher rates of mental illness, we would expect to see greater shares of mentally ill people among the African American homeless, but this is not the case. In many local studies, Latino and African American homeless people demonstrate lower levels than Whites of current mental illness symptoms, as well as less psychiatric hospitalization prior to the current homeless episode. In fact, clinicians in a nationwide network of shelter-based clinics were twice as likely to diagnose psychiatric disorder for non-Hispanic White clients as for African American or Latino clients.[12]

Substance abuse. Substance abuse is the most common mental health disorder among both the homeless and the U.S. population at large, but data on racial and ethnic variation in substance abuse are surprisingly scarce. Still, some information comes from two sources: substance abuse treatment caseloads and self-reported drug use in the general population. Both African Americans and Latinos were overrepresented in treatment units in 1984, constituting 15% and 9% of alcohol abuse clients, and 29% and 16% of drug abuse clients, respectively. Self-report data show that alcohol use is most prevalent among non-Hispanic Whites. Both Latinos and African Americans report higher use of crack cocaine than non-Hispanic Whites, and young Latinos were more likely than young African Americans to use powder cocaine.[13]

These racial and ethnic patterns also appear in homelessness research. Whites report more alcohol abuse and treatment than either Latinos or African Americans, but other drug use is more common among the two minority groups. Thus, while some evidence suggests higher rates of drug abuse among the minority homeless,

none of these patterns explains the underrepresentation of Latinos.[14]

Structural Explanations

Poverty. African American homeless people are more likely than White homeless people to cite economic reasons for their homelessness, and African Americans are also more likely to be poor than Whites. In 1984, around the time that most local studies of homelessness were being conducted, African American per capita income was half that of non-Hispanic Whites.[15]

Latinos are also concentrated in the lowest income stratum. In 1980, 22.9% of the Latino population of Mexican origin fell below the poverty line, versus 29.9% of African Americans and 9.4% of non-Hispanic Whites. In 1984, Mexican American per capita income, like African American income, was half that of non-Hispanic Whites, and Puerto Rican income was even lower. In short, poverty profiles do not untangle the Latino paradox.[16]

Housing availability. If poverty alone does not explain the Latino paradox, perhaps the answer lies in racial and ethnic variation in the relationship between poverty and housing patterns. The federal government intervenes in the low-cost housing market by supplying housing directly and by subsidizing the rents paid by poor people (see Chapter 4). Historically, both mechanisms have been most important for African Americans. In 1979, African Americans represented nearly half the residents of public housing units, whereas 12% of those units were occupied by Latinos. In 1987, nearly a third of African American renters relied on public or subsidized housing, versus 16% of Latino renters.[17]

Thus, a period of federal retrenchment in housing assistance may have affected African Americans disproportionately. From 1980 to 1988, the nationwide supply of low-income housing declined by approximately 2.5 million units. In 1986, due to huge backlogs, 17 of the 25 cities covered in a U.S. Conference of Mayors report on homelessness had stopped accepting housing assistance applications. The same report noted that only 30% of qualified low-income families in major U.S. cities were served by housing programs. Although we cannot document the racial or ethnic composition of these waiting lists, it is reasonable to believe that historical patterns of housing program use and worsening poverty profiles throughout the 1980s made African Americans the minority group most vulnerable to a more stringent housing policy.[18]

The housing that is available to poor Latinos and African Americans is often physically substandard, and African Americans are more likely than either Latinos or non-Hispanic Whites to live in housing of inadequate quality. In Houston, the African American probability of living in substandard housing exceeds the Latino probability by a factor of four. In addition, African Americans are the most likely racial/ethnic group to pay more than 30% of income for rent. Not surprisingly, African Americans report higher levels of dissatisfaction with their housing than do either Latinos or non-Hispanic Whites.[19]

Residential segregation. The link between housing and African American homelessness may be found in another feature of the African American experience: pervasive residential segregation. Unlike Latinos, Asian Americans, and Whites, African Americans continue to experience extraordinary levels of housing discrimination and residential segregation. Denton and Massey examined residential segregation patterns for 60 Standard Metropolitan Statistical Areas (SMSAs) and found African American segregation to be high and nearly impervious to change across class lines. In the 20 SMSAs with the largest African American populations, roughly 80% of African Americans with less than a high school education would have to move to a less African American-dominated census tract in order to produce a pattern where the entire SMSA was made up of census tracts that reflected the overall racial/ethnic SMSA composition. Roughly 70% of African Americans with some college education would have had to do so, as well. Latinos were less segregated from non-Hispanic Whites than were African Americans, and they were more likely to achieve integration with rising economic status. African

American college graduates were more segregated from non-Hispanic Whites than were Latinos with less than a fourth-grade education.[20]

Independent audits of housing discrimination in the rental and purchase markets continue to reveal discrimination against African Americans. In a review of housing audits conducted since 1980, Turner and Reed report an incidence of housing discrimination against potential renters of 44% for African Americans versus 24% for Latinos. These figures show little improvement over the original housing audits conducted by the Department of Housing and Urban Development in the 1970s. As housing availability has deteriorated, both poverty and racial discrimination have persisted for the African American community. Links between these trends and homelessness cannot be disregarded.[21]

The Importance of the Social Network

Portrayed as both help and hindrance, the social network is crucial in understanding psychological well-being, social service use, and employment patterns. Attempts to explain Latino underrepresentation among the homeless have been couched cautiously in social network terms, implying that Latino kinship and support patterns may mitigate homelessness.[22] Often, these patterns are referred to as "cultural" differences. But what is it about "culture" that mitigates homelessness for one group and not for another? Do the structural features of social networks differ? Or does the content of "support" flowing through the network constitute the key differences among groups?

Network structure. By "structure," network researchers mean those properties of a social network that describe its form. Key variables include size, density or connectedness, and diversity or difference among members along dimensions like kinship, gender, or ethnicity.[23]

Racial/ethnic differences exist on each dimension, but they generally distinguish non-Hispanic Whites from both Latinos and African Americans. Non-Hispanic Whites tend to have larger social networks than either minority group, reporting more people when asked to list everyone they are linked to on some measure of closeness. This difference seems due to their inclusion of unrelated network members— friends and colleagues, for example. Minority networks largely reflect family-based ties.[24]

Both Latino and African American networks are smaller and more dense than non-Hispanic White networks. Mindel found Mexican Americans more likely than non-Hispanic Whites to have kin households living in the same community, to have frequent contact with kin, and to migrate to communities where kin already were resident. Keefe found non-Hispanic Whites more likely to interact socially with friends, whereas Mexican Americans were more likely to report social interaction with kin.[25]

In short, Latino and African American social networks seem to be more alike than different when compared with those of non-Hispanic Whites. They are smaller, more kin-based, and more dense (meaning that the members of a person's network also have relationships with one another). The social networks of Latinos and African Americans are less likely than those of non-Hispanic Whites to reflect the presence of "weak ties" with people like friends and colleagues. Still, even if network structures are similar for the two groups, perhaps the content of support flowing through those networks differs in ways that might affect homelessness.

Social support. Close-knit, family-based social networks are key sources of emotional aid in times of crisis. However, social support also involves the exchange of guidance, useful information, personal services, and material assistance. Small, tightly interconnected social networks are not well-suited to some of these tasks. Wide-ranging, diverse networks are much more likely to provide individuals with new information, access to influential people, and experience in negotiating to achieve objectives. The presence of such diverse "weak ties" in non-Hispanic White networks is advantageous, for there is a strong correlation between the presence of "weak ties" and higher earnings and

educational attainment. The lack of such social resources affects fundamental opportunities like employment.[26]

Based on our current knowledge about network structure and race/ethnicity, we might expect both Latinos and African Americans to be overrepresented among the homeless because they share small, kin-dependent networks. But similarity in form does not mean similarity in function. For instance, while active family networks provide enabling information and assistance to African Americans seeking social services, the family network itself may substitute for Latino use of such services. Green and Monahan found elderly Latinos in Tucson, Arizona, more likely than non-Hispanic Whites to rely on family caregivers for personal services like household chores and cooking, even though both groups of respondents were drawn from the rolls of a public program in which community volunteers provided such services. In contrast, Mindel and Wright found that the family network served as a necessary "enabling" factor steering African American elderly people toward social services. For African Americans, active family networks were positively associated with social service utilization, while such networks did not predict use rates for other racial/ethnic groups. If social networks serve different purposes among racial/ethnic groups with respect to housing, these differences may be related to their differential use of shelters. While supportive African American networks may facilitate the use of shelters when network resources are scarce, active Latino networks may minimize such use.[27]

Further evidence for such a difference exists in housing statistics. The one measure of housing inadequacy on which Latinos consistently outpace African Americans is overcrowding. Latinos are twice as likely as African Americans to live in housing units defined as "overcrowded" by the U.S. Bureau of the Census— meaning a density of over 1.5 persons per room. Although this difference can be accounted for, in part, by a higher birthrate among Latinos, it is not the whole story. Rather, it appears that

Latinos are more likely to engage in a variety of residential arrangements, including young adults living with parents, unrelated adults sharing housing, multiple families doubling up, and in the case of immigrants, parents living with adult offspring over age 45. Interestingly, the Latino-origin group in which Bean and Tienda found multiple adults sharing housing to be least common—Puerto Ricans—is also the group for which we see the closest parallel between representation among the homeless (Latinos in New York City) and their share of the MSA population.[28]

There is a lively and continuing debate as to whether culture, economic need, or some interaction best explains Latino housing arrangements.[29] Compared to African Americans, Latinos appear more likely to use diverse housing arrangements orchestrated within personal networks to avoid the streets and shelters. Thus, the Latino paradox might be explained, in part, by how Latino populations have adapted to impoverishment. But as Hopper and Milburn emphasize in Chapter 11, the depletion of African American network resources by persistent unemployment, welfare cutbacks, and the loss of affordable housing may have undone a response to residential instability that was historically similar to what we see today among Latinos. Poor, urban African Americans seem to have absorbed shelters into their usual strategies for managing chronic residential instability. The shelter thus augments network resources rather than replacing them. Furthermore, setting aside all cultural differences in help-seeking, Latinos simply are not as likely to find homeless shelters readily at hand.

CONCLUSION

We cannot rule out the possibility that research design accounts in part for the Latino paradox and biases our understanding of the relationship between homelessness and race or ethnicity. Certain regions of the United States, like the Southwest, include "hidden" communities of Latino homeless. Incorporating such areas into homelessness research likely would increase the representation of Latinos.

However, the pervasiveness and magnitude of the difference between Latino and African American homelessness rates, given similar impoverishment, strongly suggest that something more than methodological bias is at work. Just what this is remains problematic, but it is not reducible to vague attributions of "cultural differences." Beliefs, values, and norms governing a group's housing strategies emerge from geography, historical migration and settlement patterns, responses to the demands of housing and welfare authorities, persistent unemployment, and racial and ethnic discrimination. Latino and African American experiences may indeed have differed in ways that have led to different housing profiles and differential vulnerability to homelessness. These experiences may have not yet led Latinos in great numbers to homeless shelters, but continued economic strain places them at risk of higher levels of dislocation and literal homelessness. It is not hard to imagine circumstances under which Latinos would become fully represented among the homeless, a dubious equality indeed.

Put another way, to evaluate the origins of complex social problems like homelessness inevitably broaches the age-old social science conundrum: the relative contributions of culture and social structure to the creation of social conditions. Cultural constructs like values, belief systems, shared norms, and behavioral patterns are central to the study of human experience. However, social scientists also recognize that these lived experiences are contoured by social structures such as governments, labor markets, and education and health care systems. The analytic problem derives from the fact that cultures shape society's institutions, and institutional structures shape cultural beliefs and practices. It is thus impossible to attribute findings such as racial or ethnic differences in homelessness to either set of influences exclusively, despite the impulse in social science to identify clear causal relationships. A fruitful path for research in view of the systematic racial/ethnic patterns discussed here may be to focus on the historical and adaptive dynamics of cultures "in" poverty rather than assuming the existence of static, self-perpetuating cultures "of" poverty. This will require greater attention to specific aspects of culture over time, and how they serve or fail people in the crucible of persistent suffering. Such understanding would go far in guiding effective interventions.

The lesson of the Latino paradox, then, is not that social policy should expect African Americans to do what Latinos do. Whatever their structural and cultural origins, Latino patterns that have led to overcrowding in often substandard housing should not be construed as the most durable or desirable alternatives to dislocation. Such alternatives of necessity are no substitute for housing subsidies, tax and wage policies that bolster working-class earnings, or aggressive antidiscrimination policies that open up new sectors of the labor and housing markets still closed on the basis of race.

PART
3
· · · · · · · · · ·

RESPONSES TO HOMELESSNESS

CHAPTER 13

Public Attitudes and Beliefs about Homeless People

Bruce G. Link
Jo C. Phelan
Ann Stueve
Robert E. Moore
Michaeline Bresnahan
Elmer L. Struening

During the 1980s, and for the first time since the Great Depression, homeless people entered the daily experience of millions of Americans. Even those who had no personal contact with homeless people were exposed to extensive media coverage of homelessness. Americans were challenged, if not forced, to reflect on the phenomenon and to consider how they felt and what they thought.

Public attitudes about homelessness and homeless people have two important consequences. First, understandings about a problem shape how people behave toward those who embody the problem. For example, a widespread perception that homeless people are lazy will not only inhibit volunteerism and monetary donations, but will increase the likelihood that homeless people are exposed to such derisive comments as, "Get a job!" Second, the judgments of Americans influence public policies affecting homeless people. Whether a policy concerns restrictions on panhandling, construction of low-income housing, or the involuntary commitment of people to mental hospitals, public support must make it politically feasible and morally legitimate. While media reports and highly vocal constituencies are influential, particularly when a social problem is first being defined, in the long run an accurate understanding of broader public opinion helps policy makers achieve some sustainable balance of what is rational, humane—and popular.

For these reasons, we conducted a comprehensive and systematic survey of American attitudes, beliefs, and feelings about homelessness and homeless people during the fall of 1990.[1] In this chapter, we relate Americans' answers to the following questions: Who are the homeless? What are homeless people like? What causes them to become homeless? How do they make you feel? What should be done about homelessness? What can you do? Taken together, the answers describe homelessness and homeless people as understood by the American public. In the results section, we briefly discuss the data from our survey relevant to each question. Because our comprehensive survey was conducted in 1990, and because changes in attitudes toward homeless people are a much-debated topic, we also consider trends in public attitudes toward homeless people.

METHOD

We collected our data through telephone interviews. To select individuals to be interviewed, we used a random-digit-dialing technique in which telephone numbers are selected by creating sequences of random digits. This allows telephone numbers to be picked at random and ensures that the sample includes unlisted as well as listed numbers. Once a number was reached, a respondent was randomly selected from among the adult members of the household. These randomization techniques help assure that our findings are based on a representative sample of American adults.

Telephone interviews averaging 40 minutes in length were conducted with 1,507 adult residents of the continental United States between 1 August 1990 and 20 November 1990. The response rate was 65% among English-speaking persons and 63% if non-English-speaking respondents are included in the denominator used to calculate the response rate. The response rate was achieved with considerable effort. Once a respondent was identified within a household, it took an average of 9 calls to obtain an interview with that respondent, and 5% of the interviews required 33 or more calls. All initial refusals were recontacted in an attempt to obtain an interview; 140 respondents (9.3% of the sample) were converted refusals.

We weighted the results of the study to account for how we drew our sample. Because we wanted to ensure that our sample included an adequate number of people who had frequent contact with homeless people, we oversampled telephone exchanges in the 20 largest urban areas in the United States, and the results are weighted to take account of that oversampling. Also, because we sampled telephone numbers rather than individuals or households, we weighted the results to take into account the number of persons in a household and the number of telephone numbers within a household. Our weighting scheme further ensures that the results we report are representative of the adult population of the United States.

To check the representativeness of the sample, we compared it to the 1990 United States Census, with the following results: (1) our sample slightly overrepresents women, people between the ages of 25 and 54, and married people; (2) since the interview was conducted in English, it underrepresents Latinos; and (3) the biggest discrepancy concerns education—our sample overrepresents by 10% those with more than a high school education. Even so, there are no large discrepancies between our sample and the census due to nonresponse or omission of people without telephones, at least with regard to the variables we examined.

RESULTS

Who Are the Homeless?

A major feature of the debate about homelessness has concerned the characteristics of homeless people. Conservatives, for example, have criticized liberals, advocates, and the media for creating and perpetuating the "myth" that homeless people are normal, upstanding folks down on their luck.[2] What does the public think? Do Americans believe that homeless people represent a cross section of society, or is it believed that they come disproportionately from certain demographic groups? Are homeless people the sort who engender sympathy, compassion, and a helping response, or are they people whose attributes elicit quite the opposite?

To ascertain public beliefs about the characteristics of homeless people, we asked a series of questions: "In your opinion, out of 100 homeless adults, about how many do you think are mentally ill?" "How many do you think are addicted to drugs or alcohol?"—and so on. Our results reveal a strong tendency for the public to link homelessness to deviant status—the average respondent believes that 54.5% of homeless people are addicted to drugs or alcohol, that 45.1% have been in jail or prison, and that 31.5% are mentally ill. The public also views the problem as one largely afflicting racial minorities and those with little education. The average respondent believes that 43.3% of homeless people are African American, that 31.5% are Latino, and that only 38.2% have completed high school. Homeless people are also thought to be primarily male (59.0%) and unmarried (64.9%), and they are viewed as about equally split in proportions above and below 40 years of age. Together, these results suggest that when the American public is asked who the homeless are, the profile that emerges deviates greatly from that of the average (White) American, down on his or her luck.

What Are Homeless People Like?

Throughout the interview, respondents were asked a variety of questions eliciting their beliefs about what homelessness and homeless people are like. As would be expected given the results reported above, many Americans attribute undesirable qualities to homeless people in the aggregate. Sixty-five percent or more believe that the presence of homeless people threatens the quality of life in America's cities, hurts local businesses, spoils parks for families and children, and makes neighborhoods worse.[3] But at the same time, the public may not blame the undesirable effects of homelessness on homeless people themselves. For example, when asked whether most homeless people, if given the opportunity, could take care of a home and would respect their neighbor's property, three-quarters or more responded "probably" or "definitely true." Thus, it is possible that for many Americans, what is repellent about homelessness is seeing people in such destitute and disorderly conditions. If the conditions changed, the repugnant nature of the problem would change.

Consistent with this, most Americans were optimistic about the impact of policies to reduce homelessness. Asked about the likely effectiveness of several potential policy initiatives, more than two-thirds of our respondents rated building more low-income housing, raising the minimum wage, and establishing child-care programs so that homeless mothers could work, as likely to be very effective or somewhat effective.[4] It seems, then, that relatively few Americans have concluded that homeless people are hopeless ne'er-do-wells.

We also asked people about one important negative quality often attributed to homeless people: dangerousness. Most respondents did not endorse statements describing homeless people as more dangerous or violent than other people. Only between one-fourth and one-third of respondents agreed that homeless people are more dangerous than other people (31.3%), are more likely to commit violent crimes than other people (26.7%), or should be kept from congregating in public places in the interest of public safety (26%).[5] Still, these are significant minorities, and a majority (53.5%) endorsed at least 1 of these statements.

In sum, Americans do tend to link homelessness with disabilities, character flaws, and undesirable qualities. There are substantial minorities who view homeless people as dangerous, incompetent, or irresponsible. However, the majority of Americans appear optimistic about the tractability of the people and the problem.

What Causes Homelessness?

Of all the controversies surrounding homelessness, the most contentious concerns its causes. It is a pivotal question, since the answer—or what we believe to be the answer—shapes our ideas about what can effectively reduce homelessness and whether homeless people deserve our help and sympathy.

To assess public beliefs about the causes of homelessness, we asked respondents to what extent ("a lot," "some," "a little," or "not at all") they thought homelessness resulted from each of 13 possible causes. These included structural factors such as a shortage of affordable housing and government aid, inadequate schools, and an economic system that favors the rich over the poor; individual factors such as mental and physical illness, laziness and irresponsibility, and drug and alcohol abuse; and, finally, bad luck.

We found that the public believes many factors contribute to homelessness. In fact, each cause we proposed was perceived to contribute "a lot" or "some" to homelessness by a majority of respondents. Moreover, both structural and individual causes were assigned important roles.

Among the specific causes we proposed, respondents assigned the most importance—by a wide margin—to drug and alcohol abuse: 90.8% thought these problems contributed a lot or some to homelessness. Next to drug and alcohol abuse, structural factors concerning housing (81.7%), the economic system (79.1%), and a lack of government aid (73.8%) were viewed as the most important causes. However, closely following these structural factors was irresponsible behavior on the part of the homeless themselves (72.1%). These findings suggest that the American public shares the view of most scholars that the causes of homelessness are complex and include both structural and individual factors (see Chapter 3).

How Do Homeless People Make You Feel?

Feelings evoked by homeless people are another critical aspect of public consciousness. Potentially, these emotions are more important in motivating public reactions to homelessness and homeless people than are more reasoned evaluations.

The mass media have asserted that public sentiment toward homeless people is characterized by "compassion fatigue." That is, initial feelings of compassion have yielded to indifference or outright hostility toward homeless people.[6] However, the compassion-fatigue argument is based on impression and anecdote rather than systematically acquired evidence.

Contrary to the compassion-fatigue argument, a vast majority of our respondents endorsed feelings of sadness and compassion for homeless people (85.8%) and said they feel angry that so many are homeless in a country as rich as the United States (88.9%). Further, most (76.8%) reported feeling no less compassion than previously.[7]

But these feelings of compassion did not stand alone. Only 34.6% agreed with the statement, "When you think about a homeless person, the only feeling you ever have is compassion." Other responses suggest limitations on the public's ability or willingness to empathize with homeless people. A significant minority of respondents (38.5%) agreed with the statement, "It is hard to understand how anyone could become homeless." Sixty-two percent said it is hard to imagine what homeless people do with all their free time, and 37.1% thought homelessness frees a person from wor-

ries that other people have about jobs and families. Thus, the public's feelings about homeless people are complex. While nearly all respondents indicated that they feel compassion, these sentiments frequently are alloyed with a distinct lack of empathy.

What Should Be Done?

Perhaps the bottom line in any assessment of public knowledge, attitudes, and beliefs is what people conclude should be done. Are there policies that the public would find intolerable? Are there any they strongly endorse? We assessed public opinion on two broad types of policy initiatives—interventions the federal government should pursue, and restrictions that might be placed on the behavior of homeless people.

The vast majority of respondents (73.4%) believed that the Bush administration was doing too little to help homeless people in the late 1980s, some thought the administration was doing the right amount, and only a tiny minority (2.1%) thought it was doing too much.

This assessment is consistent with responses to another set of questions that reveal just how important Americans consider the problem of homelessness to be. We asked our respondents whether reducing homelessness was more important, equally important, or less important than several other pressing national problems. On average, homelessness was deemed less important than dealing with the nation's drug problem, but it was given equal priority with cleaning up the environment, and given more importance than improving highways and bridges, strengthening the national defense, or reducing the national debt.

If the public thinks homelessness is an important problem about which too little has been done, what specifically does the public think the federal government should do? Of 7 options we provided, the most popular was for the federal government to offer free drug and alcohol treatment; 83.1% favored such a policy.[8] This was followed by building more shelters and other temporary housing (82.6%), building more public housing for poor people (78.9%), giving tax breaks to private developers to build housing for poor people (76.1%), giving rent subsidies to homeless people (73.3%), and raising the minimum wage (69.7%). The least popular option was for the federal government to spend more on welfare benefits for homeless people, but even this was endorsed by 54.4%.

At the same time, our respondents endorsed restrictions on the behavior of homeless people. Half thought that homeless people should not have the right to sleep overnight in public places like parks or bus and train stations (50.8%). A distinct majority thought that homeless people should not be allowed to set up tents or other temporary shelter in public parks (69.1%) or to panhandle in public places (69.9%).[9] (For a discussion of these legal issues, see Chapter 14.) The vast majority (86.6%) endorsed hospitalizing mentally ill homeless people, even against their will.

In sum, the American public views homelessness as an important problem and believes that too little was done by the Bush administration. They endorse both "structural" solutions focused on housing and income support as well as "individualistic" approaches focused on people's substance abuse and/or mental illness. A substantial majority support restrictive policies intended to control the public behavior of homeless people.

What Can You Do?

An obvious corollary to the question of what the federal government should do is the question of what individuals are willing to do. Are Americans willing to commit personal resources of time or money to reduce homelessness?

We asked respondents whether they personally would be very willing, somewhat willing, or not willing to do a number of things to reduce homelessness. A large majority (81.8%) said they would be very or somewhat willing to pay $25 a year more in taxes to reduce homelessness. Fewer, but still a majority (53.5%), were willing to pay $100 more. Many people also said they would be willing to volunteer 2 hours a month (84.6%), to have housing for homeless people in their neighborhood (76.6%), and to have a shelter for homeless people located near their home (73.6%). A large majority (81%) reported having donated food, money, or cloth-

ing during the past year to a charitable organization that helps homeless people. At the end of the interview, 18.3% of respondents spontaneously offered to donate their respondent fee of $10 to an organization devoted to helping homeless people. Thus, it seems that Americans agree not only hypothetically that homeless people should be helped in a variety of ways, but seek ways to contribute.

HAVE ATTITUDES TOWARD HOMELESS PEOPLE CHANGED?

Our portrait of public opinion is based on data collected in late 1990. The media have repeatedly asserted that "compassion fatigue" set in during the late 1980s and early 1990s, so it is important to ask whether our picture is still accurate. We are confident that it is, for when we examine empirical indicators of attitude, we find very little change—and none that supports the notion of compassion fatigue. For example, we tracked two critical issues through public opinion studies conducted between 1985 and 1994: willingness to have government spending increased (24 studies), and willingness to pay higher taxes to help homeless people (23 studies). We found no trend whatsoever; public opinion remained stable and strongly supportive of both proposals.[10]

Other evidence concerning attitude change comes from a 1995 nationwide study conducted by the Gallup Organization for the Los Angeles Mission. Although this study considered far fewer and different dimensions of public opinion than our study, the findings are consistent with it. Three of Gallup's findings warrant mention here. First, like our study, the Gallup study found that the public links homelessness to such stigmatized conditions as alcoholism and drug abuse. Gallup respondents rated alcoholism as just as important a cause of homelessness as a lack of affordable housing, and fully 75% believed that alcohol and drug treatment was very important in helping a homeless person become self-sufficient and productive. Second, and again similar to our findings, 86% of Gallup's respondents reported either a "great deal" or "some" sympathy for homeless people, as opposed to only 14% who indicated "little" or "none." Finally, Gallup asked respondents about their "level of sympathy compared to five years ago," and found that 58% felt the same, 31% felt "much more" or "a little more" sympathetic, and 10% felt "a little less" or "a lot less" sympathetic (these figures do not total 100% because of rounding). Thus, the Gallup study suggests that if public opinion changed between 1990 and 1995, it became somewhat more compassionate—not somewhat less.[11]

In sum, evidence suggests that public opinion has not changed markedly since late 1990. This being so, we feel confident in drawing conclusions about public sentiment from the results of our survey, which provides the most comprehensive data on public opinion about homelessness gathered to date.

CONCLUSION

Our most striking finding concerns the mixed sentiments of Americans regarding homelessness and homeless people. Viewed from one angle, the public appears concerned—even compassionate. An overwhelming majority saw homelessness as a significant social problem and stated that the Bush administration was not doing enough to end it. Many were willing to make personal commitments of time and money to help homeless people. Some spontaneously offered to donate their $10 respondent fee to an organization that helps the homeless. Most told us that the federal government should do things like build more housing for poor people and expand rent subsidies, and they believed that such policies would be effective.

Viewed from a different angle, however, public attitudes are not nearly so positive. Americans tend to associate the homeless population with other stigmatized groups—they estimate that a large proportion of homeless people abuse drugs and alcohol, are mentally ill, or have been in jail. In the public's estimation, the most im-

portant cause of homelessness is drug and alcohol abuse; and closely related, the public perceives irresponsible behavior more generally to be a leading cause.

Further, many people agreed with statements that indicate a lack of sympathy for the circumstances of homeless people: a majority agreed that homeless people have a lot of free time, and over a third thought that homelessness relieved people from worries about jobs and family. Most agreed that the presence of homeless people makes neighborhoods worse, spoils parks for families and children, and threatens the quality of urban life. A majority approved of restrictions on such survival strategies as sleeping overnight in public places, panhandling, and erecting temporary shelters in parks.

It seems, then, that as in other matters where self-control and individual responsibility appear in doubt, or where public order is threatened, Americans are simultaneously sympathetic and judgmental, compassionate and admonitory. While the public wants something done, consistent with America's long history of impulses to both help and control, public opinion is compatible with policies of both sorts.

However, some policy makers seem to believe that order and discipline are all the public wants, a perception fueled by the lack of widespread resistance to public order initiatives like antibegging and anticamping laws (see Chapter 14), and by the unsubstantiated but nearly unanimous assertion in media accounts that American compassion has been fatigued. But as our findings show, compassion fatigue is mere surmise; in fact, Americans are willing to spend more money and pay more taxes to address the problems of homeless people. Americans do want greater public civility, but it is simply wrong to conclude that repressive policies are the only ones sufficiently consistent with public opinion to be morally legitimate and politically viable.

CHAPTER 14

Municipal Regulation of the Homeless in Public Spaces

Harry Simon

Over the past decade, the increased presence of homeless people in the public spaces of American cities has engendered bitter legal controversy. As shantytowns have popped up in Los Angeles, Miami, Dallas, Atlanta, and New York, among other cities, and as citizens have become fed up with being hassled for spare change and confronting the squalor of encampments of "filth[y], flea infested, disease ridden people," city councils and county supervisors have passed laws against begging and against camping and sleeping in public places. In response, advocates for homeless people have challenged these as unlawful manifestations of official desires to drive the homeless from public view.[1]

These are high-stakes legal battles. Aggressive enforcement of public-order laws can force homeless people to choose between incarceration and banishment. In Sparks, Nevada, a homeless man was sentenced to six months in jail under an antibegging ordinance for standing by the side of the road with a sign that read, "Homeless vet will work for food—God bless you." Over a 6-month period in 1988, San Diego police cited 1,705 people in the city's downtown area under a state law that bans lodging in public or private places without permission. During that same period, 247 people were jailed in San Diego County on the same charge.

In city after city, municipal decisions to use criminal sanctions to protect public spaces have come into conflict with efforts by civil rights advocates to prevent the criminalization of homelessness. Ironically, cities traditionally identified as liberal or progressive have seen some of the most bitter struggles. In Santa Monica, California, the city council fired longtime city attorney Robert Myers over his refusal to draft and enforce ordinances against camping in public places and feeding homeless people in city parks. In San Francisco and New York, recent mayoral candidates won election based, in part, upon promises to get tough with the homeless. San Francisco's Mayor Frank Jordan's Matrix program focused considerable police resources on citing homeless individuals for a variety of petty offenses. Between August 1993, when Matrix was initiated, and the end of 1995, when newly elected Mayor Willie Brown formally abolished it, over 30,000 citations were issued for 5 "quality of life" crimes: public drinking, littering or urinating in public, blocking sidewalks, camping in city parks, and sleeping in city parks. Ironically, during Brown's first month in office (January 1996), more citations for public drinking (1,200) were issued than at any time during Jordan's tenure, and in January and February 1996, the number of citations issued for the 5 offenses was greater than in the same months of the previous year, when Jordan was in office. Far more citations for sleeping and camping in parks were issued under the "more liberal" Brown regime (144) than a year earlier under Jordan (89).[2]

CONCERNS PROMPTING OFFICIAL CRACKDOWNS ON HOMELESS PEOPLE

Advocates of such stringent policies have justified them in several ways. They have described how the use of public spaces by the homeless can adversely affect the quality of urban life:

Each spring, the army [of homeless people] migrates to the parks. . . . Sandboxes become urinals. Swings are broken. Every park bench seems to be owned by a permanently curled-up dozing alcoholic or perhaps a street schizophrenic. When the cycle is complete, the community withdraws, serious drugs and criminals move in, and you have what Los Angeles and Washington, DC, are now calling "dead parks."[3]

Defending San Francisco's Matrix program, city officials described appalling conditions in and around encampments of homeless people:

Civic Center Plaza provides a graphic example of . . . refuse problems. The above-ground air vents have been used as toilets by plaza residents. . . . The plaza has been infected with fleas, lice, mice and rats as a result of discarded food and garbage. A gardener in Civic Center has spent his first three hours each day cleaning before he can begin gardening. Each day the encampment existed he found broken glass in the Plaza.[4]

City officials and academics alike have suggested that the presence of homeless people in public spaces may contribute to a cycle of deterioration that gives rise to criminal activity. In a particularly influential article, Professors James

Wilson and George Kelling compared "vagrants" to broken windows in a building. When a piece of property is left untended it "becomes fair game for people out for fun or plunder." By analogy, they argued that while the arrest of "a single drunk or a single vagrant who has harmed no one seems unjust . . . failing to do anything about a score of drunks or a hundred vagrants may destroy an entire community." Justifying a police round-up of homeless residents in Santa Ana, California, Police Chief Paul Walters explicitly referred to the "broken window" theory set forth by Wilson and Kelling (Kelling also used the analogy when he testified in the New York City subway case, discussed below).[5]

Advocates for the "communitarian movement," founded by Professor Amitai Etzioni of George Washington University, have defended laws against begging and sleeping in public as necessary to preserve the safety, civility, and attractiveness of public spaces. These advocates recall a time when "American urban centers . . . enjoyed proud reputations as homes of civilization, public spirit and diversity." In their view, the increasing presence of homeless people in public spaces constitutes a menace: "parks, plazas and streets where citizens from all walks of life once spent their leisure hours are being abandoned by local citizens and becoming the preserve of those on the margin of society."[6]

Concerns with image also have fueled municipal crackdowns on the homeless. Supporting a recent anticamping ordinance enacted by Santa Ana, California, Councilmember Lisa Mills admitted that she was concerned primarily with the image that Santa Ana's large and visible homeless population presented to residents of surrounding cities.[7]

Not surprisingly, cities that rely heavily on tourist trade have been very concerned about image and public order. Defending Miami's arrests of homeless residents, attorneys for the city observed: "It does not take a scholar to recognize that tourists do not want to pay money to vacation in Miami and be forced to walk through homeless encampments to enjoy a city park."[8] Thus, crackdowns on the homeless often accompany major events and conventions that draw out-of-town visitors to urban public areas. In Miami, police engaged in systematic sweeps of homeless areas prior to Pope John Paul II's visit to the city in 1987 and the Orange Bowl in 1988. In a study of this subject, the Atlanta Task Force for the Homeless noted a striking correlation between jailings of homeless persons on charges of disorderly conduct and the commencement dates of major conventions.[9]

In sum—and whether or not it represents real "compassion fatigue" (see Chapter 13)—many Americans are disturbed by the disorder associated with homelessness. Their frustration was stated bluntly almost a decade ago by a commentator in *Newsweek*:

> I am about to be heartless. There are people living on the streets of American cities, turning sidewalks into dormitories. They are called the homeless, street people, vagrants, beggars, vent men, bag ladies, bums. Often they are called worse. They are America's living nightmare—tattered human bundles. They have got to go. I don't know, exactly, when they got the *right* to live on the street. I don't know, exactly, when I *lost* the right to walk through town without being pestered by panhandlers. I do know I want them off my sidewalk. If you think I am heartless for saying that, can I send them to live on *your* sidewalk?[10]

These views are not universally shared by the public at large. A poll by *Parade* magazine in July 1993 found that 82% of respondents opposed barring homeless people from libraries, parks, mass transit, and other public places.[11] Nevertheless, the public's growing frustration with the disorder associated with homelessness is undeniable.

OBJECTIONS TO MUNICIPAL POLICING OF PUBLIC SPACES

Advocates for the homeless have vigorously challenged arrests of homeless people for petty offenses such as begging, loitering, and sleeping in public. By and large, critics of these laws have rejected the notion that they are defending the rights of poor people to be homeless or disorderly. Instead, they criticize what they see as official persecution of homeless persons based upon their poverty.

In attacking anticamping and antisleeping ordinances, critics note that in many American cities, the number of people who are homeless at any given time far exceeds the number of available shelter beds. When shelters turn away homeless people for lack of space, arresting the homeless for sleeping in public punishes them for conduct they are often helpless to avoid. In a recent law review article, Jeremy Waldron observed that combined restrictions on the use of private and public property can leave homeless men and women with literally no place where they may lawfully be:

> There is no place governed by a private property rule where [a homeless person] is allowed to be whenever *he* chooses, no place governed by a private property rule from which he may not at any time be excluded as a result of someone else's say-so. As far as being on private property is concerned—in people's houses or gardens, on farms or in hotels, in offices or restaurants—the homeless person is utterly and at all times at the mercy of others.[12]

Professor Waldron points out that homeless people are saved from criminalization of their very existence merely "by virtue of the fact that some land is held as collective property and made available for common use." As cities make it illegal to engage in essential life activities in public spaces, "what is emerging—and it is not a matter of fantasy—is a state of affairs in which a million or more citizens have no place to perform elementary human activities like urinating, washing, sleeping, cooking, eating and standing around."[13] Thus, while city officials assert that public parks and plazas are "inappropriate" places to sleep and live, critics of anticamping laws observe that those who lack the present means to put a roof over their heads have little choice.[14]

While some advocates have insisted that homeless individuals should be allowed to live wherever they choose as a matter of personal liberty, this position has not been widely adopted in the antihomelessness movement. By and large, advocates for the homeless and city officials have agreed that living on the streets is detrimental both to the homeless and to society at large. Most critics of camping bans have observed that, at any given time, large numbers of homeless people lack reasonable, safe, and legal alternatives to living in public spaces. This fact has led them to condemn camping bans as punishment for poverty rather than as assaults on liberty.

In addition, advocates for the homeless argue that as a practical matter, municipal anticamping laws are futile. At its most effective, critics argue, the enforcement of such laws simply shifts problems of homelessness to surrounding communities. (This concern led one city official to describe anticamping laws as "a leafblower approach" to law enforcement.[15]) Indeed, advocates have characterized citywide camping bans as "socio-economic cleansing," noting that these laws create an unhealthy competition among cities to be inhospitable to the homeless, each community trying to avoid becoming a refuge for homeless people driven from elsewhere.[16]

Events in Orange County, California, illustrate how passage of anticamping ordinances can create a domino effect. Immediately after city officials in Santa Ana announced that they were contemplating the adoption of a citywide anticamping law, the nearby cities of Fullerton and Orange enacted similar laws. Explaining this action, Fullerton city attorney Kerry Fox frankly admitted: "We're trying to protect ourselves so that when Santa Ana throws out their 1,300 [homeless people], they don't all come over here."[17] Four months later, with four neighboring cities within Orange County considering similar measures, advocates for the homeless filed lawsuits challenging all of these laws.

To critics of anticamping laws, arresting and jailing homeless people for the "crime" of using a blanket in a public park or leaving a bedroll under a bush is simply morally wrong. An appellate court that recently overturned one such law observed:

> It simply is not a crime to be unemployed, without funds, and in a public place. To punish the unfortunate for this circumstance debases society. The comments of Justice Douglas are still relevant, "How can we hold

our heads high and confuse with crime the need for welfare or the need for work?"[18]

Advocates scoff at the notion that prohibitions on sleeping in public spaces are not discriminatory because they apply to homeless and non-homeless people alike. A century ago, an Anatole France character quipped sarcastically that "the majestic equality of the laws . . . forbid rich and poor alike to sleep under bridges, to beg in the streets, and to steal their bread."[19] Similarly, critics of anticamping laws point out the apparent speciousness of the suggestion that a law that makes it a crime to use blankets in public spaces affects homeless and non-homeless persons equally. They insist that the constitutionality of anticamping laws can only be judged by measuring their effect on homeless people for whom they constitute significant restrictions, not on housed people for whom they are irrelevant.

Critics of begging laws have focused on the discriminatory nature of antipanhandling measures. While cities permit and even encourage organized charities to solicit funds on behalf of the destitute in public places, destitute persons who request funds on their own behalf are subject to arrest and incarceration. In the view of many advocates, the suggestion that it is somehow wrong to give funds directly to the homeless is a paternalistic assault on the autonomy of the homeless. They criticize the notion that there is something inherently immoral in allowing homeless people to use alms to meet their own perceived needs as they see fit. As one commentator noted:

> Street beggars may be rude and insolent, self-abusive and unwilling to seek the treatment they obviously need, but that does not give us "a license to dismiss" these individuals with whom we share the sidewalk. The fact that we as Americans have institutionalized our approach to every social problem affords a most comforting (and deceptive) rationalization for ignoring panhandlers. "How much better it would be to teach a person to fish so that he or she eats for a lifetime, rather than to give the person a fish to eat for a day," writes Catholic scholar Ed Wojcicki, "but not every moment is a teachable moment."[20]

Moreover, in the view of critics of anti-panhandling laws, the fact that some members of the public find the presence of beggars in public places to be disturbing is no basis for criminalizing begging, since beggars, as much as anyone else, are entitled to freedom of speech. One court recently observed:

> A peaceful beggar poses no threat to society. The beggar has arguably only committed the offense of being needy. The message one or a hundred beggars sends society can be disturbing. If some portion of society is offended, the answer is not in criminalizing these people, debtors' prisons being long gone, but addressing the root cause of their existence. The root cause is not served by removing them from our sight, however; society is then just able to pretend that they do not exist a little longer.[21]

Challenges to laws against begging and sleeping in public areas have been controversial, even among advocates for the homeless. Vivian Rothstein, the director of a social services agency that runs emergency shelters in Santa Monica, California, has accused critics of these laws of fighting for the rights of homeless people "to live marginalized lives in public spaces." She has suggested that legal challenges to such laws may actually act to "institutionalize homelessness."[22] To some, this fear has been substantiated by a court decision requiring the city of Miami to set aside certain "safe zones" where homeless people may stay without being arrested for living or sleeping in public spaces. Some advocates have complained that the prospect of homeless ghettos inherent in the Miami decision is worse than the official crackdown on the homeless that the court sought to alleviate. Proponents of the Miami decision have pointed out that the litigation has had beneficial results for Miami's homeless community. The court's decision prompted the City of Miami to raise funds to aid its homeless population, a step that it had resisted until that time. Soon after the "safe zones" decision, the city imposed a 1% tax on restaurant meals, designed to raise several million dollars for the construction of shelter for the homeless. In the end, neither city officials nor advocates for the homeless found creation of the safe zones proposed by the court to be acceptable. As a result, the city of Miami stopped arresting homeless persons for sleeping in public areas throughout the city.

POLICING THE HOMELESS IN PUBLIC SPACES

Spurred on by sympathetic court decisions, anti-homelessness advocates in California, Nevada, New York, New Jersey, Maryland, Oregon, Washington, Florida, and Alabama have brought numerous suits to challenge laws and official practices that regulate the use of public spaces in ways that disadvantage their homeless clients. Reflecting the political and social views of the judges involved, courts have been sharply divided over the legality of anticamping and antibegging laws. A federal trial court struck down, and an appeals court later upheld, a municipal law that made it a crime to beg in New York City's subways. A federal trial court struck down, and an appeals court later upheld, local regulations designed to keep the homeless out of a public library in Morristown, New Jersey. A California trial court upheld, an appeals court later struck down, and the state supreme court then reinstated, a municipal law that made it a crime punishable by six months in jail to use a blanket or sleeping bag in any public space in the city of Santa Ana, California.

While generally growing more punitive, official responses to homeless people's use of public spaces have varied. The cities of Fullerton, California, and Missoula, Montana, made it a jailable offense to sleep, to possess property, or simply to linger in every public space within their respective cities. The city council of Seattle imposed more limited restrictions, making it a misdemeanor to sit or lie on public sidewalks in downtown areas during daylight hours. As part of Baltimore's Downtown Partnership plan, official guides in that city's downtown district urge homeless people to move along. El Cajon, California, created a "superblock" district covering that city's downtown and civic center, where camping is strictly prohibited.

Official responses to begging have varied as well. Officials in New York and San Francisco have enforced laws that make it a crime for beggars to solicit money from strangers in all public places under any circumstances. Seattle and Atlanta have prohibited only aggressive or coercive panhandling. Las Vegas, Nevada, has sought to prohibit begging on private property; near vehicles, bus stops, and automatic teller machines; and in those areas of the city most frequented by tourists.

The law regarding official efforts to regulate public spaces is in a state of flux, and it is unclear whether city officials or the homeless targets of these laws ultimately will prevail. However, two examples usefully illustrate the complexity of the legal and social questions underlying these conflicts. For the past six years, city officials in Santa Ana, California have been locked in an unresolved struggle with advocates for the homeless over that city's efforts to clear homeless people from public spaces. In the late 1980s and early 1990s, city officials in New York experienced both triumphs and setbacks in their efforts to crack down on panhandling. The remainder of this chapter describes the uneven course of these efforts to regulate the conduct of homeless people in public spaces.

The Struggle over Santa Ana's Homeless

Events in Santa Ana provide an extreme example of the conflicts that can arise when public opinion turns against the homeless.

Santa Ana is the county seat of Orange County, California, a county with a politically conservative, affluent population and the second highest housing costs in the nation. Like the rest of California, Orange County suffered from the recent recession, and now struggles with the uncertainties of its highly publicized bankruptcy; in recent decades, however, the county has experienced explosive growth. Over the past 30 years, the county's orange groves and farms have yielded to corporate headquarters and multi-million-dollar residences.

Santa Ana has not enjoyed the newfound affluence of other parts of Orange County.

While corporations have flocked to the nearby cities of Irvine, Costa Mesa, and Newport Beach, office buildings lie vacant on Santa Ana's Main Street. Santa Ana suffers from gang violence and elevated high school dropout rates. A conservative, White-majority city council governs Santa Ana's increasingly Hispanic population. As homelessness has worsened in Orange County, Santa Ana has developed its greatest concentration. More specifically, the homeless have tended to concentrate in Santa Ana's Civic Center, near the government agencies and social services upon which they depend.

Federal, state, and local officials—city councilmembers, county supervisors, judges, attorneys, and policemen—all work in the Civic Center and encounter homeless people on a daily basis. The reaction of these public employees to the homeless has become increasingly negative, and city officials have been determined to clear the homeless out. Homeless advocates, alarmed at the prospect that the homeless may be driven from Santa Ana entirely, have fought city officials at every turn. The result has been a bitter struggle that shows no signs of abating in the near future.

In the summer of 1988, city officials formed a Vagrancy Task Force to implement city council policy that "vagrants are no longer welcome in the City of Santa Ana." The stated mission of this task force was "to move all vagrants and their paraphernalia out of Santa Ana by continually removing them from places that they are frequenting in the city, such as Civic Center, Center Park, the mission, the Hospitality House on the east side of town, and other City facilities which offer refuge to them."[23] To carry out this plan, the Vagrancy Task Force recommended that city officials put pressure on charitable organizations to end distribution of free food to the homeless, leave sprinklers running for extended periods on public land, and conduct sweeps through city parks to confiscate and destroy bedrolls and other property of the homeless found there. Litigation resulting from Santa Ana's property confiscations resulted in a settlement under which the city agreed to store and safeguard property found on public land.

Soon after this settlement agreement was signed, Santa Ana officials adopted new methods to accomplish their ends. On the evening of August 15, 1990, Santa Ana police officers conducted Operation Civic Center. In the course of 3 hours, police arrested 63 homeless individuals in the Civic Center on a variety of minor charges, including littering, jaywalking, and destroying vegetation. Police officers stationed atop buildings in the Civic Center spotted homeless individuals with binoculars and radioed their locations to officers on the ground. Officers on the ground arrested homeless individuals, handcuffed them, and drove them to a nearby stadium for booking and fingerprinting. At the stadium, police officers used markers to write numbers on the arms of the arrestees and chained them to benches for up to six hours without food or water. Finally, the police filed their captives into vans, drove them to the edge of the Central Command Area of the Santa Ana Police Department, and unloaded them.

At the conclusion of a 7-day hearing on the events surrounding these arrests, Judge Barbara Tam Nomoto dismissed criminal charges against 28 defendants arrested during Operation Civic Center. The court concluded that in conducting the operation, the Santa Ana Police Department illegally targeted the homeless. Judge Nomoto found it inconceivable that the method of arrest used in Operation Civic Center would be conventional for a person whose only offense was jaywalking or dropping a match, a leaf, or pieces of paper. In civil litigation arising from this same mass arrest, the city of Santa Ana agreed to entry of an order restraining city officials from taking individual or concerted action to drive homeless individuals from Santa Ana and paid more than $400,000 to homeless individuals arrested during the sweep.

Following these rulings, homeless residents of Santa Ana erected a tent city in the Santa Ana Civic Center. In response, the city council made it a crime punishable by six months in jail to erect or maintain tents or other structures, to use sleeping bags and blankets, to possess property or to live temporarily outdoors in any public space within the city. At that time, according to the city's own statistics, Santa Ana had a population of 3,000 homeless people and 332 available shelter beds. Shelter providers later testified that they were turning away homeless people on a daily basis.

In the fall of 1992, at the insistence of city officials, homeless residents took down the tents and structures they had erected in the Civic Center. Police noted that the numbers of homeless in the Civic Center decreased dramatically. In January and February 1993, the police began to enforce the anticamping law, issuing more than 100 citations to homeless people found using blankets and sleeping bags on public land.

At a hearing on the legality of Santa Ana's anticamping law, Judge James Smith admitted that he and his fellow judges had met to discuss the problem of the homeless in the Santa Ana Civic Center. (In fact, at one time, the presiding judge of the Orange County Superior Court threatened to issue his own anticamping order to alleviate the judges' concerns about the use of the Civic Center.) After considering the arguments of homeless advocates, Judge Smith upheld the anticamping ordinance. Addressing the potential impact of the ordinance on Santa Ana's homeless population, Judge Smith concluded:

> This has an impact on people who want to establish housekeeping in a sense in a public place. If you don't want to establish housekeeping in a public place, you're not impacted by this statute. If you do, you are. If you want to define yourself as homeless because that's your preference, then we are impacting the homeless, or the City of Santa Ana is impacting the homeless through this statute.[24]

However, the city's victory was short-lived. The homeless appealed Judge Smith's ruling, and three months later the California Court of Appeal enjoined the city from enforcing its ordinance while it considered the appeal. In February 1994, the court of appeal struck down Santa Ana's anticamping law. The court concluded that the ordinance was "a transparent manifestation of Santa Ana's policy, adopted five years ago, to expel the homeless." After recounting in detail "the history of the city's war on its own weakest citizens," the court invalidated the ordinance on various constitutional grounds.[25]

Citing the federal court decision in the Miami "safe zones" case, the California Court of Appeal held:

> The camping ordinance leaves persons "no place where they can be without facing the threat of arrest." Given the vast number of homeless individuals and the disproportionate lack of shelter space, the [homeless] truly have no place to be. Simply put, as in some vintage oater, petitioners are to clear out of town by sunset; and that, of course, is what the ordinance is all about, a blatant and unconstitutional infringement of the right to travel.[26]

The court of appeal also concluded that the ordinance unlawfully criminalized the status of homelessness, in violation of constitutional guarantees against cruel and unusual punishment. The court observed that "the camping ordinance, if allowed to stand, would turn the county jail into a poor house, and thus . . . destroy liberty. Punishment for poverty—which the camping ordinance surely is—is cruel and unusual punishment."[27]

In May 1994, the California Supreme Court granted review of this decision, an opportunity that attracted the attention of advocates on both sides of the issue. A number of conservative groups, including the Pacific Legal Foundation, the American Alliance for Rights and Responsibilities, and the Criminal Justice Legal Foundation, joined more than 90 city attorneys from localities throughout California to urge the state's supreme court to uphold Santa Ana's ordinance. The United States Justice Department, 3 retired justices of the state supreme court, more than 40 professors of constitutional law, and a coalition of religious, mental health, child welfare, and homeless advocacy groups urged the court to strike down the camping ban.

In April 1995, the California Supreme Court handed advocates for the homeless a stinging defeat. By a vote of six to one, the court upheld Santa Ana's law. Writing on behalf of the majority, Justice Marvin Baxter concluded that there is no "constitutional mandate that sites

on public property be made available for camping to facilitate a homeless person's right to travel, just as there is no right to use public property for camping or storing property."[28] While the majority recognized that Santa Ana's law would have the effect of "deterring travel by persons unable to afford or obtain other accommodations," the court found that this "incidental impact" on the rights of homeless persons did not justify striking down Santa Ana's camping ban.[29]

In a lone dissent from this decision, Justice Stanley Mosk concluded:

> Although a city may reasonably control the use of its parks and other public areas, it cannot constitutionally enact and enforce an ordinance so sweeping that it literally prevents indigent homeless citizens from residing in its boundaries if they are unable to afford housing and unable to find a space in the limited shelters made available to them. The City cannot solve its "homeless problem" simply by exiling large numbers of homeless citizens to neighboring localities.[30]

This ruling notwithstanding, the struggle between city officials and homeless advocates in Santa Ana is far from over. Advocates may seek to relitigate these same issues within the federal court system, where legal challenges to anticamping laws have been more successful. In addition, each homeless defendant charged with violating Santa Ana's camping ban is entitled to a jury trial over the issue of whether his or her violation of the law was prompted by economic necessity. While local officials have insisted that "cost is not an issue" in prosecuting these cases, Orange County's recent bankruptcy may make serious efforts to enforce this law impossible.[31]

In the meantime, the presence of homeless people in Santa Ana's public spaces continues to be a source of tension between public officials and homeless advocates. While the parties continue to argue over the city's power to drive its homeless residents from public spaces, the underlying message of this litigation is plain: the city will never escape from the negative consequences of having homeless people living in its parks and plazas until something tangible is done to solve the problem of homelessness. In public hearings over a second anticamping ordinance, city officials reluctantly admitted as much. Former mayor Daniel Young described the city's ongoing litigation over these issues as "a wake-up call to this Council that we need to look at our policies. We're going to see litigation forever and ever, and we need to see if maybe there is now time and opportunity for a better solution."[32] As a first step, city officials proposed to spend more than $300,000 to build shelter for the homeless as part of a coordinated, countywide approach to dealing with problems of homelessness.

New York City's
Battle against Panhandlers

The city of New York has engaged in a similar battle with advocates for the homeless over the presence of beggars in the city's public spaces. A high-profile campaign to drive beggars and panhandlers from the city's subways and bus stations has met with success, while more discreet efforts to move beggars along on city streets have been declared illegal.

In 1988, the New York City Transit Authority initiated a study of "quality of life" problems experienced by riders in the huge and ancient New York City subway system.[33] Those surveyed identified the presence of beggars in the subways as a serious problem—they felt that beggars pervaded the system and that their presence contributed to the respondents' perception that the subway was fraught with hazard. Two-thirds of the riders surveyed stated that they had been intimidated into giving money to beggars.

In the fall of 1989, the transit authority commenced Operation Enforcement, a program designed to end begging and panhandling in the subways. The transit authority distributed 1.5 million pamphlets warning that anyone caught panhandling in the system would be subject to arrest, fine, and ejection. Simultaneously, the city put up 15,000 posters in the system containing the same warning.

The transit authority allowed charities to solicit money for charitable causes in certain designated areas of subway stations. In a lawsuit filed against the transit authority, homeless advocates argued that beggars should be afforded the same rights.

Judge Leonard Sand, who heard the case, agreed with them:

> Both solicitors for organized charities and beggars approach passers by, request a donation, and perhaps explain why they want money. The conduct of both types of solicitors, as well as what they actually say, may often be quite similar. Although the beggar's entreaties may be more personal, emotionally charged, and highly motivated, the substance is in essence a plea for charity.[34]

In addition, Judge Sand recognized that the information conveyed by begging can convey a powerful, if disturbing, message about the plight of the poor:

> The simple request for money by a beggar or panhandler cannot but remind the passerby that people in the city live in poverty and often lack the essentials for survival. Even the beggar sitting in Grand Central Station with a tin cup in his hand conveys the message that he and others like him are in need. While often disturbing and sometimes alarmingly graphic, begging is unmistakably informative and persuasive speech.[35]

In contrast, the court of appeals that reviewed Judge Sand's opinion viewed begging in the subway as "a menace to the common good."[36] Two of the three judges who considered the appeal concluded that begging from "captive" passengers in the close confines of the subway system amounted to nothing less than an assault. They viewed the begging prohibition as a necessary measure to protect "literally millions of people of modest means, including hard-working men and women, students, and elderly pensioners who live in and around New York City and who are dependent upon the subway for the conduct of their daily affairs."[37]

The court rejected the argument that the city's differential treatment of beggars and private charities was unfair. First, there was no evidence that passengers considered solicitations from private charities to be a nuisance. In addition, the court's decision reflected the well-entrenched notion that while charitable solicitation is virtuous, begging is base: "while there can be no doubt that giving alms is virtuous, there can also be no doubt that the virtue is best served when it reflects an 'ordered charity.'"[38]

While the court permitted city officials to punish begging in its subway system, they were not allowed to punish the same conduct above ground.[39] In invalidating the state's antibegging law, the federal trial court and the court of appeals recognized the obvious distinction between begging in the subways and on the streets: pedestrians on the streets, unlike passengers in a subway or bus terminal, are free to leave. However, both courts rejected the suggestion, made by the court of appeals in the subway begging case, that the mere act of begging constitutes a "menace to the common good." Echoing Judge Sand's decision, the courts recognized that begging sends the message that social and economic conditions have deteriorated to the point where many people are unable to support themselves and must rely upon charity to survive.

Both courts were troubled by the unfairness of singling out homeless beggars for special punishment. At trial, Judge Robert Sweet noted:

Walking through New York's Times Square, one is bombarded with messages. Giant billboards and flashing neon lights dazzle; marquees beckon; peddlers hawk; preachers beseech; the news warily wraps around the old Times Building; and especially around holidays, the Salvation Army band plays on. One generally encounters a beggar too. Of all these solicitations, though, the only one subject to a blanket restriction is the beggar.[40]

Judge Sweet rejected the notion that giving to charities designed to aid the homeless is legally different from giving alms directly to homeless persons who ask for help themselves. Both are charitable acts intended to provide someone with food, clothing, or shelter. In the words of Judge Sweet, giving directly to the beggar "just saves on administrative expenses."[41]

Both courts rejected the city's argument that the begging prohibition was necessary to preserve order in the city. The court of appeals dismissed as "ludicrous" the city's suggestion that only the antibegging law "stands between safe streets and rampant crime in the city."[42] While Judge Sweet admitted that begging has long been viewed as "the archetypical expression of disorder," he observed that "suppressing speech and conduct deemed contrary to society's sense of order merely masks the underlying disorder" inherent in the growing presence of homeless beggars.[43]

The decisions in these cases reflect a deep division over government efforts to shield "normal" members of the general public from encounters with the homeless. In upholding the ban on begging in the subways, the federal court of appeals sought to protect passengers using the New York transit system from conduct that riders found to be intimidating, threatening, and harassing. In striking down New York State's generalized criminalization of begging, the federal courts sought to ensure that government officials did not attempt to preserve public order by criminalizing homeless beggars and driving them from public view. The inherent tension between these two goals makes continued conflict over these issues inevitable.

CONCLUSION

The increasing presence of homeless people in public spaces has led to acrimonious conflict between advocates for the homeless and municipal officials. Local officials correctly perceive that homelessness has begun to adversely affect not merely the homeless, but society at large.

Regulating the conduct of individuals on public land is necessary to preserve the civility of those common areas that all citizens enjoy. On the other hand, broad prohibitions on the use of public lands by homeless people can prove futile; they simply shift the homeless to other areas, where the same complaints inevitably arise. The strategy is akin to rearranging the deck chairs on the *Titanic*. In the long run, municipal regulation of public places can satisfy neither the needs of the homeless nor the concerns of the public over the disorder associated with homelessness. Until society alleviates homelessness, the continued occupation of public spaces by the homeless will continue to afflict our cities—with all the squalor, misery, and conflict it entails.

CHAPTER 15

The Federal Response: The Stewart B. McKinney Homeless Assistance Act

Maria Foscarinis

INTRODUCTION

The Stewart B. McKinney Homeless Assistance Act was the first major federal legislative response to homelessness and, to date, it has been the only one. Enacted on July 22, 1987, the McKinney Act marked the federal government's recognition that homelessness is a national problem requiring a federal response. Initially, it authorized just over $1 billion, to be spent over a period of two years, to fund state, local, and private nonprofit programs to aid homeless people. Since that time, it has been extended and expanded four times, with Fiscal Year 1995 funding at over $1.4 billion.

The McKinney Act established 15 new federal funding programs. In addition, it amended seven existing programs to include, improve, or expedite access for homeless people. As omnibus legislation, the McKinney Act established or affected programs within eight different federal agencies. In addition, it created a new, independent federal agency, the Interagency Council on the Homeless, to oversee federal aid to homeless people.

The McKinney Act was intended to provide emergency relief to the nation's homeless population. The statute noted that "the Nation faces an immediate and unprecedented crisis" and stated as one of its purposes the intention to "to meet the critically urgent needs of the homeless of the Nation." Efforts by advocates to move beyond the emergency relief provided by the McKinney Act to longer-term solutions are now underway. These efforts have found some allies within the Clinton administration, and before the 1994 election, in Congress, as well.[1]

The 1994 election and the resulting shift in the composition of Congress presents some serious threats to the continuation of the McKinney Act programs, however, along with new challenges in moving forward an agenda for long-term solutions to homelessness. Additionally, proposals now being made or considered in Congress could alter the existing programs significantly.

BACKGROUND

In the early 1980s, as homelessness increased dramatically across the country, the response was primarily local. The position of the Reagan administration was that homelessness was not a federal concern.[2] Indeed, the Federal Inter-agency Task Force on Food and Shelter for the Homeless, created in October 1983, based its charter on the assumption that homelessness was a local problem and that new federal programs were not the answer. Instead, the role of the task force was to respond to requests by communities for information on obtaining surplus federal resources such as blankets, cots, and clothing.[3]

In 1983, in response to testimony that homelessness was becoming a serious problem nationally, Congress appropriated a total of $140 million in federal funds for emergency food and shelter.[4] This appropriation, made within an existing disaster relief program, was administered by the Federal Emergency Management Agency and was not accompanied by any authorizing statute: no new law or program was created. In 1984, an additional $70 million was appropriated, extending funding through Fiscal Year 1985.[5]

In 1986, comprehensive federal legislation to address homelessness was introduced in both houses of Congress. Known as the Homeless Persons' Survival Act, the proposed legislation was based on measures drafted by a working group of advocates; it proposed emergency relief, preventive measures, and long-term solutions. Advocates pressed for passage of the entire act, while also lobbying for adoption of its component sections. Consistent with this strategy, small pieces of the larger bill were enacted into law in October 1986.[6]

This new law, the Homeless Eligibility Clarification Act, primarily reformed existing laws. The act removed permanent address requirements and other barriers to participation by homeless people in five existing aid programs: Supplementary Security Income, Aid to Families with Dependent Children, Veterans benefits, food stamps, and Medicaid. It amended the Food Stamp program to allow the purchase of prepared meals served by nonprofit providers. In addition, the Homeless Eligibility Clarification Act created a prerelease program designed to help prevent institutionalized indigent people from becoming homeless.[7]

Also in 1986, the Homeless Housing Act was passed, which created 2 small funding programs: an Emergency Shelter Grants (ESG) program, funded at $10 million, and a transitional housing demonstration program funded at $5 million, with funds distributed in 1987. Both were to be administered by the Department of Housing and Urban Development (HUD). The ESG program allocated funds to states, cities, and localities according to a specified formula; recipients could use their allocations to provide shelter themselves, or they could distribute the funds to nonprofit shelter providers.[8] The transitional housing demonstration program distributed funds by HUD-sponsored competition to states, local governments, and nonprofits.[9]

During the winter of 1986–87, advocates mounted an intensive legislative campaign. Legislation introduced as part of that campaign by then-majority leader Tom Foley, and reflecting Title I of the earlier Homeless Persons' Survival Act, contained emergency relief provisions including shelter, transitional housing, mobile health care, and food. Following expedited legislative procedures, the Urgent Relief for the Homeless Act was passed by large, bipartisan majorities in both houses of Congress in the spring of 1987.[10] Following the death of Stewart B. McKinney, its chief Republican sponsor, the bill was renamed in his memory. On July 22, 1987, with an official White House statement of reluctance, President Reagan signed the Stewart B. McKinney Homeless Assistance Act into law.[11]

THE McKINNEY ACT

As originally enacted, the Stewart B. McKinney Homeless Assistance Act authorized expenditures just over $1 billion: $438 million for 1987 and $615 million for 1988. The amounts actually appropriated were substantially less: $350 million for 1987 (by supplemental appropriation) and $362 for 1988. In subsequent years, authorization levels and appropriations increased.[12] For Fiscal Year 1995, McKinney Act appropriations totalled over $1.4 billion. Tables 15.1 and 15.2 illustrate the changes in appropriations from 1987 to 1996.

TABLE 15.1

FISCAL YEAR 1987: MCKINNEY ACT AUTHORIZATIONS AND APPROPRIATIONS (IN MILLIONS OF DOLLARS)

Agency	Program	Authorized	Appropriated
FEMA	Emergency Food and Shelter	15	10
HUD	Emergency Shelter Grant	100	50
	Transitional Housing	80	65
	Permanent Housing	15	15
	Single-Resident-Occupancy	35	35
	Supplemental Assistance (SAFAH)	25	15
IA	Interagency Council	0.2	0.2
HHS	Primary Health Care	50	46
	Emergency Community Services Homeless Grant	40	36.8
	Mental Health Block Grant	35	32.2
	Mental Health Demonstration	10	9.2
DOE	Education of Homeless Children and Youth	5	4.6
	Adult Literacy	7.5	6.9
VA	Domiciliary Beds	20	1
TOTAL FOR FISCAL YEAR 1987		437.7	326.9

TABLE 15.2

FISCAL YEAR 1996: MCKINNEY ACT APPROPRIATIONS (IN MILLIONS OF DOLLARS)

Agency	Program	Appropriated
FEMA	Emergency Food and Shelter	100
HUD	Homeless Assistance Grants	823
DVA	Homeless Chronically Mentally Ill	40.5
	Domiciliary Care	41
DOE	Education for Homeless Children and Youth	23
	Adult Literacy	0
HHS	Health Care for the Homeless	65.4
	PATH	20
	ACCESS	17*
	Emergency Community Services Homeless Grant	0
	Family Support Centers	0
DOL	Homeless Veterans Reintegration Project	0
TOTAL FOR FISCAL YEAR 1995		1129.9

*Estimate. For Fiscal Year 1996, ACCESS was combined with several other mental health demonstration programs and did not receive a specific line-item appropriation. Final funding for the ACCESS program will be determined by the Substance Abuse and Mental Health Services Administration.

Title I: General Provisions

Title I of the McKinney Act includes a statement of six findings by Congress:

1. The Nation faces an immediate and unprecedented crisis due to the lack of shelter for a growing number of individuals and families, including elderly persons, handicapped persons, families with children, Native Americans, and veterans;

2. The problem of homelessness has become more severe and, in the absence of more effective efforts, is expected to become dramatically worse, endangering the lives and safety of the homeless;

3. The causes of homelessness are many and complex, and homeless individuals have diverse needs;

4. There is no single, simple solution to the problem of homelessness because of the different subpopulations of the homeless, the different causes of and reasons for homelessness, and the different needs of homeless individuals;

5. Due to the record increase in homelessness, States, units of local government, and private voluntary organizations have been unable to meet the basic human needs of all the homeless and, in the absence of greater Federal assistance, will be unable to protect the lives and safety of all the homeless in need of assistance; and

6. The Federal Government has a clear responsibility and an existing capacity to fulfill a more effective and responsible role to meet the basic human needs and to engender respect for the human dignity of the homeless.

Title I states the purpose of the act as follows:

1. To establish an Interagency Council on the Homeless;

2. To use public resources and programs in a more coordinated manner to meet the critically urgent needs of the homeless of the Nation; and

3. To provide funds for programs to assist the homeless, with special emphasis on elderly persons, handicapped persons, families with children, Native Americans, and veterans.

Title I provides the following definition of "homeless individual":

1. An individual who lacks a fixed, regular, and adequate nighttime residence; and

2. An individual who has a primary nighttime residence that is—

   A. Supervised publicly or privately operated shelter designed to provide temporary living accommodations (including welfare hotels, congregate shelters, and transitional housing for the mentally ill);

   B. An institution that provides a temporary residence for individuals intended to be institutionalized; or

   C. Public or private place not designed for, or ordinarily used as, a regular sleeping accommodation for human beings.

The statute specifies, however, that homeless individuals are eligible for assistance under the act only if they meet income eligibility requirements. This provision was intended to exclude individuals who might have income or assets that would ordinarily make them ineligible for assistance under federal antipoverty programs. The statute also specifically excludes imprisoned persons.

Title II: The Interagency Council on the Homeless

Title II establishes the Interagency Council on the Homeless as an independent entity within the executive branch of the federal government. As defined in the statute, this council is composed of the heads of 15 federal agencies, including 10 cabinet departments. Defined duties of the council include reviewing federal aid to homeless people; monitoring, evaluating, and recommending improvements to federal, state, local, and private programs to aid homeless people; and providing technical assistance to such programs. The act also requires the coun-

cil to prepare annual reports to the president
and to Congress, assessing the needs of homeless people, describing the activities of the federal government and of the council, assessing
the level of federal aid necessary, and specifying any recommendations for legislative and
administrative actions to meet those needs.

The statute requires the council to appoint
an executive director, and permits the appoint-
ment of additional staff. In addition, it terminates the Federal Interagency Task Force on
Food and Shelter for the Homeless (which had
previously existed within the Department of
Health and Human Services), designates the
council as its successor, and requires the transfer of records and other property from the task
force to the council.

Title III: The FEMA Emergency Food and Shelter Program

Title III authorizes and defines the emergency
food and shelter grants program within the Federal Emergency Management Agency (FEMA).
It requires the director of FEMA to establish a
national board to administer the program, and
specifies as members of the board the director
and representatives from six private organizations.[13] Localities designated by the national
board must create local boards, consisting of
representatives from the same organizations,
with the mayor or other head of local government in place of the FEMA director. Local
boards are charged with determining which local government or private nonprofit entity will
receive grants to provide services under the program.

Under the statute, the FEMA director must
award all funds appropriated by Congress for
the program to the national board, which must
then distribute them to local boards, which then
allocate them to local service providers. Funds
may be used for three purposes:

- To supplement and expand ongoing efforts
  to provide shelter, food, and supportive services to homeless people

- To fund more effective and innovative local
  programs

- To conduct minimum rehabilitation of existing mass shelters and feeding facilities

In addition, in its explanatory statement accompanying the McKinney Act, the congressional committee responsible for the act
encourages the national and local boards to prevent homelessness by providing rent and utility
assistance if more urgent needs are being met
by other resources in a community.

The statute sets short timetables for distribution of the funds: within 30 days of their appropriation by Congress, the FEMA director
must award funds to the national board, which
must disburse funds within 3 months of appropriation. Not more than 5% of total funds appropriated may be used for administrative costs.
The national board must establish written program guidelines, including methods for identifying localities with the highest need for
emergency food and shelter assistance and
methods for determining the amount and distribution to such localities. Overall, however,
the statute leaves much discretion to the board
in implementing the program.

Title IV: Housing Assistance

Title IV focuses primarily on emergency shelter and transitional housing; it also includes a
small program for permanent, single-room-occupancy housing. Title IV's programs are administered by HUD, which distributes funds to
states, local governments, and private nonprofits.

Subtitle A of Title IV stipulates that all
states, as well as larger cities and counties, must
prepare overall plans for addressing their region's
homelessness, as a condition of HUD's distribution of Title IV funds to any provider in the
jurisdiction.[14] These Comprehensive Homeless
Assistance Plans, which require HUD approval,
must describe the needs of the homeless population, existing resources, and strategies for using federal funds to meet those needs.

Subtitle B, the Emergency Shelter Grants
(ESG) Program, provides funds to cities, counties, and states, according to a formula based
on population and poverty (defined in another

federal statute).[15] The Homeless Housing Act had created a small ESG Program earlier; the McKinney Act incorporated and greatly expanded it. Recipients of ESG Program funds must meet a 50% matching requirement.[16] Local governments receiving these funds may distribute all or part of them to private nonprofit organizations assisting homeless people. ESG funds may be used for three purposes related to the provision of emergency shelter:

- To renovate or convert buildings to be used as emergency shelters

- To provide "essential services" including employment, health, drug abuse, or education services[17]

- To maintain and operate (but not to staff) shelter facilities

Subtitle C, the Supportive Housing Demonstration Program, provides funds for "supportive housing" for homeless families with children, deinstitutionalized people, people with mental disabilities, and "other handicapped homeless people." Supportive housing is defined as housing with "supportive services" that are designed to address the special needs of the homeless persons to be served by the project. The Supportive Housing Demonstration Program includes two parts. The first, transitional housing, is defined as housing primarily designed to serve deinstitutionalized and other mentally disabled homeless people and homeless families with children, and to facilitate their movement to "independent living" within "a reasonable amount of time." The second, "permanent housing for handicapped homeless people," is defined as community-based, long-term housing with supportive services.[18]

Funds for the Supportive Housing Demonstration Program are distributed by HUD directly to applicants following a national competition. Eligible applicants are states, cities, counties, tribes, and nonprofits; in the case of "permanent housing for handicapped homeless people," only states may apply, but they must transmit the funds to a private nonprofit to operate the project. Supportive Housing Demonstration Program funds may be used for the acquisition and/or the rehabilitation of buildings to provide supportive housing, for some of the operating costs of such housing, and for technical assistance to establish and operate supportive housing projects. The statute earmarks portions of the funds specifically for transitional housing projects serving homeless families with children, and for projects providing permanent housing for handicapped homeless people. Recipients must meet a 50% matching requirement.

Subtitle D, Supplemental Assistance for Facilities to Assist the Homeless, provides funds to states, cities, counties, tribes, and private nonprofit organizations for two main purposes. First, the assistance can be used to cover costs beyond what is provided under the ESG or Supportive Housing Demonstration Program, in order to meet the special needs of homeless families with children, or elderly or handicapped homeless people, or to facilitate the transfer and use of public buildings to assist homeless people. Second, the funds can be used to provide comprehensive assistance for "particularly innovative" programs to meet the immediate and long-term needs of homeless people through the purchase, lease, renovation, or conversion of facilities or the provision of supportive services. There is no requirement to provide matching funds.[19]

Subtitle E, Miscellaneous Provisions, provides assistance for moderate rehabilitation of single-room-occupancy dwellings for occupancy by homeless people. On the basis of a national competition, funds are distributed by HUD to applicants that best demonstrate need and ability to carry out a program. Local public housing authorities are eligible applicants. The subtitle limits per-unit costs to $14,000, plus the costs of meeting fire codes and other safety requirements.[20]

Title V: Identification and Use of Surplus Federal Property

Title V requires federal agencies to make suitable unused and underused federally owned buildings and land available to states, local governments, and private nonprofits for use at no cost as "facilities to assist the homeless." The Surplus Federal Property program amends existing law governing the use and disposition of unused or under-used federal property; in general, it grants priority to uses for homeless people. Property is made available by leases of at least one year.[21]

Title VI: Health Care for the Homeless

Title VI's Subtitle A establishes a grant program to provide for the delivery of health services to homeless individuals. Funds are distributed to successful applicants by the Secretary of Health and Human Services (HHS); eligible applicants are public and private nonprofits, who may provide services directly or through contracts. Health services are defined as primary health care and substance abuse services; grantees may provide mental health care at their option. Grantees must adhere to a defined set of requirements in providing health services to homeless people:[22] they must provide services without regard to ability to pay, and they may not impose any charge on homeless individuals with incomes less than the official poverty level. Federal funds must be matched at 25% of the grant, with some exceptions. The Secretary of Health and Human Services may use a portion of the funds to provide technical assistance to grantees.

Subtitle B, Community Mental Health Services, creates a block grant program under which HHS distributes funds to states.[23] States must use the funds to provide community mental health services to chronically mentally ill homeless people, including outreach, outpatient mental health services, referrals to necessary hospital, primary health and substance abuse services, case management, and supportive and supervisory services.[24] The statute limits states' administrative expenditures to 4% of their grant amount and contains a 25% fund-matching requirement.

Subtitle B also creates two demonstration programs. One funds projects to assure community-based mental health services to homeless individuals who are chronically mentally ill. The other provides grants to community-based public and private nonprofits to develop and expand alcohol and drug abuse treatment services for homeless people (see Chapter 17).

Title VII: Education, Training, and Community Services Programs

Title VII creates programs for the education of homeless adults and children, job training, and community services.

Subtitle A, Adult Education for the Homeless, creates a grant program to fund literacy education and skills training for homeless individuals. State educational agencies apply to the Secretary of Education for funds. Programs must include outreach and must be coordinated with existing community resources.

Subtitle B states that it is the "policy of Congress" that states must provide homeless children access to a free, appropriate public education, and that any residency requirements that may act as barriers to enrollment in school by homeless children must be reviewed and revised. Funds are also provided to states to carry out these policies, to establish an Office of Coordinator of Education of Homeless Children and Youth, and to develop and carry out a plan to ensure that homeless children have access to public school education, including school programs and services. Local educational agencies must comply with requirements to determine the best interests of each homeless child in making school placements and must ensure that records are transferred in a timely manner when a homeless child moves to a new school district. Subtitle B also creates a grant program to fund exemplary programs for homeless children and the dissemination of information about such programs. Finally, it requires the Secretary of Education to monitor compliance, report to Congress, and prepare a report on the number of homeless children in all states.

Subtitle C creates a demonstration program to fund job training projects for homeless people. Funds are distributed by the Secretary of Labor to eligible applicants, including public agencies, private nonprofits, and private businesses. Recipients must provide outreach and coordinate their efforts with other services for homeless people. Funds may be used for basic skills and literacy instruction, remedial education, job preparatory training, job search activities, and job counseling. The Secretary of Labor must evaluate each project annually and must report to the Interagency Council on the Homeless and to Congress. A grant program is also created to fund reintegration projects for homeless veterans, to be conducted directly by the Secretary of Labor or indirectly through a grant or contract.

Subtitle D, the Emergency Community Services Homeless Grant Program, creates a grant program administered by the Secretary of the Department of Health and Human Services to expand comprehensive services to homeless people, to provide assistance to homeless people in obtaining social and income support services, and to promote private-sector assistance to homeless people. States receive grants under the program according to a formula and must award them to community action agencies, organizations serving migrant farmworkers, and certain other groups. Ninety percent of funds must be awarded to groups already working to meet the critically urgent needs of homeless people. In the event a state does not apply, HHS must make grants directly to eligible organizations.[25]

Title VIII: Food Assistance for the Homeless

Title VIII's Subtitle A amends the Food Stamp Program. Eligibility is extended to doubled-up families.[26] The cap is raised on the excess shelter deduction,[27] which makes eligibility easier by excluding from an applicant's income any housing assistance payments made directly to providers of temporary housing without cooking facilities, such as welfare hotels. States are allowed to claim partial (50%) federal reimbursement for conducting outreach on the Food Stamp Program to homeless people. The Food Stamp Program is also required to expedite the processing of applications by households consisting of people who are homeless or at imminent risk of homelessness.

Subtitle B expands the Temporary Emergency Food Assistance Program (TEFAP), under which the Secretary of Agriculture distributes surplus commodities to the states,

by requiring that additional commodities be included and by allowing additional quantities to be distributed. States then distribute the commodities to needy individuals or to local organizations for distribution.

Title IX: Veterans' Provisions

This title simply extends the Veterans' Job Training Act. However, companion legislation to the McKinney Act required the Veterans Administration to fund the conversion of surplus space in VA hospitals and health facilities to provide beds for homeless veterans.[28]

MCKINNEY ACT AMENDMENTS
The 1988 Amendments

In 1988, Congress made relatively minor amendments to the McKinney Act. Among the more significant changes:

- Funds allocated under the Emergency Shelter Grant program could be used to prevent homelessness by providing financial assistance to families facing eviction or termination of utility services.

- Funds allocated under the Supportive Housing Demonstration Program could be used to provide employment assistance to residents of such housing.

- The matching requirement under the Health Care for the Homeless program was increased from one-quarter to one-third.

- Community Mental Health Services block grant funds could be distributed directly to public and private nonprofit entities if states failed to apply.

- Funds allocated under the Emergency Community Services Homeless Grant Program could be used to provide assistance to persons facing eviction, foreclosure, or termination of utility services.

The 1990 Amendments

In 1990, Congress amended the McKinney Act more significantly:

- The Emergency Shelter Grant program was amended with the addition of a 30% cap on use of funds for prevention of homelessness, and a requirement that shelters funded under the program meet minimum standards of habitability.

- The Supportive Housing Demonstration program was amended to allow use of funds for the construction of facilities for supportive housing, and to provide child care services.

- The Comprehensive Homeless Assistance Plan requirement was made part of a broader comprehensive housing assistance strategy ("CHAS") requirement, created by the 1990 National Affordable Housing Act, governing not only the McKinney Act emergency housing programs but other housing programs as well.

- Shelter Plus Care was created as Subtitle F within the Title IV emergency housing programs. The program provides housing assistance to homeless persons with disabilities, primarily persons who are seriously mentally ill, have chronic problems with drugs or alcohol (or both), or have acquired immunodeficiency syndrome (AIDS). Funds are distributed by HUD to state and local government applicants, which must supplement those funds with an equal amount of funds for supportive services to homeless persons assisted under the program. The program funds three kinds of housing assistance: rental assistance for units in the existing housing market;[29] moderate rehabilitation of single-room-occupancy units; and rental assistance for units in existing housing for elderly or disabled low-income people.

- The Surplus Federal Property program was amended to provide that properties may be deeded, as well as leased, to public and private nonprofits aiding homeless people.

- A new grant program was created within the Health Care for the Homeless program, to fund demonstration projects providing primary health care and outreach to children who are homeless or at imminent risk of homelessness.

- The Community Mental Health Services block grant program was given a new name—Projects for Assistance in Transition from Homelessness, or PATH—and amended to add minor renovation and other small housing costs as allowable uses of funds under the program.[30]

- The Education of Homeless Children and Youth provisions were strengthened significantly by specifying in greater detail actions required to be taken by state and local educational authorities to ensure access to public school education by homeless children; they also significantly increased authorizations and required state educational agencies to make grants to local educational authorities.

- The Job Training for the Homeless provisions were amended to include a section specifying that homeless persons are eligible for the Job Corps, an existing program under the Job Training Partnership Act, and providing that Job Corps centers serving homeless persons be residential and provide room and board.

- The Emergency Community Services Homeless Grant program was amended to include as an allowable use renovation of buildings in which to provide services.[31]

The 1992 Amendments

In 1992, Congress amended the shelter and housing provisions of the McKinney Act:

- Provisions requiring the involvement of homeless persons in the programs "to the maximum extent practicable" through employment, volunteer services, or otherwise were added to each of the programs in Title IV, as well as to the FEMA Emergency Food and Shelter program.

- A provision was added, requiring the participation of at least one homeless or formerly homeless individual on the policy-making board of each funding recipient.

- The Supportive Housing Demonstration Program was amended to include leasing, operating costs of supportive housing, and provision of supportive services (within or apart from supportive housing) as eligible uses of funds under the program.

- The single-room-occupancy housing program was amended to allow nonprofits to apply for funds under the program.[32]

- A new demonstration program was added to Title IV to fund "safe havens" for homeless persons "who, at the time, are unwilling or unable" to participate in mental health or other supportive service programs. Safe havens, described in the statute as "very low-cost housing," are facilities that provide 24-hour residence for unspecified duration, provide private or semi-private accommodations, and have an overnight occupancy limited to 25 persons. Funds may be used for acquisition, construction, renovation, or leasing of facilities; operating costs; outreach activities; and the provision of "low-demand" services and referrals for residents. Projects may not require residents to participate in services. Residents must pay an occupancy charge determined by formula; these payments may be specially held, to be applied toward their costs of moving into more permanent housing. Projects must meet a 50% matching requirement.

- Subtitle G was added to Title IV, creating a Rural Homeless Housing Assistance grant program, administered by HUD, to provide emergency assistance, homelessness prevention assistance, and assistance in obtaining access to permanent housing and supportive services. Through an application process, funds are distributed by HUD to local and county governments and to private nonprofits. The program requires a 25% match. Subtitle G also requires the Secretary of Agriculture to make available on a priority basis certain properties acquired through foreclosure[33] for use as transitional housing and turnkey housing (housing that the resident will eventually own) for homeless and other inadequately housed people.

- Appropriations for two programs—the mental health services demonstration program and the alcohol and drug abuse treatment demonstration program—were combined to fund a new, administratively created initiative, Access to Community Care and Effective Services and Supports (ACCESS). The new demonstration program awards grants to states to fund projects that integrate services—including shelter, food, clothing, and mental health care—for severely mentally ill homeless people (see Chapter 17).

The 1994 Amendments

In 1994, Congress amended the Education for Homeless Children and Youth provisions of the McKinney Act:

- Local flexibility in using McKinney Act education funds was increased.

- The application of the McKinney Act education provisions to preschoolers was clarified.

- Local educational authorities were required to comply with parents' wishes "to the extent feasible" in making school placement decisions.

- State and local educational authorities were required to coordinate with state and local housing authorities.

- McKinney Act education funds were to be made available for programs operating at religious facilities.

- The data-collection obligations of the states, requiring an estimate of the number of homeless children every three years, were loosened.

The Surplus Property Program was also amended:

- Military bases closed under base-closure laws were removed from the McKinney Act process.

- The Surplus Property Program was amended to remove bases closed under the base closure laws from the McKinney Act process. At the same time, a new law was enacted that created a process through which providers of services to homeless persons may apply to Local Redevelopment Authorities (entities created by the Base Closure Act to coordinate the conversion of closed bases) to use the property at closed bases.[34] Under the new law, Local Redevelopment Authorities are required to consider the interests of service providers in using base property for homeless persons in preparing conversion plans; these plans must be reviewed and approved by HUD.

Finally, the authorization for the PATH program (authorized by amendments in 1990) expired at the end of 1994. The program continued to operate in the following year, however, through a Fiscal Year 1995 appropriation.

RECENT AND PROPOSED CHANGES

In addition to changes made through amendments to the authorizing statute, some substantial changes to the McKinney Act were made through the appropriations process. As noted above, overall funding for the act increased significantly over the years, from $350.2 million appropriated for Fiscal Year 1987 to $1.49 billion appropriated for Fiscal Year 1995. Recently, however, overall funding has been cut, and some McKinney Act programs have had their funding eliminated (see Table 16.2 for comparison of Fiscal Year 1995 and Fiscal Year 1996 appropriations). In addition, some efforts have been made to repeal or narrow certain McKinney Act programs, but to date, these have not been successful.

Notably, beginning in Fiscal Year 1994, the Interagency Council on the Homeless lost its funding; however, it was made part of the White House's Domestic Policy Council, arguably boosting its stature.[35] In addition, beginning in Fiscal Year 1995, funding for the Job Training for the Homeless program was ended. However, the Congressional committee responsible for

overseeing the Department of Labor stated that it expects Labor to use expertise acquired from the McKinney Act job training program to assist the system funded by the Job Training Partnership Act (a program for economically disadvantaged people generally) to "build an enhanced capability to serve homeless persons."[36] Also in 1995, amendments were proposed in Congress to repeal two McKinney Act programs: the Education for Homeless Children program and the Surplus Federal Property program. Both proposals were defeated.

Under the 1996 appropriations, four programs, in addition to Job Training for the Homeless, would receive no funding for Fiscal Year 1996: Adult Education for the Homeless, the Homeless Veterans Reintegration project, the Emergency Community Services Homeless Grant program, and the Family Support Centers.[37] However, to the extent that the statutes authorizing the programs are not affected, the programs could be revived if later given an appropriation by Congress. Under pending legislation passed by both houses of Congress (the Job Training Consolidation Act)—but not yet enacted and likely to be vetoed—the Adult Education for the Homeless and the Job Training for the Homeless programs would be eliminated. In addition, an amendment has been introduced to narrow significantly the surplus property program.

The size and nature of the McKinney Act programs over the next few years is now somewhat unclear. For 1997, appropriations bills passed to date would maintain funding at 1996 levels. In addition, legislation is likely to be proposed to consolidate the McKinney Act shelter and housing programs administered by HUD into a single fund.[38] But funding and program changes probably will depend to at least some extent on the results of the November 1996 elections.

CONCLUSION

When initially enacted in 1987, the Stewart B. McKinney Homeless Assistance Act was a major step forward; indeed, it was landmark legislation. It constituted a recognition by the federal government that homelessness was a national crisis, and it was an acknowledgment of federal responsibility in addressing the situation. It provided concrete emergency aid to thousands of homeless people across the country. Almost certainly, the McKinney Act saved lives.

But the McKinney Act also has important flaws. First, implementation by the federal agencies charged with carrying out the programs has been uneven. Indeed, successful enforcement litigation has been filed under three of the programs;[39] additionally, through oversight hearings and other action, Congress has identified and sought to correct other instances of agency noncompliance.[40]

A more fundamental problem has been that the McKinney Act was intended only as a first step toward a more comprehensive federal response. While some of the amendments to the McKinney Act have enabled longer-term solutions, the statute still fosters primarily emergency relief. Because emergency relief does not address the causes of homelessness—but instead merely ameliorates its symptoms—it cannot solve it. The predictable result is that homelessness continues to grow across the country.[41] In response, national and local advocates began work to move beyond emergency relief to long-term solutions.[42]

The advocacy agenda centers on four main areas: housing, income, social services, and civil rights. It calls for measures to increase the availability of affordable housing in the public and private markets; for income sufficient to meet basic needs (including housing) through job training, jobs, and adequate wages for those able to work and income support for those unable; for access to health and mental health care, substance abuse treatment, and child care; and for civil and political rights, including the right to vote.[43]

In December 1993, the now-inactive Speaker's Task Force on Homelessness published a report, making findings and recommendations for action.[44] The report described homelessness as an extreme form of poverty and focused its recommendations on long-term solutions: increasing access to affordable housing; ensuring economic security through an adequate minimum wage and improved job training and employment; providing necessary services, including physical and mental health care and education for homeless children; and ensuring the rights of people who become homeless.[45]

In May 1994, the Clinton administration published *Priority Home! The Federal Plan to Break the Cycle of Homelessness*, including a comprehensive analysis of the nature and extent of homelessness in America, as well as its underlying causes. The plan recommended increased funding for, and consolidation and restructuring of, the McKinney Act shelter and housing programs. It recommended increased coordination between housing programs and services for health, mental health, and substance abuse for the "chronically disabled." It called for increased housing aid and greater efforts to fight discrimination. The plan also recommended more emphasis on the linkages between job training, employment, education, and economic development, and a new "social contract" that recognizes mutual rights and responsibilities between government and needy individuals.[46]

The November 1994 election and the resulting change in the composition of Congress presented new challenges, however. Indeed, actions of the 104th Congress now threaten the McKinney Act programs. While advocacy for longer-term solutions continues, much advocacy work now focuses on preserving the existing programs. Overall, both the McKinney Act programs and longer-term aid for homeless people face uncertainty.

At the same time, however, the current focus on welfare reform has the potential to bring renewed attention to the inadequacies of the "safety net," on the need for job assistance and jobs, and more generally on basic issues of equity in American society. Such a focus may create some new opportunities for debate, advocacy, and social change. Ultimately, implementing solutions to homelessness may transcend party and political lines.[47]

CHAPTER 16

Responses by the States to Homelessness

Vicki Watson

With the growing number of homeless families and individuals in America, states have developed policies and programs to address the problem. Working through local governments and nonprofit organizations, states distribute funds—often, funds granted to them by the federal government—to an array of programs and services to help homeless people. This chapter describes the role of state governments in assisting the homeless and in reducing and preventing homelessness, and it explores the probable impact on states if federal programs are reconfigured. In particular, it examines the proposed consolidation of McKinney Act housing programs; if enacted, the consolidated federal program will provide less federal funding to the states to address the problem of homelessness, but will permit greater flexibility in how that funding is used.

BACKGROUND

Well before the federal government enacted comprehensive legislation in 1987, the states had been compelled to act, if only in emergency fashion initially. In 1983, the National Governors' Association released the report of its Task Force on Homelessness, documenting a problem so widespread that (the report argued) nothing short of a national response would suffice. By the mid-1980s, a number of states had already taken independent action that went beyond the disaster relief approach favored by the federal government until late in the decade. As early as 1983, for example, Massachusetts and New York enacted legislation expanding state funding for low-income housing; New York's initiative was the first capital grants program for supportive housing (in which on-site services are included in the design) targeted for homeless people.

In 1987, the U.S. Congress considered several bills to broaden the federal role in assisting the homeless. The legislation that became law on 22 July 1987 was H.R. 558, the Urgent Relief for the Homeless Act, subsequently renamed in honor of Representative Stewart B. McKinney (Foscarinis discusses the history and significance of the McKinney Act in Chapter 15). The McKinney Act authorized new programs to provide homeless people assistance with health care, mental health services, emergency shelter, transitional housing, supportive services, and job and literacy training, along with programs to provide permanent housing for handicapped homeless persons and grants to enable group homes to renovate, convert, purchase, lease, or construct facilities for the homeless. Indeed, the act authorized numerous assistance programs for the homeless for Fiscal Years 1987 and 1988. The McKinney Act required state and local governments requesting federal assistance to prepare plans documenting their needs and assessing their existing antihomelessness resources. Although there had been substantial local activity by antihomelessness advocates before 1987 (see Introduction and Chapter 19), most state governments became involved primarily as the result of McKinney Act fiscal incentives and planning requirements.

THE FEDERAL EMERGENCY SHELTER GRANTS PROGRAM

One of the McKinney Act's programs, Emergency Shelter Grants (ESG), is the primary mechanism used by states to assist the homeless. Administered by the U.S. Department of Housing and Urban Development (HUD), it was established by the Homeless Housing Act of 1986 to help states and localities provide shelter for homeless people and assist homeless people in their efforts to move to permanent housing. The ESG program's main features are:

• Eligible grant recipients (grantees) are: states and territories, large cities, and urban counties.

• Eligible grantees receive a direct annual grant from HUD.

• Funds are allocated by formula.[1]

• Grantees disburse the federal funds received from HUD to local government and nonprofit organizations, either to deliver services directly or for further distribution to service providers.

• Each dollar of ESG funding must be matched, by either grantees or providers, with another dollar of funding from other public or private sources. For states, allocations must be matched after the first $100,000 received. In calculating the match, grantees may include the value of in-kind donations, such as buildings or materials, leases on buildings, staff salaries and time, and services contributed by volunteers.

The ESG program is broad in scope and provides funds to a large number of organizations. Because ESG funds are distributed by the federal government to eligible grantees on a formula basis, competition for funds is reduced. Over the years, ESG has funded diverse antihomelessness efforts, including the conversion, renovation, and rehabilitation of buildings for use as emergency shelters; operation of shelter facilities; supportive services; and homelessness prevention efforts. Across the United States, in Fiscal Year 1991 alone, between 3,000 and 3,500 providers received ESG funding to provide shelter and services to the homeless and to offer prevention assistance to households at risk of becoming homeless.[2] The following table shows the funds appropriated by Congress for the ESG program for Fiscal Years 1987–94.[3]

TABLE 16.1

FUNDS APPROPRIATED FOR ESG FOR FISCAL YEARS 1987–1994 (MILLIONS OF DOLLARS)

	1987	1988	1989	1990	1991	1992	1993	1994
Funding	60.0	8.0	46.5	73.2	73.2	73.2	50.0	115.0

ESG Program Grantees

The 382 grant recipients that have received funds under the ESG program include 55 states and territories, 220 metropolitan cities, and 107 urban counties. Federal resources in general, and ESG resources in particular, provide the majority of the funding for many of these ESG grantee agencies. On average, ESG program grantees reported that 82% of their Fiscal Year 1991 antihomelessness funding came from the federal government.[4] In addition to distributing federal ESG funds to eligible local activities and among local providers, grantees can also play a vital role in the planning and coordination of antihomelessness resources and programs in their regions.

Comprehensive Planning: A Federal Requirement

Title I of the National Affordable Housing Act of 1990 required state and local governments to have an approved Comprehensive Housing Affordability Strategy (CHAS) in order to qualify for certain HUD programs, including all ESG and other McKinney Act programs. A Comprehensive Housing Affordability Strategy identifies the affordable housing needs of low-income persons, the homeless, and populations with special needs in a given region. It also specifies the resources and programs that the state and local governments plan to use to provide housing assistance for these populations. When entities other than state or local governments (e.g., nonprofit organizations) sought HUD funds, their applications had to be certified by the state or local government as consistent with the CHAS.

In 1994, the CHAS was replaced with the Consolidated Plan. The new plan combines in a single document the planning and application requirements for several of HUD's formula-based programs: ESG, the Community Development Block Grant (CDBG) Program, the HOME Investment Partnerships Program, and Housing Opportunities for Persons with AIDS (HOPWA).[5] Similar to the planning requirements under the CHAS, the Consolidated Plan requires a state or local government seeking federal funds to have a three- to five-year general plan, a one-year action plan, an assessment of need, a listing of priorities, and an identification of resources. It also contains a citizen input/participation component that requires all grantees to at least hold public hearings on the Consolidated Plan and to place the Plan in public libraries so that the citizenry can provide their input. Some states have also surveyed low-income residents to ascertain their needs. The Consolidated Plan has more specific requirements with respect to homelessness than did the CHAS, stipulating that grantees describe:

- How they will help low-income families avoid becoming homeless

- How they will reach out to homeless persons and assess their individual needs

- How they will address the emergency shelter and transitional housing needs of homeless persons

- How they will help homeless persons make the transition to permanent housing and independent living

Funding of Supportive Services and Homeless Prevention Services

ESG funds have greatly increased supportive services provided by states to homeless people. Among the types of services showing the greatest increases (and being supported in whole or in part by ESG) are child care, support groups, basic skills development (e.g., personal budget management), and counseling or treatment for medical or psychological conditions or substance abuse. The development of homelessness prevention programs under ESG has given a new dimension to the program and has added a new population. States and other grantees can allocate up to 30% of their ESG funds to homelessness prevention, and some grantees have received waivers from HUD to devote an even greater portion of their funding to prevention efforts. Under the ESG program, prevention efforts can take one of two forms: (1) homeless individuals and families can be assisted in obtaining permanent housing by use of ESG funds for a first month's rent and security deposit, or

(2) individuals and families at risk of becoming homeless can be assisted in retaining their permanent housing through assistance in paying back rent and utilities (see Chapter 18). In Fiscal Year 1991, 55% of ESG grantees allocated funds to supportive services, and 38% disbursed funds to homelessness prevention services (up from 9% in Fiscal Year 1989).[6]

STATEWIDE COLLABORATION AND COORDINATION

As states have experienced growth in the number of homeless and have obtained increased funding to assist them and to prevent homelessness, they have also focused more on statewide collaboration among various anti-homelessness agencies and services, notably through state councils, task forces, and committees. Some states' councils are composed of representatives from various levels of the public sector and the nonprofit community, others are limited strictly to representatives of state agencies concerned with housing and community development, mental health, education, economic development, and human services. Whatever their composition, the goal of these state councils, task forces, and committees is to identify the state's magnitude of homelessness, coordinate resources, and suggest and promote policy changes that will benefit homeless people.

Many state councils prepare and submit annual reports to their governor, state legislature, and certain state agencies, enumerating the homeless receiving services, summarizing the types of programs and services available to assist the homeless, and describing unmet needs. By providing such assessments, the councils are able to make policy recommendations and advocate for change in existing programs and for the development of new programs and services. The councils help sustain collaboration by promoting the coordination of state antihomelessness policies, programs, and resources; the active coordination of state agencies, local governments, and local nonprofit organizations; and the sharing of information among all levels of government and the nonprofit community.

Innovative State Initiatives

Many states have undertaken or planned innovative initiatives to address the problem of homelessness. Some programs focus on providing shelter along with supportive services. Others provide homelessness prevention assistance. Some states thread housing counseling into these programs. A few examples of such initiatives are described briefly below:[7]

- The state of Louisiana is considering the use of advanced technology to coordinate the delivery of services at the local level. Through interactive video, video conferencing, and electronic data transmission, information on clients and resources are entered, shared, and stored. Linked to this electronic network are software programs that quickly determine eligibility for programs and services and update case files.

- Maryland and other states employ housing counselors to move households out of shelters and into permanent, affordable housing. The counselors are charged with securing permanent housing and assisting the households in gaining access to community resources.

- Michigan, recognizing the importance of local collaboration, gives special consideration to applications from local service providers that have collaborated on state applications.

- The state of Minnesota funds local advisory committees made up of cross sections of local communities. These committees are given flexibility in planning how to address homelessness within their communities.

Future State Initiatives

The states continue to face many pressing homelessness issues. As noted by some members of the Council of State Community Development Agencies in a June 1994 survey, the most important are:

- Creating decent, affordable housing

- Linking housing and services to assist homeless people

- Assisting homeless children and youth

- Developing alternatives to shelter-type facilities

- Addressing the needs of increasing numbers of homeless families

- Addressing the needs of people with disabilities

- Addressing the needs of people with AIDS

- Integrating homeless persons into job training programs

Many state councils plan to lobby their legislatures for new programs to address these problems. Some plan to pursue the development of state housing trust funds to assist the homeless, utilizing funds from a check-off on the state income tax form. Others plan to establish metropolitan and rural hotlines with local community action agencies to assist homeless people in crisis situations. In some states, efforts will be concentrated on providing the rural homeless with outreach, transportation, and other services. Some states plan to encourage local determination of antihomelessness services with a focus on "continuum" building (see below), including the prevention of homelessness and the inclusion of homeless persons in mainstream social service programs. States without councils in place plan to create them in the future. However, the character of future state initiatives hinges on the outcome of plans to consolidate the federal McKinney Act housing programs.

CONSOLIDATION OF MCKINNEY ACT HOUSING PROGRAMS: CONSEQUENCES FOR THE STATES

Homeless assistance programs funded under the McKinney Act have been the principal monetary resource for states, cities, and local nonprofit organizations. The majority of McKinney Act funds are administered by HUD through several independent programs, each with separate appropriations and their own eligibility and reporting requirements. Each program requires a separate application, and except for ESG, all make grants on a competitive basis.

This array of independent programs is administratively burdensome and costly for applicants, and it has been widely criticized as wasteful and biased toward applicants able to employ highly skilled grant writers. Under the proposed consolidation, HUD's antihomelessness programs will be merged into a single grant program with funds distributed to states and localities by formula.[8] This consolidation would eliminate the complexity and uncertainty of providing funds through independent programs making competitive awards. This new initiative, which calls for a "bottom up" approach to policy and program planning, gives states and localities greater flexibility, but requires increased coordination and planning. State and local boards will design, plan, and deliver programs supported by the consolidated funds.

A cornerstone of the planned consolidation is the concept of a continuum of care: a comprehensive, coordinated approach to meeting the needs of homeless people. The continuum of care would emphasize comprehensive antihomelessness systems at both state and local levels to focus on:

- Outreach and assessment

- Emergency shelters

- Transitional facilities with supportive services

- Permanent housing with supportive services

- Homelessness prevention activities

The idea is that homeless people will move along this continuum of care from homelessness to full independence or self-sufficiency, and people at risk of homelessness will be kept in their homes.[9]

CONCLUSION: THE OUTLOOK FOR FEDERAL FUNDS

The congressional elections of November 1994 saw the Republicans become the majority on Capitol Hill, and the freshman Republicans came to Congress determined to cut the fed-

TABLE 16.2

FEDERAL ANTIHOMELESSNESS APPROPRIATIONS FOR FISCAL YEARS 1995 AND 1996

Program	Administering Agency	Fiscal Year 95 (Millions of Dollars)	Fiscal Year 96 (Millions of Dollars)	Percent Change
HUD McKinney Act Programs (includes Section 8 SRO Moderate Rehabilitation; Supportive Housing; Emergency Shelter Grants; Shelter plus Care)	U.S. Department of Housing and Urban Development (HUD)	1,120	823	-27
PATH Block Grant (block grants to states for mental health services to homeless people)	U.S. Department of Health and Human Services (HHS)	29.5	20	-32
ACCESS (demonstration program on how to integrate services for homeless people)	HHS	18.6	17*	-9
Health Care for the Homeless	HHS	65.4	65.4	0
Adult Education for the Homeless (literacy program)	U.S. Department of Education	9.5	0	-100
Education of Homeless Children and Youth	U.S. Department of Education	28.8	23	-20
Emergency Food and Shelter Program	Federal Emergency Management Agency	130	100	-23
Veterans Reintegration Projects	U.S. Department of Labor	5	0	-100
Emergency Community Services Homeless Grant Program (set-aside in the Community Services Block Grant)	HHS	19.8	0	-100
Housing Opportunities for Persons with AIDS (HOPWA)	HUD	186	171	-8
Runaway and Homeless Youth Program	HHS	40.5	43.5	+7
Drug Abuse Prevention Program for Runaway and Homeless Youth	HHS	14.5	0	-100
Transitional Living Program for Homeless Youth	HHS	13.7	13.6	-1
Family Support Centers	HHS	7.4	0	-100
Chronically Mentally Ill Veterans Program	U.S. Department of Veterans Affairs (VA)	27.5	40.5†	+32
Domiciliary Care	VA	31.1	41†	+24
Comprehensive Community Treatment (Dual Diagnosis Demonstration)	HHS	3	0	-100
Research on Homeless	HHS/National Institutes of Health	18	18.6	0
Soup Kitchens	U.S. Department of Agriculture	40	40	0
Comprehensive Work Therapy	VA	3.5	3.5	0
HUD-VA Supportive Housing	VA	5.3	5.3	0
Comprehensive Services	VA	8.5	8.5	0

*Source: U.S. Department of Health and Human Services, Substance Abuse and Mental Health Services Administration, Center for Mental Health Services. For Fiscal Year 1996, the ACCESS program was combined with several other mental health demonstration programs into the Mental Health Demonstration Program, which was funded at $38.1 million for FY 96. The ACCESS program did not receive a specific line-item appropriation for FY 96. Instead, the final amount for the ACCESS program will be administratively determined by the Substance Abuse and Mental Health Services Administration. The Center for Mental Health Services, which administers the ACCESS program, anticipates the program's funding for FY 97 will be $17 million.

†Source: U.S. Department of Veterans Affairs, Office of Budget.

eral government and balance the budget. During 1995, they developed legislation to dismantle some agencies and drastically downsize others. Although the outcome of their proposals is not clear at this writing, there is no doubt that federal housing programs will be restructured and reduced.

In the Fiscal Year 1996 budget, HUD's antihomelessness programs are to be reduced to their Fiscal Year 1994 level of $823 million, a 27% drop from Fiscal Year 1995, and several other federal antihomelessness programs are slated to be cut or eliminated altogether. Table 16.2 summarizes the changes from Fiscal Year 1995 to Fiscal Year 1996.

House congressional staff have predicted that HUD's McKinney Act programs—along with several other programs—will be rolled into a special needs block grant. But whether converted to so-called "stand alone" block grants, or block grants that represent combinations of programs, the McKinney Act programs—and perhaps other federal antihomelessness efforts—probably will be converted to some form of block grant in the near future. If this happens, states will assume a much greater role in administering antihomelessness money; unfortunately, there will be much less of it to administer.

CHAPTER 17

Responding to the Needs of Homeless People with Alcohol, Drug, and/or Mental Disorders

Deirdre Oakley
Deborah L. Dennis

Homeless people with alcohol, drug, and/ or mental disorders (ADM disorders) are particularly disfranchised. They are often excluded from programs that assist homeless people because of their mental illness or substance use, and from mental health and substance abuse treatment programs because of their homelessness. Their presence on the streets and in the shelters of our nation indicates how poorly our housing, health care, and social service systems are working.[1]

As emphasized in Chapter 3, there is a great deal of controversy about prevalence rates of ADM disorders among homeless populations; however, it is fair to say that such problems— singly or together—are far more common among homeless people than in the general population. In this chapter, we will discuss what kinds of programs work for homeless people with ADM disorders—and what is still needed to make proven interventions more accessible.

LESSONS FROM FEDERAL DEMONSTRATION PROGRAMS

In 1982, the National Institute of Mental Health (NIMH) funded 10 studies intended to increase knowledge about effective services for homeless individuals with serious mental illness and to provide technical assistance to states and other localities in their efforts to provide such services. Similarly, in 1984, the National Institute on Alcohol Abuse and Alcoholism (NIAAA) began to support research on programs for homeless individuals with drinking problems. These federal projects were built upon earlier research and advocacy efforts that had raised awareness and established the importance of crucial questions about welfare insufficiency, housing problems, and the fragmentation and inaccessibility of services afforded to homeless people with ADM disorders.[2]

The initial NIMH studies were designed to answer pressing questions about the service and treatment needs of homeless persons with serious mental illnesses. With one exception (a statewide study of homelessness in Ohio), they were conducted in large metropolitan areas. By the mid-1980s, this body of research had established that the lack of an accessible, comprehensive system of community care meant that many people who would have been institutionalized in an earlier era were ending up living on the streets or in shelters. In 1992, a federal task force concluded that improving the accessibility and availability of community mental health services was more appropriate than reinstitutionalization. Findings from NIAAA-supported research pointed in the same direction. Further, the federally supported research underlined the striking heterogeneity of homeless persons with ADM disorders, a fact with important implications for the design and delivery of services.

In 1987, the Stewart B. McKinney Homeless Assistance Act (see Chapter 15) became the first federal legislation to address the multiple health and social welfare needs of the homeless population. Under Title VI, Section 612, the McKinney Act authorized nine demonstration projects to develop comprehensive mental health service systems for homeless adults with serious mental illnesses. Key components in the development of such systems included outreach to clients in nontraditional settings, mental health treatment and rehabilitation services, long-term case management, staffing and operation of supportive living programs, and management and administrative activities designed to link these services. Several issues were emphasized in the findings of the demonstration projects:

• The importance of the outreach and engagement process in establishing a therapeutic relationship

• The need for a wide range of housing options

• The need for intensive and long-term follow-up

In 1990, five more McKinney demonstration projects were funded by the federal Center for Mental Health Services (CMHS). Building on the previous demonstration projects, these new efforts were required to provide four basic services: outreach, mental health treatment, intensive case management, and housing. In addition, each project conducted a longitudinal, experimentally designed evaluation of their housing and service interventions. These projects found:[3]

• Homeless people with serious mental illnesses use accessible and relevant community mental health treatment services

• Appropriate services decrease homelessness

• Advocacy increases access to entitlement income

• Formerly homeless people with serious mental illnesses are an important resource in engaging those who are currently homeless

• Substance abuse is a major problem among homeless people with serious mental illnesses

• Housing stability, appropriate mental health treatment, and increased income lead to an improved quality of life

Throughout much of the 1980s, NIAAA supported research that was aimed at understanding homelessness and substance abuse. Under Section 613 of the McKinney Act, NIAAA, in consultation with the National Institute on Drug Abuse (NIDA), funded two rounds of demonstration projects. These programs were to provide and evaluate community-based alcohol and other drug abuse treatment and rehabilitative services for individuals who were homeless or at imminent risk of becoming so. Many of the findings paralleled those of the NIMH and CMHS projects for homeless persons with mental illnesses. Indeed, both populations share many of the same treatment and service needs; in particular, carefully designed client engagement and case management processes, housing options, and long-term follow-up and support services. Findings indicated that shelter, sustenance, and security needs should be met before addressing an individual's need for treatment. Additionally, services must be tailored to the experiences and capacities of the target population. Effective interventions combined structure and flexibility to meet individual client needs, particularly in residential programs.[4]

The NIAAA projects produced several findings specific to the homeless substance-abusing population. Perhaps most important was the finding that traditional, abstinence-oriented treatment programs were ineffective with this population. (Many programs discontinue treatment if clients refuse to be completely abstinent, or if they relapse.) These findings suggest that treatment for homeless, substance-abusing individuals should:

- Focus initially on modifying the course of substance abuse and alleviating suffering, rather than on requiring total abstinence

- Be based on a realistic assessment of the characteristics and needs of the individual undergoing treatment

- Be flexibly responsive to client needs and level of motivation, rather than committed to a particular treatment philosophy

- Be realistic in terms of goals and expectations, allowing for relapses

These studies also found that the most effective interventions provided long-term, comprehensive services, rather than the usual regimen of 28 days of inpatient care.[5]

CO-OCCURRING MENTAL HEALTH AND SUBSTANCE USE DISORDERS

The NIMH and NIAAA demonstration programs found that mental illness and substance abuse frequently were concurrent. Clinicians refer to this as co-occurring disorders or dual diagnosis. Homeless people with such co-occurring disorders frequently are excluded from mental health programs because of treatment problems created by their substance abuse, and from substance abuse programs because of treatment problems created by their mental illness. Because of the important role of substance abuse (especially drug abuse) in the loss of housing among people with serious mental illness, treatment for these individuals is critical to any effort to keep them housed. Indeed, the lack of an integrated system of care for dually diagnosed persons plays a major role in their recurrent homelessness.[6]

Integrated treatment programs address substance abuse and mental illness simultaneously. Typical program components include: individu-

alized assessment of mental health and substance abuse problems, interdisciplinary case management, individual counseling, and peer or professionally led group interventions. Several consistent findings concerning dual diagnosis and integrated treatment emerged over the course of the demonstration projects:

- Individuals with a dual diagnosis experienced little or no change in their substance abuse over time without integrated treatment

- The great majority of dually diagnosed patients could be engaged in substance abuse treatment provided in an integrated context that includes outreach, a gradual engagement process, and motivational counseling that helped them recognize and acknowledge their problems

- Patients in integrated treatment programs recovered steadily from substance abuse over time; after three or four years, about half of the patients were stably abstinent[7]

Although all of the demonstration projects confirmed the need for comprehensive, community-based services to meet the housing, treatment, and support needs of homeless people with ADM disorders, most communities find this difficult to achieve. In particular, administrative fragmentation and competition for scarce resources are powerful barriers to service integration. Thus, despite the demonstrated need for comprehensive and integrated service systems, the 1992 federal task force found that the burden of integration usually falls on the consumer, not the system. Or, as Baumohl and Huebner observe: "While clinical practice is grounded in the wisdom of working with the 'whole person,' 'beginning where the client is,' and 'partializing' complex problems for systematic attention, labyrinthine structures of human services virtually guarantee that clients, rather than problems, will be partialized."[8]

The 1992 federal task force recommended a new demonstration program specifically designed to test whether states and local communities could develop integrated systems of treatment, housing, and support services for homeless persons with serious mental illnesses. In October 1993, CMHS awarded ACCESS (Access to Community Care and Effective Services and Supports) grants to 9 states to test systems integration strategies in 18 communities. A national evaluation of these projects is currently underway.[9]

WHAT WORKS? SERVICE AND POLICY IMPLICATIONS

The federal demonstration projects confirmed the pressing need to integrate service systems from the highest levels of administration to the front lines of service provision, in order to remove barriers to care and promote efficient use of resources. Ideally, homeless people should be able to enter any service "door," be assessed, and obtain access to all services they need and want. To accomplish this, there must be an individual or team responsible for each client's need for treatment and other services, a "no-reject" policy, and programs must be accountable for individual outcomes.[10]

Integration of the systems for mental health, social services, and criminal justice is particularly critical for people discharged from hospitals and jails who are otherwise homeless (see Chapter 18). Individuals are frequently discharged from these institutions without a solid connection to community-based treatment or housing, and many subsequently move among shelters, hospitals, detoxification facilities, jails, and street life—at high cost to themselves and society.

Research also has shown that in addition to the importance of integrating service systems, particular service elements are essential to constructive work with homeless people with ADM disorders. While the emphasis on individual service components may vary, the underlying principles are the same.

The Importance of Outreach and Engagement

Engagement with services and treatment compliance can be dramatically improved through outreach. Working out of drop-in centers, mo-

bile units, soup kitchens, and shelters, outreach workers use a variety of techniques to engage people in services and treatment.[11] These include:

- A nonthreatening approach

- Flexibility in the menu of services offered and the manner in which they are provided

- Repeated contact over extended periods of time, achieved by bringing services to clients rather than waiting for them to come to the services

- Responsiveness to individuals' perceived needs for food, money, and housing as quickly as possible

- Patience in motivating clients to accept treatment and services

Using Case Management to Negotiate Systems of Care

Although there are many models of case management, all involve "a continuous helping relationship that supports and facilitates [clients'] effective use of environmental resources."[12] Case management has developed over the last 15 years in direct response to the fragmentation of human services, and its importance in helping homeless people with ADM disorders negotiate systems of care cannot be overstated.

Perhaps most important, case management establishes a single point of responsibility (and contact) for each individual. Case managers:[13]

- Train clients in daily living skills

- Link them to other needed services and monitor their provision

- Help them secure entitlements

- Assist them in applying for housing and in adjusting to a new residence once they have moved

Case managers sometimes also provide crisis intervention services; particularly for people in independent housing, a quick and appropriate response to crisis can make the difference between residential stability and homelessness.[14]

Intensive case management of about six months is critical to stabilize clients' psychiatric symptoms and/or substance abuse and their residential situation. Several demonstration projects noted that after about six months of intensive case-management services, about one-third of study participants could make the transition to relative independence. The remainder needed additional, less intensive support for a longer period.[15]

Offering a Range of Supportive Housing Options

Secure housing that affords privacy and safety is an attainable goal for nearly all homeless people with ADM disorders, but they need a range of options. One of the best mechanisms for creating various alternatives for independent living is "Section 8 housing," so-called because of its provenance in Section 8 of the U.S. Housing Act (as revised in 1974). As Dolbeare discusses in detail in Chapter 4 (note 2), project-based subsidies or tenant rental certificates have the potential to help many homeless people get a place of their own, whether in an apartment or in a single-room-occupancy hotel. Most demonstration project participants who were offered Section 8 certificates were still in their own places after one year and were significantly more positive about their lives and their living arrangements than were other participants.[16] Unfortunately, many of these tenant-based programs for homeless persons with disabilities are in jeopardy in the current conservative political climate.

With appropriate levels of support, particularly during the critical transition from homelessness to residential stability, many people with ADM disorders can live successfully in independent housing. Independent living does not serve the needs or correspond to the preferences of everyone, however. When asked about their housing preferences prior to assignment, 22% of the participants in one demonstration project said they preferred group living to living alone.[17]

Housing models for homeless substance abusers must address the issues of whether or not to require abstinence and how relapse will be handled. Among researchers and providers,

positions on these issues vary. Those in favor of abstinence-oriented residential settings argue that allowing people to use drugs and/or alcohol while providing them with safe, secure shelter, only "enables" them to continue their substance abuse. Others view "recovery" as an incremental process that does not necessarily begin with abstinence. Instead, abstinence is seen as the last of a series of steps that begin by seeking to reduce the harm that substance abuse causes. Both options are probably necessary to a comprehensive system of care. Housing models that do not require abstinence can be "damp" (residents do not have to be abstinent, but cannot drink or use drugs on the premises) or "wet" (residents are permitted to drink on the premises, but cannot use illegal drugs), but the latter form is rare.[18]

Responding to Consumer Preferences

The federal demonstration projects found that when homeless people with ADM disorders are taught the skills and given the support necessary to achieve their goals, most are willing and able to live in community settings. Providers need to learn more about—and be more responsive to—consumer perceptions of need and the ways in which they evaluate and choose among competing alternatives. Most systems respond to clients who cannot accept traditional mental health and/or substance abuse treatment by trying to limit their choices. Research and experience suggests that greater benefits would be achieved through flexible services tailored to the needs and preferences of these clients.

But empowering clients in this way is not a simple matter. Inevitably, client choice operates within an existing resource environment that often has little flexibility; thus, there is limited opportunity for individual choice or institutional innovation. The matter of innovation is especially important because the traditional institutional requirements for medication compliance and treatment participation, or abstinence from substance use, effectively preclude the most vulnerable and needy subgroups of homeless people with ADM disorders from involvement in housing and service programs. However, innovations that place minimal demands on substance abusers (such as sobering stations and needle exchanges) create opportunities to engage people gradually and to direct them gently toward sobriety.

Providing Mental Health and Substance Abuse Treatment

Involving clients in the assessment of their needs and the development of a treatment plan is an effective way to engage them in treatment. Likewise, educating clients regarding the cause and nature of their symptoms and helping them understand when and how to use medication and other treatment interventions has also proven effective.[19] Peer groups can also help sustain treatment by creating a supportive network and a sense of empowerment. Formerly homeless individuals who are in varying stages of recovery from mental illness and/or substance abuse have been extremely effective in both engaging and maintaining others in treatment.[20]

While medication is an important and effective intervention, many homeless people with ADM disorders are initially reluctant to take medication, or may discontinue its use because of negative side effects or because they do not understand their condition and the need for medication. Premature or overly aggressive attempts to address pathology with medication or other intrusive treatments may recreate earlier negative experiences and convince a client that the clinician is no more helpful or understanding than previous providers. Thus, clinicians must work closely with clients to establish what dosage of which medication is most effective and tolerable.[21]

The Need for Harm Reduction Approaches to Substance Abuse

No discussion of treating substance-abusing homeless individuals is complete without attention to methods of "harm reduction." For our purposes, harm reduction refers to attempts to minimize the damage from conditions that are unlikely to change in the short run. Recovery from substance abuse is a lengthy, stepwise process that begins with people who are not ready to be abstinent but who can benefit from ser-

vices. Harm reduction techniques encourage substance abusers to cut down on their use, to switch substances, to use less dangerous modes of ingestion, or to adopt more healthful ways of living. For example, the distribution of bleach kits or clean needles to intravenous drug users is a harm reduction tactic in an overall strategy of reducing the spread of HIV infection—and it has been shown to be extremely effective.[22] Similarly, "low-demand" services (services that make few demands of clients) attempt to improve the quality of life for people who are, at least temporarily, unwilling or unable to meet the demands of more traditional services. As noted above, the federal demonstration projects have shown that low-demand services are very useful.

The biggest barrier to increasing the availability of low-demand, harm reduction services is the notion that such efforts "enable" people to continue their substance abuse. Indeed, in many treatment settings, there is reluctance even to help nonabstinent people deal with survival needs, because such help is regarded as enablement. This objection is based on the assumption that people will change their behavior if they are fearful and ostracized; however, research indicates that people are actually more *likely* to accept treatment once their basic needs have been met.

The Importance of Meaningful Daily Activity

Demonstration projects have repeatedly found that meaningful daytime activity to combat isolation is crucial to housing stability. This underscores the need for pre- and post-housing counseling to anticipate and address the isolation and attendant psychological distress caused by the transition to new living situations. Housing support groups, tenant associations, "community livingrooms," and other associations can be helpful in this connection, while also creating opportunities for employment.[23]

Flexible employment opportunities are especially important but difficult to develop.[24] Enterprises that capture the purchasing power of the recovering-consumer market is one possibility among many. Consumer-owned enterprises that could serve the consumer community and benefit from its spending power include:

- Consumer-cooperative pharmacies

- Treatment-related services for other clients

- Housing cooperatives

- Cafeterias

- Courier and transportation services

Providing Culturally Competent Care

Cultural differences can determine how individuals define their problems and how they express them, the treatment strategies they prefer, and from whom they seek help. Practitioners, too, perceive clients through their own cultural lenses unless they have become adept at seeing in other ways. To be effective with homeless people with ADM disorders, mental health and substance abuse professionals must alter their practices and the service delivery system to become compatible with cultural expectations of care.[25] Culturally sensitive service professionals must arrange:

- A language and culture match between providers and clients

- Provision of the needed services in racial, ethnic, or other minority communities

- Flexible hours and accommodation of walk-ins

- Provision of (or referral to) services for social, economic, legal, and medical problems

- Use of family members in the treatment process

- Use of (or referral to) clergy and/or traditional healers in the treatment process

Putting the Need for Involuntary Treatment in Perspective

Homeless individuals with ADM disorders have always been susceptible to involuntary civil commitment. Recently, administrative and procedural changes in many state laws have led to broader interpretation of involuntary commitment statutes. This, in turn, has increased the frequency of the use of involuntary commitment in many jurisdictions. Many mental health and substance abuse professionals question the efficacy of involuntary commitment, which often serves only to bring homeless people with ADM disorders into a system where they continue to be unlikely to obtain access to the long-term care, housing, and other support services they need. Research indicates that only between 5% and 7% of the single, adult homeless population needs acute inpatient psychiatric care—the permission for most of which could be given voluntarily.[26]

Resisting "Easy" Solutions

In recent years, a number of cities have become overtly hostile to homeless individuals (see Chapter 14). They have launched efforts to remove homeless people from certain areas, restricted sleeping in parks and other public places, enacted antipanhandling ordinances, enforced vagrancy laws against homeless people, and turned zoning laws against shelters and other forms of group housing. Such actions make it even more difficult to find those homeless people who have ADM disorders and to engage them in appropriate services; often, all that is accomplished is to temporarily shift responsibility for their care to the criminal justice system.[27]

CONCLUSION

With more than a decade of experience devoted to designing and studying services for homeless persons with ADM disorders, we have some clear ideas about what works and what does not. Homeless people with serious mental illnesses, substance use disorders, or co-occurring disorders are willing to use mental health and substance abuse treatment services that are easy to enter and that meet their needs as they perceive them. While they can be successfully treated in the community, reaching them depends on integrating existing services and entitlements more effectively.

Documented successes point to the need for specific changes in the delivery of mental health, substance abuse, and social services to homeless people:

- Systems of care must be comprehensive and integrated

- Clinicians must recognize the importance of the engagement process

- Referrals and transitions must be handled with care

- Case management should be utilized to assist in the negotiation of systems of care

- A range of supportive housing options should be offered

- Consumer preferences need to be incorporated in services

- Appropriate and client-centered mental health and substance abuse treatment must be provided

- Harm reduction approaches should be part of a comprehensive approach to substance abuse treatment and housing

- Meaningful daily activity and opportunities for employment must be provided

- Preventive health care and education should be incorporated into any treatment plan

- Treatment must be culturally sensitive

- Involuntary treatment should only be used when absolutely necessary

- Seemingly easy solutions, such as laws to repress homelessness, make treatment less accessible

As a society, we must decide what we will do with this knowledge. On the one hand, we have never been better positioned to utilize solid findings about what works and what does not in terms of treatment, housing, and supports for homeless individuals with ADM disorders. On the other hand, the 1990s have ushered in perhaps the most restrictive era of resource allocation and program support in recent history.

CHAPTER 18

Preventing Homelessness

Eric N. Lindblom

With its implicit promise of both budgetary and humanitarian savings, the prevention of homelessness attracts a lot of rhetorical support—but implementing prevention initiatives that will actually realize such savings is tricky. Nevertheless, helping homeless people without preventing homelessness is like bailing a boat without fixing the leaks: it might keep things from getting worse, but it will never solve the problem.

Fixing the leaks—or preventing new entries and reentries into the homeless population—can take a variety of forms. Most broadly, creating more job opportunities, increasing income supports, and expanding public housing assistance would inevitably prevent homelessness, as would successful large-scale efforts to improve health, education, and employability among the poor. This chapter, however, focuses on efforts of more modest scope: practical, cost-effective ways to keep individuals and families at imminent risk of becoming homeless from ending up on the streets or in shelters.[1]

To target prevention efforts effectively, we need to know which people or groups are most at risk of becoming homeless and how they can be identified. To locate the best sites for pre-vention efforts, we need to know the places where these most-at-risk persons are housed immediately prior to becoming homeless. And to develop the best ways to help, we need to understand better the events and situations that precipitate or cause homelessness for those at-risk individuals and families.

COST EFFECTIVENESS AND TARGETING THOSE MOST AT RISK

A homelessness prevention program is "cost effective" when the total new costs it incurs are less than the costs it avoids (that is, the costs that would have been incurred if the people assisted had, instead, become homeless). The cost of prevention efforts can usually be determined quite precisely by adding together the prevention program's budget and the cost of any other new assistance it channels to its clients. Costs *avoided* by a program's efforts are calculated by multiplying the estimates of: (1) the number of prevention-assistance recipients who would otherwise have become homeless; (2) the number of days they would have spent homeless had they not been helped; and (3) the cost (if they had become homeless), per person per day, of providing them with food, shelter, and other assistance, along with the other substantial social costs associated with homelessness.[2]

While the estimates for these factors can be highly imprecise, the overall formula for calculating avoided costs clearly tells us two things: first, assisting people who would have avoided homelessness without the help reduces a program's cost effectiveness; and second, targeting people most at risk of becoming homeless repeatedly or for long periods of time will accrue the largest prevention savings. Because those at risk of repeated or long periods of homelessness are much more disabled and disadvantaged than those at risk of only temporary, brief episodes, helping them to avoid homelessness is, generally, more difficult and costly. Nevertheless, the per-person savings achieved by helping them dwarfs the savings from helping the others—especially when adding in the costs avoided for not having to treat the considerable physical and mental damage caused over time by the experience of homelessness. Presently, however, only a small portion of the persons targeted by many prevention programs are actually at risk of repeated or prolonged homelessness.[3]

Who Are the "Most At Risk of Becoming Homeless"?

Although extreme poverty is the common denominator among people who become homeless, most extremely poor persons somehow avoid repeated or prolonged homelessness. Accordingly, we need to consider the additional characteristics that correlate with increased risk of chronic or long-term homelessness among extremely poor persons:

- A history of prior homelessness

- Social isolation (having few or no friends or family able or willing to provide support)

- Serious physical or mental health problems (including substance abuse)

- A history of institutionalization (especially for mental illness, inpatient alcohol or other drug abuse treatment, foster care, jail, or prison)[4]

Not all extremely poor people with one or more of these risk characteristics become homeless, but they are substantially more likely to experience homelessness than similarly situated persons who do not have them. Indeed, virtually all chronically homeless persons have several of the risk characteristics, and the likelihood that a housed extremely poor person will become homeless repeatedly or for long periods of time increases with the number of risk characteristics they have (see Chapter 3).

Where Have Homeless Persons Been Living Prior to Homelessness?

Research shows that homeless people in most areas are "locals"—not new arrivals—and that they come disproportionately from deeply impoverished neighborhoods. Studies have also identified several settings through which people are likely to pass either immediately prior to homelessness, at some earlier point, or between episodes of homelessness. These sites offer the best places to seek and identify persons most at risk of becoming homeless.

Mental hospitals. Available research studies indicate that roughly one-quarter of all homeless people were previously in mental institutions, and many spend time in mental hospitals between bouts of homelessness. In fact, a significant portion of all extremely poor discharged mental patients experience homelessness either immediately or at some later point.[5]

Substance-abuse treatment facilities and other health institutions. Similarly, about 30% of homeless persons have been in inpatient chemical dependency or detoxification programs prior to their current episode of homelessness, and up to half of the persons in inpatient alcohol or drug treatment programs for the indigent would otherwise be homeless. Physical health problems are also important contributors to homelessness, and temporary stays in health facilities for the treatment of physical problems occur in the midst of some persons' periods of homelessness. Shelters for battered women also serve as temporary residences for some otherwise-homeless or soon-to-be-homeless women.[6]

Prisons and jails. Studies have found that more than half of all homeless persons have previously been in jail and (with some overlap) about one-fifth have been in prison, with prior incarceration highest among homeless men. In addition, some studies have found an especially significant link between past prison time and future homelessness.[7]

Foster care. Although only about 2% to 3% of the general adult population has experienced foster care or childhood out-of-home care, studies have found levels of prior foster care among the homeless to range from 14.5% to 39%. Moreover, in a study of youths emancipated from the foster care systems in San Francisco and Sacramento, 29% reported periods when they either had no home or were moving at least every week, and 39% reported sometimes or often having had problems with housing. Since this study could not locate about one-quarter of the sample, the actual percentage of emancipated foster care youths who become homeless might be significantly higher.[8]

Rental units and shared housing. Although most homeless people have been in foster care, jail, prison, a state hospital, or some other kind of institution at some time prior to becoming homeless, some studies of homeless people in New York City and Chicago found that none of them had been in institutional care *immediately* before becoming homeless. These studies suggest that the path to homelessness after discharge from institutional living typically includes an interim period of housing with friends or family, in single-room-occupancy hotels (SROs), or in other cheap rental housing.[9]

The New York City study found that 20% of families seeking shelter for the first time (who were not already homeless) had been in their own apartments the night prior to seeking shelter, and 80% had been in a doubled-up situation with family or friends (with over half of this latter group never having had their own home). Similarly, the Chicago study found that virtually all homeless families and about one-third of homeless adults without children were living with others immediately prior to becoming homeless, with the remainder living on their own (usually in day-to-day or week-to-week SROs or similar accommodations). Most families and unattached adults became homeless after informal evictions, often sparked by arguments with their hosts—or due to formal evictions, mostly because they or their hosts failed to pay the rent. Severe problems with the prior residence (such as no heat, condemnation of the building, or its destruction by fire) were also significant factors.[10]

PREVENTING HOMELESSNESS AT THE SOURCES

Promising ways to locate potentially at-risk individuals and families in rental units or shared housing include advertising prevention services in those neighborhoods that produce a disproportionately large amount of homeless people, and directly contacting poor, housed persons who are due to lose various forms of public assistance because of state or federal welfare "reforms," have been served with eviction notices, or have had their heat or other utilities shut off for nonpayment. Additional at-risk persons can be found at the other "sources" of homelessness. The next step is to provide these people with effective prevention assistance.

Preventing Evictions

As many as half of all homeless adults (well over half of unattached homeless adults, and over one-fifth of homeless families), whether living alone or with others, make the final move from housed living into homelessness because of an eviction or some other landlord or rent problem. Moreover, a significant portion of the families who enter homelessness from shared housing for reasons unrelated to evictions had previously been forced into the shared housing situation because of an eviction or other landlord or rent problem (usually within the previous month).[11] Accordingly, helping most-at-risk families and individuals (or the people putting them up) to avoid eviction could reduce the flow of persons into homelessness by more than half.

For organizations wanting to provide eviction prevention assistance, getting sufficient advance notice might be the trickiest problem: few evicted individuals or families contact any public or private social service agencies or government officials prior to losing their residence. While formal eviction papers filed with the courts could provide some notice, most evictions of low-income tenants never get to that stage.[12] By encouraging tenants facing informal eviction to make landlords go through the formal court proceedings, homelessness prevention agencies could increase both their chances of learning about the evictions and the tenants' ability to assert their legal rights.

Informing tenants of their rights under the formal eviction process—and telling them where they can get help—would most likely reduce the number willing to leave merely because their landlords ask or threaten them, and would increase the proportion of eviction attempts that would go through the formal process. At the same time, the existing notice procedures in many areas need to be amended to provide tenants and support agencies with adequate time to respond.[13] Prevention programs must also develop effective ways to help those tenants at risk of both eviction and homelessness to stay housed. Current efforts break down into two basic types: providing legal assistance and providing cash assistance.

Legal assistance programs. Only about 20% to 30% of all tenants in formal eviction proceedings have legal representation (as opposed to over 80% of landlords), and roughly one-third to one-half of all tenant defendants never file any responding papers and lose simply by default. Addressing this lack of legal assistance would prevent a lot of homelessness. A Berkeley study, for example, determined that tenants in eviction proceedings won less than 6% of the time when they did not have legal representation, but won 58% of the time when they had it. Four legal-assistance eviction-prevention projects in New York City kept low-income clients in their apartments in 84% of the first 675 cases they completed.[14]

Using conservative estimates of how many clients would have otherwise become homeless, and how much it would have cost to house them in New York City's emergency shelter system, the Bar Association of New York City estimated that during the first 2 years of operation, a group of New York City legal-assistance eviction prevention projects saved $8 in federal, state, and local expenditures for every $1 spent.[15] These programs maintained this cost effectiveness despite (or maybe because of) the added costs of providing comprehensive legal assistance from the beginning to the end of the eviction process, along with other services such as helping clients get public assistance benefits. Many other legal assistance programs do not have the resources to provide such intensive assistance, however, or have chosen to provide less intensive assistance in order to reach more people. Typically, these programs only provide tenants with advice so that they can represent themselves in court, which, in many cases, only buys them a little time before eviction.

Nevertheless, the potential savings from delaying a household's entry into the emergency assistance network can be substantial, especially when compared to the very small per-client costs of low-intensity legal assistance programs (usually well under $100 per household). A federal survey of shelter costs found that keeping a single person out of the shelters for a month could save $225 to $375, and keeping a family out of the shelters could save $675 to $1,500. In some cities, such as New York, the savings could be three times as large. Avoiding these costs, however, depends on how well the assistance programs target households truly at risk of becoming homeless: at present, most simply help any low-income household faced with eviction, regardless of their future possibilities.[16]

The greater success rates of tenants with full legal representation and the achievements of the New York City projects suggest that the more comprehensive eviction-defense programs offer the most productive way to prevent homelessness. At the same time, the New York projects serve only families, and similar programs to serve single-person households faced with eviction might not be as cost-effective. Unattached adults usually have more disadvantages and less access to resources such as public assistance than homeless or at-risk families (see Chapter 6), which makes it harder to keep them in their rental units. It is also much cheaper to house single persons in shelters, as opposed to families, which reduces the savings from preventing their eviction and subsequent homelessness.

On the other hand, because single persons tend to spend more time homeless than families and have more disadvantages and disabilities, on a per-person basis they will still cause larger costs if they become homeless. In addition, well over one-third of all single persons who become homeless are veterans with unique access to extensive health care and, to a lesser extent, cash benefits from the U.S. Department of Veterans Affairs (see Chapter 9). Single persons also can be housed in cheaper rental units than families (for example, SROs). More important, significant reductions in the size of the homeless population will be impossible without aggressive efforts to prevent homelessness among single adults. Throughout the country, unattached homeless adults are not only the largest segment of the homeless and at-risk populations but also the most likely to become homeless because of an eviction. Accordingly, legal services–based eviction prevention for single adults remains a constructive prevention tool—especially if combined with increases in other assistance.

Cash assistance programs. Despite their power, legal assistance efforts still cannot reach the large number of persons evicted into homelessness outside of formal legal proceedings. In addition, many tenants facing eviction (including some of those who receive legal assistance) will not be able to pay their current and past-due rent without new income. These two problems can be addressed by programs that provide financial help.

Several programs of this type exist, but their homelessness prevention impact is unclear. For example, the state of New Jersey's Homeless-ness Prevention Program, which has been copied by other states and private organizations, provides one-time financial assistance to applicants who have experienced a loss of income because of an emergency and need money for rent, past rent, utility bills, or mortgage payments. Although New Jersey officials estimate that its interventions are 3 times cheaper than putting families up in a shelter and 30 times cheaper than putting them in a welfare hotel, many of the program's clients would have avoided homelessness without its assistance.[17]

Most significantly, the New Jersey program exclusively targets the working poor who will be able to resume paying rent once assistance ends—but only a tiny portion of most-at-risk households are among the regularly working poor, and by definition, the vast majority of the most-at-risk are unlikely to be able to resume paying full rent on their own unless they secure a new source of income or a less expensive residence. Most other cash-assistance eviction-prevention programs have similarly poor targeting. An evaluation of eight such programs, both public and private (but not including the New Jersey program), noted that each was restricted to serving families with a reasonable prospect of resuming a self-sufficient status, that most of the assisted families had incomes over $615 per month, that almost half of the households included someone who was employed, and that all were functional families that had experienced a severe economic disruption. In contrast, at-risk households are much poorer, often dysfunctional, and rarely self-sufficient.[18]

By meeting some of the enormous need for one-time cash assistance from basically functional families facing isolated emergencies, these cash assistance programs probably have some indirect impact on preventing homelessness. To prevent homelessness more directly and powerfully, however, these programs must change their eligibility criteria and begin to help poorer, more disadvantaged households, including those consisting of single persons. More assistance would thus be provided to people who would actually become homeless without it, thereby increasing the amount of averted homelessness-related costs. In addition, because of the lower rental costs of poorer households, especially those with only one person, their one-time cash assistance amounts would, on average, be much smaller than those the programs currently provide.[19]

At the same time, the majority of most-at-risk households are, virtually by definition, in a continuing state of emergency, and providing them with one-time cash assistance is likely only to delay their entry into homelessness for a month or so rather than prevent it. Given the frequently higher per-month cost of homeless shelters, simply delaying homelessness by providing the cash assistance might still be cost effective. Moreover, even the most-at-risk households must have been paying their rent somehow at some point prior to receiving the cash assistance, and they might be able to do so again. By buying them some time, the cash assistance could enable household members to obtain other public assistance, to get help from family or friends, or even to find employment, especially if they are given some help. Extending the one-time cash assistance to some form of longer-term rental assistance would, of course, provide even more time for this process to work. In fact, the difference between those who become homeless and similarly disadvantaged people who do not often boils down to only very small differences in available cash.[20]

More broadly, providing most-at-risk families and individuals with additional time and social service assistance gives them the essential opportunity to address some of their core problems, become more self-sufficient, and avoid housing emergencies for extended periods. Connecticut's statewide eviction-prevention program, for example, refers tenants to other social services and helps them obtain available income-maintenance benefits and housing subsidies. This enables tenants to stay current with their rent while improving their basic situations through job training and placement, family counseling, alcohol or other drug treatment, and other services. Developing the most effective mix of available cash assistance, social services, and other help for each at-risk

household is difficult, but it must be done to use resources most efficiently.[21]

To improve its cost effectiveness, Connecticut's program also uses a relatively inexpensive mediation component. By helping tenants to negotiate with landlords, the program significantly reduces the amount of money paid for overdue rent and sometimes even lowers future rent levels, thereby reducing the program's cash assistance outlays and making future tenant payments less likely. Landlords are willing to make such concessions through mediation in order to receive at least some of the past-due rent and to avoid the considerable time and expense of both formal eviction proceedings and having to find a new tenant.

Direct payment and voucher programs. Although not designed to respond to eviction threats, programs that make portions of public assistance payments directly to landlords can eliminate nonpayment problems and related evictions. Because landlords need a reliable cash flow, tenants are often able to negotiate greater forgiveness of overdue rent and even lower future rents in exchange for direct payment. For example, with the permission of its clients (single adults living in SROs), the Tenderloin Housing Clinic's SRO program in San Francisco receives their monthly General Assistance (GA) and Supplemental Security Income (SSI) checks, deducts the monthly rents, forwards payments to the hotels, and then pays the remainder to the clients. This system helps to keep GA and SSI recipients from becoming homeless because of end-of-the-month cash shortages. Moreover, because the housing clinic works as its clients' advocate, this system also produces lower rents and gives the tenants greater leverage over their landlords.

Expanding and developing similar voluntary direct payment systems for all forms of public assistance could produce similar prevention benefits. However, government agencies should not deliver rent payments directly to the landlords, but should include some kind of intermediary to serve as the tenants' advocate and help protect their rights. A less administratively cumbersome alternative would be for public assistance programs to provide a portion of housed recipients' benefits as vouchers that could be used only to pay rent, but such an arrangement lacks the negotiating power that comes from directing numerous tenant payments through one advocate intermediary.

Keeping People in Shared Housing

As discussed above, over one-fifth of unattached homeless adults and over three-quarters of homeless single-parent families were in some kind of shared housing immediately prior to becoming homeless. Some lost this housing because their hosts were evicted—which the eviction-prevention initiatives described above could address. However, over two-thirds of the families and over half of the unattached adults who were in shared housing immediately prior to becoming homeless leave because of problems with their hosts. A significant portion of these problems concern the guests' rent or other contributions to the household, some relate to personality conflicts, and others involve abuse or mistreatment.[22]

It is not easy to find most-at-risk persons living in shared housing. Although the most likely neighborhoods can be targeted, service providers usually hear of specific shared housing problems only when the newly homeless persons come for help. Apart from some cases of child abuse or domestic violence, there is usually no discernible event that can notify providers of shared housing problems leading to informal eviction. Thus, providers must rely primarily on advertising, outreach, and word of mouth to try to make sure that people in shared housing know to go to them before it is too late.

Personality conflicts and minor mistreatment problems in shared housing can sometimes be resolved through family counseling or third-party mediation. Unfortunately, handling more severe conflicts, especially those that give rise to mistreatment and abuse, is much more complicated. Although local providers could address some of the money and contribution issues by providing one-time or periodic cash assistance, these problems cry out for public

action. Existing law should be changed, for example, to allow public assistance recipients to live in shared housing (either as hosts or guests) without a corresponding reduction in their benefit levels. Similarly, GA and Aid to Families with Dependent Children (AFDC) recipients should no longer have their benefits reduced if they bring someone else into their home (to help with the rent, for instance). Likewise, public housing and the Section 8 rent assistance program (see Chapter 4) should lift their prohibitions on subsidized tenants having non-family members live with them. Allowing heads of low-income households that house certain at-risk adults to list them as dependents for income tax purposes, or to take a refundable tax credit, could also reduce the economic burden on the hosts in shared housing situations. Some homelessness experts have even suggested a new Aid to Families with Dependent Adults program to reduce the burden on low-income parents and others who house adult at-risk persons.[23]

Assisting Those Displaced from Condemned or Destroyed Buildings

Perhaps as many as 10% of homeless people lose their previous place to stay because their building is condemned, destroyed by fire, or otherwise made or decreed uninhabitable.[24] In these three cases, prevention takes the form of transition assistance, which is discussed below. With the first two, better advance warning should be possible so that the assistance can begin before the forced eviction. The government agencies in charge of formally condemning buildings could be required not only to notify the tenants of the building, but also to notify the relevant assistance organizations. As with formal eviction notices, condemnation notices could be required to contain an emergency phone number through which tenants could get transition help. Such advance notice could also enable tenants and support organizations to block landlords from improperly having their buildings condemned or declared uninhabitable so that they can get rid of their current tenants and put the properties to some other use. Although advance notice is not possible when a building is lost through fire or some other calamity, it would certainly help if fire and police departments provided the displaced tenants with transition assistance information immediately.

TRANSITION ASSISTANCE

Regardless of how they lose their existing housing, displaced individuals and families at high risk of homelessness cannot make a successful transition into sustainable replacement housing without a considerable amount of help.

Security Deposit and Rent Guarantees

Obviously, lack of money is an enormous problem for at-risk persons seeking housing. More than 70% of the evicted at-risk population in a Chicago study did not look for alternative housing—or were not able to find any—because of inadequate funds.[25] Although this fundamental problem cannot be significantly reduced without expanded public assistance programs or other antipoverty efforts, several locally based strategies can provide some help. For example, many of the eviction prevention programs discussed earlier also provide funds to pay past-due rent (often necessary to qualify for new housing) and to cover a security deposit or first and last months' rent. Other special security deposit programs guarantee landlords that they will pay up to the amount of the security deposit if the tenant defaults on rent or damages the apartment. The tenant usually pays into the landlord's security deposit account each month until the full amount is reached and the guarantee removed. Expedited bankruptcy procedures for deeply indebted tenants looking for new housing could also facilitate their transition.

Information and Referral Services

Information and referral programs address the fact that even with some money and time, finding affordable, available housing can still be difficult. These programs often keep computerized records of low-cost housing available in various neighborhoods and offer detailed rental information on telephone hotlines to help match at-risk households with appropriate housing. Other programs, such as the San Francisco Sheriff's Eviction Assistance Program, link evicted households with alternative housing and support services as part of the formal eviction process. To meet current needs, such transition services should be expanded and better publicized.

One inexpensive model is the Homelessness Prevention Directline and Network in Alameda County, California, which provides information and referrals through a system of recorded messages on a 24-hour computerized phone line. Similar systems could be established by other networks of homelessness prevention services, or by social service agencies without sufficient staff to answer the phones—much less provide after-hours assistance.

Developing a Model Program of Transition Assistance

The Los Angeles Early Intervention Demonstration Project for Recently Homeless and At-Risk Families (EIDP), run by Beyond Shelter, coordinates government and community-based resources in the Los Angeles area to stabilize at-risk or recently homeless families in permanent housing. Unlike many of the previously described eviction-prevention programs, EIDP explicitly targets families that need more than one-time emergency assistance. Besides providing crisis intervention to address immediate needs, EIDP also provides 12 full months of intensive case management and other assistance. EIDP neither maintains families in inappropriate situations (such as SROs or shared housing) nor places them in transitional housing, which must inevitably be followed by further transitions. Instead, EIDP works to establish families quickly in permanent, long-term housing where they can eventually thrive without program assistance. The children are placed in neighborhood schools, and the program works to make sure that the families meet their neighbors, make friends, and become part of the new community.

In its first year, 143 families (mostly single mothers with children) were referred to the program: 38 found alternative housing, moved out of state, or otherwise disappeared; the remaining 105 were placed in permanent housing (65% in subsidized housing). After 18 months, 10 of these 105 families had left permanent housing, 80 were still working with the program, and the remaining 15 had successfully completed the 12-month program and were considered no longer at risk. The program cost less than $3,350 per family for over a year of assistance—which can be compared with annual shelter costs in the tens of thousands.[26]

Although almost a model transition assistance program for prevention purposes, EIDP does not serve single, at-risk persons and frequently refuses to assist those at-risk families the program considers too dysfunctional or uncooperative. Expanding the EIDP model to reach single adults or childless couples would be much more difficult and costly for the program than placing families, despite the typically lower rents for smaller rental units. Adults without children in custody are not eligible for AFDC (see Chapter 6) and have a much lower priority than families for HUD's Section 8 rental subsidies (see Chapter 4). Moreover, GA (basically the only public assistance available to nonelderly, able-bodied adults without children), where available at all, is almost never enough to cover housing costs (see Chapter 6). Veterans' benefits are more generous, but only about one-tenth of all homeless or at-risk single persons qualify for them. These problems could be addressed partially by placing some single adults together in group living (such as in group homes or SROs), which could reduce per-person rents and facilitate the pooling of available resources, but without new income or housing assistance for single adults, fully serving them would likely increase an EIDP-type program's costs per household assisted.

Modifying such a program to include more dysfunctional or most-at-risk families and individuals would certainly increase its per-household costs because of the additional expense of attending to those clients' more extensive needs. Even with a full range of services, the program's

success rate probably would decline—even if the program continued to screen out some of the most dysfunctional and expensive cases in order to refer those persons with severe mental illness, substance abuse problems, and the like to more appropriate treatment settings. At the same time, however, the program would increase the amount of homelessness-related costs avoided per person assisted.

Ultimately, the success of any comprehensive programs like EIDP will hinge on their ability to access the dwindling supply of housing, income assistance, and supportive services available from other sources. Accordingly, any prevention strategy based on such program access will be severely limited until the existing public assistance network is fortified and expanded.[27]

A bare-bones version of EIDP that did not directly require access to other supportive services was the state of California's recently discontinued Homeless Assistance Program (HAP). It provided shelter and move-in costs for newly homeless families, but no casework, and only the most basic referrals. HAP cost about $700 per family, and more than 60% of the families it served were still in their new permanent housing 6 months after receiving the move-in assistance. Although much more limited than the EIDP model, HAP-type programs that targeted those less-dysfunctional at-risk families and individuals that might be capable of at least temporarily maintaining independent housing might offer a cheaper, quicker way to provide at least some transition assistance to a greater number of needy at-risk households—perhaps as the first stage in developing a full-scale EIDP-type system that could provide the more comprehensive assistance that the majority of most-at-risk households need.[28]

PREVENTION STRATEGIES FOR INSTITUTIONAL RELEASES

As discussed earlier, institutional settings can offer stable, accessible environments in which to reach and assist people most at risk of homelessness, including the most "troubled and troublesome." An effective prevention strategy at these settings would:

- Use the most-at-risk profile to identify people most likely to become homeless after release. Assistance could then be provided to those who exhibit both extreme poverty and some number of the other major risk characteristics. Although this screening might miss some people who would become homeless after discharge, because of their relative lack of risk characteristics they would be among the most functional of the homeless and the most likely to leave homelessness quickly with minimal help or on their own.

- In institutional settings where longer-term predischarge assistance is possible, provide the vocational, educational, mental health, and substance abuse services that will improve the targeted persons' chances of avoiding homelessness.

- Prior to discharge, provide transition assistance, such as connecting most-at-risk persons with available public assistance and other benefits; developing firm referrals to appropriate housing, other support services, and employment; and contacting potentially helpful friends and family members.

- When appropriate, offer most-at-risk persons the option to extend their stay until adequate housing or—when necessary—further institutional care is secured. Some Department of Veterans Affairs medical centers have been working with nonprofit providers to develop facilities on VA hospital grounds where homeless and at-risk veterans can stay and continue receiving other VA assistance after leaving VA inpatient programs while they work to find more permanent housing. The Haven, administered by the Salvation Army at the West Los Angeles VA Medical Center, is one already-established example.

Many institutions (such as prisons, mental hospitals, and foster care facilities) already have some kind of rehabilitative and discharge planning systems that could be expanded to provide this more comprehensive assistance for departing most-at-risk persons, with each adapted to the special needs of the different institutions' clients or inmates.

Discharges from Mental Hospitals

Although homeless and at-risk persons with a history of mental hospitalization basically require the same kinds of assistance as other homeless or at-risk persons, they also have clinical needs that usually require continued treatment, and their mental illness can make it more difficult to obtain required assistance (see Chapter 17). Accordingly, it is especially important that mental hospitals ensure that discharged most-at-risk patients have a stable, housed situation to go to, with access to community-based treatment. Unfortunately, mental hospitals are not always so careful, and there is a critical shortage of community-based treatment linked with affordable housing for the indigent mentally ill. Developing more subsidized supported housing and special transitional programs would help, as would more staff to do post-discharge follow-up and case management. In the meantime, laws governing the use of federal funds for mental health care by the states could be amended to prohibit states from discharging patients without their permission unless housing and any necessary community-based treatment have been ensured. Putting this burden on the states without any financial assistance, however, could simply jam up the system or prompt a return to the "warehousing" of mental patients in crowded and inadequate facilities.

Emancipation from Foster Care

Foster care can be a valuable refuge (and sometimes a tremendously positive experience) for neglected, abandoned, or abused children, but foster care systems throughout the country are in a shambles. More than half of all foster youths never graduate from high school, many suffer from emotional and physical health problems, and many do not develop the most basic life skills.[29] While much should be done to improve the entire foster care experience, the focus here is on what could be done during the final stages of placement to help foster youths at risk of homelessness make successful transitions from foster care to independent living.

Foster care is supposed to be formally terminated at a court hearing when the youth reaches the age of emancipation (usually 18), but sometimes no official termination notice comes until the foster parents stop getting the checks and begin making inquiries. In many cases, foster youths are suddenly responsible for their own care and feeding, with hardly anyone to turn to and very little preparation. Along the lines of the institutional release assistance discussed above, much could be done to improve this situation (with similar targeting to the most-at-risk). Possible supplementary measures might include:

- Train foster parents better to help prepare youths to be on their own, and provide more family counseling and mediation to prevent the early departures that put foster youths on the streets utterly unprepared.

- Where appropriate, develop ways to strengthen any continuing, constructive relationships foster children have maintained with natural parents or other relations as part of a broader effort to help create helpful post-emancipation support structures for the youths.

- Raise the maximum age of emancipation to 21 (as some states have done) so that foster parents and other foster care facilities can continue receiving compensation for housing and caring for foster youths beyond their 18th birthdays. Besides being a relatively inexpensive way to provide an additional three years of housing to foster youths who want it, the extended time is especially important to youths who are completing high school or continuing their education, are not yet ready to be on their own, or simply cannot afford other housing. (Some states in which the age of emancipation is 18 already allow foster children to stay in the system until 19 if still in high school or vocational training.)

- Provide at least two years of comprehensive independent living skills training (for example, money management, job search skills, cooking, and health care). Some current living skills programs are only two weeks long.

- Raise the current ceiling on the savings foster children are allowed to have at emancipation so that they can better afford rent and move-in costs.

- Provide Section 8 rental subsidies to all emancipating poor foster youths. (There are usually no special funds to help emancipated foster children afford housing.)

- Develop transitional housing for emancipated foster youths that will offer continuing life skills training, casework assistance, and a support structure.

The federal government could prompt many of these changes through regulations associated with its Social Security Act Title IV-E foster care maintenance payments and, more directly, through the Department of Health and Human Services (HHS) Independent Living Program, which provided $70 million in Fiscal Year 1995 to local programs that assist foster youths in making the transition to independent adult living and avoid homelessness.

One especially promising homelessness prevention model is the Foster Youth Connection (FYC) of Los Angeles County, a nonprofit organization created in 1989 by current and former foster youth to assist others with the transition from foster care. Among other things, FYC has already:

- Established an emergency toll-free phone number, tended by foster youth, that provides information and referrals

- Created support groups and transition teams for foster youth approaching or undergoing emancipation

- Increased public awareness of the problem and prompted governmental responses

- Initiated a program to encourage senior citizens to provide housing to emancipated foster youth in exchange for support services

- Begun to develop new transitional housing for foster children

Another strategy is to avoid unnecessary foster care placements, especially when the foster home is likely to subject the child to more risk than his or her own family. Some states, for example, have developed family preservation strategies, whereby social workers use intensive family counseling, when possible and appropriate, to try to remove the risk presented to the child, rather than to remove the child from the family. Similarly, the federal Runaway and Homeless Youth program provides about $30 million annually to support over 330 transition shelters in all 50 states that work to prevent runaway youths from becoming homeless by reuniting them with their families or, when that is not practical, placing them in foster care. In some cases, providing income or other assistance so that the original family can secure decent housing is a major factor in enabling a child to live safely at home rather than enter the foster care system.[30]

CONCLUSION

The interventions discussed here offer a variety of community-based approaches that could be put to use immediately to prevent people from becoming homeless. There are obstacles, of course. Most notably, the majority of existing homelessness-related grant programs will not fund prevention programs, and those that do usually have restrictions that rule out the strategies discussed here.

For example, the Federal Emergency Management Agency (FEMA) regularly directs more than one-third of its Emergency Food and Shelter Program funding ($130 million in FY 1995) to homelessness prevention—mostly for one-time rent, mortgage, or utility assistance. The AFDC-related Emergency Assistance Program of the Department of Health and Human Services provides participating states with a 50% financial match for temporary financial assistance and services to eligible families experiencing an emergency, and HHS is permitted to direct a maximum of 25% of its Emergency Community Services Homeless Grant Program ($19.8 million in FY 1995) to prevention. Similarly, HUD may direct as much as 30% of its Emergency Shelter Grant program funds ($156 million in FY 1995) to support such efforts as

emergency rent assistance and mediation for landlord-tenant disputes.

However, because of the overwhelming demand from regular homeless assistance programs, the HUD and HHS programs do not actually provide anywhere near the maximum permitted amounts for prevention, and all the programs face threatened budget cuts or elimination. Moreover, they all support mainly one-time cash assistance efforts and are restricted to funding prevention activities that help families with prospects of resuming their rent payments or otherwise escaping their emergency situation on their own within a short time. Consequently, these federal programs offer virtually no help to community-based prevention programs that provide more comprehensive assistance or that target either single persons or poorer, more disadvantaged families—that is, those who are most at risk. Most state prevention programs have similar limitations.

A good first step toward expanding assistance to properly targeted and effective homelessness prevention efforts would be simply to change the rules governing existing prevention grant programs so that they can fund efforts to assist the most-at-risk population directly and through a full range of strategies. These rule changes would not require any new prevention funding, but they would shift assistance away from those current beneficiaries who face little (or even no) risk of homelessness and toward those most likely to suffer repeated or prolonged periods of homelessness.

Other strategies to increase funding for prevention efforts are far more complicated. Given current political realities, obtaining funding for new social programs is extremely difficult, especially when they are directed at helping the most miserable (and least politically powerful) in our society. Accordingly, most proposals for new programs raid existing social welfare budgets. Following suit, prevention interventions could be made eligible for funding from all existing federal homeless assistance grant programs. These existing programs, however, already fail to provide anywhere near what is needed to address the desperate needs of already-homeless persons, much less help them to secure appropriate housing. Shifting existing funding from direct homeless assistance to prevention efforts would inevitably make the situation worse for already-homeless people.

Nevertheless, a properly done shift toward prevention within existing funding could be justified as a way to reduce homelessness more quickly and cost effectively. By targeting at-risk people while they are still housed and before they have suffered the ravages of homelessness, prevention interventions can both be cheaper per person than efforts that help already-homeless people and could experience greater success. Done right, they should keep more people out of homelessness, per dollar, than after-the-fact efforts to feed, shelter, and, ultimately, remove people from homelessness.

Balancing this strategic preference for prevention against the inhumanity of weakening an already inadequate system of emergency assistance and rehabilitation for homeless persons raises extremely difficult ethical issues and politically complicated policy questions. Taking desperately needed assistance from Peter is never pleasant, even if it can more effectively help a similarly needy Paul. The only humane way to avoid this dilemma is to increase funding for prevention without reductions in existing homeless assistance programs, which is unlikely to happen.

Less gloomily, many of the low-cost prevention approaches outlined here would also benefit many poor and needy individuals and families beyond the targeted group of those most at risk of becoming homeless. Those measures directed at such educational or informational goals as improving the notice system for evictions, providing information about tenants rights, or establishing databases on available low-cost rental units would inevitably go beyond assisting the targeted population and simultaneously help many other low-income households. Moreover, with relatively small amounts of additional resources, even those programs that provide their most-at-risk clients with the fullest assistance could also help less-at-risk households by providing them with similar assistance, but less intensively.

The cash assistance programs, for example, could provide one-time, low-interest loans—without case management or other assistance—to less-disadvantaged, low-income households. Similarly, the eviction prevention programs could provide less-disadvantaged clients only with guidance and information, rather than full representation with case management. Following this two-tiered approach, prevention programs would still target and efficiently assist those people truly at risk of homelessness, but they would also, on the side, help to stabilize and support other low-income households—thereby strengthening their ability to house and otherwise assist their more-at-risk relatives and friends.

Even with this two-tiered strategy, however, new investments in prevention interventions cannot, by themselves, reduce homelessness substantially. As discussed briefly above, most prevention efforts ultimately must rely heavily on linking at-risk persons with other locally based social services, treatment programs, employment opportunities, and the like (as well as to various forms of public assistance payments), and will need to refer their most severely troubled and damaged clients to various forms of institutional inpatient treatment. Such resources are already scarce, and new prevention programs will increase the demands on them. At the very least, effectively expanding targeted prevention efforts requires a similar expansion in the capacity of these supportive local services and treatment facilities.

More broadly, homelessness cannot be largely prevented unless we also attack some of its fundamental causes more directly. The incomes of most-at-risk persons must be increased, and overall poverty in the United States reduced, through such strategies as jobs programs, changes in macroeconomic policy, tax code modifications, and even increased public assistance. The quantity of available, low-cost housing must be increased through changes in building codes and zoning laws, expansion of rental assistance programs, the removal of barriers (and the development of incentives) to shared housing, the preservation and renovation of the existing stock of low and lowest-cost housing, and the construction of new lowest-cost housing. More community-based supported housing for low-income persons with serious mental illness or chronic substance abuse must also be created. And the problem of damaging childhood experiences, which often produce youth and adult homelessness, should be directly reduced by measures to decrease the number of teen pregnancies, support and maintain two-parent families, hold absent fathers more responsible for their children, make day care more available, and improve foster care.[31]

As usual, it all boils down to political will, and each reader will have to do his or her own moral arithmetic. In my view, if we are really serious about eliminating homelessness as a significant national problem, a prevention-based strategy offers the most practical and promising way to proceed.

CHAPTER 19

Dilemmas of Local Antihomelessness Movements

Rob Rosenthal

While the national antihomelessness movement has been directed and staffed largely by people I call *housed advocates*, local[1] antihomelessness movements—involving *homeless activists* as well as housed advocates—appeared by the early 1980s.[2] Santa Barbara, California, where I was involved with such a movement, had four major antihomelessness organizations: the Homeless People's Association (HPA), which consisted exclusively of homeless "street people," mainly men; the Single Parent Alliance (SPA), almost exclusively "hidden homeless" women with children; the Santa Barbara Homeless Coalition, which (for a time) united the HPA and the SPA with housed advocates; and the Interfaith Task Force on Homelessness, exclusively made up of housed church leaders. This chapter is based on my experience with these groups, and on accounts of local antihomelessness movements in other places.

I will highlight in this chapter the various problems faced by local antihomelessness movements and the organizations within them. Some of these problems are typical of social movement organizations in general, and some are due to the special conditions of homelessness. In

particular, I will explore the dilemmas that confront local antihomelessness movements, which typically operate from a position of weakness along many dimensions. But this is not to say that such movements follow an inevitable course. Like the humans who make them up, social movements have room to maneuver, and understanding their constraints is one way to increase their agency.

That agency is first apparent in the rise of local antihomelessness movements. While the existence of a sizable local homeless population appears to be a necessary condition for a movement to develop, it seems not to be sufficient. Most local movements have been sparked by homeless people's response to suddenly imposed deprivations, such as police sweeps of previously "safe" areas, or the closing of emergency shelters.[3]

Of course, homeless people's grievances do not automatically lead to collective resistance. Another response may be acquiescence, or initial acquiescence that develops into individual resistance.[4] When resistance does become collective, however, it is typically initiated by homeless people in relatively spontaneous ways, often without input from housed advocates.

How and why collective resistance develops (in any social movement) is much debated and beyond the scope of this chapter, but certainly among the important factors are the availability of resources, and developments that increase interaction and communication. Crucially (and a reflection of the factors just mentioned), there must be a change in the consciousness of homeless people from a degree of acceptance of their fate as just, individual, and/or inevitable, to a belief that their situation is unjust, imposed upon them collectively, and possible to change. The creation, diffusion, and nurturing of this consciousness is a central contribution of social movement organizations.

GETTING AND STAYING ORGANIZED

Shared frames of reference and experience support the sense of collective agency necessary for organized resistance to develop, while ties of friendship mitigate the "free rider" problem; that is, the reluctance of some to become active participants if the fruits of victory will be theirs whether they personally fought for them or not.[5] In Santa Barbara, political groups were formed by homeless people with preexisting social ties. The Homeless People's Association was built by street people who spent most of their time in the same two or three parks in the downtown area; many already were friends. The Single Parent Alliance mainly consisted of long-term Santa Barbara residents; some knew one another before becoming homeless, while others developed enduring relationships in the process of political action. Organizational work and friendship networks are mutually reinforcing: political involvement often leads to stable ties.[6] By contrast, more socially isolated homeless subgroups and individuals ("transitory workers" constantly looking for greener pastures, youths unaccompanied by adults, and people with discernible mental illnesses) were by and large absent from movement activities.[7]

Some minimal level of pooled resources is also necessary for a group to organize, a prerequisite more difficult for homeless people than for any other group in our society to achieve. Not only do homeless people control few material resources, their links to people who do are often attenuated or nonexistent. Although some homeless people have ample free time (an essential resource for organizing), others are fully occupied by daily survival routines (see Chapter 8). Further, how do people create and sustain an organization when no one has an office or a living room? How can people be notified to attend a meeting or demonstration if they have no phone and an uncertain address? In sum, the "profound uncertainties" of homeless life make regular political commitment extremely difficult.[8]

Homeless activism also requires identifying oneself as homeless, a public declaration many people are unwilling to make, given the extra difficulties it may create with potential employers and landlords, with friends who do not know their "secret," or for their children's relations with peers. And insofar as activism undermines the strategic peace that typically exists between visible homeless groups and those charged with containing them—above all, the police—some homeless people see activism by *any* homeless people as a threat to a stable, if impoverished, life.

Finally, organization is complicated by tensions between groups in the homeless population. These undermine the necessary reciprocal expectations and obligations that allow groups to collaborate. In Santa Barbara, the single male "street people" of the Homeless People's Association and the "skidders" of the Single Parent Alliance (women with children who had "skidded down" into homelessness from working-class or middle-class lives) repeatedly clashed within the Homeless Coalition on issues of principles, tactics, and goals. These conflicts often reflected differences of gender, class, work background, child-care responsibilities, and sources of income. Even within a group, interpersonal tensions can make political work difficult. Although this is true of all political organizations, it is even more likely in homeless groups; limited resources heightens concerns that they may be diverted by leaders for individual use.

Serious problems also can develop because of the inherent tensions in the relationship between homeless activists and housed advocates. Advocates have played important parts in creating and sustaining local antihomelessness movements, particularly in securing resources and providing political clout with public officials and connections to media. In some cases, the writings of advocates have reinforced the "realness" of a movement to participants as well as to outsiders. Additionally, some advocates have played important roles as organizers.[9] However, when housed advocates take leading roles, they usually encounter mixed reactions from homeless activists and homeless people generally. Activists often resent the advantages of the advocates: their access to resources; their relatively stable personal lives; their class, race, and/ or gender privileges; and, due to their connections, their tendency to be recognized as spokespeople for the movement when elites or the media want to "talk with the homeless."

The explanation for such friction should not be reduced simply to status resentment, turf battles, or matters of ego, however. Activists often note that advocates "lack the urgency that we have," as one put it. "They go home at five. Our troubles just begin at that time."[10] Some criticism goes further, charging that advocates who are social service providers are merely using homeless people for their own purposes, typically for the financial gain of the organizations for which they work.[11]

Many homeless people feel that advocates would just as soon carry on the struggle in their name, but without their input. They believe that organizing other "respectable" supporters is more important to advocates than organizing homeless people—or aiding the activists' organization of them. Thus, the movement becomes *for* the homeless, rather than *with* homeless people or *of* homeless people. Wright's account of the squatters of "Tranquility City" in Chicago illustrates how some advocates may distance themselves from homeless people, while at the same time speaking for them in negotiations with city officials.[12] In sum, homeless activists often feel that housed advocates are doing both too little and too much.

Activists also criticize the strategies of advocates. They observe, for example, that the success of advocates in the 1980s in securing greatly increased levels of emergency shelter and

aid was based on appealing to the charity of housed people, often by "medicalizing" the problem; painting homeless people as innocent and defenseless victims to be cared for in paternalistic ways. Some activists charge advocates with helping to maintain the social relations that create homelessness in the first place, claiming that emergency assistance serves as a form of social control intended to contain dissent. Many advocates refute such charges of conscious pacification, though some acknowledge unintended consequences of advocacy that amount to the same thing.[13] Indeed, the tendency of advocates to channel a local movement's activities into the conventional politics they know best does tie homeless activists to the political and economic structure that creates mass homelessness in the first place, and the frustration of activists with such "business as usual" often leads them to accuse advocates of merely "managing" homelessness.[14]

For many activists (and the scholars and advocates who agree with them), a key issue is the "empowerment" of homeless people. Genuine empowerment results in homeless people controlling decision making within homeless coalitions, but reaching that level of empowerment—indeed, reaching anything like it—is quite difficult. The need for outside resources "paradoxically reduc[es] the autonomy and independence of the [homeless] members of the homeless union."[15] Even if advocates made no assumptions of superiority (which are endemic), those with resources to give—from funding to political experience—naturally want some say in how those resources are used. Yeich suggests that professional supporters of homeless organizations should refrain from trying to influence activists' strategic decisions; however, advocates may see this not as a sign of respect for equals, but as paternalism.[16]

Advocates often regretfully conclude that they must sacrifice the empowerment of homeless activists for the sake of efficiency. They may choose to control an organization's decision making or carry out political tasks—lobbying city council members or seeking funds from prospective supporters—because they genuinely believe (based on their experience in politics, their previous ties to donors, or the greater comfort benefactors feel with housed people) that the chances of success are greater if advocates are in the lead.[17] As persistent failure drives homeless people away from the movement, even advocates who want to hand over the reins to homeless people find themselves appropriating the bulk of political responsibilities in the name of the *future* empowerment of homeless people.

The most important barriers to the empowerment of homeless activists, however, probably are in the structural context of homelessness and any movement growing from it. The very notion of empowering someone else assumes a hierarchical arrangement in which one party has power to give away—and that arrangement reflects a structure which does not disappear, whatever the desires of advocates and activists, since it is based on factors outside of their relationship with each other. Within unequal power relationships, anything given remains a gift. As Frantz Fanon observed many years ago (regarding colonized peoples), to be truly empowered, oppressed people have to *take* the power themselves.[18]

Of course, groups dominated by advocates, or composed solely of them, *have* scored significant gains for homeless people on both the local and national levels, but whether the gains won outweigh the problems of empowerment has a great deal to do with what a local antihomelessness movement hopes to win.

WHAT DOES WINNING MEAN? GOALS OF LOCAL MOVEMENTS

In their formative stage, most local movements assume that something would be done about homelessness if only the public and/or officials knew how big and serious the problem is. By this logic, "winning" only requires drawing public attention to the problem. But most local antihomelessness organizations soon realize that they also need to formulate demands and targets of those demands; if this is not recognized when they begin to organize, then certainly it becomes evident the first time they are dismissed by public officials because they have asked for nothing specific.

In the early stages of a movement, demands usually focus on emergency aid: the creation of an emergency shelter, the expansion of a soup kitchen, or the inclusion of previously excluded groups in existing services, for example. Groups often feel most successful when their actions result in winning immediate aid, such as when the homeless protesters who erected "Tranquility City" got Chicago public housing, "apartments which normally take years to receive."[19]

Often a concurrent thrust is to ensure homeless people of civil rights that have been stripped away by their status: the rights to vote, walk the streets without police harassment, or sleep on public lands (see Chapter 14). Here, the demand is "that accepted principles be consistently applied; the appeal is to equity not innovation."[20] Modest though this goal may seem, success in such campaigns has important symbolic effects, as homeless people receive the message that they do not have to accept being treated as noncitizens.[21]

Yet activists and advocates soon realize that even the most successful campaigns to reestablish lost rights or lay new claims to emergency aid only mean "the temporary continuation of unsatisfactory outcomes."[22] Many have argued, therefore, that real "winning" requires identifying the underlying structural sources of homelessness—racism, poverty, redevelopment, and so forth—and eradicating these conditions through structural reforms.[23] By this logic, winning no longer means merely that some individuals escape from homelessness or even poverty, but that homelessness and poverty are eliminated.

Whatever the success of establishing structural links in the *minds* of policy makers and the general public, there has been virtually no structural reform at the national level, and little more at the local level. Local elite "solutions" still emphasize providing for individual escape from homelessness and amelioration of pressing needs; for example, the opening of another shelter instead of, say, neighborhood redevelopment to link the fortunes of housed and homeless people.[24] Local movements have found it easier to call for increased housing support and entitlement levels, which local governments have some ability to provide, than to demand job or housing *creation*, which during the 1980s especially fell almost entirely into the hands of the private sector, a complex and resistant political target. Acquiescence in such piecemeal gains may have important costs to a movement, however. Indeed, as Wagner argues, individual solutions offered to homeless people typically *fracture* whatever collective structure they have established while homeless.[25] But homeless activists often "win" individual benefits through movement activity (as well as producing gains for homeless people as a group). Cohen and Wagner, for instance, report that the activists who erected and maintained Portland, Maine's "Tent City" were much more likely to receive income entitlements, help with legal problems, and housing after the demonstrations than before.[26]

The effect of the *struggle*, rather than merely the *outcome*, is also important in local antihomelessness movements. Participants gain skills, from learning to write to learning about political practice.[27] There is also evidence that political involvement produces psychological changes that help individuals fight their homelessness and the sense of paralysis it can induce. Observers note less fatalism and growing feelings of personal agency among activists.[28] Crucially, many begin to construct or reconstruct a much more positive identity, often based on the homeless status that previously caused them shame.[29] In some cases, this apparently results in salutary changes in behavior, including abatement of substance abuse and increased motivation to find employment.[30]

This change in individuals' self-perception clearly emanates from a new sense of group feeling that is difficult to sustain in homeless life, but that is strong among movement activists. Activists usually are firmly located in social networks, and their relationships appear far more durable than most on the streets.[31] While the collective identity developed though political work is typically built upon a previous (though far weaker) social kinship, in some cases it is political work itself that creates a collective identity among people who previously had only superficial connections. Such was the case with some of the homeless mothers in Santa Barbara, who experienced "little solidarity—though much empathy" for one another until the establishment of the Single Parent Alliance.[32] Often, activists develop a sense of responsibility toward other homeless people that extends far beyond the local movement in which they are involved—though not often across subgroup lines.[33] And despite the many problems in the advocate-activist relationship, the struggle often engenders in homeless activists greater feelings of connection to housed advocates and other housed people.[34]

Yet, as in other social movements—and more than in most—the likelihood of individual escape is so much greater than the prospects of collective victory that it is hard to find much evidence to support Wright's view that "collective gains were not simply individual gains, but social gains leading to new beliefs in the legitimacy of organizing,"[35] or Wagner's faith that local antihomelessness movements can "build on existing social networks to assist poor people in obtaining housing and other benefits *collectively.*"[36] It may be that the goal most easily and often attained is simply the personal empowerment of activists through their struggle. This sobering conclusion leads again to the "efficiency versus empowerment" dilemma.

However, Wagner and Cohen have argued that there is no dilemma: "the use of disruptive strategies by the very poor [is] arguably quicker and more sweeping than advocacy . . . [while also engendering] the consciousness raising and empowerment necessary for solidarity ties."[37] Cress's account of several local movements similarly implies that their greatest successes came *after* homeless people assumed leadership of the movement.[38] These observers suggest that protests by activists are likely to be effective as well as empowering, although they do not address the efficiency versus empowerment dilemma when it arises because an organization decides that more conciliatory tactics (historically linked to advocates) are called for.

SOME BARRIERS TO WINNING

Given so many possible goals, both narrow and broad definitions of victory, and usually little time to reflect on and debate such matters, it is small wonder that the tactics of local antihomelessness movements vary widely. If personal empowerment is the goal, the process of the struggle is more important than its objects. But if winning is defined as gaining concessions from targets (as it almost always is), all local antihomelessness organizations begin with some common structural and tactical problems. Unlike striking workers, rent-withholding tenants, or special-interest voting blocs, homeless people lack leverage. All they can affect that is of value to their targets is civil peace and the maintenance of daily routine.[39] Further, it is difficult for antihomelessness activists and advocates to reach, let alone change, the powerful individuals and institutions that can affect homelessness as a mass phenomenon. Homeless groups "cannot make developers, builders, or landlords agree to engage in bargaining over the production or distribution of decent and affordable housing";[40] still less can they influence the processes and decision makers that shape responses to area-wide unemployment due to deindustrialization, or the destruction of affordable housing through redevelopment and gentrification.[41]

Instead, targets selected for protest and resistance are likely to be those more accessible, such as local welfare offices or the police.[42] However, such targets are charged with managing and carrying out policy rather than creating it, giving them little ability to change the basic socioeconomic and political situation. In some cases, the deflection of protest from vulnerable to insulated targets is a conscious strategy of elites; in general, however, deflection appears to be a routine consequence of the structure of local political bodies, which normally insulate decision makers. In either case, pressure that might be brought to bear against private capital (landlords who charge rents greater than impoverished people can pay, or employers who pay wages less than required by the cost of living) is diverted to organs of local government whose raison d'être is the calming of civil unrest.[43]

Even if "ultimate" targets could be reached, antihomelessness movements face another dilemma not confronted by most other social movements. We can easily think of African Americans winning civil rights and remaining African Americans and members of the civil rights movement, or women winning equal pay and remaining women and feminist activists, but homeless people can only win by escaping the category on which their solidarity is built, and most do so as soon as they are able.[44] Even the collective solutions suggested by Wagner and Wright—which would require massive, almost revolutionary, ideological and structural changes—presumably would fracture solidarity by abolishing the shared characteristic of homelessness.[45] Given the unlikelihood of such changes, the overwhelming majority understandably seek—even if they do not embrace—"individual assimilation at the expense of collective advancement."[46]

WEAPONS FOR ADVOCATES

To counter these substantial problems, local antihomelessness movements have developed or borrowed an array of weapons for wresting concessions from targets. Some depend principally on the skills, connections, and activities of housed advocates, particularly litigation and lobbying.

Litigation on the local level has sought to: (1) reestablish civil rights and entitlements withdrawn or denied due to homeless status; (2) enlarge the scope of responsibility of local governments, particularly for housing and treating members of vulnerable groups (e.g., mentally ill, HIV-positive, or substance-abusing people); and (3) ameliorate the immediate conditions of homelessness by mandating and/or protecting emergency shelters and ensuring decent conditions within them.[47] A "right to housing," an oft-declared long-range goal of many litigators, appears unlikely under existing statutes throughout the nation. While litigation has been important in its own right, it has played an indirect role in the development of local organizations. Attorneys faced with meager resources and hard choices generally have pursued legal actions with immediate impact on the conditions of life for homeless people, rather than fitting legal strategy to the needs of a local anti-homelessness movement.[48]

Lobbying is the other principal weapon of advocates. In some cases, officials feel compelled to respond because advocates are past supporters, or because they represent a constituency that cannot be ignored (a major reason for the lobbying success of religious leaders). In rare cases, lobbying may be persuasive because the arguments presented are, in themselves, convincing, as when medical outreach to homeless people or shelter creation is shown to be ultimately cost-effective for local governments.[49] Nevertheless, "rational" approaches are not likely to be politically successful in localities where aid to homeless people is unpopular with voters.

Whether local lobbying is based on personal relationships or rational appeal, it almost always includes a moral appeal to the responsibility of those with power and resources to help those with neither. As such, it almost always stresses an image of vulnerability and has worked best for groups seen as "innocent" members of the deserving poor (such as women and children), or those whose disabilities are clearly debilitating and not of their own making. Appeals on behalf of profoundly mentally ill people fare better than appeals on behalf of substance abusers, who are suspected of promoting their own ruin and of being largely incorrigible.

WEAPONS FOR ACTIVISTS

Often, the first weapon used by homeless people is to make "visible what otherwise was not seen."[50] This approach is intended to establish "a wide base of support," as one of the Tranquility City activists commented.[51] But why does simple visibility work to produce changes, and what changes are these?

Visibility was successful in garnering public sympathy and support, particularly in the 1980s, because it carried an implicit claim on the morality of viewers. Against the backdrop of the relative comfort of most Americans, the newly visible privation of other Americans fairly

shouted that something must be done; that it was *shameful* not to relieve such "an affront to commonly accepted canons of decency and justice."[52] Groups like the Community for Creative Non-Violence in Washington, DC, raised visibility to an art form by mixing in elements of celebrity and sacrifice (as in the dangerous fasts of Mitch Snyder and others) to ensure extensive media coverage. This approach was initially popular with the general public because it seemed nonadversarial; a simple matter of people of good conscience doing what needed to be done to publicize an abomination.[53] But for most local movements, visibility quickly moved from a nonadversarial tactic intended to make homelessness a *social* concern to a conflictual tactic intended to make it a *political* issue. Political officials or social service systems (under the direction of political officials) were targeted so that they would take action on the implicit or explicit demands raised by this visibility.[54]

However, shame may not be enough of a motivator, especially as time passes and the problem persists. When neither litigation and lobbying by advocate allies nor appeals to conscience lead to the changes activists believe necessary—typically, modest requests for adequate shelter or an end to police harassment—members of local antihomelessness organizations come to realize that the disruption of other people's daily lives is their greatest weapon; that civil peace is all they can deny to others (as workers withhold labor or voters withhold votes).[55]

While unplanned disruption sometimes gains resources for homeless people (such as when merchants demand the creation of day shelters because shoppers are scared away by the presence of homeless people around their establishments), disruption may also be planned. The objective may be to inconvenience citizens in general, or to disrupt specific elites; more commonly, activists attempt to clog the social control systems of a locality. In the Santa Barbara battles against laws prohibiting "illegal sleeping" on public lands, members of the Homeless People's Association deliberately overloaded the judicial system by demanding jury trials when arrested, rather than pleading guilty and being released for time served, as was customary.[56] The occupation of city offices during the Tent City protests in Portland, Maine, prevented normal city operations.[57] Especially for street populations, planned disruptions capitalize on the resources at hand—their bodies, their free time, and their willingness (especially in winter) to be arrested.[58] Although there are too few local case studies to be certain, it appears that intentional disruption or its threat often has pried loose local resources—although they have not always landed in the hands of the disrupters.[59]

Tactics that employ militant disruption flout norms and involve personal risk. As local anti-homelessness movements embrace such tactics, decision making within them tends to shift toward homeless activists, thus facilitating empowerment. Yet to the extent that a movement's policy goals remain unclear or unstated, even militant action remains, in a fundamental sense, passive and apt to be co-oped: "protests" typically remain an appeal to the public or those with power to do something. Without clear objectives, even militant antihomelessness movements leave the definition and solution of the problem in the hands of their targets.

IMAGES AND REPRESENTATION

Local antihomelessness movements, like the national movement, are continually confronted with what Hopper and Baumohl have called "persisting problems of culture and representation."[60] When homelessness re-emerged as a public issue in the early 1980s, activists and advocates were forced to confront a commonly held view that homeless people were either "skid-row bums" or slackers who refused to work and otherwise accept responsibility. In place of this view, early activists and advocates "sought to show that homelessness was a circumstance—not a personal trait,"[61] and that homeless people were "victims"—not culprits. For many advocates, particularly those from social service, mental health, and substance abuse treatment backgrounds, "victims" were those unable to fend for themselves, and the shame of the country was that we were no longer car-

ing for these incompetents. Such a "politics of compassion"[62] moved the debate "from blame the victim to pity the casualty."[63] This characterization, of course, justified growth in the funding and scope of the very enterprises these advocates worked in—a point noted by critics, including some homeless people.

In contrast, many activists (and some advocates) stressed the view that homeless people were "normal Americans" victimized by macro-level processes beyond their control (see Chapter 3). Homeless people were portrayed as innocent, even noble, victims. In a few depictions, their political resistance was emphasized, a partial corrective to their characterization as passive.[64] Clearly, those who were arguing that homeless people should be leading local efforts to end homelessness *had* to argue that homeless people were competent; otherwise, how could they be trusted with the responsibilities empowerment would thrust on them? How could they be dealt with as legitimate political actors?

This framing was strengthened by spotlighting homeless people with the fewest personal problems. Pathologies, when acknowledged, tended to be characterized as *results* of homelessness rather than causes (often with good reason). But this argument implied that homeless people who did *not* fit the image of the heroic, innocent, there-but-for-fortune-goes-you-or-I victim must not be worthy of help. The traditional distinction between the deserving and undeserving poor was reinforced, and questions of social inequality were displaced—again—by discussions of the personal defects of individual homeless people.[65] Thus, in Santa Barbara, the Single Parent Alliance quickly divorced itself from the Homeless People's Association, a group comprised of "the scuz of the earth," as one Alliance member put it, while another said: ". . . they buy drugs and drink. It seems that is their whole life. . . . I think something should be done about them." But even within the group of street people from which the Homeless People's Association grew, pressure to present a responsible face to elites constantly tempted its core of activists to renounce their associations with, and responsibility for, substance abusers, wanderers, criminals, and other ne'er-do-wells.

Thus, two related dilemmas confronted activists and their advocate allies: First, how to continue to stress the social roots of homelessness without denying that homeless people were drawn disproportionately from "categories of risk" and therefore sometimes required specialized programs?[66] And second, how to argue that homeless people deserved a place at the political table without dividing the competent and innocent from the incompetent and blameworthy?

THE FIT BETWEEN GOALS, STRATEGIES, AND REPRESENTATIONS

How homeless people are represented is related to what goals a movement has in mind. If the goal is to have powerful institutions and individuals take action to resolve an emergency situation by emergency means for a manageable number of people, the politics of compassion is a good fit, and it is most persuasive to portray homeless people as victims to be cared for, either incompetents or unfortunates. With time, however, most local antihomelessness movements have shifted to a "politics of entitlement,"[67] symbolized by a shift from demanding a right to *shelter for unfortunates* to a right to *housing for citizens*, but still essentially requiring the action of elite agents within conventional power arrangements, rather than the empowerment of homeless people. But in practice, sweeping structural changes are beyond what local targets can grant; therefore, most negotiations still revolve around emergency, or at best transitional, demands.

Recently, a number of advocates have called for moving beyond a politics of entitlement to a "politics of reciprocity," in which homeless people are represented as citizens who give as well as receive.[68] Exactly how such a politics would be undertaken is as yet unclear, but its premise suggests that it would embrace greater participation of homeless people in the political sphere, as in all others, and thus would involve the kind of empowerment called for by activists.

Other goals require different strategies (although this is not always clear to movement members in the heat of the battle). Some movements seek primarily to educate housed people about the issues—either citizens generally or government officials—assuming that knowledge will be translated into action. But as most movements come to see in a very short time that this is unlikely, they move toward political strategies. As Gamson's work on social movements predicts, groups with greater likelihood of success through conventional channels tend to work those channels, such as lobbying city councils for changes in local laws and procedures. These groups tend to be dominated by advocates, and they represent and invoke the image of more "deserving" groups. Often they have institutional sources of at least limited funding.[69] They engage in persuasion and traffic in the compromises required by conventional politics. However, activist-dominated groups, usually those representing street people, are much more likely to engage in direct action like demonstrations. Activists' demonstrations may also be thought of as persuasion, but since they typically carry at least the threat of disruption, they begin instead from a conflictual perspective.

Many local antihomelessness organizations come to believe that one of their greatest dilemmas is the fact that the weapons best suited to one kind of antihomelessness organization, strategy, or goal are ill-suited or harmful to another organization, strategy, or goal within the local movement. For "respectable" groups with insider advocates, education, compromise, and appeals to local government make sense. For street people without any other weapons, the disruption of daily life makes sense. This is one reason that the Single Parent Alliance and Homeless People's Association could not coexist in the Homeless Coalition in Santa Barbara: the Alliance believed that it could not press its moral claims on the public and city council with allies who threatened chaos.

This tactical quandary is not as injurious as it seems to many within local antihomelessness organizations. Local movements often benefit from the "good cop/bad cop dynamic,"[70] in which the actions of the militant wing of a movement generate responses from the elites, but the resulting resources are then awarded to the "respectable" moderate wing. Although moderate wings are prone to think that militancy in the streets hurts their chances in the corridors of power, local case studies repeatedly find that it is only *after* street actions begin that local governments address homeless people's concerns.[71] In short, the two approaches need not be seen as mutually exclusive, though tactical wisdom suggests that moderates act as though they are.

VICTORIES

Given the long odds against the creation, survival, and success of local antihomelessness movements, their list of victories is impressive. Further, as Cress has pointed out, to consider only the concessions shaken loose from targeted elites and institutions misses the benefits that are derived from activist participation.[72] Among the most important of these is the psychological support that comes from solidarity, the great relief that comes from sharing travails and talking about problems without fear of recrimination or ostracism. The change in homeless people's self-esteem and sense of efficacy gained through participation in an antihomelessness organization are difficult to gauge, but are doubtless of some importance to many and of great importance to some.

But more material benefits can be had as well: the use of the local office as a drop-in center and storage facility, part-time employment as a staff member, and links to other job opportunities and professionals who donate legal or medical aid. Typically, these benefits accrue most readily to actual organization members, but they are usually also available in some form to others.[73]

But even in the narrow terms of winning collective concessions from targeted elites, much has been gained, including an enormous increase in emergency shelters and food services, the creation of some transitional and permanent housing for homeless people, the reestablishment of lost civil rights, and the lib-

eralization of welfare eligibility requirements and the removal of procedural barriers intended to discourage homeless applicants.

We can begin to explain such victories by noting the importance of local political contexts, the flexibility of which are determined by supra-local events in highly particular and often unpredictable ways, and the crucial agency of activists and advocates. Whatever the local context, action by advocates and activists forces a *political* response, and where local movements weaken or die, the response to homelessness moves away from issues of political power and economic inequality, back toward police, social service, and charity responses.

Activity and success in one arena tends to reinforce activity and success in others. For instance, the judicial interpretations of local statutes most favorable to homeless people have tended to *follow* the creation of a movement that has politicized homelessness.[74] With the notable exception of New York City,[75] the localities with the strongest and most militant antihomelessness movements are those where the greatest judicial, administrative, and political gains have been made.[76] While the presence of the movement forces political institutions to treat homelessness politically, victories in these other realms strengthen the movement by protecting political rights, by guaranteeing previously denied material benefits (which frees up more time for political activity), and by emboldening activists and homeless people generally. In Santa Barbara, the success of a lawsuit by the Homeless People's Association to force the County Registrar to allow homeless people to register to vote led less to a marked increase in homeless voters than to an increased willingness of homeless people to engage in other struggles for their rights. Similarly, Wagner and Cohen note that after the Tent City "victory" in Portland, many more of those who participated began to receive welfare benefits.[77] Notably, it was not simply that welfare officials accepted more applications, but that so many more homeless people applied, reflecting a change in their view of what was rightfully theirs and/or what they could expect others to accept as rightfully theirs. But implicit in this is that *winning is important*, which again raises the dilemma of "efficiency versus empowerment."

Ironically, victories can jeopardize a movement. Co-optation is possible whenever the victory entails accepting a solution as reformulated by established political actors. Funding by local elites is especially perilous because future funding (which the movement comes to depend on) is always contingent on "acceptable" political behaviors. Thus, as Wright notes, the focus remains on "altering the behavior of the poor, not the powerful."[78]

Further, victories won through strategic acuity tend to be unstable because they rarely result from consensus among the public or political elites, but more often represent a temporary concession made to avoid political embarrassment. They often produce a backlash from various groups opposed to treating homelessness as anything other than a problem of deviance. Even without active opposition, however, such victories tend to dissipate with a new funding cycle or when the movement becomes quiet. Thus, we see an ebb and flow pattern in which victory is followed by backsliding toward neglect or repression until the movement regains momentum.[79]

Even victories that are not rolled back may be counterproductive. Wagner notes that even though movements fight to secure welfare benefits and social services for homeless people, many hate these systems once enrolled, feeling robbed of selfhood (with good reason, Wagner argues).[80] On a more systemic level, several critics have argued that movement victories often lead to the diversion of money from programs with some bearing on the structural roots of homelessness to others that instead give highly visible emergency aid while doing nothing to reduce homelessness in the long run.[81] On a national level, the very success of the politics of compassion, exemplified by the passage and progressively larger reauthorizations of the McKinney Act (see Chapter 15), arguably has led to a dissipation of energy among activists; a redefinition of the problem within public discourse, which avoids discussion of structural

roots; and an institutionalization of "emergency" aid, which now constitutes most of the societal response to homelessness.[82]

This may be the hardest dilemma for activists and advocates, nationally and locally. People are raising their children in cars, people are eating out of dumpsters, people are freezing to death on the streets. The moral imperative to do something for those in immediate peril is overwhelming—in fact, it is what made most of those active in the movement join in the first place. How can activists and advocates turn their backs on partial, co-optive, energy-dissipating solutions that relieve the extraordinary distress of real people? Yet given the limited resources available to deal with homelessness under present political conditions, emergency efforts will take up almost all of them.

Those who call for refusing palliatives may not only find themselves in an uncomfortable moral position, but in a dubious strategic position as well, one familiar to Communist Party activists in the 1930s or political radicals in the 1960s and 1970s. People join a movement wanting to "do good"; they come to believe that the condition of homeless people (or workers, or African Americans, or women) can only really be bettered by creating wide-scale, long-range structural change. But most of the people they seek to help mainly want immediate, short-term help to get out of the hole they are in. And after awhile, those people begin to feel that the activists or advocates are manipulating them in accordance with a long-range agenda instead of honorably joining their fight for immediate relief.

Given these many dilemmas, and given the state of politics today, is it likely local antihomelessness movements will make further significant progress, or have we seen their heyday? Further progress now seems possible only if antihomelessness movements, at both local and national levels, embrace coalition politics in a way they have not yet been able to do. Coalition politics offers a way for these movements to continue working on their own for the amelioration of current homelessness, while pressing for structural changes as members of coalitions dealing with basic economic and political justice. Thus, antihomelessness movements would make common cause with groups involved in labor, housing, welfare, racial, and women's issues, among others. But only formidable coalitions can hope to take up the task of basic structural change. If and where antihomelessness movements can establish meaningful links to other working-class and progressive movements around larger issues of economic and political equality—transforming movement members' defining identity from homeless to some greater identity, such as "working-class" or "progressive"—winning as a class would take on a different meaning and become more feasible.

There is little reason to believe that such coalitions are on the horizon nationally or in most localities, but there are some reasons to think such coalitions *might* form. Most important, the same structural factors that have led to the explosion of homelessness have created strain in many households yet to face such dire results. The crisis in housing has extended well into the middle class; the crisis in employment created by deindustrialization and the globalization of the economy reaches into all classes (though, of course, it is most serious among those on society's bottom rungs); the crisis in urban conditions affects all who use the cities; the crisis in health and mental health care, temporarily banished from political discourse, has returned in the fight over Medicare and Medicaid. These are universal concerns.

While efforts continue at the national level to form such coalitions, local coalition building may be more important. Ironically, while homelessness is created by national and international trends, only local political forces are really vulnerable to pressure, at least presently. But this was also the case in the 1930s, and the creation of the welfare state at the federal level was largely the result of local movements that applied pressure to local politicians and institutions who, in turn, eventually made it clear to national leaders that basic structural changes at the national level were necessary.[83] There is, at present, the possibility that pressure for a federal (and perhaps structural) response will filter up from the local level as besieged mayors, county supervisors, and state officials demand that Washington deal comprehensively with problems they cannot solve on their own. Whether the solutions that evolve will be framed by activists and advocates; whether homelessness remains an isolated issue or becomes linked to the various problems it reflects; whether these issues come to be seen as a function of the current political economy of the nation or remain largely the "fault" of the poor and homeless; whether the focus will continue to be emergency amelioration or will become structural reform—all these questions inform political dramas in which local antihomelessness movements and other social movements will play critical, if not necessarily decisive, roles.

APPENDIX

•••••••

Information Clearinghouses, National Organizations, and State Organizations

INFORMATION CLEARINGHOUSES

Health Care for the Homeless (HCH) Information Resource Center
John Snow, Inc.
44 Farnsworth St.
Boston, MA 02210-1211
Phone: (617) 482-9485
Fax: (617) 482-0617

The HCH Information Resource Center publishes the *Health Care for the Homeless Directory* and a series of free annotated bibliographies on health issues and homelessness.

National Coalition for the Homeless
1612 K St., NW, #1004
Washington, DC 20006
Phone: (202) 775-1322
Fax: (202) 775-1316
E-mail: nch@ari.net
WWW: http://nch.ari.net

The National Coalition for the Homeless (NCH) maintains and updates a library/database on homelessness. The library contains national, state, and local studies; program and training manuals; policy analyses; curriculum guides; evaluations; conference reports; literature reviews; governmental reports; advocacy manuals; and more. NCH publishes *The Essential Reference: An Annotated Bibliography on Homelessness*. Its database is accessible through the NCH home page at http://nch.ari.net.

The National Resource Center on Homelessness and Mental Illness
Policy Research Associates, Inc.
262 Delaware Ave.
Delmar, NY 12054
Phone: (800) 444-7515
Fax: (518) 439-7612
E-mail: NRC3PRA@aol.com

The National Resource Center on Homelessness and Mental Illness maintains and updates a bibliographic database on homelessness and mental illness. The Center publishes a series of annotated bibliographies, an information packet on financing services for homeless people with mental illnesses, and an organizational referral list. These materials are available free of charge.

NATIONAL ORGANIZATIONS

A regularly updated directory of national organizations can be found on the Web site for the National Coalition for the Homeless: http://nch.ari.net/direct.html.

Empty the Shelters/National Office
PO Box 8167
Philadelphia, PA 19101
Phone: (215) 387-0415
Fax: (215) 387-0417
E-mail: etsphilly@igc.apc.org

Habitat for Humanity International
121 Habitat St.
Americus, GA 31709-3498
Phone: (912) 924-6935
Fax: (912) 924-6541
E-mail: public_info@habitat.org

Health Care for the Homeless Information Resource Center
John Snow, Inc.
44 Farnsworth St.
Boston, MA 02210-1211
Phone: (617) 482-9485
Fax: (617) 482-0617

HomeBase/The Center for Common Concerns
870 Market Street, #1228
San Francisco, CA 94102-2907
Phone: (415) 788-7961
Fax: (415) 788-7965
E-mail: HN0124@handsnet.org

Housing Assistance Council, Inc.
1025 Vermont Ave., NW, #606
Washington, DC 20005-3581
Phone: (202) 842-8600
Fax: (202) 347-3441
E-mail: HN0143@handsnet.org

Interagency Council on the Homeless
451 Seventh St., SW, Ste. 7274
Washington, DC 20410
Phone: (202) 708-1480
Fax: (202) 708-3672

International Union of Gospel Missions
1045 Swift
Kansas City, MO 64116
Phone: (800) 624-5156
Fax: (816) 471-3718
E-mail: info@iugm.org
WWW: http://www.tfs.net/iugm

Legal Services Homelessness Task Force
c/o National Housing Law Project
1815 H St., NW, #501
Washington, DC 20006
Phone: (202) 783-5140
Fax: (202) 347-6765
E-mail: HN0328@handsnet.org

National Alliance of HUD Tenants
353 Columbus Ave.
Boston, MA 02116
Phone: (617) 267-9564
Fax: (617) 267-4769

National Alliance to End Homelessness
1518 K St., NW, #206
Washington, DC 20005
Phone: (202) 638-1526
Fax: (202) 638-4664
E-mail: HN0211@handsnet.org

National Coalition for the Homeless
1612 K St., NW, #1004
Washington, DC 20006
Phone: (202) 775-1322
Fax: (202) 775-1316
E-mail: nch@ari.net
WWW: http://nch.ari.net

National Coalition for Homeless Veterans
918 Pennsylvania Ave., SE
Washington, DC 20003-2140
Phone: (800) 838-4357,
   (202) 546-1969
Fax: (202) 546-2063
E-mail: NCHV@aol.com

National Health Care for the Homeless Council
PO Box 68019
Nashville, TN 37206-8019
Phone: (615) 226-2292
Fax: (615) 226-1656
E-mail: HN0621@handsnet.org

National Housing Conference
815 Fifteenth St., NW, Ste. 711
Washington, DC 20005
Phone: (202) 393-5772
Fax: (202) 393-5656
E-mail: nhc@nhc.org

National Housing Law Project
2201 Broadway, #815
Oakland, CA 94612
Phone: (510) 251-9400
Fax: (510) 251-0600
E-mail: HN0108@handsnet.org

National Law Center on Homelessness & Poverty
918 F St., NW, #412
Washington, DC 20004
Phone: (202) 638-2535
Fax: (202) 628-2737
E-mail: HN0749@handsnet.org

National Low Income Housing Coalition
1012 14th St., NW, #1200
Washington, DC 20005
Phone: (202) 662-1530
Fax: (202) 393-1973
E-mail: HN0053@handsnet.org

National Network for Youth
1319 F St., NW, #401
Washington, DC 20004
Phone: (202) 783-7949
Fax: (202) 783-7955
E-mail: NN4Youth@aol.com

National Resource Center on Homelessness & Mental Illness
Policy Research Associates, Inc.
262 Delaware Ave.
Delmar, NY 12054
Phone: (800) 444-7415
Fax: (518) 439-7612
E-mail: NRC3PRA@aol.com

National Rural Housing Coalition
601 Pennsylvania Ave., NW, #850
Washington, DC 20004
Phone: (202) 393-5229
Fax: (202) 393-3034

National Student Campaign Against Hunger & Homelessness
11965 Venice Blvd., #408
Los Angeles, CA 90066
Phone: (800) NO-HUNGR x324,
   (310) 397-5270
Fax: (310) 391-0053

Students Together Ending Poverty
8 Varney St.
Jamaica Plain, MA 02130
Phone: (617) 522-6924
Fax: (617) 983-0943
E-mail: jjones@jri.org

STATE ORGANIZATIONS

A regularly updated directory of state and local organizations can be found on the web site for the National Coalition for the Homeless: http://nch.ari.net/direct.html.

Alabama

Alabama Arise
PO Box 612
Montgomery, AL 36101
Phone: (334) 832-9060
Fax: (334) 832-4803
E-mail: Alarise@aol.com

Alabama Low Income Housing Coalition
c/o Federation of Southern Cooperatives
PO Box 95
Epes, AL 35460
Phone: (205) 652-9676
Fax: (205) 652-9678
E-mail: HN0141@handsnet.org

Alaska

Alaska Coalition on Housing & Homelessness
1057 W. Fireweed Ave., #101
Anchorage, AK 99503
Phone: (907) 272-1626
Fax: (907) 263-2001

Arizona

Arizona Coalition To End
  Homelessness
PO Box 933
Phoenix, AZ 85001-0933
Phone: (602) 340-7372
Fax: (602) 271-4930

Arkansas

Arkansas Coalition for the
  Prevention of Homelessness
c/o Union Rescue Mission
PO Box 164009
Little Rock, AR 72216
Phone: (501) 374-1748
Fax: (501) 375-5134

Arkansas Low Income Housing
  Coalition
1501 S. Main St., #100
Little Rock, AR 72202
Phone: (501) 374-6873
Fax: (501) 374-8780
E-mail: HN0132@handsnet.org

California

California Emergency Foodlink
PO Box 292700
Sacramento, CA 95829
Phone: (916) 387-9000
Fax: (916) 387-7046
E-mail: HN0066@handsnet.org
WWW: http://www.interx.com/cefl/

California Homeless & Housing
  Coalition
926 "J" St., Ste. 422
Sacramento, CA 95814-2706
Phone: (916) 447-0390
Fax: (916) 447-0458
E-mail: HN0046@handsnet.org

California Mutual Housing
  Association
2500 Wilshire Blvd., PH-B
Los Angeles, CA 90057
Phone: (213) 385-5365
Fax: (213) 385-0415
E-mail: AHeskin@UCLA.edu

Housing California
926 "J" St., Ste. 422
Sacramento, CA 95814
Phone: (916) 447-0503
Fax: (916) 447-0458
E-mail: HN0046@handsnet.org

California Coalition for Rural
  Housing
926 "J" St., Ste. 422
Sacramento, CA 95814
Phone: (916) 443-4448
Fax: (916) 447-0458
E-mail: HN0006@handsnet.org

Colorado

Colorado Affordable Housing
  Partnership
1981 Blake St.
Denver, CO 80202-1272
Phone: (303) 297-2548
Fax: (303) 297-2615
E-mail: HN1255@handsnet.org

Colorado Coalition for the
  Homeless
2100 Broadway
Denver, CO 80205
Phone: (303) 293-2217
Fax: (303) 293-2309
E-mail: HN0138@handsnet.org

Connecticut

Connecticut Coalition to End
  Homelessness
30 Jordan Lane
Wethersfield, CT 06109
Phone: (203) 721-7876
Fax: (203) 529-5176
E-mail: HN0332@handsnet.org

Connecticut Housing Coalition
30 Jordan Lane
Wethersfield, CT 06109
Phone: (203) 563-2943
Fax: (203) 529-5176
E-mail: HN0332@handsnet.org

Delaware

Delaware Housing Coalition
PO Box 1633
Dover, DE 19903-1633
Phone: (302) 678-2286
Fax: (302) 678-8645
E-mail: HN0769@handsnet.org

Delaware Task Force on Homelessness
20 East Division St.
PO Box 1653
Dover, DE 19903-1653
Phone: (302) 674-8500,
  (302) 678-2286
Fax: (302) 674-8145
E-mail: HN0769@handsnet.org

District of Columbia

Coalition of Homeless & Housing
  Organizations
c/o Hannah House
612 M St., NW
Washington, DC 20001
Phone: (202) 289-4840
Fax: (202) 289-5425

Florida

Florida Coalition for the Homeless
c/o Legal Aid Society of OCBA, Inc.
100 E. Robinson St.
Orlando, FL 32801
Phone: (407) 841-8310
Fax: (407) 648-9240

Florida Housing Coalition
PO Box 932
Tallahassee, FL 32302-0932
Phone: (904) 878-4219
Fax: (904) 942-6312
E-mail: HN0302@handsnet.org

Georgia

Georgia Coalition to End
  Homelessness
363 Georgia Ave., SE
Atlanta, GA 30312
Phone: (404) 230-5000
Fax: (404) 589-8251
E-mail: gpayne@leveller.org

Hawaii

Affordable Housing and Homeless
  Alliance
810 N. Vineyard Blvd., #12A
Honolulu, HI 96817-3540
Phone: (808) 845-4565
Fax: (808) 843-2445

Idaho

Idaho Housing Coalition
1500 N. 28th, #102
Boise, ID 83701
Phone: (208) 338-7066
Fax: (208) 338-7076

Illinois

Chicago Coalition for the Homeless
1325 S. Wabash Ave., #205
Chicago, IL 60605-2504
Phone: (312) 435-4548
Fax: (312) 435-0198
E-mail: HN0136@handsnet.org

**Illinois Coalition to End
  Homelessness**
PO Box 1267
Elgin, IL 60121
Phone: (708) 742-4227
Fax: (708) 742-3260

Statewide Housing Action Coalition
202 S. State St., #1414
Chicago, IL 60604
Phone: (312) 939-6074
Fax: (312) 939-6822
E-mail: HN0341@handsnet.org

Indiana

**Indiana Coalition on Housing &
  Homeless Issues**
902 N. Capitol Ave.
Indianapolis, IN 46204
Phone: (317) 636-8819
Fax: (317) 634-7947
E-mail: HN3861@handsnet.org

Iowa

**Iowa Coalition for Housing & the
  Homeless**
205 15th St.
Des Moines, IA 50309
Phone: (515) 288-5022
Fax: (515) 282-1810

Kentucky

**Homeless & Housing Coalition of
  Kentucky**
306 W. Main St., #513
Frankfort, KY 40601-1840
Phone: (502) 223-1834
Fax: (502) 226-4968
E-mail: HN0776@handsnet.org

Louisiana

Louisiana Coalition for the Homeless
c/o New Orleans Legal Assistance
  Corp.
144 Elk Pl., #1000
New Orleans, LA 70112
Phone: (504) 529-1019
Fax: (504) 529-1008

**Louisiana for Low Income Housing
  Today**
PO Box 50100
New Orleans, LA 70150-0100
Phone: (504) 482-3822
Fax: (504) 482-3901
E-mail: HN3524@handsnet.org

Maine

Maine Coalition for the Homeless
PO Box 415
Augusta, ME 04332-0415
Phone: (207) 626-3567
Fax: (207) 773-6892

Maryland

Action for the Homeless
1021 N. Calvert St.
Baltimore, MD 21202-3823
Phone: (410) 659-0300
Fax: (410) 659-0996
E-mail: HN6360@handsnet.org

**Maryland Low Income Housing
  Coalition/Information Service**
28 E. Ostend St.
Baltimore, MD 21230
Phone: (410) 727-4200
Fax: (410) 727-7515

Massachusetts

**Massachusetts Affordable Housing
  Alliance**
25 West St., 3rd Floor
Boston, MA 02111
Phone: (617) 822-9100
Fax: (617) 265-7503
E-mail: HN0334@handsnet.org

**Massachusetts Coalition for the
  Homeless**
288 "A" St., 4th Floor
Boston, MA 02210
Phone: (617) 737-3508
Fax: (617) 737-3290

Massachusetts Shelter Providers Assn.
c/o Worcester Public Inebriate
  Program
701 Main St.
Worcester, MA 01610
Phone: (508) 757-0103
Fax: (508) 753-2271

Michigan

**Michigan Coalition Against
  Homelessness**
1210 W. Saginaw
Lansing, MI 48915
Phone: (517) 377-0509
Fax: (517) 377-0382
E-mail: mcah@voyager.net

Michigan Housing Coalition
2500 Jefferson
Muskegon, MI 49444
Phone: (616) 733-4745
Fax: (616) 733-8241

Minnesota

Minnesota Coalition for the Homeless
122 W. Franklin Ave., #5
Minneapolis, MN 55404
Phone: (612) 870-7073
Fax: (612) 397-9227
E-mail: HN1104@handsnet.org

Minnesota Housing Partnership
122 W. Franklin Ave., #522
Minneapolis, MN 55404
Phone: (612) 874-0112
Fax: (612) 874-9685
E-mail: HN0335@handsnet.org
WWW: http://www.mtn.org/mhpage

Mississippi

**Mississippi United To End
  Homelessness**
c/o Multi-County Community
  Services
PO Box 905
Meridian, MS 39302-0905
Phone: (601) 483-4838
Fax: (601) 482-9861

Missouri

**Missouri Association for Social
  Welfare/Affordable Housing and
  Homeless Task Force**
308 E. High St.
Jefferson City, MO 65101-3237
Phone: (314) 634-2901
Fax: (314) 635-1648

Montana

Montana Low Income Coalition
PO Box 1029
Helena, MT 59624
Phone: (406) 449-8801

Montana People's Action
208 E. Main St.
Missoula, MT 59802
Phone: (406) 728-5297
Fax: (406) 728-5297
E-mail: HN1051@handsnet.org

Nevada

**Nevada Homeless Coalition
(Northern Nevada Contact)**
c/o Project Restart
1123 E. 6th Street, #2
Reno, NV 89512-3509
Phone: (702) 324-5166
Fax: (702) 324-0446

**Nevada Homeless Coalition
(Southern Nevada Contact)**
c/o Healthy Families Project
2500 Apricot Lane
Las Vegas, NV 89108
Phone: (702) 631-6345
Fax: (702) 631-6348

New Hampshire

**New Hampshire Coalition for the
Homeless**
PO Box 220
Concord, NH 03302-0220
Phone: (603) 228-8665
Fax:(603) 226-2752

New Jersey

**Non-Profit Affordable Housing
Network of New Jersey**
PO Box 1746
Trenton, NJ 08607-1746
Phone: (609) 393-3752
Fax: (609) 393-9016
E-mail: HN2436@handsnet.org

**Solutions to End Poverty Soon
Coalition**
2 Prospect St.
Trenton, NJ 08618
Phone: (908) 396-3400
Fax: (908) 396-1317

New Mexico

**New Mexico Coalition to End
Homelessness**
c/o Albuquerque Alliance to End
Homelessness
PO Box 325
Albuquerque, NM 87103
Phone: (505) 246-0066
Fax: (505) 766-6945

New Mexico Housing Alliance
PO Box 2047
Albuquerque, NM 87103
Phone: (505) 768-1100
Fax: (505) 767-2275
E-mail: JimR6367@aol.com

New York

**Neighorhood Preservation Coalition
of NYS**
303 Hamilton St.
Albany, NY 12210
Phone: (518) 432-6757
Fax: (518) 432-6758
E-mail: HN1018@handsnet.org

New York Rural Housing Coalition
350 Northern Blvd., #206
Albany, NY 12204
Phone: (518) 434-1314
Fax: (518) 426-1258
E-mail: HN0349@handsnet.org

**New York State Coalition for the
Homeless**
31 Maiden Lane
Albany, NY 12207
Phone: (518) 436-5612
Fax: (518) 436-5615
E-mail: HN0158@handsnet.org

**NYS Tenant & Neighborhood
Coalition/Information Service**
248 Hudson Ave.
Albany, NY 12210
Phone: (518) 465-1813
Fax: (518) 465-1815
E-mail: NYSTNC@aol.com

North Carolina

**North Carolina Low Income Housing
Coalition**
3901 Barrett Dr., #200
Raleigh, NC 27609
Phone: (919) 881-0707
Fax: (919) 881-0350
E-mail: HN0152@handsnet.org

North Dakota

**North Dakota Coalition for Homeless
People**
PO Box 473
Glen Ullin, ND 58631

Ohio

**Coalition on Homelessness &
Housing In Ohio (COHHIO)**
1066 North High St.
Columbus, OH 43201-2440
Phone: (614) 291-1984
Fax: (614) 291-2009
E-mail: HN0351@handsnet.org

Ohio Rural Housing Coalition
PO Box 787
Athens, OH 45701-0787
Phone: (614) 594-8499
Fax: (614) 592-5994
E-mail: HN1035@handsnet.org

Oklahoma

Oklahoma Homeless Network
PO Box 5885
Norman, OK 73070
Phone: (405) 232-2278

Oregon

Oregon Shelter Network
PO Box 12024
Salem, OR 97309
Phone: (503) 399-3353
Fax: (503) 375-7803

Oregon Rural Housing Coalition
310 Columbia Blvd.
St. Helens, OR 97051
Phone: (503) 397-3511
Fax: (503) 397-3290
E-mail: HN1641@handsnet.org

Oregon Housing Now
2710 NE 14th St.
Portland, OR 97212
Phone: (503) 288-0317
E-mail: HN5838@handsnet.org

Pennsylvania

**Pennsylvania Coalition to End
Homelessness**
c/o Harrisburg Center for Peace &
Justice
315 Peffer St.
Harrisburg, PA 17102
Phone: (717) 233-3072
Fax: (717) 233-3261

**Pennsylvania Low Income Housing
Coalition**
2 South Easton Rd.
Glenside, PA 19038
Phone: (215) 576-7044
Fax: (215) 572-0262
E-mail: HN0716@handsnet.org

**Philadelphia Committee to End
Homelessness**
802 N. Broad St.
PO Box 15010
Philadelphia, PA 19130
Phone: (215) 232-2300
Fax: (215) 232-1824

Puerto Rico

Coalition for the Rights of the
Homeless
Apartado 6300
Caguas, PR 00725
Phone: (809) 743-7658
Fax: (809) 743-7658

Rhode Island

Rhode Island Coalition for the
Homeless
PO Box 72841
Providence, RI 02907
Phone: (401) 421-6458
Fax: (401) 421-6426

Housing Network of Rhode Island
903 Broad St.
Providence, RI 02907
Phone: (401) 941-2495,
  (401) 941-2388
Fax: (401) 941-2497

Statewide Housing Action Coalition
  (SHAC)
c/o RIHMFC
60 Eddy St.
Providence, RI 02903
Phone: (401) 457-1285
Fax: (401) 457-1140
E-mail: HN0788@handsnet.org

South Carolina

South Carolina Citizens for Housing
PO Box 7812
Columbia, SC 29202
Phone: (803) 734-6122
Fax: (803) 734-6220
E-mail: HN2480@handsnet.org

South Carolina Coalition for the
  Homeless
3425 N. Main St.
Columbia, SC 29203
Phone: (803) 779-4706

South Carolina Low Income Housing
  Coalition
PO Box 1623
Columbia, SC 29202
Phone: (803) 776-2047
Fax: (803) 252-0034
E-mail: HN2480@handsnet.org

South Dakota

South Dakota Homeless Coalition
c/o Minnehaha County Welfare
413 N. Main
Sioux Falls, SD 57102
Phone: (605) 367-4217
Fax: (605) 367-4235

Tennessee

Tennessee Housing & Homeless
  Coalition
2012 21st Ave., South
Nashville, TN 37212-4313
Phone: (615) 385-2221
Fax: (615) 385-2157
E-mail: HN0153@handsnet.org

Texas

Texas Alliance for Human Needs
2520 Longview, #311
Austin, TX 78705
Phone: (512) 474-5019
Fax: (512) 476-0130
E-mail: HN0796@handsnet.org

Texas Homeless Network
200 East 8th St.
Austin, TX 78701
Phone: (512) 482-8270
Fax: (512) 478-9077

Texas Low Income Housing
  Information Service
1100 East 8th St.
Austin, TX 78702
Phone: (512) 477-8910
Fax: (512) 469-9802
E-mail: HN0525@handsnet.org

Utah

Salt Lake City Homeless
  Coordinating Council
c/o Volunteers of America
455 E. 400 South, #302
Salt Lake City, UT 84111
Phone: (801) 363-9414
Fax: (801) 355-3546

Utah Non-Profit Housing
  Corporation
455 S. 300 E., #104
Salt Lake City, UT 84111
Phone: (801) 364-6117
Fax: (801) 364-4256

Vermont

Vermont Affordable Housing
  Coalition
PO Box 175
Brattleboro, VT 05302
Phone: (802) 257-2005
Fax: (802) 387-4660

Vermont Coalition for the Homeless
PO Box 1616
Burlington, VT 05402-1616
Phone: (802) 864-7402
Fax: (802) 864-2612

Virgin Islands

Interfaith Coalition of St. Croix
PO Box 88
Frederiksted, St. Croix VI 00841
Phone: (809) 772-1142
Fax: (809) 772-2909

Virginia

Virginia Coalition For The Homeless
PO Box 12247
Richmond, VA 23241
Phone: (804) 644-5527

Virginia Housing Coalition
c/o VMH, Inc.
930 Cambria St.
Christianburg, VA 24073
Phone: (540) 382-2002
Fax: (540) 382-1935

Washington

Low Income Housing Institute
2326 6th Ave. #200
Seattle, WA 98121
Phone: (206) 727-0355
Fax: (206) 727-0363
E-mail: HN0304@handsnet.org

Washington Low Income Housing
  Congress
1400 Summitview Ave., #203
Yakima, WA 98902-2965
Phone: (509) 248-7014
Fax: (509) 575-3845

Washington Low Income Housing Network
107 Pine St. #103
Seattle, WA 98101
Phone: (206) 442-9455
Fax: (206) 623-4669
E-mail: HN2827@handsnet.org

Washington State Coalition for the Homeless
PO Box 955
Tacoma, WA 98401
Phone: (206) 572-4237
Fax: (206) 572-4239
E-mail: HN1021@handsnet.org

West Virginia

West Virginia Housing Coalition
408 11th Ave.
Huntington, WV 25701
Phone: (304) 525-5909
Fax: (304) 525-5909

Wisconsin

Wisconsin Coalition to End Homelessness
c/o Tellurian UCAN Inc.
310 E. Broadway
Monona, WI 53716
Phone: (608) 223-3303

Fax: (608) 223-3360
E-mail: movesaas@facstaff.wisc.edu

Wisconsin Partnership for Housing Development
121 S. Pinckney St., #200
Madison, WI 53703
Phone: (608) 258-5560
Fax: (608) 258-5565

Wyoming

Wyoming Coalition for the Homeless
PO Box 3043
Cheyenne, WY 82003-3043
Phone: (307) 634-8499,
   (307) 637-8634
Fax: (307) 637-8634
E-mail: WyoHomelss@aol.com

NOTES

· · · · · · ·

INTRODUCTION

The editorial remarks here reflect my own opinions, but I have benefitted from observant comments by Susan González Baker, Martha Burt, Kai Erikson, Maria Foscarinis, Mary Ann Gleason, Kim Hopper, Eric Lindblom, Julia Littell, Marybeth Shinn, and Liz Welsh.

1. At this writing, the Dole campaign is embroiled in controversy over its relationship with the Heritage Foundation and Citizens Against Government Waste. These two conservative advocacy organizations traded donor lists worth tens of thousands of dollars to the Dole campaign in return for the candidate's fund-raising help. This is by no means a new practice (Ronald Reagan did it, as well), but candidates technically are obliged by IRS rules to pay for such mailing lists in hard currency rather than political barter. Senator Edward Kennedy's current campaign, for instance, is buying a donor list from Handgun Control, Inc., a nonprofit that Kennedy has publicly endorsed. See Greve, "Dole's Fund."

2. On the Industrial Army Movement, see McMurry, *Coxey's Army.* On local disturbances, see Ringenbach, *Tramps and Reformers;* Keyssar, *Out of Work;* and Parker, "The California Casual." For reasons made clear in Chapter 1, it is difficult to distinguish historically the restiveness of the unemployed from that of recognizably homeless people. Demonstrations by the unemployed in the United States go back at least as far as the Panic of 1837, when demands for public works also were made upon the national government, albeit in Philadelphia rather than Washington. For a brief summary of this early history and a fine analysis of the Unemployed Workers' Movement of the Great Depression, including direct action to combat evictions, see Piven and Cloward, *Poor People's Movements,* 41–95.

3. See "A New Skid Row" (which appeared in *Time* in July 1974); and Joffee, "Down, Out, Flat Busted" (which ran in *The Washington Post* in May 1974). These were preceded by MacLeod's October 1973 article in *The Nation* ("Street People") and a United Press International article by Art McGinn that appeared in newspapers all over the country. The *Time* and *Post* articles were followed by many other newspaper stories with local angles. For example: with respect to Seattle, Washington, where the term "skid road" (later, "skid row") originated: Paul Boyd, "Rising New Breed on That Old Skid Road," *Seattle Post-Intelligencer,* undated clip [ca. July 1974] in author's possession; and for Ann Arbor, Michigan, see Gallagher, "Life on the Street." For discussions of this prelude to the mass homelessness of the 1980s, see Miller, *On the Fringe,* 108–37; and MacLeod, *Horatio Alger.*

4. The failure of early antihomelessness advocates to make the connection between White, working-class dispossession and Black, inner-city poverty probably was the result of their geographic and political isolation from what remained of urban antipoverty work, and the tendency of White and Black poverty warriors of the civil rights era to dismiss young, homeless Whites of the early 1970s as countercultural dropouts from privileged backgrounds. By contrast, the allied issue of juvenile runaways became a national *cause célèbre* during the mid-1970s, due largely to the determined work of youth advocates (mostly White) organized into the National Network of Runaway Centers

(now the National Network for Youth), who connected effectively with a broad base of juvenile justice reformers (many of them non-White) to create the Juvenile Justice and Delinquency Prevention Act of 1974, of which the Runaway Youth Act made up Title III. The so-called runaway center movement was aided as well by the grisly and highly publicized discovery in August 1973 of the serial murder of two dozen boys (some of them runaways) in Houston, Texas.

5. This paragraph and the remainder of this section draw on a draft of the national antihomelessness movement's history by Kim Hopper, a founder of both the New York Coalition for the Homeless and the National Coalition for the Homeless. Hopper's draft benefited from comments by many long-time members of the board of directors of the National Coalition.

6. Baxter and Hopper, *Private Lives/Public Spaces;* Walsh and Davenport, *The Long Loneliness in Baltimore;* Brown, Paredes, and Stark, *The Homeless of Phoenix;* and Hombs and Snyder, *Homelessness in America.*

7. CCNV would subsequently (March 1990) return the favor by refusing to allow census takers into the newly refurbished facility on the grounds that official efforts to count the homeless were a sham.

8. Conservative critics of the antihomelessness movement take the view that advocates have systematically lied to the public about the characteristics of homeless people and the nature of the problem. This controversy heated up in earnest following the publication in 1988 of Jonathan Kozol's *Rachel and Her Children,* condemned on the right as a strained exercise in apologetics, and Gina Kolata's *New York Times* "exposure" of advocacy's plot to sanitize homelessness by making homeless people appear sober and down on their luck ("Twins of the Streets," May 1989). Subsequently, Richard White (*Rude Awakenings,* 1992) and Alice Baum and Donald Burnes (*A Nation in Denial,* 1993) built widely read books around this theme of advocacy's deceits. While not entirely without foundation, claims of sanitizing were hyperbolic in the extreme. Moreover, given what we know now about the flaws of mid- and late-1980s surveys of homeless populations, the "sanitizers" were not far wrong (see Chapter 3).

9. Andrew Peyton Thomas ("The Rise and Fall," 31), a fellow at the conservative Heritage Foundation and an assistant attorney general for Arizona, asserted recently that Americans care less about homeless people these days "because we got to know them better." Thomas's article is recommended to curious readers as a first-rate bit of rightwing propaganda. As it glories in condemnation of deceitful advocates and "antisocial" homeless people who "have turned their backs on their loved ones and communities," it butchers American social and legal history and systematically misrepresents scholarly research and the 1990 findings of the Census Bureau. In short, it commits every sin against informed, civil discourse that this book aims to correct.

10. Hopper and Baumohl, "Held in Abeyance," 523.

11. For an extended discussion of the concept of social ownership, examples of it, and technical means of implementing it, see Stone, *Shelter Poverty,* 191–276. For a recent tri-country forum on social housing organized by the (U.S.) National Association of Housing and Redevelopment Officials, the Canada Housing and Renewal Association, and the Chartered Institute of Housing (U.K.), see the 12 papers in Hornburg and Pomeroy, *Social Housing,* Parts I and II.

CHAPTER 1

1. Lis and Soly, *Poverty and Capitalism;* Lees, "The Survival of the Unfit."

2. For the quoted passage, see Rossi, *Down and Out,* 11; for his historical application of the term, see 17–44. For a critique, see Bourdieu and Wacquant, *An Invitation to Reflexive Sociology,* 244–45.

3. In *The Satanic Verses,* Rushdie reminds us of the cursed nature of homelessness and the mythic link between homelessness and the devil. As an introductory quote, he uses a passage from Daniel Defoe's *Political History of the Devil* (1726): "Satan, being thus confined to a vagabond, wandering, unsettled condition, is without any certain abode . . ."

4. Luhrmann (*Persuasions,* 309) was speaking of belief, another notoriously difficult term to pin down.

5. In this discussion we draw especially on van Gennep (*The Rites of Passage*) and Turner (*The Forest of Symbols,* 93–111; *The Ritual Process,* 94–203; *Dramas, Fields, and Metaphors,* 166–271; *On the Edge of the Bush,* 158–62, 264f, 294f).

6. See, also, Erikson's discussion of the aftermath of the 1972 Buffalo Creek flood in West Virginia (*Everything in Its Path*).

7. Waddell, *The Wandering Scholars.* Carl Orff's *Carmina Burana* sets a recently discovered cache of such songs to music.

8. As Newman (*Falling from Grace,* 91f) notes with respect to displaced corporate managers, the anomalous situation represented by such "living contradiction" of the American promise (*talented* managers out of work!) may persist without structural resolution. If so, the sense of ever being in one's proper station may prove elusive, a predicament increasingly presenting itself to casualties of "downsizing," for whom reinstatement at comparable status and pay levels seems unlikely (see *The Downsizing of America*). It is this persistent state of being caught "betwixt and between," never resolved by market or abeyance, that we refer to as "limbo." According to the *Oxford Companion to English Literature* (Harvey, 479), the term "limbo" escaped its theological provenance and "came to be used to mean prison, confinement; and later for a place of rubbish and forgetfulness." In *The Divine Comedy,* Dante characterized these souls as forever "lost."

9. We draw here on Mizruchi (*Regulating Society*) and our earlier discussion (Hopper and Baumohl, "Held in Abeyance").

10. We depart from Mizruchi in our view that not all abeyance measures control surplus people directly or completely after the fashion of total institutions. Mizruchi has commented that he does not regard income maintenance programs as "directly relevant to abeyance" because they do not control their beneficiaries to any significant degree (personal communication, and Mizruchi, *Regulating Society*, 155–56). This depends on the program. In its earlier days, Aid to Families with Dependent Children allowed considerable moral oversight—surveillance—by caseworkers, who sometimes raided the houses of welfare mothers looking for cohabiting men; many General Assistance programs required that able-bodied beneficiaries turn up for, typically, agricultural labor several times each week. While court decisions of the 1960s and 1970s eroded this surveillance, recent developments in welfare reform, what Greenberg and Baumohl (Chapter 6) call "behavioral requirements" for continuing eligibility (mandatory job training and the school attendance of children, for example), have made manifest once more the confluence of social provision and social control, which is the hallmark of the abeyance function. We introduce the notion of "completeness" to distinguish fully fledged abeyance measures like standing armies from those that play a smaller role in a process that may support and control an individual from several directions at once (from, say, the welfare department and the public school), and that may promote social integration (through social provision) without a strong element of surveillance (the GI Bill, for instance).

11. Indeed, well into the 20th century it was common for the "inmates" of all manner of institutions to be regarded as members of such corporate families. The metaphor failed first in public institutions overwhelmed by growth after the Civil War, but lingered in the small, frequently evangelical institutions—often called "homes"—that reformed drunkards, prostitutes, and others. See Dwyer, *Homes for the Mad*; and Baumohl, "Inebriate Institutions in North America."

12. See Kusmer, "The Underclass"; and Lawrence, "William Cosby and the Freedom of the Press," 245.

13. See Rice, "The Homeless," and "The Failure of the Municipal Lodging House."

14. Morris, *Government and Labor in Early America*, 13. On the composition of Boston's almshouse population during the mid-18th century, see Rothman, *The Discovery of the Asylum*, 39–41.

15. As cited by Pomerantz, *New York*, 331.

16. "A Pauper Colony," *San Francisco Call*, 5.

17. Rothman, *The Discovery of the Asylum*, 182–205. By 1880, one-third of the almshouse population nationwide consisted of people at least 60 years old (Grob, *Mental Illness and American Society*, 181).

18. Boyer, *Urban Masses*; and Kusmer, "The Functions of Organized Charity."

19. Meyerowitz, *Women Adrift*, 44. Walt Whitman (1819–1892) and Jack London (1876–1916) sang in praise of the open road and its rugged sojourners. Inspired by the gritty street children of New York City, Horatio Alger (1832–1899) invented the urban fable of pluck and luck. For emancipated slaves, mobility and freedom were virtually indistinguishable (see Chapter 11).

20. The late Nels Anderson, who became a sociologist and America's foremost scholar of homelessness, worked in his late teens and early 20s (between 1907 and 1912) as a mule skinner, a track layer, a tunnel driller, a lumberjack, a miner, and a ranch hand. His Swedish-born father had done similar roving work as a young man, even taking a turn at prospecting in South Dakota. "In his own way he saw the road as an adventure," Nels recalled in 1961. Even after marriage, Anderson's parents moved 10 times in 16 years. "My mother called the halt." (See Anderson, *The Hobo*, v–x.)

21. Turner, *Dramas, Fields, and Metaphors*, 166–230; and Jusserand, *English Wayfaring Life*.

22. For whom the road proved one of the most integrated institutions of American life (Kusmer, "The Homeless Unemployed").

23. Note that this meant that under one roof were thus assembled both established order's uniformed guardians and its most benighted affront—to the great and continuing distress of the former.

24. "The point is that nobody seems to want the chronic drunkards," observed the *San Francisco Chronicle* in November 1934 (though it could as easily have been 1914). "The police are tired of housing them in the county jail where conditions are already overcrowded.... [T]he county hospital is so crowded with indigent sick that no room can be found for alcoholics. . . . [T]he state mental hospitals are being overrun with these offenders, who have a bad effect on the insane who are complaining." Most of the men in question wound up in the rescue missions and public shelters, of course. See Baumohl and Tracy, "Building Systems to Manage Inebriates"; cited passage, 583.

25. Baumohl interview on March 25, 1985, with Florette White Pomeroy, a federal relief administrator in California during the Depression; for New York, see Crouse, *The Homeless Transient*, 153–81. Until the end of 1938, even resident single men in California could get relief only in 39 State Relief Administration camps. When the SRA began to relieve them outside the camps, certain categories of troublesome men were retained: "chronic alcoholics, men with venereal disease and men who are not part of the community in which they live and have no ties or friends or family and . . . no prospects of securing employment" ("When Freedom Rings," 220).

26. "The Wino Welders," *San Francisco Chronicle*, 1.

27. The best discussions of the origins of skid row are in Lovald ("From Hobohemia to Skid Row") and Ander-

son (*Men on the Move*). Interestingly, when the *Post* ran a piece on the "homeless man" called "Will Ours be the Century of Homelessness," it meant refugees displaced by World War II and its aftermath (see Hopper, "A Bed for the Night," 24).

28. As sociologists Howard Bahr and Theodore Caplow put it, skid-row men were "poor, anomic, inert, and irresponsible." Cited in Hoch and Slayton, *New Homeless and Old,* 111.

29. Bahr (*Skid Row,* 9 and 11) writes: "The skid row men are a little-known tribe who live in seclusion in small urban enclaves. There are more than 150 distinct bands, each having its own land base and unique institutions. The skid row men have been at times quite numerous, but now students of the tribe speak of its imminent extinction." He continues, "Like many other 'primitive' tribes living in close contact with more 'civilized' peoples, the skid row men are objects of discrimination. . . ." Bahr then goes on to quote a journalist's racist description of the New Zealand Maori, a description which also "fits the skid row man perfectly."

30. Sigal, "The Unchanging Area in Transition."

31. Caplow, "The Sociologist and the Homeless Man," 6.

32. Groth, *Living Downtown,* 130.

33. A point nicely made by Bahr (*Skid Row,* 67–80) in a survey of contemporary *New Yorker* cartoons in which bums figured prominently.

34. Golden, *The Women Outside.*

35. Hopper and Hamberg, "The Making of America's Homeless,"13. Baumohl and Miller, "Down and Out in Berkeley," 62, studying the rise of young adult homelessness in Berkeley, worried that if "youth ghetto street life" represented a "terminus" on the order of the old skid row, "we have a problem of tragic dimensions." Miller (*On the Fringe,* 136) subsequently rephrased this passage, observing that such street life was a "terminus." This seems like a dubious generalization about the trajectories of young (if difficult) lives, but that we have since developed a homelessness problem of "tragic dimensions" is indisputable. Miller's fine book is unusual in its attention to this prelude to the mass homelessness to follow, but see also Blumberg, Shipley, and Barsky, *Liquor and Poverty,* 155–74.

36. At least one journalist, Camilo Vergara (see "Ghettoes," "Lessons Learned," and "Showdown"), who has documented the shifting fortunes of marginal neighborhoods for more than a decade in New York, has warned that the density of targeted relocation of homeless families may well mean that "new ghettoes" are emerging as the successors to unstable (and expensive) shelter systems. Homelessness recedes, but for all intents and purposes, the disfranchisement so painfully evident in the liminal stage persists.

37. No doubt, many self-initiated "exits" from homelessness, especially for "unattached" men and women, involve continuing makeshifts. The most recent occupancy survey of rental housing in New York City estimates that

there are 210,000 doubled-up households there; 86,000 of them harbor an illegal "sub-family," while the rest include "secondary individuals" (*Housing and Vacancy Report,* 58,157). A follow-up study by Sosin, Piliavin, and Westerfelt ("Toward a Longitudinal Analysis") of 265 single homeless individuals in Minneapolis showed that over three-quarters reported leaving the streets for at least a 2-week period during the 6-month follow-up period. Those who found housing went chiefly to the homes of friends and family. Just over half returned to the street and shelters before the 6-month period ended. A subsequent analysis of these data (Piliavin, et al., "Exits") set stricter criteria for exits—distinguishing "independent" (one's own place) from "dependent" (doubled-up, for example)—and found that recent work history and welfare receipt predicted independent exits. Men (probably because of the structure of welfare eligibility—see Chapters 6 and 8) and those with poor work histories were more likely to return to homelessness.

38. Hopper and Baumohl, "Held in Abeyance." We argue that shelters are not complete abeyance mechanisms because they have no concern with livelihood but provide merely a bed for the night.

39. Modell, *Into One's Own;* Hareven, "The History of the Family."

40. Compulsory attendance of high school was promoted during the Great Depression as an answer to unacceptably high rates of unemployment among (and the additional competition posed by) teenagers. See Kett, *Rites of Passage,* 264.

41. On the finite resources of young African American men in Boston, see Hainer, "Sharing Kith and Kin," and in New York City, Gounis, "The Domestication of Urban Marginality."

42. Weitzman, "Pregnancy and Childbirth."

43. Jonathan Kozol's characterization of one such welfare hotel in New York City, as cited by Groth, *Living Downtown,* 10. See also Kozol, *Rachel and Her Children.*

44. Parker, *Flesh Peddlers.*

45. Bogard, et al., "Surplus Mothers."

46. See Bahr, "Homelessness, Disaffiliation, and Retreatism," and *Skid Row.*

47. Geertz, *The Interpretation of Cultures,* 26.

48. Again, the analogy with "unemployment" is telling. See Hopper and Baumohl, "Held in Abeyance."

49. Gouldner, *The Coming Crisis,* 82.

50. For a critical review of ethnographic myopia in the contemporary anthropology of homelessness, see Hopper, "Limits to Witness."

51. "Transitional" stays (one or two shelter stays, less than two months total over a three-year period) account for nearly three-quarters of the single shelter users in New York City (Culhane, et al., "Public Shelter Admission Rates"; and Kuhn and Culhane, "Applying Cluster Analysis"). Data from six other jurisdictions, while not as com-

pletely analyzed, are consistent with this finding (Burt, "Comment"). So are the findings of Link and his colleagues which document past homelessness in a national sample of currently housed telephone respondents (see Chapter 2).

52. Marybeth Shinn, unpublished data, presented at the Nathan S. Kline Institute, February 5, 1996.

53. "Demoralization" was a term commonly used by Victorian charity workers to describe the lassitude and corrupt discipline of poor people, frequently brought on, in their view, by relief arrangements that sapped initiative. "Shelterization," coined by Sutherland and Locke (*Twenty Thousand Homeless Men*), was essentially an adaptation of the term to describe the intervention-induced torpor and dissipation of warehouse shelter residents of the Depression. See also Gounis, "The Manufacture of Dependency."

54. Milofsky, et al., "Small Town in Mass Society." This is also apparent from ongoing research on Westchester County, New York's antihomelessness system conducted under Hopper's direction at the Nathan S. Kline Institute. Preliminary report delivered at Annual Research Conference of the New York State Office of Mental Health, Albany, New York, December 1995.

55. Hainer, "Sharing Kith and Kin."

56. Schwartzman and Lewis, "Gimme Shelters." Formally obligated kinship was last tried in New York in 1937, with some success in decreasing intake rates for homeless relief.

57. As quoted by Stark, "Gore and Gingrich." Cultural conservatives in the GOP, especially, seem as nostalgic about the moral order of the immediate post–World War II era as late Victorians were about the tranquility of early 19th-century hamlets. Ironically, listening to Newt Gingrich (who has a Ph.D. in history, remarkably enough) it is often not clear whether he is exalting the 1950s or, like Ronald Reagan (a Calvin Coolidge devotee), the 1920s, or even the 1880s. Put another way, it is hard to know whether Gingrich rejects merely the premises of the Great Society, the whole legacy of the New Deal, or the entire structure of economic and social regulation that began to emerge in the 1890s.

58. Orwell, *Down and Out in Paris and London*, 119.

CHAPTER 2

1. Burt, *Alternative Methods.*

2. Burt, *Practical Methods.* A Comprehensive Housing Affordability Strategy (CHAS) or Consolidated Plan is a planning document that all jurisdictions must complete to receive HUD funds for housing, community development, and assistance to the homeless.

3. Burt, *Practical Methods.*

4. A voucher arrangement is a common way for communities without shelters, or without enough shelter space, to accommodate fluctuating numbers of homeless persons or families. It is usually a formal payment arrangement whereby the local welfare or community action agency, or a private nonprofit agency, arranges to place a homeless person or family in a hotel or motel room or in an apartment maintained for the purpose, and pays the hotel or motel owner or apartment operator through a voucher system. Individuals or families staying temporarily in other arrangements to shelter the homeless would also be included in this category (e.g., when church members affiliated with a church-sponsored program take homeless persons into their homes as a temporary shelter arrangement, with or without payment).

5. The two categories listed are subsets of the larger category commonly referred to as "the doubled up." If being doubled up means that a dwelling unit is occupied by two or more subhouseholds, then the very large majority of doubled-up households are voluntary arrangements and do not imply homelessness or an imminent risk of homelessness; e.g., a teen mother and her child living with her mother, an elderly couple residing in the home of their adult child, or a roommate or group-house arrangement. The definition given here of people at imminent risk is designed to identify the people in doubled-up situations who might be considered most likely to find themselves literally homeless; that is, residing on the streets or in shelters.

6. If the person in question is a youth (unaccompanied minor) who would not normally be expected to pay for his or her own housing, the emergency might include being a runaway, a pushout, or a throwaway.

7. The following section draws heavily from Burt, "Studies That Try to Count the Homeless." The eight studies are reported in: Lee, "Stability and Change"; Rossi, et al., *The Condition of the Homeless*; Burt and Cohen, *Feeding the Homeless*; Vernez, et al., *Review of California's Program*; James, *Numbers and Characteristics*; Taeuber and Siegel, *Counting the Nation's Homeless*; Dennis, et al., *Prevalence of Drug Use*; and Hutcheson, "Rural Kentucky Study."

8. During the 1990 decennial census, the night and early morning of March 20–21 was designated as "street and shelter night," which came to be known as S-night. On this night, Census Bureau employees enumerated everyone they found in shelters for the homeless and in pre-identified street locations, in an effort to include in the census people who would most likely not be counted in the usual household enumeration. The results of this special effort are usually dealt with as the Census Bureau's "count of the homeless." For a critique, see the collection of studies in Wright, "Counting the Homeless."

9. An official count was released of the street and shelter enumerations, and this figure was widely and incorrectly reported by the media as the official federal estimate of the size of the homeless population.

10. Resource Group, *Homelessness in Houston, Harris County and Gulf Coast United Way Delivery Areas.*

11. During every decennial census, data collection is divided into two enumerations: the household enumeration with which everyone is familiar, and the group quarters enumeration. There are over 90 types of group quarters, from jails and prisons to hospitals and nursing homes, to hotels and motels, to college dormitories and boarding schools, to residential treatment programs for people with various conditions. The Census Bureau uses a special, truncated version of the census short form to enumerate people in all of these group quarters as part of each decennial census. Shelters for the homeless are considered to be a group quarter, and the shelter enumeration on S-night was reported as part of the Census Bureau's report on group quarters.

12. Culhane, et al., "Public Shelter Admission Rates."

13. Link, et al., "Lifetime and Five-Year Prevalence of Homelessness."

CHAPTER 3

For assistance in rehabilitating the structural approach, we thank Kim Hopper.

1. Baum and Burnes, *A Nation in Denial;* for a sharp critique, see Baumohl, "A Dissent."

2. Baumohl, "A Dissent," 333–34.

3. Apgar, et al., *The State of the Nation's Housing.*

4. As we use the term, a "tight" market is one with high demand relative to supply. This is the typical lay understanding. Many housing economists use the term to mean precisely the opposite, however; that is, a market is "tight" when demand is readily absorbed, when there is no slack.

5. Wolch and Dear, *Malign Neglect.*

6. See Groth, *Living Downtown;* Hoch and Slayton, *New Homeless and Old;* Hamburger, *All the Lonely People;* Winberg and Wilson, *Single Rooms;* Stephens, *Loners, Losers, and Lovers;* and Shapiro, *Communities of the Alone.*

7. Hopper and Hamberg, "The Making of America's Homeless"; Rossi, *Down and Out;* and Wolch and Dear, *Malign Neglect.* See Hoch and Slayton, *New Homeless and Old* for the experiences of other cities.

8. Burt, *Over the Edge.*

9. Subsequent studies indicated that most of these latter individuals, among whom the mentally ill were overrepresented, were terminated largely because their impairments made it difficult for them to challenge erroneous decisions, not because they were ineligible for benefits. About half of those who managed to mount appeals were eventually successful in having their entitlements reinstated (Hopper and Hamberg, "The Making of America's Homeless," 27).

10. Indeed, drunks and addicts were among the first groups to be barred from state hospitals; virtually every state with a commitment law affecting chronic substance abus-

ers in the early 1960s had repealed it by the mid-1970s. See Baumohl and Huebner, "Alcohol and Other Drug Problems."

11. Other forms of temporary work—in clerical services, for instance—have also become dominated by the temp industry, but historically these have been less important to poor or homeless people living from day to day. On trends in the temporary help industry, see Parker, *Flesh Peddlers and Warm Bodies.*

12. "Shelter poverty," as defined by Michael Stone (*Shelter Poverty*), refers to the inability of households, regardless of income, to meet essential needs because of the burden of housing costs. For many purposes, it is thus a more sensitive measure of "affordability" (conventionally set at "30% of gross income," based upon the standard of "what most households pay"). (The shelter poverty index is more sensitive to household size, for example.) This approach suggests strongly that any program of housing support can only be designed or evaluated with reference to parallel programs for meeting other essentials at some minimal level of decency. A "shelter poor" household may have its housing costs reduced to zero through subsidy and still not be able to meet other necessities.

13. See discussions in Burt, *Over the Edge;* Wolch and Dear, *Malign Neglect;* and Chapter 4.

14. The myth persists that recipients of Aid to Families with Dependent Children (AFDC) are "dependent" on welfare. In fact, the maximum amount a family could receive in 1993 in combined cash and food stamps in an average (median) state was less than 70% of the official poverty line; no state paid enough to lift a family above that line (see Chapters 4 and 6). A close study of over 200 welfare recipients in 4 cities found that benefits alone do not provide a livelihood; instead, "recipients must supplement their welfare income with unreported work or covert contributions from boyfriends, friends, or relatives" (Edin, "The Myths of Dependence and Self-Sufficiency," 1; see also Edin and Lein, *Making Ends Meet*). To survive, that is, they must contrive to cheat.

15. Koegel, "Through a Different Lens."

16. Link and Phelan, "Social Conditions." For a fine example of the approach we have in mind, see Sullivan, *Getting Paid.*

17. Culhane, et al., "Public Shelter Admission Rates."

18. Kuhn and Culhane, "Applying Cluster Analysis."

19. Burt, "Comment."

20. Burt, "Thoughts on Solving the Problem of Homelessness."

21. While rates of substance abuse would certainly be lowered by the inclusion of children, rates of depression and anxiety might be another matter. Along with developmental and academic delay, these are common problems among homeless children, a fact attributable to the backgrounds of poverty and relentless stress from which they

come, and to the unique stressors associated with homelessness itself. See Chapter 10 for a discussion.

22. In Koegel and Burnam's Los Angeles research, for instance, the lifetime prevalence of depression was 21%, while the current (within the last 6 months) prevalence was 16%; with respect to schizophrenia, 7% and 5%, respectively; for substance use disorder, 71% and 48%. The sample consisted primarily of single men.

23. For the best review of this literature, see Lehman and Cordray ("Prevalence of Alcohol, Drug, and Mental Disorders").

24. See Fischer ("Estimating the Prevalence of Alcohol, Drug, and Mental Health Problems"); Fischer and Breakey, "The Epidemiology of Alcohol, Drug, and Mental Disorders."

25. In an earlier study, for example, Koegel, Burnam, and Farr ("The Prevalence of Specific Psychiatric Disorders") found that homeless adults in the downtown area of Los Angeles, when compared with a domiciled sample drawn from the more general community (i.e., not a sample of poor people), were 38.3 times more likely to suffer from schizophrenia and 37.5 times more likely to have experienced a manic episode within the last 6 months. Interestingly, while recent alcohol dependence and drug dependence were both highly prevalent (27.1% and 10.1%, respectively)—much more prevalent than schizophrenia and mania (11.5% and 7.5%, respectively)—homeless adults were only 2.7 times more likely than those in the general community to be experiencing substance use disorders. This was because these disorders were also highly prevalent among housed individuals. These figures make it clear that successful attempts to understand the magnitude of a problem in a homeless population must employ a community comparison. Without a standard against which to compare results, we are prey to making the mistake of assuming that problems that are pervasive throughout the general population are unique to homeless individuals.

26. Koegel and Burnam, "Issues in the Assessment of Mental Disorders."

27. Mangine, et al., "Homelessness among Adults"; and Susser, Struening, and Conover, "Childhood Experiences of Homeless Men."

28. See Weitzman, Knickman, and Shinn, "Predictors of Shelter Use"; Bassuk, Rubin, and Lauriat, "Characteristics of Sheltered Homeless Families"; Bassuk and Rosenberg, "Why Does Family Homelessness Occur?"; Susser, et al., "Childhood Antecedents"; Caton, et al., "Risk Factors"; and Wood, et al., "Homeless and Housed Families."

29. Koegel and Burnam studied a probability sample of 1,563 adults who had been homeless within the last 30 days. The sample was drawn from two sections of Los Angeles where homeless people tend to congregate. Compared with the general Los Angeles population, the sample is disproportionately male (80%), African American (over half), concentrated between the ages of 29 and 48, and more poorly educated (nearly 40% had not finished high school).

Nearly three-quarters suffered from a major mental illness (4%), a substance use disorder (52%), or both (17%). Two-thirds of the men, and almost half (44%) of the women had been incarcerated as an adult. Strikingly, nearly half of the sample (45%) had been homeless multiple times that added up, on average, to more than a year. (For details, see Koegel, Burnam, and Mclamid, "Childhood Risk Factors.")

30. To take one example: In a comparison of two groups of vulnerable adults (all of whom made use of the same free meal programs in Chicago)—one group homeless, the other domiciled—Sosin found relatively few statistically significant differences, and argues that differential access to protection for "problem-ridden adults" is what best explains why some become homeless (Sosin, "Homeless and Vulnerable").

31. Studies comparing homeless families with their poor, but housed, counterparts typically find a real, but relatively small gradient of difference. As Shinn and Weitzman report (Chapter 10), 69% of the homeless mothers in a Boston study reported a major family disruption during childhood, but so did 57% of the comparison group. Out-of-home placements during childhood do appear to be more common among homeless than among domiciled mothers, but a close study of domestic violence revealed no difference between homeless and housed mothers in New England. Generally speaking, Shinn and Weitzman also note, the histories of homeless mothers tend to reveal less disruption than those of women in shelters for single adults.

32. Sosin, Colson, and Grossman, *Homelessness in Chicago),* for example, found that half of an "extremely poor" (but not homeless) comparison group in Chicago had been homeless in the past, some of them repeatedly. In Los Angeles, researchers found that 39% of a comparison group of welfare families had been forced to double up with "strangers" at some point in the past five years; one-fifth had been literally homeless (Wood, et al., "Homeless and Housed Families").

33. Rock, "The Sociology of Deviance," 143.

34. Rosenheck and Fontana, "A Model of Homelessness," 427.

CHAPTER 4

Much of the information in this chapter is based on studies of HUD and Census Bureau data by the author for the Low Income Housing Information Service. Raw data from the American Housing Survey was the primary source of information on housing and household characteristics in 1989 and 1993.

1. The 1950 census was the first to tabulate metropolitan area residents by location within or outside of central cities. The 1990 census found that the proportion of metropolitan population outside of central cities was still 60%.

2. "Section 8" refers to Section 8 of the U.S. Housing Act of 1937 as revised in 1974, the enabling legislation for

this program. The subsidy under the program covers the difference between the "tenant contribution" toward rent and utilities and the "fair market rent" for the housing. With some exceptions, the tenant contribution was initially 25% of adjusted income; this was increased to 30% of income in 1981. Fair market rents (FMRs) are supposed to be what the market rent for a comparable unit would be if there were no subsidy. The Section 8 program includes both project- and tenant-based subsidies. Project-based subsidies have been provided under the program for new construction, substantial or moderate rehabilitation and, more recently, single-room-occupancy (SRO) housing.

Tenant-based rental assistance, a second major part of the Section 8 program, supplements the amount paid by households subsidized. This program is administered by local or state public housing agencies (PHAs). The subsidy is based on covering the difference between the required tenant contribution and an amount based on the FMR for the unit. FMRs are based on estimates of the rent and utility costs, by number of bedrooms, for housing occupied by recent movers (within two years) to rental housing, excluding new construction and public housing. They are set annually by HUD for each metropolitan area and nonmetropolitan county.

Once a household reaches the top of the waiting list, it receives a certificate or voucher. Essentially, this is a notice from the PHA stating that it will contract with the owner to pay the applicable subsidy. Units occupied must meet HUD's housing quality standards. In the case of certificates, they must cost no more than an approved rent (which may be a market rent lower than the FMR or may be an "exception rent" above the FMR). In the case of vouchers, the subsidy is the difference between the tenant contribution (generally 30% of adjusted income) and the applicable "payment standard" set by the PHA, which may be no lower than 80% of the FMR. A household finding a unit for less than the payment standard benefits by paying less than 30% of income; a household finding a unit for more than the payment standard obviously pays more than 30% of income.

The two separate programs are the result of a compromise in the early 1980s between Congress and the Reagan administration. Essentially, the certificate program was developed during the 1970s and the voucher program is the version that the Reagan administration was unable to substitute for it in the early 1980s. There have been numerous efforts to combine the two programs.

3. Two factors lay behind this increase: (1) the overhang of units approved prior to 1980 but not completed until afterward, and (2) Congress's refusal to approve many of the cuts proposed by the Reagan administration. In contrast, since 1988, Congress has tended to reduce presidential budget requests for low-income housing.

4. The number of units covered by HUD low-income housing payments in fiscal 1994 was 4.74 million. As of March 1996, HUD was estimating levels of 4.72 million in fiscal 1995 and 4.75 million in fiscal 1996.

5. Gross rents, now termed "housing costs," is used by the Bureau of the Census and others to include what are considered to be the normal costs of occupying rental housing, whether these costs are included in the rent payment or not. As defined by the Census Bureau, rental housing costs "include the contract rent plus the estimated average monthly cost of utilities (electricity, gas, and water) and fuels (oil, coal, kerosene, wood, etc.); property insurance, mobile home land rent, and garbage and trash collection if these items are paid for by the renter (or paid for by someone else, such as a relative, welfare agency, or friend) in addition to rent" (U.S. Bureau of the Census, "American Housing Survey for the United States in 1989," App.–20). Unless otherwise stated, the terms "rents" and "housing costs" are used interchangeably with gross rents.

6. Fair market rents (FMRs) are estimated annually by HUD for each metropolitan area and nonmetropolitan county, primarily for use in setting subsidies under Section 8. The concept was developed as a proxy for the concept of modest, but adequate housing. FMRs are the estimated rents, by number of bedrooms, for units occupied by households moving within the past two years, excluding new construction and public housing. FMRs do not reflect submarket rent levels, which may vary widely.

7. Author's tabulations of raw 1993 American Housing Survey data.

8. Data on housing costs cited here follow the definitions used by HUD and the Census Bureau for the American Housing Survey; generally, rent, fuel, and utilities for renters, and mortgage payment, taxes, fuel, utilities, and insurance costs for owners.

9. The following comparisons are based on 30% of income as reported in the American Housing Survey (AHS). In other words, this is gross income, not the adjusted income levels used under HUD programs for determining eligibility and setting subsidy levels. This difference in definition is probably more than offset by under-reporting of income in the AHS.

10. Christopher Jencks is frequently cited by those who downplay the role of housing affordability. Yet Jencks's analysis rests on changes in *median* rents and incomes, not on those at the bottom of the market. For those whose incomes kept pace with rising housing costs, the quality of rental housing did increase, but this did not affect the situation of households with incomes so low that they became homeless or were threatened with homelessness. Jencks also cites the increased number of subsidized housing units, while ignoring the far greater increase in the need for them, as demonstrated by the housing gap analysis. More significant than his view of changes in the housing market as a cause of homelessness, in his first chapter on partial solutions to homelessness, Jencks identifies better housing "as the first step in dealing with the problem. Regardless of why people are on the streets, giving them a place to live that offers a modicum of privacy and stability is usually the most important thing we can do to improve their lives. Without stable housing, nothing else is likely to work" (Jencks, *The Homeless*, 107).

11. Generally speaking, all very-low-income renter households (incomes below 50% of area median) are eligible for housing assistance. Depending on the program, some households with higher incomes are eligible as well. Thus, in addition to very-low-income renters, 7% of "lower income" renter households (incomes between 50% and 80% of median), 3% of middle-income renter households (incomes between 80% and 120% of median), and 2% of upper-income renter households (incomes above 120% of median) lived in federally assisted housing. Households in the latter groups are those remaining in assisted housing after their incomes increased.

12. After-tax income, instead of gross income, is the relevant measure to use for this example. It is assumed that most households unable to meet their basic nonhousing needs would not have taxable income.

13. This analysis is based on adjusting the lower level Bureau of Labor Statistics (BLS) City Worker's Family Budget, last issued in 1981, by subsequent changes in the Consumer Price Index and then calculating the cost of nonhousing items. If housing costs in relation to income are inadequate to cover these items, the household is considered "shelter poor." If income is below the cost of the nonhousing items, the household is considered extremely shelter poor, as any housing expenditures reduce the income available for other purposes. The term "shelter poverty" was first used by Michael Stone (*One-Third of a Nation*). The factors I used to adjust the 1981 BLS levels differ somewhat from Stone's, and the figures on renter shelter poverty are based on raw data from the 1989 American Housing Survey.

14. As of March 1996, these "federal preferences" had been suspended for a year, and legislation was pending in Congress to repeal them entirely.

15. U.S. Department of Housing and Urban Development, *Budget Summary: Fiscal Year 1997*.

16. The HUD analysis of worst case needs (U.S. Department of Housing and Urban Development, *Budget Summary: Fiscal Year 1997*) contains a wealth of data on the nature of these needs and their policy implications. As of March 1996, information on obtaining copies, as well as the report itself and key additional data, will be posted on the Internet at http://www.hud.gov.

17. Dolbeare, *Out of Reach*.

18. For detailed tables on FMRs and affordability, by state and metropolitan area, see Dolbeare, *Out of Reach*. For more recent information, contact the National Low Income Housing Coalition, 10112 14th Street, NW, Washington, DC 20005.

19. Information from data contained in federal budget documents, with inflation adjustments to 1996 dollars based on price index for Gross Domestic Product (see: Executive Office of the President of the United States, *The Budget of the United States Government: Fiscal Year 1997*).

20. HUD has released a series of documents on the problem and evolving refinements of the mark-to-market approach. The information here comes from *Multifamily Portfolio Re-Engineering: HUD's Subsidy and Affordability Considerations*, an undated HUD memorandum distributed in February 1996.

21. In the Congressional appropriations process, HUD's funds are in the same appropriation as Veterans Affairs, the Environmental Protection Agency, NASA, and a number of other independent agencies. The budget process limits total appropriations for all of these agencies and programs. Thus, low-income-housing funding has to compete with veterans, the environment, and the space program for a share of the diminishing pot of money.

CHAPTER 5

The author thanks Jim Baumohl for many helpful comments on earlier drafts.

1. Hombs, "Reversals of Fortune," 114.

2. Katz, *The Undeserving Poor*, 238. As Katz quotes the renowned Swedish social scientist Walter Korpi, "the European observer finds lively debates [in the United States] on issues that he or she has previously met only in the more or less dusty pages of historical accounts of the development of social policy at home."

3. Cross-national summaries of these trends include International Labor Organization (*World Employment 1995*); Organisation of Economic Cooperation and Development (*The OECD Jobs Study*); McFate ("Joblessness in the Nineties"); and Gottschalk and Joyce ("The Impact"). Summaries of these trends in the U.S. include Mishel and Bernstein (*The State of Working America 1994–95*); and Burtless (*A Future of Lousy Jobs?*).

4. It should be emphasized that these are average rates. That is, they indicate the average portion of the workforce and number of workers unemployed for the year. Far higher percentages and numbers of workers were unemployed at some point during the year.

5. People are considered unemployed only if they did not work at all during the period under review, were available for work (i.e., were not sick, caring for another household member, or attending school), and made specific efforts to find employment in the month preceding the review period. Thus, those working as little as one hour a week or who have given up looking for a job are not considered unemployed. See United States Department of Labor, *Report on the American Workforce*, 4.

6. McFate, "Joblessness in the Nineties," 1.

7. McFate, "Joblessness in the Nineties," 1.

8. In this context, "developed" denotes those nations with the highest levels of economic development as indicated by gross domestic product per capita.

9. Organisation of Economic Cooperation and Development, *The OECD Jobs Study*, 7. For assessments of these same developments, as well as analysis of those in the "de-

veloping" countries, see International Labor Organization, *World Employment 1995.*

10. Organisation of Economic Cooperation and Development, *The OECD Jobs Study*, 9.

11. United Nations Development Programme, *Human Development Report 1995*, 35 and 33.

12. Council of Economic Advisors, *Economic Report of the President*, 172.

13. Calculated from Mishel and Bernstein, *The State of Working America 1994–95*, 112, Table 3.

14. Mishel and Bernstein, *The State of Working America 1994–95*, 73, Table 1.31.

15. Council of Economic Advisors, *Economic Report of the President*, 114.

16. Mishel and Bernstein, *The State of Working America 1994–95*, 64, Table 1.25.

17. Mishel and Bernstein, *The State of Working America 1994–95*, Table 3.10.

18. See Ruggles (*Drawing the Line*) for an assessment of alternative measures of poverty. When it was conceived in the 1960s, the poverty line was based on the finding that food expenditures comprised one-third of the average family's budget. Subsequent updates in the poverty line assumed this proportion remained static. But as Schwarz and Volgy note, by 1990 nutrition expenditures comprised only one-sixth of the average family budget. Revising the poverty line to reflect this change in 1990 would yield an income level some 67% higher for a family of 4 (1992, 35–36). Schwarz and Volgy cite various survey data indicating that Americans believe "an income at or perhaps somewhat above 150% of the present official poverty line is required to achieve self-sufficiency" (1992, 40–41). The 1996 poverty level for a family of four is $15,600.

19. Davis, "Cross-Country Patterns," 289.

20. International Labor Organization, *World Employment 1995*, 28, Table 2.

21. Harrison and Bluestone (*The Great U-Turn*); and Harrison (*Lean and Mean*).

22. Blank, "The Employment Strategy," 173.

23. Blank, "The Employment Strategy," 173. An article in the *New York Times* of 21 February 1996 (D1) highlighted these trends in different segments of the textile industry, which traditionally has provided jobs to relatively unskilled workers. While "American apparel makers are surviving by hiring cheap labor overseas," it reported, "the other big component of the textile industry, the companies that weave cloth and fabric, is thriving by applying the latest technology at home." Imports share of the apparel market increased from 20% to 50% during the last 20 years, when nearly 500,000 of the industry's U.S. jobs were eliminated. Job losses have accelerated since the enactment of NAFTA, as 100,000 jobs were lost in 1995 and another 40,000 to 50,000 are slated to be lost in 1996. The fabrics industry lost 42,000 jobs in 1995 alone, in large part because of technological advances such as those in a factory described in the *Times* article: with recently installed machines, *20 workers can now produce 50% more fabric than 400 workers could previously.*

24. Shelley, "More Job Openings."

25. Blank ("The Employment Strategy"); and Mishel and Bernstein (*The State of Working America 1994–95*).

26. According to the National Bureau of Economic Research, the official scorekeeper on such matters in the United States, there have been nine U.S. business cycles since WWII. See McNees, "The 1990–91 Recession." Useful discussions of these broader issues include Gordon ("Stages of Accumulation"); Mandel (*Long Waves*); Goldstein (*Long Cycles*); and Kennedy (*The Rise and Fall of Great Powers*).

27. The unique combination of factors that created hothouse conditions for capitalist development and individual opportunity in the United States included the absence of entrenched feudal social structures, a continental land mass providing abundant land and other unparalleled natural resources, a relatively weak indigenous population, an oceanic moat affording protection from foreign enemies, and the diverse and ever-growing labor force provided through slavery and successive waves of immigrants. See Dowd (*U.S. Capitalist Development*); DuBoff (*Accumulation and Power*); and the sources cited therein.

28. Armstrong, Glyn, and Harrison (*Capitalism Since 1945*), and the sources cited therein, provide a useful introduction. In addition, see Piore and Sabel (*The Second Industrial Divide*); Harrison and Bluestone (*The Great U-Turn*); Kolko (*Restructuring the World Economy*); Bowles, Gordon, and Weisskopf (*After the Waste Land*); and Harrison (*Lean and Mean*).

29. For an informative overview, see Garraty, *Unemployment in History.*

30. United States Department of Labor, *Report on the American Workforce*, 28–29.

31. Przeworski, "Less Is More," 12. See also Rifkin, *The End of Work.*

32. Currie, *Reckoning*, 145–46.

33. The major components of the supply-side policy mix included major reductions in spending on social programs, tax cuts for the wealthy and corporations, and reduced environmental and workplace regulations. Major increases in military spending were a fundamental if implicit additional element of these policies. The literature on these policies and their effects is vast. Useful discussions include Harrison and Bluestone (*The Great U-Turn*); Bowles, Gordon, and Weisskopf (*After the Waste Land*); and Armstrong, Glyn, and Harrison (*Capitalism Since 1945*).

34. Thurow, "Why Their World Might Crumble," 78.

35. Shelley, "More Job Openings," 154.

36. OECD study cited in the *New York Times*, October 27, 1995, D2.

37. Mead *(The New Politics of Poverty)*; and Murray *(Losing Ground)*.

38. The classic on this is Polanyi *(The Great Transformation)*. Useful recent discussions include Kuttner *(The Economic Illusion)*, Block *(Postindustrial Possibilities)*, and Alvater *(The Future of the Market)*. As Alvater observes (page 238), "A pure market economy has never existed in history; it has always been politically regulated by society. The invisible hand of the market has to be regulated by the visible hand of state intervention, and both require the 'third hand' of a network of social and economic institutions."

39. Employment and export data provide striking indices of the impacts of these policies on different social groups. Between 1977 and 1986, for example, U.S. transnational corporations created less than 600,000 domestic jobs but eliminated another 3.3 million, for a net loss of 2.7 million (Glickman and Woodward, *The New Competitors*). And while the share of world manufactured exports produced in the United States fell from 17.1% in 1966 to 13.4% in 1985, the share of U.S. corporations increased from 17.3% to 18.3% (Kwan, "Footloose and Country Free," 7).

40. Standing, "Labor Insecurity," 153 and 185.

41. Informative discussions of the causes and consequences of the Fed's policies include Greider *(Secrets of the Temple)*; Snyder ("Bad Medicine"); and Michl ("Assessing the Costs").

42. Goldfield *(The Decline of Organized Labor)* provides the most useful discussion of these issues.

43. Piven, "Is It Global Economics," 111. The literature on this is vast. Useful introductions include Ferguson and Rogers *(Right Turn)*; Harrison and Bluestone *(The Great U-Turn)*; Piven and Cloward *(The New Class War)*; Bowles, Gordon, and Weisskopf *(After the Waste Land)*; and Akard ("Corporate Mobilization").

44. Piven and Cloward, *The New Class War*, 346.

45. Thurow, "Why Their World Might Crumble," 78.

46. United States Department of Labor, *Report on the American Workforce*, Table 1.8.

47. Unpublished data from the U.S. Bureau of Labor Statistics indicate that the 1995 average unemployment rate for college graduates 25 years and older was 2.5% for Whites, 3.4% for Blacks, and 3.6% for Hispanics (Latinos). Unpublished Census Bureau data reveal that the 1994 median earnings of White workers 25 years old and over with a bachelor's degree or more was $35,613, while the median earnings for their Black and Hispanic counterparts were $31,186 and $30,194, respectively.

48. See Oliver and Shapiro, *Black Wealth/White Wealth*.

49. The changing mainstream state-of-the-art knowledge in the U.S. about these matters is chronicled in the volumes produced during the past 20 years by the Institute for Research on Poverty. See Plotnick and Skidmore *(Progress against Poverty)*; Haveman *(A Decade)*; Danziger and Weinberg *(Fighting Poverty)*; and Danziger, Sandefur, and Weinburg *(Confronting Poverty)*. The article by Havemen in the final volume summarizes current research wisdom about these issues.

50. This panoply of policy measures is needed because the wage and related trends discussed above make it "more difficult to implement an employment strategy as a way to reduce poverty than it has been at any time in the recent past" ("The Employment Strategy," 1994, 177–78). This does not mean that improving employment opportunities should not be the centerpiece of antipoverty and antihomelessness strategies, as Hopper and Baumohl ("Held in Abeyance") have argued. But given the limited job opportunities currently available in the labor market to less-skilled workers, to say nothing of workers' other needs for housing, health care, and so forth, employment alone is very unlikely to reduce poverty and homelessness appreciably.

51. International Labor Organization, *World Employment 1995*, 25.

52. See, for example, Harvey *(Securing the Right to Employment)*; Danzinger, Sandefur, and Weinberg *(Confronting Poverty)*; McFate, Lawson, and Wilson *(Poverty, Inequality, and the Future)*; and International Labor Organization, *World Employment 1995*).

53. Standing ("Labor Insecurity"). We should note that the differences between the United States and Western European countries in terms of their levels of unemployment and wages—the United States has lower unemployment rates but lower relative wages among the employed—are directly related to the differences in the extent of labor market regulation and the generosity of the social wage. The United States has far less regulation and far less generous assistance programs.

54. Michl, "Assessing the Costs."

55. Glyn, "Social Democracy," 35–38.

56. See Stein *(The Fiscal Revolution)*; and Lekachman *(The Age of Keynes)*.

57. See Hardin, ("The Militarized Social Democracy"); Lekachman *(The Age of Keynes)*; and Weir ("The Federal Government").

58. Center for Defense Information, *CDI Military Almanac*, 17.

59. The House Republicans' proposals would offset cuts in social spending (especially in programs benefiting low-income people) with increases in military spending and tax cuts advantaging corporations and the wealthy. The proposed military spending increases—despite the clear absence of any military threat—reveal, on one hand, the need for and attractiveness of stimulus, and, on the other, the difficulty of ending long-standing policy approaches, however dubious they may be.

60. United States Department of Labor *(What's Working, 1)*.

61. United States Department of Labor (*What's Working,* 61–62).

62. Data for Fiscal Year 1996 levels and cut from Fiscal Year 1995 are from U.S. Department of Labor, Employment and Training Administration (ETA). Reductions since Fiscal Year 1979 are author's calculations based on ETA data and data in: Executive Office of the President, *The Budget of the United States Government Fiscal Year 1997,* Tables 3.2 and 10.1.

63. McDermott, "Bare Minimum."

64. Center on Budget and Policy Priorities, "7.7 Million Households."

65. Katznelson (*City Trenches*) provides a useful introduction to this issue. Quadagno *(The Color of Welfare)* contains a fine analysis of the way racism shaped the development of the U.S. welfare state.

66. Among others, see Rubin, *Families on the Fault Line;* and Edsall, *Chain Reaction.*

CHAPTER 6

1. It is impossible to state precisely what percentage of homeless people nationwide currently receive cash assistance; findings vary from place to place and by the aid program in question. In 1987, Burt and Cohen (*America's Homeless*) found that 20% of the 1,704 homeless people in a national survey received Aid to Families with Dependent Children, Supplemental Security Income, or General Assistance. Since that time, the share of the homeless comprising families has increased, and homeless families appear more likely to receive aid than do other homeless persons. Over the same period, however, the availability of General Assistance—the principal source of aid to nondisabled, non-elderly single persons and couples without children—has sharply contracted.

2. In the legal sense, "entitlement" also means that, under decisions of the United States Supreme Court, a recipient of assistance is entitled to due process protections; i.e., that assistance may not be reduced or terminated without advance written notice and without providing a right to be heard in cases of dispute about a proposed action to reduce or terminate aid. *Goldberg v. Kelly,* 397 U.S. 254 (1970).

3. It has been estimated that in 1992, the number of persons in poverty in the United States would have been 14.6 million greater but for the availability of Social Security benefits. In contrast, the availability of means-tested cash benefits only reduced the number of persons in poverty by 2.8 million persons (U.S. House of Representatives, Committee on Ways and Means, *Overview of Entitlement Programs,* 1171). While the antipoverty effects of Social Security are important, one should also keep in mind that in 1990, more than $8 billion in Social Security benefits were received by families with incomes above $100,000 (Congressional Budget Office, *Reducing Entitlement Spending,* 8).

4. See Congressional Budget Office, *The Economic and Budget Outlook,* 41. More specifically, AFDC represented about 2% of entitlement spending, and Food Stamps and SSI each represented about 3%.

5. See Burke, *Cash and Noncash Benefits.*

6. The Earned Income Tax Credit (EITC) is a refundable tax credit available to low-income workers. "Refundable" means that if a taxpayer's credit is greater than his or her tax liability, the government will make a payment for the difference. Under recent expansions, the EITC for a family with children can be quite substantial. In 1996, a parent with two or more children could qualify for a maximum EITC of approximately $3,576, based on a credit of 40% of the family's initial earnings. The EITC for families with only one child is smaller, and the EITC for childless workers is considerably smaller. For childless workers, the maximum EITC is set at 7.65% of the first $4,100 of earnings—a maximum of $314.

For parents with earnings, the EITC has become an increasingly important part of national antipoverty policy. However, the EITC is of very limited assistance to working individuals without children, and provides no assistance to individuals without earnings. Recent legislative proposals have sought—unsuccessfully, to date—to eliminate the portion of the EITC for individuals without children.

7. AFDC (originally Aid to Dependent Children, as there was no specific grant for the parent) was created by the Social Security Act of 1935, although it grew out of Mothers' Aid or Widows' Pension programs mounted between 1911 and 1935 by all but two states (Georgia and South Carolina).

8. The waiver process occurs under Section 1115 of the Social Security Act. This decades-old provision authorizes the Secretary of Health and Human Services to waive AFDC state-plan requirements (and certain requirements of the Social Security Act) to permit a state to test an experimental or demonstration program intended to further the objectives of the act. While historically intended as a provision to authorize research activities, the Bush and Clinton administrations have used it to permit states to depart from virtually any state-plan requirement, so long as the state program is evaluated and does not result in new costs to the federal government. For more detail on the content of state waiver initiatives, see Savner and Greenberg, *The CLASP Guide to Welfare Waivers.*

9. More precisely, AFDC earnings rules allow for a $90 work expense deduction and a deduction of $30 and one-third of the remainder of earnings for the first four months of employment. In the next eight months of employment, the rules allow for a $90 work expense deduction and a deduction of $30 of the remainder. After 12 months of employment, only the $90 work expense deduction is allowed. Throughout employment, a working family also is allowed to deduct actual dependent care expenses not to exceed $200 a month for a child under age two, and $175 a month for a child age two or older.

10. U.S. House of Representatives, Committee on Ways and Means, *Overview of Entitlement Programs,* 374. The falling value of AFDC was partially offset by adjustments in Food Stamps, but even when Food Stamp assistance is considered, the combined value of AFDC and Food Stamps for a three-person family fell 27% from 1972 to 1993.

11. Some observers suggest that procedural barriers are only partly explained by concerns for payment accuracy, and should be partly understood as a vehicle to make access to assistance more difficult. It is suggested that in looking to limit expenditures and discourage defection from the low-wage labor market, governments impose requirements that they know will deter applications. Such practices have a long history in public welfare, and descend from the Victorian principle of "less eligibility." This holds that relief benefits should be lower than the prevailing minimum wage, and that relief should be administered under onerous (deterrent) conditions. In other words, relief should always be "less eligible" (less attractive) than the most ill-paid and menial labor. While modern public assistance administration does not use the specter of the workhouse to deter the poor from seeking assistance, the barriers presented by the administrative complexity and demeaning nature of the application process may accomplish the same end.

12. In Fiscal Year 1993, 55% of all AFDC application denials were for failure to comply with procedural requirements. More than half (52%) of all AFDC discontinuances were due to "family request or initiative" or for reasons "other" than exceeding income or resource limits or no longer having an eligible child. See U.S. Department of Health and Human Services, *FY 1992–93 Quarterly Public Assistance Statistics,* 460–61.

13. Common new behavioral requirements include school attendance (in which the family's grant is reduced if school-age children do not meet state-specified attendance standards); use of grant reductions for families in which children do not have all required immunizations; and implementation of requirements that individuals participate in available substance abuse programs.

As to exemptions, the principal exemption for adults under current federal law is a prohibition on requiring participation of those with children under the age of one. Federal law also bars requiring full-time participation by those with children under age six. (An exception to both of these is made for teen parents in high school completion activities.) A number of state waivers reduce or eliminate these and other exemptions.

As to penalties, some state waiver proposals increase the portion of the grant that can be reduced; some also make use of "full-family sanctions"; i.e., complete elimination of all cash assistance to the family for a period of time.

One further waiver approach does not actually reduce assistance but may have the same practical effect. A set of states have received approval to operate a family cap or child exclusion provision, under which a family receives no additional assistance for a child who was conceived during the time in which the family was receiving AFDC.

14. A federal study in 1992 found that 69% of homeless families interviewed in homeless family shelters were already receiving AFDC benefits at the time of interview (U.S. Department of Health and Human Services, Office of Inspector General, *Homeless Families and Access to AFDC*).

15. Families who receive aid for longer periods of time are most likely to have had less than a high school education and no recent work experience at the point they began receiving AFDC. See Pavetti, "Who Is Affected by Time Limits?"

16. Some time-limited proposals expressly recognize this issue. Florida's legislation to impose time limits in a two-county demonstration explicitly provided that aid to the entire family would not be terminated if such termination would result in a risk of shelter care or out-of-home placement of children.

17. FS was created in 1964 to replace a commodities distribution program established by the Agriculture Act of 1949. This earlier program paid less attention to the nutritional needs of poor people than to the economic needs of farmers with surpluses to sell off. In other words, poor people were the incidental beneficiaries of a program intended mainly to support farm commodity prices.

18. See Trippe, *Trends in FSP Participation Rates.* It is important to keep in mind, however, that not all poor individuals will qualify for Food Stamps. For example, a household may have a car that exceeds the Food Stamp asset limit; or a poor individual may be residing with, and purchasing and preparing food with, other non-poor persons. The Department of Agriculture estimates that in January 1992, 74% of all eligible persons were participating in the Food Stamp program.

19. Countable income is gross non-excluded income, less allowable deductions. Certain forms of income are excluded by federal law; e.g., tax refunds or payments of the Earned Income Tax Credit. A household is entitled to certain deductions from income: a standard deduction for all households; 20% of earned income; a medical expense deduction for the elderly and disabled; and a deduction for "excess shelter costs" if shelter costs exceed more than half of a household's income after all other deductions are allowed.

20. Gross and net income limits vary with household size. For a household of four, the gross income limit is $1,642 and the net income limit is $1,263.

21. For example, suppose the FS benefit level for a household is $200 and that the household has $300 in countable income. Since 30% of $300 is $90, the Food Stamp allotment would be $110 ($200 – $90 = $110).

22. The Food Stamp Act defines a "homeless individual" as (1) an individual who lacks a fixed and regular nighttime residence; or (2) an individual who has a primary nighttime residence that is (a) a supervised publicly or privately operated shelter (including a welfare hotel or congregate

shelter) designed to provide temporary living accommodations; (b) an institution that provides a temporary residence for individuals intended to be institutionalized; (c) a temporary accommodation in the residence of another individual; or (d) a public or private place not designed for, or ordinarily used as, a regular sleeping accommodation for human beings.

23. Bartlett, Burstein, and Pan, *Evaluation of Expedited Service*.

24. SSI was created in 1972 (to take effect in 1974) to consolidate and standardize under federal administration existing needs-based programs for the elderly, blind, and disabled. These existing programs were Old Age Assistance and Aid to the Blind, created in 1935, and Aid to the Permanently and Totally Disabled (later Aid to the Disabled), created in 1949 to take effect in 1950.

25. Correspondence from Congressional Budget Office to Alice M. Rivlin (Director, Office of Management and Budget), April 3, 1996.

26. According to data published in May 1994, the GA programs in California and Illinois appear to be in for a run of applications by terminated substance abusers, the vast majority of whom, nationwide, are heavy drinkers rather than habitual users of other drugs. See U.S. General Accounting Office, *Social Security: Major Changes Needed*, 15–16 especially.

27. See Advisory Council on Unemployment Compensation, *Unemployment Insurance in the United States*, 230.

28. UC was a provision of the 1935 Social Security Act. By this time, Germany's UC system was 50 years old. Although various American states had debated the merits of UC for over a generation, only Wisconsin had such a program before 1935, and Wisconsin's unemployment insurance scheme took effect only in 1934.

The federal role in UC is somewhat different than in the previously described programs. The Federal Unemployment Tax Act imposes a 6.2% gross tax on the first $7,000 paid by a "covered" employer to each employee. However, if the state operates an approved UC program and has no delinquent federal loans, the state may credit 5.4 percentage points against the 6.2% tax rate, making the effective federal tax rate 0.8%. The federal revenue finances program administration, half the cost of federal-state extended benefits, and a federal account for loans to states. The state, in turn, is supposed to use the revenue from the 5.4% credit to finance its regular state program, and half the cost of extended benefits.

29. Three states stand out for particularly high requirements: Montana ($5,400), Oklahoma ($4,160), and Virginia ($3,250).

30. For example, in New Mexico, the total base-period earning requirement is only $1,284.72, but the individual must have earned at least $1,027.78 in one quarter. Similarly, in the District of Columbia, the base-period earning requirement is $1,950, but the individual must have earned at least $1,300 in one quarter. See U.S. Department of Labor, *Comparison of State Unemployment Insurance Laws*, Table 301.

31. See Falk, *The Uncompensated Unemployed*.

32. GA programs have vastly different histories. The oldest programs of local, public "home relief" (as opposed to relief by residence in institutions like almshouses) go back to the colonial era, but most of these were interrupted for long periods between 1880 and the early years of the Great Depression, during which time most cash relief was distributed by private charities on a highly discretionary basis. Further, many public programs did not dispense cash benefits until the Depression, but rather distributed commodities like coal, clothing, and food.

33. Center on Budget and Policy Priorities and National Conference of State Legislatures, *National General Assistance Survey, 1992*.

34. A set of reductions in program availability since 1992 are discussed in Center on Budget and Policy Priorities, *The Conference Agreement on the Welfare Bill*.

35. Burt, *Over the Edge*, 173–78.

36. See Hauser and Freedman, *Jobless, Penniless, Often Homeless*; and Nichols and Porter, *General Assistance Programs*.

37. For more detail on the 1994 Clinton Plan, and on issues presented by attempts to structure work requirements for families receiving cash assistance, see Greenberg, *Two Years and Work*; and Greenberg, *The Devil Is in the Details*.

38. For an overview of the provisions of H.R. 4, see Center on Budget and Policy Priorities, *The Conference Agreement on the Welfare Bill*.

39. Over the last 20 years, there have been a total of 4 occasions where states reduced AFDC benefits by at least 10%; since the beginning of 1995, 5 governors have proposed to do so. Since the November 1994 elections, 11 states have submitted proposals to implement a time limit in which all cash aid to affected families would be cut off after a period of less than 5 years; 7 have submitted proposals for a statewide time limit of 2 years or less (Greenberg, *Racing to the Bottom?*).

40. Correspondence from Alice M. Rivlin (Director, Office of Management and Budget) to Sam Gibbons (Committee on Ways and Means, U.S. House of Representatives), December 6, 1995.

CHAPTER 7

The Rural Homelessness Committee of the National Coalition for the Homeless, and Sue Watlov Phillips in particular, are thanked for their comments on an earlier draft of this chapter.

1. A 1989 collection of studies from 15 states gave scarce notice to rural homelessness, save for the occasional mention, e.g., of people (in Missouri) "living in cars along

county roads or staying in public campgrounds beyond the normal season." Elsewhere, it was claimed that homelessness was not "a major problem in rural areas," based on the dubious evidence of the small number of homeless families showing up at the local department of social services for shelter assistance (see Momeni, *Homelessness,* 59, 95, 135).

2. Harrington, *The Other America,* 2–3.

3. See Gorham and Harrison, *Working Below the Poverty Line;* Deavers and Hoppe, *Rural Poverty in America;* and Lichter, McLaughlin, and Cornwall, *Investing in People.*

4. Housing Assistance Council, "Rural Homelessness." The United Nations, for example, recognizes a condition of "relative homelessness." This refers to housing that does not meet minimal standards of affordability, protection from the elements, access to safe water and sanitation, secure tenure and personal safety, and that lies within easy reach of employment, education, and health care.

5. Burt, "Findings and Implications from RECD's Rural Homelessness Conferences."

6. Kondratas, "Estimates and Public Policy."

7. See Ohio Department of Mental Health, *Homelessness in Ohio;* Stasny, Toomey, and First, "Estimating the Rate of Rural Homelessness"; and First, Rife, and Toomey, "Homelessness in Rural Areas."

8. Corrected for poor methods in one county, that urban rate rose to 30.5 per 10,000.

9. Burt, "Findings and Implications from RECD's Rural Homelessness Conferences."

10. Fitchen, "On the Edge of Homelessness" and *Poverty in Rural America.*

11. But note that home ownership is still more common among the rural poor (55%) than among the urban poor (32%).

12. Burt, "Findings and Implications from RECD's Rural Homelessness Conferences."

13. Harvard University Joint Center on Housing Studies, *State of the Nation's Housing, 1991.* Data are for 1989 and exclude households with reported housing costs of $0.

14. New York and a few other states already have taken steps to give the owners of mobile homes more security, setting aside loan funds to create tenant-owned, cooperative trailer parks should landlords decide to sell out.

CHAPTER 8

The research on which this chapter is based was supported in part by grants from the Hogg Foundation for Mental Health in Austin, Texas, and the National Science Foundation (SES-9008809).

1. For examples of the first genre of research, see Baumann, et al., *The Austin Homeless;* Fischer and Breakey, 1991; LaGory, et al., "Homelessness in Alabama"; Lee, "Homelessness in Tennessee"; Rossi, *Down and Out;*

and Wright and Weber, *Homelessness and Health.* For examples of the second genre, see Burt, *Over the Edge;* Elliot and Krivo, "Structural Determinants"; and Ringheim, *At Risk of Homelessness.* Jencks's recent analysis *(The Homeless)* can be construed as a synthesis of the two.

2. When applied to human behavior, the term "survival" clearly is multidimensional. It encompasses not only material subsistence but also social or interpersonal and psychological needs. Maslow *(Toward a Psychology of Being),* among others, has suggested as much with his well-known hierarchy of needs, which holds that the emergence and gratification of social and psychological needs, such as the need for self-esteem, are contingent on the prior satisfaction of physiological and safety needs. We agree that there are basic human needs, but we contend that they typically are integrated into a seamless whole rather than arrayed hierarchically (see Snow and Anderson, "Identity Work" and *Down on Their Luck).* Nonetheless, for analytic purposes, they can be examined separately, which is what we do in this chapter by focusing on material survival strategies.

3. For a more detailed discussion of the methodology associated with this study, see Snow and Anderson, *Down on Their Luck,* 19–34.

4. Proceeding in this fashion is consistent with the logic of what we call "niche" sampling. Lifestyle niches rather than individuals are the initial sampling unit. The construction of such a sample is pursued through a maximum variation sampling strategy. It is a kind of Darwinesque strategy wherein one samples as widely as possible within a given sociocultural context until redundancy is reached with respect to types of niches, patterns of adaptation, and the like. If the range of niches in a given context has been uncovered, then a sample of such niches can be assembled. This, in turn, provides a basis for examining concretely, and with some degree of confidence, behavioral repertoires and adaptive strategies across the individuals that populate the sampled niches, although it does not provide a basis for making claims about the representativeness of the individuals in the niches. This, in effect, is what we tried to do in the three cities. By scouting the cities during the course of our fieldwork, and by conferring with the array of agencies and organizations that had contact with the homeless, we identified a range of niches in each city and attempted to interview homeless individuals within a sample of those niches.

5. See, in particular, Burt and Cohen, *America's Homeless;* and Shlay and Rossi, "Social Science Research." In spite of the consistency in the demographic portraits of the homeless produced by cross-sectional studies that aggregate their findings across cities, it is important not to overlook the diversity among homeless people both within and across cities. In our sample, for example, there were striking differences in the racial/ethnic composition of the samples in the three cities, with Tucson being 70% White, and Detroit and Philadelphia being 91% and 99% Black. For a detailed demographic profile of our samples of the

homeless in the three cities, write to David A. Snow, Department of Sociology, University of Arizona, Tucson, AZ 85721.

6. Running through much of the literature is an assumption that homeless people who sleep in shelters are different from those who sleep "rough." Our data suggest that this neat division is uncommon. When asked where they slept during the last 30 days, 88% of our 400 interviewees indicated shelters; 73% outdoors, in cars, in abandoned buildings, and in public places; 26% with family and friends; 9% in motels and hotels; 7% in hospitals and jails; and 4% in rented apartments. All together, they averaged 2.1 different sleeping arrangements during the previous 30 days.

7. Hopper, Susser, and Conover, "Economics of Makeshift," 195.

8. For a discussion of criminal activity among the homeless and its relationship to city ordinances, see Snow and Anderson, *Down on Their Luck*, 95–102, 165–67; and Snow, Baker, and Anderson, "Criminality."

9. For an elaboration of this context in one city, see Snow and Anderson, *Down on Their Luck*, 73–109.

10. Wiseman's field study of skid-row alcoholics in the 1960s *(Stations of the Lost)* yielded similar observations about mission employment. Indeed, this has been a complaint of homeless men since the era of the charity woodyard.

11. Burt and Cohen, *America's Homeless*, 43. Shlay and Rossi ("Social Science Research," 136–37) report similar findings from 60 local and national studies.

12. As discussed in Chapter 6, there are two other notable reasons for the poor benefit coverage of homeless people. First, most do not have the recent work histories that establish eligibility for unemployment compensation; second, the lack of a stable address, a telephone, safe storage for personal papers, or reliable transportation often make it difficult for homeless people to qualify procedurally for initial or continuing eligibility. Such obstacles to eligibility were clearly operative in Austin (see Snow and Anderson, *Down on Their Luck*, 138–41), as they are elsewhere. For example, in 1986 in Alameda County, California, 98% of GA denials resulted from missed appointments, failure to provide necessary documents, the incorrect completion of forms, and so forth (Barnes, Baumohl, and Hopper, "The New Paternalism," 8).

13. This is hardly surprising given that most of the homeless come from poverty-level backgrounds. See Rossi, *Down and Out;* Shinn and Gillespie, "The Roles of Housing and Poverty"; and Shlay and Rossi, "Social Science Research" for discussion of this relationship.

14. Shlay and Rossi ("Social Science Research," 136) report that unemployment averaged 81% in the studies they examined, with "unemployment rates of 75% or more . . . found among the homeless in three-quarters of these investigations."

15. The finding that around one-third of our three-city sample had worked for pay during the past month is consistent with most research on the employment status and income sources of the homeless. In his 1985–86 survey of 722 homeless in Chicago, Rossi found that 32% counted some form of wage labor as a source of income during the past month (*Down and Out*, 108–09). Similarly, in the Urban Institute's 1987 survey of 1,704 homeless adults in 20 cities, 25% reported employment as a source of income during the preceding 30 days (Burt and Cohen, *America's Homeless*, 43). There was, however, significant variation across some of the cities in both the Urban Institute study (Burt and Cohen, *America's Homeless*, 74) and in our research (see Table 8.1).

16. See, for example, Southern Regional Council, *Hard Labor;* and Weigand, "Sweat and Blood."

17. The term shadow work is borrowed from Ivan Illich *(Shadow Work),* who uses it more expansively to include such unpaid work as housework, grocery shopping, and commuting.

18. Space does not permit us to provide a detailed consideration of the ins and outs of these various types of shadow work, but see Snow and Anderson, *Down on Their Luck*, 145–70, for such a discussion.

19. The attitudes of homeless people who profitably collect and sell used aluminum cans (and the like) may differ, of course. But whatever their attitudes toward scavenging, it might be thought of as a "recycling" activity that in some instances constitutes a community service of sorts.

20. Levi-Strauss, *The Savage Mind*, 12.

21. Wiseman, *Stations of the Lost*, 27. See also Hopper, Susser, and Conover ("Economics of Makeshift") who argue that homelessness and its makeshift survival strategies constitute but one element in an overall subsistence pattern among a segment of the poor.

22. See Snow and Anderson, *Down on Their Luck*, especially pages 132–34, for empirical documentation of this pattern.

23. Burt and Cohen, "Differences," 520–21.

24. This raises the question of why so few elderly are homeless in comparison to previous eras. The answer no doubt has to do with the existence of various federal assistance programs, such as OASDI and SSI, for which people become eligible at age 65.

25. This finding is consistent with research on the distribution of crime in general: most types of violent and property crimes are concentrated heavily among males between the ages of 15 and 25 (see Hirschi and Gottfredson, "Age and the Exploration of Crime").

26. We used this dichotomy because of the small number of Latinos (14) and Native Americans (5) in the sample. Moreover, a separate analysis incorporating Latinos yielded no significant correlations. See Chapter 12 for a discussion of Latino homelessness.

27. In time, however, as individuals' networks of street associates expand and deepen, they are likely to find themselves engaged in peer-group activities more congruent with shadow work than regular work, making withdrawal from these activities difficult. For a discussion of the "pull" of street-based, peer-group activities, see Snow and Anderson, *Down on Their Luck,* 291–92.

28. This argument underlies many attempts to account for the persistence of poverty, ranging from Lewis's "culture of poverty" thesis *(The Culture of Poverty)* to recent neoconservative works that attribute urban poverty and inner-city "pathologies" to the confluence of cultural factors and various dysfunctional "liberal" social policies (see Murray, *Losing Ground).* Although it has received a wide hearing, particularly since the early 1980s, the argument also has been soundly challenged (see Wilson, *The Truly Disadvantaged;* Katz, *The Undeserving Poor).*

29. Leibow, *Tally's Corner,* 64–65.

30. Coles, "The Children of Affluence."

31. We highlight individual action here because our research on collective mobilization among the homeless in 18 of the nation's largest cities suggests that many of the homeless participating in these actions believe that they can make a difference collectively. See also Wagner, *Checkerboard Square,* and Chapter 19.

CHAPTER 9

1. Adkins, *Medical Care for Veterans.*

2. Veterans Administration, *Annual Report 1987.*

3. On homelessness and PTSD, see Robertson, "Homeless Veterans"; and Goldin, *Soldiers of Misfortune.* USA Today: Edmonds, "Lost Paths."

4. Robertson, "Homeless Veterans."

5. Rosenheck, Frisman, and Chung, "The Proportion of Veterans" (1994).

6. Burt and Cohen, *Feeding the Homeless.*

7. U.S. Bureau of the Census, *1987 Survey of Veterans.* Among 19,000 homeless veterans assessed in a national VA program, 1.6% were women, but adjustment for the specific age distribution of homeless persons and for the lower risk for homelessness among women indicates that the risk of homelessness among female veterans is similar to that among female nonveterans. See Leda, Rosenheck, and Gallup, "Mental Illness."

8. Kulka, et al., *Trauma and the Vietnam War.*

9. See Rosenheck, Frisman, and Chung, "The Proportion of Veterans"(1994). The methodological foundation of case control studies such as these is the fact that the "exposure odds ratio" (the odds of exposure to the risk factor among "cases" relative to the odds of exposure to the risk factor among "controls") provides an accurate estimate of the "disease odds ratio" (the odds of developing the dis-

ease among "exposed" subjects relative to the odds of developing the disease among "nonexposed" subjects).

10. North and Smith, "Posttraumatic Stress Disorder."

11. Blake, et al., "Prevalence of PTSD"; and Hamilton and Canteen, "Post-traumatic Stress Disorder."

12. The following discussion draws on Rosenheck and Fontana, "A Model of Homelessness."

13. Rosenheck, Frisman, and Chung, "The Proportion of Veterans among the Homeless."

14. No differences were noted in the risk of homelessness between Black and White veterans in most of the age groups represented in Table 9.3 (as evidenced by overlapping 95% confidence intervals). However, in the post-Vietnam age group, the group at highest risk for homelessness, White veterans were at significantly *greater* relative risk for homelessness as compared to White nonveterans (odds ratio=4.76) than were Black veterans as compared to Black nonveterans (odds ratio=2.13). In spite of this difference, both Black and White veterans of the post-Vietnam generation were at significantly greater risk for homelessness (as compared to their nonveteran peers) than were veterans of other generations. See further exploration of the relationship of race to homelessness among veterans below. On African American homelessness more generally, see Chapter 11.

15. Office of the Assistant Secretary of Defense, *Population Representation.*

16. Rosenheck, Frisman, and Chung, "The Proportion of Veterans."

17. Rosenheck, Frisman, and Chung, "The Proportion of Veterans."

18. Janowitz, "The All-Volunteer Military."

19. Cooper, *Military Manpower;* Kim, et al., *National Longitudinal Survey;* and Office of the Assistant Secretary of Defense, *Population Representation,* 55.

20. Laurence, Ramsberger, and Gribben, *Effects of Military Experience;* and Eitelberg, et al., *Screening for Service.*

21. Cahalan, et al., *Drinking Practices,* iv; Bray, et al., *1985 Worldwide Survey;* and Polich, "Epidemiology of Alcohol Abuse."

22. Detailed information on veterans who entered the military from 1971 to 1975 are not available, but are presumed to reflect similar characteristics. Data from the NVVRS suggest that these late-entry Vietnam era veterans represent less than one-fourth of all Vietnam era veterans and less than 10% of those who served in the Vietnam theater (Kulka, et al., *The National Vietnam Veterans Readjustment Study).*

23. Eitelberg, et al., *Screening for Service.*

24. See Terry, *Bloods;* and Parson, "Ethnicity and Traumatic Stress," for discussions of the experiences of Blacks in the military.

25. Burt and Cohen, *Feeding the Homeless.*

26. These studies were conducted in Ohio (Roth, "Homeless Veterans"), Boston (Schutt, "A Short Report"), New York (Struening and Rosenblatt, *Characteristics of Homeless Veterans*), and Los Angeles (Robertson, "Homeless Veterans").

27. See Rosenheck and Koegel, "Characteristics of Veterans and Nonveterans," for comparative data on homeless veterans and nonveterans.

28. Knight, *Health Care Issues.*

29. Winkelby and Fleshin, "Physical, Addictive, and Psychiatric Disorders."

30. Leda, Rosenheck, and Gallup, "Mental Illness."

31. This section is based on studies of VA homeless programs conducted at the Northeast Program Evaluation Center, including the following: Rosenheck, et al. ("Initial Assessment Data"); Rosenheck and Leda ("Who Is Served?"); Leda and Rosenheck ("Impact of Staffing" and "Mental Health Status"); Rosenheck and Gallup ("Involvement"); Rosenheck, Gallup, and Frisman ("An Outcome Study"); Leda, Rosenheck, and Medak *(Progress Report);* Rosenheck and Frisman *(Preliminary Report).*

32. Smith and Yates, "The New England Shelter."

33. Rosenheck, Leda, and Gallup, "Combat Stress"; and Smith and Yates, "The New England Shelter."

34. Veterans Administration, *Annual Report 1987.* Even so, we have been less enthusiastic about providing benefits to veterans whose health problems do not derive directly from combat or other service-related activities. National leaders from Alexander Hamilton to Franklin Roosevelt argued that such expenditures were unwarranted burdens on the federal budget. See Ross, *Preparing for Ulysses;* and Severo and Milford, *The Wages of War.*

35. See Katz, *The Underserving Poor,* on the importance of historical distinctions among categories of the poor. See Hopper and Baumohl, "Held in Abeyance," on the unintended but invidious consequences of defining homelessness in certain ways.

CHAPTER 10

Preparation of this chapter was funded, in part, by National Institute of Mental Health Grant R01MH46116. We thank Jim Baumohl, Carolyn Berry, Kirsten Cowal, Lisa Duchon, Faith Gruelich, Yvonne Rafferty, and Daniela Stojanovic for comments on an earlier version. In addition, collaborations with Colleen Gillespie, James Knickman, and Yvonne Rafferty have enriched our understanding of the issues.

1. Rossi, "Troubling Families."

2. U.S. Conference of Mayors, "A Status Report." The Conference of Mayors publishes an annual survey of member cities in which city officials estimate the size and characteristics of the homeless population using whatever data are available to them. The quality of these data varies from city to city, and, most experts believe, exaggerate the proportion of homeless families; they are more likely than single people to use city services. The figure of 43% is also substantially larger than figures for the previous 6 years (32%–36%), and so should be viewed with skepticism. Burt and Cohen show that homeless families are far more likely than homeless single adults to use shelter. Their data are based on a systematic sample of shelters and soup kitchens in 1987 and are far more accurate, although, we shall suggest, biased in the opposite direction.

3. Burt and Cohen, "Differences," and Jencks, *The Homeless.* See Burt and Cohen's Table 2 for relative duration of homelessness. The numerator for the proportion of families among those who become homeless is the proportion of families who are homeless for one night (.18) times the ratio of the length of time individuals are homeless to the length of time families are homeless (2.75). The equivalent numerator for single adults is just their proportion homeless for one night (.82). The denominator for both fractions is the sum of these numbers. Thus for families, the proportion is:

$$(.18 \times 2.75) \div [(.18 \times 2.75) + .82] = .38$$

We are indebted to Helen Seitz for the river analogy.

4. Data on number of children per family are from Burt and Cohen, "Differences." The HUD report is cited in Rossi, "Troubling Families." Jacobs ("Defining a Social Problem") discusses the exclusion of people who are separated from their families from the count of family members. In a survey of 59 shelter facilities nationwide reported by Jacobs, Little, and Almeida, "Supporting Family Life," the number of families served ranged from 2 to 200 with a median of 10; a substantial portion of the sample would not have been eligible by Burt and Cohen's size criterion.

5. Jacobs, "Defining a Social Problem," and Mills and Ota, "Homeless Women." According to the U.S. Conference of Mayors, 16 of 25 cities surveyed reported that families may have to break up to be accommodated in emergency shelter. This does not count New York City, where families must prove their legal or biological ties to be housed as a unit. Three surveys of individual shelters found that 21%–40% excluded adolescent boys. Weinreb and Rossi ("The American Homeless Family") found that 21% of 646 shelters that replied to a survey conducted by the Better Homes Foundation excluded adolescent males, and an overlapping 23% had restrictions on family size. Earlier and smaller surveys found higher proportions of shelters with restrictions: Jacobs, Little, and Almeida, "Supporting Family Life," found that 40% excluded adolescent males; U.S. General Accounting Office, in a 1989 report cited by Solarz ("To Be Young and Homeless"), found that 33% excluded adolescent males.

6. For New Jersey, see U.S. House of Representatives Select Committee on Children, Youth, and Families, *No Place to Call Home.* For both the effects of economic stressors and the bias in ratings by income of families, see McLoyd, "The Impact of Economic Hardship." For discus-

sion of model welfare guidelines and decisions regarding child placement, see Williams, "Child Welfare Services."

7. Williams, "Child Welfare Services."

8. For New York City, see New York City Commission on the Homeless, *The Way Home*, B-5; and D'Ercole and Struening, "Motherhood." For Maryland, see DiBlasio and Belcher, "Keeping Homeless Families Together." For Washington, see Dockett, *Street Homeless People*. For Chicago, see Rossi, *Down and Out*, 131–33. For Travelers Aid, see Maza and Hall, *Homeless Children*.

9. Unpublished data from our study with James Knickman (Shinn, Knickman, and Weitzman, "Social Relations").

10. Jacobs, "Defining a Social Problem"; Rossi, "Troubling Families"; and Weinreb and Rossi, "The American Homeless Family."

11. Weitzman, Knickman, and Shinn, "Predictors." This policy is undergoing change.

12. Shinn, "Homelessness," 14.

13. Surprisingly, findings from comparisons of homeless families with those who are housed but poor have been less consistent across cities, suggesting that local conditions affect a family's vulnerability to homelessness. But it should be noted that different studies have defined their comparison group—housed families—in different ways. For example, in a comparative study in Boston, female-headed families were sampled from among those at home during the day in neighborhoods with high proportions of poor families headed by women, regardless of the individual household's financial status (Bassuk and Rosenberg, "Why Does Family Homelessness Occur?"). In Philadelphia, comparison families were selected from the waiting room of a pediatric clinic (Rescorla, Parker, and Stolley, "Ability, Achievement, and Adjustment"). In one study in New York City, the housed comparison group was randomly sampled from among all welfare families (Knickman and Weitzman, *A Study of Homeless Families*). In Los Angeles, a welfare sample also was used, but was designed so that the housed families were matched to the homeless families with regard to neighborhood (Wood, et al., "Homeless and Housed"). These differences in definitions and sampling methods may account for contradictory findings across cities.

14. On the general characteristics of homeless mothers, see Rossi, "Troubling Families." Bassuk and Rosenberg ("Why Does Family Homelessness Occur?"), Goodman ("The Prevalence of Abuse"), Rescorla, Parker, and Stolley ("Ability, Achievement, and Adjustment"), and Wood, et al. ("Health of Homeless Children") found homeless mothers to be the same age as housed but poor mothers; Knickman and Weitzman (*A Study of Homeless Families*) and Schteingart, et al. ("Homelessness and Child Functioning") found homeless mothers to be younger. Burt and Cohen ("Differences") and the New York City Commission on the Homeless, *The Way Home*) found homeless mothers to be younger than homeless single adults.

15. Burt and Cohen, "Differences."

16. Goodman ("The Relationship between Social Support and Family Homelessness"), Masten, et al. ("Children in Homeless Families"), Schteingart, et al. ("Homelessness and Child Functioning"), and Wood, et al. ("Health of Homeless Children") did not find differences, although in two cases it is not clear whether the comparison group was intentionally matched on race, and in a third, the comparison group was matched on neighborhood. Knickman and Weitzman (*A Study of Homeless Families*) found overrepresentation of African Americans among homeless families.

17. Rossi, "Troubling Families," and Jencks, *The Homeless*.

18. Goodman, "The Relationship between Social Support and Family Homelessness"; Rescorla, Parker, and Stolley, "Ability, Achievement, and Adjustment"; and Schteingart, et al., "Homelessness and Child Functioning."

19. Shinn, et al., "Social Relations" and Wood, et al., "Homeless and Housed." We initially greeted with skepticism our finding (Shinn, et al., "Social Relations") that 21.9% of 677 women on public assistance who requested shelter, but only 6.5% of 495 women randomly drawn from the public assistance caseload, reported being married or living with a partner, thinking that housed respondents might be reluctant to acknowledge the presence of a man for fear they would lose eligibility for welfare. The problem of getting accurate reports of marital status is probably common to most data sets on homeless and housed poor families, and even the meaning of marital status may be different in different economic strata. For example, divorce is a costly legal process that makes most sense when there are assets to divide, so poor families may be more likely to separate informally, and possibly to engage in new committed relationships without the formality of divorce and remarriage. For several reasons, we are now inclined to take more seriously the finding that the presence of a man increases a family's risk for homelessness: first, domestic violence is often a precursor of homelessness for families; second, the high rates of unemployment and low earnings of young minority men with poor education (Rossi, "Troubling Families"), who are most likely to be fathers in families who are homeless, mean that men may be more of an economic drag than an economic support to their families; and third, except in a few states, two-parent families are less likely to be eligible for welfare. Even where they are eligible, families may not be aware of this, and workers may deny benefits.

20. Burt and Cohen, "Differences," and Shlay and Rossi, "Social Science Research."

21. Homeless mothers in New York City (Weitzman, "Pregnancy and Childbirth") were less likely than housed poor mothers to have given birth to their first children prior to age 18 (37% versus 24%); however, a Boston study (Bassuk and Rosenberg, "Why Does Family Homelessness Occur?") found no difference between housed and home-

less mothers in mean age at the birth of their first children. Average numbers of children per homeless family were 1.7 in New England (Goodman, "The Relationship between Social Support and Family Homelessness"), 2.2 in a national sample (Burt and Cohen, "Differences"), 2.3 in Northern California (Stanford Center, *The Stanford Studies*), 2.4 in Boston (Bassuk and Rosenberg, "Why Does Family Homelessness Occur?"), 2.7 in Los Angeles (Wood, et al., "Homeless and Housed"), and 3.3 in Minneapolis (Masten, et al., "Children in Homeless Families"), where the sampling requirement that families have a school-age child meant that mothers were older and the families were less likely to have additional children in the future. In our New York study, families had an average of 2.2 children but only 1.8 with them. For comparison with housed families, see Weitzman, "Pregnancy and Childbirth."

22. Comparable high school graduation rates were found by Goodman ("The Relationship between Social Support and Family Homelessness"), Knickman and Weitzman (*A Study of Homeless Families*), and Schteingart, et al. ("Homelessness and Child Functioning"). Of note, Bassuk and Rosenberg ("Why Does Family Homelessness Occur?") found homeless mothers to be more likely than housed mothers to be high school graduates, while Wood, et al. ("Homeless and Housed") found the reverse.

23. Bassuk and Rosenberg ("Why Does Family Homelessness Occur?"), Burt and Cohen ("Differences"), and Wood, et al. ("Homeless and Housed") all found the vast majority of homeless families to be receiving public assistance. It is critical, however, that in most localities shelter policies limit access to those currently receiving or potentially eligible for such economic assistance.

24. Knickman and Weitzman, *A Study of Homeless Families,* for New York data. Bassuk and Rosenberg ("Why Does Family Homelessness Occur?") found that in Boston, housed mothers had slightly worse job histories, while Goodman ("The Relationship between Social Support and Family Homelessness") found no differences in New England.

25. For national data: Burt and Cohen, "Differences." For New York City data: New York City Commission on the Homeless, *The Way Home.*

26. Bassuk and Rosenberg, "Why Does Family Homelessness Occur?"

27. For family separation, see Shinn, Knickman, and Weitzman, "Social Relations" and Wood, et al., "Homeless and Housed." For abuse, see Bassuk and Rosenberg, "Why Does Family Homelessness Occur?"; Shinn, Knickman, and Weitzman, "Social Relations"; and Wood, et al., "Homeless and Housed." The more detailed New England study is by Goodman, "The Prevalence of Abuse."

28. New York City Commission on the Homeless, *The Way Home,* B-6, for homeless families versus homeless single adults; Shinn, Knickman, and Weitzman, "Social Relations," for homeless versus housed poor families.

29. Very high rates of foster care experience and lifetime prevalence of physical or sexual abuse have also been noted in other studies of homeless single men and women; e.g., D'Ercole and Struening ("Victimization"); McChesney ("Characteristics"); Sosin, Colson, and Grossman (*Homelessness in Chicago);* Susser, et al. ("Childhood Antecedents"); and Susser, Struening, and Conover ("Childhood Experiences"). See Shlay and Rossi ("Social Science Research") for a summary. On the crudeness of measures of abuse and violence, and the resulting underestimates of prevalence, see Browne, "Family Violence."

30. On Los Angeles, see Wood, et al., "Homeless and Housed." On New York, Weitzman, Knickman, and Shinn, "Predictors." For other studies reporting hospitalization rates for homeless mothers, see Bassuk and Rosenberg, "Why Does Family Homelessness Occur?" (8%); Johnson and Kreuger, "Toward a Better Understanding" (6%); and Mills and Ota, "Homeless Women" (9%). On rates for homeless single adults, see Weitzman, Knickman, and Shinn, "Predictors," and Shlay and Rossi, "Social Science Research." See also Burt and Cohen, "Differences," and, for St. Louis, see Johnson and Kreuger, "Toward a Better Understanding."

31. For Boston, see Bassuk and Rosenberg, "Why Does Family Homelessness Occur?" For Minneapolis, see Masten, et al., "Children in Homeless Families." For New York, see Schteingart, et al., "Homelessness and Child Functioning."

32. Burt and Cohen ("Differences") compare homeless individuals and families.

33. The higher incidence of depressive symptoms in women has been found repeatedly (e.g., Kessler, et al., "Lifetime and 12-Month Prevalence"). On poverty and mental illness, see Dohrenwend, et al., "Socioeconomic Status"; and McLoyd, "The Impact of Economic Hardship."

34. For New York: Knickman and Weitzman, *A Study of Homeless Families.* For Los Angeles: Wood, et al., "Homeless and Housed." For Northern California: Stanford Center, *The Stanford Studies.* For comparisons of homeless families and single adults, see New York City Commission on the Homeless, *The Way Home,* for New York, and Burt and Cohen, "Differences," for national figures. For problems in measuring substance abuse and problems of causal interpretation, see Baumohl and Huebner, "Alcohol and Other Drug Problems."

35. Studies finding differences include Wood, et al. ("Homeless and Housed") in Los Angeles, and Bassuk and Rosenberg ("Why Does Family Homelessness Occur?") in Boston. Studies finding no differences include Goodman ("The Relationship between Social Support and Family Homelessness") in Boston, and Molnar, et al. (*Ill Fares the Land*) in New York. These studies sampled cross sections of families. The New York study finding that homeless families had more extensive networks with fewer housing resources than housed families (Shinn, Knickman, and Weitzman, "Social Relations") sampled families requesting shelter. Both it and Stanford Center (*The Stanford Studies*) suggest the exhaustion of resources.

36. For Boston, see Bassuk, "Women and Children." For Los Angeles, see Wood, et al., "Homeless and Housed." For New York City, see Knickman, et al., *A Study of Homeless Families.*

37. For the comparison of homeless families with housed families, see Knickman, et al., *A Study of Homeless Families.* For the comparison with single women, see New York City Commission on the Homeless, *The Way Home.*

38. For New York City, see Knickman, et al., *A Study of Homeless Families,* who also found crowding among homeless families. For other findings of crowded conditions, see Dehavenon and Boone, *Out of Sight!* and Stanford Center, *The Stanford Studies.*

39. For California: see Stanford Center, *The Stanford Studies.* For New York City: Weitzman and Berry, *Formerly Homeless Families.* Although in other cities public housing has often deteriorated, in New York it is reasonably managed and among the best options available to poor families.

40. Shinn and Gillespie ("The Roles of Housing and Poverty") provide more information on many of the issues in this section. See also McChesney, "Family Homelessness."

41. For national data: see Ringheim, *At Risk of Homelessness,* 48. For New York City: see Knickman and Weitzman, "A Study of Homeless Families."

42. For the improvement in housing conditions, see Jencks, *The Homeless.* For the tradeoff between adequacy and affordability still faced by many families, see the Joint Center for Housing Studies, *The State of the Nation's Housing,* 32. For the housing conditions of families in New York City, see Knickman, et al., *A Study of Homeless Families.*

43. Jencks, *The Homeless.*

44. Yinger, *Housing Discrimination Study.* Rates of discrimination against Latino testers were similar.

45. For an example of the criticism, see Stegman and Keyes, "Housing, Poverty, and Homelessness." For trends in poverty, see U.S. Bureau of the Census, *Poverty in the United States,* x; and U.S. House of Representatives Committee on Ways and Means, *Overview of Entitlement Programs,* 1275. The latter source also contains information on incomes of the poorest 20% of different demographic groups, 1376–77.

46. U.S. House of Representatives Committee on Ways and Means, *Overview of Entitlement Programs,* 1323. These analyses included the value of food and housing subsidies as well as cash benefits. Among married couple families with children, changes in welfare programs accounted for 24% of the increase in the number of people in poverty, and changes in other social insurance programs accounted for 31% of the increase. Changes in market income were especially adverse, but were offset by demographic changes. For cuts in benefits see Lav, et al., *The States and the Poor,* viii.

47. Of note, similar criticism has also been leveled at measures of income for people in other economic strata. For example, some argue that perquisites of employment, such as frequent-flier miles or subsidized housing, should be calculated into income statistics. Further, government benefits in the form of tax deductions (for health insurance, mortgage interest, etc.) might also be included.

48. Watts, "Have Our Measures of Poverty Become Poorer?"

49. For the shortfall in family income, see Littman, "Poverty in the 1980s." Calculations of average family incomes among poor families are based on U.S. Bureau of the Census, "Poverty in the United States," 145.

50. Lazere, et al., *A Place to Call Home.*

51. Jencks, *The Homeless,* 88.

52. Edin, "The Myths of Dependence and Self-Sufficiency."

53. For the National Health Interview Survey data on residential mobility, see Simpson and Fowler, "Geographic Mobility," and Wood, et al., "Impact of Family Relocation." The latter authors showed that the relationships held up controlling for children's age and a number of other variables. For research on ordinary school transitions, see Eccles and Midgley ("Stage/Environment Fit"). Felner, Primavera, and Cauce ("The Impact of School") and Levine, Wesolowski, and Corbett ("Pupil Turnover") review problems associated with school mobility, and a recent study by the U.S. General Accounting Office *(Elementary School Children)* showed that third graders who had attended three or more schools since first grade were more likely than their peers to be below grade level in reading and math and to have repeated grades. Peterson and Crockett ("Pubertal Timing") found effects of school mobility on adolescents' self-esteem. For research on stability in day care, see Howes, "Relations"; Howes and Hamilton, "The Changing Experience"; and Howes and Stewart, "Child's Play."

54. Molnar, Rath, and Klein, "Constantly Compromised"; Molnar and Rubin, "The Impact of Homelessness," and Rafferty and Shinn, "The Impact." The remainder of this section relies heavily on, but updates, the last reference.

55. Studies of homeless children may underestimate the extent of their problems because most of what we know comes from studies of children in shelters with their families. One study that included children in families who were not sheltered found more serious health problems among this group (Stanford Center, *The Stanford Studies*). Two other groups of children are excluded from this chapter: children and adolescents who are homeless on their own and children separated from homeless parents. The latter simply have not been studied.

56. See Alperstein and Arnstein, "Homeless Children" and Alperstein, Rappaport, and Flanigan, "Health Problems," regarding hospitalization, immunization, and lead levels; Chavkin, et al., "Reproductive Experience," regarding prenatal care; and Wright, "Poverty, Homelessness,

Health, Nutrition, and Children," regarding clinic users. Health studies are summarized in Rafferty and Shinn, "The Impact."

57. Bassuk and Rosenberg, "Psychosocial Characteristics"; Stanford Center, *The Stanford Studies* (with data on medical services); Wood, et al, "Health of Homeless Children" (with data on diet and obesity).

58. In 48% of cities surveyed by the U.S. Conference of Mayors (*A Status Report*), families had to leave shelter during the day.

59. Studies showing that homeless children fared worse than housed poor children include Rescorla, Parker, and Stolley ("Ability, Achievement, and Adjustment"), who noted that problems were most severe for preschool children, and Wood, et al. ("Health of Homeless Children"), who used parental reports rather than direct measures. Bassuk and Rosenberg ("Psychosocial Characteristics") found nonsignificant trends in the same direction only for school-aged children; Fox, et al. ("Psychopathology") and Zima, Wells, and Freeman ("Emotional and Behavioral Problems") had no housed comparison groups, but found that homeless children had elevated scores compared to the general population samples for whom test scores were normed. Rescorla, Parker, and Stolley ("Ability, Achievement, and Adjustment") and Bassuk and Rosenberg ("Psychosocial Characteristics") also found that housed poor children fared poorly compared to these general population samples. For effects of maternal depression, see Downey and Coyne, "Children of Depressed Parents," but homeless mothers are not consistently more depressed than housed poor mothers.

60. For Minneapolis: Masten, et al., "Children in Homeless Families." For New York: Schteingart, et al., "Homelessness and Child Functioning."

61. Stanford Center, *The Stanford Studies*.

62. For studies with comparison groups see Bassuk and Rosenberg, "Why Does Family Homelessness Occur?" (Boston); Rescorla, Parker, and Stolley, "Ability, Achievement, and Adjustment" (Philadelphia); and Schteingart, et al., "Homelessness and Child Functioning" (New York). For studies without comparison groups see Fox, et al., "Psychopathology"; Whitman, et al., "Homelessness and Cognitive Performance"; Wood, et al., "Health of Homeless Children"; and Zima, Wells, and Freeman, "Emotional and Behavioral Problems." Note that Rescorla and her colleagues found early childhood education to be rare among homeless children.

63. Wood, et al. ("Health of Homeless Children") found effects for both attendance and repeating grades. Rafferty and Rollins (*Learning in Limbo*) found these effects as well as differences in test scores. Bassuk and Rosenberg ("Psychosocial Characteristics") found a nonsignificant trend in the same direction for repeating grades, while Rescorla, Parker, and Stolley ("Ability, Achievement, and Adjustment") did not. Masten ("Homeless Children") and Stanford Center (*The Stanford Studies*) found differences in

regard to expectations for the future. Fox, et al. ("Psychopathology"), without a comparison group, found high rates of repeating grades and failing to attend school. Rafferty ("The Legal Rights and Educational Problems") provides an excellent summary of educational problems for homeless children.

64. Rafferty, "The Legal Rights and Educational Problems"; Rafferty and Shinn, "The Impact."

65. Rafferty and Rollins, *Learning in Limbo*; Rafferty, *And Miles to Go*; and Stanford Center, *The Stanford Studies*.

66. U.S. Department of Labor, Bureau of Labor Statistics, unpublished tabulations.

67. Weitzman and Berry, *Formerly Homeless Families*.

68. See parallel argument by McChesney, "Family Homelessness."

69. See Wittman, "Affordable Housing," for a discussion of some of these options. Of note, supported and/or sober housing for adults with children is a much more expensive and complex enterprise than development of such housing for single adults.

CHAPTER 11

1. There has been much debate over the years about the appropriate labels for racial and ethnic groups within the United States. We believe "African American" is most appropriate, since it reflects ethnic origins. However, terms such as "Black American" and "Black" are in common use among commentators of all colors, appear throughout the literature on homelessness, are preferred by substantial proportions of surveyed African Americans (Hochschild, *Facing up to the American Dream*, 271), and so are used here, as well.

2. Specifics of shelter use over a 3-year period—for Blacks: 6.2% Philadelphia, 5.6% NYC; for Whites (not of Hispanic origin): 0.42% Philadelphia, 0.28% NYC. (Race-specific poverty rates for NYC, 1990: 27.2% of Black households and 12.1% of White households (Stegman, "Housing and Vacancy Report," 219). For specific studies, see: Shlay and Rossi ("Social Science Research"); Barrett, et al. ("The 1990 Census Shelter and Street Night Enumeration"); and Culhane, et al. ("Public Shelter Admission Rates").

3. See Burt and Cohen, *America's Homeless*; Knickman and Weitzman, *A Study of Homeless Families*; Wood, Valdez, Hayashi, and Shen, "Homeless and Housed Families"; and Rossi, "Troubling Families."

4. As Wilson (*The Truly Disadvantaged*) argues. "When the underclass surfaced in *Time*, other magazines, and Auletta's book [Ken Auletta: *The Underclass*, 1982]," Michael Katz has argued, few liberal social scientists objected. "They had no alternative framework" (*Improving Poor People*, 75). See Gans (*The War against the Poor*) for a recent critique.

5. See Landry, "The Enduring Dilemma"; Gregory and Sanjek, *Race*; Kusmer, "African Americans in the City"; and DeMott, *The Trouble with Friendship*.

6. Note that for the most part, this historical account is restricted to men, with a few exceptions. Intersection of the trade of prostitution and the literal homelessness it made it possible for women to avoid has only begun to be studied (e.g., Golden, *The Women Outside*). Nothing to our knowledge has been published regarding African American women in this respect.

7. So much so, in fact, that the earliest New York City poorhouse (1734) also served as a jail for runaway slaves (Booth, *History of the City of New York*, 347). For the more general point, see Kusmer, "The Underclass."

8. For sources in addition to those cited below, see Kusmer, "The Underclass: Tramps and Vagrants," 223; Jones, "Southern Diaspora"; Monkkonen, "Introduction," 14; and Bahr, *Disaffiliated Man*.

9. Blumberg, et al., *Liquor and Poverty*; Schneider, "Tramping Workers," 213–15; and Kusmer, "The Underclass," 22.

10. Anderson, *The Hobo*, 8; Frazier, *The Negro Family*, 118. Formed in 1906, the National Urban League soon became the premier social service agency for urban Blacks, and the chief source of assistance to migrating newcomers in cities like Chicago (Grossman, *Land of Hope*, 134, 142–43).

11. Even then, it was one astute observer's impression that "the Negro drifter" typically avoided both public shelter and hobo "jungles," preferring to rely upon friends, odd jobs, and improvised shelter (LeCount, as cited by Anderson, *The Homeless*, 135).

12. The quote is from Turkel, *Hard Times*, 58–59. Other sources for information in the paragraph: Anderson, *The Homeless*; Schubert, *Twenty Thousand Transients*; Sutherland and Locke, *Twenty Thousand Homeless Men*; Webb, *The Transient Unemployed*; Crouse, *The Homeless Transient*, 9; Caplow, "Transiency as a Cultural Pattern," 737; and Peery, *Black Fire*, 89–129.

13. Borchert, *Alley Life*; Grossman, *Land of Hope*; and Trotter, "Blacks in the Urban North."

14. For Rochester: Pittman and Gordon, *Revolving Door*. For New York City: Bigart, "Grim Problems"; Levinson, "The Homeless Man"; and Kean, "A Comparative Study." For Chicago: Bogue, *Skid Row in American Cities*; and Hoch and Slayton, *New Homeless and Old*. For Philadelphia: Rooney, "Race Relations in Skid Row."

15. See Clines, "Study Finds Bowery Losing Derelicts," 21; and Bahr and Caplow, *Old Men*; Table 2-1. One study by P. Nash estimated that the percentage among *new* arrivals on the Bowery (a better indicator of contemporary trends, as most Bowery men at that time tended never to leave under their own power) had more than doubled between 1955 and 1964, from 18% to 39% (as cited by Rooney, "Race Relations in Skid Row," footnote 2). Regarding the

younger age among Black homeless men, Chase is quoted as observing: "Negro derelicts reach the last stop quicker" (as quoted by Clines, "Study Finds Bowery Losing Derelicts").

16. Sigal, "The Unchanging Area in Transition," 284–93.

17. Blumberg, et al., *Liquor and Poverty*, 175; see also Liebow, *Tally's Corner*; and Anderson, *A Place on the Corner*. In an early study of Berkeley's street population, Baumohl and Miller (*Down and Out in Berkeley*) found that Black men made up 12% of the patrons of the local breadline in an index week of March 1973; compared to White patrons, they were older, less educated, less transient and more likely to be working in the shadow economy. Half of them (vs. 70% of Whites) reported paying no rent where they currently lived.

18. Crystal and Goldstein, *New Arrivals*; Shlay and Rossi, "Social Science Research."

19. Proportional representation in these nine studies ranged from 10% to 91%; see Rossi "Troubling Families." Men are often present in these family units, but are discouraged from declaring themselves by the current social welfare system. No doubt their contributions are often sporadic. But studies do not support their wholesale absence (Milburn and D'Ercole, "Homeless Women"; Sullivan "Absent Fathers"; MacLeod, *Ain't No Makin' It*).

20. Stack, *All Our Kin, Call to Home*; and Billingsley, *Climbing Jacob's Ladder*.

21. "Social capital" refers to resources available to someone through connections and group membership. Specifically, the term designates those social linkages made through family, neighborhood, work affiliations, civic and religious groups, professional and trade associations, and the like. These can play all-important roles in gaining access to scarce slots in education, the job market, professional placement, etc. Bourdieu and Wacquant defined it as ". . .the sum of the resource, actual or virtual, that accrue to an individual or a group by virtue of possessing a durable network of more or less institutionalized relationships of mutual acquaintance and recognition" (*Invitation to Reflexive Sociology*, 119). For a critique, see Stack, "Second Thoughts on Social Capital." For its application to homelessness, see Blumberg, et al. on "social credit" (*Liquor and Poverty*, 175); and Wiseman (*Stations of the Lost*) on "social margin." To the extent that Black homeless men come from families among the ghetto poor, they are deficient in stocks of more broadly defined social capital (Wilson, et al., "The Ghetto Underclass," 22–23). See also Putnam, "The Prosperous Community" and "The Strange Disappearance of Civic America." Knowledge about local resources does not appear to be a problem. A California study found that, relative to Anglos and Mexican Americans, African Americans were more likely to be knowledgeable about services for homeless families (Dornbusch, "Some Political Implications").

22. On African American poverty, see Bane, "Household Composition and Poverty"; on the informal economy,

see Sassen, *The Mobility of Labor and Capital*. On Bowery flophouses, see Cohen and Sokolovsky, *Old Men of the Bowery*; and Tierney, "Save the Flophouse," 16. Discrimination is emphatically *not* the case in public shelters serving the Bowery clientele, nor (if photographic evidence tells the story) in the missions (Bonner, *Jerry McAuley*).

23. See Kuhn and Culhane, "Applying Cluster Analysis" (for a summary, see White, "Perception vs. Reality," 110–12). Preliminary findings from a five-year follow-up of sheltered families also show remarkably high and stable relocation rates (M. Shinn, personal communication).

24. See Groth, *Living Downtown*. For an argument that shelters are functional substitutes for such places, see Hopper and Baumohl, "Held in Abeyance."

25. Two recent doctoral dissertations offer especially good discussions of these issues: Hainer, "Sharing Kith and Kin," and Gounis, "The Domestication of Urban Marginality."

26. Bogard, et al., "Surplus Mothers."

27. So pronounced and stable is this pattern that some political theorists have argued that it constitutes a necessary third criterion (in addition to desert and need) when judging the fairness of employment policies (e.g., Gutman, "Justice across the Spheres"). For an especially moving account of the situation of African American men in postwar Washington, DC, see Leibow, *Tally's Corner*.

28. Jencks, *Rethinking Social Policy*, Table 5.3. For detailed documentation of the trends summarized in this section, see Hopper, "Margins within Margins."

29. Tilly and Tilly, "Capitalist Work and Labor Markets," 306. Note that this isn't simply a matter of "misunderstandings" between boss and employee (as Jencks suggests), but a severely constrained sphere of service work vs. old blue-collar settings and dirty work. As Fine nicely documents, for example, the cramped quarters of kitchen work still allow for a good deal of horseplay, pranks, teasing and "deviance" (Fine, *Kitchens*, 118f). See also Jencks, *Rethinking Social Policy*, 128; MacLeod, *Ain't No Makin' It*, 179, 227, 243; and Bourgois, *In Search of Respect*.

30. See, for example, Billingsley, *Climbing Jacob's Ladder*; Stack, "Second Thoughts on Social Capital."

31. Grossman, *Land of Hope*; and Liebow, *Tally's Corner*. The quote is from Hans Medick, as cited by Hareven, "The History of the Family," 103.

32. Stern, "Poverty and Family Composition."

33. See Milburn and D'Ercole, "Homeless Women," 1164.

34. See Shinn, et al., "Social Relationships": 1183–85. Compared to poor housed Black women, more homeless Black women had been homeless within the past year, were currently pregnant or had given birth in the past year, had parents on public assistance, and had experienced social disruptions (such as having parents tell them to leave their house). See also Krueger, et al., *Ethnic Differentials*.

35. Jackson, *Crabgrass Frontier*; and Massey and Denton, *American Apartheid*. Rainwater ("The Revolt of the Dirty Workers") referred to the tacit containment policy as "dirty work"—deemed necessary, but just as surely disavowed and preferably out of sight.

36. Lazere. et al., *The Low Income Housing Crisis Continues*; and Stone, *Shelter Poverty*, 147f.

37. Groth, *Living Downtown*, 133.

38. Groth, *Living Downtown*, 283; Hartman, et al., *Displacement*. See also Chapter 4.

39. Mead, *The New Politics of Poverty*, is emblematic.

40. Hochschild, "The Politics of the Estranged Poor," 565.

41. Wilson, *The Truly Disadvantaged*, 138.

42. Anderson, "Sex Codes and Family Life," 65; and Sullivan, "Absent Fathers."

43. Ogbu, "The Consequences of the American Caste System"; and Fine, *Framing Dropouts*.

44. MacLeod, *Ain't No Makin' It*. For the Black teens he followed, race both explained past familial failures to achieve while serving notice that the achievements of the civil rights movement had removed former barriers and expanded one's own individual potential. The converse also applies: among White teenagers, the absence of race as an exculpatory device helps explain their diminished aspirations (MacLeod, *Ain't No Makin' It*, 129–35). It is worth noting that all three studies are set against the background of three decades of sustained improvement in Black educational attainment and performance on standardized achievement tests (Carnoy, *Faded Dreams*).

45. MacLeod, *Ain't No Makin' It*, 243.

46. Hochschild, "The Politics of the Estranged Poor," 573. Nor, Hochschild also points out, is there always a bright line between legal and illegal work, *Facing Up to the American Dream*, 193f. See also Currie, *Reckoning*, 143f; Nightingale, *On the Edge*, 135–65; and MacLeod, *Ain't No Makin' It*, 231.

47. See Luhrmann, *Persuasions of the Witch's Craft*, for the general argument; Hochschild, *Facing Up to the American Dream*: 218f, for application to American Blacks.

48. This can mean, variously, retreat to "shadow values" (Liebow, *Tally's Corner*), maddening attempts to marry the dictates of foreign "respectability" with the demands of local repute (Wilson, *Oscar*), open repudiation of standards of class-based expected performance (Willis, *Learning to Labor*), subtle efforts at subterfuge and insubordination (Scott, *Domination and the Arts of Resistance*), and reinterpretation of dominant values in terms that make sense on the home front, however alien they may seem from without (Hainer, "Sharing Kith and Kin").

49. Bourdieu and Wacquant, *Invitation to Reflexive Sociology*, 80; and Sennett and Cobb, *The Hidden Injuries of Class*. These are not, in the main, original observations;

nor are they specific to the present age. In his classic analysis of deviance, Merton *(Social Theory and Social Structure)* long ago pointed out that (when it doesn't retreat or turn in on itself) frustrated ambition will seek the spoils of success via forbidden channels.

50. See Kessler and Neighbors, "A New Perspective"; Thomas and Hughes, "The Continuing Significance of Race"; Ulbrich, et al., "Race, Socioeconomic Status, and Psychological Distress."

51. See Milburn and D'Ercole, "Homeless Women."

52. Critical outside support—such as federal community development grants—is needed effectively to translate social capital into a substantial force locally. Stack, "Second Thoughts on Social Capital," is especially instructive on this point.

53. See Anderson, *Streetwise*; and Hainer, "Sharing Kith and Kin."

54. See Sullivan, *Getting Paid*; and Fagan, "Crime, Drugs, and Neighborhood Change."

55. Kessler and Neighbors, "A New Perspective."

56. See Currie, *Reckoning*, 11; Fagan, "Crime, Drugs, and Neighborhood Change"; MacLeod, *Ain't No Makin' It*, 179f; and Bourgois, *In Search of Respect.*

57. See Wallace's discussion of "urban desertification" ("A Synergism of Plagues").

58. The combination of deindustrialization in the north and the pull of home roots has led to a reversal of the postwar African American migration north; see Stack, *Call to Home*. A curious side note may be of interest here: African American communities of rural, north-central Pennsylvania have also played host to a recent influx of migrants disenchanted with city life. This flow has been abetted by the aftercare strategies of some big-city substance abuse treatment programs (which prescribe a profound change of scenery to sustain sobriety and drug-free living), complemented by a thriving "recovery industry" in places like Williamsport. While only a few wind up settling there, those who do frequently bring their families. See Milofsky, et al., "Small Town in Mass Society."

59. See Anderson's discussion of the declining moral authority of "old heads" in poor African American neighborhoods *(Streetwise)*.

60. Although not reviewed in this chapter, much evidence points to the poor job done by community resources in adapting to the markedly changed landscape of the late 1970s and the 1980s—particularly with respect to ensuring basic survival resources for persons with severe mental illness, and alcohol and drug problems (see Chapter 17).

61. See Snow and Anderson, *Down on Their Luck*, for discussion of this point.

62. See Bahr, "Introduction," xxi.

63. Early students of Washington, DC's Black poor noted that "the strong community spirit in the alleys is their most notable attribute. They feed their own hungry, house their own homeless, lend to their penniless, and shelter their own refugees from the law" (Forestall, "Trends in Housing," 32).

64. "Faced with an increasing number of individuals and families unable to survive on their own resources, urban jobless householders opened their homes to friends and kin even though it did nothing to improve the economic status of their immediate family" (Stern, "Poverty and Family Composition," 248).

65. Of the 7 Black teenagers MacLeod followed into their mid-20s, almost all of whom paid their cultural dues and played by the rules, only 2 have managed to establish their own household.

66. We have in mind the behavioral accompaniments of a serious drug (and especially crack) habit, the ways in which it squanders social capital as well as liquid funds. Hartwell's ("Track Marks and Pipe Dreams") doctoral dissertation is filled with rueful recollections of such damage on the part of currently homeless junkies.

67. Recall that it was the fluid reshuffling of residential arrangements that so impressed earlier students of the African American extended family. See Stack, *All Our Kin*, 61 (that kin live in proximity to one another is key to their effectiveness in mutual aid networks); and Hainer, "Sharing Kith and Kin," 297 (housing surplus must exist to accommodate changing family rosters and preserve family unity as "a movable feast").

68. As Wallace and Bassuk argue, "as the housing famine progesss, social networks become 'congested' as virtually everybody who can house a displaced friend or relative does so" ("Housing Famine and Homelessness," 489).

69. Williams, "There Goes the Neighborhood."

70. See Fischer, "Estimating the Prevalence of Alcohol, Drug and Mental Health Problems," 366. Psychiatric hospitalization and victimization, however, figure more highly in their pre-homeless careers. The rise of crack cocaine may have already weakened some of these sex differences by the time they were reported (Burt, *Over the Edge*, 111–16). If early accounts are borne out, the subsequent increase in virtually abandoned kids, a kind of forced fosterage, has placed great strains on grandmothers in Black communities (see Minkler, Roe, and Robertson-Beckley, "Raising Grandchildren").

71. In discussing the preventive role played by enduring kinship resources, an early observation by Crystal merits note. In examining intake assessments of a 1982–83 cohort of shelter applicants in New York, he found that the women were more than twice as likely as the men (7.4% vs. 2.8%) to have had institutional or foster care placements as the *"principal* living arrangement in which they grew up" ("Homeless Men and Homeless Women," 4). Many more, Crystal adds, had spent at least part of their childhood in such settings. He also found that severe psychiatric disorder was more common among the women, a finding since replicated in other studies as well (Fischer and

Breakey, "The Epidemiology of Alcohol, Drug, and Mental Disorders").

72. See Duneier, *Slim's Table*; and Burton, "Teenage Childbearing." "On the street and in the shelters, one meets many homeless women who had been kept afloat by family members until, for one reason or another, the family had to let go. For most women, living with relatives or receiving significant financial or other support from them was the last stage in their descent into homelessness" (Liebow, *Tell Them Who I Am*, 81–82; see also Golden, *The Women Outside*).

73. Or, as Gounis ("The Domestication of Urban Marginality") argues, public shelter itself may be converted into a kind of respite service in the makeshift economies of the marginally situated.

74. Requirements for the military have also changed with an all-volunteer force in terms of literacy and a high school diploma. Nonetheless, it remains one of the most integrated institutions in American life (*New York Times*, 5 April 1995: A1).

75. *New York Times*, 11 January 1989: B3. For further discussion of this point, see Hopper, "The New Urban Niche of Homelessness."

76. Struening and Pittman, *Characteristics of Residents*.

77. Stern, "The Emergence of the Homeless," 301.

78. Blumberg, et al., *Liquor and Poverty*, 122.

79. White, "Representing 'The Real Deal.'"

80. Gates, *Loose Canons*, 193.

81. "When they approach me they see only my surroundings, themselves, or figments of their imagination—indeed, everything and anything except me" (Ellison, *Invisible Man*, 3).

CHAPTER 12

1. On the presence of African Americans among the homeless, see Hopper and Milburn, Chapter 11. On Los Angeles, see Ropers, *The Invisible Homeless*. On San Antonio and New York, see Freeman and Hall, "Permanent Homelessness."

2. African American and Latino MSA totals derived from U.S. Bureau of the Census, *Population Estimates by Race and Hispanic Origin for States, Metropolitan Areas, and Selected Counties: 1980 to 1985*. Non-Hispanic White totals derived from U.S. Bureau of the Census, *Patterns of Metropolitan Area and County Population Growth: 1980 to 1987*. Albuquerque: Wright, "The Johnson-Pew Health Care for the Homeless Program." Austin: Snow, et al., "The Myth of Pervasive Mental Illness." Baltimore: Clark, "Health Care Needs of Homeless Women in Baltimore"; and Wright, "The Johnson-Pew Health Care for the Homeless Program." Birmingham: Wright, "The Johnson-Pew Health Care for the Homeless Program." Boston: Wright, "The Johnson-Pew Health Care for the Homeless Program." Chicago: Wright, "The Johnson-Pew Health Care for the Homeless Program"; and Rossi, et al., *The Condition of the Homeless in Chicago*. Detroit: Mowbray, et al., *Mental Health and Homelessness in Detroit*; and Wright, "The Johnson-Pew Health Care for the Homeless Program." Los Angeles: Robertson, et al., *The Homeless of Los Angeles County*. Milwaukee: Rosnow, et al., *Listening to the Homeless*; and Wright, "The Johnson-Pew Health Care for the Homeless Program." Nashville: Wright, "The Johnson-Pew Health Care for the Homeless Program." New York: Crystal, *New Arrivals*; Hoffman, et al., *Who Are the Homeless?*; and Wright, "The Johnson-Pew Health Care for the Homeless Program." Philadelphia: Wright, "The Johnson-Pew Health Care for the Homeless Program." Phoenix: Brown, et al., *The Homeless of Phoenix*. Portland: Multnomah County, *The Homeless Poor*; and Multnomah County, *Homeless Women*. San Antonio: Wright, "The Johnson-Pew Health Care for the Homeless Program." San Francisco: Wright, "The Johnson-Pew Health Care for the Homeless Program." St. Louis: Morse, *A Contemporary Assessment*. Washington, DC: Wright, "The Johnson-Pew Health Care for the Homeless Program."

Readers wanting a detailed comparative display of the data from these studies, and discussion of the technical considerations involved in classifying people by race and/or ethnicity, may write the author: Susan González Baker, 336 Burdine, University of Texas, Austin, TX 78712.

3. For Los Angeles, see Ropers, *The Invisible Homeless*. For age breakdowns across ethnic categories, see Rossi, "Minorities and Homelessness." For Ohio, see First, Roth, and Arewa, "Homelessness." For Texas, see Andrade, *Living in the Grey Zone*.

4. See Andrade, *Living in the Grey Zone*.

5. First, Roth, and Arewa, "Homelessness"; Andrade, *Living in the Grey Zone*; and Rossi, "Minorities and Homelessness."

6. Rossi, "Minorities and Homelessness."

7. On African American single adults, see First, Roth, and Arewa, "Homelessness"; and La Gory, et al., "Homelessness in Alabama." On single mothers, see Burt and Cohen, "Differences."

8. See First, Roth, and Arewa, "Homelessness"; Andrade, *Living in the Grey Zone*; and Garrett and Schutt, "Homelessness in Massachusetts." For Austin, see Snow, et al., "The Myth."

9. Rossi, *Down and Out*; and Snow and Anderson, "Identity Work."

10. Chavez, *Shadowed Lives*.

11. Bean and Tienda, *The Hispanic Population*; and Rodriguez and Hagan, "Apartment Restructuring."

12. On tests of the general population, see Umberson, "Sociodemographic Position"; Warheit, et al., "Interpersonal Coping Networks"; and Dohrenwend, "Social Status." On current symptoms in homeless populations, see Davis and Winkleby, "Sociodemographic." On comparative diagnoses, see National Academy of Science, *Homelessness*.

13. On the scarcity of studies, see Trimble, Padilla, and Bell, *Drug Abuse*. Treatment data come from 4,232 treatment units participating in the National Drug and Alcoholism Treatment Utilization Survey. Each unit provides extensive information on its clientele, staffing, funding levels, funding sources, and treatment modalities (i.e., inpatient hospital-based, outpatient hospital-based, or community-based center). On the comparative use of forms of cocaine, see U.S. Department of Health and Human Services, *National Household Survey*.

14. Koegel, Burnam, and Farr, "The Prevalence"; Rossi, *Down and Out*; and National Academy of Science, *Homelessness*.

15. Tienda and Jensen, "Poverty and Minorities."

16. Tienda and Jensen, "Poverty and Minorities."

17. Kolodny, *Exploring New Strategies*; and O'Hare, *America's Minorities*.

18. See National Academy of Science, *Homelessness*.

19. See Weicher, "Housing Quality"; James, McCummings, and Tynan, *Minorities in the Sunbelt*; and Turner and Reed, *Housing America*.

20. Denton and Massey, "Residential Segregation."

21. Turner and Reed, *Housing America*.

22. On the importance of social networks, see Warheit, et al., "Interpersonal Coping Networks"; Greene and Monahan, "Comparative Utilization"; Mier and Giloth, "Hispanic Employment"; and Granovetter, "The Strength." On social networks and homelessness, see Burt, *Over the Edge*; Rossi, "Minorities and Homelessness"; and Hopper and Milburn, Chapter 11.

23. Campbell, Marsden, and Hurlburt, "Social Resources."

24. Marsden, "Core Discussion Networks"; Vernon and Roberts, "A Comparison"; Warheit, et al., "Interpersonal Coping Networks."

25. Mindel, "Extended Familialism"; Keefe, "Personal Communities."

26. On social networks and emotional support, see Wellman and Wortley, "Different Strokes"; Griffith, "Social Support Providers"; and Blazer, "Impact of Late-Life Depression." On "the strength of weak ties," Mark Granovetter's wonderful phrase, see Granovetter, "The Strength"; Campbell, Marsden, and Hurlburt, "Social Resources"; and Mier and Giloth, "Hispanic Employment."

27. Greene and Monahan, "Comparative Utilization"; and Mindel and Wright, "The Use of Social Services."

28. For the census data, see Weicher, "Housing Quality." On Latino residential arrangements, see Valdivieso, "High School and Beyond"; O'Hare, *America's Minorities*; Bean and Tienda, *The Hispanic Population*; and Jasso and Rosenzweig, "The New Chosen." Puerto Ricans: Bean and Tienda, *The Hispanic Population*; and Crystal, *New Arrivals*.

29. See Angel and Tienda, "Determinants."

CHAPTER 13

1. To accomplish this, we built on two local studies of such public attitudes, one conducted in Buffalo, New York, and the other in Nashville, Tennessee. For Buffalo, see Toro and McDonnell, "Beliefs, Attitudes and Knowledge." For Nashville, see Lee, Hinze-Jones, and Lewis, "Public Beliefs."

2. See White, *Rude Awakenings*, and Baum and Burnes, *A Nation in Denial*, for good examples of this.

3. That is, they responded that these statements were "definitely true" or "probably true," rather than "definitely false" or "probably false."

4. The remaining respondents said these policies would be "a little effective" or "not at all effective."

5. These respondents answered "definitely true" or "probably true," rather than "definitely false" or "probably false," to statements describing homeless people as being "more dangerous than others."

6. See Wilkerson, "Shift in Feelings," and more recently, Smolowe, "Giving the Cold Shoulder."

7. They "strongly agreed" or "agreed" with these statements, rather than "disagreed" or "strongly disagreed."

8. That is, when asked whether the federal government should adopt this policy, these respondents answered "definitely yes" or "probably yes," rather than "definitely no" or "probably no."

9. These respondents answered "definitely no" or "probably no," rather than "definitely yes" or "probably yes," to statements affirming these rights.

10. Link, et al., "Public Knowledge, Attitudes, and Beliefs about Homeless People."

11. Gallup Organization, *Homeless but Not Hopeless*.

CHAPTER 14

1. "One police captain described the police's mission [in enforcing San Francisco's Matrix Program] as a 'no tolerance program' against the 'filth, flea infested, desease [sic] ridden people' of San Francisco." *Joyce v. City and County of San Francisco*, Case No. C93 4149 DLJ (N. D. Cal., February 17, 1994), *Plaintiffs' Reply to Defendant's Memorandum in Opposition to Motion for Preliminary Injunction*, 19–20.

2. However, the volume of citations under Brown was substantially smaller than during Jordan's unsuccessful re-election campaign from August through October, 1995. For a detailed comparison, see Lynch, "Matrix Gone."

3. Leo, "Homeless Rights," 56.

4. *Joyce v. City and County of San Francisco*, Case No. C93 4149 DLJ (N. D. Cal., February 9, 1994), *City's Memorandum of Points and Authorities in Opposition to Motion for Preliminary Injunction*, 29–30.

5. Wilson and Kelling, "Broken Windows," 35; Walters, "Fixing," B9.

6. *Joyce v. City and County of San Francisco*, C93 4149 DLJ (N. D. Cal., February 9, 1994), *Amicus Memorandum of American Alliance for Rights and Responsibilities in Opposition to Motion for Preliminary Injunction*, 2.

7. Santa Ana City Council, *Transcript*, 17–18.

8. *Pottinger v. City of Miami*, Case No. 88-2406-Civ-Atkins (S. D. Fla., August 21, 1992), *Defendant City of Miami's Post-Trial Memorandum*, 48.

9. Atlanta Task Force for the Homeless, *The Criminalization of Poverty*.

10. Byofsky, "No Heart," 12.

11. Tyson, "Cities Crack Down."

12. Waldron, "Homelessness," 299.

13. Waldron, "Homelessness," 300–01.

14. "Inappropriate" places: Santa Ana City Council (1993), remarks of Councilmember Lisa Mills, 17.

15. Gurza, "Police Enforcing Ban."

16. In challenging the validity of citations issued under Santa Ana's camping ban, the Orange County Public Defender questioned "whether the city['s] . . . latest attempt at socio-economic cleansing is constitutional." [*People v. Zuckernick*, Orange County Municipal Court Case No. 93CM02631 (April 12, 1993), *Demurrer*, 2].

17. Shaffer, "Tent Cities."

18. *Tobe v. City of Santa Ana* (Cal. Ct. App. 1994), 27 Cal. Rptr. 2d 386, 394.

19. France, *The Red Lily*, 95.

20. Burns, "Fearing the Mirror," 801.

21. *Loper v. New York City Police Department*, 802 F. Supp. 1029, 1037 (S.D.N.Y. 1992) *aff'd* 999 F. 2d 699 (2nd Cir. 1993).

22. Rothstein, "Is There a Right?" 19.

23. *Tobe*, note 18, above, 387–88. The California Court of Appeal noted that "the municipal memoranda [describing these events] can only be characterized as astonishing."

24. *Tobe v. City of Santa Ana*, Orange County Superior Court Case No. 696000 (April 8, 1993), *Reporter's Transcript*, 75.

25. *Tobe*, note 18, above, 395, 392 n. 4.

26. *Tobe*, note 18, above, 393.

27. *Tobe*, note 18, above, 394.

28. *Tobe v. City of Santa Ana*, 9 Cal. 4th 1069, 1103 (1995).

29. *Tobe*, note 28, above, 5247.

30. *Tobe*, note 28, above, 5251.

31. Gurza, "Camping Crackdown."

32. Santa Ana City Council, *Transcript*, 24-25.

33. According to the federal court of appeals: "The New York City Subway System transports approximately 3,500,000 passengers on an average workday, operates twenty-four hours a day, seven days a week, and consists of 648 miles of track, 468 subway stations, and over 6,000 subway cars. Many parts of the subway system are almost one hundred years old. In a timeworn routine of New York City life, each day a multitude descends the steep and long staircases and mechanical escalators to wait on narrow and crowded platforms bounded by dark tunnels and high power electrical wires." [*Young v. New York City Transit Authority*, 903 F. 2d 146, 149 (2nd Cir. 1990).]

34. *Young v. New York City Transit Authority*, 729 F. Supp. 341, 352 (S.D.N.Y. 1990) *rev'd* 903 F. 2d 146 (2nd Cir. 1990).

35. *Young*, note 34, above, 729 F. Supp. at 352.

36. *Young*, note 34, above, 903 F. 2d at 156.

37. *Young*, note 34, above, 903 F. 2d at 158.

38. *Young*, note 34, above, 903 F. 2d at 156. The third judge on the three-judge panel, Judge Meskill, dissented: "Begging is indistinguishable from charitable solicitation for First Amendment purposes. To hold otherwise would mean that an individual's plight is worthy of less protection in the eyes of the law than the interests addressed by an organized group. No court has ever so ruled. Defendants therefore may not open the door to the latter while slamming the door in the face of the former." (*Young*, note 34, above, 903 F. 2d at 167)

39. *Loper*, note 21, above. Since the state's establishment in the 18th century, New York has criminalized the act of begging. In the decade prior to the *Loper* decision, police made few arrests under New York State's antibegging law, but they did use the law as a mechanism to compel beggars to stop begging and to move along. (802 F. Supp. at 1032–34)

40. *Loper*, note 21, above, 802 F. Supp. at 1039.

41. *Loper*, note 21, above, 802 F. Supp. at 1037.

42. *Loper v. New York City Police Dept.*, 999 F. 2d 699, 701 (2nd 1993).

43. *Loper*, note 21, above, 802 F. Supp. at 1030–31.

CHAPTER 15

I am grateful to Laurel Weir for her research assistance with this chapter.

1. For Clinton administration support, see Interagency Council on the Homeless, *Priority Home! Federal Plan to Break the Cycle of Homelessness;* for congressional support, see Speaker's Task Force on Homelessness, *Report*.

2. In 1982, a Reagan administration official stated publicly that "no one is living on the streets" (in the *Bos-*

ton Globe, June 17, 1982, then cited in Hopper and Hamberg, "The Making of America's Homeless"); in 1983, presidential advisor Edwin Meese claimed that soup kitchens were a "free lunch" for persons not truly in need (see Engel and Sargent, "Meese's Hunger Remarks"); in 1984, President Reagan expressed the opinion that some of those living on the streets were doing so "by their own choice" (see Green and MacColl, *Reagan's Reign of Error*).

3. General Accounting Office, *Homelessness: A Complex Problem and the Federal Response,* 40.

4. General Accounting Office, *Homelessness: A Complex Problem and the Federal Response,* 32.

5. General Accounting Office, *Homelessness: A Complex Problem and the Federal Response,* 32–33. The McKinney Act incorporated and formally authorized the program. *U.S. Code,* vol. 42, sec. 11331 (1987).

6. *Homeless Eligibility Clarification Act,* Public Law 99-570, Title XI, October 27, 1986.

7. *Homeless Eligibility Clarification Act,* Public Law 99-570, Title XI, October 27, 1986, amending *U.S. Code,* vol. 17, sec. 2020.

8. *Homeless Housing Act of 1986,* Public Law 99-500, sec. 101(g), October 18, 1986.

9. *Homeless Housing Act of 1986,* Public Law 99-500, sec. 101(g), October 18, 1986.

10. *Congressional Record,* daily ed., March 5, 1987, House vote, 264–121; *Congressional Record,* daily ed., April 9, 1987, Senate vote, 85–12.

11. Pear, "President Signs $1 Billion."

12. Authorizations refer to amounts that *may* be allocated by Congress through a separate appropriations process by which funds are *actually* allocated. Supplemental appropriations are appropriations made after the usual appropriations process, generally because of special urgency.

13. These organizations are specified by the statute: United Way, the Salvation Army, the National Council of Churches of Christ, Catholic Charities, The Council of Jewish Federations, and The American Red Cross.

14. The statute makes an exception for nonprofit applicants for aid under subtitles C and D, provided that the applicable state has an approved plan.

15. This is the Community Development Block Grant statute, which distributes funds based on population and poverty. If the amount that would be allocated under the formula falls under a certain minimum, HUD must, in most cases, reallocate it to the state.

16. Recipients must also certify that: buildings renovated with the funds will continue to be used for low-income people for a period of 3 or 10 years, depending on how the funds were used; that safe and sanitary conditions will be provided; and that they will assist homeless people in obtaining other services and assistance.

17. However, not more than 15% of the total allocation may go to local government for provision of such services. Moreover, funds may be granted to local government to support such services only if the services had not been provided by the local government in the preceding year.

18. Under the statute, up to eight handicapped homeless persons may live in such housing.

19. Applicants must agree to continue to use any facilities purchased, leased, renovated, or converted with the funds for homeless or lower-income people for a period of at least 10 years; and they must demonstrate that they have made reasonable efforts to use local resources and resources available under other provisions of Title IV of the McKinney Act, and that those resources are not sufficient or are not available. In addition, in distributing the funds, the Secretary must, "to the maximum extent practicable," set aside 50% of the funds for facilities designed primarily to benefit homeless elderly individuals and homeless families with children, and to use a portion of those funds for child care facilities; the Secretary must also, "to the extent practicable," distribute funds equitably across geographic areas.

20. No single city or county may receive more than 10 percent of the total amount of funds made available under this program.

21. Title V has been the subject of much litigation to require the federal agencies to comply with its provisions, and to defend use of the program at the local level. The National Law Center on Homelessness and Poverty is engaged in an ongoing monitoring and litigation effort to ensure that the agencies comply with the statute, permanent injunction and enforcement orders obtained to date. See National Law Center on Homelessness and Poverty, *To Protect and Defend.*

Title V also contains a provision relating to surplus personal property, directing the General Service Administration to require certain state agencies to inform providers of services to homeless people about the availability of surplus personal property under existing federal law.

22. In particular, grantees providing health services to homeless people must provide health services at locations accessible to homeless persons; provide homeless persons emergency health services at all hours; refer homeless persons for necessary hospital services as appropriate; refer mentally ill homeless persons for mental health services (or provide such services); provide outreach to inform homeless people of the availability of health services; and aid homeless people in establishing eligibility for assistance, and in obtaining services, under entitlement programs.

23. Allocations are determined by formula, based on the state's relative urban population, or at a certain minimum amount, whichever is higher.

24. Services must be provided in residential settings not supported under the supportive housing or the 1986 transitional housing program. Funds may not be used for inpatient services, for purchase or major improvement of real property, or for purchase of major medical equipment.

25. A fifth part, Subtitle E, "Miscellaneous Provisions," includes a requirement that HHS make research demonstration grants to study the causes of youth homelessness.

26. The provision amends the law by allowing related families living together as separate households to qualify separately.

27. This refers to a rule under the Food Stamp Act that allows applicants, for purposes of establishing income eligibility, to deduct shelter expenses (e.g., rent costs) that exceed 50% of income, but caps allowable deductions at a certain dollar amount.

28. Homeless Veterans Act of 1987.

29. Such assistance is provided through existing housing programs designed to close the gap between prevailing market rents and payments that low-income tenants can afford, both as defined by HUD.

30. Other allowed costs added include housing planning, technical assistance in applying for housing assistance, costs of matching homeless people with housing, one-time rent payments to prevent eviction, and security deposits.

31. The amendments also added two new subtitles to Title VII. The first, Family Support Centers, creates a grant program within HHS to distribute funds to state or local entities or private nonprofits to provide intensive and comprehensive support services to very low income individuals and families living in government subsidized housing, with priority to those who were previously homeless or who are at imminent risk of homelessness. It also provides for demonstration grants by HHS to local educational authorities to provide services to economically disadvantaged residents of public housing. The second new subtitle, "Preventive Services Regarding Children of Homeless Families or Families at Risk of Homelessness," creates a demonstration grant program within HHS to prevent the separation of children from their families because of homelessness. Funds are distributed to state and local child welfare authorities; there is a 25% matching requirement.

32. The amendments changed the Shelter Plus Care program, creating separate provisions for tenant-based rental assistance, project-based rental assistance, and sponsor-based rental assistance, and moderate rehabilitation assistance for single-room-occupancy units.

33. This provision applies to properties with mortgages guaranteed by the federal government through the Farmers Home Administration.

34. Base Closure Community Redevelopment and Homeless Assistance Act of 1994.

35. Guggliota, "Federal Council for Homeless Dies." In addition, the McKinney Act provisions authorizing the council contain a "sunset" clause in accordance with which the council technically ceased to exist in October 1994; language reauthorizing the council failed to pass when the housing bill they were part of died in the Senate. Nevertheless, despite these problems, the council has continued to operate with funding provided by HUD, and arguably

received a boost in stature when it was made part of the Domestic Policy Council within the White House, following its loss of funding. See Guggliota, "Resurrected Homeless Council."

36. This language is in the conference committee report accompanying legislation authorizing Department of Labor programs for Fiscal Year 1995 (the "School-to-Work" Bill), Public Law 103-239.

37. Welfare legislation passed by Congress but vetoed by the president would have repealed the Family Support Centers demonstration program (see note 31 for further explanation of the Family Support Centers demonstration program).

38. A proposal to consolidate the programs was made in 1994, but the bill was not enacted.

39. The three suits were to enforce the SAFAH program under Title IV, the Education for Homeless Children and Youth provisions under Title VII, and the surplus property program under Title V.

40. Oversight hearings reviewed programs including the surplus property program under Title V, the education of homeless children under Title VII, and the performance of the Interagency Council on the Homeless.

41. Perhaps less predictable are some of the negative effects that emergency relief has had in the absence of longer-term measures. See Foscarinis, "Beyond Homelessness."

42. National Law Center on Homelessness and Poverty, et al., *Beyond McKinney.*

43. National Law Center on Homelessness and Poverty, et al., *Beyond McKinney.* See also the campaign of the National Coalition for the Homeless, "You Don't Need a Home to Vote"; and United States Conference of Mayors, *Ending Homelessness in America's Cities.*

44. Speaker's Task Force on Homelessness, "Report."

45. Speaker's Task Force on Homelessness, "Report."

46. Interagency Council on the Homeless, *Priority Home! The Federal Plan to Break the Cycle of Homelessness.* The administration's effort to amend the McKinney Act to consolidate the HUD programs and require communities applying for the consolidated funds to ensure a "continuum of care"—that is, the coordination of emergency, transitional, and permanent housing, with any needed services—for their homeless populations, passed the House but died in the Senate when that body failed to pass major housing legislation that was before it prior to the end of the 103rd Congress.

47. Enacted in October 1986, the Homeless Eligibility Clarification Act, the first federal legislation aimed at a systemic response to homelessness, had Senator Pete Domenici (R-NM) as its primary sponsor. The McKinney Act, named in memory of its chief Republican sponsor, Stewart B. McKinney (R-CT), was passed with bipartisan support and signed into law—albeit reluctantly—by President Ronald Reagan. President George Bush made full funding of the

McKinney Act a campaign promise, which he fulfilled (see DeParle, "Bush Homeless Plan"). During his confirmation hearings, Jack Kemp, Secretary of Housing and Urban Development under President Bush, stated that homelessness was his top priority (see Ifill, "Kemp Pledges").

CHAPTER 16

1. A "formula" is a set standard for allocating funds to eligible applicants. In the case of ESG, HUD determines the formula.

2. U.S. Department of Housing and Urban Development, *Evaluation of the Emergency Shelter Grants Program*, Executive Summary.

3. U.S. General Accounting Office, *Homelessness: McKinney Act Programs and Funding through Fiscal Year 1993*, 26.

4. U.S. Department of Housing and Urban Development, *Evaluation of the Emergency Shelter Grants Program*, Executive Summary.

5. U.S. Department of Housing and Urban Development, *Consolidated Submission for Community Planning and Development Programs, Proposed Rule*, 40148.

6. U.S. Department of Housing and Urban Development, *Evaluation of the Emergency Shelter Grants Program*, Executive Summary.

7. *Council of State Community Development Agencies, survey to members, June 1994.*

8. U.S. Senate, Committee on Banking, Housing and Urban Affairs, *The Housing Choice and Community Investment Act of 1994*, 5.

9. Ibid., 6.

CHAPTER 17

1. On exclusion from services, see Lamb (*The Homeless Mentally Ill*); and Lamb, et al., (*Treating the Homeless Mentally Ill*).

2. For the earlier literature which helped set the agenda for the NIMH/NIAAA studies, see Baumohl and Miller (*Down and Out in Berkeley*); Segal, Baumohl, and Johnson ("Falling through the Cracks"); Reich and Siegel ("The Emergence of the Bowery"); Segal and Baumohl ("Engaging the Disengaged" and "The New Chronic Patient"); Baxter and Hopper (*Private Lives/Public Spaces*); Estroff (*Making It Crazy*); Lipton, Sabatini, and Katz ("Down and Out in the City"); and Bassuk, Rubin, and Lauriat ("Is Homelessness a Mental Health Problem?"). For an overview and synthesis of the 10 NIMH studies, see Tessler and Dennis ("Mental Illness among Homeless Adults"); Morrissey and Levine ("Researchers Discuss Latest Findings"); National Institute of Mental Health (*Two Generations of NIMH-Funded Research*); and Levine and

Rog ("Mental Health Services for Homeless Mentally Ill Persons").

3. For more detailed information concerning the interim findings of the third-round McKinney Demonstration Projects, see Center for Mental Health Services, *Making a Difference*.

4. For a complete review of the NIAAA demonstration project findings, see National Institute on Alcohol Abuse and Alcoholism, *Community Demonstration Grant Projects*.

5. For a review of effective treatment interventions for homeless persons with substance use disorders, see Willenbring, et al., "Community Treatment."

6. Findings concerning appropriate services and treatment outcomes for homeless persons with co-occurring mental health and substance use disorders can be found in Drake, et al., "The Course, Treatment, and Outcome"; and Osher, "A Vision for the Future."

7. For a complete review of longitudinal data concerning persons with co-occurring mental health and substance use disorders over the past decade, see Drake, et al., "The Course, Treatment, and Outcome."

8. Baumohl and Huebner, "Alcohol and Other Drug Problems," 852. For a discussion of integrated systems of care, see Federal Task Force on Homelessness and Severe Mental Illness, "Outcasts on Main Street."

9. For a brief description of the ACCESS Program, see Randolph, "Improving Service Systems."

10. For further discussion, see Federal Task Force on Homelessness and Severe Mental Illness, "Outcasts on Main Street"; and Center for Mental Health Services, *Lessons Learned*.

11. For an in-depth examination of the outreach and engagement process, see Interagency Council on the Homeless (*Reaching Out*); Axleroad and Toff (*Outreach Services*), and Rog (*Engaging Homeless Persons*). The five outreach programs studied by Barrow, et al. ("Evaluating Outreach Services") were developed in response to the failure of the more traditional mental health providers to reach, engage, and serve homeless individuals with serious mental illnesses. While the specifics of each program varied, they all shared certain features that departed from more traditional mental health services including: (1) they defined as their target population homeless individuals with chronic psychiatric disabilities not served by the existing mental health programs; (2) they worked in nontraditional settings (e.g., the streets, parks, transportation terminals, shelters, and food programs), using outreach and other active efforts to contact and engage clients in services; (3) they addressed a broad range of emergency and basic needs; and (4) they combined this with direct services their clients often required.

12. Baumohl and Huebner, "Alcohol and Other Drug Problems," 852.

13. Housing-related activities often consume a substantial proportion of case managers' time, for they must become familiar with housing authority approval requirements and processes; establish working relationships with housing specialists; assess clients' eligibility and readiness for housing; find appropriate housing for clients; negotiate agreements with landlords, housing specialists, and clients; move clients and help furnish apartments; and help clients adjust to new settings.

14. For further discussion of housing-related activities conducted by the case managers on behalf of their clients, see the project descriptions and interim findings for the San Diego, Baltimore, and Boston projects in Center for Mental Health Services, *Making a Difference*.

15. With appropriate case management services, most of the McKinney projects found that participants increased their use of community-based mental health treatment and other services over time. Often, this was coupled with a decrease in the use of expensive inpatient services. In Baltimore, Assertive Community Treatment (ACT) team participants used the emergency room and hospital less often then the usual care group after six months. In San Diego, the mean number of inpatient days for all participants declined from 7.2 days at the start of the study to 3.3 days after 12 months, representing significant cost saving (see Center for Mental Health Services, *Making a Difference*). For a review of the ACT model, see Bond, et al. ("Assertive Community Treatment"). For a complete review of site descriptions and findings of the NIAAA Community Demonstration Grant Projects for Alcohol and Drug Abuse Treatment of Homeless Individuals, see National Institute on Alcohol Abuse and Alcoholism (*Community Demonstration Grant Projects*).

16. For further discussion of empowerment in housing stability and the importance patients attach to private space, see Ware, et al. ("Empowerment"). The McKinney Act projects found that successful housing arrangements may require different options depending on the client. While the Boston project found that those participants residing in group homes were more likely than those in independent housing to remain housed after 18 months, the San Diego project found that two-thirds of their participants receiving Section 8 certificates were still in an apartment after one year with the support of an intensive case manager (see Center for Mental Health Services, *Making a Difference*).

17. On housing preferences among mental health consumers, see Schutt, Goldfinger, and Penk ("The Structure and Sources"); and Tanzman ("An Overview of Surveys").

18. For a thorough consideration of supported housing models for homeless people with ADM disorders, see Wittman ("Affordable Housing").

19. For discussion of the importance of informing the client about the nature of their illness and actively involving them in their treatment plan, see Susser, Goldfinger, and White ("Some Clinical Approaches"). Also see Susser, Goldfinger, and White for issues concerning empowerment

and advocacy as a method of engaging the client. For a discussion of what constitutes coercion in the outreach and engagement process, see Lopez ("The Perils of Outreach Work").

20. For examples of peers groups, consumer-run programs and the employment of consumers as providers, see Van Tosh (*Working for a Change*).

21. According to Susser, Goldfinger, and White ("Some Clinical Approaches"), it is important for clinicians to involve patients in their treatment plan and also to be responsive to patient concerns regarding medications, whether about adverse side effects or simply an unwillingness to take them. It is possible, with gentle encouragement and perhaps a period of experimentation, to see which medicine is best tolerated. Rarely does forced compliance work.

22. For a discussion of harm reduction approaches, see Strang ("Harm Reduction for Drug Users") and Heather, et al. (*Psychoactive Drugs and Harm Reduction*).

23. For discussion of the importance of meaningful daily activity, see Dixon, Friedman, and Lehman ("Housing Patterns"). On "community livingrooms," see Segal and Baumohl ("The Community Living Room").

24. For a discussion of the value of employment for persons with ADM disorders, see Warner (*Recovery from Schizophrenia*); Bachrach ("Perspective on Work and Rehabilitation"); Bond and McDonel ("Assertive Community Treatment"); and Fabian ("Work and the Quality of Life").

25. For a more detailed review of the components of culturally competent treatment, see Flaskerud ("The Effects of Culture-Compatible Intervention").

26. See Tessler and Dennis ("Mental Illness among Homeless Adults"); and Putnam, Cohen, and Sullivan ("Innovative Outreach Services").

27. The National Law Center on Homelessness and Poverty (*No Homeless People Allowed*) report provides descriptions of antihomeless ordinances in cities and towns across the nation.

CHAPTER 18

1. This chapter defines being homeless as sleeping in shelters or on the streets, and does not include staying with friends or living in doubled-up situations.

2. Clean-up costs made necessary by homeless persons' use of New York City transit centers, for example, total more than $20 million each year. See Machalaba, "Mobile Homes."

3. Many prevention programs claim cost effectiveness by simply assuming that all their clients would have become homeless for extended periods without their assistance. This assumption is rarely warranted, especially because many prevention programs "cream": they select cli-

ents—intentionally or not—who are considerably less disadvantaged than other candidates, easier to successfully assist, and, consequently, less likely to become homeless.

4. For a detailed discussion of these risk characteristics, see Lindblom, "Toward a Comprehensive Homelessness Prevention Strategy," which includes extensive citations to supportive studies and data. These risk factors can be gathered in checklist form for use in screening potential prevention clients. The first section of such a form would screen out those with greater than minimal incomes or economic resources. The second section would determine the number of additional risk factors for each of the remaining applicants. Helping those with the greatest number of risk factors would target assistance to those most at risk of lengthy or chronic homelessness.

5. On mental institutionalization prior to homelessness, see Rossi (Down and Out and Homelessness in America) and Burt and Cohen (America's Homeless); on discharge into homelessness, see, for example, Toomey, et al. ("Evaluating Community Care"); Marcos, et al. ("Psychiatry Takes to the Street"); see also Sosin, Colsen, and Grossman (Homeless in Chicago); Drake, et al. ("Housing Stability and Homelessness among Rural Schizophrenic Patients"); Drake, Wallack, and Hoffman ("Housing Instability and Homelessness among Aftercare Patients"); and Piliavin, et al. (The Duration of Homeless Careers).

6. On prior inpatient substance abuse treatment, see Rossi (Homelessness in America), and Burt and Cohen (America's Homeless); on the proportion of homeless persons in various treatment programs, see Sosin, Colsen, and Grossman (Homeless in Chicago); on homelessness and health, see Wright and Weber (Homelessness and Health).

7. On prisons and jail histories, see Rossi (Down and Out and Homelessness in America), and Burt and Cohen (America's Homeless); on prison and future homelessness, see Piliavin, et al. (The Duration of Homeless Careers).

8. On foster care histories of homeless persons, see Piliavin, et al. (The Duration of Homeless Careers); Knickman and Weitzman (A Study of Homeless Families); Wood, et al. ("Homeless and Housed Families"); Barth ("On Their Own"); and Susser, Struening, and Conover ("Childhood Experiences of Homeless Men"). For San Francisco and Sacramento findings, see Barth ("On Their Own").

9. For New York study, see Knickman and Weitzman (A Study of Homeless Families); for Chicago studies, see Rossi (Down and Out), and Sosin, Colsen, and Grossman, Homeless in Chicago).

10. For New York study, see Knickman and Weitzman (A Study of Homeless Families), and see also Weitzman, Knickman, and Shinn ("Pathways to Homelessness"); for Chicago study, see Sosin, Colsen, and Grossman (Homeless in Chicago). See also Rossi (Down and Out).

11. Knickman and Weitzman (A Study of Homeless Families); Bueno, et al. (When the Rent Comes Due); and Committee on Legal Assistance (Report on the Prevention of Homelessness).

12. Sosin, Colsen, and Grossman, Homeless in Chicago.

13. For a more detailed discussion of how notice and eviction procedures could be altered to protect against illegal or improper evictions and to give tenants adequate time to assert their rights and defenses, see Lindblom, "Toward a Comprehensive Homelessness Prevention Strategy."

14. On legal representation percentages and Berkeley data, see Hall (Homelessness and Preventing Evictions); on New York City legal assistance projects, see Committee on Legal Assistance (Report on the Prevention of Homelessness) and New York State Department of Social Services (The Homeless Prevention Program).

15. Given the projects' guidelines, which explicitly target families on public assistance who are not only threatened with eviction but also are considered at risk of entering the city's shelter system, these savings are reasonable and not substantially inflated by "creaming" (see note 3, above), especially since none of the savings from avoided public and social costs other than shelter expenses are included in the savings calculations (see note 2 and accompanying text). On the New York eviction prevention projects and their estimated savings, see Committee on Legal Assistance (Report on the Prevention of Homelessness); see also New York State Department of Social Services (The Homeless Prevention Program).

16. For New York City projects, see Committee on Legal Assistance (Report on the Prevention of Homelessness), and New York Department of Social Services (The Homeless Prevention Program); information on other legal assistance prevention programs based on interviews with Roderick T. Field (attorney, Legal Aid Foundation of Los Angeles, interviewed 21 February 1991) and Cathy Mosbrucker (staff attorney, Tenderloin Housing Clinic, Eviction Defense Office, San Francisco, interviewed 13 February 1991); shelter cost data from Office of the Inspector General, HHS (Homeless Prevention Programs), and Committee on Legal Assistance (Report on the Prevention of Homelessness).

17. On the New Jersey program, see Bureau of Housing Services (1993 Annual Report); New Jersey Statutes 52:27D 280–87; U.S. General Accounting Office (Homelessness—Too Early to Tell); and Ifill ("New Jersey Is Blunting the 'Knife Edge of Homelessness'").

18. For the eight-program evaluation, see Office of the Inspector General, HHS, Homeless Prevention Program.

19. The existing cash assistance programs could expand their scope to reach the most-at-risk households without requiring significant new funding if they converted their current cash assistance to the basically functional families into low-interest or no-interest loans.

20. On the small income differences between otherwise similar housed and homeless persons, see, for example, Sosin, Colsen, and Grossman (Homeless in Chicago). The power of small increases in income is also reflected in the fact that many solitary adults living in SROs become home-

less for some short time at the end of each month when their monthly public assistance checks run out, and then return to the SROs when their next assistance check arrives.

21. On Connecticut's eviction prevention program, see Connecticut Department of Human Resources, *(Eviction Prevention Program Guidelines)*, Bureau of Evaluation and Review *(Evaluation Report)*, State of Connecticut *(An Act Concerning Programs to Prevent Homelessness)*, and Connecticut General Statutes VI:176–804,80.

22. On homeless families and individuals coming from shared housing, see Knickman and Weitzman *(A Study of Homeless Families)*, and Sosin, Colsen, and Grossman *(Homeless in Chicago)*.

23. On Aid to Families with Dependent Adults, see, for example, Rossi *(Without Shelter)*, and Wright *(Address Unknown)*.

24. Sosin, Colsen, and Grossman, *Homeless in Chicago*.

25. Sosin, Colsen, and Grossman, *Homeless in Chicago*.

26. EIDP data from Tanya Tull, president and chief executive officer of Beyond Shelter, Los Angeles, interviewed 20 February 1991. See also "Application for Federal Assistance," Beyond Shelter.

27. For further examples of the many different kinds of community-based prevention programs, see HomeBase *(Preventing Homelessness—Bay Area Programs)*; and Schwartz, et al. *(Preventing Homelessness: A Study of State and Local Homelessness Prevention Programs)*. Note, however, that some of the programs described therein should not be considered true prevention efforts without improved client targeting.

28. On the HAP program, see Statistical Services Bureau, *AFDC Survey*.

29. On the problems with foster care, see, for example, Wexler ("Beware of Pitfalls of Foster Care"); Barth ("On Their Own"); and Barden ("When Foster Care Ends").

30. Family preservation is fraught with controversy. For a good overview of the research, see Schuerman, Rzepniki, and Littell *(Putting Families First)*. For useful debate, see Bath and Haapala ("Family Preservation Services" and "Evaluation Outcomes"), and Littell ("Evidence or Assertions?").

31. These kinds of approaches are discussed in more detail in Lindblom, "Toward a Comprehensive Homelessness Prevention Strategy."

CHAPTER 19

1. "Local" here means at most covering a metropolitan region, though some groups are loosely affiliated with regional or national organizations.

2. Rosenthal, *Homeless in Paradise*; Kessler, "After Charity"; Wagner and Cohen, "The Power of the People"; Wagner,

Checkerboard Square; and Yeich, *The Politics of Ending Homelessness*.

3. Suddenly imposed deprivations: McAdam, "Micromobilization Contexts." Police sweeps: Ropers, *The Invisible Homeless*; Ruddick, "Heterotopias"; and Rosenthal, *Homeless in Paradise*. The closing of shelters: Wagner and Cohen, "The Power of the People," 546.

4. Ruddick, "Heterotopias"; Wagner, *Checkerboard Square*; and Wright, "Homeless Collective Empowerment."

5. See McAdam, "Micromobilization Contexts," 136; Olson, *The Logic of Collective Action*, 21. Not all of the functions of preexisting networks described by Tierney, "The Battered Women Movement," and McAdam, "Micromobilization Contexts," translate that well into homeless organizations. Tierney emphasizes *already politicized* networks based on past organizational work, shared frames of reference, and experienced leaders who may transfer to the new movement in blocs. McAdam cites Oberschall's description of "bloc recruitment" (Oberschall, *Social Conflict*, 125, cited in McAdam, "Micromobilization Contexts," 142) of entire political groupings from one movement to the other, but given homeless people's unlikelihood of already existing in political organizations, this does not occur among them. It *does*, however occur among housed advocates, one example being the Community for Creative Non-Violence's collective conversion to a focus on poverty and homelessness.

6. In Santa Barbara, there was an important exception to this relationship. What I have called "Latino Families" had by far the strongest preexisting social networks, yet they did not, by and large, take part in political struggles around homelessness. I attribute this primarily to the undocumented status of many, which made political involvement extremely hazardous. Other factors may be their greater loyalty to Chicano/Mexicano struggles, and their ongoing greater contact with housed than homeless people. For more on this subgroup (as well as others mentioned in this paper), see Rosenthal, *Homeless in Paradise*.

7. While a literature has appeared in recent years calling into question the "isolated loner" image of homeless people common in disaffiliation models (Rosenthal, "Homelessness and Isolation"; La Gory, et al., "Homelessness and Affiliation"; Snow and Anderson, *Down on Their Luck*; and Cohen and Sokolovsky, *Old Men of the Bowery*), most researchers in the newer tradition would still agree that networks and individual relationships tend to be fragile and contingent, given the uncertainties of homeless life. Yet they apparently are strong enough in some cases to sustain homeless organizations.

8. Hoch and Slayton, *New Homeless and Old*, 211.

9. This role is sometimes minimized in accounts of local movements due to romanticization regarding activists' roles, political correctness, or modesty (since the authors of the accounts are often among the housed advocates). Note, too, that the line between activist and advocate is not always clear: was the late Mitch Snyder (of the Com-

munity for Creative Non-Violence), who chose homelessness, a homeless activist or a housed advocate?

10. Cress, "Look Out World," 16.

11. Wright, "Homeless Collective Empowerment," 23–24.

12. Wright, "Tranquility City," 26–27. Note that Wright's account contains no such complaints by squatters against housed people who simply supplied resources but did not attempt to speak for them or decide policy: "for many of the squatters these outside supporters, bringing food, clothing, blankets, pots, pans and conversation, were not simply attempting to do good, but in the squatters' eyes, 'they became a part of us'" (Wright, "Homeless Collective Empowerment," 24).

13. On the ties of activists to the conventional political system, Wagner, Checkerboard Square; and Ruddick, "Heterotopias," 188. On the frustration of activists, Hopper and Baumohl, "Held in Abeyance."

14. Wright, "Homeless Collective Empowerment"; Yeich, The Politics of Ending Homelessness; and Hopper and Baumohl, "Held in Abeyance," 544.

15. Hoch and Slayton, New Homeless and Old, 216.

16. Yeich, The Politics of Ending Homelessness.

17. Rosenthal, Homeless in Paradise, Chapter 5.

18. Fanon, Wretched of the Earth.

19. Wright, "Tranquility City," 1. Hopper and Baumohl argue that victories that result in "privileging access to a scarce good in this way raises vexing questions of equity" ("Held in Abeyance," 527). I have seen only a few reports of this privileging leading to friction with other poor people (e.g., Tierney, "Using Housing Projects"), but it could certainly become an impediment to the kinds of coalitions I call for in the last part of this chapter.

20. Hopper, "Girding for the Long Haul," 2, cited in Hombs, "Reversals of Fortune," 114.

21. Rosenthal, Homeless in Paradise.

22. Hombs, "Reversals of Fortune," 117.

23. See Mair, "The Homeless and the Post-industrial City"; Deutsche, "Architecture of the Evicted"; and Hopper and Baumohl, "Held in Abeyance." The most important of these is usually said to be closing the income/rent (or mortgage) gap by preserving, rehabilitating, and creating massive amounts of affordable housing, including housing with special services for those with physical or mental illnesses or substance abuse problems. Many local antihomelessness movements have also emphasized broadening and raising the safety net of entitlements; Hopper and Baumohl, "Held in Abeyance," have recently suggested placing the emphasis on employment.

24. Hopper and Baumohl, "Held in Abeyance."

25. Wagner, Checkerboard Square.

26. Cohen and Wagner, "Acting on Their Own Behalf."

27. Wagner and Cohen, "The Power of the People"; and Rosenthal, Homeless in Paradise.

28. Wagner and Cohen, "The Power of the People"; Rosenthal, Homeless in Paradise; Cress, "Look Out World"; and Wright, "Tranquility City" and "Homeless Collective Empowerment."

29. See Wright, "Tranquility City"; Wagner and Cohen, "The Power of the People"; and Cohen and Wagner, "Acting on Their Own Behalf." Some researchers have suggested strong ties among homeless people may actually prolong homelessness (Snow and Anderson, Down on Their Luck). Wagner and Cohen, however, found that activists retained a homeless allegiance while escaping literal homelessness (Wagner and Cohen, "The Power of the People," 556).

30. Wagner and Cohen, "The Power of the People"; and Wright, "Tranquility City."

31. For example, 85% of the Portland (Maine) Tent City "veterans" could name 3 close friends, and more than 80% were in a long-term relationship of some kind (Cohen and Wagner, "Acting on Their Own Behalf," 26–28). Further, "more than 80 percent of located subjects maintained close social relationships with their comrades from tent city after three years" (Wagner and Cohen, "The Power of the People," 547–48); many were still involved in political work several years later (Cohen and Wagner, "Acting on Their Own Behalf," 32).

32. Rosenthal, Homeless in Paradise and "Skidding/Coping/Escaping."

33. Wright, "Tranquility City"; and Rosenthal, Homeless in Paradise.

34. Wright, "Tranquility City"; and Rosenthal, Homeless in Paradise.

35. Wright, "Tranquility City," 3.

36. Wagner, Checkerboard Square, 19.

37. Wagner and Cohen, "The Power of the People," 557.

38. Cress, "Look Out World."

39. Rosenthal, "Good Cop/Bad Cop" and Homeless in Paradise.

40. Hoch and Slayton, New Homeless and Old, 216.

41. These metropolitan-wide trends are themselves reactions to still larger forces of national and international developments, although some room for maneuvering exists within local parameters. For a review of the literature debating the extent of structure and agency within localities, see Flanagan, Contemporary Urban Sociology.

42. This may also explain why shelters and advocacy groups are so often the types of organizations most criticized by homeless people (e.g., Wright, "Homeless Collective Empowerment," 12): they are accessible.

43. On conscious strategy: Wright, "Homeless Collective Empowerment," 31. On routine consequence: O'Connor, The Fiscal Crisis of the State; and Ruddick,

"Heterotopias," 195. On diversion to local government: Piven and Cloward, *Regulating the Poor*.

44. Rosenthal, *Homeless in Paradise*, 96.

45. Wagner, *Checkerboard Square*; and Wright, "Tranquility City" and "Homeless Collective Empowerment."

46. Wright, "Homeless Collective Empowerment," 34.

47. Blasi, "Litigation"; Hombs, "Reversals of Fortune"; and Barak, *Gimme Shelter*.

48. See Blasi, "Litigation"; and Barnes, Baumohl, and Hopper, "The New Paternalism." There are certainly exceptions to this. In Santa Barbara, for instance, at some points the Homeless Coalition had a committee that discussed legal strategies in the context of general strategies, but there was no guarantee that the local legal aid firms involved would abide by Coalition decisions.

49. Rosenthal, "Homeless People's Project" and *Homeless in Paradise*.

50. Hombs, "Reversals of Fortune," 111.

51. Wright, "Homeless Collective Empowerment," 30. This strategy may be created by homeless people themselves, or by advocates (Hombs, "Reversals of Fortune," 111), or worked out jointly. What is important is that it requires the activity of homeless people.

52. Hopper, "Girding for the Long Haul," quoted in Hombs, "Reversals of Fortune," 112.

53. Rader, *Signal Through the Flames*.

54. Ruddick, "Heterotopias," 196; Wright, "Homeless Collective Empowerment," 21; and Wagner and Cohen, "The Power of the People," 551.

55. Piven and Cloward, *Poor People's Movements*.

56. Rosenthal, *Homeless in Paradise*, Chapter 5.

57. Wagner and Cohen, "The Power of the People."

58. Where disruption is *combined* with perceived vulnerability, it is particularly powerful. Hoch and Slayton note, for example, that "arresting poor people because they have illegally occupied vacant public housing units in order to escape the cold undermines the legitimacy of local government caretaking efforts while mobilizing public support for the homeless" (Hoch and Slayton, *New Homeless and Old*, 215). But this combination is rare in practice: those most likely to be seen as vulnerable, such as women with children, are the least likely to engage in disruptive activities.

59. Rosenthal, "Good Cop/Bad Cop" and *Homeless in Paradise*; Cress, "Look Out World"; Wagner and Cohen, "The Power of the People"; and Wright, "Tranquility City" and "Homeless Collective Empowerment."

60. Hopper and Baumohl, "Held in Abeyance," 536.

61. Hombs, "Reversals of Fortune," 113.

62. Hoch and Slayton, *New Homeless and Old*.

63. Hopper, "Advocacy for the Homeless," 168.

64. Ruddick, "Heterotopias"; Wagner, *Checkerboard Square*; Snow and Anderson, *Down on Their Luck*; and Rosenthal, *Homeless in Paradise* and "Homelessness and Isolation."

65. Hopper and Baumohl ("Held in Abeyance," 541) further note that the representation of homeless people as "just like you and me" "may have served to sanction the old division of the urban poor into deserving and undeserving, but this time along implicitly racial lines."

66. Hopper and Baumohl, "Held in Abeyance," 528.

67. Hoch and Slayton, *New Homeless and Old*.

68. Hoch and Slayton, *New Homeless and Old*, 215; and Hopper and Baumohl, "Held in Abeyance."

69. Gamson, *The Strategy of Social Protest*.

70. Rosenthal, *Homeless in Paradise* and "Good Cop/Bad Cop."

71. Cress, "Look Out World," 10; for discussions of *why* this occurs, unfortunately too detailed for present purposes, see Rosenthal, "Good Cop/Bad Cop," and *Homeless in Paradise*, Chapter 5. There may be a limit to how productive this dynamic is. Martin Luther King, Jr., argued that even if violence resulted in immediate gains for African Americans, the long term bitterness engendered would result in a counterproductive backlash ("The Power of Nonviolent Action"). Wright has argued that activists' greater militancy has led public attitudes to "harden" ("Homeless Collective Empowerment," 7), but there is little firm evidence that it is the militancy of activists, rather than despair at the intractability of the problem, that has led to a loss of public support for homeless groups—if in fact there has been such a decline in support (see Chapter 13).

72. Cress, "Look Out World," 6.

73. Cress, "Look Out World," 20–22; services: Wagner and Cohen, "The Power of the People," 553.

74. For examples: Cress, "Look Out World," 19; and Barak, *Gimme Shelter*, Chapter 7.

75. While New York has an extensive advocacy community, perhaps the strongest in the nation, it has never had a coherent movement of homeless activists.

76. For comparative examples, see Cress, "Look Out World."

77. Wagner and Cohen, "The Power of the People."

78. Wright, "Homeless Collective Empowerment," 13.

79. Rosenthal, *Homeless in Paradise*.

80. Wagner, *Checkerboard Square*.

81. Hopper, "Advocacy for the Homeless"; Hoch and Slayton, *New Homeless and Old*; and Hopper and Baumohl, "Held in Abeyance."

82. Hombs, "Reversals of Fortune"; and Hopper and Baumohl, "Held in Abeyance."

83. Piven and Cloward, *Regulating the Poor*.

REFERENCES

• • • • • • •

Adkins, R. *Medical Care for Veterans.* Washington, DC: Government Printing Office, 1968.

Advisory Council on Unemployment Compensation. *Unemployment Insurance in the United States: Benefits, Financing, Coverage: A Report to the President and Congress.* Washington, DC: Advisory Council on Unemployment Compensation, February 1995.

Akard, Patrick J. "Corporate Mobilization and United States Economic Policy in the 1970s." *American Sociological Review* 57, 5 (1992).

Alperstein, Garth; and Ellis Arnstein. "Homeless Children: A Challenge for Pediatricians." *Pediatric Clinics of North America* 35 (1988): 1413–25.

Alperstein, Garth; Claire Rappaport; and Joan M. Flanigan. "Health Problems of Homeless Children in New York City." *American Journal of Public Health* 78 (1988): 1232–33.

Alvater, Elmar. *The Future of the Market.* London and New York: Verso, 1993.

American Psychiatric Association. *Diagnostic and Statistical Manual of Mental Disorders.* 3rd ed. Washington, DC: American Psychiatric Association, 1980.

Anderson, Elijah. *A Place on the Corner.* Chicago: University of Chicago Press, 1978.

———. "Sex Codes and Family Life among Poor Inner-City Youths." *Annals of the American Academy of Political and Social Science* 501 (1989): 59–78.

———. *Streetwise.* Chicago: University of Chicago Press, 1990.

Anderson, Nels. *The Hobo.* 2nd ed. Chicago: University of Chicago Press, 1961 (originally published in 1923).

———. *The Homeless in New York City.* New York: Welfare Council, 1934.

———. *Men on the Move.* Chicago: University of Chicago Press, 1940.

Andrade, Sally J. *Living in the Grey Zone: Health Care Needs of Homeless Persons.* Austin, TX: Benedictine Health Resource Center, 1988.

Angel, Ronald; and Marta Tienda. "Determinants of Extended Household Structure: Cultural Pattern or Economic Need?" *American Journal of Sociology* 87 (1982): 1360–83.

Apgar, William C., Jr.; Denise DiPasquale; Nancy McArdle; and Jennifer Olson. *The State of the Nation's Housing.* Cambridge, MA: Joint Center for Housing Studies of Harvard University, 1989.

"Application for Federal Assistance." Los Angeles: Beyond Shelter, May 1, 1990.

Armstrong, Philip; Andrew Glyn; and John Harrison. *Capitalism Since 1945.* Oxford, England, and Cambridge, MA: Blackwell, 1991.

Atlanta Task Force for the Homeless. *The Criminalization of Poverty: City Ordinances Unfairly Target Homeless People for Arrest.* Atlanta: Atlanta Task Force for the Homeless: September 1993.

Auletta, Ken. *The Underclass.* New York: Random House, 1982.

Axleroad, S. E.; and G. E. Toff. *Outreach Services for Homeless Mentally Ill People*. Washington, DC: George Washington University, 1987.

Bachrach, Leona. "Perspective on Work and Rehabilitation." *Hospital and Community Psychiatry* 42, 9 (1991): 890–91.

Bahr, Howard M., ed. *Disaffiliated Man: Essays and Bibliography on Skid Row Vagrancy, and Outsiders*. Toronto: University of Toronto Press, 1970.

Bahr, Howard M. "Homelessness, Disaffiliation, and Retreatism." In *Disaffiliated Man*, edited by Howard M. Bahr, 39–50. Toronto: University of Toronto Press, 1970.

———. "Introduction." In *Homelessness in the United States*, edited by J. Momeni, xvii–xxv. New York: Greenwood Press, 1989.

———. *Skid Row: An Introduction to Disaffiliation*. New York: Oxford University Press, 1973.

Bahr, Howard M.; and Theodore T. Caplow. *Old Men Drunk and Sober*. New York: New York University Press, 1973.

Bane, Mary Jo. "Household Composition and Poverty." In *Fighting Poverty: What Works and What Doesn't*, edited by S. H. Danziger and D. H. Weinberg, 209–231. Cambridge: Harvard University Press, 1986.

Barak, Gregg. *Gimme Shelter*. New York: Praeger, 1991.

Barden, J. C. "When Foster Care Ends, Home Is Often the Street." *The New York Times* January 6, 1991: 1.

Barnes, Ed; Jim Baumohl; and Kim Hopper. "The New Paternalism in American Public Welfare: General Assistance Reform in Alameda County, California." Paper presented at the Conference on Justice and Human Rights Advocacy, Montreal, Quebec, March 2–3, 1992.

Barrett, D. F.; I. Anolik; and F. H. Abramson. "The 1990 Census Shelter and Street Night Enumeration." Paper presented at the annual meeting of the American Statistical Association, Boston, August 1992.

Barrow, S. M.; F. Hellman; A. M. Lovell; J. D. Plapinger; and E. L. Struening. "Evaluating Outreach Services: Lessons from a Study of Five Programs." In *Psychiatric Outreach to the Mentally Ill*, edited by N. Cohen, 29–45. *New Directions for Mental Health Services* 52 (1991).

Barth, Richard P. "On Their Own: The Experiences of Youth after Foster Care." *Childhood and Adolescent Social Work Journal* 7, 5 (October 1990): 419–40.

Bartlett, Susan; Nancy R. Burstein; and Elsie C. Pan. *Evaluation of Expedited Service in the Food Stamp Program, Volume I*, United States Department of Agriculture, Food and Consumer Service. Cambridge: Abt Associates, Inc., June 1995.

Bassuk, Ellen L. "Women and Children without Shelter: The Characteristics of Homeless Families." In *Homelessness: A National Perspective*, edited by Marjorie J. Robertson and Milton Greenblatt, 257–64. New York: Plenum Press, 1992.

Bassuk, Ellen L.; and Lynn Rosenberg. "Psychosocial Characteristics of Homeless Children and Children with Homes." *Pediatrics* 85 (1990): 257–61.

———. "Why Does Family Homelessness Occur? A Case-Control Study." *American Journal of Public Health* 78 (1988): 783–88.

Bassuk, Ellen L.; Lenore Rubin; and Alison S. Lauriat. "Characteristics of Sheltered Homeless Families." *American Journal of Public Health* 76 (1986): 1097–1101.

———. "Is Homelessness a Mental Health Problem?" *American Journal of Public Health* 141 (1984): 1546–55.

Bath, Howard I.; and David A. Haapala. "Evaluation Outcomes of Family Preservation and the Way Ahead: A Reply to Littell." *Social Service Review* 69 (1995): 351–58.

———. "Family Preservation Services: What Does the Outcome Research *Really* Tell Us?" *Social Service Review* 68 (1994): 386–404.

Baum, Alice S.; and Donald W. Burnes. *A Nation in Denial: The Truth about Homelessness*. Boulder, CO: Westview Press, 1993.

Baumann, Donald J.; Cheryl Beauvais; Charles Grigsby; and F. D. Schultz. *The Austin Homeless: Final Report Provided to the Hogg Foundation for Mental Health*. Austin, Texas: Hogg Foundation for Mental Health, 1985.

Baumohl, Jim. "A Dissent from the Manichees." *Contemporary Drug Problems* 20 (1993): 329–53.

———. "Inebriate Institutions in North America, 1840–1920." In *Drink in Canada*, edited by Cheryl Krasnick Warsh, 92–114 and 218–31 (notes). Montreal: McGill-Queens University Press, 1993.

Baumohl, Jim; and Robert B. Huebner. "Alcohol and Other Drug Problems among the Homeless: Research, Practice, and Future Directions." *Housing Policy Debate* 2, 3 (1991): 837–66.

Baumohl, Jim; and Henry Miller. *Down and Out in Berkeley*. Report prepared for City of Berkeley-University of California Community Affairs Committee, May 1974.

Baumohl, Jim; and Sarah Tracy. "Building Systems to Manage Inebriates: The Divergent Paths of California and Massachusetts, 1891–1920." *Contemporary Drug Problems* 21 (1994): 557–97.

Baxter, Ellen; and Kim Hopper. *Private Lives/Public Spaces: Homeless Adults on the Streets of New York City*. New York: Community Service Society, 1981.

Bean, Frank D.; and Marta Tienda. *The Hispanic Population of the United States*. New York: Russell Sage Foundation, 1987.

Bigart, H. "Grim Problems of the Bowery Complicate Clean-Up Drive." *New York Times* November 20, 1961: 1 and 36.

Billingsley, Andrew. *Climbing Jacob's Ladder*. New York: Simon and Schuster, 1992.

Blake, D. D.; T. M. Keane; P. R. Wine; and C. Mora. "Prevalence of PTSD Symptoms among Combat Veterans Seeking Medical Treatment." *Journal of Traumatic Stress* 3 (1990): 15–27.

Blank, Rebecca. "The Employment Strategy: Public Policies to Increase Work and Earnings." In *Confronting Poverty: Prescriptions for Change*, edited by Sheldon Danziger, Gary Sandefur, and Daniel Weinburg. Cambridge, MA: Harvard University Press, 1994.

Blasi, Gary L. "Litigation on Behalf of the Homeless: Systematic Approaches." *Journal of Urban and Contemporary Law* 31 (1987): 137–42.

Blazer, Dan G. "Impact of Late-Life Depression on the Social Network." *American Journal of Psychiatry* 140 (1983): 162–65.

Block, Fred. *The Origins of International Economic Disorder.* Berkeley: University of California Press, 1977.

———. *Postindustrial Possibilities.* Berkeley: University of California Press, 1990.

Blumberg, Leonard U.; Thomas F. Shipley, Jr.; and Stephen F. Barsky. *Liquor and Poverty: Skid Row as a Human Condition.* New Brunswick, NJ: Rutgers Center of Alcohol Studies, 1978.

Bogard, Cynthia J.; J. Jeff McConnell; Naomi Gerstel; and Michael Schwartz. "Surplus Mothers: Assessing Family Shelters as Gendered Abeyance Structures." Paper delivered at the annual meeting of the Eastern Sociological Association, Philadelphia, March 1995.

Bogue, Donald J. *Skid Row in American Cities.* Chicago: University of Chicago Press, 1963.

Bond, G. R.; and E. C. McDonel. "Vocational Rehabilitation Outcomes for Persons with Psychiatric Disabilities: An Update." *Journal of Vocational Rehabilitation* 1, 3 (1991): 9–20.

Bond, G. R.; T. F. Witheridge; J. Dincin; and D. Wasmer. "Assertive Community Treatment: Correcting Some Misconceptions." *American Journal of Community Psychology* 19, 1 (1991): 41–51.

Bonner, Arthur. *Jerry McAuley and His Mission*, rev. ed. Neptune, NJ: Loizeaux Brothers, 1990.

Booth, Mary L. *History of the City of New York.* New York: W.R.C. Clark and Meeker, 1859.

Borchert, James. *Alley Life in Washington.* Chicago: University of Illinois Press, 1980.

Bourdieu, Pierre; and Loïc J. D. Wacquant. *An Invitation to Reflexive Sociology.* Chicago: University of Chicago Press, 1992.

Bourgois, Philippe. *In Search of Respect: Selling Crack in El Barrio.* New York: Cambridge University Press, 1995.

Bowles, Samuel; David Gordon; and Thomas Weisskopf. *After the Waste Land.* Armonk, New York: M. E. Sharpe, 1990.

Boyer, Paul. *Urban Masses and Moral Order in America, 1820–1920.* Cambridge, MA: Harvard University Press, 1978.

Bray, R. M.; M. E. Marsden; L. L. Guess; S. C. Wheeless; D. K. Pate; G. H. Dunteman; and V. G. Iannacchione. *1985 Worldwide Survey of Alcohol and Nonmedical Drug Use among Military Personnel.* Research Triangle Park, NC: Research Triangle Institute, 1986.

Brown, Carl E.; S. MacFarlane; R. Paredes; and L. Stark. *The Homeless of Phoenix: Who Are They and What Should Be Done?* Phoenix: Phoenix South Community Mental Health Center, 1983.

Brown, Carl; Ron Paredes; and Louisa Stark. *The Homeless of Phoenix: A Profile.* Phoenix: Phoenix Consortium for the Homeless, September 1982.

Browne, Angela. "Family Violence and Homelessness: Avenues for Research." Paper presented at National Institute of Mental Health and National Institute of Alcohol Abuse and Alcoholism sponsored conference, Cambridge, MA, February 1991.

Buckner, J. C.; E. L. Bassuk; and B. T. Zima. "Mental Health Issues Affecting Homeless Women: Implications for Intervention." *American Journal of Orthopsychiatry,* 63 (1993): 385–99.

Bueno, Irene; Maureen Brown Parton; Steven Ramirez; and Dan Viederman. *When the Rent Comes Due: Breaking the Link between Homelessness and Eviction—An Eviction Prevention Action Plan.* San Francisco: HomeBase Regional Support Center for Homelessness Policy and Programs, March 1989.

Bureau of Housing Services, Division of Housing and Community Resources, Department of Community Affairs, State of New Jersey. *1993 Annual Report of the Homeless Prevention Program.* Trenton: Dept. of Community Affairs, State of New Jersey, 1994.

Burke, Vee. *Cash and Noncash Benefits for Persons with Limited Income: Eligibility Rules, Recipient and Expenditure Data, FY 1992–94.* No. 96-159 EPW. Washington, DC: Congressional Research Service, Library of Congress, December 19, 1995.

Burns, Michael. "Fearing the Mirror: Responding to Beggars in a 'Kinder and Gentler' America." *Hastings Constitutional Law Quarterly* 19 (1992): 783–844.

Burt, Martha R. *Alternative Methods to Estimate the Number of Homeless Children and Youth.* Report to Congress from the Department of Education, July 1991. Washington, DC: The Urban Institute, 1991.

———. "Comment." *Housing Policy Debate* 5 (1994): 141–52.

———. "Findings and Implications from RECD's Rural Homelessness Conferences." Report to Congress. Washington, DC: U.S. Department of Agriculture, Rural Economic and Community Development Administration, December 1995.

———. *Over the Edge: The Growth of Homelessness in the 1980s.* New York: Russell Sage Foundation, 1992.

———. *Practical Methods for Counting Homeless People: A Manual for State and Local Jurisdictions.* Washington, DC:

Interagency Council on the Homeless and Department of Housing and Urban Development, 1991.

———. "Thoughts on Solving the Problem of Homelessness." Paper presented at Russell Sage Foundation meeting on Policy Approaches to Homelessness, January 31, 1994.

———. "What to Look for in Studies That Try to Count the Homeless." In *Enumerating Homeless Persons: Methods and Data Needs—Conference Proceedings,* edited by Cynthia M. Taeuber. Washington, DC: Bureau of the Census, 1991.

Burt, Martha R.; and Barbara E. Cohen. *America's Homeless: Numbers, Characteristics, and Programs that Serve Them.* Urban Institute Report 89-3. Washington, DC: Urban Institute Press, 1989.

———. "Differences among Homeless Single Women, Women with Children, and Single Men." *Social Problems* 36, 5 (December 1989): 508–24.

———. *Feeding the Homeless: Does the Prepared Meals Provision Help?* Volumes 1 and 2. Washington, DC: The Urban Institute, 1988.

Burtless, Gary, ed. *A Future of Lousy Jobs?* Washington, DC: Brookings Institution, 1990.

Burton, L. M. "Teenage Childbearing as an Alternative Life-Course Strategy in Multigeneration Black Families." *Human Nature* 1 (1990): 123–43.

Byofsky, Stuart. "No Heart for the Homeless." *Newsweek* December 1, 1986: 12.

Cahalan, Donald; Ira A. Cisin; G. L. Gardner; and G. C. Smith. *Drinking Practices and Problems in the U.S. Army.* Final Report of a Study Conducted for the Deputy Chief of Staff, Personnel Headquarters, Department of the Army. Contract No. DAHC15-72-CO346/72Jun30. 1972.

Campbell, Karen E.; Peter V. Marsden; and Jeanne S. Hurlburt. "Social Resources and Socioeconomic Status." *Social Networks* 8 (1986): 97–117.

Caplow, Theodore. "The Sociologist and the Homeless Man." In *Disaffiliated Man,* edited by Howard M. Bahr, 3–12. Toronto: University of Toronto Press, 1970.

———. "Transiency as a Cultural Pattern." *American Sociological Review* 5 (1940): 731–39.

Carnoy, M. *Faded Dreams.* New York: Cambridge University Press, 1994.

Caton, Carol L. M.; Patrick E. Shrout; Paula F. Eagle; Lewis A. Opler; Alen Felix; and Boanerges Dominguez. "Risk Factors for Homelessness among Schizophrenic Men: A Case-Control Study." *American Journal of Public Health* 84 (1994): 256–70.

Center on Budget and Policy Priorities. "7.7 Million Households—Including 3.9 Million Families with Children—Would Be Worse Off Due to Conference EITC Cuts, Even after the Benefits from the New Child Tax Credit Are Considered." Washington, DC: Center on Budget and Policy Priorities, 1995.

Center for Defense Information. *CDI Military Almanac.* Washington, DC: Center for Defense Information, 1995.

Center for Mental Health Services. *Lessons Learned: A Final Look at the First-Round McKinney Service Demonstration Projects for Homeless Adults with Severe Mental Illness.* Rockville, MD: Center for Mental Health Services, 1994.

———. *Making a Difference: Interim Status Report of the McKinney Research Demonstration Program for Homeless Mentally Ill Adults.* Rockville, MD: Center for Mental Health Services, 1994.

Center on Budget and Policy Priorities. *The Conference Agreement on the Welfare Bill.* Washington, DC: Center on Budget and Policy Priorities, January 16, 1996.

Center on Budget and Policy Priorities and National Conference of State Legislatures. *National General Assistance Survey, 1992.* Washington, DC: CBPP and NCSL, December 1992.

Chavez, Leo R. *Shadowed Lives: Undocumented Immigrants in American Society.* Fort Worth: Harcourt Brace Jovanovich College Publishers, 1992.

Chavkin, Wendy; Alan Kristal; Cheryl Seabron; and Pamela E. Guigli. "Reproductive Experience of Women Living in Hotels for the Homeless in New York City." *New York State Journal of Medicine* 87 (1987): 10–13.

Clark, A. L. "Health Care Needs of Homeless Women in Baltimore." Unpublished manuscript. University of Maryland, College Park, 1985.

Clines, F. X. "Study Finds Bowery Losing Derelicts." *New York Times* January 27, 1969: 21.

Cohen, Barbara E.; and Martha R. Burt. "The Homeless: Chemical Dependency and Mental Health Problems." *Social Work Research and Abstracts* 26, 1 (1990), 8–17.

Cohen, Carl I.; and Jay Sokolovsky. *Old Men of the Bowery.* New York: Guilford, 1989.

Cohen, Marcia B.; and David Wagner. "Acting on Their Own Behalf: Affiliation and Political Mobilization among Homeless People." *Journal of Sociology and Social Welfare* 19, 4 (1992): 21–40.

Coles, Robert. "The Children of Affluence." *The Atlantic Monthly,* September 1977.

Committee on Legal Assistance, Association of the Bar of the City of New York. *Report on the Prevention of Homelessness by Providing Legal Representation to Tenants Faced with Eviction Proceedings.* New York: Association of the Bar of the City of New York, November 1988.

Congressional Budget Office. *The Economic and Budget Outlook: Fiscal Years 1996–2000, Spending.* Washington, DC: U.S. Government Printing Office, January 1995.

———. *Reducing Entitlement Spending.* Washington, DC: U.S. Government Printing Office, September 1994.

Connecticut Department of Human Services, Bureau of Evaluation and Review. *Evaluation Report: Community Mediation, Inc. Eviction Prevention Program.* Hartford: Connecticut Department of Human Services, December 1990.

Cooper, R. V. L. *Military Manpower and the All-Volunteer Force.* Santa Monica, CA: Rand, 1977.

Council of Economic Advisors. *Economic Report of the President.* Washington, DC: U.S. Government Printing Office, 1995.

Cress, Dan. "Look Out World, the Meek Are Getting It Ready: Implications of Mobilization among the Homeless." Paper presented at the American Sociological Association annual meeting, Washington, DC, August 13, 1990.

Crouse, Joan M. *The Homeless Transient in the Great Depression: New York State, 1929–1941.* Albany: State University of New York Press, 1986.

Cruikshank, Barbara. "The Will to Empower: Technologies of Citizenship and the War on Poverty." *Socialist Review* 23, 4 (1994): 29–56.

Crystal, Stephen M. "Homeless Men and Homeless Women: The Gender Gap." *Urban and Social Change Review* 17 (1984): 2–6.

Crystal, Stephen M.; and Merv Goldstein. *New Arrivals: First-Time Shelter Clients.* New York: Human Resources Administration, 1982.

Crystal, Stephen M.; Merv Goldstein; and R. Levitt. *Chronic and Situational Dependency: Long-Term Residents in a Shelter for Men.* New York: Human Resources Administration, 1982.

Culhane, Dennis P.; Edmund F. Dejowski; Julie Ibanez; Elizabeth Needham; and Irene Macchia. "Public Shelter Admission Rates in Philadelphia and New York City: The Implications of Turnover for Sheltered Population Counts." *Housing Policy Debate* 5, 2 (1994): 107–40.

Currie, Elliot. *Reckoning: Drugs, the Cities, and the American Future.* New York: Hill and Wang, 1993.

D'Ercole, Ann; and Elmer Struening. "Motherhood within the Shelters for the Homeless: Some Important Implications." Paper presented at Research on Homeless Families, Implications for Public Policy, New York, NY, December 1985.

———. "Victimization among Homeless Women: Implications for Service Delivery." *Journal of Community Psychology* 18 (1990): 141–52.

Danziger, Sheldon; Gary Sandefur; and Daniel Weinburg, eds. *Confronting Poverty: Prescriptions for Change.* Cambridge, MA: Harvard University Press, 1994.

Danziger, Sheldon; and Daniel Weinberg, eds. *Fighting Poverty: What Works and What Doesn't.* Cambridge, MA.: Harvard University Press, 1986.

Davis, Laurie A.; and Marilyn A. Winkleby. "Sociodemographic and Health-Related Risk Factors among African-American, Caucasian, and Hispanic Homeless Men: A Comparative Study." *Journal of Social Distress and the Homeless* 2 (1993): 83–101.

Davis, Steven J. "Cross-Country Patterns of Change in Relative Wages." Working Paper No. 4085. Cambridge, MA: National Bureau of Economic Research, 1992.

Deavers, Kenneth; and Robert A. Hoppe. "Overview of the Rural Poor in the 1980s." In *Rural Poverty in America*, edited by C. M. Duncan, 4–20. New York: Auburn House, 1992.

Dehavenon, Anna Lou; and Margaret Boone. *Out of Sight, Out of Mind: Or How New York City and New York State Tried to Abandon the City's Homeless Families in 1993.* New York: Action Research Project on Hunger, Homelessness, and Family Health, 1993.

DeMott, Benjamin. *The Trouble with Friendship: Why Americans Can't Think Straight about Race.* New York: Grove/Atlantic, 1996.

Dennis, Michael L.; Ronaldo Iachan; Jutta S. Thornberry; and Robert M. Bray. *Prevalence of Drug Use in the Washington, DC, Metropolitan Area Homeless and Transient Population: 1991—The Washington, DC, Metropolitan Area Drug Study.* Rockville, MD: National Institute on Drug Abuse, 1993.

Denton, Nancy A.; and Douglas S. Massey. "Residential Segregation by Socioeconomic Status and Generation." *Social Science Quarterly* 69 (1988): 797–817.

DeParle, Jason. "Bush Homeless Plan: 'Godsend' or False Hopes." *New York Times* February 12, 1990: A1.

Department of Human Resources, State of Connecticut. *Eviction Prevention Program Guidelines.* January 1991.

Deutsche, Rosalyn. "Architecture of the Evicted." *Strategies* 3 (1991): 159–83.

DiBlasio, Frederick A.; and John R. Belcher. "Keeping Homeless Families Together: Examining Their Needs." *Children and Youth Services Review* 14 (1992): 427–38.

Dixon, L.; N. Friedman; and A. Lehman. "Housing Patterns of Homeless Mentally Ill Persons Receiving Assertive Treatment Services." *Hospital and Community Psychiatry* 44, 3 (1993): 286–89.

Dockett, Kathleen H. *Street Homeless People in the District of Columbia: Characteristics and Service Needs.* Washington, DC: University of the District of Columbia, 1989.

Dohrenwend, Bruce P. "Social Status and Psychological Disorder: An Issue of Substance and an Issue of Method." *American Sociological Review* 31(1966): 14–34.

Dohrenwend, Bruce P.; Itzhak Levav; Patrick E. Shrout; Sharon Schwartz; Guedalia Naveh; Bruce G. Link; Andrew E. Skodol; and Ann Stueve. "Socioeconomic Status and Psychiatric Disorders: The Causation-Selection Issue." *Science* 255 (1992): 946–52.

Dolbeare, Cushing N. *At a Snail's Pace, FY 1995: A Source Book on the Proposed 1995 Budget and How It Compares to*

Prior Years. Washington, DC: Low Income Housing Information Service, 1994.

——. *Low Income Housing Needs.* Washington, DC: Low Income Housing Information Service, 1989.

——. *The Widening Gap: Housing Needs of Low Income Families: Findings from the American Housing Survey, 1989.* Washington, DC: Low Income Housing Information Service, 1992.

——. *The Widening Gap Sourcebook: A Collection of Graphs on the Housing Needs of Low Income Families.* Washington, DC: Low Income Housing Information Service, 1992.

——. *Working Paper on Federal Housing Trust Fund Proposal.* Washington, DC: National Low Income Housing Coalition, 1994.

Dornbusch, S. "Some Political Implications in the Stanford Studies of Homeless Families." In *American Women in the Nineties: Critical Issues,* edited by S.-M. Matteo. Boston: Northeastern University Press, 1993.

Dowd, Douglas. *U.S. Capitalist Development Since 1776.* Armonk, NY: M. E. Sharpe, 1993.

Downey, Geraldine; and James C. Coyne. "Children of Depressed Parents: An Integrative Review." *Psychological Bulletin* 108 (1990): 50–76.

The Downsizing of America. New York: Times Books, 1996.

Drake, Robert E.; et al. "Housing Stability and Homelessness among Rural Schizophrenic Patients." Paper presented at the 143rd annual meeting of the American Psychiatric Association in New York. New Hampshire-Dartmouth Psychiatric Research Center, Concord, NH, May 1990.

Drake, Robert E.; K. T. Mueser; R. E. Clark; and M. A. Wallach. "The Course, Treatment, and Outcome of Substance Disorder in Persons with Severe Mental Illness." *American Journal of Orthopsychiatry* 66, 1 (1996): 42–51.

Drake, Robert E.; Michael A. Wallach; and J. Schuyler Hoffman. "Housing Instability and Homelessness among Aftercare Patients of an Urban State Hospital." *Hospital and Community Psychiatry* 40, 1 (January 1989): 46–51.

DuBoff, Richard. *Accumulation and Power: An Economic History of the United States.* Armonk, NY: M. E. Sharpe, 1989.

Duneier, Mitchell. *Slim's Table.* Chicago: University of Chicago Press, 1992.

Dwyer, Ellen. *Homes for the Mad: Life inside Two Nineteenth-Century Asylums.* New Brunswick, NJ: Rutgers University Press, 1987.

Eccles, Jacquelynne S.; and Carol Midgley. "Stage/Environment Fit: Developmentally Appropriate Classrooms for Early Adolescents." In *Research on Motivation in Education,* edited by Russell E. Ames and Carole Ames, vol. 3, 139–86. San Diego: Academic Press, 1989.

Edin, Kathryn J. "The Myths of Dependence and Self-Sufficiency: Women, Welfare and Low-Wage Work." *Focus* 17 (1995): 1–9.

Edin, Kathryn J.; and Laura Lein. *Making Ends Meet: How Single Mothers Survive Welfare and Low-Wage Work.* New York: Russell Sage, forthcoming.

Edmonds, P. "Lost Paths, New Beginnings." *USA Today* 10 November 1993: 7A.

Edsall, Mary; and Thomas Edsall. *Chain Reaction.* New York: Norton, 1992.

Eitelberg, M. J.; J. H. Laurence; B. K. Waters; and L. S. Perelman. *Screening for Service: Aptitude and Education Criteria for Military Entry.* Alexandria, VA: Office of the Assistant Secretary of Defense (Manpower, Installations and Logistics),1984.

Elliot, M. E.; and L. J. Krivo. "Structural Determinants of Homelessness in the United States." *Social Problems* 38 (1991): 113–31.

Ellison, Ralph. *Invisible Man.* New York: Random House, 1989 (originally published in 1952).

Engel, M.; and E. Sargent. "Meese's Hunger Remarks Stir More Outrage among Groups." *Washington Post* December 11, 1983: A1.

Erikson, Kai T. *Everything in Its Path.* New York: Simon and Schuster, 1976.

Estroff, Susan E. *Making It Crazy.* Berkeley: University of California Press, 1981.

Executive Office of the President of the United States. *The Budget of the United States Government: Fiscal Year 1997.* CD-ROM. Washington, DC: 1996.

Executive Office of the President of the United States, Office of Management and Budget. *The Budget of the United States Government Fiscal Year 1997, Historical Tables.* Washington, DC: Government Printing Office, 1996.

Fabian, E. S. "Work and the Quality of Life." *Psychosocial Rehabilitation Journal* 12, 4 (1989): 39–49.

Fagan, J. "Crime, Drugs and Neighborhood Change." Background memorandum prepared for the SSRC Policy Conference on Persistent Urban Poverty, November 9–10, 1993, Washington, DC.

Falk, Gene. *The Uncompensated Unemployed: An Analysis of Unemployed Workers Who Do Not Receive Unemployment Compensation.* Washington, DC: Congressional Research Service, Report. No. 90-565 EPW, November 15, 1990.

Fanon, Frantz. *Wretched of the Earth.* New York: Grove, 1963.

Federal Task Force on Homelessness and Severe Mental Illness. "Outcasts on Main Street: Report of the Federal Task Force on Homelessness and Severe Mental Illness." Washington, DC: Interagency Council on the Homeless, 1992.

Felner, Robert D.; Judith Primavera; and Ana M. Cauce. "The Impact of School Transitions: A Focus for Preventive Efforts." *American Journal of Community Psychology* 9 (1981): 449–59.

Ferguson, Thomas; and Joel Rogers. *Right Turn: The Decline of the Democrats and the Future of American Politics.* New York: Hill and Wang, 1986.

Fine, Gary Alan. *Kitchens.* Berkeley: University of California Press, 1996.

Fine, Michelle. *Framing Dropouts: Notes on the Politics of an Urban Public High School.* Albany: State University of New York Press, 1991.

First, Richard J.; John C. Rife; and Beverly G. Toomey. "Homelessness in Rural Areas: Causes, Patterns, and Trends." *Social Work* 39, 1 (1994): 97–108.

First, Richard J.; Dee Roth; and Bobbie Darden Arewa. "Homelessness: Understanding the Dimensions of the Problem for Minorities." *Social Work* 33 (1988): 120–24.

Fischer, Pamela J. "Estimating the Prevalence of Alcohol, Drug, and Mental Health Problems in the Contemporary Homeless Population." *Contemporary Drug Problems* 16 (1989): 333–89.

Fischer, Pamela J.; and W. R. Breakey. "The Epidemiology of Alcohol, Drug, and Mental Disorders among Homeless Persons." *American Psychologist* 46 (1991): 1115–28.

Fitchen, Janet M. "On the Edge of Homelessness: Rural Poverty and Housing Insecurity." *Rural Sociology* 57 (1992): 173–93.

———. *Poverty in Rural America: A Case Study.* Boulder, CO: Westview Press, 1981.

Flanagan, William G. *Contemporary Urban Sociology.* New York: Cambridge University, 1993.

Flaskerud, J. H. "The Effects of Culture-Compatible Intervention on the Utilization of Mental Health Services by Minority Clients." *Community Mental Health Journal* 22, 2 (1986): 127–41.

Forestall, M. R. "Trends in Housing: Delinquency and Health in the Central Northwest Area in Washington, D.C." Master's thesis, Catholic University, 1938. Courtesy of James Borchert.

Foscarinis, Maria. "Beyond Homelessness: Ethics, Advocacy and Strategy." *St. Louis University Public Law Review* 12, 1 (1993): 37–67.

Fox, Sarah J.; R. Joffree Barrnett; Mark Davies; and Hector R. Bird. "Psychopathology and Developmental Delay in Homeless Children: A Pilot Study." *Journal of the American Academy of Child and Adolescent Psychiatry* 29 (1990): 732–35.

France, Anatole. *The Red Lily.* London: John Lane, 1925.

Frazier, E. Franklin. *The Negro Family in Chicago.* Chicago: University of Chicago Press, 1932.

Freeman, Richard B.; and Brian Hall. "Permanent Homelessness in America?" *Population Research and Policy Review* 6 (1987): 3–27.

Frisman, Linda K.; Robert Rosenheck; and Janine DeLisa Chapdelaine. *Health Care for Homeless Veterans Programs: The Eighth Annual Report.* West Haven, CT: Northeast Program Evaluation Center, U.S. Department of Veteran Affairs, March 13, 1995.

Frisman, Linda K.; R. Rosenheck; C. L. Leda; and D. DiLella. "Make or Buy? A Comparison of Two VA Programs for Homeless Veterans." Paper presented at the 9th Annual VA Health Services Research Conference, Washington, DC, April 25, 1994.

Gallagher, Jim. "Life on the Street for Teen Hoboes." *Detroit Free Press* September 8, 1974: D1, D8–D9.

Gallup Organization. *Homeless but Not Hopeless.* Princeton, NJ: Gallup Organization, 1995.

Gamson, William A. *The Strategy of Social Protest.* Homewood, IL: Dorsey, 1975.

Gans, Herbert J. *The War against the Poor.* New York: Basic, 1995.

Garraty, John. *Unemployment in History: Economic Thought and Public Policy.* New York: Harper and Row, 1986.

Garrett, Gerald R.; and Russell K. Schutt. "Homelessness in Massachusetts: Description and Analysis." In *Homelessness in the United States: State Surveys*, vol. 1, edited by Jamshid A. Momeni, 57–72. Westport, CT: Greenwood Press, Inc., 1989.

Gates, Henry Louis. *Loose Canons: Notes on the Culture Wars.* New York: Oxford, 1992.

Geertz, Clifford. *The Interpretation of Cultures.* New York: Harper, 1973.

Glickman, Norman; and Douglas Woodward. *The New Competitors.* New York: Basic, 1989.

Glyn, Andrew. "Social Democracy and Full Employment." *New Left Review* 211 (1995): 33–55.

Golden, Stephanie. *The Women Outside.* Berkeley: University of California Press, 1992.

Goldfield, Michael. *The Decline of Organized Labor in the United States.* Chicago: University of Chicago Press, 1987.

Goldin, H. J. *Soldiers of Misfortune.* New York: Office of the Comptroller, 1982.

Goldstein, Joshua. *Long Cycles: Prosperity and War in the Modern Age.* New Haven: Yale University Press, 1988.

Goodman, Lisa A. "The Prevalence of Abuse in the Lives of Homeless and Housed Poor Mothers: A Comparison Study." *American Journal of Orthopsychiatry* 16 (1991): 489–500.

———. "The Relationship between Social Support and Family Homelessness: A Comparison Study of Homeless and Housed Mothers." *Journal of Community Psychology* 19 (1991): 321–32.

Gordon, David. "Stages of Accumulation and Long Economic Cycles." In *Process of the World System*, edited by T. Hopkins and I. Wallerstein. Beverly Hills, CA: Russell Sage, 1980.

Gorham, Leslie; and B. Harrison. *Working Below the Poverty Line*, Washington, DC: The Aspen Institute, 1990.

Gottschalk, Peter; and Mary Joyce. "The Impact of Technological Change, Deindustrialization, and Internationalization of Trade on Earnings Inequality: An International Perspective." In *Poverty, Inequality and the Future of Social Policy*, edited by Katherine McFate, Roger Lawson, and William J. Wilson. New York: Russell Sage Foundation, 1995.

Gouldner, Alvin W. *The Coming Crisis of Western Sociology*. New York: Basic Books, 1970.

Gounis, Kostas. "The Domestication of Urban Marginality: New York Shelters for Homeless Men." Doctoral dissertation, Columbia University, 1993.

———. "The Manufacture of Dependency: Shelterization Revisited." *New England Journal of Public Policy* 8 (1992): 685–93.

Granovetter, Mark S. "The Strength of Weak Ties." *American Journal of Sociology* 78 (1973): 1360–80.

Green, M.; and G. MacColl. *Reagan's Reign of Error*. New York: Pantheon Books, 1987.

Greenberg, Mark. *The Devil Is in the Details: Key Questions in the Effort to "End Welfare as We Know It."* Washington, DC: Center for Law and Social Policy, 1993.

———. *Racing to the Bottom? Recent State Welfare Initiatives Present Cause for Concern.* Washington, DC: Center for Law and Social Policy, February 1996.

———. *Two Years and Work: Understanding the Clinton Plan.* Washington, DC: Center for Law and Social Policy, 1994.

Greene, Vernon L.; and Deborah J. Monahan. "Comparative Utilization of Community-Based Long-Term Care Service by Hispanic and Anglo Elderly in a Case Management System." *Journal of Gerontology* 39 (1984): 730–35.

Gregory, Steven; and Roger Sanjek, eds. *Race*. New Brunswick, NJ: Rutgers University Press, 1994.

Greider, William. *Secrets of the Temple*. New York: Touchstone, 1987.

Greve, Frank. "Dole's Fund Appeal May Be Illegal." *The Philadelphia Inquirer* May 25, 1996: A1, A11.

Griffith, James. "Social Support Providers: Who Are They? Where Are They Met? The Relationship of Network Characteristics to Psychological Distress." *Basic and Applied Social Psychology* 6 (1985): 41–60.

Grob, Gerald N. *Mental Illness and American Society, 1875–1940.* Princeton, NJ: Princeton University Press, 1983.

Grossman, James R. *Land of Hope*. Chicago: University of Chicago Press, 1989.

Groth, Paul. *Living Downtown*. Berkeley: University of California Press, 1994.

Guggliota, G. "Federal Council for Homeless Dies." *Washington Post* October 18, 1993: A4.

———. "Resurrected Homeless Council Gains a Patron at White House." *Washington Post* November 20, 1993: A2.

Gurza, Augustin. "Camping Crackdown." *Orange County Register* April 26, 1995: Metro Section, 1.

———. "Police Enforcing Ban on Public Camping." *Orange County Register* September 12, 1992: B2.

Gutman, Amy. "Justice across the Spheres." In *Pluralism, Justice, and Equality*, edited by D. Miller and M. Walzer, 99–120. New York: Oxford University Press, 1995.

Gutman, Herbert G. *The Black Family in Slavery and Freedom, 1750–1925.* New York: Vintage Press, 1967.

Hainer, Peter. "Sharing Kith and Kin: A Study of Kinship Behavior, an Approach to Explanation." Doctoral dissertation, Brandeis University, 1991.

Hall, Rebecca. *Homelessness and Preventing Evictions: The Need for Legal Representation for Low-Income People.* Berkeley, CA: Berkeley Community Law Project, 1991.

Hamburger, Robert. *All the Lonely People: Life in a Single Room Occupancy Hotel.* New York: Ticknor and Fields, 1983.

Hamilton, J. D.; and W. J. Canteen. "Post-traumatic Stress Disorder in World War II Naval Veterans." *Hospital and Community Psychiatry* 38 (1987): 197–99.

Hardin, Bristow. "The Militarized Social Democracy." Doctoral dissertation, University of California, Santa Cruz, 1991.

Hareven, Tamara K. "The History of the Family and the Complexity of Social Change." *American Historical Review* 96 (1991): 95–124.

Harrington, Michael. *The Other America: Poverty in the United States.* New York: Macmillan, 1963.

Harrison, Bennet. *Lean and Mean.* New York: Basic, 1994.

Harrison, Bennet; and Barry Bluestone. *The Great U-Turn.* New York: Basic, 1988.

Hartman, Chester; D. Keating; and R. Legates. *Displacement: How to Fight It.* Berkeley: National Housing Law Project, 1982.

Hartwell, S. "Track Marks and Pipe Dreams: Life Histories of Homeless Substance Abusers." Doctoral dissertation, Yale University, 1995.

Harvard University Joint Center for Housing Studies. *State of the Nation's Housing, 1991.* Cambridge, MA: Harvard University Joint Center for Housing Studies, 1991.

Harvey, Paul, ed. *The Oxford Companion to English Literature.* 4th edition, revised by Dorothy Eagle. New York: Oxford University Press, 1967.

Harvey, Philip. *Securing the Right to Employment.* Princeton, NJ: Princeton University Press, 1989.

Hauser, Sandra; and Henry Freedman. *Jobless, Penniless, Often Homeless: State General Assistance Cuts Leave "Employables" Struggling for Survival.* New York: Center on Social Welfare Policy and Law, February 1994.

Haveman, Robert H., Ed. *A Decade of Federal Antipoverty Programs: Achievements, Failures, and Lessons.* New York: Academic Press, 1977.

Heather, Nick; Alex Wodak; Ethan A. Nadelmann; and Pat O'Hare. *Psychoactive Drugs and Harm Reduction: From Faith to Science.* London: Whurr Publishers, 1993.

Hirschi, Travis; and Michael Gottfredson. "Age and the Explanation of Crime." *American Journal of Sociology* 89 (1993): 552–84.

Hoch, Charles; and Robert A. Slayton. *New Homeless and Old: Community and the Skid Row Hotel.* Philadelphia: Temple University Press, 1989.

Hochschild, Jennifer L. *Facing Up to the American Dream.* Princeton: Princeton University Press, 1995.

———. "The Politics of the Estranged Poor." *Ethics* 101 (1991): 560–78.

Hoffman, S. F.; D. Wenger; J. Nigro; and R. Rosenfield. *Who Are the Homeless? A Study of Randomly Selected Men Who Use New York City Shelters.* Albany: New York State Office of Mental Health, 1982.

Hombs, Mary Ellen. "Reversals of Fortune: America's Homeless Poor and Their Advocates in the 1990s." *New Formations* 17 (1992): 109–25.

Hombs, Mary Ellen; and Mitch Snyder. *Homelessness in America: A Forced March to Nowhere.* Washington, DC: Community for Creative Non-Violence, 1982.

HomeBase. *Preventing Homelessness—Bay Area Programs and What They Do.* San Francisco: The Center for Common Concerns, 1991.

Hopper, Kim. "Advocacy for the Homeless in the 1980s." In *Homeless in America,* edited by Carol M. Caton. New York: Oxford University, 1990.

———. "A Bed for the Night: Homeless Men in New York City, Past and Present." Doctoral dissertation, Columbia University, 1987.

———. "Girding for the Long Haul: Some Notes on Advocacy for the Homeless, 1979–1984." Unpublished draft.

———. "Limits to Witness: Homelessness, Hysteresis and Ethnography." Paper presented at the annual meeting of the American Anthropological Association, Washington, DC, November 1995.

———. "Margins within Margins." In *The Security of Marginal Populations,* edited by S. Nolutshungu. Rochester: University of Rochester Press, 1996.

———. "The New Urban Niche of Homelessness." *Bulletin of the New York Academy of Medicine* 66 (1990): 435–50.

Hopper, Kim; and Jim Baumohl. "Held in Abeyance: Rethinking Homelessness and Advocacy." *American Behavioral Scientist* 37 (1994): 522–52.

Hopper, Kim; and Jill Hamberg. "The Making of America's Homeless: From Skid Row to New Poor, 1945–1984." In *Critical Perspectives on Housing,* edited by Rachel G. Bratt, Chester Hartman, and Ann Meyerson, 12–40. Philadelphia: Temple University Press, 1986.

Hopper, Kim; Ezra Susser; and Sarah Conover. "Economics of Makeshift: Deindustrialization and Homelessness in New York City." *Urban Anthropology* 14 (1985): 183–236.

Hornburg, Steven P.; and Stephen P. Pomeroy, eds. *Social Housing Toward the Year 2000, Part I. Housing Policy Debate* 6, 3 (special issue, Fall 1995).

———. *Social Housing Toward the Year 2000, Part II. Housing Policy Debate* 6, 4 (special issue, Winter 1995).

Housing Assistance Council. "Rural Homelessness: A Review of the Literature." Washington, DC: Housing Assistance Council, December 1991.

Howes, Carollee. "Relations between Early Child Care and Schooling." *Developmental Psychology* 24 (1988): 53–57.

Howes, Carollee; and Claire E. Hamilton. "The Changing Experience of Child Care: Changes in Teachers and in Teacher-Child Relationships and Children's Social Competence with Peers." *Early Childhood Research Quarterly* 8 (1993): 15–32.

Howes, Carollee; and Phyllis Stewart. "Child's Play with Adults, Peers and Toys." *Developmental Psychology* 24 (1987): 423–30.

Hutcheson, Natalie. "Toward Census 2000: Rural Kentucky Study." Paper presented at *Toward Census 2000* Conference, Alexandria, VA, September 28–29, 1993. Frankfort, KY: Kentucky Housing Corporation, 1993.

Ifill, G. "Kemp Pledges Campaign to Help Nation's Poor." *Washington Post* January 28, 1989: A4.

———. "New Jersey Is Blunting the 'Knife Edge of Homelessness.'" *Washington Post National Weekly Edition* March 19–25, 1990: 33.

Illich, Ivan. *Shadow Work.* Boston: Marian Boyars, 1981.

Interagency Council on the Homeless. *Priority Home! The Federal Plan to Break the Cycle of Homelessness.* Washington, DC: Interagency Council on the Homeless, 1994.

———. *Reaching Out: A Guide for Service Providers.* Washington, DC: Interagency Council on the Homeless, 1991.

International Labor Organization. *World Employment 1995.* Geneva: International Labor Organization, 1995.

Jackson, Kenneth T. *Crabgrass Frontier.* New York: Oxford, 1985.

Jacobs, Francine H. "Defining a Social Problem: The Case of Family Homelessness." *American Behavioral Scientist* 37 (1994): 396–403.

Jacobs, Francine H.; Priscilla M. D. Little; and Cheryl Almeida. "Supporting Family Life: A Survey of Homeless Shelters." *Journal of Social Distress and the Homeless* 2 (1993): 269–88.

James, Franklin. *Numbers and Characteristics of the Homeless: A Preliminary Application in Colorado of a New Methodology.* Denver: University of Colorado at Denver, Graduate School of Public Affairs, 1988.

James, Franklin J.; Betty L. McCummings; and Eileen A. Tynan. *Minorities in the Sunbelt.* New Brunswick, NJ: Center for Urban Policy Research, 1984.

Janowitz, Morris. "The All-Volunteer Military as a Socio-Political Problem." *Social Problems* 22 (1975): 432–49.

Jasso, Guillermina; and Mark R. Rosenzweig. *The New Chosen People: Immigrants in the United States.* New York: Russell Sage Foundation, 1990.

Jencks, Christopher. *The Homeless.* Cambridge, MA: Harvard University Press, 1994.

———. *Rethinking Social Policy.* Cambridge: Harvard University Press, 1992.

Joffee, Robert. "Down, Out, Flat Busted, Desperate: The Bloom Is off the 'Flower' Era." *The Washington Post* May 24, 1974: B1, B6.

Johnson, Alice K.; and Larry Kreuger. "Toward a Better Understanding of Homeless Women." *Social Work* 34 (1989): 537–40.

Joint Center for Housing Studies of Harvard University. *The State of the Nation's Housing, 1993.* Cambridge, MA: Harvard, 1993.

Jones, J. "Southern Diaspora: Origins of the Northern 'Underclass.'" In *The "Underclass" Debate,* edited by M. B. Katz, 27–55. Princeton: Princeton University Press, 1993.

Jusserand, J. J. *English Wayfaring Life in the Middle Ages.* Revised ed. London: Ernest Benn, 1920.

Katz, Michael B. *Improving Poor People.* Princeton: Princeton University Press, 1995.

———. *The Undeserving Poor: From the War on Poverty to the War on Welfare.* New York: Pantheon Books, 1989.

Katznelson, Ira. *City Trenches.* New York: Pantheon, 1980.

Kean, G. G. "A Comparative Study of Negro and White Homeless Men." Doctoral dissertation, Yeshiva University (New York), 1965.

Keefe, S. E. "Personal Communities in the City: Support Networks among Mexican Americans and Anglo Americans." *Urban Anthropology* 9 (1980): 51–74.

Kennedy, Paul. *The Rise and Fall of Great Powers.* New York: Random House, 1987.

Kessler, Brad. "After Charity, Start Organizing." *The Nation* April 16, 1988: 528–30.

Kessler, Ronald C.; Katherine A. McGonagle; Shanyang Zhao; Christopher B. Nelson; Michael Hughes; Suzann Eshleman; Hans-Ulrich Wittchen; and Kenneth S. Kendler. "Lifetime and 12-Month Prevalence of DSM-III-R Psychiatric Disorders in the United States." *Archives of General Psychiatry* 51 (1994): 8–19.

Kessler, Ronald C.; and H. Neighbors. "A New Perspective on the Relationships among Race, Social Class, and Psychological Distress." *Journal of Health and Social Behavior* 27 (1986): 107–15.

Kett, Joseph. *Rites of Passage: Adolescence in America, 1790 to the Present.* New York: Basic Books, 1977.

Keyssar, Alexander. *Out of Work: The First Century of Unemployment in Massachusetts.* New York: Cambridge University Press, 1986.

Kim, C.; G. Nestel; R. L. Phillips; and M. E. Borus. *National Longitudinal Survey of Youth Labor Market Experience: Military Studies.* Columbus, OH: Center for Human Resources Research, Ohio State University, 1980.

King, Martin Luther, Jr. "The Power of Nonviolent Action." In *Social Theory,* edited by Charles Lemert, 373–78. Boulder: Westview, 1993.

Knickman, James R.; and Beth C. Weitzman. *A Study of Homeless Families in New York City: Risk Assessment Models and Strategies for Prevention, Final Report to the New York City Human Resources Administration.* Vol. 1. New York: Health Research Program, Wagner Graduate School, 1989.

Knickman, James R.; Beth C. Weitzman; Marybeth Shinn; and Ellen H. Marcus. *A Study of Homeless Families in New York City: Characteristics and Comparisons with Other Public Assistance Families, Final Report to the New York City Human Resources Administration.* Vol. 2. New York: Health Research Program, Wagner Graduate School, 1989.

Knight, J. W. *Health Care Issues of Homeless Veterans.* West Roxbury, MA: Brockton West Roxbury Medical Center, 1987.

Koegel, Paul. "Through a Different Lens: An Anthropological Perspective on the Homeless Mentally Ill." *Culture, Medicine and Psychiatry* 16 (1992): 1–22.

Koegel, Paul; and M. Audrey Burnam. "Issues in the Assessment of Mental Disorders among the Homeless: An Empirical Approach." In *Homelessness: The National Perspective,* edited by Marjorie J. Roberts and Milton Greenblatt. New York: Plenum Press, 1992.

Koegel, Paul; M. Audrey Burnam; and Rodger K. Farr. "The Prevalence of Specific Psychiatric Disorders among Homeless Individuals in the Inner City of Los Angeles." *Archives of General Psychiatry* 45 (1988): 1085–92.

Koegel, Paul; M. Audrey Burnam; and Elan Mclamid. "Childhood Risk Factors for Homelessness among Homeless Adults." *American Journal of Public Health* 85 (1995): 1642–49.

Kolata, Gina. "Twins of the Streets: Homelessness and Addiction." *New York Times* May 22, 1989: A12.

Kolko, Joyce. *Restructuring the World Economy.* New York: Pantheon, 1988.

Kolodny, Robert. *Exploring New Strategies for Improving Public Housing Management: A Study for the Office of Policy Development and Research, U.S. Department of Housing and Urban Development.* Washington, DC: Government Printing Office, 1979.

Kondratas, Anna. "Estimates and Public Policy: The Politics of Numbers." *Housing Policy Debate* 2 (1991).

Kozol, Jonathan. *Rachel and Her Children: Homeless Families in America.* New York: Ballantine Books, 1989.

Kreuger, L. W.; J. J. Stretch; and A. K. Johnson. *Ethnic Differentials among the Homeless Seeking Shelter Placement of Traumatized Families.* Paper presented at the annual meeting of the National Association of Social Work Minorities Issues Conference, Washington, DC, 1987.

Kuhn, Randall; and Dennis Culhane. "Applying Cluster Analysis to Test a Typology of Homelessness by Pattern of Shelter Utilization." Unpublished manuscript, University of Pennsylvania, 1995.

Kulka, R.A.; W. E. Schlenger; J. A. Fairbank; R. L. Hough; B. K. Jordan; C. R. Marmar; and D. A. Weiss. *The National Vietnam Veterans Readjustment Study: Tables of Findings and Technical Appendices.* New York: Brunner/Mazel, 1990.

———. *Trauma and the Vietnam War Generation: Report of Findings from the National Vietnam Veterans Readjustment Study.* New York: Brunner/Mazel, 1990.

Kusmer, Kenneth. "African-Americans in the City since World War II: From the Industrial to the Post-industrial Era." *Journal of Urban History* 21 (1995): 458–504.

———. "Conceptualizing Social History: Homeless Men in America, 1865–1940, as a Case Study." In *Reconstructing American Literary and Historical Studies,* edited by G. H. Lenz, H. Keil, and S. Bröck-Sellah. New York: St. Martins, 1990.

———. "The Functions of Organized Charity in the Progressive Era: Chicago as a Case Study." *Journal of American History* 60 (1973): 657–78.

———. "The Homeless Unemployed in Industrializing America, 1865–1930: Perception and Reality." *Amerikastudien* (Germany), forthcoming.

———. "The Underclass in Historical Perspective." In *On Being Homeless: Historical Perspectives,* edited by R. Beard, 20–31. New York: Museum for the City of New York, 1987.

———. "The Underclass: Tramps and Vagrants in American Society, 1865–1930." Doctoral dissertation, University of Chicago, 1980.

Kuttner, Robert. *The Economic Illusion: False Choices between Prosperity and Social Justice.* Philadelphia: University of Pennsylvania Press, 1984.

Kwan, Ronald. "Footloose and Country Free." *Dollars and Sense* 164 (1991): 6–9.

La Gory, Mark; Ferris Ritchey; and Kevin Fitzpatrick. "Homelessness and Affiliation." *The Sociological Quarterly* 32 (1991): 201–18.

La Gory, Mark; Ferris J. Ritchey; Timothy O'Donoghue; and Jeffrey Mullis. "Homelessness in Alabama: A Variety of People and Experiences." In *Homelessness in the United States: State Surveys,* vol. 1, edited by Jamshid A. Momeni, 1–20. Westport, CT: Greenwood Press, Inc., 1989.

Lamb, H. Richard. *The Homeless Mentally Ill: A Task Force Report.* Washington, DC: American Psychiatric Press, 1984.

Lamb, H. Richard.; Leona L. Bachrach; and F. I. Kass. *Treating the Homeless Mentally Ill: A Report of the Task Force on the Homeless Mentally Ill.* Washington, DC: American Psychiatric Association, 1992.

Landry, B. "The Enduring Dilemma of Race in America." In *America at Century's End,* edited by A. Wolfe, 185–207. Berkeley: University of California, 1991.

Laurence, J. H.; P. F. Ramsberger; and M. A. Gribben. *Effects of Military Experience on the Post-service Lives of Low-Aptitude Recruits: Project 100,000 and the ASVAB Misnorming.* Alexandria, VA: Human Resources Research Organization, 1989.

Lav, Iris J.; Edward B. Lazere; Robert Greenstein; and Steven D. Gold. *The States and the Poor: How Budget Decisions Affected Low Income People in 1992.* Washington DC: Center on Budget and Policy Priorities, and Albany: Center for the Study of the States, 1993.

Lawrence, E. "William Cosby and the Freedom of the Press, 1732–1736." In J.G. Wilson, ed., *Memorial History of the City of New York,* edited by J. G. Wilson, vol. 2, 209–58. New York: New York History Co., 1892.

Lazere, Edward B.; Paul A. Leonard; and L. L. Kravitz. *The Other Housing Crisis: Sheltering the Poor in Rural America.* Washington, DC: Center on Budget and Policy Priorities, 1989.

Lazere, Edward B.; Paul A. Leonard; Cushing N. Dolbeare; and Barry Zigas. *A Place to Call Home: The Low Income Housing Crisis Continues.* Washington, DC: Center on Budget and Policy Priorities and Low Income Housing Information Service, 1991.

Leda, Catherine L.; and R. A. Rosenheck. "Impact of Staffing Levels on Transitional Residential Treatment Programs for Homeless Veterans." *Psychosocial Rehabilitation Journal* 15 (1991): 55–68

———. "Mental Health Status and Community Adjustment after Treatment in a Residential Treatment Program for Homeless Veterans." *American Journal of Psychiatry* 149 (1992): 1219–24

Leda, Catherine L.; R. A. Rosenheck; and L. Corwel. *The Pilot Evaluation of Veterans Benefits Administration's Homeless Outreach Program.* West Haven, CT: Northeast Program Evaluation Center, 1992.

Leda, Catherine L.; R. A. Rosenheck; and P. Gallup. "Mental Illness in Homeless Female Veterans." *Hospital and Community Psychiatry* 43 (1992): 1026–28.

Leda, Catherine L.; R. A. Rosenheck; and S. Medak. *Progress Report on the Veterans Industries/Therapeutic Residences Program.* West Haven, CT: Northeast Program Evaluation Center, 1993.

Lee, Barrett A. "Homelessness in Tennessee." In *Homelessness in the United States,* edited by Jamshid A. Momeni, 191–203. Westport, CT: Greenwood Press, 1989.

———. "Stability and Change in an Urban Homeless Population." *Demography* 26 (1989): 323–34.

Lee, Barrett A.; S. Hinze-Jones; and D. Lewis. "Public Beliefs about the Causes of Homelessness." *Social Forces* 69 (1990): 253–65.

Lees, Lynn H. "The Survival of the Unfit: Welfare Policies and Family Maintenance in Nineteenth-Century London." In *The Uses of Charity: Poor Relief in the Nineteenth-Century Metropolis,* edited by Peter Mandler, 60–91. Philadelphia: University of Pennsylvania Press, 1990.

Lehman, Anthony F.; and David S. Cordray. "Prevalence of Alcohol, Drug, and Mental Disorders Among the Homeless: One More Time." *Contemporary Drug Problems* 20 (1993): 355–83.

Lekachman, Robert. *The Age of Keynes.* New York: Random House, 1966.

Leo, John. "Homeless Rights, Community Wrongs." *U.S. News & World Report* July 24, 1989.

Levi-Strauss, Claude. *The Savage Mind.* Chicago: University of Chicago Press, 1966.

Levine, Irene S.; and D. J. Rog. "Mental Health Services for Homeless Mentally Ill Persons: Federal Initiatives and Current Service Trends." *American Psychologist* 45, 8 (1990): 963–68.

Levine, Murray; John C. Wesolowski; and Frank J. Corbett. "Pupil Turnover and Academic Performance in an Inner City Elementary School." *Psychology in the Schools* 3 (1966): 153–56.

Levinson, B. M. "The Homeless Man: A Psychological Enigma." *Mental Hygiene* 47 (1963): 590–600.

Lewis, Oscar. "The Culture of Poverty." *Scientific American* 215 (1966): 19–25.

Lichter, Daniel T.; D. K. McLaughlin; and G. T. Cornwell. "Migration and the Loss of Human Resources in Rural America." In *Investing in People: The Human Capital Needs of Rural America,* edited by L. J. Beaulieu and D. Mulkey, 224–46. Boulder, CO: Westview Press, 1994.

Liebow, Elliot. *Tally's Corner: A Study of Negro Streetcorner Men.* Boston: Little, Brown and Company, 1967.

———. *Tell Them Who I Am: The Lives of Homeless Women.* New York: Basic Books, 1993.

Lindblom, Eric N. *The 1990 Annual Report of the Interagency Council on the Homeless.* Washington, DC: U.S. Interagency Council on the Homeless, February 1991.

———. *The 1991–1992 Annual Report of the Interagency Council on the Homeless.* Washington, DC: U.S. Interagency Council on the Homeless, September 1992.

———. "Toward a Comprehensive Homelessness Prevention Strategy." *Housing Policy Debate* 2, 3 (Summer 1991): 957–1025.

Link, Bruce G.; and Jo Phelan. "Social Conditions as Fundamental Causes of Diseases." *Journal of Health and Social Behavior* extra issue (1995): 80–94.

Link, Bruce G.; Jo Phelan; Michaeline Bresnahan; Ann Stueve; Robert Moore; and Ezra Susser. "Lifetime and Five-Year Prevalence of Homelessness in the United States: New Evidence on an Old Debate." *American Journal of Orthopsychiatry* 65, 3 (1995): 347–54.

Link, Bruce G.; Sharon Schwartz; Robert Moore; Jo Phelan; Elmer Struening; Ann Stueve; and Mary Ellen Colten. "Public Knowledge, Attitudes, and Beliefs about Homeless People: Evidence for Compassion Fatigue?" *American Journal of Community Psychology* 23 (1995): 533–55.

Lipton, F.; A. Sabatini; and S. Katz. "Down and Out in the City: The Homeless Mentally Ill." *Hospital and Community Psychiatry* 34, 9 (1983): 817–21.

Lis, Catharina; and Hugo Soly. *Poverty and Capitalism in Pre-Industrial Europe.* Atlantic Highlands, NJ: Humanities Press, 1979.

Littell, Julia H. "Evidence or Assertions? The Outcomes of Family Preservation Services." *Social Service Review* 69 (1995): 338–51.

Littman, Mark S. "Poverty in the 1980s: Are the Poor Getting Poorer?" *Monthly Labor Review* 112, 6 (1989): 13–18.

Lopez, M. "The Perils of Outreach Work: Overreaching the Limits of Persuasive Tactics." In *Coercion and Aggressive Community Treatment: A New Frontier in Mental Health Law,* edited by D. Dennis and J. Monahan, 85–92. New York: Plenum Press, 1996.

Lovald, Keith A. "From Hobohemia to Skid Row: The Changing Community of the Homeless Man." Doctoral dissertation, University of Minnesota, 1960.

Luhrmann, T. M. *Persuasions of the Witch's Craft.* Cambridge, MA: Harvard University Press, 1989.

Machalaba, Daniel. "Mobile Homes: Transit Systems Face Burden of Providing Last-Resort Shelter." *Wall Street Journal* July 18, 1990: 1.

MacLeod, Celeste. *Horatio Alger, Farewell.* New York: Seaview, 1980.

———. "Street People: The New Migrants." *The Nation* October 22, 1973: 395–97.

MacLeod, Jay. *Ain't No Makin' It*. Revised ed. Boulder: Westview, 1995.

Mair, Andrew. "The Homeless and the Post-industrial City." *Political Geography* 5 (October 1986): 351–65.

Mandel, Ernest. *Long Waves of Capitalist Development*. New York: Cambridge University Press, 1980.

Mangine, Steven J.; David Royse; Vernon R. Wiehe; and Michael T. Nietzel. "Homelessness among Adults Raised as Foster Children: A Survey of Drop-in Center Users." *Psychological Reports* 67 (1990): 739–45.

Marcos, Luis R., Neal L. Cohen; David Nardacci; and Joan Brittain. "Psychiatry Takes to the Streets: The New York City Initiative for the Homeless Mentally Ill." *American Journal of Psychiatry* 147, 11 (Nov. 1990): 1557–61.

Marsden, Peter V. "Core Discussion Networks of Americans." *American Sociological Review* 52 (1987): 122–31.

Maslow, Abraham H. *Toward a Psychology of Being*. New York: Van Nostrand, 1962.

Massey, Douglas S.; and Nancy A. Denton. *American Apartheid: Segregation and the Making of the Underclass*. Cambridge: Harvard University Press, 1993.

Masten, Ann S. "Homeless Children in the United States: Mark of a Nation at Risk." *Current Directions in Psychological Science* 1, 2 (1992): 41–44.

Masten, Ann S.; Donna Milotis; Sandra A. Graham-Bermann; Mary Louise Ramirez; and Jennifer Neemann. "Children in Homeless Families: Risks to Mental Health and Development." *Journal of Consulting and Clinical Psychology* 61 (1993): 335–43.

Maza, Penelope L.; and Judy A. Hall. *Homeless Children and Their Families: A Preliminary Study*. Washington, DC: Child Welfare League of America, 1988.

McAdam, Doug. "Micromobilization Contexts and Recruitment to Activism." *International Social Movement Research* 1 (1988): 125–54.

McChesney, Kay Young. *Characteristics of the Residents of Two Inner-City Emergency Shelters for the Homeless*. Los Angeles: Social Science Research Institute, University of Southern California, 1987.

———. "Family Homelessness: A Systemic Problem." *Journal of Social Issues* 46, 4 (1990): 191–205.

McDermott, John. "Bare Minimum: A Too-Low Minimum Wage Keeps All Wages Down." *Dollars and Sense* 200 (July/August 1995): 26–29.

McFate, Katherine. "Joblessness in the Nineties: The Collapse in Demand for Low-Skilled Workers." Unpublished manuscript, 1995.

———. "Trampolines, Safety Nets, or Free Fall? Labor Market Policies and Social Assistance in the 1980s." In *Poverty, Inequality and the Future of Social Policy*, edited by Katherine McFate, Roger Lawson, and William J. Wilson. New York: Russell Sage Foundation, 1995.

McFate, Katherine; Roger Lawson; and William Julius Wilson, Eds. *Poverty, Inequality and the Future of Social Policy*. New York: Russell Sage Foundation, 1995.

McIntire, James L.; Jon Layzer; and Luke Weisberg. *On Firmer Ground: Housing for Homeless and Near-Homeless Families*. Seattle: Washington State Department of Community Development and University of Washington Institute for Public Policy and Management, 1992.

McLoyd, Vonnie C. "The Impact of Economic Hardship on Black Families and Children: Psychological Distress, Parenting, and Socioemotional Development." *Child Development* 61 (1990): 311–46.

McMurry, Donald L. *Coxey's Army: A Study of the Industrial Army Movement of 1894*. Seattle: University of Washington Press, 1968 (originally published in 1929).

McNees, Stephen K. "The 1990–91 Recession in Historical Perspective." *The New England Economic Review* January/February 1992: 13–20.

Mead, Lawrence. *The New Politics of Poverty*. New York: Basic Books, 1992.

Merton, Robert K. *Social Theory and Social Structure*. New York: Free Press, 1949.

Meyerowitz, Joanne J. *Women Adrift: Independent Wage Earners in Chicago, 1880–1930*. Chicago: University of Chicago Press, 1988.

Michl, Thomas R. "Assessing the Costs of Inflation and Unemployment." In *The Political Economy of Full Employment*, edited by Philip Arestis and Mike Marshall. Brookfield, VT: Edward Elgar, 1995.

Mier, Robert; and Robert Giloth. "Hispanic Employment Opportunities: A Case of Internal Labor Markets and Weak-Tied Social Networks." *Social Science Quarterly* 66 (1985): 296–309.

Milburn, Norweeta; and J. A. Booth. "Illicit Drug and Alcohol Use among Homeless Black Adults in Shelters." *Drugs and Society* 6 (1992): 115–55.

Milburn, Norweeta; and A. D'Ercole. "Homeless Women: Moving Toward a Comprehensive Model." *American Psychologist* 46 (1991): 1161–69.

Miller, Henry. *On the Fringe: The Dispossessed in America*. Lexington, MA: D.C. Heath, 1991.

Mills, Crystal; and Hiro Ota. "Homeless Women with Minor Children in the Detroit Metropolitan Area." *Social Work* 34 (1989): 485–89.

Milofsky, Carl; Anthony Butto; Michael Gross; and Jim Baumohl. "Small Town in Mass Society: Substance Abuse Treatment and Urban-Rural Migration." *Contemporary Drug Problems* 20 (1993): 433–71.

Mindel, Charles H. "Extended Familialism among Urban Mexican Americans, Anglos, and Blacks." *Hispanic Journal of Behavioral Sciences* 2 (1980): 21–34.

Mindel, Charles H.; and Roosevelt Wright, Jr. "The Use of Social Services by Black and White Elderly: The Role of

Social Support Systems." *Journal of Gerontological Social Work* 4 (1982): 107–25.

Minkler, K. M.; R. J. Roe; R. J. Robertson-Beckley. "Raising Grandchildren from Crack-Cocaine Households: Effects on Family and Friendship Ties with African-American Women." *American Journal of Orthopsychiatry* 64 (1994): 20–29.

Mishel, Lawrence; and Jared Bernstein. *The State of Working America 1994–95.* Armonk, NY: M. E. Sharpe, 1994.

Mishel, Lawrence; Jared Bernstein; and Edith Rasell. *Who Wins with the Minimum Wage?* Washington, DC: Economic Policy Institute, 1995.

Mizruchi, Ephraim H. *Regulating Society.* Chicago: University of Chicago Press, 1987 (originally published in 1983).

Modell, John. *Into One's Own: From Youth to Adulthood in the United States, 1920–1975.* Berkeley: University of California Press, 1989.

Molnar, Janice; William Rath; and Tovah Klein. "Constantly Compromised: The Impact of Homelessness on Children." *Journal of Social Issues* 46, 4 (1990): 109–24.

Molnar, Janice; William Rath; Tovah P. Klein; Cynthia Lowe; and Annelie H. Hartmann. *Ill Fares the Land: The Consequences of Homelessness and Chronic Poverty for Children and Families in New York City.* New York: Bank Street College of Education, 1991.

Molnar, Janice; and David H. Rubin. "The Impact of Homelessness on Children: Review of Prior Studies and Implications for Future Studies and Policy." Paper presented NIMH/NIAAA research conference organized by the Better Homes Foundation, Cambridge, MA, January–February 1991.

Momeni, Jamshid A., ed. *Homelessness in the United States,* vol. 1. New York: Greenwood Press, 1989.

Monkkonen, Eric H. "Introduction." In *Walking to Work: Tramps in America, 1790–1935,* edited by E. H. Monkkonen, 1–17. Lincoln: University of Nebraska, 1984.

———. "Regional Dimensions of Tramping." In *Walking to Work: Tramps in America, 1790–1935,* edited by E. H. Monkkonen, 189–211. Lincoln: University of Nebraska, 1984.

Morris, Richard Brandon. *Government and Labor in Early America.* New York: Columbia University Press, 1946.

Morrissey, J.; and I. Levine. "Researchers Discuss Latest Findings, Examine Needs of Homeless Mentally Ill Persons." *Hospital and Community Psychiatry* 38, 8 (1987): 811–12.

Morse, Gary A. *A Contemporary Assessment of Urban Homelessness: Implications for Social Change.* St. Louis: Center for Metropolitan Studies and the University of Missouri, St. Louis, 1986.

Mowbray, Carol; Sue Johnson; and Andrea Solarz. "Homelessness in a State Hospital Population." *Hospital and Community Psychiatry* 38, 8 (August 1987): 880–82.

Mowbray, Carol; Sue Johnson; Andrea Solarz; and C. J. Combs. *Mental Health and Homelessness in Detroit: A Research Study.* Lansing: Michigan Department of Mental Health, 1985.

Multnomah County, Oregon, Department of Human Services. *The Homeless Poor.* Multnomah County, Oregon: Social Services Division, Department of Human Services, 1984.

———. *Homeless Women.* Multnomah County, Oregon: Social Services Division, Department of Human Services, 1985.

Murray, Charles. *Losing Ground: American Social Policy, 1950–1980.* New York: Basic Books, 1984.

National Academy of Science. *Homelessness, Health, and Human Needs.* Washington, DC: National Academy Press, 1988.

National Alliance to End Homelessness. *The Prevention of Homelessness.* Washington, DC: National Alliance to End Homelessness, September 1992.

National Institute of Mental Health. *Deinstitutionalization Policy and Homelessness.* A Report to Congress, Washington, DC: National Institute of Mental Health, May 1990.

———. *Two Generations of NIMH-Funded Research on Homelessness and Mental Illness: 1982–1990.* Rockville, MD: NIMH, 1991.

National Institute on Alcohol Abuse and Alcoholism. *Community Demonstration Grant Projects for Alcohol and Drug Abuse Treatment of Homeless Individuals: Final Evaluation Report and Executive Summary.* Rockville, MD: NIAAA, 1992.

National Law Center on Homelessness and Poverty. *Beyond McKinney: Policies to End Homelessness.* Washington, DC: National Law Center on Homelessness and Poverty, 1992.

———. *No Homeless People Allowed: A Report on Anti-Homeless Law, Litigation and Alternatives in 49 United States Cities.* Washington, DC: National Law Center on Homelessness and Poverty, 1994.

———. *To Protect and Defend: Converting Military Housing and Other Federal Property to Help Homeless Americans.* Washington, DC: National Law Center on Homelessness and Poverty, 1994.

National Low Income Housing Coalition. *Out of Reach: Why Everyday People Can't Find Affordable Housing.* Washington, DC: National Low Income Housing Coalition, 1996.

"A New Skid Row." *Time* July 8, 1974: 76.

New York City Commission on the Homeless. *The Way Home: A New Direction in Social Policy.* New York: New York City Commission on the Homeless,1992.

New York State Department of Social Services, Office of Program Planning, Analysis and Development, and Office of Shelter and Supported Housing Programs. *The Homeless Prevention Program Outcomes and Effectiveness.* Albany: New York State Dept. of Social Services, 1990.

Newman, Katherine S. *Falling from Grace: The Experience of Downward Mobility in the American Middle Class.* New York: Free Press, 1988.

Nichols, Marion; and Kathryn Porter. *General Assistance Programs: Gaps in the Safety Net.* Washington, DC: Center on Budget and Policy Priorities, March 1995.

Nightingale, Carl Husemoller. *On the Edge.* New York: Basic, 1993.

North, C. S.; and E. M. Smith. "Posttraumatic Stress Disorder among Homeless Men and Women." *Hospital and Community Psychiatry* 43 (1992):1010–16.

Oberschall, Anthony. *Social Conflict and Social Movements.* Englewood Cliffs, NJ: Prentice Hall, 1973.

O'Connor, James. *The Fiscal Crisis of the State.* New York: St. Martin's, 1973.

O'Hare, William P. *America's Minorities: The Demographics of Diversity.* Population Bulletin 47:4. Washington, DC: Population Reference Bureau, 1992.

Office of the Assistant Secretary of Defense. *Population Representation in the Military Service: Fiscal Year 1989.* Alexandria, VA: Assistant Secretary of Defense, 1990.

Office of the Inspector General, U.S. Department of Health and Human Services. *Homeless Prevention Programs,* Washington, DC: U.S. Dept. of Health and Human Services, February 1991.

Ogbu, John U. "The Consequences of the American Caste System." In *The School Achievement of Minority Children,* edited by U. Neisser, 19–56. Hillsdale, NJ: Lawrence Erlbaum Associates, 1986.

Ohio Department of Mental Health. *Homelessness in Ohio: A Study of People in Need.* Columbus: Ohio Department of Mental Health, 1985.

Oliver, Malvin L.; and Thomas M. Shapiro. *Black Wealth/White Wealth: A New Perspective on Racial Inequality.* New York: Routledge, 1995.

Olson, Mancur. *The Logic of Collective Action.* Cambridge, MA: Harvard University, 1965.

Organisation of Economic Cooperation and Development. *The OECD Jobs Study: Facts, Analysis, Strategies.* Paris: OECD, 1994.

Orwell, George. *Down and Out in Paris and London.* New York: Harcourt Brace Jovanovich, 1933.

Osher, Fred. "A Vision for the Future: Toward a Service System Responsive to Those with Co-occurring Addictive and Mental Disorders." *American Journal of Orthopsychiatry* 66, 1 (1996): 71–76.

Parker, Carleton. "The California Casual and His Revolt." *Quarterly Journal of Economics* 30 (1915): 110–26.

Parker, Robert E. *Flesh Peddlers and Warm Bodies.* New Brunswick, NJ: Rutgers University Press, 1994.

Parson, E. R. "Ethnicity and Traumatic Stress: The Intersecting Point in Psychotherapy." In *Trauma and Its Wake,* volume I, edited by C. R. Figley. New York: Brunner/Mazel, 1985.

"A Pauper Colony." *San Francisco Call.* January 17, 1884, 5.

Pavetti, LaDonna. "Who Is Affected by Time Limits?" *Welfare Reform: An Analysis of the Issues.* Washington, DC: Urban Institute Press, 1995.

Pear, R. "President Signs $1 Billion in Homeless Aid." *New York Times* July 24, 1987: 1.

Peery, Nelson. *Black Fire.* New York: The New Press, 1994.

Peterson, Ann C.; and L. Crockett. "Pubertal Timing and Grade Effects on Adjustment." *Journal of Youth and Adolescence* 14 (1985): 191–206.

Piliavin, Irving; Michael Sosin; and Herb Westerfelt. "Tracking the Homeless" *Focus* 10 (1987): 20–25.

Piliavin, Irving; Michael Sosin; Herb Westerfelt; and Ross L. Matsueda. *The Duration of Homeless Careers: An Exploratory Study.* Madison, WI: University of Madison, August 1990.

Piliavin, Irving; Bradley R. E. Wright; Robert D. Mare; and Alex H. Westerfelt. "Exits from and Returns to Homelessness." *Social Service Review* 70 (1996): 33–57.

Piore, Michael; and Charles Sabel. *The Second Industrial Divide.* New York: Basic, 1984.

Pittman, Donald J.; and C. Wayne Gordon. *Revolving Door: A Study of the Chronic Police Case Inebriate.* New York: Free Press, 1958.

Piven, Frances Fox. "Is It Global Economics or Neo-Laissez Faire?" *New Left Review* 213 (September/October 1995): 107–14.

Piven, Frances Fox; and Richard Cloward. *The New Class War.* Revised and Enlarged Edition. New York: Pantheon, 1985.

———. *Poor People's Movements.* New York: Pantheon, 1977.

———. *Regulating the Poor.* New York: Vintage, 1971.

———. *Regulating the Poor: The Functions of Public Welfare* (Updated Edition). New York: Vintage, 1993.

Plotnick, Robert; and Felicity Skidmore. *Progress against Poverty: A Review of the 1964–1974 Decade.* New York: Academic Press, 1975.

Polanyi, Karl. *The Great Transformation.* Boston: Beacon Hill, 1957.

Polich, J. M. "Epidemiology of Alcohol Abuse in Military and Civilian Populations." *American Journal of Public Health* 71 (1981): 1125–32.

Pomerantz, Sidney Irving. *New York: An American City, 1783–1803.* New York: Columbia University Press, 1938.

Przeworski, Adam. "Less Is More: In France, the Future of Unemployment Lies in Leisure." *Dollars and Sense* 200 (July/August 1995): 12–15, 41.

Putnam, J. R.; N. L. Cohen; and A. M. Sullivan. "Innovative Outreach Services for the Homeless Mentally Ill." *International Journal of Mental Health* 14, 4 (1986): 112–24.

Putnam, R. D. "The Prosperous Community: Social Capital and Public Life." *American Prospect* 13 (Spring 1993): 35–42.

———. "The Strange Disappearance of Civic America." *American Prospect* 24 (Winter 1995): 34–48.

Quadagno, Jill. *The Color of Welfare. How Racism Undermined the War on Poverty.* New York, Oxford: Oxford University Press, 1994.

Rader, Victoria. *Signal Through the Flames: Mitch Snyder and America's Homeless.* Kansas City, MO: Sheed and Ward, 1986.

Rafferty, Yvonne. "The Legal Rights and Educational Problems of Homeless Children and Youth." *Educational Evaluation and Policy Analysis* 17 (1995): 39–61.

———. *And Miles to Go: Barriers to Academic Achievement and Innovative Strategies for the Delivery of Educational Services to Homeless Children.* New York: Advocates for Children, 1991.

Rafferty, Yvonne; and Norma Rollins. *Learning in Limbo: The Educational Deprivation of Homeless Children.* New York: Advocates for Children, 1989.

Rafferty, Yvonne; and Marybeth Shinn. "The Impact of Homelessness on Children." *American Psychologist* 46 (1991): 1170–79.

Rainwater, L. "The Revolt of the Dirty Workers." *Transaction* 5 (1967): 1, 11.

Randolph, F. L. "Improving Service Systems through Systems Integration: The ACCESS Program." *American Rehabilitation* 21 (1995): 36–38.

Reich, R.; and L. Siegel. "The Emergence of the Bowery as a Psychiatric Dumping Ground." *Psychiatric Quarterly* 50, 9 (1978): 191–201.

Reich, Robert. *The Work of Nations,* 1993.

Rescorla, Leslie; Ruth Parker; and Paul Stolley. "Ability, Achievement, and Adjustment in Homeless Children." *American Journal of Orthopsychiatry* 61 (1991): 210–20.

Resource Group. *Homelessness in Houston, Harris County and Gulf Coast United Way Service Delivery Areas: Report of Data Collection and Analysis.* Austin, TX: Resource Group, 1989.

Rice, Stuart A. "The Failure of the Municipal Lodging House." *National Municipal Review* 11 (1922): 358–62.

———. "The Homeless." *Annals of the American Academy of Political Science* 77 (1918): 140–53.

Rifkin, Jeremy. *The End of Work.* New York: Putnam, 1995.

Ringenbach, Paul T. *Tramps and Reformers, 1873–1916.* Westport, CT: Greenwood Press, 1973.

Ringheim, Karin. *At Risk of Homelessness: The Roles of Income and Rent.* New York: Praeger, 1990.

Rivlin, Alice (Director, Office of Management and Budget) correspondence to Sam Gibbons, (Committee on Ways and Means, U.S. House of Representatives) December 6, 1995.

Robertson, Marjorie J. "Homeless Veterans: An Emerging Problem?" In *The Homeless in Contemporary Society,* edited by R. D. Bingham, R. E. Green, and S. B. White, 64–82. Beverly Hills, CA: Sage Press, 1987.

Robertson, Marjorie J.; Richard Ropers; and Richard Boyer. *The Homeless of Los Angeles County: An Empirical Evaluation.* Document No. 4, Los Angeles: Basic Shelter Research Project. Los Angeles: School of Public Health, University of California, Los Angeles, 1985.

Rock, Paul. "The Sociology of Deviancy and Conceptions of Moral Order." *British Journal of Criminology* 14 (1974): 139–49.

Rodriguez, Nestor; and Jacqueline Maria Hagan. "Apartment Restructuring and Latino Immigrant Tenant Struggles: A Case Study of Human Agency." *Comparative Urban and Community Research* 4 (1992): 164–80.

Rog, D. *Engaging Homeless Persons with Mental Illness into Treatment.* Alexandria, VA: National Mental Health Association, 1988.

Rooney, James F. "Race Relations in Skid Row." Unpublished manuscript, 1969.

Ropers, Richard H. *The Invisible Homeless.* New York: Insight Books, 1988.

Rosenheck, Robert A.; and Alan F. Fontana. "A Model of Homelessness among Male Veterans of the Vietnam War Generation." *American Journal of Psychiatry* 151 (1994): 421–27.

Rosenheck, Robert A.; and L. K. Frisman. *Preliminary Report on the SSA-VA Joint Outreach Initiative for Homeless Veterans.* West Haven, CT: Northeast Program Evaluation Center, 1994.

Rosenheck, Robert A.; L. K. Frisman; and A. Chung. "The Proportion of Veterans among the Homeless." *American Journal of Public Health* 84, 3 (1993): 466–68.

———. "The Proportion of Veterans among the Homeless." In *Health Care for Homeless Veterans Program: Fifth Annual Progress Report,* edited by L. K. Frisman, R. A. Rosenheck, and D. DiLella, A1–A20. West Haven, CT: Northeast Program Evaluation Center, 1993.

Rosenheck, Robert A.; and P. Gallup. "Involvement in an Outreach and Residential Treatment Program for Homeless Mentally Ill Veterans." *Journal of Nervous and Mental Diseases* 179 (1991): 750–54.

Rosenheck, Robert A.; P. Gallup; and L. K. Frisman. "An Outcome Study of the Homeless Chronically Mentally Ill Veterans Program." In *Health Care for Homeless Veterans Programs: Sixth Annual Progress Report*, edited by L. K. Frisman, R. A. Rosenheck, and D. DiLella. West Haven, CT: Northeast Program Evaluation Center, 1994.

———. "Service Linkage and Related Costs of an Outreach Program for Homeless Mentally Ill Veterans." *Hospital and Community Psychiatry* 44 (1993): 1166–71.

Rosenheck, Robert A.; and P. Koegel. "Characteristics of Veterans and Nonveterans in Three Samples of Homeless Men." *Hospital and Community Psychiatry* 44 (1993): 858–63.

Rosenheck, Robert A.; and C. Leda. "Who Is Served by Programs for the Homeless? Admission to a Domiciliary Care Program for Homeless Veterans." *Hospital and Community Psychiatry* 42 (1991): 176–81.

Rosenheck, Robert A.; C. Leda; and P. Gallup. "Combat Stress, Psycho-Social Adjustment and Health Services Utilization among Homeless Vietnam Theatre Veterans." *Hospital and Community Psychiatry* 43 (1992):145–49.

Rosenheck, Robert A.; C. Leda; P. Gallup; B. Astrachan; R. Milstein; P. Leaf; D. Thompson; and P. Errera. "Initial Assessment Data from a 43-Site Program for Homeless Chronically Mentally Ill Veterans." *Hospital and Community Psychiatry* 40 (1989): 937–42.

Rosenthal, Rob. "Good Cop/Bad Cop: A Social Movement Dynamic." Paper presented to the Society for the Study of Social Problems annual meeting, San Francisco, August 7, 1989.

———. *Homeless in Paradise*. Philadelphia: Temple University, 1994.

———. "Homeless People's Project Interim Report 2." Santa Barbara Homeless Coalition: Santa Barbara, 1984.

———. "Homelessness and Isolation." Paper presented to the Eastern Sociological Society annual convention, Baltimore, March 19, 1994.

———. "Skidding/Coping/Escaping: Constraint, Agency, and Gender in the Lives of Homeless 'Skidders.'" In *Negotiating at the Margins: The Gendered Discourses of Power and Resistance*, edited by Sue Fisher and Kathy Davis. New Brunswick, NJ: Rutgers University, 1993.

Rosnow, M. J.; T. Shaw; and C. S. Concord. *Listening to the Homeless: A Study of Homeless Mentally Ill Persons in Milwaukee*. Report prepared by Human Services Triangle, Inc. Madison: Wisconsin Office of Mental Health, 1985.

Ross, Davis R. B. *Preparing for Ulysses: Politics and Veterans during World War II*. New York: Columbia University Press, 1969.

Rossi, Peter H. *Down and Out in America: The Origins of Homelessness*. Chicago: University of Chicago Press, 1989.

———. *Homelessness in America: Selected Topics*. Study done for the U.S. Interagency Council on the Homeless. Amherst, MA: University of Massachusetts, Social and Demographic Research Institute, September 1989.

———. "Minorities and Homelessness." In *Divided Opportunities: Minorities, Poverty, and Social Policy*, edited by Gary D. Sandefur and Marta Tienda. New York: Plenum Press, 1988.

———. "Troubling Families: Family Homelessness in America." *American Behavioral Scientist* 37 (1994): 342–95.

———. *Without Shelter: Homelessness in the 1980s*. New York: Priority Press Publications, 1989.

Rossi, Peter H.; Gene A. Fisher; and Georgianna Willis. *The Condition of the Homeless in Chicago: A Report Based on Surveys Conducted in 1985 and 1986*. Amherst, MA and Chicago: Social and Demographic Research Institute, University of Massachusetts-Amherst and National Opinion Research Center, Chicago, 1986.

Roth, Dee. "Homeless Veterans: Comparisons with Other Homeless Men." In *Homelessness: A National Perspective*, edited by M. J. Robertson and M. Greenblatt, 213–20. New York: Plenum Press, 1992.

———. "Homelessness in Ohio: A Statewide Epidemiological Survey." In *Homelessness in the United States: State Surveys*, edited by Jamshid A. Momeni, 145–63. New York: Greenwood Press.

Rothman, David J. *The Discovery of the Asylum*. Boston: Little, Brown, 1971.

Rothstein, Vivian. "Is There a *Right* to be Homeless?" *Boston Review* December/January 1993–94.

Rubin, Lillian. *Families on the Fault Line*. New York: HarperCollins, 1994.

Ruddick, Susan. "Heterotopias of the Homeless: Strategies and Tactics of Placemaking in Los Angeles." *Strategies* 3 (1990): 184–201.

Ruggles, Patricia. *Drawing the Line: Alternative Poverty Measures and Their Implications for Public Policy*. Washington, DC: Urban Institute, 1990.

Rushdie, Salman. "At the Auction of the Ruby Slippers." In *East and West*, by Salman Rushdie. New York: Viking, 1995.

———. *The Satanic Verses*. New York: Viking, 1988.

Santa Ana City Council. *Transcript of December 6, 1993 City Council Meeting Re: Santa Ana Ordinance NS-2210*.

Sassen, Saskia. "The Informal Economy." In *Dual City: Restructuring New York*, edited by J. H. Mollenkopf and M. Castells, 78–102. New York: Russell Sage, 1991.

———. *The Mobility of Labor and Capital*. New York: Cambridge, 1988.

Savner, Steve; and Mark Greenberg. *The CLASP Guide to Welfare Waivers, 1992–1995.* Washington, DC: Center for Law and Social Policy, May 1995.

Schneider, John C. "Tramping Workers, 1890–1920: A Subcultural View." In *Walking to Work: Tramps in America, 1790–1935.* edited by E. H. Monkkonen, 212–34. Lincoln: University of Nebraska, 1984.

Schor, Juliet. *The Overworked American.* New York: Basic, 1991.

Schteingart, Judith S.; Janice Molnar; Tovah P. Klein; Cynthia B. Lowe; and Annelie H. Hartmann. "Homelessness and Child Functioning in the Context of Risk and Protective Factors Moderating Child Outcome." *Journal of Clinical Child Psychology* 24 (1995): 320–32.

Schubert, H. J. P. *Twenty Thousand Transients.* Buffalo: Emergency Relief Bureau, 1935.

Schuerman, John R.; Tina L. Rzepniki; and Julia H. Littell. *Putting Families First: An Experiment in Family Preservation.* New York: Aldine de Gruyter, 1994.

Schutt, Russell K. *A Short Report on Homeless Veterans—A Supplement to Homelessness in Boston in 1985: The View from Long Island.* Boston: University of Massachusetts, 1986.

Schutt, Russell K.; Stephen M. Goldfinger; and W. E. Penk. "The Structure and Sources of Residential Preferences among Seriously Mentally Ill Homeless Adults." *Sociological Practice Review* 3, 3 (1992): 148–56.

Schwartz, David C.; Donita Devance-Manzini; and Tricia Fagan. *Preventing Homelessness: A Study of State and Local Homelessness Prevention Programs.* New Brunswick, NJ: American Affordable Housing Institute and National Housing Institute, Rutgers University, October 1991.

Schwartzman, Paul; and David L. Lewis. "Gimme Shelters to Shut: Commish." *New York Daily News* February 1, 1995: 4.

Schwarz, John E.; and Thomas Volgy. *The Forgotten Americans.* New York: W. W. Norton, 1992.

Scott, J. C. *Domination and the Arts of Resistance.* New Haven: Yale University Press, 1990.

Segal, Steven; and Jim Baumohl. "The Community Living Room." *Social Casework* 66, 2 (1985): 111–16.

———. "Engaging the Disengaged: Proposals on Madness and Vagrancy." *Social Work* 25, 5 (1980): 358–64.

———. "The New Chronic Patient: The Creation of an Underserved Population." In *Reaching the Underserved: Mental Health Needs of Neglected Populations,* edited by L. R. Snowden, 95–116. Beverly Hills: Sage Publications, 1982.

Segal, Steven; Jim Baumohl; and Elsie Johnson. "Falling through the Cracks: Mental Disorder and Social Margin in a Young Vagrant Population." *Social Problems* 24, 3 (1977): 387–400.

Sennett, Richard; and Jonathan Cobb. *The Hidden Injuries of Class.* New York: Doubleday, 1973.

Severo, R.; and L. Milford. *The Wages of War.* New York: Touchstone, 1989.

Shaffer, Gina. "Tent Cities: Laws Aim to Break Camp." *Orange County Register,* June 7, 1992: B8.

Shapiro, Joan Hatch. *Communities of the Alone.* New York: Association Press, 1971.

Shelley, Kristina. "More Job Openings—Even More New Entrants: The Outlook for College Graduates, 1992–2005." *Occupational Outlook Quarterly* Summer 1994:5–9.

Shinn, Marybeth. "Homelessness: What Is a Psychologist to Do?" *American Journal of Community Psychology* 20 (1992): 1–24.

Shinn, Marybeth; and Colleen Gillespie. "The Roles of Housing and Poverty in the Origins of Homelessness." *American Behavioral Scientist* 37 (1994): 505–21.

Shinn, Marybeth; J. R. Knickman; and B. C. Weitzman. "Social Relationships and Vulnerability to Becoming Homeless among Poor Families." *American Psychologist* 46, 11 (1991): 1180–87.

Shlay, Anne B.; and Peter H. Rossi. "Social Science Research and Contemporary Studies of Homelessness." *Annual Review of Sociology* 18 (1992): 129–60.

Sigal, N. M. "The Unchanging Area in Transition." *Land Economics* 43 (1967): 284–93.

Simpson, Gloria A.; and Mary Glenn Fowler. "Geographic Mobility and Children's Emotional/Behavioral Adjustment and School Functioning." *Pediatrics* 93 (1994): 303–09.

Smith, Ken; and Yates, James M. "The New England Shelter for Homeless Veterans: A Unique Approach." *New England Journal of Public Policy* 8 (1992): 669–84.

Smolowe, Jill. "Giving the Cold Shoulder." *Time,* December 6, 1993: 28–31.

Snow, David A.; and Leon Anderson. *Down on Their Luck: A Study of Homeless Street People.* Berkeley: University of California Press, 1993.

———. "Identity Work among the Homeless: The Verbal Construction and Avowal of Personal Identities." *American Journal of Sociology* 92 (1987): 1336–71.

Snow, David A.; Susan G. Baker; and Leon Anderson. "Criminality and Homeless Men: An Empirical Assessment." *Social Problems* 36 (1989): 532–49.

Snow, David A.; Susan G. Baker; Leon Anderson; and Michael Martin. "The Myth of Pervasive Mental Illness among the Homeless." *Social Problems* 33 (1986): 407–23.

Snyder, Bryan. "Bad Medicine: Is the 'Cure' for Inflation Worth the Cost?" *Dollars and Sense* 194 (July/August 1994): 8–11, 38.

Solarz, Andrea. "To Be Young and Homeless: Implications of Homelessness for Children." In *Homelessness: A National Perspective*, edited by Marjorie J. Robertson and Milton Greenblatt, 275–86. New York: Plenum Press, 1992.

Sosin, Michael R.. "Homeless and Vulnerable Meal Program Users: A Comparison Study." *Social Problems* 29 (1992): 170–88.

Sosin, Michael R.; Paul Colson; and Susan Grossman. *Homelessness in Chicago: Poverty and Pathology, Social Institutions, and Social Change*. Chicago: The University of Chicago, School of Social Service Administration, 1988.

Sosin, Michael R.; Irving Piliavin; and Herb Westerfelt. "Toward a Longitudinal Analysis of Homelessness." *Journal of Social Issues* 46, 4 (1990): 157–74.

Southern Regional Council. *Hard Labor: A Report on Day Labor Pools in Temporary Employment*. Atlanta, GA: Southern Regional Council, 1988.

Speaker's Task Force on Homelessness. *Report to the Speaker: Findings and Recommendations*. Washington, DC: Speaker's Task Force on Homelessness, 1993.

Stack, Carol. *All Our Kin*. New York: Harper and Row, 1974.

———. New York: Basic Books, 1996.

———. "Second Thoughts on Social Capital." Paper presented at the annual meeting of the American Anthropological Association, Washington, DC, November 1995.

Standing, Guy. "Labor Insecurity through Market Regulation: Legacy of the 1980s, Challenge for the 1990s." In *Poverty, Inequality and the Future of Social Policy*, edited by Katherine McFate, Roger Lawson, and William J. Wilson. New York: Russell Sage Foundation, 1995.

Stanford Center for the Study of Families, Children, and Youth. *The Stanford Studies of Homeless Children and Youth*. Stanford, CA: Stanford University, 1991.

Stark, Andrew. "Gore and Gingrich—Men in a Mirror." *New York Times* February 5, 1995: E17.

Starr, Paul. *The Social Transformation of American Medicine*. New York: Basic, 1982.

Stasny, Elizabeth; Beverly G. Toomey; and Richard J. First. "Estimating the Rate of Rural Homelessness: A Study of Nonurban Ohio." Columbus: Ohio State University, Department of Statistics, Technical Report 509, April 1993.

Statistical Services Bureau, California Department of Social Services. *AFDC Survey of Homeless Assistance Applications Approved in California during May 1989—Social and Economic Characteristics of Families Approved to Receive Homeless Assistance Benefits*. December 1990.

Stegman, Michael A. *Housing and Vacancy Report, New York City, 1991*. New York: City of New York, Department of Housing Preservation and Development, 1993.

Stegman, Michael A.; and Langley C. Keyes. "Housing, Poverty, and Homelessness: A Literature Review and Research Agenda." Paper presented at a National Institute of Mental Health/National Institute on Alcoholism and Alcohol Abuse sponsored conference, Cambridge, MA, January 1991.

Stein, Herbert. *The Fiscal Revolution in America*. Washington, DC: American Enterprise Institute Press, 1990.

Stephens, Joyce. *Loners, Losers, and Lovers: Elderly Tenants in a Slum Hotel*. Seattle: University of Washington Press, 1976.

Stern, Mark J. "The Emergence of the Homeless as a Public Problem." *Social Service Review* 58 (1984): 291–301.

———. "Poverty and Family Composition Since 1940." In *The "Underclass" Debate*, edited by M. B. Katz, 220–53. Princeton: Princeton University Press, 1993.

Stone, Michael E. *One-Third of a Nation: A New Look at Housing Affordability in America*. Washington, DC: Economic Policy Institute, 1990.

———. *Shelter Poverty: New Ideas on Housing Affordability*. Philadelphia: Temple University Press, 1993.

Strang, J. "Harm Reduction for Drug Users: Exploring the Dimensions of Harm, Their Measurement, and Strategies for Reductions." *AIDS and Public Policy Journal* 7, 3 (1992): 80–87.

Struening, Elmer L.; and C. Pittman. *Characteristics of Residents of the New York City Shelter System, Summer 1987*. New York: Epidemiology of Mental Disorders Dept., New York State Psychiatric Institute, 1987.

Struening, Elmer L.; and A. Rosenblatt. *Characteristics of Homeless Veterans in the New York City Shelter System*. New York State Psychiatric Institute, 1987.

Sullivan, Mercer L. "Absent Fathers in the Inner City." *Annals of the American Academy of Political and Social Science* 501 (1989): 48–58.

———. *Getting Paid: Youth, Crime and Work in the Inner City*. Ithaca: Cornell University Press, 1989.

Susser, Ezra; Elmer L. Struening; and Sarah Conover. "Childhood Experiences of Homeless Men." *American Journal of Psychiatry* 144, 12 (December 1987): 1599–601.

Susser, Ezra; S. Goldfinger; and A. White. "Some Clinical Approaches to the Homeless Mentally Ill." *Community Mental Health Journal* 26, 5 (1990): 463–80.

Susser, Ezra; Shang P. Lin; Sarah A. Conover; and Elmer L. Struening. "Childhood Antecedents of Homelessness in Psychiatric Patients." *American Journal of Psychiatry* 148 (1991): 1026–30.

Sutherland, Edwin H.; and Harvey L. Locke. *Twenty Thousand Homeless Men*. Chicago: J. P. Lipincott, 1936.

Taeuber, Cynthia M.; and Paul M. Siegel. *Counting the Nation's Homeless Population in the 1990 Census*. Washington, DC: U.S. Bureau of the Census, Population Division, 1991.

Tanzman, B. "An Overview of Surveys of Mental Health Consumers' Preferences for Housing and Support Services." *Hospital and Community Psychiatry* 44, 5 (1993): 450–55.

Terry, Wallace, ed. *Bloods: An Oral History of the Vietnam War by Black Veterans*. New York: Random House, 1984.

Tessler, R. C.; and D. L. Dennis. "Mental Illness among Homeless Adults: A Synthesis of Recent NIMH-Funded Research." In *Research in Community and Mental Health*, vol. 7, edited by J. R. Greenley and P. J. Leaf, 3–53. Greenwich, CT: JAI Press, Inc., 1992.

Thomas, Andrew Peyton. "The Rise and Fall of the Homeless." *The Weekly Standard* April 8, 1996: 27–31.

Thomas, M. E.; and M. Hughes. "The Continuing Significance of Race: A Study of Race, Class, and Quality of Life in America, 1972–1985." *American Sociological Review* 51 (1986): 830–41.

Thurow, Lester. "Why Their World Might Crumble." *New York Times Sunday Magazine* November 19, 1995: 78–79.

Tienda, Marta; and Leif Jensen. "Poverty and Minorities: A Quarter-Century Profile of Color and Socioeconomic Disadvantage." In *Divided Opportunities: Minorities, Poverty, and Social Policy*, edited by Gary D. Sandefur and Marta Tienda, 23–62. New York: Plenum Press, 1988.

Tierney, John. "Save the Flophouse." *New York Times Magazine* January 14, 1996: 16.

———. "Using Housing Projects for Welfare Angers Tenants." *New York Times* June 28, 1990, A1.

Tierney, Kathleen. "The Battered Women Movement and the Creation of the Wife Beating Problem." *Social Problems* 29 (1982): 207–20.

Tilly, Chris; and Charles Tilly. "Capitalist Work and Labor Markets," In *The Handbook of Economic Sociology*, edited by N. J. Smelser and R. Swedberg, 283–312. Princeton and New York: Princeton University Press and Russell Sage Foundation, 1994.

Toomey, Beverley G.; Richard J. First; John C. Rife; and John R. Belcher. "Evaluating Community Care for Homeless Mentally Ill People." *Social Work Abstracts and Research* December 1989: 21–26.

Toro, Paul; and Dennis McDonnell. "Beliefs, Attitudes and Knowledge about Homelessness: A Survey of the General Public." *American Journal of Community Psychology* 20 (1992): 53–80.

Trimble, Joseph E.; Amado M. Padilla; and Catherine S. Bell. *Drug Abuse among Ethnic Minorities*. U.S. Department of Health and Human Services Publication No. (ADM)87-1474. Washington, DC: Government Printing Office, 1987.

Trippe, Carol. *Trends in FSP Participation Rates: Focus on August 1993*. U.S. Department of Agriculture, Food and Consumer Service. Washington, DC: Mathematica Policy Research, Inc., December 1995.

Trotter, J. W., Jr. "Blacks in the Urban North." In *The "Underclass" Debate*, edited by M. B. Katz, 85–117. Princeton: Princeton University Press, 1993.

Turkel, Studs. *Hard Times*. New York: Avon, 1970.

———. *Race*. New York: Anchor Books, 1992.

Turner, Margery Austin; and Veronica M. Reed. *Housing America: Learning from the Past, Planning for the Future*. Washington, DC: The Urban Institute Press, 1990.

Turner, Victor. *Dramas, Fields, and Metaphors*. Ithaca, NY: Cornell University Press, 1974.

———. *On the Edge of the Bush*. Tucson: University of Arizona Press, 1985.

———. *The Forest of Symbols*. Ithaca, NY: Cornell University Press, 1967.

———. *The Ritual Process*. Ithaca, NY: Cornell University Press, 1969.

Tyson, James L. "Cities Crack Down on Homeless." *Christian Science Monitor* January 21, 1994: 4.

U.S. Bureau of the Census. "American Housing Survey for the United States in 1989." Current Housing Reports H150/89.

———. *1987 Survey of Veterans*. Washington, DC: Department of Veterans Affairs, 1989.

———. *Patterns of Metropolitan Area and County Population Growth: 1980–1987*. Current Population Reports, Series P-25, No. 1039. Washington, DC: Government Printing Office, 1989.

———. *Population Estimates by Race and Hispanic Origin for States, Metropolitan Areas, and Selected Counties: 1980 to 1985*. Current Population Reports, Series P-25, No. 1040-RD-1. Washington, DC: Government Printing Office, 1989.

———. "Poverty in the United States: 1991." In *Current Population Reports, Series P-60, No. 181*. Washington, DC: U.S. Government Printing Office, 1992.

U.S. Conference of Mayors. *Ending Homelessness in America's Cities: Implementing a Plan of Action*. San Francisco: HomeBase, 1993.

———. *A Status Report on Hunger and Homelessness in America's Cities: 1993*. Washington, DC: U.S. Conference of Mayors, 1994.

U.S. Department of Commerce, Bureau of the Census. *Current Population Reports, Consumer Income, Series P60-189*. Washington, DC: Bureau of the Census, April 1996.

———. *Current Population Survey: Annual Demographic File, 1987*. Ann Arbor, MI: Inter-University Consortium for Political and Social Research, 1987.

U.S. Department of Health and Human Services. *National Household Survey on Drug Abuse, 1988 Population Estimates*. DHHS Publication No. (ADM)89-1636. Washington, DC: Government Printing Office, 1989.

U.S. Department of Health and Human Services, Administration for Children and Families. *FY 1992–93 Quarterly Public Assistance Statistics*. Washington, DC: U.S. Department of Health and Human Services, 1995.

U.S. Department of Health and Human Services, Office of Inspector General. *Homeless Families and Access to AFDC*. Washington, DC: U.S. Government Printing Office, October 1992.

U.S. Department of Housing and Urban Development. *Budget Summary: Fiscal Year 1997*. U.S. Department of Housing and Urban Development: Washington, DC, 1996.

———. Proposed Rule. "Consolidated Submission for Community Planning and Development Programs." *Federal Register* 59, 150 (August 1994): 40148–67.

U.S. Department of Housing and Urban Development, Office of Policy Development and Research. *Evaluation of the Emergency Shelter Grants Program*. Vol. 1. Washington, DC: U.S. Department of Housing and Urban Development, September 1994.

———. *Priority Housing Problems and "Worst Case" Housing Needs in 1989: A Report to Congress*. Washington, DC: U.S. Department of Housing and Urban Development, 1991.

———. *Rental Housing Assistance at a Crossroads: A Report to Congress on Worst Case Housing Needs*. Washington, DC: U.S. Department of Housing and Urban Development, 1996.

U.S. Department of Labor. *Comparison of State Unemployment Insurance Laws*. Washington, DC: U.S. Department of Labor, January 1994.

———. *Report on the American Workforce*. Washington, DC: U.S. Government Printing Office, 1994.

U.S. Department of Labor, Bureau of Labor Statistics. *Employment and Earnings*. Washington, DC: Bureau of Labor Statistics, January 1996.

———. Unpublished tabulations from the Current Population Survey, 1992 annual averages. Washington, DC: U.S. Department of Labor, Bureau of Labor Statistics, 1993.

U.S. Department of Labor, Office of the Chief Economist. *What's Working (and What's Not): A Summary of Research on the Economic Impacts of Employment and Training Programs*. Washington, DC: U.S. Department of Labor, 1995.

U.S. General Accounting Office. *Children and Youths: About 68,000 Homeless and 186,000 in Shared Housing at Any Given Time*. Washington, DC: U.S. General Accounting Office, June 1989.

———. *Elementary School Children: Many Change Schools Frequently, Harming Their Education*. Washington, DC: General Accounting Office GAO/HEHS-94-45, February, 1994.

———. *Homelessness: A Complex Problem and the Federal Response*. Washington, DC: General Accounting Office, 1985.

———. *Homelessness: McKinney Act Programs and Funding through Fiscal Year 1993*. GAO/RCED-94-107. Washington, DC: U.S. General Accounting Office, June 1994.

———. *Homelessness: Too Early to Tell What Kinds of Prevention Assistance Work Best*. GAO/RCED-90-89. Washington, DC: General Accounting Office, April 24, 1990.

———. *Social Security: Major Changes Needed for Disability Benefits for Addicts*. Washington, DC: U.S. General Accounting Office, May 1994.

U.S. Government Printing Office. *Budget System and Concepts of the United States Government*. Washington, DC: U.S. Government Printing Office, 1994.

———. *Report of the President's Committee on Urban Housing: A Decent Home*. Washington, DC: U.S. Government Printing Office, 1969.

U.S. House of Representatives Committee on Ways and Means. *Overview of Entitlement Programs: 1992 Green Book*. Washington, DC: U.S. Government Printing Office, 1992.

———. *Overview of Entitlement Programs: 1994 Green Book: Background Material and Data on Programs within the Jurisdiction of the Committee on Ways and Means*. WMCP 103–27. Washington, DC: U.S. Government Printing Office, 1994.

U.S. House of Representatives Select Committee on Children, Youth, and Families. *No Place to Call Home: Discarded Children in America*. Report 101-395. 1990.

U.S. Senate, Committee on Banking, Housing, and Urban Affairs. *The Housing Choice and Community Investment Act of 1994*, Report 103-307. 103d Congress, 2d session, S2281. Washington, DC: U.S. Government Printing Office, July 1994.

Ulbrich, P. M.; G. J. Warheit; and R. S. Zimmerman. "Race, Socioeconomic Status, and Psychological Distress: An Examination of Differential Vulnerability." *Journal of Health and Social Behavior* 30 (1989): 131–46.

Umberson, Debra. "Sociodemographic Position, World Views, and Psychological Distress." *Social Science Quarterly* 74 (1993): 575–89.

United Nations Development Programme. *Human Development Report 1995*. New York: Oxford University Press, 1995.

Valdivieso, Rafael. "High School and Beyond: The Young Hispanic Woman." In *American Women 1988–1989*, edited by Sara Rix. New York: Norton Press, 1988.

van Gennep, Arnold. *The Rites of Passage*. Chicago: University of Chicago Press, 1960 (originally published in 1908).

Van Tosh, L. *Working for a Change: Employment of Consumers/Survivors in the Design and Provision of Services for Per-*

sons Who Are Homeless and Mentally Disabled. Rockville, MD: Center for Mental Health Services, 1993.

Vergara, Camilo. "Ghettoes: No Way Out." *New York Daily News* February 11, 1990.

———. "Lessons Learned, Lessons Forgotten." *The Livable City* 15 (1991): 2–9.

———. "Showdown in Drug City." *Village Voice* March 27, 1990.

Vernez, Georges M.; Audrey Burnam; Elizabeth A. McGlynn; Sally Trude; and Brian Mittman. *Review of California's Program for the Homeless Mentally Disabled.* Santa Monica, CA: The Rand Corporation, 1988.

Vernon, Sally W.; and Robert E. Roberts. "A Comparison of Anglos and Mexican Americans on Selected Measures of Social Support." *Hispanic Journal of Behavioral Sciences* 7 (1985): 381–99.

Veterans Administration. *Annual Report 1987.* Washington, DC: Veterans Administration, 1988.

Wacquant, Loïc J. D.; and William Julius Wilson. "The Cost of Racial and Class Exclusion," *Annals of the American Academy of Political and Social Science* 501 (1989): 8–25.

Waddell, Helen. *The Wandering Scholars.* New York: Anchor, 1927.

Wagner, David. *Checkerboard Square: Culture and Resistance in a Homeless Community.* Boulder: Westview Press, 1993.

Wagner, David; and Marcia B. Cohen. "The Power of the People: Homeless Protesters in the Aftermath of Social Movement Participation." *Social Problems* 38 (November 1991): 543–61.

Waldron, Jeremy. "Homelessness and the Issue of Freedom." *U.C.L.A. Law Review* 39 (1991): 295–324.

Wallace, R. "A Synergism of Plagues." *Environmental Research* 47 (1989): 1–33.

Wallace, R.; and E. Bassuk. "Housing Famine and Homelessness: How the Low-Income Housing Crisis Affects Families with Inadequate Supports." *Environment and Planning* A 23 (1991): 485–98.

Walsh, Brendan; and Dorothy Davenport. *The Long Loneliness in Baltimore.* Baltimore: Viva House Community, September 1981.

Walters, Paul. "Fixing Public's 'Broken Windows.'" *Los Angeles Times (Orange County Edition)* August 28, 1990: B9.

Ware, N. C.; R. R. Desjarlais; T. L. AvRuskin; J. Breslau; B. J. Good; and S. M. Goldfinger. "Empowerment and the Transition to Housing for Persons Who Are Homeless and Mentally Ill: An Anthropological Perspective." *New England Journal of Public Policy* 8, 1 (1992): 297–315.

Warheit, George; William Vega; David Shimizu; and Kenneth Meinhardt. "Interpersonal Coping Networks and Mental Health Problems among Four Race-Ethnic Groups." *Journal of Community Psychiatzry* 10 (1982): 312–24.

Warner, R. *Recovery from Schizophrenia: Psychiatry and Political Economy.* New York: Routledge, Chapman and Hall, 1994.

Watts, Harold W. "Have Our Measures of Poverty Become Poorer?" *Focus* (University of Wisconsin-Madison Institute for Research on Poverty) 9, 2 (1986): 18–23.

Webb, J. N. *The Transient Unemployed.* Washington: WPA, 1935.

Weicher, John C. "Housing Quality: Measurement and Progress." In *Housing Issues of the 1990s,* edited by Sara Rosenberry and Chester Hartman, 9–32. New York: Praeger Publishers, 1989.

Weinreb, Linda; and Peter H. Rossi. "The American Homeless Family Shelter System." Unpublished manuscript, 1994. Available from Better Homes Foundation, 189 Wells Ave., Newton Centre, MA 02159.

Weir, Margaret. "The Federal Government and Unemployment." In *The Politics of Social Policy in the United States,* edited by Margaret Weir, Ann Shola Orloff, and Theda Skocpol, 149–97. Princeton, NJ: Princeton University Press, 1988.

Weitzman, Beth C. "Pregnancy and Childbirth: Risk Factors for Homelessness?" *Family Planning Perspectives* 21, 4 (1989): 175–78.

Weitzman, Beth C.; and Carolyn Berry. "Formerly Homeless Families and the Transition to Permanent Housing: Hisk Risk Families and the Role of Intensive Case Management Services." Final report to the Edna McConnell Clark Foundation. New York: Health Research Program, Robert F. Wagner Graduate School, New York University, June 1994.

Weitzman, Beth C.; James R. Knickman; and Marybeth Shinn. "Pathways to Homelessness among New York City Families." *Journal of Social Issues* 46, 4 (1990): 125–40.

———. "Predictors of Shelter Use among Low Income Families: Psychiatric History, Substance Abuse, and Victimization." *American Journal of Public Health* 82, 11 (1992): 1547–50.

Wellman, Barry; and Susan González Baker. "Using SAS Software to Link Personal Network, Tie and Individual Level Data: A Novice's Guide." *Connections: Bulletin of the International Network for Social Network Analysis* 8 (1985): 176–87.

Wellman, Barry; and Scot Wortley. "Different Strokes from Different Folks: Which Kinds of Ties Provide What Kinds of Social Support?" Research Paper, Centre for Urban and Community Studies Paper No. 174. Toronto: University of Toronto, 1989.

Wexler, Richard. "Beware of Pitfalls of Foster Care." *New York Times* January 21, 1996: E15.

"When Freedom Rings." *The Survey* 75 (1939): 220.

White, Lucie. "Representing 'The Real Deal.'" *University of Miami Law Review* 45 (1990–91): 271–313.

White, Richard. *Rude Awakenings: What the Homeless Crisis Tells Us.* San Francisco: Center for Self Governance, 1992.

Whitman, Barbara; Pasquale Accardo; Mary Boyert; and Rita Kendagor. "Homelessness and Cognitive Performance in Children: A Possible Link." *Social Work* 35 (1990): 516–19.

Wiegand, R. Bruce. "Sweat and Blood: Sources of Income on a Southern Skid Row." In *Homelessness in the United States: Data and Issues,* edited by Jamshid A. Momeni, 111–22. Westport, CT: Greenwood Press, 1990.

Wilkerson, Isabel. "Shift in Feelings on the Homeless: Empathy Turns to Frustration." *New York Times,* September 2, 1991: 1.

Willenbring, M. L.; J. A. Whelan; J. S. Dahlquist; and M. E. O'Neal. "Community Treatment of the Chronic Public Inebriate I: Implementation." *Alcoholism Treatment Quarterly* 7, 1 (1990): 79–97.

Williams, B. "There Goes the Neighborhood." In *There's No Place Like Home,* edited by A. L. DeHavenon. Westport: Bergin and Garvey, forthcoming.

Williams, Carol W. "Child Welfare Services and Homelessness: Issues in Policy, Philosophy, and Programs." In *Homeless Children and Youth: A New American Dilemma,* edited by Julee H. Kryder-Coe, Lester M. Salamon, and Janice M. Molnar, 285–99. New Brunswick, NJ: Transaction, 1991.

Willis, P. *Learning to Labor.* New York: Columbia University Press, 1977.

Wilson, James Q.; and Paul Kelling. "Broken Windows." *Atlantic Monthly,* March 1982.

Wilson, Peter J. *Oscar.* New York: Random House, 1974.

Wilson, William Julius. *The Truly Disadvantaged: The Inner City, the Underclass, and Public Policy.* Chicago: University of Chicago Press, 1987.

Wilson, William Julius; Robert Aponte; Joleen Kirschenman; and Loïc J. D. Wacquant. "The Ghetto Underclass and the Changing Structure of Urban Poverty." In *Quiet Riots,* edited by Fred R. Harris and Roger W. Wilkins, 123–51. New York: Pantheon, 1988.

Winberg, Ellie; and Tom Wilson. *Single Rooms.* Cambridge, MA: Schenkman, 1981.

Winkelby, M. A.; and D. Fleshin. "Physical, Addictive, and Psychiatric Disorders among Homeless Veterans and Nonveterans." *Public Health Reports* 108 (1992): 30–36.

"The Wino Welders." *San Francisco Chronicle,* October 23, 1942, 1.

Wiseman, Jacqueline P. *Stations of the Lost: The Treatment of Skid Row Alcoholics.* Englewood Cliffs, NJ: Prentice Hall, 1970.

Wittman, Friedner D. "Affordable Housing for People with Alcohol and Other Drug Problems." *Contemporary Drug Problems* 21 (1993): 541–609.

Wolch, Jennifer R.; and Michael Dear. *Malign Neglect: Homelessness in an American City.* San Francisco: Jossey-Bass, 1993.

Wood, David L.; Neal Halfon; Debra Scarlata; Paul Newacheck; and Sharon Nessim. "Impact of Family Relocation on Children's Growth, Development, School Function, and Behavior." *Journal of the American Medical Association* 270, 11 (1993): 1334–38.

Wood, David L.; Robert Burciaga Valdez; Toshi Hayashi; and Albert Shen. "Health of Homeless Children and Housed, Poor Children." *Pediatrics* 86, 6 (1990): 858–66.

———. "Homeless and Housed Families in Los Angeles: A Study Comparing Demographic, Economic, and Family Function Characteristics." *American Journal of Public Health* 80, 9 (1990): 1049–52.

Wright, James D. *Address Unknown: The Homeless in America.* New York: Aldine de Gruyter, 1989.

———, ed. "Counting the Homeless." *Evaluation Review* 16, 4 (August 1992): entire issue.

———. "The Johnson-Pew Health Care for the Homeless Program." In *The Homeless with Alcohol-Related Problems,* edited by F. D. Wittman and M. Arch. Rockville, MD: National Institute on Alcohol Abuse and Alcoholism, 1985.

———. "Poverty, Homelessness, Health, Nutrition, and Children." In *Homeless Children and Youth: A New American Dilemma,* edited by Julee H. Kryder-Coe, Lester M. Salamon, and Janice M. Molnar, 71–104. New Brunswick, NJ: Transaction, 1991.

Wright, James D.; and Eleanor Weber. *Homelessness and Health.* Washington, DC: McGraw Hill's Healthcare Information Center, 1987.

Wright, Talmadge. "Homeless Collective Epowerment: San Jose, California and Chicago, Illinois." Department of Sociology and Anthropology, Loyola University, Chicago, 1994.

———. "'Tranquility City' and Shelters: Homeless Placemaking, Protest and Collective Gains within a Chicago Homeless Encampment." Department of Sociology and Anthropology, Loyola University, Chicago, 1994.

Yeich, Susan. *The Politics of Ending Homelessness.* Lanham, MD: University Press of America, 1994.

Yinger, John. *Housing Discrimination Study: Incidence and Severity of Unfavorable Treatment.* Prepared for the U.S. Department of Housing and Urban Development, contract HC-5811. Washington, DC: The Urban Institute, 1991.

Zima, Bonnie T.; Kenneth B. Wells; and Howard E. Freeman. "Emotional and Behavioral Problems and Severe Academic Delays among Sheltered Homeless Children in Los Angeles County." *American Journal of Public Health* 84, 2 (1994): 260–64.

INDEX

• • • • • • •

James Minkin